Programming Starter Kit for Macintosh

Jim Trudeau

Hayden
Books

Programming Starter Kit for Macintosh

Jim Trudeau

Hayden
Books

Programming Starter Kit for Macintosh

©**1995 Hayden Books, a division of Macmillan Computer Publishing**

Library of Congress Catalog Number: 94-73447
ISBN: 1-56830-174-X

97   96   95   4   3   2   1

Interpretation of the printing code: the rightmost double-digit number is the year of the book's printing; the rightmost single-digit number is the number of the book's printing. For example, a printing code of 95-1 shows that the first printing of the book occurred in 1995.

Dedication

To my son Jay,

who keeps my mind sharp

Credits

Publisher
David Rogelberg

Manager of Product Development
Patrick J. Gibbons

Acquisitions Editor
Oliver von Quadt

Development Editor
Kezia E. Endsley

Copy/Production Editor
Brian Gill

Marketing Manager
Andy Roth

Technical Reviewers
Tom Thompson, Brad Mohr,
Henly Wollin

Usability Reviewers
Brian Hubbard, Robert Bailey

Publishing Coordinator
Rosemary Lewis

Interior Designer
Fred Bower

Cover Designer
Karen Ruggles

Production Team
Gary Adair, Angela Calvert,
Dan Caparo, Kim Cofer,
Jennifer Eberhardt, Kevin Foltz,
David Garratt, Joe Millay, Erika
Millen, Beth Rago, Gina Rexrode,
Erich Richter, Christine Tyner,
Karen Walsh, Robert Wolf

Indexer
Brad Herriman

To Our Readers

Dear Friend,

Thank you on behalf of everyone at Hayden Books for choosing *Programming Starter Kit for Macintosh* to enable you to learn about the exciting world of programming on the Macintosh. We think you'll enjoy the examples in this book, while getting a true understanding of the conceptual nature of Macintosh programming.

What you think of this book is important to our ability to better serve you in the future. If you have any comments, no matter how great or small, we'd appreciate you taking the time to send us email or a note by snail mail. Of course, we'd love to hear your book ideas.

Sincerely yours,

David Rogelberg
Publisher, Hayden Books and Adobe Press

You can reach Hayden Books at the following:

Hayden Books
201 West 103rd Street
Indianapolis, IN 46290
(800) 428-5331 voice
(800) 448-3804 fax

Email addresses:

America Online: Hayden Bks
AppleLink: hayden.books
CompuServe: 76350,3014
Internet: hayden@hayden.com

About the Author

Jim Trudeau

Jim Trudeau is an independent programming consultant, accomplished Macintosh programmer, and writer. He is the author of commercial software and shareware, an instructor on the external faculty of Apple's Developer University, and teaches courses in Macintosh programming and debugging to both beginners and advanced professionals.

Acknowledgments

This book would not exist but for many people who gave unstintingly and selflessly of their time and ideas:

John Trudeau who had the idea, and for being a friend and teacher as well as a brother.

Brad Mohr for his creativity, and for yeoman's service as code writer, technical reviewer, and bug finder.

Bill Hofmann for giving invaluable technical feedback and encouragement in the early stages of EasyApp.

Eric Shapiro, Bill Worzel, and Steve Falkenburg for writing application shells and providing inspiration.

Neil Rhodes for lending a hand and good advice to a fellow author.

Zz Zimmerman for some intriguing insights into Clarus.

Oliver von Quadt, Kezia Endsley, and Brian Gill at Hayden (and the production team) for their invaluable assistance.

Larry Fisher for being a true gentleman and the ultimate source of much of what I know about Macintosh programming, although I'm sure he's too modest to admit that he could have had anything to do with it.

I want to thank each of you. Your insight, ideas, and support helped make this book what it is.

Most of all, I want to thank Abby Rose, who always believed in this project and who provided technical support of which other authors only dream.

Following are the people and organizations that kindly contributed materials to this book. They, individually and as a group, have my sincere thanks:

Some illustrations are from the Canvas 3.5 Clip Art Collection from Deneba Software. For product information, call (305) 596-5644.

Some images courtesy of Developer University at Apple Computer.

Some images courtesy of Image Club Graphics, Inc. For a free catalog, call: 1-800-661-9410.

Four demo applications available on the CD are courtesy of Developer University. They are HeapDemo, EventDemo, QuickDrawDemo, and ScrollDemo.

Clarus the dogcow is a trademark of Apple Computer. Images of Clarus are used with permission. Clarus doesn't mind either.

Thanks to Martin R. Wachter and Phil Kearney for permission to include MacErrors 1.2 among the tools on the CD. MacErrors is shareware ($5.00).

Thanks to *develop* for permission to use Dean Yu's zooming code and Bryan Ressler's asynchronous sound helper library. Thanks to the authors of that code, as well.

Thanks to Ladd Van Tol for the typing sounds in the Hello World program. They come from *Annoying Key Sounds*, a freeware program.

Contents

To All Budding Mac Programmers,

You want to program your Mac. You know you do. But you don't have a clue where to start, do you? I don't blame you. I teach programming for a living (my day job is as a Computer Scientist at The University of Chicago), so I know where you are coming from (pardon the dated 70's cliché).

Despite many efforts made with good intentions, most introductory programming books for the Mac have either missed the mark by being too hard or too easy or just plain too bad. Yet the ability to program (rather than to just react to others' software) your Mac is still a reasonable, even lofty goal. And now, thanks to Jim Trudeau's *Programming Starter Kit for Macintosh*, it's a goal within easy reach.

No longer will you wonder what it's like to program your Mac. No longer will you wonder how to make it jump through hoops of your own design. And no longer will you wonder what software you need to buy when you can roll your own anytime you want. Jim Trudeau's *Programming Starter Kit for Macintosh* tells you all this, and a lot more, besides giving you labs and programming exercises to make the whole thing happen in real time.

I've read too many bad Macintosh programming texts, especially introductory ones. Of all those books, this is the first one that really makes programming the Mac a reasonable proposition for mere mortals. It explains the essence of the Mac programming experience and its pitfalls while leading you around them. And it lets you put Mac programming into your skill set faster than you'd ever think possible from simply reading (and using) a book.

The simple truth is you can make your Mac do things if you can program it, that cannot be done otherwise. Jim Trudeau captures the essence of this incredible power and makes it understandable for anyone willing to try.

But don't take my word for it. Read the book and tell me what you think. The *Programming Starter Kit for Macintosh* lives in the Don Crabb Macintosh Library because it delivers the inside scoop on getting started with Mac programming. Let it be your introductory companion for creating and delivering the custom solutions you want in your Mac environment.

It's simple. Jim Trudeau's *Programming Starter Kit for Macintosh* delivers the goods of introductory Mac programming. Read it and you'll wonder why you didn't try to get REAL CONTROL over your Mac years ago.

See you on the ether,

Don Crabb

Don Crabb

decc@cs.uchicago.edu
April 1995
Chicago, IL

P.S. Send me your first working CodeWarrior program. I'm looking forward to it!

Introduction

For most people, the computer is something of a puzzle. It is a closed box, and magic happens inside. As long as the software works, most people who use computers are very happy.

You are different. You want to solve the puzzle. You want to know what's going on inside the magic box. You want to write your own software for the Macintosh! This book shows you how.

Writing good Macintosh software is not that hard. *Programming Starter Kit for Macintosh* proves this by taking you step-by-step through programming for both the Power Macintosh and the older "68K" Macs that use chips from the Motorola 68000 family.

Although the Macintosh is more than 10 years old, it has recently been reborn as the Power Macintosh. Like the original Macintosh, the Power Macintosh is a machine ahead of its time.

The Once and Future Mac

In his novel *1984*, George Orwell predicted a gray, faceless, totalitarian dystopia. As it turned out, Apple Computer had other plans. The real 1984 witnessed the birth of the Macintosh.

In sharp contrast to Orwell's predictions, the new Macintosh embodied two key utopian ideas: personal power and freedom. The new, funny-looking little computer was unlike anything seen before. The person using the computer didn't have to negotiate through all kinds of lists or type in arcane commands to make the machine work. Instead, there was a mouse, a movable arrow cursor, and a friendly looking interface that allowed the user remarkable freedom.

The original Macintosh had a new and powerful microprocessor—the remarkable Motorola 68000. This revolutionary chip gave the Macintosh unheard of power. As a result, it could successfully run a new and innovative graphical interface.

The Macintosh turned the old way of doing things upside down. The user was no longer a slave to the machine. Unlike other computers, the Macintosh was a tool to be used according to the whim and wisdom of the human being at the controls.

At the time that Apple Computer introduced the Macintosh, only a few visionaries had any idea what the new machine could do. The tasks for which it was suited hadn't been invented yet. The software hadn't been written. However, bright and imaginative programmers wrote great software, and entire new industries—such as desktop publishing—were born.

Figure 0.1 An early Macintosh

Ten years and tens of millions of computers later, Apple did it again. In 1994 Apple Computer introduced the Power Macintosh. Like its predecessor, the Power Macintosh has a new, innovative, and phenomenally powerful microprocessor that is a generation beyond anything ever seen in a desktop computer—the PowerPC chip (see Figure 0.2). The tasks for which this kind of power can be used haven't been invented yet. Much software is yet to be written.

Figure 0.2 The PowerPC 601 chip

The PowerPC chip is inside desktop computers that lead the industry in power and performance. Better still, the 601 is just the beginning of a whole family of microprocessors: the PowerPC 603, the second generation 604, and the 64-bit 620 will take the Power Macintosh over the horizon into unexplored territory.

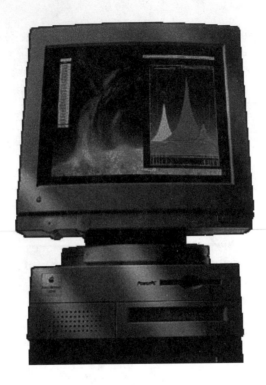

Figure 0.3 The Power Macintosh

No one knows what the Power Macintosh will give us. Somewhere, someone has an idea about how to make a computer do something in a way that no one has ever thought of before. Perhaps that someone is you.

What You Need to Know

There is a lot to learn to become a Macintosh programmer. Unfortunately, most programming books don't give you the big picture. They give you little examples and snippets of code on a wide variety of topics, but they don't show you how everything works together as a cohesive whole.

This approach works fine for expert programmers who want to master some new twist in an environment with which they are already familiar. But it does not work well for beginners trying to learn from scratch. Why? Because putting the pieces together can cause problems. You don't get any guidance in what kinds of problems might arise or how you should solve them.

Programming Starter Kit for Macintosh takes a different approach. As you go through this book, you will write a *complete* application (program) that embodies all of the common features of a good Macintosh program. You will learn and use all the skills and techniques necessary to become a Macintosh programmer. In the process, you will learn a great deal about what the Macintosh is, and why Macintosh software works the way it does.

Assuming you have a Macintosh computer with a CD-ROM drive, everything else you need to become a Macintosh programmer is in this book. The knowledge you need rests between these covers. The software you need is on the accompanying CD-ROM disk. All that's required of you is a willingness to learn. If you've read this far, you have that all-important desire.

To write Macintosh software you need four things:

- A development environment
- Reference materials
- Understanding of the Macintosh operating system—Mac OS
- Knowledge of a programming language

Figure 0.4 What you need

A development environment is the software you use to write software. A typical environment consists of three major components: a text editor to write the code, a compiler to turn that text into object code (a series of numbers the computer understands), and a debugger to test the resulting code to make sure it works correctly.

The CD in the back of this book has a modified version of the CodeWarrior development environment from Metrowerks. Chapter 2 introduces you to CodeWarrior and teaches you how to use it.

Figure 0.5 A CD-ROM disk

No Macintosh programmer gets very far without reference materials. There are many good sources of information about the technical details of programming the Macintosh.

This book includes a handy programmer's reference to each of the Toolbox managers and the calls that you use while writing code for this book. (We'll discuss what the Toolbox is in Chapter 1.) The reference section at the end of most chapters can get you started.

Inside Macintosh is the ultimate source for programming information about the Macintosh. In a real sense, *Inside Macintosh* is the user's guide to the Macintosh Toolbox. At the time of this writing, the *Inside Macintosh* series consists of 26 volumes containing thousands upon thousands of pages. New volumes are added to the series as new features are added to the Mac OS. These volumes are packed with all the nitty-gritty details of how the Macintosh works. The size of *Inside Macintosh* can be intimidating.

The good news is, you don't have to master all of *Inside Macintosh* to be a Macintosh programmer. Because the volumes in the series are organized by topic, you can study those volumes that contain the subjects of interest to you. It is also available in electronic form.

The third item you need to be a Macintosh programmer is an understanding of the Macintosh operating system—Mac OS. That's what this book is all about. By the time you reach the end of this book you'll know quite a lot about Mac OS—the philosophy behind it, what it is, how it's organized, and how to use it.

Figure 0.6 The Toolbox

Finally, you need to know a programming language. The computer code in this book uses the C programming language. Mastering the knowledge in this book will be easier if you already know or are familiar with C.

If you don't know C, don't despair. Although it is certainly harder to learn two things at once, you can learn C while working with this book. I have done three things to make this task easier:

- Use simple C syntax and avoid the strange and hard-to-read kinds of statements you frequently find in C code. I have tried to keep things straightforward and understandable.

- Every time I introduce a feature of the C language for the first time, you'll see a C Note. A C Note discusses the new feature briefly. Best of all, each C Note refers you to the third resource I have provided for you: the "Guide to C."

7

- The "Guide to C" is Appendix A in *Programming Starter Kit for Macintosh*. It gives you an overview of C and covers the features of C used in the book. The guide provides you with the C language information you need to use this book successfully.

With these tools in hand, you can begin solving the puzzle of how to be a Macintosh programmer.

Coding and Typographic Conventions

You encounter a lot of new ideas in this book. I have followed certain conventions whenever possible so that the new ideas you encounter appear in familiar ways. These conventions apply to both the text and the code you work with.

The typographic conventions help to clearly identify various elements in the text so you can more easily understand what's going on.

- All file names are in Helvetica plain, such as main.c.

- File names are followed by .c for source files, and .h for header files, .µ for CodeWarrior project files, and .rsrc for resource files.

- All code is in MCPdigital typeface.

- Function names in the text are followed by parentheses. Function names begin with a capital letter, and each subsequent natural word within the name (if any) begins with a capital letter, such as EasyCheckMemory().

- Macintosh Toolbox calls are in **bold monospace**, such as **GetNewWindow()**.

- Most routines in the EasyApp shell begin with the word "Easy," such as EasyMakeWindow().

- Default or base window behaviors begin with the word "Base," such as BaseScrollWindow().

- The names of variables begin with a lowercase letter. Each subsequent word within the name begins with a capital letter, such as thisWindow.

- The names of constants begin with a lowercase "k," such as kErrorDialogID.

- C functions and calls are in **bold monospace**.

- All code subordinate to a branch or loop appears within brackets, even if there is only one line of code. All brackets appear on separate lines, so they don't get lost. For example:

```
if (foo == 1)
{
SysBeep(30);
}
```

Code lines shown in italic (as is the first line above) indicate code that you have already seen. These lines are included only for reference. The remaining code lines are the ones that you type as you follow along in the exercises.

The coding style followed in this book follows the guidelines in Appendix C. You can refer to that appendix for information on the coding style.

Now and then you'll see icons in the margin of the text. The icons draw your attention to something of interest.

The icon in the margin indicates a C Note. When you encounter some feature of the language for the first time, a C Note refers you to the "Guide to C." If you are new to C, you can go to the guide to learn more about that particular feature of the language. You can read about the concept, and then use it right away. There's no better way to learn a programming language. You'll find more C Notes near the beginning of the book, and fewer towards the end. Of course, if you ever have a question about some feature of the language, you can refer to the "Guide to C" at any time.

This icon shows up for wizard notes. The wizard gives you insight into the subtleties of programming for the Macintosh. The wizard may give you tips and tricks that programming masters use with respect to a particular feature of the Mac. The wizard also knows the dangers facing a sorcerer's apprentice, and will warn you of hazards lurking for the unsuspecting Macintosh magician.

This is the style for notes, which inform you of important information regarding the present topic that doesn't normally come up in the regular discussion.

Overview

When starting a journey, a road map is a useful tool. This final section of the introduction provides you with a brief map of the road you travel while becoming a Macintosh programmer.

In *Programming Starter Kit for Macintosh* you write a complete, full-featured Macintosh application. You do this in two principle stages. In the first few chapters, you write core routines that you can use over and over again in future programming projects.

After you learn and master the core techniques, you write an application named EasyPuzzle that uses those core routines to create a puzzle. The puzzle window displays a picture. You can put any picture you want in the puzzle. You break the picture up into rectangular puzzle pieces, and then move the pieces around to solve the puzzle—complete with sound effects and simple animation.

Figure 0.7 The Cat and Hat

In the process of writing EasyPuzzle, you learn, practice, and master a wide variety of Macintosh programming skills.

To get you warmed up, we start with a little light reading in Chapter 1. This chapter discusses some of the key concepts underlying the Macintosh, and why it is such a cool machine for which to write software.

Chapters 2–5 ensure that you have the basic skills and knowledge necessary to write Macintosh software. Chapter 2 introduces the CodeWarrior environment. In that chapter you will write your first Macintosh program. Chapter 3 introduces the Macintosh memory architecture. Chapter 4 teaches you the joys of ResEdit, and shows you how creating resources can simplify your programs. Chapter 5 makes sure you know how to find and stomp bugs.

Chapters 6–13 teach you the core features of the Mac OS that make a program look and feel like a Macintosh program. Chapter 6 covers events on the Mac, and how to write an event loop. Chapter 7 teaches you how to create and manipulate menus. In Chapter 8, you do windows, and I don't mean that other operating system. Chapter 9 covers controls and scroll bars in a window. Chapter 10 discusses drawing in a window. Chapter 11 tells you everything you need to know about a special kind of window—the dialog box. You learn how to create, manage, and dispose of them. There are some very cool tricks in here; techniques that even some professional programmers don't know about. Chapter 12 talks about feedback—how to tell the user what's going on in a way that is familiar. Chapter 13 shows you how to make your application look cool. You'll want your application to have captivating icons to impress folks.

After that, Chapters 14–19 introduce some really fun features that you'll want to add to your applications. In Chapter 14 you add sounds to your application that play while the computer is busy doing other things. In Chapter 15 you save files to disk and open files. Chapter 16 teaches you how to print documents. Chapters 17–19 show you how to share data between windows and between applications. These chapters introduce you to the future of desktop computing: the free and easy exchange of data transparently and seamlessly in a document-centered environment.

Chapter 20 introduces you to text management in a Macintosh application. You'll learn about TextEdit, fonts, and everything you need to handle simple text.

When you reach the end of this book, you are far from the end of the road. Chapter 21 points you down the highway and shows you some of the routes you might take as you become an expert Macintosh programmer. The Macintosh universe is large and diverse. Chapter 21 also gives you a peek at some of the unexplored territories that are just over the horizon; places that you and the Macintosh will explore tomorrow and in the months and years to come.

Before you get there, you have to take the first step. And that happens when you turn the page.

1

Way Cool: The Macintosh Programming Way

Once upon a time, there was an idea. That idea still grips us today, and has become an ideal. It is a bold, innovative, even radical concept. Like all great ideas, it is really quite simple.

Computers should be easy to use.

The pursuit of this ideal gave birth to the Macintosh. Much has been written about the unique perspective that the Macintosh introduced to the computing world. The decade from 1984 to 1994 saw the rest of the industry first laughing at and then imitating Apple's bold innovations in personal computers.

Those innovations rest upon fundamentally different concepts of how a computer works and how it should be programmed. These concepts attracted some unconventional programmers who thrived on exceeding the known limits. The programmers bring a fresh outlook and a wonderful irreverence with them.

In this chapter, you are introduced to some of the fun of being a Macintosh programmer. Also discussed are several important concepts and assumptions underlying all things Macintosh. These concepts form the foundation of the Macintosh Operating System (Mac OS). Developing an understanding of these concepts is vital if you want to be a good Macintosh programmer. You will learn about events, the Macintosh Toolbox, program resources, and application frameworks.

Like many things in life, *Programming Starter Kit for Macintosh* is circular. When you have completed this book, you may want to read this chapter again. You will have learned a lot by then, and you'll be able to get a lot more out of the following discussion.

Clarus Says "Moof"™

Allow me to introduce a friend of mine. I'd like you to meet Clarus, the dogcow. You can see her picture in Figure 1.1. Do not be dismayed by her pixelated appearance. That's what Clarus looks like. Clarus is, after all, a dogcow.

Clarus is the mascot of Apple's Developer Technical Support and a trademark of Apple Computer. In fact, everything Clarus has ever said is also a trademark.

Clarus can occasionally be seen grazing the lawn at 1 Infinite Loop in Cupertino, CA— the home of Apple's research and development campus. You have to admire a computer company that not only inspires Clarus, but names the location at which it does its leading-edge development work "Infinite Loop."

Clarus is an almost mythical figure in the Macintosh developer community. While many have seen her picture, true sightings of our friend are quite rare. It's rumored that Elvis took lessons from Clarus before going into hiding.

All the same, her presence lives in every Macintosh. Her image was captured by Susan Kare and included in the Cairo font that shipped with the very first Macintosh. She was sighted again and named on October 15, 1987 by Scott "Zz" Zimmerman. He and Mark Harlan made her existence known to the rest of the world.

Since then, Clarus has had important work. If you open the Page Setup dialog for the LaserWriter or some other printers and click the Options button, you'll find Clarus there. She's ready to show you how an image will appear on paper when printed. She'll even stand on her head for you. To quote from official technical documentation, "Like any talented dog, it can do flips. Like any talented cow, it can do precision bitmap alignment."

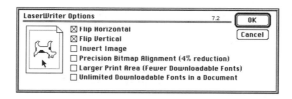

Figure 1.1 Clarus at work and play

It is rumored that she was captured once in a Microsoft advertisement, but she escaped as soon as she could. Scholarly Macintosh programming journals have published articles about Clarus. She has wandered into an official Macintosh technical note. Clarus even has a nest on the Internet's World Wide Web where you can hear her speak and become steeped in dogcow lore.

Because she is two-dimensional, Clarus can face predators head-on to avoid being seen. This may explain why Clarus can fit inside your computer. She might even be standing next to you and yet remain invisible. No wonder Elvis consulted her!

Clarus is female, of course, as are all cows. Mark Harlan wrote in *develop* magazine that "…males would be referred to as dogbulls, but none exist because there are already bulldogs and God doesn't like to have naming problems."

You encounter this light-hearted spirit throughout the Macintosh development community. Some have us believe that Clarus is a semi-official creation of a major corporation. Independent Macintosh programmers know that although she is a trademark, Clarus was discovered, not invented.

This playful spirit is one reason why developing software for the Macintosh is so much fun—the Macintosh developer community is full of renegades. Once a year, the free-spirits gather at a national event that is devoted to hacking (in the best and original sense of the word as it relates to computers). The MacHack conference celebrates independence, original thinking, and elegant solutions to complex problems. Great minds gather in search of the totally cool. More often than not, they find it.

What is it that draws such brilliant and innovative thinkers to the Macintosh? Part of the answer can be found in the design decisions made when Apple developed the original Macintosh.

Events and the Mac

What makes the Macintosh so different from other computers is that, at its heart, the Macintosh is an event-driven machine.

But what does that mean? To answer this question, you have to know something about the internal architecture of the Macintosh.

Take a look at the Macintosh in layers. First, there's the hardware layer. Included in this layer are the mouse, the CPU chip, the sound chip, disk drives, serial ports, and so on. Figure 1.2 illustrates some typical Mac hardware.

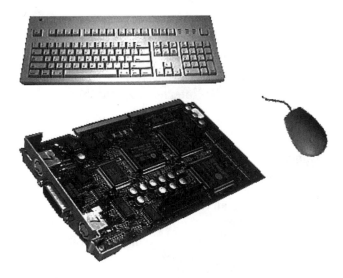

Figure 1.2 The Power Mac 7100/66 AV logic board

Then there is the famous Mac OS that controls this hardware. The operating system is located in the machine's read-only memory (ROM), and in the System file on the startup disk. The Mac OS is what makes the Macintosh look, feel, and act like a Macintosh.

Finally, on top of the hardware and system software are application programs.

Events happen at the hardware level. The user pushes the mouse button, releases the button, moves the mouse, types a key on the keyboard, and so forth. These are the events that drive a Macintosh.

Many computers look for special kinds of events in certain situations. The computer might demand a typed command, for example, to execute some operation. Typically that command must follow a precise—and not always obvious—syntax in order for the machine to work, and it must be typed at just the right moment. In this philosophy, the computer controls both the events and the user.

The Macintosh takes the opposite approach—the events control the computer. The system software communicates constantly with the hardware, taking any event as it happens in the order in which it occurs and lining them up in a queue, as shown in Figure 1.3. It is up to the software to retrieve events from the queue and interpret the event. It is not the user's responsibility to fathom what kind of event the computer requires, or the form in which the computer wants it.

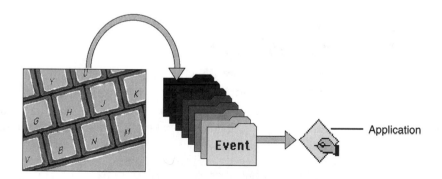

Figure 1.3 The event queue

This fundamental distinction is what makes the Mac friendly, powerful, and unbounded. You can type a key, move the mouse, click and drag, or choose a menu item; and you can do any of these things in any order. Usually you can get the same result by taking one of several different paths. For example, to choose a menu item you can use the mouse or type a keyboard command. Either one gets the job done. This concept is a fundamental in good Macintosh software. A good Mac program lets the user choose from a variety of approaches to get to the goal.

This would seem to make things more difficult for a programmer because you don't know what's going to happen, when, or in what order. This kind of chaos can be frightening or invigorating, depending upon how you look at the situation. That's why the Macintosh attracts a certain breed of programmer.

This is also part of the reason why the Macintosh has a reputation for being a challenging machine to program. This reputation is not entirely deserved, however. It is true that to write good Macintosh software you must follow strict guidelines, jump through all the right hoops, and manage the chaos. But there is another side to this coin, one that will make your life as a Macintosh programmer a *lot* easier.

One of the great advantages of Macintosh software is that most of it behaves in the same manner. Realizing that no two people—including programmers—ever do anything exactly alike, how is it that there is so much similarity in the look and feel of Macintosh programs?

The answer lies in the Mac OS. It incorporates thousands of little pieces of software that you can use to build applications. These functions are the common building blocks that most programmers use to build Mac programs. Taken together, these are called the Macintosh Toolbox.

The Macintosh Toolbox

The Toolbox is the second fundamental distinction between the Macintosh and all that came before it. If being event-driven is the heart of the Macintosh, the Toolbox is its soul. For example, if you want to use a window—and what Macintosh application doesn't—you don't have to write the code from scratch. You use a Toolbox function to create the window for you.

Inside Macintosh, the ultimate Mac reference work, organizes the Toolbox into "Managers." Each Manager is a group of conceptually related functions that focus on one particular aspect of Macintosh programming, such as handling events or working with menus. You will meet several managers in this book.

If you use the Toolbox, you don't have to reinvent the wheel every time you write a program. The Toolbox encompasses the entire Macintosh interface: windows, menus, drawing, and so on. It also provides you with hundreds of behind-the-scenes tools for manipulating data. As you read this book, you learn a lot about the Toolbox, and you will use it extensively. The Toolbox serves as the connection between applications and the operating system. Most of the code that you need to make your program look and feel like a Macintosh program has already been written for you. It's in the Toolbox.

The existence of the Toolbox means two things: Macintosh programs look the same (and thus are easier to use); and your programming efforts are simplified because you have access to a vast array of useful, professional, and thoroughly tested code.

Resources on the Mac

The Macintosh has another technique to make life easier for programmers. On the Mac you can separate program "resources" from program code. Take a brief look at what resources are, and how they are different from data. Resources are discussed in detail in Chapter 4.

A *resource* in this context is a consistent, unique, and structured bit of data used by a program. The concept of a resource is very general and extensible. Resources can be used (and should be used) to describe windows, menus, pictures, icons, buttons, scroll bars, strings of text, and much more. You can even define your own resource types if you wish. Figure 1.4 shows some application resources.

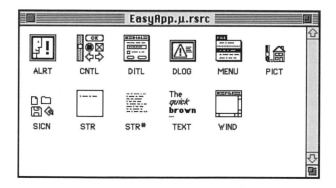

Figure 1.4 Some application resources

Following is an example of why separating resources from program code is useful. Say that at one point in a program you want to display a message to the user. In a traditional computer program, you put the message right into the code of the program. Everything works just fine, but what happens if you ever want to change the text? What if you want to translate your program into French? What if you discover a mistake in the message? What if you decide there are better words to use? You're out of luck. You have to change that little bit of code and then recompile the entire program.

Extend this problem to window definitions, menus, pictures, and so forth. Modifying these things in an old-fashioned program is a nightmare.

However, on the Macintosh you can make the text of that message a resource. A resource is something the program can use repeatedly—in this case every time you need to display the message. Instead of putting the message directly into your code, you write code that gets the resource, and then displays whatever it finds. The Resource Manager is the part of the Mac OS that takes care of resources. It lives up to its name—it manages resources.

What this means to the programmer is that life has become much easier. You can change your program by changing resources, not the controlling code. A well-designed application fetches resources when they are needed, and disposes of them when no longer needed. The content of the resources may change, but the program behaves the same.

So if you find a spelling mistake, you can fix it. If you want to translate your program into French, you can translate the text string resources and leave the code alone. You can even give the user a choice of languages by simply including text in various languages as part of the application's resources. The code that runs the program remains unchanged, but messages may appear in English, French, Spanish, German, Italian, or just about any language you want.

There are special tools in a Macintosh development environment for creating and manipulating resources. The CD accompanying this book includes Apple's own resource editor, ResEdit. You will learn all about resources—what they are and how to use them—as you read this book.

The Application Shell

As you read this book and perform the exercises in the various chapters, you will write a Macintosh application. In the process you are introduced to a fundamental and powerful concept in application programming—the application shell.

Most applications do exactly the same things to support the Macintosh interface. They create and manage windows the same way, respond to menu choices the same way, and so forth. An application shell does all these things, but the windows are empty.

An application shell is like a black box that contains all the generic code you need to create an empty application. You never change the contents of the black box. The shell provides a framework on which you hang your own application's unique behavior. You add your own code and resources to make the application uniquely yours. The shell does the rest of the work. Figure 1.5 illustrates the concept of an application shell.

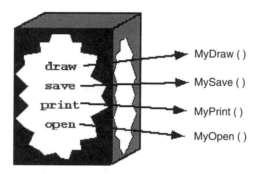

Figure 1.5 The application shell

For example, to make something appear in a window you "draw" it in the window. Take a look at how a shell written in the C language might allow you to draw the contents of your own window.

The shell cannot know in advance what will be in your window or how to draw the contents of your window. It does know *when* to draw based on the events that are happening in the application. But what function does it call?

There must be some connection between the shell and your application. This connection is called a hook function. Every time it is appropriate to draw, the shell calls a drawing "hook" function. In the raw shell, this is an empty function that does nothing because the window has no contents. However, the existence of the hook gives you one place in which you can substitute your own drawing code. Whenever it becomes necessary to draw your window, the shell calls the hook. You make the hook call your own code, and you draw the contents of the window. You don't have to worry about figuring out when to draw.

If this seems a trifle confusing, don't worry. All of this will become clear as you do the coding exercises in *Programming Starter Kit for Macintosh*. In the exercises you will write the code for significant portions of the EasyApp application shell. EasyApp is an educational programming tool designed for this book. Writing the code for EasyApp familiarizes you with the basic tasks a Macintosh program must perform, and how to perform them. This experience is vital and provides necessary background information for any Macintosh programmer.

Because you write EasyApp, you'll be very familiar with its structure and operation. In subsequent chapters you will use EasyApp as the basis for the EasyPuzzle application. Writing EasyPuzzle gives you valuable experience in how to use an application shell.

When you are finished, you will have a neat little puzzle. Better still, you will also have a simple, but fully functional C application shell for the Macintosh. You can use this shell as the basis for other application programming projects. When you gain experience as a Macintosh programmer, you will certainly graduate to a more powerful, commercial application framework. In the meantime, EasyApp should serve you well.

Once you get some experience under your belt, you can experiment with the Glypha III code on the CD to see how a top-notch game is created.

So, let's get to it. Remember to have fun along the way, and keep an eye out for Clarus! You never know when she might show up.

2

Conquering Hero: Becoming a Code Warrior

This chapter introduces you to the CodeWarrior development environment from Metrowerks. If you are already familiar with CodeWarrior, you should still read the sections on installing CodeWarrior and installing the Starter Kit software. You can then skip to Lab 2.1 at the end of the chapter. In that section, you write your first Macintosh application. Don't miss out on the fun.

If CodeWarrior is new to you, read on. CodeWarrior is a marvelous development environment, and you should enjoy learning about it.

Most development systems consist of three elements: a *source code editor,* a *code compiler,* and a *linker.* Most also include a debugger so that you can test the results of your work. The source code editor is the text processor you use when you write source code. The compiler turns that souce code into numbers the computer understands. The linker takes the various pieces of object code and ties them together.

In the bad old days, these various portions of the development system were separate programs, and using them was less than friendly. The pain involved was serious enough that bright software engineers created integrated development environments (IDEs) in which the editor, compiler, and linker are seamless pieces of the same product.

CodeWarrior is such an IDE, and it is one of the friendliest development environments around. In fact, MacUser magazine named it the software product of the year for 1994, a remarkable achievement for a programming tool.

The CD-ROM accompanying *The Macintosh Programming Starter Kit* contains a limited version of CodeWarrior. (From now on the CD-ROM will be referred to simply as "the CD.") The full CodeWarrior package includes compilers for the 68K Macintosh (those that use the Motorola 680x0 series processor) and the Power Macintosh in three languages: C, C++, and Pascal. It includes a full-featured C++ application framework for the Macintosh called PowerPlant. In addition, CodeWarrior comes with a wide variety of useful programming tools and example code.

The limited edition on the CD is missing some of these extras, but it does include everything you need to build and run the projects in this book. To familiarize you with CodeWarrior, this chapter covers the following topics:

- Installing CodeWarrior
- Installing the Starter Kit software
- Launching CodeWarrior
- Using the toolbar

- Using the project window

- Creating and editing source code

- Compiling source code

- Running with the debugger

After that, you write your first Macintosh application.

Installing CodeWarrior

First, make sure you have what it takes to run CodeWarrior. CodeWarrior comes in two flavors, one for the 68K Mac and one for the Power Mac.

Metrowerks CodeWarrior requires a Motorola 68020, 68030, or 68040, or PowerPC processor; 8 megabytes (M) of RAM; System 7.1 or later (for 68K-based Macintosh computers) or System 7.1.2 or later (for Power Macintosh computers); and a CD-ROM drive to install the software. For optimum performance, Metrowerks recommends that you use a Macintosh equipped with a 68030, 68040, or PowerPC microprocessor.

You can install CodeWarrior using one of two methods. On the CD, there is a file named CWInstaller. This utility installs everything you need. This is the simpler method, and the one I recommend you take. You will need 15M to 20M of free space on your hard drive for all the various elements of the package.

If you have limited hard drive space, you can install the software manually. You must make sure you install everything you need. Both of these approaches are covered in detail in the following text.

note
If you have the full version of CodeWarrior, follow the installation instructions that came with it.

Running CWInstaller

Put the CD in your CD-ROM drive, and then follow these steps:

1. When the icon appears on the Desktop, double-click it, opening a window that displays the CD's contents.

2. Locate the CWInstaller icon inside this window. Double-click its icon.

3. The CWInstaller program launches. An opening screen appears. Click the Continue button.

4. You should then see a second screen with last-minute information about CodeWarrior. You should read this information to be aware of any changes in the product or the installation process that might affect you.

5. When you are through reading the text, click the Continue button in this window. A third window appears (see Figure 2.1). The window may differ slightly from the illustration.

6. Click the Install button and you're on your way.

Figure 2.1 The CWInstaller window

Installing CodeWarrior Manually

This installation requires less disk space. The automatic installation installs both the 68K and Power Mac versions of CodeWarrior. If you install manually, you can pick the one you want.

The 68K version compiles code for 68K Macs. However, it runs on both the 68K Mac and Power Mac. Similarly, the Power Mac version compiles native code for Power Macintosh computers. It also runs on either a 68K or a Power Macintosh. So, pick the version that compiles code for your kind of machine. That way you can run your application and test your work.

If you are working on a 68K Macintosh, copy the MW C/C++ 68K folder to your hard drive. If you are working on a Power Macintosh, copy the MW C/C++ PPC folder to your hard drive.

After you have done that, you must install some software in your system folder. Open the folder that you copied onto your hard drive.

For the 68K Mac, locate the file named DebuggerINIT. Put that in the Extensions folder inside your system folder. If you are using System 7.1, also install the Macintosh Drag and Drop extension in the Extensions folder.

For the Power Mac, you have several files to install. Put the following file inside the Extensions folder in your system folder:

- ObjectSupportLib

If you are using System 7.1, also install these files inside the Extensions folder:

- Macintosh Drag and Drop
- PPCTraceEnabler

Finally, install Power Mac DebugServices in the Startup Items folder of your Macintosh.

Then, restart your Macintosh. That's it.

Installing the Starter Kit Software

As you read this book, you will write a real Macintosh application. All the code you need to write this application is on the CD, but you must put some of this code on your hard drive. Before copying the files, you should understand how *Programming Starter Kit for Macintosh* structures your coding.

As you read the chapters in this book, you build an application sequentially. In each chapter you learn something new about the Macintosh. Each chapter has one or more "lab exercises" that give you step by step instructions explaining the code you must write to implement the new features. Because you build the application sequentially, most of the time you build on your own code from lab to lab.

However, you will not write every single line of code necessary to complete the application. There are a few occasions when you start a lab with new code. In each case the instructions in the lab tell you whether to use your code from the previous lab or to use brand new start code. There are three reasons why you get new start code from time to time:

- The early labs are kept as simple as possible. About half-way through the book, however, you have learned enough to start doing some complicated things. At that time some additional support code is introduced. Rather than having the additional code confuse you at the beginning, you get it for free later.

- A lot of the code has nothing to do with programming the Macintosh. This code relates to generic programming problems and solutions, such as list management and the like. Because this book concentrates on Macintosh programming, for the most part you will write code related to the Mac OS, and not the ancillary code.

- After you learn something and implement it once or twice, it doesn't make a lot of sense to do the same thing over again. The code in any computer program has a lot of redundancy, and forcing you to type code that deals with topics you have already mastered is a waste of your time. *Programming Starter Kit for Macintosh* should be a fun learning experience, not drudgery.

For example, in Chapter 11 you will learn how to create and manage a dialog box. Later on in the book, if you need to add a dialog box to implement a new feature the necessary code is given to you. Why? Because you already know how to do it, and you should put your efforts into the new material.

Just remember, when the instructions tell you to use new start code, go get it. Simply copy the entire start code folder to your hard drive. This happens in Chapters 3, 10, and 20. In addition, Chapters 2 and 5 have nothing to do with the work of writing EasyApp or EasyPuzzle, so they have separate start code as well.

To implement this approach, each chapter has two sets of code: the start code on which you build and the solution code. The solution code is what your code should look like after you are through with the chapter. This gives you an "answer" to look at. You can check your work against the solution code if something doesn't work exactly right.

Because you learn new features in each chapter, *the start code for a chapter may not be identical to the solution code for the previous chapter*. Therefore, when it comes time to write code in a chapter, you need to use the start code *for that chapter*.

You can copy all the start code over to your hard drive at once, or you can copy the code one chapter at a time, as you need it. You do not need to copy the solution code to your hard drive. The solution code is just a reference. You will not modify or add to the solution code at any time.

On the CD there are two code-related folders. One is titled MPSK Code (68K). The other is titled MPSK Code (Power Mac). Choose the folder that matches the version of CodeWarrior you use.

Inside either folder there are two more folders: MPSK Start Code and MPSK Solution Code. Copy the MPSK Start Code folder to your hard drive. If you do not have room for all the start code, you can copy individual chapters from inside the MPSK Start Code folder as you begin each chapter. Instructions in each chapter remind you to use the start code for that chapter.

{

The 68K Code versus the Power Mac Code

The source code for each kind of Macintosh is identical. However, each start code folder contains two CodeWarrior project files. One project file was created using the 68K version of CodeWarrior and includes a library of 68K code for the Mac OS. The other was created with the Power Mac version and includes several libraries of support code for the Power Mac architecture.

Future versions of CodeWarrior may combine both 68K and Power Mac versions into a single application. You should still be able to open the project you want to use, either 68K or Power Mac.

}

The CD has a folder titled **MPSK Code**. If you look inside that folder you see folders for each chapter. Inside each chapter's folder is the code for the lab or labs in that chapter. There may be a start code folder. For each lab exercise there will be a file titled Step Code and a solution code folder.

The Step Code files contain code snippets that complete each particular step in the lab. If typing code is not your idea of fun, you can open this file to copy and paste the code into the lab in the locations specified by the instructions. You will learn more by actually typing the code. However, for long steps or complicated code, you may want to just copy the code from the Step Code file.

Each lab exercise also has a solution code folder. The solution code is what your code should look like after you are through with the chapter. This gives you an "answer" to look at. You can check your work against the solution code if something doesn't go exactly right.

If your code gets hopelessly messed up or you feel like skipping a chapter, you can use the previous lab's solution code as the start code for the next lab—unless that lab has a new start code, in which case you use the new start code.

In addition to the code you write, there are some programming tools you will need. Locate the Tools You Need folder on the CD and copy it to a convenient location on your hard drive. Along with some other tools, inside this folder are

- ResEdit—a resource editing tool
- ZoneRanger—a memory inspection tool

You use these tools at various times as you read this book.

Launching CodeWarrior

The moment has arrived at last. Inside the CodeWarrior folder, locate the icon for CodeWarrior, which is shown in Figure 2.2. The name of the file is either MW C/C++ PPC 1.2 or MW C/C++ 68K 1.2. Double-click the icon to launch CodeWarrior.

MW C/C++ PPC 1.2

Figure 2.2 The CodeWarrior icon

Reading this chapter will not make you an expert code warrior, but it does give you an overview of CodeWarrior's features. CodeWarrior usually has several paths to the same goal, and you get to decide which path best matches the way you like to work.

note   The illustrations in this chapter are derived from the full Power Mac version. The limited edition on the CD—either 68K or Power Mac—should be essentially identical.

When CodeWarrior launches, no window appears. It waits for you to open something. However, a toolbar appears and the menus change to reflect the many choices available in the CodeWarrior environment.

The Preferences item in the Edit menu allows you to open a series of dialog boxes to set your operating preferences for the source code editor, the linker, the project file, and many other features. You use some of these dialogs in the coding lab for this chapter and in subsequent lab exercises.

Using the Toolbar

The Toolbar is a series of small icons or buttons that correspond to various commands that you can issue in CodeWarrior. To see what each button does, just put the cursor over the icon. A description of the button appears in the area below the icons. When you click the button, the command executes. For example, in the Toolbar shown in Figure 2.3, you can click the Compile button to compile code.

Below the row of icons is the *status display*. CodeWarrior uses this area to keep you up-to-date with what's happening. When you compile code, for example, CodeWarrior displays the number of lines compiled. The status display is very useful to see how things are going in the environment.

Figure 2.3 The Toolbar

You can also modify the Toolbar to suit your own personal preferences. To delete an item from the Toolbar, press Control-⌘ and click the icon. To add an icon to the Toolbar, press Control-⌘ while choosing that item in the menu. To remove all the icons from the Toolbar (turning it into a plain status bar) press the Shift key and choose the Clear Toolbar item from the Tools menu.

Normally, the Toolbar appears automatically and is anchored to the position at the top left of the window (just under the menu bar). Using selections in the Tools menu (see Figure 2.4), you can modify this behavior to suit your fancy. You can even make the Toolbar go away.

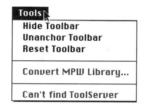

Figure 2.4 The Tools menu

The designers of CodeWarrior followed good human interface principles when creating the program. If you don't like clicking icons in the Toolbar to get things done, you have other options. You can choose items in menus, or use command-key combinations to execute many CodeWarrior commands.

Using the Project Window

CodeWarrior is a project-based environment (what that means will become clear in just a minute). Open a project to see what one looks like.

You can open a project in two ways. You can double-click a project icon, or you can choose the Open item from the File menu. When you choose the Open item, an Open File dialog box appears, as shown in Figure 2.5.

2

The Open File dialog box allows you to open either a project or a source file. You choose which type of file to open by clicking the icons at the bottom of the dialog box. The icon on the left is the project icon. The icon on the right is the source-file icon. Figure 2.5 shows the project icon selected, and a project available for opening.

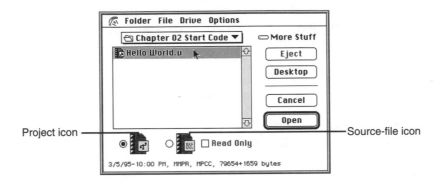

Figure 2.5 The Open File dialog

Navigate to the Lab 02.1 Start Code folder on your hard drive. Two Hello World.µ project files should appear in the dialog box. Double-click the name or click the Open button to open the project appropriate for your machine, either the 68K version or the Power Mac version. When you do, a project window appears as shown in Figure 2.6.

> The funny character at the end of the name is the "Option-m" character in most typefaces. This is a CodeWarrior naming convention. All project file names should end with this character.

File	Code	Data		
▽ **Sources**	**1K**	**317**	•	▽
HelloWorld.c	1052	317	•	▷
▽ **Resources**	**0**	**0**		▽
HelloWorld.µ.rsrc	n/a	n/a		▷
▽ **Libraries**	**3K**	**810**		▽
InterfaceLib	0	0		▷
MWCRuntime.lib	3492	810		▷

4 file(s)	4K	1K

Figure 2.6 A project window

The title of the window corresponds to the name of the project file. The project file consolidates all the source, header, library, and object code files that are used when you develop a program. Don't worry if you are unfamiliar with any of these terms. They will become clear as you continue.

n
o
t
e

> You may have only one project open at a time. If you open another project, the project that is open is automatically closed and added to the Project Switch List submenu in the CodeWarrior Window menu.

The project window is a busy place. Just below the title are some column headings: File, Code, Data, and two little icons. At the rightmost part of the project window, there is a tiny popup menu. Figure 2.7 identifies the function of each of the various parts of the project window.

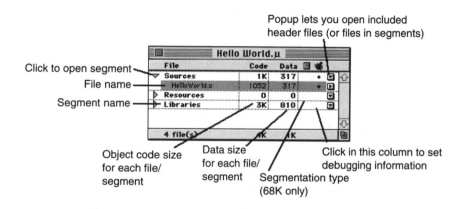

Figure 2.7 The Project window parts

In the File column are segments and files. Segment names are bold, file names are plain text. Files are grouped into segments. On the Power Macintosh, this is purely aesthetic. You can group files according to whatever pattern seems best to you. The segmentation has no effect on the final code. On a 68K Mac, segments are real. 68K segments are discussed in Chapter 4.

You can change the name of a segment by double-clicking its name. A dialog box appears that allows you to enter the new name.

At the far right of the window, each line has a tiny popup menu. If you click the popup menu for a segment, the menu lists every source file in the segment. You can open a file by choosing it from this menu. Figure 2.8 shows the file popup menu.

If you click the popup menu when a file is selected, you see that the first item in the menu is the Touch item. The menu then lists every header file included in that source file. You can open a header file by choosing it from this menu. If you choose the Touch item, the compiler will recompile the file the next time you update the code. If the file has not yet been compiled, the only item will read "Has to be compiled."

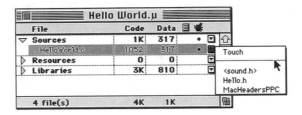

Figure 2.8 A file popup menu

For more information about header files, consult the "Header Files and Source Files" section in Appendix A.

Just to the left of the popup menus in the project window is the debugging column. If there is a dot in this column, the linker generates debugging information for the file. You can turn debugging information on or off at the file or segment level. Debugging is discussed in detail in Chapter 5.

You select a file by clicking its name in the project window. You select multiple files by Shift-clicking a file name while another file is selected. You can select discontiguous files by ⌘-clicking the file name.

You can move files between segments by dragging selected files to the segment where you want them to be. If you want to create a new segment, drag the file or files to the empty part of the project below any existing segment.

In the limited version of CodeWarrior on the CD, you cannot add or remove files from a project. In the full version, you can add files to a segment by choosing the Add Files item in the Project menu. This opens a dialog box that allows you to add several files to a project simultaneously. You may remove selected files by choosing the Remove Files item in the Project menu.

Creating and Editing Source Code

Of course, when you are writing a program you must write some actual code at some point. CodeWarrior, being an integrated development environment, provides you with a text editor designed with the features most programmers want.

The Editor Window

To see the Editor, you must open a file. You may open a source file in five ways:

- Click the Open icon in the Toolbar
- Choose the Open item in the File menu
- Choose the file from the segment's popup menu
- Press Return when the file is selected in the project window
- Double-click the file's name in the project window

Open the Hello World.c file now so you can explore the CodeWarrior Editor.

> A word about source file names. A C source-file name must end with the ".c" extension. This identifies the file as containing C source code. Without the extension, CodeWarrior won't even let you add the file to a project.

When you open the file, a fairly typical Macintosh window appears containing some text. You are now looking at the CodeWarrior Editor, shown in Figure 2.9. It has some very nice features.

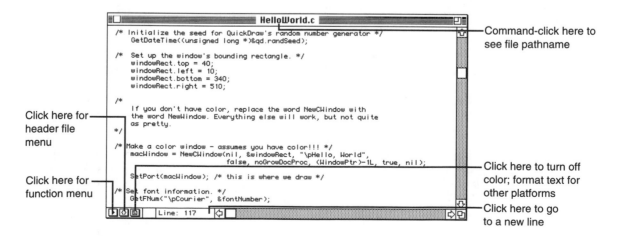

Figure 2.9 The Editor window

If you are working on a color monitor, the first thing you'll notice is that the code text is in color! This is a big help in understanding a program because color conveys a tremendous amount of information. You can set the colors by choosing the Preferences item in the Edit menu and selecting the Editor group of options. The default settings show comments in red, keywords in blue, custom keywords in green, and code in black.

> Keywords are words reserved for use by the C language. For more information about keywords, consult the "Introduction" section in Appendix A.

Navigating the Code

The Editor has some excellent navigation features.

At the lower-left corner are three popup menus. The arrow popup on the left is identical to the project window popup. It lists the included header files, and allows you to Touch the file to notify the compiler that the file has to be recompiled.

The popup menu with braces is the Function menu. This menu lists all of the source file's functions in the order of appearance in the file (see Figure 2.10). If you Option-click this popup, the names appear in alphabetical order. This tool is invaluable for rapid and painless navigation through a source file. Simply choose the function you want to see from the popup menu, and the Editor jumps to that function's name.

> Functions are C subroutines. If you don't know what a function is, consult the "What Is a Function?" section in Appendix A.

The rightmost popup menu lets you turn color off, and allows you to format the text for Macintosh, DOS, or UNIX environments.

You can also jump to a specific line of code if you wish. At the bottom of the window, a small panel tells you the line of code where the insertion point is located. If you click that panel, a dialog box appears that allows you to type in the line number to which you want to move.

Text that you enter appears at the insertion point. Pressing an arrow key moves the cursor one character left or right, or one line up or down. If you press Option and type an arrow key, you move left or right one word, or up or down one page of text. If you press ⌘ and type an arrow key, you move to the beginning or end of the line, or you move to the beginning or end of the file. If you press the Shift key for any such operation, all the text between the beginning and ending locations of the insertion point is selected.

The CodeWarrior editor also has the usual text-selection features. You click to set the insertion point, double-click to select a word, and triple-click to select a paragraph of text—in the code editor, one line of code.

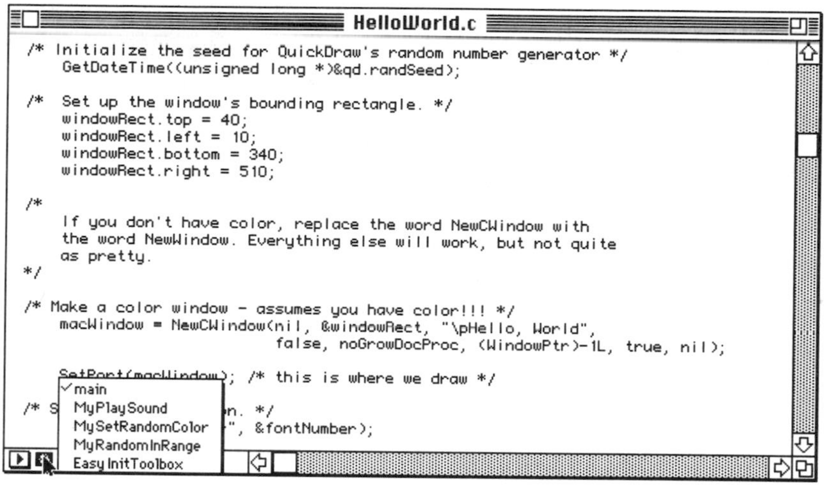

Figure 2.10 The function popup menu

Entering Code

Entering code is as simple as typing. However, the line does not automatically break after a certain number of characters or when you reach the edge of the window. Lines break only when you press the Return or Enter key. For long source lines, you sometimes have to scroll off to the right to see the end of the line. In the source code accompanying *Programming Starter Kit for Macintosh*, the lines should typically be short enough to fit in a standard-width window.

There is nothing in the C language that says a command must fit on one line. You will often see examples in the code for *Programming Starter Kit for Macintosh* where code has been broken manually so it doesn't extend too far to the right.

Likewise, there is nothing in C that says a line may have only one statement. You can enter multiple statements on a single line. However, having multiple statements per line makes the code harder to read. You won't see it done in this book. Having multiple commands also makes it harder to set breakpoints in the debugger, because you can set only one breakpoint to a line. If there are multiple statements on a line, you can't break on the individual commands. Breakpoints and the debugger are discussed a little later in this chapter.

Find and Replace

The editor has powerful search and replace features. The options are in the Search menu, as shown in Figure 2.11. Choose the Find item in the Search menu to access some powerful find and replace features for single or batch searches.

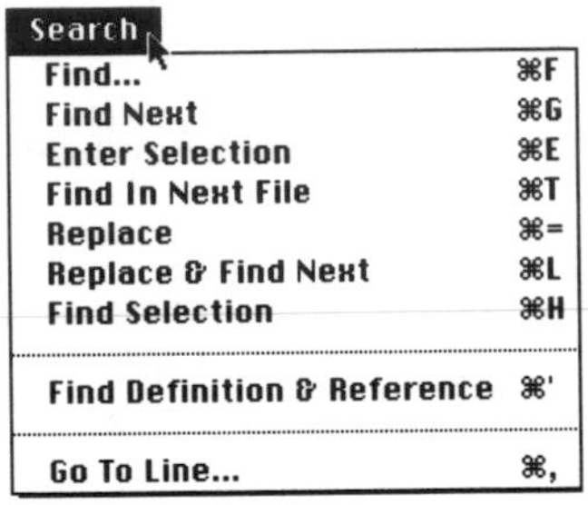

Search	
Find...	⌘F
Find Next	⌘G
Enter Selection	⌘E
Find In Next File	⌘T
Replace	⌘=
Replace & Find Next	⌘L
Find Selection	⌘H
Find Definition & Reference	⌘'
Go To Line...	⌘,

Figure 2.11 The Search menu

When you choose the Find item in the Search menu, the Find dialog box appears (see Figure 2.12). You enter the search string in the Find box, and then click the Find button. You may search in the current file, or in many files. If you want to search in many files, you can choose all the project source files, header files, or system headers with a click of the mouse.

One marvelous feature is that you can click the Others button at the bottom right of the dialog to select individual or groups of files in which to search, no matter where they are. This is extremely useful if you want to search in Apple's universal headers for the location of a function prototype for a particular Toolbox call.

Another marvelous feature is the capability to save sets of files and switch between them at will. Click the File Sets popup menu, and you can add or remove file sets.

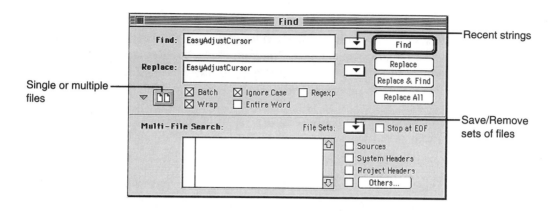

Single or multiple files

Recent strings

Save/Remove sets of files

Figure 2.12 The Find dialog box

If you enable the Batch checkbox, CodeWarrior reports all finds in a single message window. The Message window displays compiler errors, warnings, and notes (see Figure 2.13). The three checkboxes along the top of the message window allow you to control which of these messages appear. The results of a find operation appear as notes.

Figure 2.13 The Message window

Figure 2.13 shows the result of a batch search for the name EasyAdjustCursor. After you have found what you are looking for, getting to the actual text is simple. You can accomplish that goal using one of three methods. Select a note and press the Return key. You can double-click a note. Or you can use the arrow buttons at the top right of the message window. Whichever technique you use, CodeWarrior jumps immediately to the line of code in the correct source file.

If you want to replace the search string in the Find dialog box, enter the replacement text in the Replace section. If you turn off batch searching, CodeWarrior goes to each item it finds and allows you to replace the item. If you click the Replace All button, CodeWarrior automatically replaces every appearance of the search text with the replacement text. This is both powerful and dangerous.

Pay close attention to the Ignore Case and Entire Word checkboxes in the Find dialog. They allow you to narrow your search to the precise word or text you wish to replace.

Finally, the Wrap checkbox controls where CodeWarrior searches in a file. If the Wrap checkbox is disabled, the search starts at the insertion point and goes to the end of the file. If you are halfway through a file when you start searching, the top half of the file is not searched. If the Wrap checkbox is enabled, CodeWarrior goes back to the beginning and searches the whole file.

Balancing

C syntax frequently requires the use of braces (the { and } marks), brackets (the [and] marks), and parentheses. These must balance. That is, for every open brace, bracket, or parenthesis, there must be a close brace, bracket, or parenthesis. If they do not balance, the code will not compile.

The Editor automatically scans your code as you type to make sure you balance your punctuation. When you type a close punctuation mark, the editor flashes the corresponding open punctuation mark. If it cannot find one, it beeps. Before long, you will become adept at listening for the beep and fixing the balance problem immediately. Many programmers love this feature. Others hate it. CodeWarrior lets you turn it off in the Preferences, if you wish.

Wherever the insertion point is located in the code, the Balance item in the Edit menu (⌘-B) selects all the code between the nearest braces. You can use this item to help you find where your braces begin and end. If you choose Balance again, the next level out becomes selected. Figure 2.14 illustrates what happens.

You can also double-click any delimiter (parenthesis, brace, bracket) and CodeWarrior highlights the code up to the balancing delimiter.

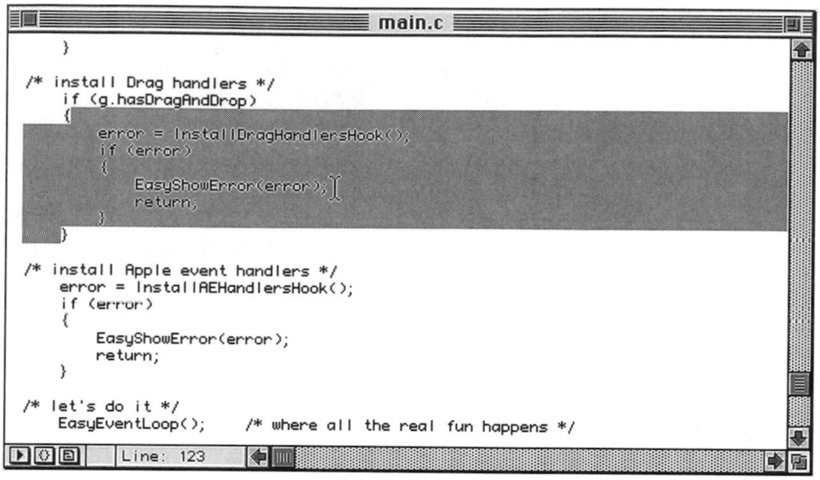

```
┌─────────────────────────────────── main.c ───────────────────────────────┐
│         }                                                                 │▲│
│  /* install Drag handlers */                                              │ │
│     if (g.hasDragAndDrop)                                                 │ │
│     {                                                                     │ │
│         error = InstallDragHandlersHook();                                │ │
│         if (error)                                                        │ │
│         {                                                                 │ │
│             EasyShowError(error);                                         │ │
│             return;                                                       │ │
│         }                                                                 │ │
│     }                                                                     │ │
│                                                                           │ │
│  /* install Apple event handlers */                                       │ │
│     error = InstallAEHandlersHook();                                      │ │
│     if (error)                                                            │ │
│     {                                                                     │ │
│         EasyShowError(error);                                             │ │
│         return;                                                           │ │
│     }                                                                     │ │
│                                                                           │ │
│  /* let's do it */                                                        │ │
│     EasyEventLoop();        /* where all the real fun happens */          │▼│
│ ▶ ◊ ▤  Line: 123     ◀ ▥                                                   │ │
└───────────────────────────────────────────────────────────────────────────┘
```

Figure 2.14 The effect of the Balance command

Compiling Source Code

Assuming you have your source code written and ready to go, you must compile the code to turn it into an application. Compilers are a gift, and developers who write compilers deserve a special place in programmer heaven. The compiler reads source code and creates "object code." Object code is the machine-level bits and bytes that the Macintosh understands. When your application runs, it is the object code that is running.

Before you compile, you may want to check your code's syntax. You can do that by choosing the Check Syntax item (⌘-semicolon) from the Project menu. The compiler goes through the code for the active editor window without actually creating any object code. However, if there are problems, the compiler will find them and alert you to them. You can then fix them before compiling.

The compiler is so fast, however, that checking syntax doesn't save you much time. You can simply compile, and the compiler will find the same mistakes and tell you about them.

Compiling Files

You can compile individual files, or you can update an entire project.

There are two ways to select an individual file to compile. You can select the file in the project window, and choose the Compile item (⌘-K) in the Project menu. Or you can make the file the active window and choose Compile.

To update the entire project, choose the Bring Up To Date item (⌘-U) in the Project menu. The compiler will compile every file in the project that needs updating.

The CodeWarrior project keeps track of the state of all the files in the project. The compiler will update only files that have changed. If the file has not been changed, the compiler skips it.

Forcing an Update

Occasionally, the project data may become confused and not realize that a file has been changed. You can mark a file as changed by "touching" it. Again, there are two ways you can do this. The simplest way is to click the popup menu to the right of the file's name in the project window, and choose the Touch item. Or you can open the file, make a do-nothing change (like add and delete a space), and save the file.

Object Code

After the compiler is through, the linker hooks all the object code from all the different source files together. The linker is very smart. If some code within a source file is never used, it does not include that code in the project.

The project stores the resulting object code (also known as "binaries") in the project. You may want to remove the object code for some reason. For example, you may want to force a complete rebuild of a project.

To remove the object code, choose the Remove Binaries item (⌘-hyphen) in the Project menu. CodeWarrior will ask you to confirm your request, because if you remove the binaries you must recompile the entire project before running it again.

Running with the Debugger

No application works right the first time. Even if it did, you wouldn't know that unless you tested it. The only safe way to test an application is to run it with a debugger. The CodeWarrior debugger is a separate application, but it meshes almost seamlessly. You may forget that the debugger is really a separate application. There are different versions of the debugger for the 68K Mac and the Power Mac.

The 68K version requires the DebuggerINIT file in the Extensions folder inside your system folder. The Power Mac version of CodeWarrior requires that the application Power Mac DebugServices be running. The best way to ensure that it is running is to put the application (or an alias) in the Startup Items folder inside the System folder. The automatic installer puts the right software in the right places for your kind of Macintosh. You cannot tell whether Power Mac DebugServices is running by looking at the Application menu at the right of the menu bar, because it is a faceless background application. It can never be brought forward and has no public interface.

One last detail. For the debugger to work correctly, it must have a "symbol" file. Choose the Preferences item in the CodeWarrior Edit menu, and select the Linker options. The linker generates the symbol file if you have the Generate SYM File option on for the linker.

Assuming that everything has been installed correctly, using the debugger is simple. Choose the Enable Debugging item in the Project menu. Then run the project.

To run your project, choose the Run item (⌘-R) in the Project menu. If debugging is enabled—and it should be—the electrons spin for a moment and then two windows appear.

> By the way, because the debugger is a separate application, you can use it even when CodeWarrior is not running! Just launch it like any application or double-click a SYM file.

The Debugger Window

The front window is the debugger window. The other window is discussed in a little while.

The window has three panes. The calling chain occupies the top-left pane. The calling chain is the list of functions that you have passed through to get to where you are in the code. The top-right pane of the debugger window contains the variables that are in scope for this function. The local variables are at the top; global and other variables come next.

> Variables that are in scope are those that the function can use. For more information about variable scope, consult the "Data Scope" section in Appendix A.

note

The bottom half of the debugger window displays your code. Figure 2.15 shows the debugger window.

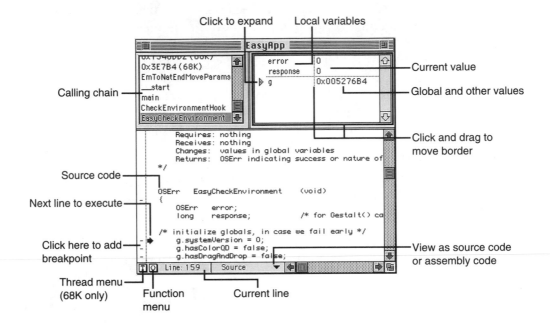

Figure 2.15 The debugger window

If you click and drag the double lines between panes, you can resize the panes to give one or another more room. There is a vertical dotted line inside the variable pane, between the names of the variables and their values—you can click and drag this line sideways to give one or the other more room.

The single dark arrow on the left side of the code section points to the line of code that executes next. If you click the little dash in the leftmost column, you set a breakpoint. The code will stop automatically at a breakpoint.

Along the bottom of the debugger window are some familiar-looking controls. The Thread popup menu works only for 68K Macs. The code in this book does not use the Thread Manager Toolbox routines. To the right of that is your friend the Function popup menu. To the right of that is the line number for the current line of code.

The rightmost control along the bottom of the debugger window lets you choose how you want to see your code. You can switch between looking at source code and looking at the same code in assembly. If you use the 68K version of CodeWarrior, you will see 68K assembly code. If you use the Power Mac version of CodeWarrior, you will see PPC assembly code in all of its glory.

Navigating Code in the Debugger

When you are working with a project in the debugger, you can do a lot of things with the code. The Control menu has the principal commands. There is also a Toolbar with buttons to accomplish the same tasks, shown in Figure 2.16.

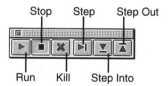

Figure 2.16 The debugger Toolbar

You can run the code, stop the code, or kill the code entirely. The Run item (⌘-R) starts the project running, just as if it was a real application (which, in fact, it is).

The Stop item (⌘-period) interrupts the application temporarily. The Kill item (⌘-K) terminates the application. The debugger is still running, but the application process is now dead. This allows you to return to CodeWarrior and change your code, update it, and run it again.

note   When you are stopped in code, you may want to proceed one line at a time to keep a close eye on what's happening. The Step Over item (⌘-S) in the Control menu lets you do just that.

The line of code about to execute may make a function call. Sometimes you want to go into the function to see what happens, sometimes you don't. The Step Over item doesn't *skip* the function call. It runs that code and then stops at the next line, so you do not see the code inside the called function.

If you want to go *into* a function when stepping, choose the Step Into item (⌘-T). For a mnemonic to help remember the command-key combination, think of this command as going *to* a function.

If you are in a function and want to get back out quickly, choose the Step Out item (⌘-U). Think of this command-key combination as meaning "Up" (because you're going back up the calling chain) and you'll remember it easily.

When you are trying to figure out what is going on in a function, many times it helps to see where you came from. The CodeWarrior debugger has a marvelous feature to help you with this. If you click the name of a function in the calling chain (in the top-left pane of the debugger window), the source code changes to that function, right at the call that took you to your breakpoint. Better still, all the local variables reflect the state of the application while it was in that function. Sometimes the local variables are unavailable, but most of the time you can see them all. This is rather like a magic window into the past. You can jump back to where you came from and see exactly what was going on while you were there. You can jump back to any function in the calling chain.

You can use the function popup menu to see the source code for any other function in the same source file. This does not change the next line of code that will execute, but it does let you see some other part of the code.

You can skip code in a function or go back and repeat code. Click and drag the statement arrow to the line you want to execute. Doing things out of order or repeating things can be helpful, but it may also cause unexpected results. If the code you skip or repeat depends on the normal flow of events, you could crash big time. Be careful.

Viewing Data

The controls for displaying data are, appropriately, in the Data menu of the debugger. The data pane in the debugger window lists all the variables available to the function, and their values.

The debugger is pretty smart about how you want to see the data. A variable is always of a particular data type, and the debugger displays the data as that type. If you want the debugger to actually show the name of the data type along with the name of the variable, choose the Show Types item from the Data menu.

For more information about data types, see the "Basic Data Types" section in Appendix A.

You do not have to accept the debugger's judgment, however. You can tell the debugger to display your data in the form you desire: decimal, unsigned decimal, or hexadecimal. You can view it as a Pascal or C string, or a floating point number, along with a few other options.

If you want to see the value of a single variable, you don't have to use the variable pane. Sometimes the particular variable that you want may be scrolled off the pane and difficult to find. In a pinch, you can select the variable name in the source code pane, and then choose the Copy To Expression item (⌘-D) in the Data menu. This opens a window for that variable and its value.

Some variables have a triangle control to the left of the name. This triangle indicates that the variable is a pointer to data, or is a structure of some kind. If you click the triangle, the variable "opens up" to display its contents. If it is a pointer, you can see what it points to. If it is a structure, you can see its fields.

> A structure is a data type in C. A pointer is the address of a variable in memory. For more information about structures, see the "Structs and Typedefs" section in Appendix A. For more information about pointers, see the "Pointers" section in Appendix A.

In Figure 2.17, the variable named theEvent is an EventRecord. This is a structure defined for the Macintosh. (Events and EventRecords are discussed in detail in Chapter 6.) By clicking the triangle and expanding the data, you can see the various fields of an EventRecord and their values. The fields include: what, message, when, where, and modifiers. The where field is also a structure that you could expand.

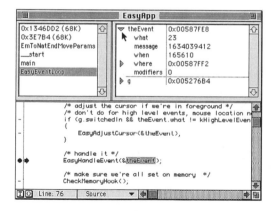

Figure 2.17 Viewing fields in a struct

Rather than viewing the data within the confines of the variable pane of the debugger window, you can open data in its own window. You can choose the Open Variable Window item in the Data menu, or double-click the variable name. Either way, a window appears displaying that data. This can be very useful when a structure has many members and they don't all fit conveniently in the variable pane.

You can even change the value of a variable if you wish. This can be very useful when a value is causing problems. To change the value of a variable, double-click the value (not the name). The displayed value becomes an editable text box in which you can enter whatever value you want. Like all powerful tools, this can be very dangerous. The value you enter may cause more problems than the value you are replacing.

Setting Breakpoints

Frequently you want your program to stop just before a particular location that you suspect causes problems. You can set breakpoints in the debugger window at places where you would like to stop. Notice that there is a dash to the left of each line of code in the debugger window. To set a breakpoint, click the dash for the line of code at which you want to stop. A large dot appears (a red ball or "stop sign" on color monitors), indicating that the debugger will stop there. Figure 2.18 illustrates this process.

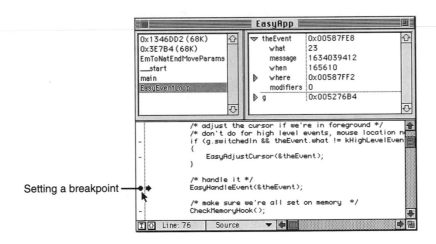

Figure 2.18 Setting a breakpoint

If you press Option and click to set a breakpoint, the application will run until that line of code is encountered and then stop, but no breakpoint appears. Option-clicking sets a temporary break that stops the application once.

When you quit the application or the debugger, breakpoints are saved. The next time you run the application, the same breakpoints are there. The only time this fails is if you change the source code where the breakpoint lives. In that case, CodeWarrior warns you that one or more breakpoints could not be restored.

Like just about everything else in the CodeWarrior environment, there are lots of other options. The most powerful of these is the SYM window. This is the second debugger window.

The SYM Window

The SYM window (see Figure 2.19) has the name of the project, followed by the extension ".xSYM" for Power Macs or ".SYM" for 68K code. This is the symbol file that the linker generates if you choose the Generate SYM File option in the project's linker preferences.

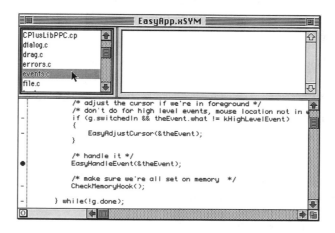

Figure 2.19 The SYM window

The top-left pane of the SYM window contains the names of all the source files in the project. If your application has global variables and you click the global variables item in the top-left pane, those variables appear in the top-right pane. The bottom pane contains the source code. There is also a function popup menu in the usual location at the bottom left of the window.

If you double-click a file name, CodeWarrior opens up the original source file in the editor. If you make changes, they will not be reflected in the running application until you quit the application and rebuild it with CodeWarrior.

A SYM file contains the mapping of individual lines of source code with the object code that the compiler creates. SYM files have a tremendous amount of information in them, including the names and data types of all your variables.

Whenever you are in the debugger, you can switch to the SYM window and set a breakpoint anywhere in your code. In the SYM window, click a file name in the source file pane and the source code for that file appears in the source code pane. If you have changed the source file after the most recent build, you may get a message that the source code is unavailable. The only cure is to quit the debugger and rebuild the application.

After the source code appears for the file you want, select the function you want with the function popup menu. Then set the breakpoint at the line of code you want.

There is a one-to-one relationship between the debugger window's breakpoints and the SYM window's breakpoints. If you create or remove a breakpoint in one window, the change appears in the other window immediately. You can use whichever window is more convenient.

You can also set conditional breakpoints. These are breaks that take effect only if a certain condition is true. For example, you can test a variable and break if it has a particular value. This is wonderful for testing inside loops, where a breakpoint might stop the program every time through the loop, but you want to see what happens the 50th time through the loop.

To set a conditional breakpoint, choose the Show Breakpoints item from the debugger's Window menu. The breakpoint window appears. It lists all your breakpoints on the left and any conditionals on the right.

To set a condition, double-click in the conditional area to the right of the breakpoint. That section becomes an editable text box. Type in the expression that you want evaluated every time the debugger encounters that line of code. Figure 2.20 displays the one breakpoint currently in this project. The condition set for that breakpoint specifies that the debugger should break if the "what" field of the local variable "theEvent" has the value of 6.

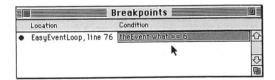

Figure 2.20 Conditional breakpoints

Finally, CodeWarrior is so friendly that you don't even have to use the CodeWarrior debugger if you don't want to. The SYM file that the CodeWarrior linker generates follows industry standards for SYM files. As a result, other debuggers can use the same information. Although the CodeWarrior debugger is excellent and powerful, as you become more experienced writing software for the Macintosh, you may decide that you prefer a third-party debugger. It is good to know that the people at Metrowerks let you choose your own tools.

During this intense whirlwind tour, you have had a glimpse of the breadth and depth of the CodeWarrior development environment. It is friendly, powerful, state of the art, and deserving of the honors it has received. Now it's time to put it to work, have some fun, and write some software.

Lab 2.1 Hello to the Mac Programming World

Just about every introductory programming book that uses the C language begins with a "Hello World" program. That tradition will not be broken in this book. However...

The Macintosh is a truly great machine, and it can do more than simply display a line of text in a console window. That's not what the Mac is about. The Mac is about brilliance and color and light and sound, all working together to help you be more productive and creative. So we're going to have some fun with Hello World.

I give you a few functions to make things a little easier, but you write the guts of the application that do the real work. And you do it with fewer than 40 lines of code. You could do drab and ugly in about 20 lines, but who wants drab and ugly?

In this lab you:

- Open the Hello World project
- Set project preferences
- Set up the application
- Create and display a window
- Display characters in a window
- Idle away some time
- Clean up after yourself

Step 1: Open the Hello World project

Lab 2.1 has a unique start code. Make sure you have copied the right start code for Lab 2.1 to your hard drive. Then double-click the project file (68K or Power Mac) to launch CodeWarrior and open the project. When you're done, you should have an open project window that looks something like Figure 2.1.1.

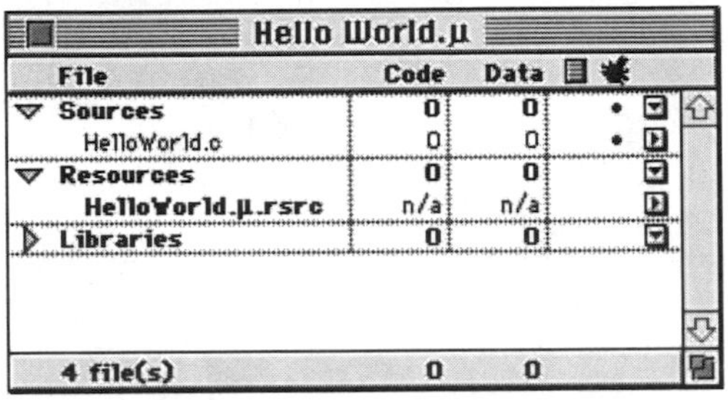

Figure 2.1.1 The Hello World project window

Step 2: Set project preferences

Modify: project data in Hello World project

The locator line right after the step title tells you what to look for and what file to open. When starting a new project, you should make sure that the project preferences are set correctly.

Choose the Preferences item in the CodeWarrior Edit menu, scroll to the Project preferences icon and click it. Make sure the settings for the project match those in Figure 2.1.2.

The project type is an application. Set the creator to "Mpsk" and the type to "APPL." Set the project name to "Hello World." The name is not critical. This will be the name of the final application. Notice the heap size and stack size settings. This is the memory partition the application gets when it runs. Chapter 3 discusses memory.

Look in the SIZE popup menu and make sure that the only item checked is the "is32BitCompatible" flag (see Figure 2.1.3). All other choices should have no check mark. The meaning of the items in the SIZE popup menu becomes clear in subsequent chapters.

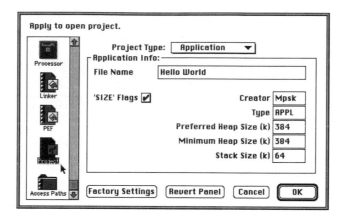

Figure 2.1.2 The project preferences

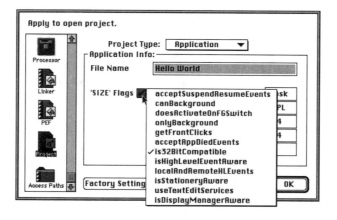

Figure 2.1.3 The SIZE flags

Feel free to examine the other preference options if you wish. There is no need to change any of them for this lab exercise.

Step 3: Set up the application

Modify: main() in HelloWorld.c

Open the HelloWorld.c file and locate the main() function. This is where you make changes.

Type this code verbatim. Be careful with those odd syntax marks (such as the amper-sand and asterisk). Existing code is in italics. It is provided so you can figure out where the new code belongs.

When you first look at `main()`, you'll see that all the local variables—like `delayTime` and `finalTicks`—have been defined for you. I want you to concentrate on writing real code.

```
long      delayTime;
long      finalTicks;

EasyInitToolbox();

GetDateTime((unsigned long *)&qd.randSeed);

windowRect.top = 40;
windowRect.left = 10;
windowRect.bottom = 340;
windowRect.right = 510;
```

When you are through typing code, choose the Check Syntax item in the CodeWarrior Project menu (⌘-semicolon) to make sure you didn't make a typing mistake. It is also wise to save your work. You can do this after each step, or at the end of the exercise.

The first line calls a function provided for you that initializes the Macintosh Toolbox for this application. You can examine the code if you want. This is a process that every Macintosh application goes through as soon as it launches.

The `GetDateTime()` Toolbox routine gets the current time—an essentially random value—and sets the random "seed" to that value so that we can generate pseudo-random numbers. As you'll see, the application uses random numbers to generate colors and positions for letters.

The next four lines set the size of the window that you are about to create.

Step 4: Create and display a window

Modify: `main()` in HelloWorld.c

In this step you create a window in memory, set a few features of the window, and display the window. If you do not have a color-capable Macintosh, replace the `NewCWindow()` call with `NewWindow()`. This looks a *lot* nicer in color, but it will work in black and white.

```
windowRect.right = 510;

macWindow = NewCWindow(nil, &windowRect,
                       "\pHello, World",
                       true,
                       noGrowDocProc,
                       (WindowPtr)-1L,
                       true, nil);

SetPort(macWindow);

GetFNum("\pCourier", &fontNumber);
TextFont(fontNumber);
TextFace(bold);
TextSize(72);

MoveTo(topMargin, topMargin + lineHeight);
```

The `NewCWindow()` call sets up a window record based on all the parameters you provide, and displays the window. The `SetPort()` call says that this is the window in which you want to draw (the graphics "port").

Then you get the number for the Courier font. The "\p" before the name tells the compiler you want the string to be a Pascal-style string, which is what the Toolbox expects to receive. You then set the font, style, and size for the type that appears in the window.

The `MoveTo()` call moves the "pen" to the spot where you want to start drawing—the left margin and one line down from the top.

Step 5: Display characters in a window and play a sound

Modify: `main()` in HelloWorld.c

In this step you write the code to display the characters in a message. The message is in the local variable `myString`, which is defined in the very first line of code in `main()`. You can change that message if you want.

```
MoveTo(topMargin, topMargin + lineHeight);

stringLength = myString[0];
for (index = 1; index <= stringLength; index++)
{
  MySetRandomColor();

  DrawChar(myString[index]);

  if (myString[index] == ' ')
  {
```

```
      MyPlaySound(kSpaceSoundID);
    }
    else
    {
      MyPlaySound(kKeyClickSoundID);
    }

    GetPen(&penLoc);
    if ( (penLoc.h + letterWidth) >
         macWindow->portRect.right)
    {
      MoveTo((leftMargin), (penLoc.v + lineHeight));

      MyPlaySound(kReturnSoundID);
    }

    delayTime = (long)MyRandomInRange(4, 25);
    Delay(delayTime, &finalTicks);

  }  /* all done typing letters */

  MyPlaySound(kHelloSoundID);
```

First, you find out how long the Pascal style string is, and set up a for loop to print each character in the string.

> For more information about Pascal strings, see Appendix B. For more information about loops, see "The for Statement" section in Appendix A.

For each character, you set a random color and draw it. `MySetRandomColor()` is provided for you. Color is discussed in Chapter 10. The call to `DrawChar()` draws the character and moves the pen to the end of the new character (in just the right spot to draw the next character). Then you play a sound—one sound for a space character, another sound for any other key. The sounds are stored as application resources in the HelloWorld.µ.rsrc file. The `MyPlaySound()` function is provided for you. Resources are covered in Chapter 4, and sound is covered in Chapter 14.

Then you check to make sure the next character fits in the window. The call to `GetPen()` gets the pen's location. You add the width of a character. If that does not fit within the window (`portRect.right`), you move the pen to the left margin, move it down one line, and play another sound.

After each key, you add a random delay to simulate the irregularity of typing. The `MyRandomInRange()` call is another function provided for you. This code says you want a delay between 4 and 25 ticks. A tick is 1/60th of a second.

When you are all through with all the keys, you play one more sound, a greeting. The braces (the { and } symbols) mark the beginning and end of the loop.

Step 6:   Idle away some time

Modify: `main()` in HelloWorld.c

This application runs until the user clicks the mouse. While waiting, let's be a little creative. The code you write in this step sprays letters all over the window.

```
MyPlaySound(kHelloSoundID);

while (!Button())
{
  MySetRandomColor();

  penLoc.h = MyRandomInRange(-10, 500);
  penLoc.v = MyRandomInRange(0, 310);
  MoveTo(penLoc.h, penLoc.v);

  randomLetter = MyRandomInRange(1, stringLength);

  DrawChar(myString[randomLetter]);
}
```

The **Button()** call tells you if the mouse button has been pressed. As long as the button has not been pressed, this loop repeats.

> For more information about while loops, see "The while Statement" section in Appendix A.

While waiting, you pick a random color, pick a random location, move the pen to that spot, pick a random letter out of the string, and draw the letter at the random location.

Step 7:   Clean up after yourself

Modify: `main()` in HelloWorld.c

When the user clicks the button, it is time to quit. You have to do some clean up work to pick up after yourself. Not only is it the polite thing to do, but there are times that if you fail to clean up after yourself, you crash the machine.

```
    DrawChar(myString[randomLetter]);
  }

  MyPlaySound(kGoodByeSoundID);

  DisposeWindow(macWindow);
}
```

On the way out, you play a "Good bye" sound. Then you dispose of the window. That's it. You have just written a complete Macintosh application. Let's see if it works.

Step 8: Run the application

Modify: none

Follow these instructions *carefully*.

Save your work and run the *project* using the debugger. In this Lab I explain what that means. In subsequent labs I'll simply tell you to save your work and run the project. At that time you should follow the detailed steps outlined here:

1. Make sure debugging is on. Choose the Enable Debugging item from the Project menu, if necessary, so that there is a check mark indicating that debugging is active.

2. Choose Run from the Project menu (⌘-R). The compiler compiles your code, the linker puts it all together, and the debugger should launch. The application is ready to go, but it is stopped at the first line of code. If there is a problem, the debugger does not appear. The message window appears with errors and warnings.

3. If there is an error or warning, compare your code to the instructions in this lab and see where they differ. Fix the problem and try again. You will learn a lot from this process, although it may not seem like it right away. If you have a problem that you can't seem to figure out, go to the solution code for this lab exercise and compare your code to the solution code to see where they differ. Then fix your code. If the problem persists, run the solution code instead.

4. When there are no problems and you run the *project*, if the debugger is already running, the SYM window appears instead of the debugger window. Just type ⌘-R again to start the project in the debugger.

When you are all set and ready to go, you should be looking at the debugger window, shown in Figure 2.1.4.

Run the application (⌘-R), and enjoy. When you're through enjoying the show, just click the mouse to quit the application. Figure 2.1.5 shows the program in action.

Figure 2.1.4 Hello World about to run

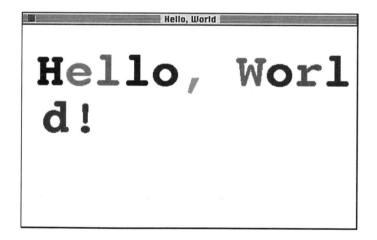

Figure 2.1.5 Hello World

You have written a real Macintosh application, complete with color, text, and sound. There are some limitations to the program. There is no menu bar, for example, and you can't move the window around. However, you see some of the power of the Toolbox in real life. With just a few calls, you have an actual Macintosh window full of stuff! In the rest of this book, you'll learn everything you need to know to write a fully functional Macintosh application. You're on your way!

3

A Moving Target: Getting a Handle on Memory

3

This chapter explores how the Macintosh uses memory. As described in Chapter 1, the Toolbox consists of a series of "managers." Each manager is a group of conceptually related routines that focuses on one particular aspect of the Mac OS. The Memory Manager takes care of—appropriately enough—memory issues.

This chapter discusses:

- The Macintosh memory map
- The application memory map
- Allocating memory
- Managing memory
- Dealing with memory shortages

This chapter has three coding labs where you implement what you learn. At the end of this chapter—as in most chapters—there is a handy reference to the Toolbox calls you use when writing code. This reference lists the C prototype for each call, describes its parameters, and discusses how to use the call.

The Macintosh Memory Map

There are two kinds of memory inside a Macintosh computer: Random Access Memory—RAM—and Read-Only Memory—ROM. See Figure 3.1.

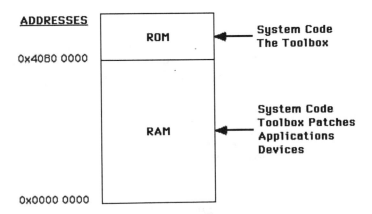

Figure 3.1 Macintosh memory

The content of ROM is static—it cannot change. You can only read what is already there—that's why it is called read-only memory. Most of the Toolbox code lives in ROM. In other respects the ROM is of little direct interest to an application programmer.

By contrast, RAM is dynamic. You can write data to RAM, so its contents can change. RAM is the place where computers get work done, and that area is a lot more interesting to us. The operating system runs here. Applications live here as well. Other parts of RAM are devoted to special purposes like the screen display or communicating with your hard drive.

Every byte in RAM has an address—a number that identifies its location. RAM addresses start at zero and are sequential. How high they go depends on how much RAM is in your machine. The maximum amount of RAM that you can have in your Macintosh (at the time of this writing) is 1 gigabyte—a billion bytes.

Figure 3.2 shows four sections of RAM: system globals, the system heap, the Process Manager heap, and device space. The principal section of RAM of interest to an application programmer is the Process Manager heap. A "heap" is simply a section of RAM, a pile of bits and bytes.

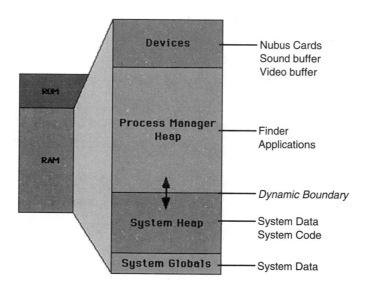

Figure 3.2 The Macintosh RAM

The system heap is where the System lives. When the Macintosh starts up, the System seizes the low addresses in available RAM, loads itself into position, and goes to work. Most applications don't do anything directly with the system heap. However, all of the system software that is not in ROM lives here. Many of the Toolbox calls use resources and code that are in the system heap. You don't have to worry about how that works because the Mac OS takes care of the details.

One of the tasks the System performs on startup is to allocate the Process Manager heap. Except for special-purpose areas of RAM, whatever the System doesn't use, the Process Manager gets. The Process Manager is the part of the Toolbox that keeps track of processes. "Process" is a generic term for some task running in the computer. An application is a process.

When an application launches, the Process Manager assigns memory for the application's use as high as possible in the Process Manager heap. In other words, applications load from the top down. How much memory the application gets depends upon how much the application asks for and how much is available. Because the Finder usually launches before other applications, it is at the top of the heap (see Figure 3.3).

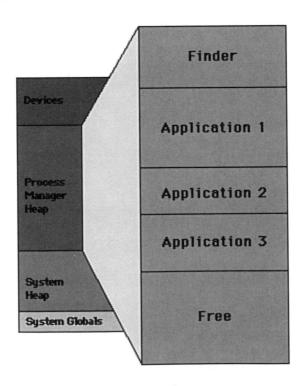

Figure 3.3 The Process Manager heap

After the Process Manager gives the application its allocated space, the application never moves. It is locked in memory until it quits. What happens inside the application's memory space is what Macintosh application programming is all about.

The Application Memory Map

The application's memory space is your territory. However, there are structures even within this space. There are three principle sections to discuss: the globals, the function stack, and the application heap. Programmers usually use the simple terms "stack" and "heap" to refer to the latter two sections. Just to add to the confusion, many programmers refer to the *entire* application memory space as the application heap. However, the term "application heap" will be used in this book to refer to that part of the application space that does not include the stack or the globals (see Figure 3.4).

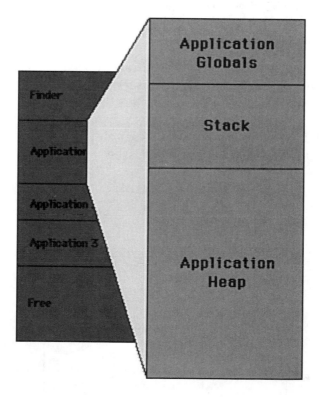

Figure 3.4 Application memory space

The Globals

The globals section holds data for the application. This includes the global variables your application defines and a whole set of information that the system software manages called the QuickDraw globals. In addition, the global space is home to the application's jump table, which keeps track of each function's actual address in memory so that function calls can jump to the right spot.

The Macintosh was originally designed to run one application at a time. As a result, the operating system has only one set of data that it uses to perform a variety of functions, like drawing. This presents a serious problem when you have two or more programs running simultaneously. One of them may change the drawing environment, and the other has no way of knowing what happened.

So that each application in a multitasking environment can rely on these system-level variables, the System stores a complete set for each application inside the application's own memory space. These are the QuickDraw globals. QuickDraw globals include such vital information as what window to draw in, how big the pen is, what color to use, and so forth.

Taken together, the application globals, QuickDraw globals, and application jump table are called the application's A5 world. This term comes from the A5 register—a special location in the 68K chip's address registers that keeps track of where this information is (see Figure 3.5). The System is usually responsible for maintaining the A5 register on 68K Macs and swapping the QuickDraw globals into play. This is called a context switch. On Power Macs this is not an issue.

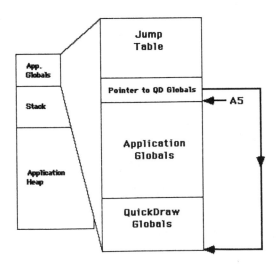

Figure 3.5 The A5 world

There are times when an application may want to do something while it is not in direct control of the computer, sort of behind the System's back. In that case you would have to set up the A5 register yourself. That is an advanced topic that is not discussed further in *Programming Starter Kit for Macintosh*.

A quick aside on terminology. After you work on a programming project for a little while, you start to identify with your code. Throughout this book you will find the terms "you," "your application," and "application" used interchangeably when talking about what the code should accomplish. In the Zen of programming, you are what you program, and your code is you.

The Function Stack

The second area in your application's memory space is the function stack. The stack contains stack frames. You create a stack frame—which is simply a series of values pushed onto the stack—every time you make a function call. The stack frame includes the function parameters and any local variables created by a function, and the return address so that the code can jump back to the calling routine. The frame stays in existence while that routine is executing. The frame is discarded by popping all of its values off the stack when the routine ends.

As a result, the stack is a dynamic data space. Every time you make a call, a new stack frame appears. Every time a function returns, a frame disappears. Curiously, the part of the stack that is lowest in memory is called the top of the stack, because that's the place where a new stack frame appears. The stack is a last-in, first-out pile. It is like a stalactite hanging from the ceiling of a cave—you add new stack frames at the tip (low in memory) making the stack a little longer, and you take them off the tip making the stack a little shorter (see Figure 3.6).

Like application context switches, for the most part stack management is transparent. When you compile your application's code, the compiler creates the necessary machine-level commands to create and destroy stack frames.

Unless you specify otherwise, the Process Manager sets the size of the stack for you. Most of the time, the default size is fine. If your application makes unusual demands on the stack, the stack can grow down to collide with the application heap. This can cause disaster as the stack frames stomp all over your application's heap. Although uncommon, stack overflow is not unheard of. You can increase the size of the stack, but that is an advanced topic that is not discussed further in *Programming Starter Kit for Macintosh*.

3

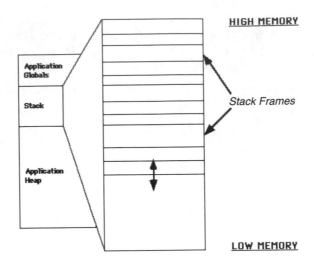

HIGH MEMORY

Application
Globals

Stack

Stack Frames

Application
Heap

LOW MEMORY

Figure 3.6 A stack in operation

The Application Heap

The third area of application memory space is the application heap. This is where
you get to play. The rest of this chapter—and indeed the rest of this book—concerns
how to use the heap.

When the Process Manager sets up your application memory space, it creates the
global space, allocates memory for the stack, and gives your application a tiny heap.
In between this tiny heap and the stack is all the rest of the memory assigned to your
application.

Some or all of your application code may live inside your application heap. On a 68K
Mac, you can separate your code into segments that load automatically. You can
unload segments if you wish. Unloading 68K segments is an advanced topic, so you
do not unload code segments in this book. On a Power Macintosh, your code loads
into the application heap as one block and stays there. If virtual memory is on, then
the Process Manager keeps your application code in virtual memory. That gives you
more room in the application heap.

When it first launches, your application must take over the heap. You do this with the
Toolbox routine `MaxApplZone()`. This call grows your heap until it reaches the bottom
of the stack area. Your heap is then as big as it can get.

If you want to resize your stack, do it before calling `MaxApplZone()`.

There is really no empty space inside your heap. The Memory Manager divides the heap into a series of blocks. Every byte of memory in your heap belongs to a block. There are three kinds of blocks: nonrelocatable, relocatable, and free. After you call `MaxApplZone()`, most of the heap consists of a few free blocks. As the application works, it creates nonrelocatable and relocatable blocks. Relocatable blocks may also be locked in place.

Figure 3.7 shows the ideal placement of memory blocks. Locked relocatable blocks are at the top of the heap. Nonrelocatable blocks are low in the heap. The center of the heap consists of unlocked relocatable and free blocks. Remember, a free block is not empty space. It is a block of memory just like any other that is controlled by the Memory Manager.

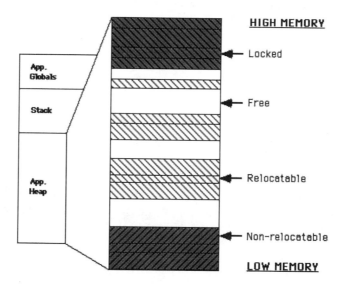

Figure 3.7 The application heap

As your application does its work, it must create and dispose of blocks of memory for its own purposes. The Memory Manager controls this process. When your application requests memory, either implicitly or explicitly, the Memory Manager takes the necessary memory from a free block, creates a new block to satisfy your request, and tells you where the new block is. The size of the free block shrinks by the amount of memory in your new block.

An application heap may have hundreds of blocks at any moment. Every byte of memory belongs to the Memory Manager at all times. The Memory Manager loans you the memory for a while. You can use it as long as you want, but you have to give it back when you're done.

Lab 3.1 Allocating Memory

In this lab you write some simple functions to allocate and dispose of memory. In subsequent labs in this chapter, you'll refine these functions so that they become more intelligent. In the process, you start building EasyApp, a Macintosh application shell. Managing memory is a basic service that the shell should provide for any application.

In addition, because this is the first EasyApp lab, there is some setup work you need to perform, just like there was for the Hello World project in the previous chapter. In this lab you:

- Set up the application
- Initialize application variables
- Allocate any handle
- Dispose any handle
- Dispose a specific handle

Lab 3.1 has a new start code. Make sure you copy the start code for Lab 3.1 to your hard drive. Then double-click the project file (68K or Power Mac) inside the start code folder to launch CodeWarrior and open the project. The project preferences are already set for you. You learned how to do that in the previous lab.

Step 1: Set up the application

Modify: `main()` in main.c

At startup, you must take all the memory you can and do other setup work. A C application always starts in the `main()` function, so that's where we begin to write code.

```
void main (void)
{
  OSErr    error;

  MaxApplZone();
```

```
    InitToolboxHook();

    error = EasyInitErrorDialog();
    if (error)
    {
      return;
    }

    error = CheckEnvironmentHook();
    if (error)
    {
      ShowErrorHook(error);
      return;
    }

    error = InitAppHook();
    if (error)
    {
      ShowErrorHook(error);
      if(error != kNoPrinterError) /* no printer not fatal */
      {
        return;
      }
    }

    error = LoadCursorsHook();
    if (error)
    {
      ShowErrorHook(error);
      return;
    }

    error = ShutdownHook();
    if (error)
    {
      ShowErrorHook(error);
    }
}
```

The `MaxApplZone()` call extends the application heap to fill all remaining memory in your application partition.

The call to `InitToolboxHook()` is your first use of the EasyApp shell architecture. The only thing the hook function does is call `EasyInitToolbox()`. The actual code for `EasyInitToolbox()` is provided for you. Examine it if you wish. It initializes all the necessary managers in the required order.

Next you set up an error dialog to report problems. Again the actual code is provided for you. Dialogs are covered in Chapter 11. If an error happens, you just return. Returning from the `main()` function means the application quits. You can't display the error because you had a problem creating the error dialog!

Then you call a hook function to examine the operating environment. Again, the actual function called from the hook—EasyCheckEnvironment()—is provided for you. It makes sure you are running System 7, among other tasks. If there is an error, you show the error and quit. You study how to check the operating environment in Chapter 19.

Next you call InitAppHook(). That hook calls EasyInitApp(), a function you'll write in the next step. If there is an error, you show the error and return. Similarly, you load cursors for use by the application.

Finally you call ShutdownHook(). In subsequent labs you'll do a lot more before shutting down.

Errors that occur while setting up the application are usually fatal. If you cannot set things up to work properly, you had better not work at all. EasyApp attempts to exit "gracefully." If at all possible, EasyApp informs the user what the problem is and why it cannot run by showing an appropriate error statement.

When you are through, you can check your syntax and save the file.

Step 2: Initialize application variables

Modify: EasyInitApp() in init.c

Like most applications, EasyApp has a series of global variables. These variables contain information used throughout the application. In this step you set up those variables.

```
OSErr   EasyInitApp  (void)
{
  OSErr    error = noErr;
  THPrint   printJob;

  g.newOnLaunch  = true;
  g.windowCount  = 0;
  g.creator      = kCreator; /* app creator */
  g.defaultType  = kGenericFileType;
  g.windowList   = (WindowPtr) nil;
  g.done         = false;
  g.switchedIn   = true;
  g.abortChar    = 0x1b; /* escape key */
  g.cmdAbortChar = '.';   /* for command-period */
  g.sleepTime    = kFrontSleepTime;
  g.mouseRegion  = nil;
  g.dragMoving   = false;

  error = EasyAllocateHandle(sizeof(TPrint),
                             (Handle*)&printJob);
```

```
if (error)
{
  return error;
}

return error;
```

EasyApp has a single global structure named "g" that contains all the global variables. Each variable is a field in this structure. The structure is declared in the EasyApp.h file.

> For more information about structures, see the "Structs and Typedefs" section of Appendix A.

In the first lines of code, you set the values for several of those fields. Constants like kGenericFileType and kCreator are declared in the application's header files, either EasyApp.h or userDeclare.h. The newOnLaunch field determines whether a new window appears automatically when you launch the application (this won't actually work until Chapter 17). The windowCount field is the number of untitled windows. The creator is the application's creator code. The defaultType field is the file type for files created by the application (this is discussed in Chapter 15). The done field is set when the application is ready to quit. You will encounter these variables as you work through the labs.

After setting the globals, you allocate memory to hold a print job record. You won't do anything with the print job until printing is covered in Chapter 16, but we talk about memory in this chapter. To allocate the memory for this record, you call the EasyApp function EasyAllocateHandle(). If there is an error, you return the error. You write EasyAllocateHandle() in the next step.

In the call to EasyAllocateHandle(), you pass two parameters. First, you tell the function that you want memory the size of a TPrint record.

> For more information about the sizeof() operator, see the "The sizeof() Operator" section of Appendix A.

Next, the (Handle *)&printJob syntax says you are passing the address of printJob—&printJob—and that the compiler should treat that as a pointer to a handle. This is a typecast. The actual variable is a THPrint type, a handle to a TPrint structure in memory somewhere. The function you're calling requires the address of a plain handle. So you typecast the value to meet the requirements of the called function.

> For more information about the "&" operator and passing an address, see the "Pointers" section of Appendix A. For more information about typecasting, see the "Typecasting" section of Appendix A.

When you are through, check your syntax and save your changes.

Step 3: Allocate a handle

Modify: `EasyAllocateHandle()` in memory.c

Allocating memory is something you'll do often. It makes sense to write the code to do that once, and call it when you need it.

```
OSErr EasyAllocateHandle(long size,
                         Handle *handleAddress)
{
  OSErr  error = noErr;

  *handleAddress = NewHandleClear(size);

  if (!*handleAddress)
  {
    error = MemError();
  }

  return error;
}
```

The function receives the number of bytes to allocate and a pointer to a Handle—the address where you want to store the new handle. The call `NewHandleClear()` allocates the memory. You specify the number of bytes. This call sets all the bytes to zero. You put the resulting handle in the location pointed to by handleAddress.

Then, being a good programmer, you check for errors. If the handle is nil, you call `MemError()` to get the error number. Existing code returns the error value.

Step 4: Dispose a handle

Modify: `EasyDisposeHandle()` in memory.c

The converse of allocating is disposing. Disposing a handle can be tricky. You must make sure it is a valid handle first.

```
void EasyDisposeHandle (Handle *handleAddress)
{
  char  flags;
```

```
Handle  theHandle = *handleAddress;

if (theHandle)
{
  DisposeHandle(theHandle);

  *handleAddress = nil;
}
}
```

In this code, you make sure that the handle is not nil. If it is not nil, you do two things. You dispose of the handle by calling **DisposeHandle()**. You also set the contents of the handle to nil for safety. If you mistakenly try to dispose of this handle again using this function, you won't be able to do it.

note | EasyApp never allocates a nonrelocatable block, so there is no EasyAllocatePointer() function. There is an EasyDisposePointer() function that parallels EasyDisposeHandle(). Feel free to examine the code if you wish.

Step 5: Dispose a specific handle

Modify: EasyShutdown() events.c

Whatever you create, you must also release. Creating and disposing should be symmetrical. In Step 2, you called EasyAllocateHandle() to allocate the default application print record. That handle is stored in the global variable g.defaultPrintJob. In this step you dispose of it when the application quits.

```
OSErr  EasyShutdown (void)
{
  CloseDialog (g.errorDialog);

  EasyDisposeHandle ((Handle *)&g.defaultPrintJob);

  DisposeRoutineDescriptor(g.modalEventFilterUPP);
  DisposeRoutineDescriptor(g.drawDefaultButtonUPP);
  return noErr;
}
```

The existing code closes the error dialog for you. You then dispose of the default print record. Because EasyDisposeHandle() expects to receive the address of a handle, and defaultPrintJob is actually a THPrint variable, you typecast it to the required type. The existing code also disposes of some other items that are called routine descriptors or UPPs. These will be discussed in due course. The code then returns noErr. At this point, it doesn't matter if an error occurs because you are shutting down the application anyway.

Step 6: Run the application

Modify: none

Save your work and run the project using the debugger. If at any point in any lab you get warnings about unused variables, go to the preferences and turn off that warning. There will be dozens of such warnings because all the variables have been defined for you, but you haven't written the code to use the variables yet.

After the debugger launches, go to the SYM window, select the memory.c file, locate the EasyAllocateHandle() function, and set a breakpoint at the call to NewHandleClear(), (see Figure 3.1.1).

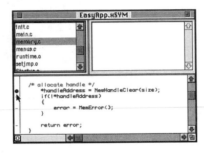

Figure 3.1.1 Set a breakpoint

Then run the application. It should stop almost immediately at your breakpoint. You are about to allocate the TPrint record. The upper-left pane of the debugger window shows you the calling chain—the functions you passed through to get to where you are.

Local variables appear in the upper-right pane of the debugger window. Examine the handleAddress variable. Click the triangle to the left of the variable name to dereference it. This allows you to see both the address itself and the contents of the variable, as shown in Figure 3.1.2. The actual numbers you see will differ from the illustration.

Figure 3.1.2 The handleAddress variable

Then step through one line of code (⌘-S) to make the actual call to `NewHandleClear()`. The *contents* of `handleAddress` (`*handleAddress`) should change. This is the new handle you just allocated. If an error occurred, the contents should be zero. Notice that the address of `handleAddress` itself doesn't change, just the contents of the address.

That's all there is to it. For now, you can run the application and it will just quit— disposing of the `TPrint` memory on the way out. You can step through the code if you want to see EasyApp dispose of the memory. EasyApp is just beginning. It won't really do anything showy for a couple of chapters.

Allocating Memory

There are two kinds of memory blocks that you create: relocatable and nonrelocatable. In this section both kinds of blocks are talked about in some detail.

Nonrelocatable Blocks

New programmers are very comfortable with nonrelocatable blocks. A nonrelocatable block never moves. You always know where it is: neat, sweet, and complete.

When you create a nonrelocatable block, you get the address in memory where it lives. The address of such a block tells you where it is. In programmer talk, the address "points" to the location in memory, and therefore the address is called a pointer. The address is the lowest number in memory that belongs to the block—the "bottom" or beginning of the block. Blocks start at low numbers and extend upward in memory. Figure 3.8 illustrates a pointer to a block that starts at address 0x001D040A. That block will remain at that location until released. It never moves.

To create a nonrelocatable block, you call `NewPtr()`. If you want the new block filled with zeroes, call `NewPtrClear()`. You tell the Memory Manager how many bytes you want. The Memory Manager creates a block of that size and returns the address (the pointer) to you. You now have a new pointer, on loan from the Memory Manager.

> You will frequently see the term "pointer" shortened to "ptr" in Toolbox routines and data structures.

While you have the block, you can put anything you want in it. When you are through with the memory, you must give it back. You call `DisposePtr()`. You give the Memory Manager the pointer, it takes care of the rest. You must be careful not to use the pointer—or the memory it points to—after you dispose of the pointer. You must also be careful not to dispose of the same pointer twice because after you release the memory the first time, the Memory Manager may use it for something else.

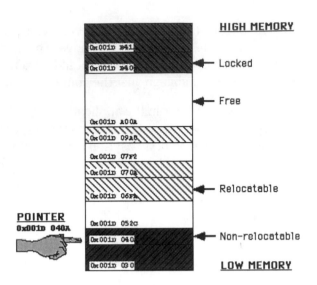

Figure 3.8 A nonrelocatable block and its pointer

Relocatable Blocks

Relocatable blocks are quite different. After you create a relocatable block, the Memory Manager can move it around in memory. Therefore the address of the block does not remain constant. You can't tell from one moment to the next where a relocatable block is.

At first glance, this seems like an insane concept. How can you work with a block of memory when you have no idea where it is? Why would anyone want to do this in the first place?

The purpose behind relocatable blocks is simple. Because an application's memory demands vary from one moment to the next, it makes sense to be able to shuffle blocks of memory to make the most efficient use of available space. There are many times when the ability to move memory around prevents a program from crashing or being unable to function. The simple truth is, if the Memory Manager didn't shuffle blocks of memory for you, you would have to do it yourself.

However useful the concept of movable memory is, the underlying problem still remains. How do you work with a moving target?

Think about nonrelocatable blocks. Remember, when you create a nonrelocatable block you get a pointer. This pointer is the address of that memory. Every *relocatable* block also has a pointer. The problem is, the address changes.

The trick to solving this problem is simple. You store the pointer to a relocatable block at a nonrelocatable special address. When you want to know where the relocatable block is in memory, you look at your special address. The number at that special address may change as the block moves around, but the *location* of that special address never changes.

The special location where the Memory Manager stores a pointer to a relocatable block is called a master pointer. When you look at the contents of a master pointer, the number stored there is the current address of the relocatable block. Whenever the Memory Manager moves a block, it keeps the stored address updated. In other words, you access the address of the relocatable block indirectly, by looking at the master pointer (see Figure 3.9).

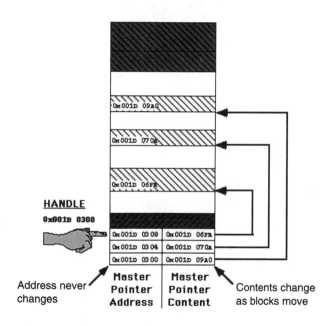

Figure 3.9 Tracking a relocatable block

When you ask the Memory Manager to create a relocatable block, the Memory Manager stores the pointer to the relocatable block in a master pointer. It then tells you the address of the master pointer, so you'll know where to look for the relocatable block. In other words, the Memory Manager gives you a pointer to the master pointer. A pointer to a master pointer is called a handle. Handles are everywhere in the Toolbox. Every relocatable block has a handle.

If this seems a trifle obscure, think about how call forwarding works. If you have call forwarding on your telephone, people can call you no matter where you are. A friend dials your phone number. Your telephone knows where you are, and forwards the call to the correct number. Your public phone number is an address of sorts. It is constant, it doesn't change, and all your friends, neighbors, and business associates know your number. They can call you at any time. You, however, move around. You can be in the car, at the office, at home, or visiting relatives. You still get your phone calls, because the telephone knows where you really are and sends the message to the right spot (see Figure 3.10).

Figure 3.10 Call forwarding

To allocate memory for a relocatable block, you call `NewHandle()`. If you want the new block to be filled with zeroes, call `NewHandleClear()`.

When allocating memory, you tell the Memory Manager how many bytes you want. The Memory Manager creates a block of that size. Because it is relocatable, the Memory Manager takes the address of that block and stuffs it into a master pointer. The Memory Manager then returns the address of the master pointer to you—the handle to your new relocatable block. You now have a new handle on loan from the Memory Manager.

You may ask yourself, where does the Memory Manager get the master pointers? When the application launches, the Memory Manager automatically creates a master pointer block containing 64 master pointers at the bottom of the application heap. If the Memory Manager runs out of master pointers, it allocates another block of 64 new master pointers in your application heap. This topic will be revisited when a common problem with memory management—heap fragmentation—is discussed.

Just like pointers, when you are through with a handle you must give it back. You call `DisposeHandle()`. You give the Memory Manager the handle, it takes care of the rest.

You must be careful not to use the handle—or the memory to which it refers—after you dispose of the handle. After you give the memory back, the Memory Manager can do whatever it wants with it. Like a pointer, you must be careful not to dispose of a handle twice. You must also be careful not to call `DisposeHandle()` with anything other than a handle.

Managing Memory

The problem with relocatable blocks is that they move around. In this section you learn when they move, how to lock them in place when you want to, and how to avoid heap fragmentation.

When Do Relocatable Blocks Move?

Relocatable blocks may move any time the Memory Manager receives a request for memory in your application heap.

Memory requests may come from either you or the operating system. Toolbox routines call each other all the time. You may make a seemingly innocuous Toolbox call that apparently has nothing to do with memory. However, that Toolbox call may use another Toolbox routine, and that routine calls `NewPtr()` or `NewHandle()` to allocate a block of memory in your heap. This sort of interaction happens all the time because the Toolbox is highly interconnected.

Unless you know for sure that a Toolbox routine does not allocate memory, you should assume that it does. So the safe answer to the question is, memory may move every time you make a Toolbox call. In fact, there are many Toolbox routines that do not allocate (and therefore do not move) memory.

Requests for new memory may move existing blocks because of the way the Memory Manager does its magic. When the Memory Manager receives a request for a new block, it examines the available free blocks. It looks for one that is the right size or larger. If it finds such a free block, it creates the new block out of the free block.

If it does not find an acceptable free block, the Memory Manager moves all the relocatable blocks to a place that is low in the heap in an attempt to put all the free blocks together into one big contiguous block. It also releases the memory allocated to any purgeable blocks. (Purgeable blocks may be removed from memory temporarily. Purgeable blocks are discussed in detail in Chapter 4.) This process is called compacting the heap. If compacting the heap creates a free block large enough to meet your request, the Memory Manager creates the new block and returns a pointer or handle. Otherwise, it returns a zero value.

Notice in Figure 3.11 that after compacting the heap, the contents of the master pointers have changed to reflect the new locations of each relocatable block. The Memory Manager keeps these addresses updated automatically for you.

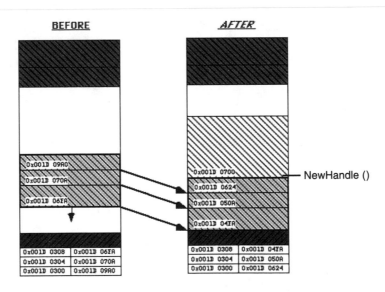

Figure 3.11 Compacting the heap

Locking Relocatable Blocks

There are times when you do *not* want a relocatable block to move. For example, you may be passing the actual address of the block to some routine that relies on the block staying in one place. You will encounter this situation on a regular basis when programming the Macintosh.

The Memory Manager provides utility routines to take care of this problem. First you call **HGetState()**. You specify the handle and the Memory Manager returns a byte of information that reflects the current state of that block's attributes (whether it is locked, purgeable, and so forth). You then call **HLock()** to lock the block. You specify the handle. When you are through working with the block you call **HSetState()**. You provide the preserved state information from the original **HGetState()** call. If the block was locked before you did anything to it, it remains locked when you restore its state. If the block was unlocked to begin with, this unlocks it.

> The contents of a locked block can be changed. In fact, the block can be disposed of while locked. It just cannot be moved.

You can also call **HUnlock()** to unlock a block directly, but this is usually unwise. Assume that routine "A" locks a block, then calls routine "B" to do something. Routine "B" wants to make sure the block is locked. So it locks the block (a redundant call), does its thing, and then unlocks the block and returns to routine "A." What happens back at routine "A"? Disaster may strike because you have unlocked a block that routine "A" still thinks is locked.

If routine "B" uses the **HGetState()** and **HSetState()** technique this problem doesn't happen. You preserve the state, do what you will to the block, and when you are through you restore the original state. Because you restore the original state, you have left no footprints and have not permanently changed the state of the block.

Heap Fragmentation

The memory map is getting crowded. You have nonrelocatable blocks, relocatable blocks, free blocks, and locked relocatable blocks. In the ideal application heap, all the locked and nonrelocatable blocks are tucked away at either end of the heap. There should be one large free block sitting right in the middle of the heap. This arrangement gives the Memory Manager maximum flexibility when allocating memory. If you need a single large block of memory, the Memory Manager can find it.

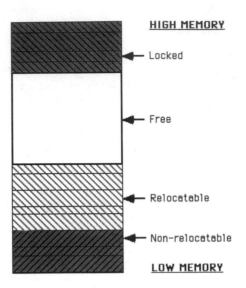

Figure 3.12 The ideal heap

Every time you create a nonrelocatable block or lock a relocatable block, you put up a barrier in the heap. If this barrier is in the middle of the heap, it causes problems for the Memory Manager. You may have two midsized blocks of free memory divided by the immovable block. If there is a memory request bigger than either of your free blocks, the Memory Manager can't meet the request. It cannot put the two free blocks together because the immovable block sits in between. This is heap fragmentation (see Figure 3.13).

Heap fragmentation is bad because it interferes with the Memory Manager's work. There are ways to minimize or prevent heap fragmentation. They are simple techniques, and make good sense.

First, try to allocate nonrelocatable blocks when you have no locked blocks around. When you ask the Memory Manager for a pointer to memory—a nonrelocatable block—it tries to allocate that memory as low in the heap as possible. In order to do this, it will move everything that's moveable out of the way.

Second, before you lock a block of memory for an extended period of time, call `MoveHHi()`. This moves the handle's block high in the heap, out of the way of the Memory Manager. After you have moved the block, then you can lock it. You can move and lock the block with a single call, `HLockHi()`.

So far, so good. You create pointers low in the heap, you lock handles high in the heap. That leaves the middle full of free or movable blocks. What's left?

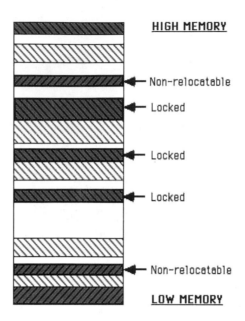

Figure 3.13 A fragmented heap

Remember master pointer blocks? If the Memory Manager runs out of master pointers, it creates a new, nonrelocatable block. If that happens at a moment when you're heap is full of stuff, that nonrelocatable block may end up right in the middle of the heap. If it does, the presence of the nonrelocatable block can hinder compaction.

The solution to this problem is to explicitly allocate all the master pointers you need at a moment when the application heap is well-ordered. Because a master pointer block is nonrelocatable, the Memory Manager will put it as low in the heap as possible. To allocate a master pointer block, you call `MoreMasters()`. Every time you call `MoreMasters()` another block of 64 master pointers appears in your application heap.

How do you know how many master pointers you need? The only real way to answer the question is to test your program. You run it wide open, doing as much as you possibly can. Then you use a memory inspection utility like ZoneRanger to see how many handles the Memory Manager created. Double that number and you should be safe. You are introduced to ZoneRanger in Chapter 5.

Lab 3.2 Heap Fragmentation

The goal of this lab is to help you understand what causes heap fragmentation and how to avoid it. There's nothing like a little hands-on experience to see how all this works. Richard Clark—formerly with Developer University at Apple Computer—has created a wonderful application named HeapDemo that shows how memory allocation works in the application heap.

In this lab you:

- Use HeapDemo to study memory allocation
- Allocate master pointer blocks
- Move and lock handles

Use your code from the previous lab as the starting point for your work in this lab. Also, locate the HeapDemo application in the DU Demos folder on the CD. You can run it from the CD or copy it to your hard drive.

Step 1: Explore HeapDemo

Double-click HeapDemo to launch the application. When you do, a window titled "Heap Display" appears. There are two active buttons, NewHandle and NewPtr. To the right of each is an editable text box that allows you to set how large a block you want to create.

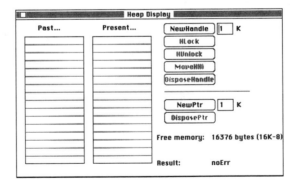

Figure 3.2.1 The heap display window

Before you start clicking buttons, the first thing you should do is choose the About HeapDemo item in the Apple menu. A help window appears with instructions. Read it, but don't worry if some of it goes over your head.

When you are through reading, create and dispose of a pointer. In the Heap Display window, click the NewPtr button. Observe what happens in the heap titled "Present." The lowest block in the heap is allocated to the new pointer. Select the block and click the DisposePtr button. The block is removed from the heap. The "Past" heap reflects the former condition.

Now create and dispose of a handle. Click the NewHandle button. A 1K relocatable block appears low in the heap. Now click the MoveHHi button. The block moves to the top of the heap. Now click the HLock button. The block becomes locked. Notice that the MoveHHi button becomes disabled. You cannot move a locked block. Finally, click the DisposeHandle button. The block is released, even though it is locked.

Now watch what happens when you mix pointers and handles. Create a 1K pointer. It appears low in the heap. Then create a 1K handle. It appears right above the nonrelocatable block. Now create a second 1K pointer and observe what happens. The relocatable block moves up, and the new nonrelocatable block appears low in the heap. The Memory Manager always places nonrelocatable blocks as low in memory as possible. It moved the relocatable block out of the way.

Now observe heap fragmentation. Create a 3K pointer and then a 3K handle. Select the relocatable handle and click the HLock button to lock it in place. Then, create a second 3K pointer. The Memory Manager puts the nonrelocatable block as low in memory as possible, but it cannot move the locked block. As shown in Figure 3.2.2, the new nonrelocatable block appears on top of the locked relocatable block in the heap.

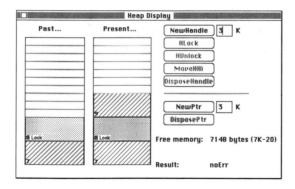

Figure 3.2.2 Incipient heap fragmentation

Select the relocatable block (the handle) and click the DisposeHandle button. A hole appears in the middle of the heap. Create a 4K Handle. It cannot fit in the hole, so it goes above the higher nonrelocatable block. You have 6K of memory left available in two 3K chunks. Try to create a second 4K handle. You can't, because the Memory Manager cannot put the two free blocks together into a single block. Why? Because there is a nonrelocatable block stuck in the middle of the heap. You have 6K free, but the largest contiguous block is only 3K. Figure 3.2.3 shows this heap fragmentation.

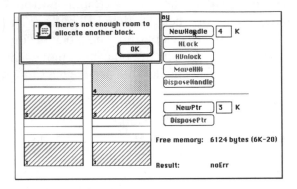

Figure 3.2.3 Heap fragmentation

HeapDemo has several more features. Choose the Advanced Display item in the Window menu to see them. In the advanced mode, you can purge blocks, compact the heap, and so forth. Explore HeapDemo for a while until you get a feel for the way that relocatable and nonrelocatable blocks work together.

Notice that if you move relocatable blocks high in the heap before locking them, they never cause heap fragmentation. Also notice that no matter what you do, if you allocate a series of nonrelocatable blocks and then dispose of some in the middle, you end up with a hole in the heap. If you allocate a block small enough, the Memory Manager will take advantage of the hole.

The lessons to be learned from this are simple: move relocatable blocks high before locking, and allocate nonrelocatable blocks carefully. Let's use these lessons in some real code.

Step 2:   Allocate master pointer blocks

Modify: `main()` in main.c

Modify: `EasyGetMoreMasters()` in memory.c

Every handle requires a master pointer. Master pointers must be in nonrelocatable blocks because the handle always points to the master pointer. If the Memory Manager runs out of master pointers, it will allocate a new block. This may result in a nonrelocatable block appearing in the middle of your heap. To avoid this problem, you should allocate all the necessary master pointer blocks on launch.

In main(), call EasyGetMoreMasters() as soon as you maximize the heap.

```
MaxApplZone();
EasyGetMoreMasters(kNumberMasters);
InitToolboxHook();
```

EasyGetMoreMasters() is a function to allocate master pointers. The kNumberMasters constant is the number of master pointer *blocks* to create. It is defined in userDeclare.h.

In memory.c, locate EasyGetMoreMasters() and finish that function.

```
void EasyGetMoreMasters (short numberMasterBlocks)
{
  while (numberMasterBlocks > 0)
  {
    MoreMasters();
    numberMasterBlocks--;
  }
}
```

This function uses a while loop to call **MoreMasters()** repeatedly—in this case kNumberMasters times.

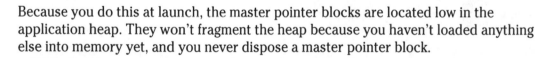

For more information about while loops, see "The while Statement" section of Appendix A.

Because you do this at launch, the master pointer blocks are located low in the application heap. They won't fragment the heap because you haven't loaded anything else into memory yet, and you never dispose a master pointer block.

For 68K Macs, the EasyGetMoreMasters() function should be in the same code segment as main(). If it is not, when you call EasyGetMoreMasters(), the segment containing that function loads into memory first and the master pointer blocks come in after. This may fragment the heap if you later unload the segment containing EasyGetMoreMasters().

Step 3: Move and lock a handle

Modify: EasyLockHandle() in memory.c

When locking a handle, it is usually wise to move it out of the way, high in the heap. This function handles the task.

```
SignedByte  EasyLockHandle (Handle h)
{
  SignedByte  state;

  state = HGetState(h);
  HLockHi(h);
  return state;
}
```

First, **HGetState()** gets the block's current state. Then you call **HLockHi()** to move the block high in the heap and lock it. The existing code returns the state to the calling function so that the caller can ultimately restore the block's original state.

These two tricks—allocating all master pointer blocks early and keeping locked handles out of the way—give you everything you need for basic heap management.

Save your changes. You will run the project after the next lab exercise.

Dealing with Memory Shortages

No matter how much you plan or how much RAM you have, the chances are pretty good that your program will run out of memory sometime. Running out of memory means that the Memory Manager was unable to fulfill a request for a block of memory, either because there is insufficient memory, or because heap fragmentation prevented it from meeting your request.

If you ignore a memory shortage, your program will crash and burn. In a good program you should plan for memory shortages. It is easy to do. You must look for problems, then respond if you find them. How to do that is what this section is all about.

Looking for Memory Manager Problems

Every time you make a memory request, you should check for failure by looking at the new pointer or handle. On every request for memory, the Memory Manager returns a pointer or a handle to the new block. If the request fails, the returned value will be nil—that is, zero. Such failed results are called nil handles or nil pointers.

If you get a nil value back from the Memory Manager, the request failed utterly. You did *not* get a good memory block at address zero! Treating address zero as a valid address is very very bad. The Macintosh stores machine-critical information in low memory, right after address zero. These are called the low-memory globals.

If you accept address zero as a *pointer* and start writing data to the nonexistent block at that address, you will overwrite all those critical values and the machine will crash. It may even reboot automatically.

If you accept address zero as a *handle*, you will treat whatever random number happens to be at address zero as a pointer to some location in memory. If you try to write to the nonexistent block at that "address," you will be writing into a more or less random location in memory. This may or may not cause a crash, depending on where that address points. You may get lucky. On the other hand, you may not. That "address" may point to something critical, and if you overwrite it you end up in big trouble. If you do crash, you may crash with spectacular results—weird screen effects, strange sounds, and so forth.

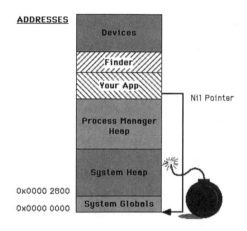

Figure 3.14 Writing to address zero

Reading data from or writing data to a zero address is the single most common insidious bug in Macintosh applications. This problem will be revisited in Chapter 5 on debugging.

If you make a request to the Memory Manager and receive a nil pointer or handle, call `MemError()` to get an error number. Knowing what went wrong might help you deal with the problem. `MemError()` returns a value of type OSErr. This is a Macintosh data type used for operating system errors. The System Errors and MacErrors applications in the Tools You Need folder provide a handy reference to the error numbers and what they mean.

Responding to Memory Shortages

All right. You're a good programmer and you check carefully for nil handles and pointers. What do you do when you get one?

There are four things you can do when the Memory Manager cannot find the memory you need. Each is a valid and reasonable memory management strategy. In EasyApp you will use three of them. The fourth is a more advanced technique of which you should be aware, but you will not implement it in this book.

The strategies you may follow are

- Alert the user

- Preflight memory requests

- Maintain an emergency memory reserve

- Create a `GrowZone()` function

These strategies may all work together, they are not mutually exclusive.

The first strategy is the simplest and is always required of a good Macintosh program. If a memory request fails, you should not go blithely on about your business. You must stop, alert the user to what happened, and recover gracefully. You must do this not only for memory shortages, but for any kind of operating system error your program encounters. You must always implement this strategy because it is your final recourse. If the other strategies fail, you must fall back to this one and let the user know you have run out of memory (see Figure 3.15).

Figure 3.15 A memory alert

The second strategy—preflighting memory requests—is a defensive approach. Before you make a memory request, you look to see if you have enough memory.

To do this, call `PurgeSpace()`. The Memory Manager reports back to you how many free bytes are available in the heap and the size of biggest free block if you made a memory request. This is called the largest contiguous free block.

In Figure 3.16, the largest contiguous block would be the total number of bytes available in the two free blocks higher in the heap. If the Memory Manager compacts the heap, it could put those two blocks together. The total number of bytes available would also include the three small blocks toward the bottom of the heap. Those could not be put together with the other free blocks because there is a locked block in the way.

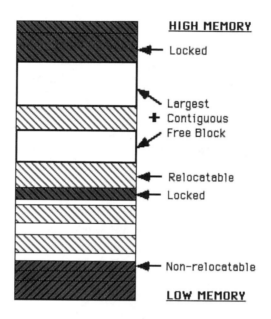

Figure 3.16 Preflighting memory requests

The largest contiguous block is more important than the total number of free bytes. The largest contiguous free block reflects the size of the biggest block the Memory Manager can allocate. If the size of your request is greater than the largest contiguous free block, your request will fail. Calling PurgeSpace() gives you advance warning of an impending memory shortage.

The third strategy—maintaining a memory reserve—works hand in hand with preflighting memory requests. Here's how it works.

When your program launches, you grab a block of whatever size suits your needs and save it as an emergency reserve. For this discussion, assume you reserve a block that's 40K in size. Later on, your preflighting strategy discovers an impending memory shortage. You can release your reserve. Suddenly your application has 40K additional space in which to work.

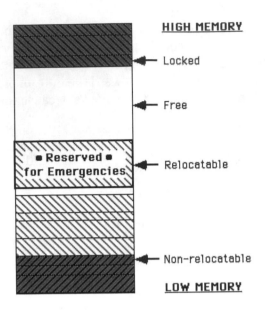

Figure 3.17 The memory reserve

In a real program, you would size the memory reserve based upon your assessment of the likely emergency memory needs of the application. You would also make attempts to reestablish the emergency reserve if adequate memory becomes available once again (so that releasing the reserve is not a one-shot solution). You will do this in the next lab.

The fourth strategy—the GrowZone() function—is similar to the emergency memory reserve. If you have a GrowZone() function, you tell the Memory Manager where this function is. If the Memory Manager runs out of memory it will call your GrowZone() function. The GrowZone() function then does what it can to create enough memory for the Memory Manager, such as release an emergency memory reserve or dispose of unnecessary memory structures.

You will not implement a GrowZone() function in EasyApp. This is one of those situations that involves setting up the A5 world on a 68K Mac.

Lab 3.3 Managing Memory

In this lab you implement two strategies for dealing with memory shortages—a memory reserve and preflighting memory allocation. To accomplish this, you will:

- Create a memory reserve
- Preflight memory requests
- Examine the heap
- Check the memory reserve

Use your code from this chapter's previous lab as the starting point for your work in this lab.

Step 1:   Create a memory reserve

Modify: EasyInitApp() in init.c

This is as easy as allocating a handle of the required size. You do this when initializing the application, after allocating all the master pointers.

```
g.canReceive   = false;
g.moving       = false;

error = EasyAllocateHandle(kMemoryReserveSize,
                                &g.memoryReserve);
if (error)
{
  return error;
}

error = EasyAllocateHandle(sizeof(TPrint),
                                (Handle*)&printJob);
```

Already you can take advantage of EasyApp services. To allocate a handle, just call EasyAllocateHandle(). You specify the size of the block and the address of the handle. The kMemoryReserveSize constant is declared in userDeclare.h. It sets aside 40K of memory. The handle to the memory reserve is in a field in the application global structure. As always, you check for errors.

Step 2:   Preflight memory requests

Modify: EasyAllocateHandle() in memory.c

Before you allocate memory, make sure you have enough room. EasyAllocateHandle() is the EasyApp service for allocating memory, so this is where you make a preflight check.

```
OSErr  error = noErr;

error = EasyCheckMemory(size);
```

```
  if (error)
  {
    *handleAddress = nil;
    return error;
  }

  *handleAddress = NewHandleClear(size);
```

You call EasyCheckMemory(). You write this function in the next step. It returns an error
if memory is unavailable. If there is an error, you set the new handle to nil—just to be
safe—before returning. Notice that the preflight request occurs before the existing
call to **NewHandleClear()**. You don't ask for memory unless you know that it is available.

Step 3: Examine the heap

Modify: EasyCheckMemory() in memory.c

To determine whether you have enough memory, you must examine the heap. That's
what EasyCheckMemory() does.

```
OSErr  EasyCheckMemory (long numberBytes)
{
  OSErr  error = noErr;
  long   totalSize, contigSize;

  PurgeSpace(&totalSize, &contigSize);

  if (contigSize < numberBytes)
  {
    if (g.memoryReserve)
    {
      EasyDisposeHandle(&g.memoryReserve);
      ShowErrorHook(kReleaseMemoryError);
      error = EasyCheckMemory (numberBytes);
    }
    else  /* no reserve left */
    {
      error = memFullErr;  /* so we're out of memory */
    }
  }
  return error;
}
```

This function receives the desired number of bytes. The call to **PurgeSpace()** tells you
both the total number of free bytes and the potential largest contiguous free block
available in the heap. You then check to see whether the contiguous block is big
enough. If it is not big enough, you may *not* be out of luck.

If you have a memory reserve, you can release it. The call to EasyDisposeHandle() does
that. The call to ShowErrorHook() displays a message to the users that they are running

out of memory. Finally, releasing the reserve may not release enough memory. You call EasyCheckMemory() again to make sure that there is enough memory. This is a *recursive call*—the function is calling itself! This is not only legal, it is very cool. You already have a function to check memory, why write another one?

On the other hand, if there is no reserve, you're out of luck. You post a memFullErr back to the caller. The caller is usually EasyAllocateHandle(), which then does not make the memory request because you know in advance that it will fail.

Step 4: Check the memory reserve

Modify: EasyCheckMemoryReserve() in memory.c

The memory reserve should be dynamic. You may release it at need, but you should also try to restore it when you can. That way the reserve is more than a one-shot defense against memory shortages.

When you check the reserve, it would be good to do two things. First, if there is a reserve and the user is very low on memory, release the reserve. This warns the user that memory is getting low, even if a memory request is not being made. Second, if there is no reserve, try to restore it.

```
void EasyCheckMemoryReserve(void)
{
  if (g.memoryReserve)
  {
    EasyCheckMemory(kMinimumMemory); /* ignore error */
  }
  else
  {
    EasyAllocateHandle (kMemoryReserveSize,
                        &g.memoryReserve);
  }
}
```

The call to EasyCheckMemory() ensures that there is a minimum amount of memory available. The kMinimumMemory constant is declared in userDeclare.h. If it is not available, EasyCheckMemory() releases the reserve. You can safely ignore any error because EasyCheckMemory() handles it.

If there is no reserve, you call EasyAllocateHandle() to build one. If there isn't enough room, that call will fail. However, you can ignore the error again because EasyCheckMemory() takes care of it.

In a subsequent lab, you call EasyCheckMemory() every time through the EasyApp main event loop.

Step 5:   Run the application

Modify: none

Save your work and run the project using the debugger. When the debugger window appears, do *not* run the program! If you run the program it just quits and you don't see anything.

Because we are still working at a basic level, there isn't much to see, but there is a lot going on. To see what's happening, switch to the SYM window. In the upper-left pane, select the init.c file. Locate the code for the EasyInitApp() function. You can use the function popup menu to locate it quickly, or you can scroll through the code. Set a breakpoint next to the first call to EasyAllocateHandle(), which is the call that establishes the memory reserve.

After you have the breakpoint set, run the application. It should stop almost immediately at your breakpoint. Take a look around. The calling chain of functions that led you here is in the top-left pane. The local variables are in the top right pane.

Issue a trace command (⌘-T) to step *into* the EasyAllocateHandle() function. Then trace into the EasyCheckMemory() function. Step through that code line by line. Watch what happens as EasyApp inspects the heap to ensure that there is available space. Check the value of the local variable contigSize as you walk through the function.

When you are through with EasyCheckMemory(), step out of the function and go back up to EasyAllocateHandle(). Step through this code. Because there was no error in EasyCheckMemory(), you call NewHandleClear() to actually allocate memory.

You may now run the application (⌘-R). When you do, it just quits.

The code you have written in the three labs in this chapter constitute a complete, basic memory-management strategy. Every time you make a memory request, EasyApp goes through this process. You preflight every memory request, maintain an emergency reserve, keep your pointers low in memory, keep your locked handles high, and warn the user when things go wrong.

This is the minimum behavior that any good Macintosh program should implement. It is not a guarantee of safety, because this strategy handles memory requests only from your application. The System also allocates memory inside your heap. The GrowZone() strategy discussed earlier in this chapter handles memory shortages when the System requests memory.

Memory Manager Reference

This section summarizes the basic Memory Manager calls you use in a standard Macintosh application. For full details on all the Memory Manager calls, consult Chapter 1 of *Inside Macintosh: Memory*.

You should always remember that Memory Manager calls that allocate memory may not work because the Memory Manager cannot create a contiguous free block big enough to meet your request. This situation becomes fatal—that is, the machine crashes—only when you ignore it. So, don't ignore it. To catch errors, you should do two things:

- Check for nil handles and pointers
- Call `MemError()`

note

The word "pascal" at the start of each function prototype simply tells the compiler to use Pascal language conventions when passing parameters. The Mac OS was originally written in Pascal, and the Toolbox functions expect Pascal conventions to be used.

```
pascal OSErr MemError(void);
```

Parameters	none
Returns	error value, zero if no error
Description	Call this routine if the return value from `NewHandle()` or `NewPtr()` is nil to find out what went wrong, or after other Memory Manager calls that allocate memory, such as `HandAndHand()` or `SetHandleSize()`.

```
pascal void MaxApplZone(void);
```

Parameters	none
Returns	void
Description	Increase the size of the application heap to maximum limit, so it just reaches the bottom of the stack. Make this call once as the application launches, before allocating any memory. (If you expand the size of your stack, do that before calling `MaxAppleZone()`.)

```
pascal void MoreMasters(void);
```

Parameters	none
Returns	void
Description	Each call allocates one block of 64 master pointers. Typically you should allocate as many master pointers as you will ever need as the application launches. This helps avoid heap fragmentation.

```
pascal Ptr NewPtr(Size byteCount);
```

Parameters	byteCount	the number of bytes you want in the new nonrelocatable block
Returns	A pointer to the new block, nil if error occurs.	
Description	Creates a nonrelocatable block as low in the application heap as possible. Returns the address of that block to you.	

```
pascal Ptr NewPtrClear(Size byteCount);
```

Parameters	byteCount	the number of bytes you want in the new nonrelocatable block
Returns	A pointer to the new block, nil if error occurs.	
Description	Same as `NewPtr()`, but fills the block with zeroes.	

```
pascal void DisposePtr(Ptr p);
```

Parameters	p	address of a nonrelocatable block
Returns	void	
Description	Returns block to the Memory Manager, releasing it for other uses. Do not use the pointer to this block after this call, and do not dispose of the same pointer twice. Formerly known as `DisposPtr()`.	

```
pascal Size GetPtrSize(Ptr p);
```

Parameters	p	address of a nonrelocatable block
Returns	The size in bytes of the block	
Description	Use this routine if you need to know how many bytes are in a nonrelocatable block.	

```
pascal void SetPtrSize(Ptr p, Size newSize);
```

Parameters p address of a nonrelocatable block

newSize new size of block in bytes

Returns void

Description Changes the size of a block. You may increase or decrease the size. If increasing the size, the block immediately above the target block must be moveable or the operation will fail. You should call **MemErr()** to determine the success of this operation.

```
pascal Handle NewHandle(Size byteCount);
```

Parameters byteCount the number of bytes you want in the new nonrelocatable block

Returns Handle to the relocatable block—a pointer to a master pointer. **Returns** nil if allocation fails.

Description Creates a relocatable block somewhere in the application heap.

```
pascal Handle NewHandleClear(Size byteCount);
```

Parameters byteCount the number of bytes you want in the new nonrelocatable block

Returns Handle to the relocatable block—a pointer to a master pointer. **Returns** nil if allocation fails.

Description Same as **NewHandle()**, but fills the block with zeroes.

```
pascal void DisposeHandle(Handle h);
```

Parameters h handle to a relocatable block

Returns void

Description Returns block to the Memory Manager, releasing it for other uses. Do not use the handle to this block after this call, and do not dispose of the same handle twice. Do not use this routine to dispose of resource handles! Use **ReleaseResource()** for that purpose. Formerly known as **DisposHandle()**.

```
pascal void SetHandleSize(Handle h, Size newSize);
```

Parameters   h   handle to a relocatable block

                      newSize   new size of block in bytes

Returns   void

Description   Changes the size of a block. You may increase or decrease the size. If
                      increasing the size, the block immediately above the target block must
                      be moveable or the operation will fail. You should call `MemErr()` to
                      ensure success of this operation. You are more likely to succeed if the
                      block you are resizing is unlocked, because the Memory Manager will
                      move it if necessary.

```
pascal Size GetHandleSize(Handle h);
```

Parameters   h   handle to a relocatable block

Returns   The size in bytes of the block

Description   Use this routine if you need to know how many bytes are in a
                      relocatable block.

```
pascal Handle RecoverHandle(Ptr p);
```

Parameters   p   the master pointer to a relocatable block

Returns   Handle to the block. If the parameter is not a master pointer, the
                      return value is undefined, so be sure you pass in a valid master pointer.

Description   Returns handle to a relocatable block when you have the master
                      pointer.

```
pascal char HGetState(Handle h);
```

Parameters   h   handle to a relocatable block

Returns   A char value reflecting the state of the block, whether it is
                      locked, purgeable, or a resource.

Description   Call this routine to get the current state of a block. Typically you do this
                      before changing the state of a block so you can restore it later using
                      `HSetState()`.

```
pascal void HSetState(Handle h, char flags);
```

Parameters	h	handle to a relocatable block
	flags	a char value reflecting the state of the block, whether it is locked, purgeable, or a resource
Returns	void	
Description		Typically you use this call to restore the state of a block, using a value obtained previously from `HGetState()`.

```
pascal void HLock(Handle h);
```

Parameters	h	handle to a relocatable block
Returns	void	
Description		Locks the relocatable block. This means the Memory Manager will not move the block. You can still change the contents of the block or dispose it. Typically you do this for very brief periods of time. If you want to lock a block for an extended period, move it high in the heap first using `MoveHHi()`.

```
pascal void HUnlock(Handle h);
```

Parameters	h	Handle to a relocatable block
Returns	void	
Description		Unlocks the relocatable block. Generally you use `HGetState()` and `HSetState()` to manipulate block state. Unlocking a block directly can cause hard-to-locate bugs if you unlock a block that some other routine expects to remain locked.

```
pascal void HPurge(Handle h);
```

Parameters	h	handle to a relocatable block
Returns	void	
Description		Marks the relocatable block as purgeable. This call does not actually purge the block. Generally it is advisable to use `HGetState()` and `HSetState()` to preserve and restore block state.

```
pascal void HNoPurge(Handle h);
```

Parameters	h	handle to a relocatable block
Returns	void	

Description   Marks the relocatable block as not purgeable. You may still dispose of it. Generally it is advisable to use `HGetState()` and `HSetState()` to preserve and restore block state.

```
pascal void MoveHHi(Handle h);
```

Parameters	h	handle to a relocatable block
Returns	void	

Description   Moves a block high in the heap. Typically called just before locking a block for a long period of time.

```
pascal void HLockHi(Handle h);
```

Parameters	h	handle to a relocatable block
Returns	void	

Description   Moves a block high in the heap and locks it. This is a convenience routine and accomplishes the same task as sequential calls to `MoveHHi()` and `HLock()`.

```
pascal void PurgeSpace(long *total, long *contig);
```

Parameters	total	address of a long value to receive total free bytes available
	contig	address of a long value to receive largest contiguous free block of memory
Returns	void	

Description   This call returns the total number of free bytes and the size of the largest contiguous block that would be available if memory were purged and compacted. This call does not actually purge or compact the application heap.

```
pascal long StackSpace(void);
```

Parameters	none	

Returns   The number of bytes between the top of the application heap and the bottom of the stack.

Description   If you're worried about stack overflow, you can use this call during development to monitor the space left for the stack.

```
pascal void BlockMove(const void *srcPtr, void *destPtr, Size byteCount);
```

Parameters   srcPtr   address of the source data

                   destPtr   address of the destination data

                   byteCount   the number of bytes you want to move

Returns   void

Description   Copies bytes from one location to another. This call works even if the source and destination overlap.

```
pascal OSErr HandToHand(Handle *theHndl);
```

Parameters   theHndl   address of a handle to a relocatable block

Returns   Value indicating whether an error occurred

Description   Use this call to duplicate the contents of a relocatable block into a new relocatable block. This call is a trifle dicey, so pay attention. You provide the address of a handle to an *existing* relocatable block. The Memory Manager makes a new block, copies the data, and returns the handle to the new block *in the same address you passed in*, overwriting and destroying your original handle. You must retain a copy of the original handle before calling **HandToHand()**, or you will lose it forever. That's life. Hey, even the wizards who wrote the Toolbox had an off day now and again.

```
pascal OSErr HandAndHand(Handle hand1, Handle hand2);
```

Parameters   hand1   handle to a relocatable block

                   hand2   handle to a second relocatable block

Returns   Value indicating whether an error occurred

Description   Appends the contents of hand1 onto the end of hand2. As a result, hand2 grows. The hand1 block remains unchanged. Because hand2 grows, this call allocates memory. Make sure you check the error value, as neither handle will be nil.

4

Marshal Your Resources: ResEdit Is Your Friend

This chapter introduces the basics of resources and resource management on the Macintosh—matters of concern to the Resource Manager in the Toolbox.

This chapter discusses:

- What a resource is
- The data and resource forks
- The resource map
- Working with resources
- Working with purgeable resources
- Where the Resource Manager finds resources

In this chapter you also use a resource editing tool—ResEdit—to modify existing resources in the EasyApp project. At the end of the chapter, you write code to work with resources.

What Is a Resource?

A resource is data of any kind stored in a structured format. That's pretty general—let's get a little more specific.

The designers of the Mac OS realized that much of what a computer program uses are definable tidbits of data that can be stored in standard formats. The information required to draw a window, create a menu, or display a dialog box has constant elements. The data in those elements may vary depending upon what the window looks like, how the menu operates, or the contents of the dialog box. However, each of these items has certain features that can be defined and stored in a set format.

Any data organized and stored in such a structured format can be a resource.

Resource Types and IDs

Each kind of resource has a particular assigned type. A resource type is a unique sequence of four characters. Apple Computer has defined many of the common resource types for features of the Macintosh interface, such as windows and menus. Legal characters in a resource type include letters, numbers, the space, and other symbols like the pound sign.

Examples of some common Macintosh resource types include:

- WIND—data that describes a window
- MENU—data that describes a menu
- CNTL—data for control items like buttons
- DLOG—dialog window data
- DITL—dialog item list
- ICON—a 32×32 pixel bitmap
- PICT—data that defines a picture
- snd—data that defines a sound (ends with a space)

The resource type code is case-sensitive. Most of these examples came into existence early in the history of the Macintosh. At that time, Apple Computer used all capital letters for its own resource types. The 'snd ' resource type is of more recent vintage. Currently, Apple Computer uses all lowercase letters. This bit of trivia is important when you define your own resource types, as you'll see in a little while.

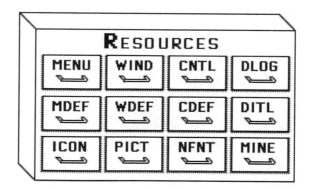

Figure 4.1 Structured resources

Most resources contain structured data. For example, the MENU resource contains the title of the menu, the names of the items in the menu, any associated command-key equivalents, and some other information. Because this data is structured, the same kind of data appears in the same place in every MENU resource. You can change them easily without having to rewrite or recompile your code.

Some resources contain executable code that defines the look and behavior of standard desktop objects. These resources are generally located in the System file.

The resource type for definition resources generally ends with the letters "DEF." For example, a resource of type MDEF is a menu definition resource. The operating system executes code found in the MDEF resource to draw and manage a menu. Similarly, the WDEF resource defines the appearance of one or more windows. A CDEF resource defines the appearance of a control item like a checkbox, button, scroll bar, or popup menu.

The existence of definition resources in the System file simplifies your life as a Macintosh programmer. You don't have to worry about how to draw windows, menus, or controls. The operating system takes care of all that drudgery for you.

Advanced programmers occasionally substitute their own definition resources so that they can create unique and sometimes extraordinary behavior for windows, menus, and controls. Generally, it is wise to use the standard definitions. Then, your application behaves exactly the way millions of Macintosh owners expect it to behave. Besides, if Apple improves the standard definitions, you get the benefit without changing a thing in your program.

Resource ID Numbers

As there are different types of resources, you may have several different resources of the same type. For example, an application may have several different MENU resources, one for each menu in the application.

You identify individual resources of a given type with an ID number. For example, each MENU resource must have a unique ID number to distinguish it from the other MENU resources. Figure 4.2 shows some typical MENU ID numbers.

The full range allowed for resource ID numbers is –32768 to 32767. However, all numbers less than 128—including negative numbers—are reserved for special purposes. Some specific resources have further restrictions on their resource ID numbers, but the details are beyond the scope of this book. In general, when you create resources you should assign ID numbers greater than 127.

Besides type and ID number, resources may also have names. Very few applications use names to access resources except for fonts. Fonts should be accessed by name because the same font resource may have different numbers on different machines. You must use Pascal-style strings when working with names. See Appendix B for a discussion of the differences between Pascal and C strings.

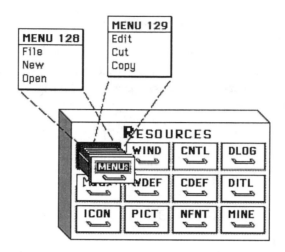

Figure 4.2 MENU ID numbers

Custom Resource Types

You are not limited to Apple-defined resource types. You can define your own resource types. There are no limits to the kind of data you include in a resource, or how you structure that data.

If you create your own resources, you must assign a resource type. That type must not impinge on any existing standard resource types. In addition, the resource type should use capital letters. This ensures that you will not interfere with any new resource types that may be created by Apple Computer in the future. Apple Computer reserves all resource types that consist of lowercase letters.

In Figures 4.1 and 4.2, the bottom-right drawer of the cabinet contains resources of type MINE. This is a fictitious resource type created to illustrate the fact that you can create your own resource types. There is no standard resource of type MINE.

Resource Attributes

The Resource Manager routines are responsible for manipulating resources. So that the routines can do their work, resources have attributes. Resource attributes are bit flags that tell the Resource Manager how to handle a resource.

Each resource has six attributes, as shown in Figure 4.3. When speaking of attributes, if the attribute is "set," it means that the option is on or active. If the attribute is "clear" it means that the option is off or inactive. Figure 4.3 shows the resource attributes.

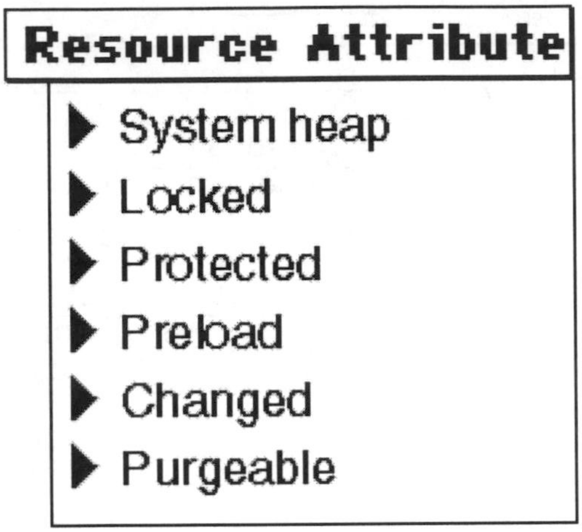

Resource Attribute

▶ System heap
▶ Locked
▶ Protected
▶ Preload
▶ Changed
▶ Purgeable

Figure 4.3 Resource attributes

You may set or clear these attributes using a resource editor like ResEdit. You may also change some of these attributes at runtime—while a program is running—using Toolbox calls. The two attributes you are most likely to set using Toolbox calls are the *locked* and *purgeable* attributes.

If the load into system heap attribute is set, the Resource Manager puts the resource in the system heap. Normally, you want an application's resources loaded into the application's own heap, so you clear this attribute for typical application resources.

Resources are always loaded into relocatable blocks by the Resource Manager, so you access a resource through a handle. Some of the Memory Manager routines that operate on handles work for resource handles as well.

For example, you use the Memory Manager calls `HLock()` and `HUnlock()` to set or clear the *locked* attribute of a resource, just like you do for any other handle. If the resource is locked, the resource cannot be moved in memory, nor can it be purged (even if the *purgeable* flag is set).

If the *protected* attribute is set, the resource cannot be changed. This means you cannot change the resource ID, the name, the contents of the resource, or remove the resource from the resource fork. Normally, you don't need to set this attribute.

If a resource's *preload* attribute is set, the Resource Manager loads the resource into memory automatically when your application launches. If this attribute is clear, the Resource Manager loads the resource when you ask for it. On occasion you may want to have a resource preloaded, but most of the time this attribute is clear.

The *changed* attribute tells the Resource Manager that this resource has changed. Usually, the Resource Manager takes care of this attribute for you. You can explicitly set this attribute by calling `ChangedResource()`.

If the *purgeable* attribute is set, you are telling the Memory Manager that it can dispose of this resource any time it needs memory. This can optimize your application's use of memory, but it has to be done correctly or the results will be fatal. This topic will be discussed in detail in the section titled "Working with Purgeable Resources" later in this chapter.

The `HPurge()` and `HNoPurge()` Memory Manager routines mark a handle as purgeable or not purgeable. These calls work for resource handles.

In summary, each resource has a type, ID, a set of attributes, and may have a name. You usually create or modify resources with a resource editor application. In this book you use ResEdit.

Lab 4.1 An Introduction to ResEdit

This lab introduces ResEdit, Apple's resource editing application. You will use ResEdit in several labs. If you are already familiar with ResEdit, you can skip this lab. If you are unfamiliar with ResEdit, in this lab you:

- Launch ResEdit

- Open a resource file

- Open an existing resource

- Make a resource purgeable

- Save changes and quit ResEdit

In subsequent chapters, you create several resources of various types.

A copy of ResEdit is in the Tools You Need folder on the CD. If you have not already done so, copy ResEdit to your hard drive. Use your code from the previous lab as the starting point for your work in this lab.

The illustrations in this lab may differ slightly from the version of ResEdit you use. You can find the latest version of ResEdit online in many places and on many services.

Step 1: Launch ResEdit

Double-click the ResEdit icon on your hard drive to launch the application. A window may appear with a cute jack-in-the-box (see Figure 4.1.1). If this happens, click the window and it disappears. You can modify preferences to see this window and select other default settings for ResEdit by choosing the Preferences item in the File menu.

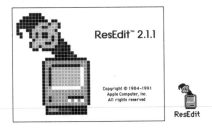

Figure 4.1.1 ResEdit splash screen and icon

Step 2: Open a resource file

Modify: none in EasyApp.μ.rsrc

Choose the Open item from the File menu. In the resulting dialog box, navigate to the Easy Source folder inside your project folder. This folder contains all the source, resource, and header files for EasyApp. Inside that folder, locate the EasyApp.μ.rsrc file. This file contains the EasyApp resources. Double-click this file name in the dialog box, or click the Open button to open the file. Figure 4.1.2 shows the open dialog box.

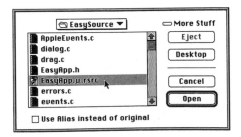

Figure 4.1.2 Opening a resource file

The resource window for this file appears, listing all the types of resources available. In the View menu, you can choose to view the available resources by icon or by type. Figure 4.1.3 shows both views. You decide which suits you best.

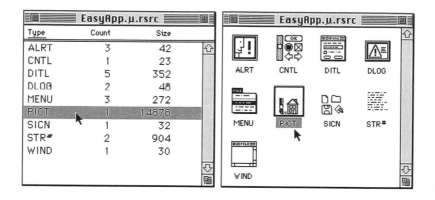

Figure 4.1.3 The resource window

Step 3: Open an existing resource

Modify: none in EasyApp.µ.rsrc

To open an existing resource, double-click the type of resource you want to open. For this exercise, double-click the PICT resource type. You may also select the PICT type and choose the Open PICT Picker item in the Resource menu.

A new window appears. This is the PICT picker. The picker allows you to select a particular PICT resource. In this case there is only one PICT resource. Once again, the View menu gives you options for how to view the resource. Figure 4.1.4 illustrates the PICT view. The View menu is dynamic, it changes depending upon the nature of the resource at which you are looking. In this case you have the option of viewing a thumbnail of the PICT resource itself.

With most resources you double-click the individual resource in the picker window to open and edit the resource. If you double-click a PICT resource, you can view the PICT at actual size. You cannot change the PICT.

Figure 4.1.4 The PICT picker

Step 4:   Make a resource purgeable
Modify: `PICT resource` in EasyApp.μ.rsrc

In this step you modify a resource's attributes. Click once on the PICT in the picker window to select it. Then choose the Get Resource Info item (⌘-I) from the Resource menu. The resource information window appears, shown in Figure 4.1.5.

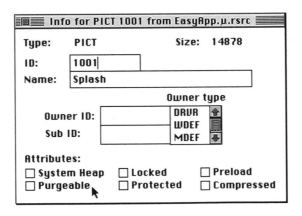

Figure 4.1.5 Resource information window

You can set the resource ID number and resource name here. In this case those items are all right, so don't change them. You will not use the Owner ID and Sub ID items at any time in this book. Along the bottom of the window are the resource attributes.

Click the Purgeable checkbox to make this resource purgeable. An "x" should appear in the checkbox. Then close the information window.

With the PICT picker window as the active window, use the View menu to view the PICT resources by ID number. In this view the picker window displays the current state of the resource attributes. In Figure 4.1.6, notice that the Purge column has a dot indicating that this attribute is now set.

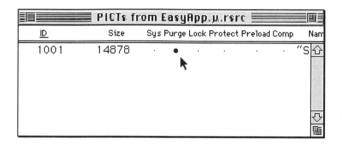

Figure 4.1.6 The picker window revisited

Step 5:   Save changes and quit ResEdit

Save the changes you have made to the resource file. Choose the Save item (⌘-S) in the File menu. Choose the Quit item (⌘-Q) in the File menu to quit ResEdit.

This exercise is just a brief introduction to ResEdit. In subsequent labs, you use ResEdit to create new resources for EasyApp and EasyPuzzle. If you want more information about ResEdit and other resource editors, consult Appendix D.

The Data and Resource Forks

The concept of resources gave the Macintosh designers a problem. Where do you store this information? Resources are highly structured, and you want to get at them more or less randomly. There is no way to know what resource you may want next.

The solution to this problem is both elegant and powerful. The Macintosh operating system separates data from resources, and provides a map to the resources. As a result, every Macintosh file has two parts, or "forks," the data fork and the resource fork, either of which can be empty. Figure 4.4 illustrates this idea.

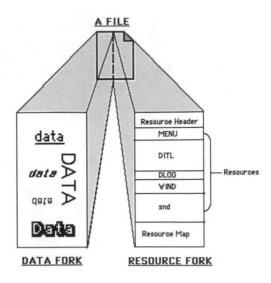

Figure 4.4 Data and resource forks

The *data fork* is a closet with no shelves, dividers, or hangers. It can contain any kind of data organized in any fashion. Your application must manage the exact byte location of each particular piece of data that it saves in the data fork so that you can locate the right data when you need it.

In contrast to the unstructured nature of the data fork, the *resource fork* is a file cabinet with a series of drawers, each of which contains a certain type of data, as illustrated in Figures 4.1 and 4.2. You access resources by their type and ID number.

Different kinds of files tend to use the two forks differently. For this discussion, three kinds of files are considered: a document, a 68K application file, and a Power Mac application file. Table 4.1 summarizes how the different kinds of files use the data and resource forks. An explanation of the table's contents follows the table.

Table 4.1: Fork Contents

File Type	Data Fork	Resource Fork
Document	store data	document-related resources
68K Application	empty	resources & code resources
Power Mac Application	code	resources

Typically, a document file's data fork holds the contents of the document in a form that the creating application understands. There are no limits to this format. Your application can store data in whatever way it deems appropriate. However, the data in a document may take a highly structured form. For example, one type of resource on the Macintosh is a PICT resource. It defines a picture. If the document contains a PICT, the application may store the PICT data in the resource fork of the document file rather than the data fork.

Applications may have some data, but typically applications consist of executable code (the code that actually runs in the computer) and application resources. Power Mac and 68K application files store this information differently.

The data fork for a 68K application file is usually empty. The resource fork for a 68K application file contains both code and resources. The application's code is stored in one or more resources of type CODE. Other application resources are also in the resource fork.

The data fork for a Power Mac application contains the application's executable code. Power Mac applications store other application resources in the resource fork. Power Mac applications do not typically have CODE resources unless they are "fat binary." A fat binary application has code for both the 68K Mac and Power Mac.

The Resource Map

Built into every resource fork is a special data structure known as the resource map. The Resource Manager creates and maintains this important structure. The resource map contains the resource type, ID number, name, attributes, and location of each and every resource in the resource fork.

When the map is stored in a file on-disk, the location contains the number of bytes between the start of the resource fork and the start of the particular resource. Using this offset information, the Resource Manager can locate the correct resource when you ask it to get a resource for you.

The map does double duty, however. When the Resource Manager opens the resource fork of a file, just about the first thing it does is read this map into memory. The map remains in memory until the fork is closed.

When you get a resource for the first time, the Resource Manager puts the resource handle in the resource map as the location of that resource. If the resource has not been loaded into memory, the handle is nil. Unless the *preload* attribute is set, resources are not read into memory until you ask for them.

Figure 4.5 illustrates some parts of the resource map in memory. Note that the two MENU resources have the preload attribute set, so they have been loaded into memory. Their handles are stored in the location area of the resource map. The other resources have not been loaded into memory yet. The two PICT resources are marked as purgeable. The WIND resource is not purgeable.

TYPE	ID	ATTRIBUTES Pre Lock Pur			HANDLE
MENU	1000	X			124C
MENU	1001	X			128A
WIND	1000				NIL
PICT	1000			X	NIL
PICT	1001			X	NIL

Figure 4.5 Resource map in memory

Whenever you ask for a resource, the Resource Manager first looks at the resource map. If there is a handle, it gives you the handle. If the handle is nil, it knows that the resource has never been loaded. It goes to disk and gets the resource for you, puts it in memory, returns the handle to you, and stores the handle in the resource map for future reference.

This makes your work with resources as efficient as possible.

Working with Resources

You should always remember that Resource Manager calls *may not work*. Any number of things can go wrong. For example, there may not be enough memory to load the resource, the Resource Manager cannot find the file it wants to read, or the resource itself does not exist.

Very few of these problems are initially fatal. They become fatal—that is, the machine crashes—when you ignore them. So, don't ignore them. To catch Resource Manager errors, you should do two things:

- Call ResError()
- Check for nil handles

The Resource Manager does not report errors directly. You should call ResError() after *every* Resource Manager call that can result in an error.

However, ResError() is not foolproof! Some calls—like Get1Resource()—return a nil handle when they fail, but ResError() may return no error! You should look for *both* an error and a nil handle. Never trust one or the other alone. Keep this error checking in mind every time you make a Resource Manager call.

Why doesn't ResError() always work? The Macintosh has a single location in memory to store the latest resource error. If Get1Resource() fails, for example, it sets the error. However, before it returns to you, it makes another internal Resource Manager call. If that call succeeds, it clears the error and you miss the error completely. Bad design? You bet. Just remember to look for errors *and* nil handles; then you will be safe.

To work with resources, you must know how to create, open, and close a resource fork. While the resource fork is open, you may also read resources from disk, write resources to disk, modify, add, release, or remove resources.

You do not need to open or close your application's resource fork. The Mac OS handles that for you when it launches your application and when your application quits. If you use the resource fork of a document file, you *do* need to open and close the resource fork for that file. Saving and opening files—including resource forks—is discussed in detail in Chapter 15. At that time you will learn about how to specify with which file to work. A brief overview here helps you understand how the Resource Manager works with files and the resource map.

When you save a new document, you may want to create a resource fork for the file. Call FSpCreateResFile(). This creates an empty resource fork. This does not open the fork, it merely creates the fork and writes an empty resource map to disk.

To open a resource fork, you call FSpOpenResFile(). You specify which file you want to open and whether you want to read or write data, or both. You can then use Resource Manager calls to work with the open resource fork. This is discussed in a little bit.

To close a resource fork when you are through with it, call CloseResFile().You specify the file. This call updates the resource fork of the file on-disk if you have changed resources.

While the resource fork is open, you can read resources into memory. When you want a handle to a resource, you call GetResource(). You provide the resource type and ID number to the Resource Manager. It returns a handle to the resource data.

There are several routines similar to GetResource() that make this process easier for particular kinds of resources. For example, the Menu Manager routine GetMenu()

requires a resource ID only because it knows you want a MENU resource. Using `GetMenu()` has the same effect as calling `GetResource()` with a resource type MENU and the resource ID.

Similar calls from other managers include `GetNewControl()`, `GetCursor()`, `GetNewDialog()`, `GetIcon()`, `GetPattern()`, `GetPicture()`, `GetString()`, and `GetNewWindow()`. Each requires a simple resource ID number because it knows the type of resource you want to use. Many perform additional tasks besides simply getting the resource for you.

To release memory allocated to a resource, call `ReleaseResource()`. You provide the resource handle. This invalidates the resource handle, sets the master pointer to nil, clears the resource map, and releases the memory occupied by the resource. If you subsequently get the resource again, the Resource Manager reads it from disk and creates a new handle.

> Do not call `DisposeHandle()` with a resource handle. If you do, the handle in the resource map for that block remains in place, although the memory it points to is now free and the handle is invalid. In essence, the Resource Manager doesn't know that you have dumped the memory. If you attempt to access the resource using that handle, you are in for big trouble. Using `DisposeHandle()` on a resource handle qualifies as an official Bad Thing.

After you obtain a resource, sometimes you want to use that data independently of the Resource Manager. To convert a resource handle to a regular handle, call `DetachResource()`. You specify the resource handle. The Resource Manager sets the handle in the resource map to nil. This makes the Resource Manager think that the data is no longer in memory. However, the memory is not released. The handle remains valid. The data is no longer a resource, however, and you are responsible for maintaining and disposing of the data. Use `DisposeHandle()` to release blocks that are detached from the Resource Manager.

On occasion, you may want to convert a regular handle to a resource so that you can add it to the resource fork of a file. To do this, call `AddResource()`. You provide the handle to the data, the desired resource type, the desired ID number, and a name. This adds the resource to the resource map in memory for the current resource file. *It also converts the handle to a resource handle.* What does that mean? Don't use `DisposeHandle()` on this handle, because it is now a resource.

You have to be careful using AddResource(). You don't want to use a handle to an existing resource. The handle must be to data that is not already a resource. There is a second pitfall, as well. The Resource Manager does not ensure that the ID number you provide is not already in use. If you use a duplicate ID number, you will overwrite the existing resource with the same type and ID, with potentially evil consequences. You can use UniqueID() to get a unique ID number.

If you modify a resource and you want to let the Resource Manager know it has changed, call ChangedResource(). This sets the resource's changed attribute.

You may also remove a resource from the resource map permanently. Call RemoveResource(). This detaches the resource and removes information about the resource from the resource map. When you update or close the resource file, *the resource is removed from disk.*

RemoveResource() does not release memory occupied by the resource handle. You must call DisposeHandle() to do that. You cannot use ReleaseResource() because the handle is no longer a resource handle. It has been detached as well as removed from the resource map.

If you want to write the entire resource map and all changed data to disk, call UpdateResFile(). This happens automatically when you close the resource file.

If you want to write a specific resource to disk, use WriteResource(). You provide the resource handle. This writes the data only if the changed attribute is set. Of course, you must make sure the resource hasn't been purged before you write it. Purgeable resources can be a conundrum. However, working with them is simple if you understand and follow the rules.

Working with Purgeable Resources

Of all the resource attributes, the one of greatest concern is the purgeable attribute. If a resource is purgeable, the Memory Manager may remove it from memory without warning and is sure to do so at the most inopportune moment. If you attempt to use a resource after it has been purged, you could be in for big trouble.

Some resources must never be purgeable. MENU resources are the prime example. The Menu Manager expects them to be in memory at all times, so they must never be purged.

However, most other resources may be purgeable. There are methods for dealing with purgeable resources, which will be discussed in just a bit, but most of the time you can avoid problems altogether with a simple trick.

Don't make your resources purgeable unless you must.

The whole idea behind purgeable resources dates back to the time when the Macintosh had 128K of memory. With space that tight, programmers had to be very careful what went where, and how long it stayed around. With purgeable resources, the Memory Manager could remove them from precious memory while they were not in use, and put something else in their place.

Times have changed. Most Macintosh computers have lots of memory. Most resources can hang around in memory without causing you to suffer a memory shortage. Most resources are very small. A DLOG resource occupies 24 bytes. A WIND resource requires 30 bytes. These are not memory monsters.

Considering the hazards of purgeable resources, it is generally advisable to make all small and basic resources nonpurgeable. You avoid a lot of problems, and the only penalty is that you lose a little memory.

All the same, some resources do take up a lot of room. For example, PICT, 'snd ', and QuickTime movie resources can occupy enormous amounts of space. It doesn't make a lot of sense to move a 400K sound into memory, play it once, and then leave it in memory in case you need it again later. If it's purgeable, the Memory Manager can get rid of the resource to reclaim the memory.

You get a purgeable resource like any other resource. You call `GetResource()`. This loads the resource into memory and gives you a handle to the resource. At that point you know the purgeable resource is in memory, but it might be purged immediately if the next thing you do allocates memory. The Memory Manager may purge the resource without warning. When a resource is purged, its *master pointer* is set to nil. The handle still points to the correct master pointer, but the master pointer is invalid because it points to zero.

> Remember, using address zero is a Very Bad Thing! If you attempt to read data pointed to by an invalid master pointer, you get garbage and may crash the machine. If you attempt to write data to a purged resource, you will *certainly* crash the machine, thoroughly and completely, because you are writing to a zero address.

Before using a purgeable resource, you have to exercise some caution. You must do two things:

- Make sure the resource is in memory
- Make sure it stays in memory while you use it

The first task is easy to accomplish. Always assume the resource is purged. If you already have a handle to the resource, call LoadResource(). If the resource has been purged, LoadResource() loads it back into memory. *Always make this call before performing any operation on a purgeable resource.*

When you call LoadResource(), the Resource Manager looks at the master pointer. If the master pointer is nil, the Resource Manager goes to disk to read the resource back into memory. If the master pointer is valid, the Resource Manager does nothing, because both the handle and the master pointer are valid.

To ensure that the resource stays in memory, use the Memory Manager routine HNoPurge(). This makes the resource nonpurgeable. *Do this before performing any operation on a purgeable resource.*

The safe way to use this routine is with two other Memory Manager routines, HGetState() and HSetState(). These routines were discussed in Chapter 3 in connection with locking a handle. Use HGetState() to get and preserve the current state of the memory block (in this case, a resource). Then call HNoPurge() to make the resource nonpurgeable. When you are through working with the resource, restore the original state of the handle with HSetState(). Doing so ensures that you leave things exactly as you found them.

If you do not make the resource nonpurgeable, you could be in for immediate trouble. For example, assume you have a purgeable PICT resource, and you call LoadResource() to make sure you have the PICT in memory. Then you call DrawPicture() with that resource handle. The resource may disappear! The call to DrawPicture() may cause the resource to be purged from memory. If it does, your application will crash. You must make the resource nonpurgeable before any operation that may move or purge memory.

In summary, the procedure for working with purgeable resources is simple. Before doing *anything* with a purgeable resource, call LoadResource(), and then make the resource nonpurgeable. When you are through, restore the resource's original state. If you follow these steps, purgeable resources will cause you no problems.

Where the Resource Manager Finds Resources

When you ask for a resource, the Resource Manager follows a clear path to locate it. You can control that path to a certain extent.

The search begins in the current resource file. Unless you tell the Resource Manager otherwise, the current resource file is the most recently opened resource fork. This may be your application's resource fork, or a document's resource fork.

If the Resource Manager does not locate the resource in the current resource file, it looks in the next most recently opened resource fork—perhaps another document or your application. If the requested resource is not found, the search continues to the next most recent resource fork, and so on.

In short, resource files are connected in a linked list. The start of the list is the current resource file. The end of the list is the System file. Figure 4.6 shows the resource search path.

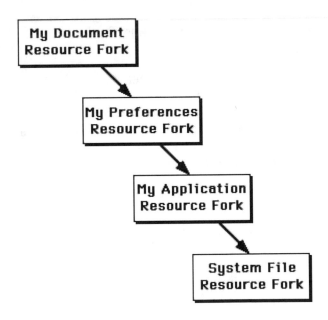

Figure 4.6 Default resource search path

The search stops when the Resource Manager finds a resource of the specified type and ID. The default search path allows you to put a resource in a document, open the document, and have that resource override a resource with the same type and ID in your application. Likewise, your application resources can override resources in the System file, because your application is normally searched first.

You can control where the search begins. You may specify the file where the search starts by calling UseResFile(). This sets the current resource file to the file you specify. The search starts there and continues down the linked list.

In a typical Macintosh application, one of the first things you do is get a reference number for your own application's resource file. (The File Manager assigns every resource file a unique reference number.) To do this, call CurResFile(). This call returns the file reference number to the current resource file. Because you just opened your application, it is the current resource file.

Then, when you want to load a resource that you know is in your own application, you call UseResFile() to specify your file as the current resource file (see Figure 4.7). Doing so can make the search more efficient because files higher in the resource path are not searched.

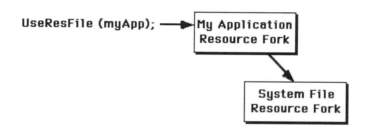

Figure 4.7 Specified search path

To further increase the efficiency of the search, the Resource Manager has some "1-deep" routines that parallel routines that have already been discussed (see Figure 4.8). These routines search the current resource file only. No other resource files are examined.

For example, you can use Get1Resource() as an alternative to GetResource(). Unique1ID() parallels UniqueID().

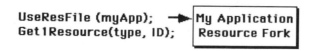

Figure 4.8 One-deep resource search

4

Lab 4.2 Managing Resources

In this exercise, you write code to get resources. In addition, you modify `EasyDisposeHandle()` to dispose of resource handles properly.

There are certain steps you must take to get a resource. You can follow those steps every time you want a resource—but that means you write a lot of redundant code, and you increase the likelihood of making a mistake. The EasyApp approach to Toolbox calls that require such care and feeding is to write a function that takes care of the details. These are called "wrappers" because the function wraps some application code around the Toolbox call.

In this lab you write the EasyApp wrapper for the **Get1Resource()** Toolbox routine. Every time you need a resource, call `EasyGet1Resource()`. This function takes care of all the Resource Manager details. You write it once, you do it right, and then you don't have to worry about how to get resources. In this lab you:

- Get a resource from a file

- Dispose of a resource handle

- Use the new `EasyGet1Resource()` function

Use your code from the previous lab (Lab 4.1) as the starting point for your work in this lab.

Step 1: Get a resource from a file

Modify: `EasyGet1Resource()` in file.c

In this step, you write the code for a 1-deep search of a single file's resource fork. As usual, the function title and local variables are provided for you. This function receives three parameters: the file ID number that specifies the file in which to search, the resource type to look for, and the resource ID to get.

```
OSErr      error;


saveResFile = CurResFile();
UseResFile(fileID);
error = ResError();
if (error)
{
  UseResFile(saveResFile);
  return resource; /*set to nil already */
}

resource = Get1Resource(resType, resID);

error = ResError();  /* look for resource error */
if (error || resource == nil) /* and nil handle */
{
  resource = nil;  /* make sure it is nil */
}

UseResFile(saveResFile);
return(resource);
```

The call to CurResFile() preserves the current resource file, because we may be changing it. The call to UseResFile() tells the Resource Manager to start searching in the specified file. You check for an error and restore things if an error occurs.

You then call Get1Resource() to perform a 1-deep search of the resource file for the resource of the specified type and ID number. The results of the search end up in the local variable, resource.

As always, check for errors. Notice that the error-checking code calls ResError() *and* checks for a nil handle. If there is an error, the handle returned is set to nil.

Before returning the resulting handle, the function restores the original resource file. The state of the machine is the same after the call as it was before the call.

Step 2: Dispose a resource handle

Modify: EasyDisposeHandle() in memory.c

If a handle is a resource handle, you should call ReleaseResource(), not DisposeHandle(). The EasyDisposeHandle() function should take care of this for you. The existing code (in italics) makes sure the handle is valid before disposing of it. You should also determine whether the handle is a resource handle.

```
if (theHandle)
{
  flags = HGetState(theHandle);  /* get the handle flags */
  if (flags & 0x0020)     /* it is a resource */
  {
    ReleaseResource(theHandle);
  }

  else  /* not a resource */
  {
    DisposeHandle(theHandle);
  }

  *handleAddress = nil;
}
```

The new code gets the state of the handle, which includes a bit that identifies the handle as a resource handle. Rather than simply calling DisposeHandle(), the new code tests the resource bit. If the handle is a resource handle, you call ReleaseResource(). If not, you call DisposeHandle().

Now EasyDisposeHandle() can take care of any handle.

Step 3: Use the EasyGet1Resource() function

Modify: EasyGetDialog() in dialog.c

In its current stage of development, the only function in EasyApp that gets resources is EasyGetDialog(). You won't learn about dialogs until later, but EasyGetDialog() is necessary so that the shell can display error messages at this early stage.

The code in EasyGetDialog() does not call EasyGet1Resource() because that function hasn't existed until now. In this step you replace some of the original code in EasyGetDialog() with calls to EasyGet1Resource().

There are two existing calls to Get1Resource() in EasyGetDialog(). The first checks for the existence of a 'DLOG' resource, the second for the associated 'DITL' resource. You replace them both. A 'DLOG' is a dialog window resource. A 'DITL' is a dialog item list—the items in the dialog.

First, make the call for the 'DLOG' resource. In the following listing, you must delete the existing code and replace it with the new code. Make sure you delete the existing code (existing code is in italics).

```
dlog = (DialogTemplate**) Get1Resource('DLOG', resID);
error = ResError();
if(error)
{
  return error;
}
dlog = (DialogTemplate**)EasyGet1Resource(g.appResFile,
                                  'DLOG', resID);
```

Make sure you delete all the existing code listed previously. Then make your new call to EasyGet1Resource(). The remaining existing code checks the dlog handle to ensure that the call to EasyGet1Resource() was successful.

Repeat the process for the DITL resource. Remember, delete all this existing code.

```
ditl = Get1Resource('DITL', (**dlog).itemsID);
error = ResError();
if(error)
{
    return error;
}

ditl = EasyGet1Resource(g.appResFile, 'DITL',
                    (**dlog).itemsID);
```

Make sure you delete all the code listed previously. The remaining existing code checks the validity of the ditl handle to ensure that everything is OK.

You accomplish several things here. The new calls to EasyGet1Resource() make this function a lot simpler to understand. They also make your code more efficient because you reuse the code in EasyGet1Resource() instead of writing redundant code. Your code is less prone to error because you don't have to repeat every step required to get a resource successfully.

In addition, the EasyGet1Resource() function is more robust than the original code, because it ensures that you use the correct resource file.

Finally, if you discover some unforeseen problem in the resource-fetching code, or you decide to modify how you get resources (perhaps to hunt more deeply than one file), you have to fix only one function.

Step 4: Run the application

Modify: none

Save your work and run the project using the debugger.

In the SYM window, select the dialog.c file in the upper-left pane of the window. Locate the `EasyGetDialog()` function in the source code and set a breakpoint at the first call to `EasyGet1Resource()`. Then run the application.

When the code stops at the breakpoint, take a look around. In the debugger window, the top-left pane has the calling chain. You can see the names of the functions you passed through to get to where you are. The top-right pane has the local variables.

Now, step into `EasyGet1Resource()` (⌘-T for trace). Then issue a series of step commands (⌘-S) to walk through the code you wrote. Watch how the code works. Study the local variable `resource` to see how the handle changes at the call to **`Get1Resource()`**.

When you are through, type ⌘-R to resume the program. It just quits right away. It still doesn't do much, but you're making substantial progress. Thanks to you, EasyApp now handles memory and resources quite well.

In the next chapter, we take a short side trip into the entomology of the code jungle— bugs. Then we get to the main event—creating an event loop.

Resource Manager Reference

This reference summarizes the basic Resource Manager calls you use in a standard Macintosh application. For full details on all the Memory Manager calls, consult Chapter 1 of *Inside Macintosh: More Macintosh Toolbox*.

```
pascal short ResError(void)
```

Parameters	none
Returns	A value indicating an error
Description	Make this call after every Resource Manager call that may cause an error. Don't forget to also check for a nil handle when getting a resource.

```
pascal void FSpCreateResFile(const FSSpec *spec, OSType creator, OSType
fileType, ScriptCode scriptTag)
```

Parameters	spec	address of a file specification for the new file
	creator	creator signature of creating application
	fileType	file type of the new file
	scriptTag	script system, usually roman
Returns	void	
Description	Creates an empty resource fork for the file specified. Does not open the file. Call `ResError()` to check for errors.	

```pascal
pascal short FSpOpenResFile(const FSSpec *spec, SignedByte permission)
```

Parameters	spec	address of file specification for file to open
	permission	flag indicating read/write permissions
Returns	A file reference to the newly opened file. If it fails, return value is –1	
Description	Open the resource fork of the specified file. Makes file the current resource file. Use `ResError()` to check for errors.	

```pascal
pascal void CloseResFile(short refNum)
```

Parameters	refNum	file reference number for this resource fork
Returns	void	
Description	Closes the resource fork of the file. Use `ResError()` to check for errors.	

```pascal
pascal short CurResFile(void)
```

Parameters	none
Returns	The file reference number for the current resource file
Description	Call this routine to get the file reference number for the current resource file.

```pascal
pascal void UseResFile(short refNum)
```

Parameters	refNum	file reference number for file you want to be the current resource file
Returns	void	
Description	Sets current resource file to file specified. Usually you want to preserve the current file before changing it so you can restore it.	

```
pascal Handle GetResource(ResType theType, short theID)
```

Parameters   theType   the four-character resource type
                          theID   the ID number of the desired resource

Returns   A handle to the desired resource, nil if error occurs

Description   Returns the handle to the resource from the resource map. Loads the resource from disk if necessary. Use **ResError()** to get actual error if result is nil.

```
pascal Handle Get1Resource(ResType theType, short theID)
```

Parameters   theType   the four-character resource type
                          theID   the ID number of the desired resource

Returns   A handle to the desired resource, nil if error occurs

Description   Same as **GetResource()** but searches current resource file only.

```
pascal void LoadResource(Handle theResource)
```

Parameters   theResource   handle to the desired resource

Returns   void

Description   If the resource is not in memory, this loads it into memory. **ResError()** tells you if this call fails.

```
pascal void ChangedResource(Handle theResource)
```

Parameters   theResource   handle to the desired resource

Returns   void

Description   Sets the resource's changed attribute. The data is not written immediately. Call **ResError()** because the Resource Manager checks to make sure the data fits on-disk. If it does not, the call fails.

```
pascal void AddResource(Handle theData, ResType theType, short theID,
ConstStr255Param name)
```

Parameters   theData   handle to the data you want to become a resource
                          theType   the resource type to assign to this data
                          theID   the resource ID for this data
                          name   the name for this resource, typically blank

Returns	void
Description	Converts a handle to a resource handle, adds it to the resource map for the current resource file, marks it as changed. Does not write data to disk immediately. Call `ResError()` to check for failure. Does not verify unique ID number.

```pascal
pascal void UpdateResFile(short refNum)
```

Parameters	refNum	file reference number for the resource file
Returns	void	
Description	Writes resource map and all changed resources to disk. Use `ResError()` to check for errors.	

```pascal
pascal void WriteResource(Handle theResource)
```

Parameters	theResource	handle to the resource to write to disk
Returns	void	
Description	If the resource is changed, writes it to disk. Does not write resource map. `UpdateResFile()` is usually better. Use `ResError()` to check for errors.	

```pascal
pascal short UniqueID(ResType theType)
```

Parameters	theType	resource type for which you want a unique ID
Returns	A unique ID value	
Description	In system 7, returns random ID number >=128 not in use in any open resource file.	

```pascal
pascal short Unique1ID(ResType theType)
```

Parameters	theType	resource type for which you want a unique ID
Returns	A unique ID value	
Description	Same as `UniqueID()`, but looks in current resource file only.	

```pascal
pascal void ReleaseResource(Handle theResource)
```

Parameters	theResource	handle to the resource in question
Returns	void	
Description	Releases memory allocated to a resource handle.	

```
pascal void DetachResource(Handle theResource)
```

Parameters   theResource   handle to the resource in question

Returns   void

Description   Sets value for this handle in resource map to nil, but handle remains valid and your responsibility. Handle is no longer a resource handle.

```
pascal void RemoveResource(Handle theResource)
```

Parameters   theResource   handle to the resource in question

Returns   void

Description   Entirely removes entry for this handle from the resource map. When data is written to disk, resource is removed from the resource fork of the file.

5

Bug Hunting: Finding Bugs in Code

You have already come a long way. In Chapter 3, you learned about how the Macintosh manages memory. In Chapter 4, you learned about the concept of resources on the Macintosh, and how to use the Resource Manager. There is a lot of information in both chapters. You don't have to memorize it all. These chapters familiarize you with fundamental principals that derive from the design of the Mac OS. If you feel confused right now, don't worry about it. Because these are basic concepts, you encounter them again and again. You have many opportunities to grasp the details, and ultimately they will become an integral part of your programming skills.

You can categorize all of this material as background knowledge. Before you get to the real meat of Macintosh application programming, there is one more background skill you should become familiar with—finding bugs.

In this chapter, you read about the different kinds of common bugs you may encounter. Then you learn how to sneak up on a bug—compiler in hand—ready to squash it. At the end of this chapter you go on a bug hunt to find a memory leak.

Types of Bugs

Computer entomology is a rich and varied field. Any attempt at classifying bugs is sure to miss quite a few species hiding in the code jungle. Nevertheless, into the jungle we go.

You can generally classify bugs as falling into two categories: logic bugs and coding bugs.

Logic Bugs

An algorithm, in its most general sense, is a series of steps you follow to reach a solution. An algorithm is not necessarily mathematical. A recipe for making chocolate fudge is an algorithm that produces a tasty solution.

A logic bug is a problem with the algorithm. Logic bugs are mistakes in the way you solve a problem. In a logic bug, the code is absolutely perfect, it just does the wrong thing. If your algorithm for chocolate fudge neglects to consider the temperature of the oven, you might end up creating a charcoal brick.

Finding a logic bug can be difficult. You have already thought the problem through and developed a solution. Clearly you thought it was the right solution. Because you "know" the solution is right, it's hard to find out what is wrong with the algorithm. It is up to you to study the routine where the problem crops up, and rethink exactly what is happening.

Later on in this chapter you learn techniques for sneaking up on bugs. You can apply those techniques to locate the general area of a logic bug. The same tricks you use for coding bugs apply; you're just looking for a different variety of beast.

Coding Bugs

The existence of a coding bug is usually easy to recognize because a coding bug usually makes unexpected things happen. Finding the bug is another matter. In this section you learn about five types of coding bugs:

- Syntax errors
- Unintentional syntax
- Overstepping array bounds
- Using nil pointers and handles
- Memory leaks

Syntax Errors

Syntax errors are easy to find. When the compiler encounters text that it can't understand, the compiler chokes and displays a message. (Programming is full of precise and evocative technical terminology like "choke," which means that instead of swallowing your code, the compiler coughs up an error.)

The Metrowerks compiler is very helpful. It displays all the errors it finds in the message window as a list—you don't have to find them one-by-one. The message tells you the line on which the compiler thinks the error occurs. Sometimes the compiler is off by a line or two, but it usually gets you very close to the real error. If it is off, the real error is always on a line *before* the one flagged by CodeWarrior. If you double-click the message, CodeWarrior opens that file exactly at the line specified in the message. Figure 5.1 shows one such syntax error.

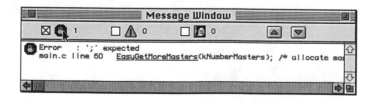

Figure 5.1 A syntax error

Figure 5.1 tells you that there is a missing semicolon on line 60 of the file main.c. If you look closely, you'll see that the semicolon is present. What gives? The semicolon is actually missing from the previous line of code. Messages aren't always perfect or precise, but they usually get you close to where you want to be.

Sometimes a minor syntax error can generate hundreds of spurious errors because—after encountering the first problem—the compiler becomes confused. Don't be alarmed. Fixing the first bug on the list may make many other "errors" go away. As you gain experience, you can detect the kinds of bugs that cause a cascade of spurious errors. Frequently, a cascade occurs when you are missing a closing brace, bracket, or parenthesis.

On the bug scale, syntax errors are trivial. You can't even run your code until you fix them, so you aren't going to miss them.

Unintentional Syntax

More subtle is the case where the code compiles because it is syntactically correct. However, what it does is not what you intended. For example, you may use the assignment operator (the equal sign) instead of the identity operator (the double equal sign), or include a semicolon at the end of a conditional statement.

For more information about these two subtle bugs, refer to the "Problems with the Identity Relational Operator" and "The if Gotcha" sections in Appendix A. Note the use of another highly technical bit of programming jargon, the "gotcha."

A really good compiler (and that includes CodeWarrior) can spot some of these problems and warn you about them. In CodeWarrior you control what warnings you receive in the Warnings section of the Preferences dialog box.

The message window in Figure 5.2 lists two such problems. There is a spurious and unintentional semicolon on line 68, and an unintended assignment on line 80. Let's look at the assignment problem.

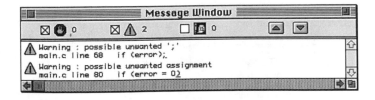

Figure 5.2 Unintended syntax warnings

The programmer's intent is to test the value in the variable `error` to see if it is zero. If it is not zero, there is an error. The code doesn't do that. It *sets* the value in `error` to zero, guaranteeing that no error is detected even if one occurred.

The code for line 80 should be:

```
if(error == 0)
```

It should have a double equal sign—the identity operator.

The problem with this kind of bug is that everything works—it just doesn't work right. Finding such a bug can be difficult. The bug is usually a tiny little punctuation mark that falls beneath notice. This is a really good reason to not turn off compiler warnings. If you turn them off, the compiler doesn't warn you. Then you have to walk painstakingly through the code, step-by-step, to locate the problem and fix it.

Overstepping Array Bounds

When you define an array, the compiler allocates enough memory for exactly as many elements as you request, no more. However, when you want to put something in the array, the compiler does not make sure that the index value you use is really inside the array. You can use an incorrect value and write a value to a location in memory that is outside the bounds of the array.

> For more information about arrays and problems with array bounds, see the "Defining Arrays" and "Array Gotchas" sections in Appendix A.
>
> *note*

Figure 5.3 shows what happens. The code allocates enough room for a four-element array, with elements numbered zero through three. The code does not set the contents of the array, so the values inside the array are random. The code also sets up a variable named `vitalData` into which you put the secret of the universe—42.

Then the code loops to set the values in the array to zero. Unfortunately, the code loops for elements from zero to four, and element four does not exist! The compiler lets this slip by without error or warning. As a result, when the index reaches four it stomps all over the next item in memory after element 3—in this case the `vitalData` variable. Bummer. Your secret is gone forever.

Overstepping array bounds can be a tricky problem. If you read from an invalid location, you get unpredictable data—and equally unpredictable results. If you write to an invalid location, you replace whatever is supposed to be there. This is a Bad

Thing. If you're lucky, the location where you write might be unused at the moment, so you escape unharmed. If the location contains an important value, the program may die quickly. You might even crash the computer.

You commonly encounter this kind of problem inside loops—where the index value controlling the loop gets out of control. Typically you go one element too far, the infamous "off by one" error illustrated in Figure 5.3.

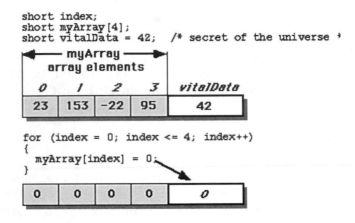

Figure 5.3 Exceeding array bounds

Using Nil Pointers and Handles

You learned about this problem in Chapter 3 on memory. But what was said there is worth repeating. A nil handle or pointer is one that points to address zero. Using address zero is a Very Bad Thing (even worse than the earlier Bad Thing).

The Macintosh stores machine-critical information in low memory, right after address zero. These are called the *low-memory globals*. If you accept address zero and start writing data to the nonexistent block at that address, you overwrite all those critical values and the machine will crash for sure. Figure 5.4 illustrates what to do with nil addresses.

Reading data from, or writing data to, a zero address is the single nastiest bug in Macintosh applications. Whenever you get a new handle or pointer, always make sure it is valid.

There are debugging tools to help you discover this problem. Chief among them is a marvelous little utility named EvenBetterBusError, affectionately known as EBBE. This gem puts a thoroughly illegal address at location zero. If you make any attempt to write to a zero address, you immediately get a kind of fault known as a bus error. EBBE doesn't prevent the problem, it just catches it immediately (instead of a thousand operations later). This makes finding the cause of the problem a *lot* easier.

Figure 5.4 Don't use nil addresses

A *bus error* simply means you are trying to use an illegal address that the computer's CPU does not know how to access. To use EBBE, you should have a debugger installed and running on your computer. Otherwise your computer crashes when it hits the bus error.

EvenBetterBusError is widely available through various online services. EBBE is a development tool, not something you use all the time. You use it to test your software to make sure you don't use address zero. No Macintosh programmer should be without it.

Memory Leaks

When you are through with a block of memory, you return the memory to the Memory Manager by "disposing" it with `DisposePointer()`, `DisposeHandle()`, or `ReleaseResource()`. If you do not return the memory when you are through, you may create a memory leak.

A memory leak occurs when you lose track of memory without giving it back to the Memory Manager. You no longer maintain a pointer or handle to the memory, so you don't know where it is. However, because you did not dispose of the memory, the Memory Manager thinks you are still using it and cannot allocate it for other purposes.

A memory leak will not immediately crash your program or the computer. However, a leak does represent a loss of memory. If a leak occurs often enough, it can swallow large amounts of memory. That can make it difficult for your program to accomplish work and can ultimately lead to more serious difficulties, including crashes.

In the exercise at the end of this chapter, you track down and stomp a memory leak.

Stalking Bugs

You develop your own debugging style as you become adept at programming. You learn the kinds of things that seem to go wrong with the code you write, and learn where to look for problems. However, I can generalize to a certain extent about the kinds of things programmers do while on a bug hunt.

First, you should understand the distinction between symptoms and bugs. The computer crashing is a symptom. Memory disappearing is a symptom. The screen going crazy is a symptom. The bug is the mistake in code that causes the symptoms to appear.

Sometimes a bug makes things go wrong immediately. This kind of bug is easy to find. There is a direct correlation between the bug and the symptom. You "walk" the code using the debugger's step or trace commands to approach the problem point. When you reach the problem point, you find the bug staring you in the face. It may be a brazen bug (see Figure 5.5), but it is now short-lived.

Figure 5.5 A brazen bug

Unfortunately, most of the time a bug is more subtle. A subtle bug doesn't cause problems right away, it just sets you up for a fall later on. When symptoms appear, the real cause of the problem—the bug—is hiding far away. So, how do you track the little bugger down? Follow these basic steps:

1. Appreciate what the bug really does. Study the symptoms. Determine whether the problem is repeatable. Reproducible bugs are much easier to find, because they happen every time you follow the right steps. Intermittent bugs are harder to find because you are never quite sure what sets them off.

2. Narrow the search. Make a reasonable guess as to where in the code a problem that generates the observed symptoms might exist. For example, if the user clicks an object onscreen but the object does not become selected, that might indicate that your selection-handling code or your click-handling code might be the cause. Or it might be that your screen update routine isn't drawing selected shapes correctly. This bug probably has nothing to do with saving files. Note the use of the word "probably." Nothing is impossible in the code jungle.

3. Then use the debugger to step through your code. Sneak up on the bug carefully. Set breakpoints at significant locations and examine the pertinent variables that affect how that piece of code works. (Refer to Chapter 2 for a discussion of breakpoints.)

4. Focus on the bug. As you move closer and closer to the suspected location of the bug, watch carefully and keep an open mind. The bug may slip by you a couple of times, but ultimately you will find it.

The first few times you do this, you will find the process difficult and slow. Experience is a great teacher, however. You will become familiar with the natural history of electronic bugs. Before long, you will be able to drop into your code at the debugger level, quickly zip through the sections that are likely to be trouble-free, and focus your efforts on the typical places where bugs try to hide.

Sometimes the search is hard because the bug is very subtle and well-camouflaged. Eventually you will spot it. When you do, you will feel a real sense of accomplishment as you type the change that sends the bug into electronic oblivion forever, making the code jungle a little safer for ordinary electrons.

Lab 5.1 A Real Bug Hunt

This lab gives you some practice finding and eliminating a bug. Of the many species of bugs, the memory leak is one of the safest to play with. It is usually not lethal to an application; it simply eats memory.

In the process of developing an application, at some point you start testing. To discover a leak, you usually have to go looking for it, although bad leaks may suck up all your memory and cause problems that alert you to their existence. To go hunting for leaks, you need the right tools for exploring your heap. CodeWarrior comes with a free memory-inspection tool, ZoneRanger.

In this lab you:

- Launch ZoneRanger and explore the heap
- Discover a memory leak
- Find the code that causes the leak
- Plug the leak

Lab 5.1 uses a separate little application called "Leaky," and its associated CodeWarrior project and source code. This is the only lab that uses this code. For Chapter 6 you return to your own code from the end of Chapter 4, so don't throw that away. Leaky isn't really start code because you aren't adding code to this project. You are hunting for a bug inside the code. For the same reason, there isn't any solution code either.

Make sure you copy the Leaky folder for Chapter 5 to your hard drive. Then double-click the project file (68K or Power Mac) inside the Leaky folder to launch CodeWarrior and open the project. If you have not already done so, you should copy the ZoneRanger application from the Tools You Need folder on the CD.

This lab assumes you're using ZoneRanger 1.1. The latest CodeWarrior includes version 1.5 of ZoneRanger, and has a different interface than the steps shown in this lab. Make sure you use version 1.1 from the Tools You Need folder on the CD.

Step 1: Launch ZoneRanger and explore the heap

In this step you become familiar with some of ZoneRanger's many features. Launch ZoneRanger. When you do, an "Overview" window appears (see Figure 5.1.1) that lists every running process.

Name	Free Blocks	Pointers	Handles...	🔒	🗑	📑
System	266244	921120	1716620	920432	544820	243932
MultiFinder	2068540	4480	6572620	5464028	1101496	0
Finder	6168	6032	89492	55868	17420	40540
QuicKeys™ Tool...	119328	772	171376	40716	10012	74584
Microsoft Word	843608	272604	972136	909112	3076	20812
MW C/C++ 68K 1...	1174280	12376	834828	653160	4584	760936
ZoneRanger 1.1	228184	1752	119688	102928	70200	93572

Figure 5.1.1 The ZoneRanger overview window

For each process, the window displays information about the free blocks, pointers, and handles. For handles you also get information about the state of the handle—locked, purgeable, and resource.

In the ZoneRanger Configure menu, you can choose to display block size, block count, or block usage. Block size displays the total number of bytes in each category. Block count displays the number of blocks in each category. Block usage displays bar graphs representing the percentage of the heap devoted to each category of block.

Name	Free Blocks	Pointers	Handles...	🔒	🗑	📑
System	259	328	1677	243	129	158
MultiFinder	7	2	387	25	315	0
Finder	18	10	111	13	29	49
QuicKeys™ Tool...	10	4				
Microsoft Word	91	28				
MW C/C++ 68K 1...	421	9				
ZoneRanger 1.1	18	9				

Zone: Finder
Count: 111
Size: 89492

Type	Size	Attr	Type	ID	Name
Handle	80	● L.R	'CURS'	006506	
Handle	48	● L.R	'acur'	006500	
Handle	92	● L.R	'CURS'	006505	
Handle	80	● L.R	'CURS'	006504	
Handle	80	● L.R	'CURS'	006503	
Handle	88	● L.R	'CURS'	006502	
Handle	88	● L.R	'CURS'	006501	
Handle	88	● L.R	'CURS'	006500	
Handle	14060	● L.R	'CODE'	000003	%EntryVector
Handle	6696	● L.R	'CODE'	000004	Main
Handle	16	. ...	......	......	
Handle	16	. ...	......	......	
Handle	8572	. ...	......	......	
Handle	28				

Figure 5.1.2 ZoneRanger block data

In any display, if you click a number, a popup window appears that displays information about each individual block within that category. Figure 5.1.2 shows an example.

The block data display identifies the type of the block, the number of bytes, and whether the block is locked, purgeable, or a resource. If the block is a resource block, you also get the resource type, the resource ID, and the name (if any) of the resource.

Step 2: Discover a memory leak
Modify: none

If you have not already done so, open the CodeWarrior project for this lab and run the Leaky application. Leaky has a Memory menu with two items: Allocate Handles and Dispose Handles.

After Leaky is running, switch to ZoneRanger. A line has appeared in the Overview window for Leaky. Choose the Display Block Counts item in the Configure menu. Then note the number of handles in Leaky.

Now switch to Leaky. Choose the Allocate Handles item in the Memory menu. In the ZoneRanger window, notice that the number of handles for Leaky has gone up.

Choose the Dispose Handles item in the Memory menu and watch the number of handles in ZoneRanger. The number of handles goes down, but not to what it was before you chose the Allocate Handles item. Repeat this a few times—choose Allocate Handles, and then choose Dispose Handles. Each time you do, the number of handles increases. You have discovered a memory leak with the help of ZoneRanger.

Step 3: Find the leak
Modify: none

The key to finding a problem is to think about when it appears. In this case, it's pretty obvious. Either the function that allocates the handles is making too many, or the function that disposes of the handles is disposing too few.

You can track the leak down by following two paths. You might look through the menu-dispatch code that responds to the user's menu choice. You can start this hunt in the `MenuDispatchHook()` function in the menu.c file. EasyApp always passes through this function for menu dispatching tasks. Follow the chain of function calls until you arrive at your destination.

Alternatively, you can use the CodeWarrior Find command to look for calls to `EasyAllocateHandle()` or `EasyDisposeHandle()`. If you're having a problem with memory, it might be in a function that makes a call to one of these functions. There is clearly some disparity between how the handles are allocated and how they are disposed.

Good luck hunting. If you can't find the bug, proceed to Step 4 to find out where it is. Step 4 provides the fix and, in the process, identifies the exact nature of the problem.

Step 4:   Plug the leak

Modify: `LeakyDisposeHandles()` leaky.c

This leak is caused by an "off-by-one" error in the loops that allocate and dispose handles. `LeakyAllocateHandles()` allocates five handles, and `LeakyDisposeHandles()` disposes of four.

Look at the loop that creates the handles, and the loop that disposes of them.

```
for(index = 0; index <= 4; index++) /* creating handles */
for(index = 0; index < 4; index++)  /* disposing handles */
```

The code that allocates the handles loops as long as `index` is less than 5 (less than or equal to 4). The code for disposing handles loops while `index` is less than 4.

The fix is to make them loop the same number of times. To dispose five handles instead of four, you use this code:

```
for(index = 0; index <= 4; index++)  /* disposing handles */
```

Apply this change to the code in `LeakyDisposeHandles()`.

Step 5:   Run the application

Modify: none

Save your work and run the project using the debugger.

Repeat Step 2. Use ZoneRanger to observe the number of handles in the Leaky heap. When you dispose handles, the number should return to what it was before you created them, because the leak has been plugged. Congratulations!

In a "real" application—one that has a lot more complexity than our leaky friend—finding leaks and other types of bugs is difficult, frustrating, and time-consuming. Nevertheless, hunting bugs is a task that you must perform on all your projects. No one writes perfect code. As you find and stomp bugs, your expertise will grow and the task will become easier.

6

The Main Event: Events and Event Loops

Now it's time to get to the heart of every Macintosh application—events.

Events drive the Mac. The Mac OS continually polls the hardware to generate a stream of events. It is your responsibility to dip into the stream of events, take out the events that mean something, and respond appropriately.

There are two tasks here. First, you must get the event. Then, you must decide what to do with the event. The first task is the responsibility of the application's main event loop. The second task is called *event parsing*.

This chapter discusses:

- Kinds of events
- The event queue
- The main event loop
- Parsing events

In the first lab exercise you write the event loop for the EasyApp shell. In a second lab exercise, you write the principal event parser for EasyApp.

This type of code—event loops and event parsing—is almost universal among Macintosh applications. In fact, you may never write this kind of code again. Every decent Macintosh application shell or framework provides this kind of code for you. However, to be a good Macintosh programmer you need to know how it works.

Kinds of Events

You might expect that there would be dozens or even hundreds of different kinds of events on the Macintosh. In fact, there are eleven:

- Activate event
- Mouse-down event
- Mouse-up event
- Key-down event
- Key-up event
- AutoKey event
- Disk event
- Update event

- Operating system event

- High-level event

- Null event

Keep in mind that this discussion of the kinds of events is background information. You do not need to memorize this material. Each kind of event is discussed in turn, but first a little history.

These events can be grouped as low-level events, operating system events, and high-level events. The different groups of events are reflections of the history of the Mac OS.

The first nine events in the previous list are called low-level events. Low-level events are the "original" Macintosh events.

The operating system event—osEvt—came on the scene with MultiFinder and System 6. There are three different events hidden inside the osEvt type. These events relate to applications suspending or resuming activity as they move to the background or foreground in a multitasking environment.

High-level events appeared when System 7 introduced Apple events for inter-application communication. Whenever your application is the target for an Apple event, the application receives a high-level event and processes it. For example, if you double-click a document icon, the Finder sends an Apple event to your application telling it to open the document. Chapter 17 discusses Apple events in detail.

The operating system stores information about each of these events in a data structure named an EventRecord. This data structure is identical for each kind of event. Figure 6.1 illustrates an EventRecord and the kind of data stored inside.

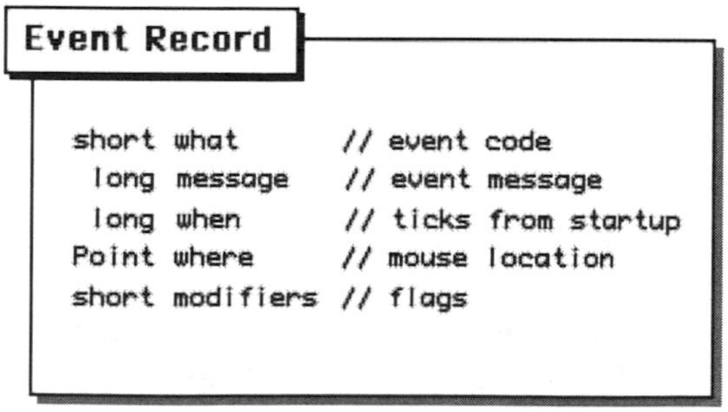

```
Event Record

    short what      // event code
     long message   // event message
     long when      // ticks from startup
    Point where     // mouse location
    short modifiers  // flags
```

Figure 6.1 An EventRecord

The contents of the fields in an EventRecord vary depending upon the kind of event this record represents:

- The what field specifies the kind of event.

- The message field contains additional information about the event.

- The when field holds the time when the event occurred, measured in ticks on the Macintosh clock.

- The where field holds the mouse location for mouse-related events.

- The modifiers field contains bit flags used to represent the state of various modifier keys on the keyboard.

Some events use various bits in the modifiers field to flag other situations besides the keyboard. Figure 6.2 identifies the purpose of each bit in the modifiers field. The identified key is pressed if the bit is true. The mouse button is up if bit seven is true. The deactivate flag (bit one) is true if the event is a deactivate event.

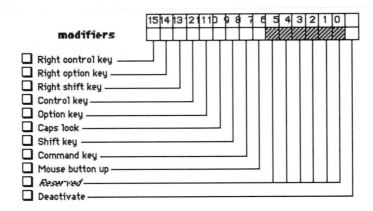

Figure 6.2 Modifier bit flags

Now that we've covered the EventRecord, let's discuss each of the events.

Activate Event

The activate event controls both *activating* and *deactivating* a window. To keep things clear, the activate event will be referred to as either an activate or a deactivate event. Figure 6.3 illustrates the contents of an EventRecord for an activate event.

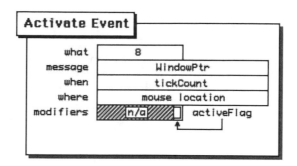

Figure 6.3 Activate event

When the user selects a window, the system generates two activate events—a deactivate event for the current active window and then an activate event for the newly selected window. The message field of the EventRecord contains the pointer to the window affected. The lowest bit of the modifiers field is a flag that tells the application whether to activate or deactivate the window involved.

When the application receives the event, it responds by turning scroll bars off or on, hiding or showing the current selection, and performing any other deactivate/activate tasks.

Mouse Events

There are two kinds of mouse events, mouse-down and mouse-up. When the user pushes down on the mouse button, you get a mouse-down event. When the user releases the mouse button, you get a mouse-up event.

Most applications receive but ignore mouse-up events because they are usually insignificant. Yes, it is safe to ignore events sometimes. When it is important to know whether the user has released the mouse, WaitMouseUp() and StillDown() let you know.

The mouse-down event, however, is very important. This event drives most of a typical application (see Figure 6.4).

The critical item here is the where field of the EventRecord. The application's actions depend entirely on the mouse location. If the click is in the menu bar, you manage menus. If it is in a scroll bar, you scroll. If it is in the title bar of the window, the zoom box, the grow box, or in your window's contents, your program responds appropriately.

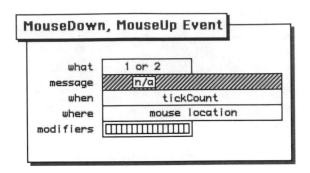

Figure 6.4 MouseDown Event

{
Where Is the Double-Click Event?
There is no double-click event! Your application determines if there is a double-click by checking the when field of two sequential mouse-down events and seeing whether they happened close enough together to constitute a double-click. How close is close enough? Call `GetDblTime()` to find out.
}

The modifiers field tells you whether the user pressed the command, control, or option keys while clicking the mouse.

Key Events

There are three key-related events: key-down, key-up, and autoKey.

Like the mouse-up event, the key-up event is usually insignificant. Most applications are concerned with when the user presses a key, not when the user releases a key.

The System generates an autoKey event if the user holds a single key down for a period of time. A typical application looks for key-down and autoKey events, and ignores key-up events. The data inside each kind of key event is the same, except for the value of the what field (see Figure 6.5).

Other than the kind of event, the important information about the event is in the message field. The lowest byte contains the ASCII code for the character typed. Usually, this is the only information you need. The next byte of the message field contains the virtual key code for the key pressed. This may vary from keyboard to keyboard. The third byte contains the ADB (Apple Desktop Bus) address of the keyboard that caused the event. The fourth and highest byte is officially reserved. However, if the keyboard in use can generate more than 256 characters, this byte contains the high byte of a two-byte character.

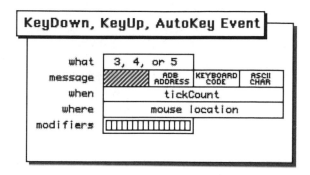

Figure 6.5 Key events

The modifiers field tells you whether the user pressed the command, control, or option keys while typing. This information is critical to the proper handling of a key-down or autoKey event. If the command key is pressed, for example, you check whether the keypress represents a menu command.

Disk Event

If the user inserts a disk into a drive, the system generates a disk event. A good application should respond to disk events (see Figure 6.6). If the disk is uninitialized, you can initialize the disk. Otherwise, you can ignore the event.

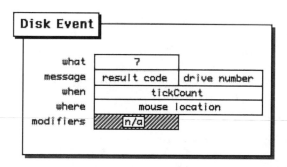

Figure 6.6 Disk event

The important information is in the result code stored in the high word of the message field—the two high bytes. This is where the File Manager reports an error when the disk mounts. If there is an error, you can give the user the opportunity to initialize the disk.

Update Event

When a window moves or becomes active, parts of a window that had been concealed by other windows may be revealed, in which case the newly exposed parts of the window must be redrawn. The Mac OS tells you when you must redraw the window. The System tracks all windows and generates an update event whenever some portion of a window should be redrawn (see Figure 6.7).

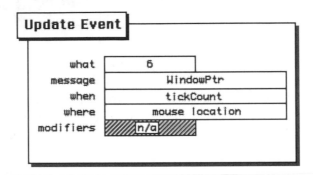

Figure 6.7 Update event

The message field identifies the window in need of updating. Information in the window record itself tells you what part of the window needs updating. Chapter 8 discusses window records.

The search for windows in need of updating goes from front window to back window, so updating occurs in front to back order. This works well because the front window is updated first, and that is most likely where the user is looking.

Update events occur for both background and foreground windows, and for background and foreground applications. This is one of the few events that a background application can receive.

> When you receive an update event, you *must* respond to it immediately. This is not an event you can ever ignore, because if you do, the System won't allow time for other tasks to run.

Operating System Events

There is only one operating system event. However, there are three kinds of events hiding inside this one event type: the resume event, the suspend event, and the mouse-moved event.

The System sends a suspend event to your application just before it sends your application to the background. The System sends a resume event just after it brings your application to the foreground. In either case, you can perform necessary processing to switch gracefully.

The System generates a mouse-moved event if the mouse moves outside of a specified region. This allows you to change the cursor so that it is appropriate for its location onscreen. The section on polling for events later in this chapter discusses this topic more fully.

All the information identifying the precise nature of the event—suspend, resume, or mouse-moved—is in the message field of the operating system event record (see Figure 6.8).

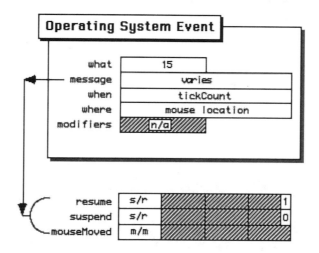

Figure 6.8 Operating system event

For suspend or resume events, the high byte contains a constant that identifies the event as a suspend/resume event. Bit zero of the message field distinguishes the two events. If the bit is set, the event is a resume event. If the bit is clear, the event is a suspend event. Your application determines which event it is and responds accordingly.

A constant in the high byte of the message field indicates whether the operating system event is a mouse-moved event. The other parts of the message field are either reserved or undefined. The where field tells you the mouse location, so you can decide what kind of cursor you want to use.

High-Level Event

Your application receives high-level events—Apple events—via the System from other applications (or sometimes from itself). For example, your application may receive Apple events from the Finder that tell it to quit, open a document, or print a document. An application may receive high-level events when it is in the foreground or background.

Each Apple event has an event class and event ID that uniquely identifies the nature of the data you are receiving. The System puts that information in the event record for the high-level event (see Figure 6.9).

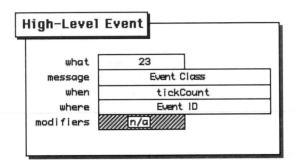

Figure 6.9 High-level event

Notice in Figure 6.9 that the where field is not a point and does not refer to the mouse location. When parsing an Apple event, you look to the message field for the event class, and the where field for the event ID. This is a good example of software engineers having to stuff new information into old data structures.

Apple events are discussed in detail in Chapter 17.

Null Event

When there are *no* events waiting and you ask for an event, the System creates a null event and gives that to your application. Your application can use the null event as a signal that the machine is idle. You can then perform "idle-time" tasks. Idle-time tasks are things that you do not have to handle right away, so you can put off doing them until more time is available.

Like update and high-level events, your application may receive a null event while in the foreground or backbroumd. Null events give a background application the opportunity to perform background processing.

Most of the information in the event record is meaningless for null events. The null event is really a signal that time is available (see Figure 6.10).

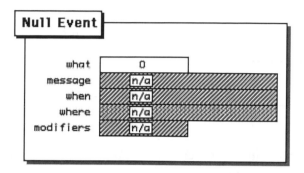

Figure 6.10 Null event

Table 6.1 summarizes the various kinds of events and what the fields of an EventRecord mean for each event.

Table 6.1: Macintosh Events

Event	What	Message	When	Where	Modifiers
null	0	n/a	n/a	n/a	n/a
mouse-down	1	n/a	ticks	mouse	flags
mouse-up	2	n/a	ticks	mouse	flags
key-down	3	key info	ticks	mouse	flags
key-up	4	key info	ticks	mouse	flags
autoKey	5	key info	ticks	mouse	flags
update	6	window	ticks	mouse	n/a
disk	7	result/drive	ticks	mouse	n/a
activate	8	window	ticks	mouse	flags
operating system	15	type	ticks	mouse	n/a
high-level	23	class	ticks	ID	n/a

Null, update, and high-level events may go to background applications. All other events go to the foreground application only. Events numbered 9-14 and 16-22 are undefined and reserved for future use by Apple Computer, as are all other event numbers.

The Event Queue

Now things start to get interesting. Events happen fast and furious on the Macintosh. Events may happen faster than an application can respond to them, so the System maintains an event queue. The queue is the line of events waiting to be processed.

In fact, the System maintains two event queues, the operating system event queue (of low-level and operating system events) and the high-level event queue.

There is one operating system event queue for the entire machine. All applications share this same queue. It can hold a maximum of 20 events. If the queue becomes full, the System discards the oldest event (whatever it is) to make room for the new one. This happens without warning. Events that the System discards are lost forever. For example, if you type while a word processing application is busy saving a lengthy file, you might generate so many key-down events that the event queue overflows and keystrokes are lost. You should keep this fact in mind and design your application to be responsive. Applications can usually process events much faster than the user can generate them, so queue overflow is not usually a problem.

There is a separate high-level event queue for each application. High-level events destined for your application are placed in this queue. There may be any number of events in this queue, restricted by available memory only.

Event Priority

You do not receive events in the order in which they happen. You receive events according to rules of priority built into the Event Manager.

An activate event—bringing a window to the foreground or sending it to the background—has the highest priority. If there is an activate event, it goes to the front of the line for immediate pickup. There can be one, and only one, activate event in existence at any moment.

After that, mouse-down, mouse-up, key-down, key-up, and disk events go into the queue in chronological—first-in first-out—order. That means that the event at the front of the queue has been waiting longest. Next come autoKey events.

The System generates update events separately. If an update event is lost, the System recognizes that there is still a need for an update event and recreates the event when it has time to do so.

The operating system event type comes after the low-level events in the queue.

You reach high-level events only when all other events have been processed. The System doesn't start pulling from the high-level event queue until the low-level event queue is empty.

If there are no events in either queue, the System generates a null event.

The Main Event Loop

One of the first things an application does as it launches is call **FlushEvents()**. This cleans out any leftover events in the operating system event queue. This does *not* wipe out high-level events, an important fact because a high-level event may be why your application launches in the first place. You wouldn't want to lose the data in the high-level event.

After initializing the Toolbox and performing its own setup tasks, the application falls into the event loop. The application gets an event, handles it, checks to see whether the user has quit, and if not, gets the next event (see Figure 6.11).

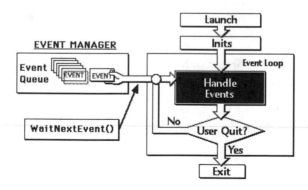

Figure 6.11 The event loop

Polling for Events

The central Event Manager routine at the heart of most applications is **WaitNextEvent()**. This is the axle on which the entire application turns.

```
Boolean WaitNextEvent (short       eventMask,
                       EventRecord *theEvent,
                       long        sleep,
                       RgnHandle   mouseRgn);
```

The return value is a `Boolean` value. Applications generally ignore the return value because it doesn't tell us anything significant. The return value from this call is `false` if the event retrieved is a null event, `true` otherwise.

In this context, a `Boolean` value is a Macintosh-declared data type that may have one of two values: `true` or `false`. The value 0 means `false`, the value 1 means `true`. Many Toolbox routines return `Boolean` values. This is part of the Macintosh's Pascal language heritage.

The `Boolean` data type is not the same thing as a boolean logic operation. Boolean logic is heavily used in C. For more information about Boolean operations in C, see the "Logical Operators" section of Appendix A.

Here is a snippet of real code that calls `WaitNextEvent()`

```
WaitNextEvent(everyEvent, &theEvent, 6, nil);
```

When you call `WaitNextEvent()`, the first parameter is an event mask. The event mask indicates what kinds of events you want returned. The typical value for the event mask parameter is the declared constant `everyEvent`. This tells the System to give you every event that appears.

The second parameter is a pointer to an `EventRecord`. In the previous example, this is the address of a local `EventRecord` variable, `theEvent`. The System fills in all the data for the event. You use the data in the `EventRecord` when you process the event.

The third parameter is the sleep time in clock ticks—about 1/60th of a second. This is the amount of time you are willing to surrender to background applications. In the example code, that's six ticks. When you call `WaitNextEvent()` and there are no events waiting for your application, the System surrenders control to background applications. They in turn should regularly call `WaitNextEvent()` so that the System can return control to you after the specified sleep time has expired. System 7 is a cooperative multitasking environment. This is where you cooperate.

There is no guarantee that a background application will call `WaitNextEvent()` often. If someone in the background keeps control for a long time, the System will not be able to return control of the computer back to you within your specified sleep time. This process requires that every application cooperate by calling `WaitNextEvent()` regularly.

The sleep time you set in your call to `WaitNextEvent()` should normally be greater than zero, and less than the caret flashing interval. The caret flashing interval is how fast the text insertion caret flashes. You want to get control back at least that often so you can make sure the caret blinks correctly. You can get the caret flashing interval by calling `GetCaretTime()`.

You can modify the sleep time value depending upon what your application is doing. If you are busy, you can reduce the sleep time (which means you surrender less time). If you are not busy, you can increase the sleep time. If you are in the background and don't have anything to do, set the sleep time value to –1. The value –1 means you surrender all your time to other processes.

The final parameter in the call to `WaitNextEvent()` is a `RgnHandle`—a handle to a Region. If the mouse is outside of the bounds of the specified region, the System generates a mouse-moved event. If you receive such an event, you could update your cursor. You might want the cursor to be an arrow when it is near some items, a text cursor when it is inside text items, and so forth. In the example code, the handle is nil. In that case the System never generates a mouse-moved event.

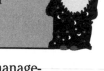

A Region is a Macintosh-defined data structure that describes an area or areas with arbitrary bounds. A region may have any shape, geometric or irregular, as long as it consists of one or more closed loops. Chapter 10 discusses regions in more detail.

EasyApp supports, but does not use, the mouse-moved approach to cursor management. Instead, EasyApp calls a hook function every time through the event loop, and lets the front window manage the cursor based on mouse location.

Beyond fetching the event, the main event loop in a typical application usually performs other incidental processing. For example, in EasyApp the main event loop gets the event, updates the cursor, calls a function to handle the event, and checks the memory situation.

Old Systems and the SIZE Resource

Over the years, the Mac OS has gone through several incarnations. *Programming Starter Kit for Macintosh* is written for System 7. Earlier systems had different routines for polling events. They are still available if you wish to write software for older operating systems.

Because one of the guiding principles of the Macintosh has always been backwards compatibility, most software written for old systems still works, even if it can't take advantage of all of the features of System 7 such as high-level events. How does the System know whether it should send high-level and other advanced events to your application?

You tell the System what you can handle by setting flags in the application's SIZE resource. The SIZE resource tells the Memory Manager how much memory to allocate for your application. It also tells the System what kinds of advanced events your application can handle.

In a System 7 application, you use the SIZE resource to tell the System that the application can accept suspend/resume events, can handle background null events, is 32-bit compatible, and is high-level event aware. You will set the SIZE resource for EasyApp in the next lab exercise.

Lab 6.1 Writing an Event Loop

The principle task of the event loop is to retrieve an event from the event queue. In addition, there are a few other event-related tasks that you perform in this lab.

In this lab you:

- Set the SIZE resource flags for EasyApp
- Flush events as the application launches
- Call the main event loop
- Write the main event loop

Use your code from the end of Lab 4.2 as the starting point for your work in this lab. *Do not use your code from lab 5.1.* If you have thrown away your earlier code from Chapter 4, use the Lab 4.2 solution code as your starting point for Lab 6.1.

Step 1: Set the SIZE resource flags

Modify: `project data` in EasyApp project

Choose the Preferences item in the CodeWarrior Edit menu and then select the Project preferences. Set the items in the SIZE menu so that they look like Figure 6.1.1. Do not set the high-level event flag. You work with high-level events later in this book.

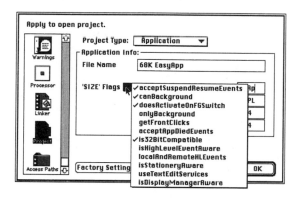

Figure 6.1.1 The EasyApp SIZE flags

Step 2: Flush events at launch

Modify: `EasyInitToolbox()` in init.c

You want to avoid getting leftover low-level events created by some other application. A good place to handle this task is when you initialize the Toolbox. The existing code initializes all the necessary Toolbox managers.

```
InitDialogs(0L);
InitCursor();
FlushEvents(everyEvent,0);
```

The parameters in the call to **FlushEvents()** clean out every low-level event on the queue. However, this call does not remove any events from the high-level event queue—those should remain available for your application.

Step 3: Call the main event loop

Modify: `main()` in main.c

The main() function simply sets up the application and quits. Event handling happens in a new function that you write in the next step, EasyEventLoop().

```
error = LoadCursorsHook();
if (error)
{
  ShowErrorHook(error);
  return;
}

EasyEventLoop();  /* where all the real fun happens */
```

When the application is set up and ready to go, you call EasyEventLoop(). Control does not return to main() until the user quits the application.

Step 4:   Write the main event loop

Modify: EasyEventLoop() in events.c

This is the heart of any Macintosh application.

```
void EasyEventLoop(void)
{
  EventRecord      theEvent;

  g.done = false;     /* just to be safe */

  do
  {
    WaitNextEvent(everyEvent, &theEvent,
                  g.sleepTime, g.mouseRegion);

    if (g.switchedIn &&
        theEvent.what != kHighLevelEvent)
    {
      EasyAdjustCursor(&theEvent);
    }

    EasyHandleEvent(&theEvent);

    CheckMemoryHook();
  } while(!g.done);
}
```

You start out by setting the global done flag to false. Then the code goes into a do loop.

> For more information about do loops, see "The do...while Statement" section of Appendix A.

First you call **WaitNextEvent()** to get any kind of event. The call fills in the data for the local variable theEvent. You also pass global values for sleep time and a mouse region.

The default mouse region in EasyApp is nil, but you can use this region to generate mouse-moved events.

The next bit of code allows the application to adjust the cursor on a regular basis. The if statement tests two conditions: if the application is in the foreground, and if the event is not a high-level event. If both conditions are true, you call EasyAdjustCursor(). You should not adjust the cursor if you are in the background, and the necessary mouse information is not present in a high-level event.

Next you call a function, EasyHandleEvent() to take care of the event. You'll work on that function in the next lab.

There is a reason why event handling is a separate function. There are times when your application will retrieve events from outside the main event loop. The fact that it is the *main* event loop does not make it the *only* event loop. For example, you may call WaitNextEvent() periodically during a long operation like saving a lengthy file. If you factor-out (separate) the event handling code, you can use it to handle all events.

Every time through the event loop you check your memory state. You wrote EasyCheckMemory() in Chapter 3. If you are low on memory, it releases the memory reserve. If the reserve has already been released, it attempts to rebuild the reserve.

Finally, at the end of the do loop you put in a "while" test. As long as the global done flag remains false, go back and do it all over again. This assumes that some code somewhere inside the application sets the done flag to true at the correct moment. In EasyApp that happens when the user chooses the Quit item in the File menu.

Step 5: Run the application
Modify: none

Save your work and run the project using the debugger.

When the debugger window appears, switch to the SYM window and set a breakpoint just after the call to WaitNextEvent() in EasyEventLoop(). Then run the application.

The application should stop at your breakpoint. In the variable pane, click the little triangle to the left of the variable theEvent to view its fields. The data in the event record is what drives the Macintosh (see Figure 6.1.2). Note the value of the what field. This is the type of event you have retrieved from the queue. Notice also the when field. This was the moment when the event occurred. Click the Go button, and you will break again at the same point. Note the values for the what and when fields again. The what field may be the same, but when has surely changed.

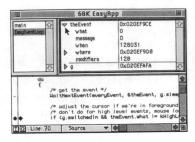

Figure 6.1.2 The event record fields

When you are through observing, quit the application by typing any key. Things are starting to get good, but the application still doesn't do much. Now that you have events, the next step is to do something with them.

Parsing Events

Now that you have finished writing an event loop, you see how simple it really is. The real work begins with the event parser. The main event loop you just wrote calls EasyHandleEvent() to do preliminary event parsing.

To parse an event, you look inside the EventRecord. First, you identify what kind of event the EventRecord represents. Based on the kind of event, you switch to other code to pull more information out of the event.

Parsing an event is really quite simple. You're growing an event tree. The main event loop is the trunk of the tree. When you write the event parser you add the important branches of the tree. In subsequent chapters, you will further refine the branches until you reach the outermost leaves of the tree.

For example, if you identify a mouse-down event, you then look to see where the mouse was when the user clicked the button. You may do any number of tasks based on the mouse location. If the event is an activate event, you look to see what window is involved, and whether you are activating or deactivating the window. Based on what you discover, you perform the tasks necessary to respond appropriately to the event.

In the next lab, you run a neat event-parsing demo that shows you how event parsing works in a simple drawing application. Then you write the real code to parse events for EasyApp. After you complete this lab, your next venture is into the world of menus.

Lab 6.2 Writing an Event Parser

The goal of this lab is to identify the different kinds of events in the event queue. To make sure you have a clear understanding of event parsing, the first thing you do in this lab is play around with EventDemo, a very nice demonstration of how event parsing works. Larry Fisher—formerly of Developer University at Apple Computer— wrote this little gem.

After exploring EventDemo, you write the code to parse low-level and operating system events. You take care of high-level events in Chapter 17. In this lab you:

- Play with the EventDemo application
- Parse low-level events
- Parse operating system events
- Handle a disk event

You find EventDemo in the DU Demos folder. You can run it from the CD, or copy it to your hard drive. For the code-related steps, use your code from the previous lab as the starting point for your work in this lab.

Step 1: Play with EventDemo

Modify: none

EventDemo graphically demonstrates event parsing. Double-click EventDemo to launch the application. Three windows appear. At the top left of your monitor are two overlapping windows named Target1 and Target2. At the bottom-left corner of your monitor is a window titled Target Event Monitor that has a series of checkboxes.

Choose the About EventDemo item in the Apple menu. Read the short help file that appears with instructions about the demo.

When you are through reading the instructions, click the Event Record checkbox. When you do, a new window appears next to the Target Event Monitor, as shown in Figure 6.2.1.

The Event Record window details the contents of each event record as it arrives. It identifies the type of event, the message, when it occurred, where it occurred, and the state of the modifier flags.

Do something to generate an event. Click in a Target window, press a key, activate Target1, and so forth. Watch what happens in the Event Record window. Study the various fields to see how they change. Each event has its own record, and the contents of each record are unique.

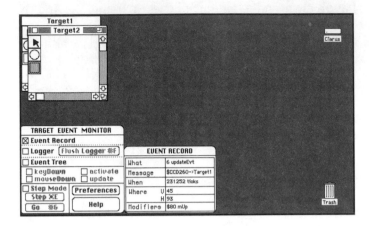

Figure 6.2.1 The Event Record window

Now look at event parsing. Click in the Event Tree checkbox of the Target Event Monitor window. Another window appears, the Event Diagram. Also click the keyDown, mouseDown, activate, and update checkboxes in the Target Event Monitor window. When you do, the four branches of the event tree appear in the Event Diagram window—the branches that handle key-down, mouse-down, activate, and update events.

Observe that the bounding rectangle around the `WaitNextEvent()` box in the Event Diagram window is flashing. The Target application is repeatedly polling the System looking for events. Click the mouse in the Target2 window, and watch what happens in the Event Diagram window. There is a cascade of activity as Target parses the mouse-down event, as shown in Figure 6.2.2.

Click and drag the Target2 window. Observe what happens in the Event Diagram window. The Target application parses the event and ultimately calls a Toolbox routine named `DragWindow()`.

Now click the Target1 Window to bring it to the foreground. As you do, observe the Event Diagram window carefully. You will see that this one click generates a series of events. The first thing that occurs is a mouse-down event that ultimately calls `SelectWindow()`, which makes Target1 the front window. Then an activate event arrives to deactivate Target2. A second activate event arrives to activate Target1. Finally, an update event arrives to update Target1.

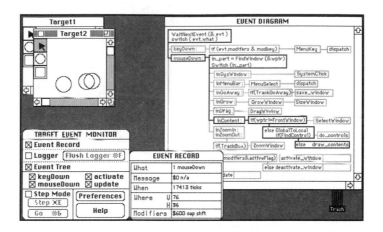

Figure 6.2.2 Parsing a mouse-down event

EventDemo has several other features, such as a log window and the capability to step through the event tree one function at a time. Continue to explore the various features of EventDemo and watch how a typical Macintosh application parses and handles events. You should open and close windows, make menu choices, drag and zoom windows, and so forth. Have a good time.

The four events displayed in the Event Diagram are the principle low-level events. There are several other kinds of events whose branches are not displayed, such as disk events, operating system events, and high-level events.

As you study the event tree, you will notice that there are several Toolbox calls that you haven't encountered yet. You will encounter everything you see in the Event Diagram window, starting with the next step. However, you should realize that—like nature—there is more than one way to grow a tree. The EasyApp tree closely resembles the Target tree, but does not match it precisely.

When you are through playing with EventDemo, quit the application. Feel free to come back and play some more whenever you want. As you fill out the EasyApp tree, you can come back to EventDemo and compare the two trees.

Step 2: Parse low-level events

Modify: `EasyHandleEvent()` in events.c

The principle task of event parsing is to identify the nature of the event and to dispatch control to a function that handles that particular kind of event. `EasyHandleEvent()` performs that task for EasyApp. It receives a pointer to an event record from which it extracts the necessary information.

```
/* delete this code for lab 6.2 step 2 */
    if(theEvent->what == keyDown)
    {
            g.done = true;
    }

  switch(theEvent->what)
  {
    case mouseDown:
      MouseDownEventHook(theEvent);
      break;

    case keyDown:
    case autoKey:
      KeyDownEventHook(theEvent);
      break;

    case updateEvt:
      EasyUpdate((WindowPtr)theEvent->message);
      break;

    case activateEvt:
      EasyActivate((WindowPtr)theEvent->message,
              (theEvent->modifiers & activeFlag) != 0);
      break;

    case diskEvt:
      EasyDisk(theEvent);
      break;

    case osEvt:
      EasyParseOSEvent(theEvent);
      break;

    case kHighLevelEvent:
      EasyAppleEvent(theEvent);
      break;

    case nullEvent:
      NullEventHook();
      break;
  }
}
```

The existing code quits the application when it identifies a key-down event. Delete that code.

After that, you switch based on the type of event. For each kind of event, you call an appropriate function—either a hook or some other EasyApp function—and pass the correct parameters.

> For more information about switch statements, see "The switch/case Statements" section of Appendix A.

In most cases you pass theEvent—a pointer to the event record. For the update and activate events, you pass the window pointer for the window involved. For the activate event, you also pass whether to activate or deactivate the window. Window pointers and windows are discussed in detail in Chapter 8. At this time EasyUpdate() and EasyActivate() don't do anything because there are no windows in EasyApp.

For the operating system event, you call EasyParseOSEvent() to do further parsing. You write this new function in the next step.

Step 3:   Parse operating system events

Modify: EasyParseOSEvent() in events.c

There are really three kinds of operating system events. Using the information in the event record, you can determine which of the three events a particular operating system event record represents.

```c
void EasyParseOSEvent(EventRecord *theEvent)
{
  char   eventType;

  eventType = theEvent->message >> 24; /* high byte */
  if (eventType & mouseMovedMessage)
  {
    MouseMovedHook(theEvent);
  }

  else if (eventType & suspendResumeMessage)
  {
    if (theEvent->message & resumeFlag)  /* resume event */
    {
      g.switchedIn = true;
      g.sleepTime = kFrontSleepTime;
      EasyActivate(FrontWindow(), true);
    }
    else  /* suspend event */
    {
      g.switchedIn = false;
      g.sleepTime = kBackSleepTime;
      EasyActivate(FrontWindow(), false);
    }
  }
}
```

The first thing you do is get the event type—this is stored in the high byte of the message field of the event record for operating system events. If the event is a mouse-moved event, you call MouseMovedHook().

If the event is a suspend/resume event, you check the resume flag in the message field. If it is a resume event, that means your application has just come to the foreground. You set the switchedIn flag to true, and set the sleepTime variable to kFrontSleepTime. You also activate the front window by calling EasyActivate(). The call to **FrontWindow()** returns a pointer to the front window. The second parameter is a Boolean value, true. That means you want to activate the window.

If the event is a suspend event, the application is about to go to the background. You perform the converse tasks. You set switchedIn to false and sleepTime to kBackSleepTime because you are going into the background. You also deactivate the front window by calling EasyActivate() with the second parameter as false.

Step 4: Handle a disk event

Modify: EasyDisk() in events.c

Other events, such as the mouse-down event, are significant branches in the event-parsing tree. The disk event is just a twig, so you can handle the event completely with just a few lines of code. If the user inserts a disk and an error results—such as from an uninitialized disk—you display the standard disk initializing dialog.

```
void EasyDisk (EventRecord *theEvent)

{
  Point  ignored; /* in system 7, centered automatically */
  ignored.h = ignored.v = 90;

  if (HiWord(theEvent->message) != noErr)
  {
    DILoad();  /* load the disk initialization package */

    DIBadMount(ignored, theEvent->message);

    DIUnload();  /* unload the disk initialization package */
  }
}
```

You examine the high word of the message field of the event record. If it is nonzero, an error occurred. In that case, you make three Toolbox calls. **DILoad()** loads the disk initialization package. **DIBadMount()** displays and manages the dialog. **DIUnload()** unloads the package.

Step 5: Run the application

Modify: none

Save your work and run the project using the debugger.

Before actually running the application, let's take a quick look at where we are. EasyApp successfully identifies the nature of each event and dispatches control elsewhere. Most of those functions don't do anything constructive yet. A mouse-down event results in a beep. A key-down event causes the application to quit—code to do this has been provided for you. You'll see it in the next chapter. Operating system, activate, update, high-level, and null events don't do anything. The only event that is fully functional is the disk event.

Now, launch the application. After it is running, click the mouse in the menu bar, even though there are no menus there. (A click anywhere else will switch applications.) You should hear a beep.

If you have an uninitialized floppy disk handy, put it in your floppy drive. This generates a disk event. If the disk is uninitialized you should get the standard dialog asking you if you want to initialize the disk, shown in Figure 6.2.3.

Figure 6.2.3 The disk initialization dialog

When you have completed your observations, type a key to quit the application.

You have successfully identified a key-down event, a mouse-down event, and a disk event. You have completely handled the disk event. In subsequent labs, you extract more information from other kinds of events and act accordingly. In the end, everything that happens is event driven.

Event Manager Reference

This section summarizes the basic Event Manager calls you use in a standard Macintosh application, including several mouse- and timing-related calls in addition to the calls discussed previously in this chapter. For full details on all the Event Manager calls, consult Chapter 2 of *Inside Macintosh: Macintosh Toolbox Essentials*.

This section also includes calls for initializing disks.

```
pascal void FlushEvents(short whichMask, short stopMask)
```

Parameters	whichMask	mask identifying what kinds of events to flush, usually constant `everyEvent`
	stopMask	pass zero to remove all events specified in `whichMask`
Returns	void	
Description		Cleans out the event queue as you launch your application. Does not remove activate, update, operating system or high-level events.

```
pascal Boolean WaitNextEvent(short eventMask, EventRecord *theEvent,
                            unsigned long sleep, RgnHandle mouseRgn)
```

Parameters	eventMask	what kind of events to return, usually constant `everyEvent`
	theEvent	address of an `EventRecord` to store results
	sleep	ticks to surrender to background when null events received
	mouseRgn	handle to region, if mouse moves outside this region, `mouseMoved` event generated
Returns		Boolean value that is typically ignored. False for null events, true otherwise.
Description		Gets the next event in the event queue. When you make this call, you are at the very heart of all things Macintosh. You are expected to be appropriately reverent.

```
pascal void GetMouse(Point *mouseLoc)
```

Parameters	mouseLoc	address of a point to store location of mouse
Returns	void	

Description	Puts the current location of the mouse in mouseLoc, in "global" coordinates. This is the actual pixel location on the monitor, with (0,0) being the top left corner of the main monitor.

```
pascal Boolean Button(void)
```

Parameters	none
Returns	Boolean value, true => there is a mouse-down event in the event queue
Description	Does not mean that the button is currently down, only that it was down quite recently.

```
pascal Boolean StillDown(void)
```

Parameters	none
Returns	Boolean value, true => there *is not* a mouse event in the queue, that is, the button is still down
Description	Call after receiving a mouse-down event, confirms that there is no mouse event (up or down) in the queue.

```
pascal Boolean WaitMouseUp(void)
```

Parameters	none
Returns	Boolean value, true => there *is* a mouse-up event in the queue
Description	If there is a mouse-up event in the queue, this call removes the event from the queue and returns true. (**StillDown()** returns false and does not remove the event.) Typically you use this call to determine whether a drag has started, or whether the mouse-down event is just a click.

```
pascal unsigned long TickCount(void)
```

Parameters	none
Returns	Number of ticks since the machine last started up
Description	Ticks are in 60th of a second. Result is usually accurate to one tick, but not guaranteed.

```
pascal long GetDblTime(void);
```

Parameters	none
Returns	Number of ticks that define a double-click

Description   Any number of ticks between mouse-down events less than this value implies a double-click.

```
pascal long GetCaretTime(void);
```
Parameters   none

Returns   Number of ticks between blinks of the caret

Description   The sleep time in your `WaitNextEvent()` call should be greater than zero and less than this value, if you have a caret displayed somewhere. Otherwise the caret does not blink steadily.

```
pascal void DILoad(void);
```
Parameters   none

Returns   void

Description   Reads in resources necessary to initialize a disk.

```
pascal void DIUnload(void);
```
Parameters   none

Returns   void

Description   Releases resources used to initialize a disk

```
pascal short DIBadMount(Point where, long evtMessage);
```
Parameters   where   top left corner where dialog should appear, ignored in System 7

     evtMessage   message field of event record

Returns   an error code

Description   Displays and manages disk initializing dialog.

7

One from Column A: Creating and Using Menus

This chapter answers the question, "Now that I have an event, what do I do with it?" Menus are a good place to begin for two reasons. First, the user drives your program by choosing menu items. Second, the Mac OS gives you just about everything you need to handle menus in the Menu Manager.

This chapter discusses the different kinds of menus you encounter in the Macintosh human interface. Then the chapter discusses how to use menus. There are two principle tasks you perform with menus.

First, you respond to menu choices. The user makes a choice with the mouse, or by typing a command-key combination. You parse the event and respond accordingly.

Second, you keep menus updated. Menus change to reflect the state of the application. Menu items may be disabled or enabled, the text in the items may change, and you may even add or remove menu items. Before displaying a menu, you must make sure that all the menu items are up to date.

In the first lab for this chapter, you use ResEdit to create MENU resources for EasyApp, and you add menus to the application. In the second lab, you respond to menu choices. In the third lab, you update menus before responding to a menu choice.

How Menus Behave

A menu is an interface element. A menu allows the user to see and choose an item from a list of commands or options in your program. An MDEF (Menu DEFinition) resource controls the appearance of the menu. The basic MDEF resource is part of the System file. You do not have to provide one, unless you wish to create a menu that has a custom appearance or behavior.

Menu Features

There are three principal kinds of menus in the Macintosh human interface: pull-down menus, popup menus, and hierarchical menus (see Figure 7.1).

Figure 7.1 shows the Finder's Edit menu as an example of a pull-down menu; the Scramble dialog box from the EasyPuzzle application with an example of a popup menu; and a portion of the Apple menu displaying recently used applications as an example of a hierarchical menu.

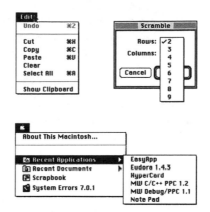

Figure 7.1 Menus

n
o
t
e A quick note on terminology. Technically, in Figure 7.1 the hierarchical menu is the highlighted "Recent Applications" item in the Apple menu. The menu off to the side that lists those applications is a submenu. In effect, the hierarchical menu is the title of the submenu.

The Finder's File menu illustrates the important features of a menu (see Figure 7.2).

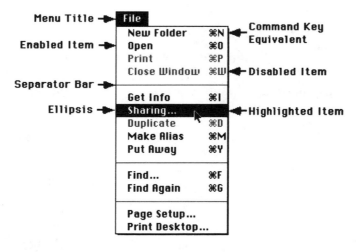

Figure 7.2 Menu features

Items in the menu may be enabled or disabled. The Menu Manager greys-out (or dims) disabled items. As the user drags the cursor over menu items, the Menu Manager highlights enabled items.

Items that have a logical relationship are grouped together between separator bars. The bars are menu items that the Menu Manager always treats as disabled, so the user can never choose one.

Menu items may have command-key equivalents to the right of the item text. Menu items may also have a marking character to the left of the item. Figure 7.1 shows a check mark before one item in the Scramble dialog box popup menu. The marking character indicates that a menu item reflects the current state of affairs in the application.

Although not illustrated, you may change the style of text used for a menu item. You may make the text bold, italic, underline, outline, shadow, condensed, extended, or any combination of these options.

Menu items that end with an ellipsis (the … character) indicate that if you choose the item, a dialog box appears that requests additional information.

Menu items may also have icons associated with them, although most Macintosh applications do not avail themselves of this feature.

You set most of these features in a MENU resource, and the Menu Manager takes care of the rest. You make a few well-placed Menu Manager calls, and correct menu behavior is automatic—a gift from the Mac OS.

Pull-Down Menus and Menu Bars

Pull-down menus have a title that appears in a menu bar. The menu bar extends across the top of the main monitor (see Figure 7.3). Unless your application does something unusual, you should always have a menu bar and you should never hide it. When the user clicks on the title of a menu in the menu bar, the menu items appear to drop down from the title.

Figure 7.3 Menu bar

Every application has its own menu bar. Figure 7.3 is the Finder's menu bar. Notice that entire menus may be disabled in the menu bar, as is the View menu in Figure 7.3. You learn how to do that later on in the "Updating Menus" section of this chapter.

You create a menu bar for your application in one of two ways:

- You use an MBAR resource that contains the menus in your menu bar.

- You add individual menus and build the menu bar on the fly as the application launches.

You create an MBAR resource for the application. The MBAR resource has the ID number of each MENU resource for the pull-down menus in the menu bar. You do not add the menus that appear at the right end of the menu bar—the help, keyboard, and application menus—the Menu Manager takes care of them for you. To use an MBAR resource, you call `GetNewMBar()`. You provide the resource ID number for your MBAR resource. When finished, the call returns a handle to the menu list. After you have the handle, call `SetMenuBar()` to copy the list into the current menu list for your application. You provide the handle to the menu list, the Menu Manager does the rest. To make the menu bar actually appear onscreen, call `DrawMenuBar()`.

EasyApp adds individual menus on the fly. For this approach, you first call `GetMenu()`. This call loads the data from the application's MENU resource in the resource fork of the file. You provide the resource ID for the MENU resource. The call returns the resource handle to the menu data. Remember to check for a nil handle!

You then call `InsertMenu()`. You provide the handle to the menu data. You also provide the menu ID for the menu before which to insert the new menu. (In other words, you can add a menu into the middle of an existing menu list.) If you use the number zero, the new menu appears at the end of the existing list. This is the typical value when you launch an application. You must make these two calls for each of your application's menus.

After you have obtained and inserted each of your application's menus, you call `DrawMenuBar()` to draw the menu onscreen.

There is no practical difference between these two approaches. The first approach—using an MBAR resource—is essentially an automatic way of accomplishing what EasyApp does in the second approach. The reason EasyApp uses the second approach is that it is a little more flexible, as you'll see in the coding labs. Because EasyApp is a shell, flexibility is very important.

After you have installed a menu, if you need to retrieve the menu handle, you can call `GetMenuHandle()`. You provide the menu ID. It returns the handle from the menu list. This call works only after you have installed the menus in the menu list with either `SetMenuBar()` or `InsertMenu()`.

7

The menu ID is not the same as the MENU resource ID. You should always set your menu ID to the same value as your resource ID to avoid confusion. You do so in Lab 7.1 when you build MENU resources.

Popup Menus

Popup menus usually appear inside dialog boxes. Most of the items in a dialog box are control items—usually referred to simply as controls. Examples of common controls include scroll bars, checkboxes, radio buttons, push buttons, and so forth. Popup menus are also controls.

The default control definition procedure for popup menus is in a CDEF resource in the System file. The CDEF handles the appearance and behavior of the popup menu. It draws the border, title, drop shadow, and the triangle that identifies the control as a popup menu (see Figure 7.4). The CDEF code opens the menu, highlights choices, handles check marks, and so forth. This is a gift to you from the Mac OS.

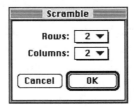

Figure 7.4 Popup menus

Handling a popup menu is no more difficult than creating the resources for it—a CNTL resource, and a MENU resource. You create the CNTL resource, tell it what CDEF to use, and what MENU to use. It's that easy.

The popup menu behaves like any other menu. You won't work with popup menus until subsequent chapters, after you have learned how to work with dialog boxes and controls.

Hierarchical Menus

A hierarchical menu is a menu item that has a submenu attached to it. You can identify a hierarchical menu because there is a triangle to the right of the menu item text.

Creating a hierarchical menu is trivial with ResEdit. You create a MENU resource for the submenu. Then you create the pull-down menu resource and specify that the heirarchical item has a submenu. You provide the resource ID for the submenu.

After you have created a submenu, you must install it in the menu list for the application. You call `GetMenu()` to get a handle to the menu data, just like you do for a pull-down menu. You then call `InsertMenu()` and pass –1 as the position for the new menu. The Menu Manager adds the menu to the menu list as a submenu rather than as a menu that appears in the menu bar.

The Menu Manager knows what submenu to draw when you pause over a hierarchical menu item because the menu item has the submenu's resource ID attached to it. After you install it, a hierarchical menu behaves exactly like any other menu.

Hierarchical menus are useful for displaying lists of related items. However, they can be difficult to navigate for people with hand disabilities. You should never use more than one level of hierarchical menu. If you find yourself doing so, consider your human interface carefully. There may be a reasonable way to simplify your design. Neither EasyApp nor EasyPuzzle use a hierarchical menu.

Building Standard Menus

Every Macintosh application should have three menus at the left end of the menu bar: Apple, File, and Edit. After that, you're on your own.

If you support text, you should provide three more menus. In left-to-right order, they are the Font, Style, and Size menus. If at all possible, these should be separate menus. If you do not have enough space in your menu bar, you can make Style and Size appear as submenus from hierarchical items at the top of the Font menu.

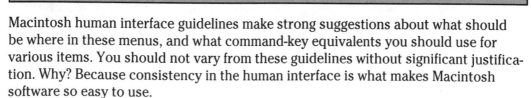

> The recommended order of text-related menus was Font, Size, and Style until recently. With the advent of QuickDraw GX and the proliferation of font styles, the Style menu has become significant in font selection. The interface designers decided that the Font and Style menus should be side by side.

Macintosh human interface guidelines make strong suggestions about what should be where in these menus, and what command-key equivalents you should use for various items. You should not vary from these guidelines without significant justification. Why? Because consistency in the human interface is what makes Macintosh software so easy to use.

Standard Menus and Items

The Apple menu should have an About item as its first item. This item opens a dialog providing information about the application. Then there should be a separator bar. After that, all the usual Apple menu items appear.

Table 7.1 lists the standard File menu items and, when applicable, their keyboard equivalents. You may add other items to this menu, but the typical Macintosh user expects to see every one of these items on the menu.

Table 7.1: Standard File Menu

Command	Key	Purpose
New	⌘-N	Open a new untitled document
Open...	⌘-O	Open an existing saved document
Close	⌘-W	Close the active window
Save	⌘-S	Save the active window to its current file
Save As...		Save the active window to a named file
Page Setup		Display the Page Setup dialog box
Print One		Print one copy of a document
Print...	⌘-P	Display the Print dialog box
Quit	⌘-Q	Quit the application

Separator bars should appear around the printing-related items. Other than that, use your judgment as to the use and placement of separator bars.

The requirements for a standard Edit menu appear in Table 7.2. You should include all of these items in the Edit menu, even if you don't support them. Some Dialog Manager routines work only if these items are present in the order described. They might also be necessary to support a desk accessory inside your application's partition.

Table 7.2: Standard Edit Menu

Command	Key	Purpose
Undo	⌘-Z	Reverse the previous action
Cut	⌘-X	Remove the current selection, put it on the Clipboard

Command	Key	Purpose
Copy	⌘-C	Put a copy of the current selection on the Clipboard
Paste	⌘-V	Copy data from the Clipboard into the active window, replacing any current selection
Clear		Delete the current selection
Select All	⌘-A	Select all data in the item or the document

There should be a separator bar after the Undo item. You may add additional items to this menu. Many applications put the Find and Find Again commands in the Edit menu. If you support Publish and Subscribe, those menu items belong in the Edit menu, as well.

The standard Font menu should list all fonts available on the machine. You learn how to add fonts in just a bit.

The Style menu for a QuickDraw application (as distinguished from QuickDraw GX) should have the menu items shown in Table 7.3.

Table 7.3: Standard Style Menu

Command	Key	Purpose
Plain		Remove all styles from selected text
Bold	⌘-B	Set selected text to bold
Italic	⌘-I	Set selected text to italic
Underline	⌘-U	Underline selected text
Outline		Set selected text to outline
Shadow		Set selected text to shadow

The keyboard equivalents for the Style menu items listed here are not part of the official human interface guidelines. They are common keys widely used in text-related applications. There are many variations on this theme.

The standard Size menu should list the common font sizes that the user would expect in your application. You should also provide an item that allows the user to make the text larger or smaller by one-point increments; and you should provide an Other item that displays a simple dialog box to set the size of the text to some arbitrary value.

> ## When to Bend the Menu Guidelines
>
> Having said all this about menus, remember that these are *guidelines*, not laws. You can bend them for a good cause.
>
> The CodeWarrior debugger is a perfect example. The interface for the debugger uses ⌘-S as the equivalent for stepping a line of code instead of saving a file. That's a bold departure from the guidelines, but absolutely correct. You do not normally save files in a debugger, but you step through code all the time. This interface decision simplifies the debugger, even though it violates human interface guidelines. Using ⌘-S to step through code is intuitive and friendly.
>
> Remember, it is not your goal to follow the rules. Your goal is to write great software that is both powerful and easy to use. The human interface guidelines *serve* that purpose—they are not the purpose itself. However, you should violate them only for Very Good Reasons, and you had better be prepared to take the heat from the users if they disagree.

Now that you know what standard menus look like, you can see how to create the Apple and Font menus.

Creating the Apple and Font Menus

Everybody's machine has a different set of Apple menu items and fonts. So how do you know what to include in the menus? This one is easy, yet another gift from the Mac OS.

You call `AppendResMenu()`. This call has two parameters. The first parameter is a handle to the menu to which you want to add items (obtained from `GetMenu()` or `GetMenuHandle()`). The second parameter is the resource type you want to add.

To add Apple menu items, you use a handle to the Apple menu and the constant 'DRVR.' The code looks like this:

```
AppendResMenu(myAppleMenu, 'DRVR');
```

The Mac OS takes care of everything else. It adds an item to the menu for each file in the Apple Menu Items folder. It really is that easy.

> The 'DRVR' constant is really a resource type that dates back to the original Macintosh. At that time, desk accessories actually lived as resources of type 'DRVR' inside the System file. The same call still works, even though Apple menu items now may be applications, documents, aliases, or anything else you put inside the Apple Menu Items folder.

To add all the fonts in the Fonts folder to the Font menu, follow this code:

```
AppendResMenu(myFontMenu, 'FONT');
```

You can use the same trick to create other kinds of menus. For example, if you want to create a menu of all available 'snd' resources, the code would look like this:

```
AppendResMenu(mySoundMenu, 'snd ');
```

It's really that easy, and it really works. You'll prove it in the lab exercise.

Lab 7.1 Creating Menus

In this lab you add a menu bar to EasyApp. EasyApp is simply an application shell, so it has the three standard menus: Apple, File, and Edit. Applications that use this shell can add other menus as needed.

To add menus to an application, you need MENU resources and some code to read those resources into memory. In this lab you:

- Create an Apple MENU resource
- Create a File MENU resource
- Call to add menus to the application
- Add menus to the application

Use your code from the previous lab as the starting point for your work in this lab.

Step 1: Create an Apple MENU resource
Modify: resources in YourApp.rsrc

When you open the resource file, you'll see that there is already a MENU resource that appears in the list of resource types. Double-click this item to open the MENU picker (see Figure 7.1.1). The existing MENU resource is for the Edit menu. In this step you add an Apple menu, and in the next step you add the File menu.

To create a new MENU resource, choose the Create New Resource (⌘-K) item in the ResEdit Resource menu. The MENU template window appears. Click the Apple menu radio button to set the Apple symbol as the title of this menu (see Figure 7.1.2). You also want to make sure the entire menu is enabled by clicking the Enabled checkbox in the upper-right corner of the window.

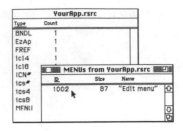

Figure 7.1.1 The MENU picker

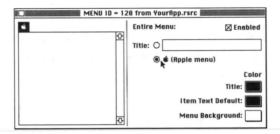

Figure 7.1.2 Setting the Apple title

Press the Return key to accept the title and enter the first item. Enter the text "About EasyApp" and press Return to enter the second item. The second item is a separator bar, so just click the separator line item. Figure 7.1.3 shows the complete Apple MENU resource.

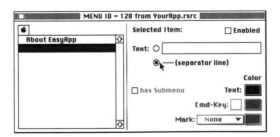

Figure 7.1.3 The Apple MENU resource

Finally, you must set the correct ID number. Choose the Get Resource Info item (⌘-I) from the Resource menu. Set the ID number to 1000. You can name the resource if you wish. Providing a name can be helpful when viewing a list of resources in the picker window. Leave all the resource attributes clear. Figure 7.1.4 shows your result.

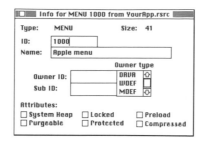

Figure 7.1.4 Info for the Apple MENU resource

When you close the window, a warning dialog will appear. It tells you that the menu's internal ID number no longer matches the resource ID number. It asks you whether you want to update the internal menu ID number. Click the OK button to do so. See Figure 7.1.5.

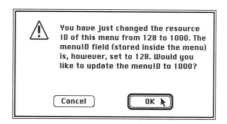

Figure 7.1.5 Updating the MENU ID

You should always keep the resource ID number and the menu's internal ID number consistent. Inconsistent menu ID and resource ID numbers are a common source of problems. Menu Manager calls rely on the *internal ID number*. That number is not obvious. The resource ID number is obvious. If they are the same, you can simply use the resource ID number.

You can modify the internal menu ID number manually if you choose the Edit Menu & MDEF ID item in the ResEdit MENU menu. This menu appears only when a MENU template is open.

Step 2:   Create a File MENU resource

Modify: resources in YourApp.rsrc

Repeat the process you followed in Step 1 to create a File menu. Create the resource, enter File as the title, enable the menu, and then enter the items.

193

The items and the associated command keys are:

- New   ⌘-N
- Open...   ⌘-O
- Close   ⌘-W
- Save   ⌘-S
- Save As...
- Revert...
- separator
- Page Setup...
- Print One
- Print...   ⌘-P
- separator
- Quit   ⌘-Q

You create the ellipsis punctuation (looks like three periods) by typing option-semicolon. *Do not use three periods.* Specify the command-key equivalents for those items that have them. When the menu item is active, fill in the desired key in the ⌘-Key editable text box at the lower-right side of the MENU template window. See Figure 7.1.6 for the complete File MENU.

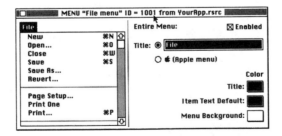

Figure 7.1.6 The File MENU resource

After creating the menu items, change the resource ID and menu ID to 1001.

When you are through, save your changes. You may quit ResEdit if you wish, we're through with it for now.

Step 3: Call to add menus to the application

Modify: `main()` in main.c

Now that you have the necessary resources, it's time to add a menu bar to EasyApp. If you have not already done so, launch the CodeWarrior project for this lab and open the main.c file.

In this step you simply call the EasyApp function that sets up menus—that is where the real work happens.

```
error = LoadCursorsHook();
if (error)
{
  ShowErrorHook(error);
  return;
}

error = EasySetupMenus();
if (error)
{
  ShowErrorHook(error);
  return;
}
EasyEventLoop();   /* where all the real fun happens */
```

After loading the cursors and before going to the main event loop, you call `EasySetupMenus()`. This function returns an error value. If there is an error, you display the error and exit the application by returning from `main()`.

Step 4: Add menus to the application

Modify: `EasySetupMenus ()` in inits.c

This function should get the menu resources, add the Apple menu items to the Apple menu, create the menu bar, allow for additional menus, and draw the menu bar.

```
OSErr EasySetupMenus(void)
{
  OSErr  error;

  g.appleMenu = GetMenu(kAppleMenuID);
  g.fileMenu  = GetMenu(kFileMenuID);
  g.editMenu  = GetMenu(kEditMenuID);

  if (!g.appleMenu || !g.fileMenu || !g.editMenu)
  {
    error = kNoResourceError;
    return error;
  }
```

```
        AppendResMenu(g.appleMenu, 'DRVR');

        InsertMenu(g.appleMenu, 0 );
        InsertMenu(g.fileMenu, 0 );
        InsertMenu(g.editMenu, 0 );

        error = SetupAppMenusHook();
        if (error)
        {
           return error;
        }

        DrawMenuBar();

        return(error);
     }
```

First you call GetMenu() three times to get MENU resources for each of the three standard menus. The constants used as parameters are defined in EasyApp.h. Then you check for errors by looking for nil handles for each menu. If there is an error, you return kNoResourceError. After you have the handles, you don't have to worry about the resources disappearing from memory because they are nonpurgeable.

Next, you add items to the Apple menu by calling AppendResMenu(). After that, you call InsertMenu() for each of the three standard menus to put the menu titles in the menu bar.

Because applications that use EasyApp are likely to add their own menus, you call SetupAppMenusHook(). When you want to install additional menus, you can modify the SetupAppMenusHook() function to install your own menus, knowing that the standard menus have been taken care of for you.

If the application suffers an error installing its own menus, it returns an error value. If there is an error, you return it to the caller.

Finally, if all goes well, you draw the menu bar. A simple call to DrawMenuBar() handles that task.

Step 5: Run the application

Modify: none

Save your work and run the project using the debugger.

When the debugger window appears, launch the application. A menu bar should appear with the three menus: Apple, File, and Edit.

If you click in the menu bar, you hear a beep, but nothing else happens. The menus don't pull down yet because you aren't fully parsing the mouse-down event. You'll take care of that problem in the next lab.

When you are through observing, quit the application by pressing any key.

Handling Menu Choices

Now you have created MENU resources, and you have successfully compiled and run EasyApp in its current state. You have already taken significant steps. You retrieve and parse events, and you display the menu bar. The next step is to make the menus work.

You must respond to mouse and key events. When there is a mouse click, you get its location and look to see if it is in the menu bar.

The first thing you do with a mouse-down event is extract the coordinates where the click occurred from the `where` field of the EventRecord. Then call `FindWindow()`. This is a Window Manager call that takes the point you pass to it and then identifies what window was hit (if any). It also returns a "part code" that identifies what part of the screen or window was hit.

One possible value for the returned part code is the menu bar. If the click is in the menu bar, call `MenuSelect()`. You pass in the point of the mouse click. It does all the work: highlights the menu title, drops the menu, tracks the mouse, highlights the correct item in the menu, and ultimately returns a value to you. This is a long value (four bytes). The top two bytes of the value (the high word) contain the menu ID. The lower two bytes (the low word) contain the number of the item that the user ultimately chose (if any). If the user drags the mouse off the menu or doesn't choose an item, the returned result is zero.

Based on that information (menu and item number) you can dispatch control to the appropriate function to handle the command.

After you are through, the Menu Manager leaves one detail for you to take care of. Call `HiliteMenu()` to remove the highlighting from the menu bar. Pass zero as the only parameter, and the Menu Manager removes highlighting from whatever menu happens to be highlighted.

For key commands, the process is similar. First, determine whether the command key was down at the time of the event. You check the correct bit of the `modifiers` field of the `EventRecord`.

If that bit is true, the command key was down. Extract the key itself from the message field of the EventRecord. Then call MenuKey(). You pass in the key.

MenuKey() looks for a menu item whose keyboard equivalent matches the key it receives. If it finds a match, it highlights the menu title and returns a long value with the menu ID in the high word and the menu item in the low word of the result. If there is no match, the return value is zero.

Based on that information (menu ID and item number), you can dispatch control to the appropriate function to handle the command. When you are through, you call HiliteMenu() to remove the highlighting from the menu bar.

And that's all there is to it. A few Menu Manager calls, one Window Manager call, and the Mac OS does all the hard work.

Launching an Apple Menu Item

Once again, the Mac OS comes to the rescue. Assuming you have identified a selection in the Apple menu, you dispatch control to a function to handle that type of command. In this function, you must do two things.

First, get the actual text for the item selected. Call GetMenuItemText(). You provide three pieces of data: the handle to the menu, the number of the item, and the address of an Str255 variable to hold the name. The Menu Manager fills in the name for you.

> Str255 is a data type defined for the Macintosh. It is a Pascal type string with a maximum length of 255 characters. Like all Pascal strings, the first byte is the length of the string, so the entire data structure occupies 256 bytes of memory. Refer to Appendix B for more information on strings.

After you have the text for the chosen item, call OpenDeskAcc(). This works for anything in the Apple menu—old-fashioned desk accessories, applications, aliases, you name it. All you do is provide the text for the menu item. The system does the rest. It immediately launches the "desk accessory" as an application, but leaves it in the background. The next time your application calls WaitNextEvent(), the System sends you a suspend event and then sends the "desk accessory" a resume event.

Lab 7.2 Menu Choices

The user can make a menu choice with the mouse or by typing a command-key equivalent. You must write code to support both paths. In this lab you start filling out the branches of the event parsing tree for both mouse-down and key-down events.

In this lab you:

- Respond to clicks in the menu bar
- Respond to command-key (⌘) equivalents
- Handle choices in the Apple menu

Use your code from the previous lab as the starting point for your work in this lab.

Step 1: Respond to clicks in the menu bar

Modify: EasyMouseDown() in events.c

In the EasyHandleEvent() function that you wrote in the previous chapter, you identified mouse-down events and called MouseDownEventHook(). That function, in turn, calls EasyMouseDown() to further parse the mouse-down event. EasyApp calls through a hook to allow an application to override the default mouse-down behavior. In this step you create some of the default behavior.

This function should determine whether the click is in the menu bar. If it is, pull down the menu and dispatch control to the function that is designed to handle the chosen menu item.

```
SysBeep(30);  /* delete me in lab 7.2 step 1 */

windowPart = FindWindow(theEvent->where, &hitWindow);

switch (windowPart)
{
  case inMenuBar:
    menuChoice = MenuSelect(theEvent->where);

    if (menuChoice)
    {
      MenuDispatchHook(frontWindow, menuChoice);
    }

    HiliteMenu(0);
    break;

}  /* end switch on window part */

if (error)
{
  ShowErrorHook(error);
}
```

The existing code beeps for every mouse-down event. Delete the call to SysBeep().

You call FindWindow() to identify where the click occurred. This call returns a part code that you put in the local variable windowPart. This call also puts a window pointer to the clicked window—if any—in the local variable hitWindow. This may not be the same as the front window. You work with windows in Chapter 8.

The windowPart is the critical value here. There are several possible values, one of which is inMenuBar. If the user clicks in the menu bar, the call to FindWindow() returns this value.

You switch based on the value in windowPart. In the case of inMenuBar, you perform a series of tasks.

First, you call MenuSelect(). This call highlights the menu title and actually runs the menu. The resulting choice—if any—returns in menuChoice.

Second, if there is a choice you call MenuDispatchHook() to dispatch control to the appropriate function. The menuChoice parameter contains both the menu and the item chosen by the user.

Third, you call HiliteMenu() to turn off the highlighting turned on by MenuSelect().

That's all you have to do to respond to a mouse click in any menu. Now let's implement command-key equivalents.

Step 2: Respond to command-key equivalents

Modify: EasyKeyDown() in events.c

Processing a keystroke is similar to processing a click. When the user presses a key, EasyHandleEvent() identifies the event as a key-down event and calls KeyDownEventHook(). That function in turn calls EasyKeyDown() to further parse the event.

To properly respond to command-key equivalents, you must determine whether the command key is pressed. If it is, you may have a command-key equivalent to a menu choice.

```
g.done = true;  /* delete me in lab 7.2 step 2 */

if (theEvent->modifiers & cmdKey)
{
  theKey = (char)(theEvent->message & charCodeMask);
  menuChoice = MenuKey(theKey);
  if (HiWord(menuChoice))
```

```
    {
      MenuDispatchHook(frontWindow, menuChoice);
      HiliteMenu(0);
    }
  }
}
```

Delete the existing line of code that sets `g.done` to `true`. That's how you have been able to quit the program until now.

Instead, test to see whether the command key is pressed. You examine the `modifiers` field of the event record and perform a bitwise and (&) with the constant `cmdKey`. If the result is true, the command key is pressed.

> For more information about bitwise and (&), see the "Bitwise Operators" section of Appendix A.

If the command key is pressed, you perform a series of tasks.

1. Extract the actual key pressed by performing a bitwise and between the `message` field of the event record and the constant `charCodeMask`.

2. Call **MenuKey()** to determine whether this is a command-key equivalent. The corresponding menu item—if any—returns in `menuChoice`. If there is a menu item, this call also highlights the menu title.

3. Examine the high word of `menuChoice` to see whether the user really chose an item. If there is a choice, you call `MenuDispatchHook()` to dispatch control to the appropriate function. The `menuChoice` parameter contains both the menu and the item chosen by the user. You also call **HiliteMenu()** to turn off the highlighting turned on by **MenuKey()**.

Step 3: Handle choices in the Apple menu

Modify: `EasyHandleAppleMenu()` in menus.c

Both the mouse-down and key-down branches call `MenuDispatchHook()` to dispatch control. Dispatch is based on the user's choice of menu and item. Through a series of simple functions provided for you that identify the menu, control ultimately proceeds to `EasyHandleAppleMenu()`, `EasyHandleFileMenu()`, and `EasyHandleEditMenu()`, depending upon the menu containing the chosen item.

You refine the File and Edit menu handling process in subsequent labs. In this step you handle the Apple menu.

```
GrafPtr  oldPort;

switch(menuItem)
{
  case kAboutItem:
    AboutBoxHook();
    break;

  default:
    GetPort(&oldPort);

    GetMenuItemText(g.appleMenu, menuItem, itemName);
    OpenDeskAcc(itemName);

    SetPort(oldPort);
    break;
}
```

This function receives a single parameter, the item number of the item selected. You switch based on that value. If it is the first item in the menu, kAboutItem, you call the AboutBoxHook() function. This function should display the application's about box. For now it does nothing.

You handle every other item in the default case. All items are "desk accessories" from the code point of view. First you call **GetPort()** to get the current "graphics port" (a topic discussed in Chapters 8 and 10). This is where the Macintosh does its drawing. Like preserving a handle's state, you want to preserve the port so you can restore it later.

Then you get the name of the item chosen. You call **GetMenuItemText()** to do that. After you have the name in itemName, you call **OpenDeskAcc()** to open that item. This launches the Apple menu item in the background. Your application remains in the foreground, for the moment, and control returns immediately to you. However, you will soon receive a suspend event, as the System sends you to the background and brings the desk accessory to the foreground.

Finally, you restore the original graphics port—just in case the desk accessory changed it.

Step 4:   Run the application

Modify: none

Save your work and run the project using the debugger. When the debugger window appears, launch EasyApp.

Click in the Apple menu. The menu should pull down and be fully functional. Choose any item (other than the About EasyApp item) in the Apple menu, and the corresponding file or folder will open. If you choose the About EasyApp item, nothing happens. The About box is a dialog. You work with dialogs in Chapter 11.

The File and Edit menus are also functional, but choosing an item in the menu doesn't accomplish the intended task (except for the Quit item in the File menu). Implementing the functionality represented by the menu items is simply a matter of writing the code that does the work.

When you are through observing, quit the application. Now you can accomplish this task in the normal way. You can choose the Quit item from the File menu, or type ⌘-Q. The quitting code has been provided for you. Feel free to step through it to study how it works.

EasyApp is really starting to cook. However, there is one more menu-related topic to consider. Menus are dynamic. In the right circumstances, you should enable or disable items to give the user feedback about the state of the application. This process is called menu updating.

Menu Updating

Menus are a two-way street. You have seen how the user issues commands to your application, and how your application responds. That's one direction—the user gives you information.

In the other direction, you should use menus to give information back to the user. As users look at your menus, they can learn things about the application. You can provide two kinds of information: what choices are appropriate, and what is going on in the application.

When you enable or disable menus and/or menu items, you tell the user what choices are available/appropriate at any moment. When you put check marks in front of menu items or change the text of a menu item, you tell the user what the current state of affairs is in the application.

For example, if there is no window open, the Save item in the File menu should be disabled. Why? Because there is nothing to save. A second example: if some selected text has a particular font, style, and size, you should put check marks before the appropriate menu items. The users can look in the menu to determine what the settings for the selected text are. They don't have to guess, they can just look. In either case you tell the users something helpful.

Of course, when you should put check marks, change text, or disable or enable menu items depends entirely upon your application and what is happening at any moment.

You can update menus every time through the event loop, just in case the next event involves a menu. This, however, is very inefficient. Most events have nothing to do with menus.

A better approach is to update the menus when you receive a menu-related event. You update the menus before acting on the event. Then the state of the menus is current when the user looks inside them. You do not have to update them at any other time, because no one is looking at them.

It's rather like the light inside the refrigerator. It doesn't stay on all the time (at least so they tell us), because most of the time no one needs the light. When the door opens, the light goes on. When the user wants to make a menu choice, you update the menus.

The two Menu Manager calls that start menu handling are `MenuSelect()` and `MenuKey()`. Update your menus before you make those Toolbox calls.

To enable a menu item, call `EnableItem()`. To disable an item, call `DisableItem()`. In either case, you provide a menu handle and the item number you want to work on. If the item is already in the desired state, the calls have no effect. When you disable a menu item, the Menu Manager dims it and does not allow the user to choose the item.

You may enable or disable an entire menu by passing zero as the menu item. If you do, call `InvalMenuBar()` right away to update the appearance of the menu bar. Enabling or disabling the entire menu changes the appearance of the menu title. The `InvalMenuBar()` call tells the System to redraw the menu bar.

This is an exception to the "wait until the user looks" rule. The menu bar is always visible, so you should update it immediately if you enable or disable a menu title. You don't want a situation where the user clicks what looks like an active menu, only to have it suddenly become disabled.

To set or clear a check mark for a menu item, call `CheckItem()`. You provide the menu handle, the item number, and a Boolean value. If the Boolean value is true, a check mark appears. A false value clears any check mark.

You can get or set other marks besides a check mark with `GetItemMark()` and `SetItemMark()`. You will use these calls much less frequently than `CheckItem()`.

To get the current text of an item, call `GetMenuItemText()`. You provide three pieces of data: the handle to the menu, the number of the item, and the address of an Str255 variable to hold the text. The Menu Manager fills in the text in your Str255 variable.

To set the current text for an item, call `SetMenuItemText()`. You provide the same information as in `GetMenuItemText()`. With this call, the Menu Manager reads the contents of the Str255 variable that you provide and puts it in the menu item.

Finally, you can use `GetItemStyle()` and `SetItemStyle()` to get or set the text style for a menu item. You pass the menu handle, the item number, and a third parameter. To get the style, you pass the address of a Style variable. (A Style is a Macintosh-defined data type.) To set the style, you pass in the Style variable by value.

> For more information on the difference between passing an address and passing a value, see the "What Is a Pointer?" section of Appendix A.

Lab 7.3 Menu Updating

As with other parts of EasyApp, menu updating passes through hook functions. Hook functions give an application based on EasyApp the opportunity to replace default behavior. Most of the time default behavior is just fine, and in this lab you continue to write the code that implements default behavior.

In this lab you:

- Update menus before displaying them
- Enable all items in a menu
- Disable all items in a menu
- Update the Apple menu
- Update the File menu
- Update the Edit menu

Use your code from the previous lab as the starting point for your work in this lab.

Step 1: Update menus before displaying them

Modify: `EasyHandleMousedown()` in events.c

Modify: `EasyHandleKeydown()` in events.c

Recall from the previous lab that the user can choose a menu item with a mouse click or a command-key (⌘) combination. The mouse click results in a call to MenuSelect(). The command key results in a call to MenuKey(). Before making either call, you should update the menus.

This is the code for EasyHandleMousedown().

```
case inMenuBar:
    UpdateMenusHook(frontWindow);

    menuChoice = MenuSelect(theEvent->where);
```

This is the code for EasyHandleKeydown().

```
theKey = (char)(theEvent->message & charCodeMask);
UpdateMenusHook(frontWindow);
menuChoice = MenuKey(theKey);
```

In each function, you call UpdateMenusHook(). You do this *before* handling the menu choice. You pass a pointer to the front window. This could be nil if there is no front window. Although EasyApp doesn't have windows yet, it will. The existence of a window makes a difference in the menus, as you see in this lab.

UpdateMenusHook() calls EasyUpdateMenus() to implement default behavior. In turn, EasyUpdateMenus() calls a series of additional hook functions: UpdateAppleMenuHook(), UpdateFileMenuHook(), UpdateEditMenuHook(), and UpdateAppMenusHook(). An application built on EasyApp can substitute its own updating behavior for all menus, or for individual menus as necessary. In addition, the UpdateAppMenusHook() allows the application to update its own menus.

Each hook function for the individual standard menus calls a corresponding EasyApp function to implement default updating for that menu. You write EasyUpdateAppleMenu(), EasyUpdateFileMenu() and EasyUpdateEditMenu() in subsequent steps in this lab.

Step 2: Enable all items in a menu

Modify: EasyEnableMenu() in menus.c

This is a utility function to enable every item in a menu. Frequently, the most straight-forward way to handle menu updating is to enable every item and then disable those few items that should be disabled. Then you don't have to worry about the prior state of any item.

```
void EasyEnableMenu(MenuHandle theMenu)
{
  short     thisItem;

  thisItem = CountMItems(theMenu);

  while (thisItem >= 0)
  {
    EnableItem(theMenu, thisItem--);
  }
}
```

This function receives a single parameter, the handle to the menu involved. You call **CountMItems()** to get the number of the last item in the menu. Then you use a while loop to step backwards through the items one by one. For each item, you call **EnableItem()** and then decrement thisItem to do the next item up the menu. Notice that the code also enables item zero. This is the menu title itself. If you enable items in the menu, the title must be enabled as well.

Step 3: Disable all items in a menu

Modify: EasyDisableMenu() in menus.c

This is a utility function to disable every item in a menu. It is the converse of EasyEnableMenu().

```
void EasyDisableMenu(MenuHandle theMenu)
{
  short     thisItem;

  thisItem = CountMItems(theMenu);

  while (thisItem > 0)
  {
    DisableItem(theMenu, thisItem--);
  }
}
```

This code is the same as EasyEnableMenu() with two exceptions. First, you call **DisableItem()** to disable the menu item. Second, you do not disable item zero—the menu title. It is up to the calling function to decide whether to disable the menu title. The caller may use this function to disable all items before enabling one or two of the items. Disabling the menu title would be the wrong thing to do in that case.

Step 4: Update the Apple menu

Modify: EasyUpdateAppleMenu() in menus.c

As described earlier, the dispatch mechanism ultimately calls individual functions to update the individual standard menus. In this step you update the Apple menu. This one is easy.

```
void    EasyUpdateAppleMenu  (WindowPtr macWindow)
{
  EasyEnableMenu(g.appleMenu);
}
```

At this stage in EasyApp's development, the Apple menu items are always enabled. Just call the EasyEnableMenu() utility function for the Apple menu. When I introduce dialog windows in Chapter 11, you will disable Apple menu items in some cases.

Step 5: Update the File menu

Modify: EasyUpdateFileMenu() in menus.c

If there is no window open, several items in the File menu should be disabled, including the Close, Save, Save As, Revert, Print One, and Print items. Why? There is no window to close, and no file to save, revert, or print.

```
void    EasyUpdateFileMenu  (WindowPtr macWindow)
{

  EasyEnableMenu(g.fileMenu);

  if (!macWindow)
  {
    DisableItem(g.fileMenu, kCloseItem);
    DisableItem(g.fileMenu, kSaveItem);
    DisableItem(g.fileMenu, kSaveAsItem);
    DisableItem(g.fileMenu, kRevertItem);
    DisableItem(g.fileMenu, kPrintOneItem);
    DisableItem(g.fileMenu, kPrintItem);
  }
}
```

You take the "enable everything" approach and call EasyEnableMenu() for the File menu. Then, if there is no window, you call DisableItem() for those items that should be disabled. You can find the constants in userDeclare.h.

Step 6: Update the Edit menu

Modify: `EasyUpdateEditMenu()` in menus.c

Finally, you must update the Edit menu. If there is no window open, all items in the menu should be disabled. If there is a window open, all items should be enabled.

```
void    EasyUpdateEditMenu  (WindowPtr macWindow)
{
  if (!macWindow)
  {
    EasyDisableMenu(g.editMenu);
  }
  else
  {
    EasyEnableMenu(g.editMenu);
    DisableItem(g.editMenu, kUndoItem);
  }
}
```

If there is no window open, you call `EasyDisableMenu()` for the Edit menu. This disables all the items.

Otherwise, you enable all the items by calling `EasyEnableMenu()`. You then disable the Undo item. EasyApp does not implement Undo, although it provides support for an application to do so.

> Actually, even when there is a window open, some Edit menu items might be disabled. For example, you should disable the Paste item if there is nothing on the Clipboard to be pasted. We discuss the Clipboard in Chapter 18.

Step 7: Run the application

Modify: none

Save your work and run the project using the debugger.

When the debugger window opens, launch the application. Everything should behave as before, except that some items in the File menu and all the items in the Edit menu are disabled. There is no window open. Given the current operating state of the application, these items are inappropriate and should be disabled.

When you are through observing, quit the application.

EasyApp now has fully functional menus. They transmit user commands to the application, and the application uses them to provide feedback to the user.

In the next chapter, you add windows!

Menu Manager Reference

The Menu Manager is a basic part of the Macintosh Toolbox. You haven't seen very many Macintosh applications without menus, have you? This section summarizes the basic Menu Manager calls you use in a standard Macintosh application. For full details on all the Menu Manager calls, consult Chapter 3 of *Inside Macintosh: Macintosh Toolbox Essentials.*

```
pascal void InitMenus (void);
```

Parameters   none

Returns   void

Description   Initialize the Menu Manager for your application. Call at application launch.

```
pascal MenuHandle GetMenu (short resourceID);
```

Parameters   resourceID   The resource ID of a MENU resource

Returns   MenuHandle to the menu data, a resource handle. Value will be nil if an error occurs.

Description   Call to load a MENU resource from disk. Usually called at application startup. Equivalent to calling `GetResource()` with resource ID and type MENU. If you ever want to dispose of this handle, use `ReleaseResource()`.

```
pascal void InsertMenu (MenuHandle theMenu, short beforeID);
```

Parameters   theMenu   A handle to the menu data for the menu in question.

                   beforeID   Menu ID of the menu before which this new menu should be inserted. A value of zero adds the menu to the end of the menu list.

Returns   void

Description   Add a menu to the application's menu list so it appears in the application's menu bar.

```
pascal MenuHandle GetMenuHandle (short menuID);
```

Parameters   menuID   Menu ID of the MENU resource. In a resource editor, set the menu ID to be the same as the MENU resource ID to avoid confusion and resulting bugs.

Returns   A handle to the menu data

Description   Use this call to retrieve a handle to the menu data after the menu has been loaded into memory with `GetMenu()`.

```
pascal Handle GetNewMBar (short menuBarID);
```

Parameters   menuBarID   Resource ID of the MBAR resource.

Returns   A handle to the menu list

Description   Loads all of the menus in the MBAR resource into memory and creates a menu list. Equivalent to calling `GetMenu()` and `InsertMenu()` for each application menu. Call `SetMenuBar()` after calling `GetNewMBar()` to copy the menu list to the current menu list for this application. Then dispose of this list with `DisposeHandle()`.

```
pascal void SetMenuBar (Handle menuList);
```

Parameters   menuList   A handle to a menu list, usually obtained from `GetNewMBar()`.

Returns   void

Description   Copies the given menu list to the application's current menu list.

```
pascal short GetMBarHeight (void);
```

Parameters   none

Returns   A value in pixels for the height of the menu bar

Description   Use this if you need to know how tall the menu bar is onscreen. In Roman script systems, it is usually 20 pixels. It may vary in other script systems, so don't automatically assume it is 20 pixels high.

```
pascal void DrawMenuBar (void);
```

Parameters   none

Returns   void

Description   Draws the menu bar onscreen. Call this routine or `InvalMenuBar()` if you change the menu bar in any way.

```pascal
pascal void InvalMenuBar (void);
```

Parameters   none

Returns   void

Description   Invalidates the area of the menu bar. Next time your application calls `WaitNextEvent()`, the System calls `DrawMenuBar()` for you. This technique avoids multiple drawing of the menu bar if you do a lot of menu adjusting.

```pascal
pascal long MenuSelect (Point startPt);
```

Parameters   startPt   The location of a mouse click in global coordinates, usually obtained from an EventRecord in response to a mouse-down event.

Returns   A long value, high word containing the menu ID, the low word containing the item number of the menu hit. If the user did not choose an enabled menu item, the return value is zero.

Description   Implements all standard menu behavior. Call this routine to highlight and pull a menu down, and get a user choice. Call `HiliteMenu()` to clear the highlighting when through.

```pascal
pascal long MenuKey (short ch);
```

Parameters   ch   A character, usually retrieved from a key-down event.

Returns   A long value, high word containing the menu ID, the low word containing the item number of the menu hit. If there is no menu item corresponding to this key, the return value is zero.

Description   Call this routine if the user types a command key. It searches all keyboard equivalents for a match. If it finds a match, it highlights the menu title. Call `HiliteMenu()` to clear the highlighting.

```pascal
pascal void HiliteMenu (short menuID);
```

Parameters   menuID   Menu ID of the menu title you want to highlight. Value zero turns off any highlighted menu.

Returns	void	
Description	Highlight or remove highlighting from a menu title in the menu bar.	

```
pascal void AppendResMenu (MenuHandle theMenu,ResType theType);
```

Parameters	theMenu	Handle to the menu to which you wish to append items
	theType	A four-character type to identify what kinds of items to add to the menu. Typically, the value is 'DRVR' for Apple menu items, or 'FONT' for Font menu items.
Returns	void	
Description	Use this routine to build the Apple menu and the Font menu. Create the menus using **GetMenu()**, and then call this routine to add the necessary items.	

```
pascal void EnableItem (MenuHandle theMenu,short item);
```

Parameters	theMenu	Handle to the menu containing the item
	item	Number of the item in the menu you want to enable
Returns	void	
Description	Sets the menu item to enabled status. If already enabled, this has no effect.	

```
pascal void DisableItem  (MenuHandle theMenu,short item);
```

Parameters	theMenu	Handle to the menu containing the item
	item	Number of the item in the menu you want to disable
Returns	void	
Description	Set the menu item to disabled status. If already disabled, this has no effect. The Menu Manager draws disabled items in grey text, or "dimmed."	

```
pascal void GetMenuItemText (MenuHandle theMenu, short item,
                   Str255 itemString);
```

Parameters	theMenu	Handle to the menu containing the item
	item	Number of the item in question

	itemString	String to hold text of item
Returns	void	
Description	This call fills in the contents of itemString with the text of the requested menu item.	

```
pascal void SetMenuItemText (MenuHandle theMenu, short item,
                    ConstStr255Param itemString);
```

Parameters	theMenu	Handle to the menu containing the item
	item	Number of the item in question
	itemString	String with new text of item
Returns	void	
Description	This call sets the menu item to the contents of the itemString.	

```
pascal void GetItemStyle (MenuHandle theMenu, short item,
                    Style *chStyle);
```

Parameters	theMenu	Handle to the menu containing the item
	item	Number of the item in question
	chStyle	Address of a Style variable to hold current style. A Style is a Macintosh defined type that is the same length as a short
Returns	void	
Description	Fills in the chStyle variable with the item's current text style such as bold, italic, and so forth.	

```
pascal void SetItemStyle (MenuHandle theMenu, short item,
                    short chStyle);
```

Parameters	theMenu	Handle to the menu containing the item
	item	Number of the item in question
	chStyle	A value indicating the desired type style for the item
Returns	void	
Description	The style may be normal or any combination of bold, italic, underline, outline, shadow, condense, or extend. These constants are defined in Types.h.	

```
pascal void CheckItem    (MenuHandle theMenu, short item,
                          Boolean checked);
```

Parameters	theMenu	Handle to the menu containing the item
	item	Number of the item in question
	checked	Boolean value true => check the item, false => clear any check mark

Returns void

Description Use this routine to either set or clear a check mark to the left of a menu item.

```
pascal short CountMItems (MenuHandle theMenu);
```

Parameters	theMenu	Handle to the menu in question

Returns A short value containing the number of items in the menu

Description Call this routine if you need to know how many items there are in the menu.

Windows on the World: Making and Managing Windows

Everything that you have read and done in this book has been getting you ready for the big picture, and this is it. A window is the most important element in the Macintosh human interface. It is the portal through which you look at data. This chapter and the next three chapters—on controls, drawing in windows, and dialog boxes—are devoted to windows in one form or another.

This chapter begins with a look at the various kinds of windows you can create. In the first lab for this chapter, you create a WIND resource for EasyApp.

Next, the chapter discusses the details of how windows exist in memory. It talks about the graphics port and the window record. This discussion is followed by some important concepts in software design relating to window behavior, and a review of the basic Window Manager calls that you use to create windows. In the second lab, you actually make windows in EasyApp.

Then you'll learn about handling events in windows. You must identify and handle clicks in various parts of the window. In the third coding lab you implement standard behaviors for the EasyApp window.

We've got a lot of territory to cover, so let's get to it!

Kinds of Windows

Figure 8.1 illustrates the important parts of a typical Macintosh window. These elements do not appear in every Macintosh window, but they all appear in one type of window or another.

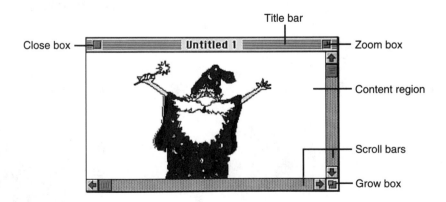

Figure 8.1 Window parts

The content region of the window is everything within the bounds of the window *below the title bar.* The application is completely responsible for the content region of the window. This includes the scroll bars. Scroll bars are control items added to the window by the application. Controls are discussed in Chapter 9.

The Window Manager defines nine standard window types that you can use to handle just about any situation. The types of windows include document, dialog, and rounded-corner windows. There are four document windows, four dialog windows, and one rounded-corner window. Figure 8.2 illustrates the four document window types.

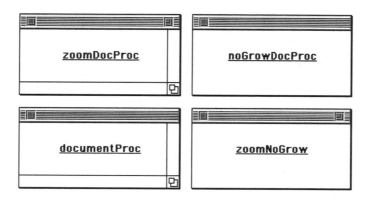

Figure 8.2 Document windows

The names in the illustration are the Window Manager's defined constants for windows of that type. Usually, you set a window type with a resource editor (a task you perform in the first lab of this chapter), so you don't have to use the names very often.

Each of the document window types has its uses. All four have close boxes. They vary with respect to the zoom and grow boxes.

Most document windows are of the zoomDocProc type. Programmers use the noGrowDocProc window most commonly for modeless dialog boxes. It has neither the zoom nor the grow box. You work with dialog boxes in Chapter 11. The zoomNoGrow and documentProc window types are uncommon. One type can grow but not zoom, the other can zoom but not grow. Generally, if a window can change size, it should be able to change size by zooming and growing.

There are also four types of modal dialog box windows (see Figure 8.3). None of these windows has any of the three document-window boxes—close, zoom, or grow. The difference among these windows is the border.

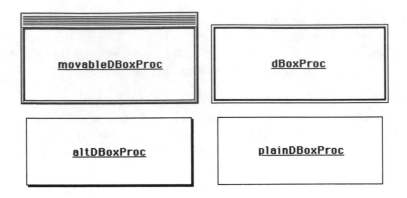

Figure 8.3 Dialog box windows

The content area of each of the four windows in Figure 8.3 is identical. The actual area of the window—the content area plus border—varies. The Window Manager is responsible for the border of the windows. It puts the border on the outside of the window content.

The movableDBoxProc window is a movable modal dialog window. You create one of these in Chapter 11. The dBoxProc is the most common type of dialog box window. The altDBoxProc and plainDBoxProc window types are less common.

The rounded-corner window type is uncommon today (see Figure 8.4). It was much more common in the early days of the Macintosh. This is the "desk accessory" window. It has rounded-corners and a black title bar. With the advent of System 7, the distinction between desk accessories and applications has largely disappeared.

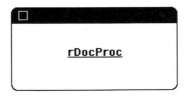

Figure 8.4 The desk accessory window

You can set all of these window features using a resource editor. Before getting into the details of windows in an application, let's make a WIND resource.

Lab 8.1 Making WIND Resources

You may recall from the Hello World exercise in Chapter 2 that you made a call to `NewCWindow()` that had a long list of parameters. By putting all that information—and more—into a WIND resource, you can simplify your programming tasks. You also make your code more flexible because you can change the nature of the window without changing code.

In this brief lab, you use ResEdit to create a WIND resource. In this lab you:

- Create a WIND resource
- Set WIND information

Use your code from the previous lab as the starting point for your work in this lab.

Step 1: Create a WIND resource

Create: `WIND resource` in EasyApp.µ.rsrc

In this step you create a WIND resource that EasyApp uses to create generic window.

Choose the Create New Resource item (⌘-K) in the resource menu. A dialog box appears in which you enter a new resource type or select a type from a scrolling list of standard resource types (see Figure 8.1.1).

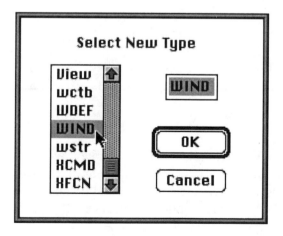

Figure 8.1.1 The Create Resource dialog box

Scroll down the list to the WIND name and double-click WIND (or you can type WIND into the text item in the dialog box and click the OK button). Either way, a new window appears (see Figure 8.1.2).

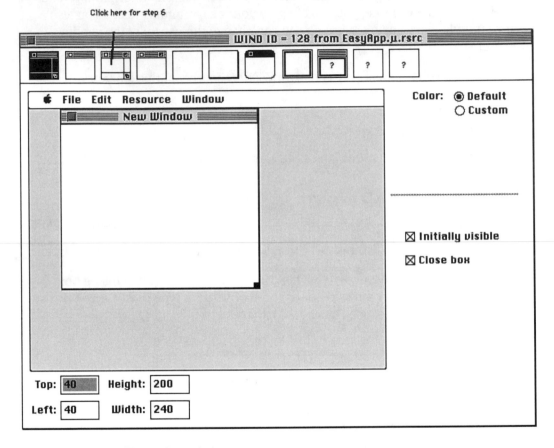

Figure 8.1.2 WIND template window

The central part of the WIND template window displays a mini-version of your Desktop with the new window on it. This gives you an idea of the window's size. EasyApp uses the default window size created by ResEdit. The dimensions are in the bottom-left portion of the WIND template window. You can set the window size to any reasonable value.

Along the top of the window is a series of icons representing different kinds of windows. The default window type is the first icon on the left. Click the third icon from the left to change the window type to a window that has a title bar, grow box, *and* zoom box, as illustrated in Figure 8.1.2.

On the right side of the WIND resource window, there are two checkboxes. Click the "Initially visible" checkbox to turn it *off*. You want the window to be invisible to start so you can adjust the window before the user sees it. The EasyApp shell makes the window visible when necessary.

Finally, in the WIND menu (it appeared in the menu bar when you opened the WIND template) select the Auto Position item. In the dialog box that appears, set the window to appear staggered on the main screen (see Figure 8.1.3). By setting the auto-position, EasyApp doesn't have to worry about where to place the window that it creates.

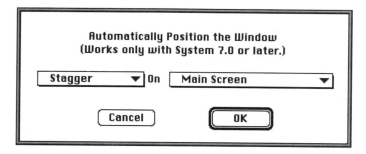

Figure 8.1.3 Auto position a window

That's it. Everything else you can leave as is. Close the WIND template window.

Step 2:   Set WIND information

Modify: WIND resource in EasyApp.μ.rsrc

EasyApp uses the ID number 1000 as the base for most of its resources. In this step you change the resource ID number for the new WIND resource to 1000. By default, ResEdit assigns the lowest allowable unique ID number to a new resource. Because there was no other WIND resource, the default ID number is 128.

Open the resource information window for the WIND resource. Choose the Get Resource Info (⌘-I) item from the ResEdit Resource menu. In the resulting dialog, change the ID number to 1000. Figure 8.1.4 also illustrates giving a name to the resource. Names help you identify which resource is which when you have several resources of the same type in a picker window.

The default values for the attributes are fine. They should all be clear. When you have completed this step, save your changes. You may quit ResEdit; we are through with it for this chapter.

```
┌─────────────────────────────────────────────────┐
│ ▓▓▓    Info for WIND 1000 from EasyApp.µ.rsrc  ▓▓▓ │
│                                                   │
│   Type:    WIND              Size:   30           │
│                                                   │
│   ID:     ┌──────────────┐                        │
│           │ 1000         │                        │
│   Name:   ┌──────────────────────────────┐        │
│           │ Base Window│                  │        │
│           └──────────────────────────────┘        │
│                              Owner type           │
│                            ┌──────────┬──┐         │
│          Owner ID:         │ DRVR     │▲▓│         │
│                            │ WDEF     │▓▓│         │
│          Sub ID:           │ MDEF     │▼▓│         │
│                            └──────────┴──┘         │
│                                                   │
│   Attributes:                                     │
│   ☐ System Heap   ☐ Locked      ☐ Preload         │
│   ☐ Purgeable     ☐ Protected   ☐ Compressed      │
└─────────────────────────────────────────────────┘
```

Figure 8.1.4 Changing WIND information

The Port

Before you move on to actually displaying a window onscreen, it's time we talked a little about how the Macintosh draws. All drawing on the Macintosh occurs in a *graphics port*.

There are two kinds of graphics ports, a CGrafPort and a GrafPort. The GrafPort supports black and white drawing. The CGrafPort supports color drawing. Each of these is a formal data structure that has many fields.

> For more information about structs, see the "Structs and Typedefs" section of Appendix A.

Happily, you don't need to know the ins and outs of everything in a graphics port to be a Macintosh programmer. Table 8.1 lists some important fields of a CGrafPort, and their purposes. A plain GrafPort has these same members.

Table 8.1: Important GrafPort Fields

Field	Data Type	Description
portRect	Rect	size of the port
visRgn	RgnHandle	visible part of the port

Field	Data Type	Description
clipRgn	RgnHandle	part of port available for drawing
pnLoc	Point	location of pen
pnSize	Point	size of pen
txFont	short	font for text
txFace	Style	style for text (bold, outline, and so on)
txSize	short	size for text

The graphics port includes information about the size of the drawing area, what parts are visible, what parts you can draw in, the pen, and so forth. There is more information in a graphics port that relates to all sorts of deep magic, most of which you can ignore as a beginning programmer.

Every window has its own graphics port. Most of the Window Manager routines use a pointer to a graphics port as the principle parameter. This is how the Window Manager knows what port to draw in.

The pointer to a window's graphics port is a WindowPtr. This is a formal data type declared for the Macintosh. WindowPtrs are everywhere in the Window Manager. Before long, you'll be tossing WindowPtrs around like confetti. For easy reading, we will refer to them from here on in as window pointers, not WindowPtrs.

However, a window pointer—despite its name—is not really a pointer to a window! It is a pointer to the graphics port associated with the window. A graphics port is a generic structure used for all sorts of rendering, including printing. Windows are more specialized. They include a graphics port, but they also include additional window-specific information.

The Window Record

No matter what kind of window you create, the Window Manager represents that window in memory as a data structure, either a CWindowRecord for color windows, or a WindowRecord for black and white windows.

Here's the complete declaration of a color window record.

```
struct CWindowRecord {
CGrafPort                               port;
short                                   windowKind;
Boolean                                 visible;
Boolean                                 hilited;
Boolean                                 goAwayFlag;
Boolean                                 spareFlag;
RgnHandle                               strucRgn;
RgnHandle                               contRgn;
RgnHandle                               updateRgn;
Handle                                  windowDefProc;
Handle                                  dataHandle;
StringHandle                            titleHandle;
short                                   titleWidth;
ControlHandle                           controlList;
struct CWindowRecord                    *nextWindow;
PicHandle                               windowPic;
long                                    refCon;
};
```

The most important field in this struct is the port field—a graphics port! This is the graphics environment in which your window draws. Because this is the first field in the window record, the pointer to that port (the window pointer) is, for all intents and purposes, the pointer to the window.

> The differences between a color window and a black-and-white window are in the port and nextWindow fields. In a CWindowRecord, the data types are a CGrafPort or CWindowRecord, respectively. In a black-and-white window the data types are a GrafPort and WindowRecord. The CGrafPort has additional information related to color display. Everything else is the same.

Every window has two main structures: a window record and—as part of the window record—a graphics port. You use a window pointer with Window Manager calls, and to access fields of the graphics port. You cannot use the window pointer to access the fields of the window record. Why? Because a window pointer is a pointer to a graphics port, not a pointer to a window record.

A pointer to a window record is called a WindowPeek. You can typecast the window pointer as a WindowPeek and peek at the contents of the window record. You use the same address for both purposes, but you tell the compiler that in one case you want that address interpreted as a window pointer, and in the other case as a WindowPeek.

> For more information about typecasting, see the "Typecasting" section of Appendix A.

EasyApp uses the WindowPeek in special functions called "accessors." An accessor retrieves or sets information in a data structure for you. The function name for an accessor usually takes the form of GetSomething() or SetSomething(). Rather than accessing the window record information directly, you call accessor functions to do it for you. This approach reflects the latest developments in system software design.

Private Data Structures

There is a trend in Macintosh system software to make data structures like the window record "private." A private structure is one where the fields are not accessible directly through a pointer. If a structure is private, you *must* use accessors to get or set information.

There are very good reasons for doing this. Chief among them is that system engineers can change a private data structure without breaking every piece of software known to humanity.

In the very near future, window records will become private, and you will no longer be able to access window information directly. Using the EasyApp accessors will get you accustomed to this process.

Now that the port field of the window record has been covered, let's take a quick look at some of the other data. This is the data you manipulate while working with windows. Table 8.2 lists the more important fields of a window record, and their purposes.

Table 8.2: Important Fields of a Window Record

Field	Data Type	Description
port	CGrafPort	graphics port for the window
windowKind	short	dialog, DA, or user window
visible	Boolean	if this window should be invisible or not
hilited	Boolean	draw lines in the title bar or not
goAwayFlag	Boolean	does this window have a close box
spareFlag	Boolean	does this window have a zoom box
updateRgn	RgnHandle	the area of the window in need of update
titleHandle	StringHandle	handle to the window's title string
controlList	ControlHandle	handle to the first control item in the window
nextWindow	CWindowRecord*	address of the next window behind this one in this app
refCon	long	a field you can use to store data

Most of these items are related to housekeeping details concerning what kind of window this is and what its features are. EasyApp provides accessors for several of these fields. The Window Manager provides accessors to some others. These details are discussed a little later.

The nextWindow field points to the window behind this window. As a result, all windows form a linked list. In the last window in the list, this field is nil. The System uses this feature to keep track of the visual order of windows.

The last item in Table 8.2—the refCon field—deserves special mention (see Figure 8.5). This field is critical to how your code uses windows. You attach data to the window by putting a handle or pointer to the data in the refCon field. The refCon field is the critical link between what appears onscreen and your data in memory. This is how you know what data is attached to what window in a multiwindow environment.

In fact, you can use the refCon field for anything you want, but this is the standard way most applications use it, and it is a *very* good approach.

Data

```
63BC000000000 1060
10300 1 102FF0C00FF
FFFFFF00000000000
000000 10300000 106
00000000000000 1E0
00 1000A000000000 1
060 10300988 10A008
C00B 10 1920 1BB0000
00000000000000480
```

Figure 8.5 The refCon field

If you use the refCon field this way, the window itself "knows" what data you have attached to it. Then you can rely on the *window* to manipulate the data for you.

How is this possible? The designers of the Mac OS certainly had no advance knowledge of what data you intend to put in your window, or how you intend to manipulate it.

Before we get deep into the technical details of how to make a window manipulate data, let's take a step back up the ladder and look at this problem from a broader perspective. Let's talk a little bit about software design.

Window Behavior

You display data in a document window. In fact, the data defines the nature of the window. How you want the window to behave depends on the nature of the data and what you want to do with it.

For example, most—but not all—windows zoom. If the data is a constant dimension and fits in a small window, the window can remain one size and have no zoom box. So, whether a window should zoom really depends on the nature of the data in the window.

The concept of window behavior goes much further. Figure 8.6 shows how the same window type might have radically different contents, depending upon the application using the window. So how do you draw the contents of the window?

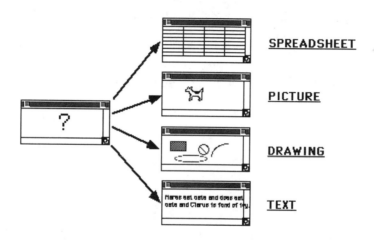

Figure 8.6 How do I draw thee?

There are two strategies for drawing window contents. In one, the central control system of the application is responsible for drawing. In the second strategy, the window is responsible for drawing its own contents.

Here's a code example for the application-level strategy. In the following scenario, the window is not responsible for its own behavior. It is simply a repository for information.

```
windowType = MyGetWindowType(windowPtr);

switch(windowType)
{
    case type1:
      DrawType1Window(windowPtr);
      break;

    case type2:
      DrawType2Window(windowPtr);
      break;

    case type3:
      DrawType3Window(windowPtr);
      break;
}
```

Using this strategy, you figure out what type of window you are about to draw. Based on the window type, you call the right function to draw that kind of window. This is a perfectly valid way to write code, but it isn't the most efficient or flexible.

For example, if you add a new type of window you have to add a new case to handle the window. While that might seem simple enough, remember that you have to do that not only for drawing, but for zooming, updating, scrolling, printing, resizing, and a dozen other common window behaviors that are controlled from a dozen different places in your code. Suddenly it's not so simple.

Now take a look at a different approach, one where the window takes care of itself. When it is time to draw a window, you can draw any window with one line of code.

```
myWindow->DrawYourself(windowPtr);
```

You no longer care what kind of window it is—the window knows that. Because the window knows how to draw itself, you just send it a message to do so. It takes care of the rest.

This strategy goes beyond drawing contents. The window should be responsible for all events that concern its own contents—printing, saving, zooming, cut, copy, paste, and so forth.

Don't misunderstand. You still must write the code to implement the window behavior—in this case to draw the contents. The point of this discussion is that by attaching behavior directly to the window, you enhance flexibility. If you want to add a new kind of window, you can do so by modifying the window behavior, rather than changing all the dispatch and control code that runs the program.

Flexibility is critical to an application shell. This concept—making objects responsible for themselves—is central to the design of EasyApp, and to good software design in general.

Basic Window Manager

So much for theory. What you really want to know is, how do I get a window onscreen?

At application startup, call `InitWindows()` to initialize the Window Manager for your application. You must also call `InitGraf()` and `InitFonts()` before calling `InitWindows()` because the Window Manager is dependent upon those other managers.

You can create a window two ways. You can create a window by passing in a long list of parameters to `NewCWindow()`—`NewWindow()` for black and white.

An easier way to accomplish your goal is to create a window based on a WIND resource. Call `GetNewCWindow()`—`GetNewWindow()` for black and white. You provide the resource ID for a WIND resource, the address in memory where you want the window record placed, and the window pointer for the window in front of the new window. If you pass nil as the address for the window record, the Window Manager allocates memory for you. If you want the new window to appear in front of all others (the usual case), pass the value –1 as the window behind which you want it to appear.

If the window is set to invisible in the WIND resource, you can resize and position the window before the user sees it. Generally, you display the window only when it is finished and ready to be seen. To display an invisible window, you call `ShowWindow()`. To hide a visible window, call `HideWindow()`. In either case, you provide the window pointer.

When you are through with a window, you must dispose of it. How you do that depends on how you created it.

If you allocated your own storage for the window record, call `CloseWindow()`. You must then dispose of the memory you allocated yourself, using either `DisposePtr()` or `DisposeHandle()` as appropriate. This is the approach used in EasyApp.

If, on the other hand, the Window Manager allocated the storage, call `DisposeWindow()`. The Window Manager disposes of everything.

Recall that one of the features of a window record is a title string. The Window Manager provides accessors for the purpose of getting and setting the window title.

To get the current window title, call `GetWTitle()`. You provide the window pointer, and an `Str255` variable to hold the result. To set the title, call `SetWTitle()`. You provide the window pointer and an `Str255` variable that contains the new title.

The Window Manager also provides accessors for the all-important `refCon` field. To get the current `refCon`, call `GetWRefCon()`. You provide the window pointer. The call returns a `long` value. Typically, you typecast the return value to some other data type to match what you stored in the `refCon` field. To set the `refCon` field, call `SetWRefCon()`. You provide both the window pointer and a `long` value that you want stuffed into the `refCon` field. You typically typecast your original value to be a type `long` to match the calling parameters.

Recall that the grow box is inside the content area of the window. That means that you are responsible for drawing the grow box. To do that, call `DrawGrowIcon()`. You provide the window pointer for the window. This also draws the lines that define where the scroll bars appear.

If you want to know what the active window is at any moment, call `FrontWindow()`. This call returns the window pointer for the frontmost visible window—that is, the active window. If there are no visible windows, this call returns nil.

These Window Manager calls give you the basics of how to get a window onscreen. Let's put that to knowledge into practice.

Lab 8.2 Making Windows

This is a critical lab exercise. In this lab you accomplish two principle tasks. First, you open and close a window. Second, you learn how to attach behaviors to a window so that it responds to generic messages.

Every Macintosh window you create is really a `WindowRecord` in memory. This lab refers to a `WindowRecord` as a Mac window. In EasyApp, each Mac window is attached to an `EasyWindow` data structure through the `refCon` field. This lab refers to the `EasyWindow` data structure as an Easy window.

In this lab you:

- Study the `EasyWindow` data structure
- Create a new window
- Make a window structure in memory

- Attach the Easy window to the Macintosh window

- Get the Easy window pointer

- Close a window

- Implement the close behavior

- Attach the close behavior to a window

Use your code from the previous lab as the starting point for your work in this lab.

Step 1: Study the EasyWindow data structure

Study: EasyWindow in EasyApp.h

Because it is central to EasyApp's power and functionality, the first thing you do in this lab is take a close look at the EasyWindow data structure.

This is an EasyApp structure. Some of the code is presented here for reference. This already exists. Do not type it into EasyApp.h.

```
typedef struct
{
    WindowPtr       itsMacWindow;
    WindowPtr       nextMacWindow;
    WindowPtr       prevMacWindow;
    THPrint         printJob;
    OSType          fileType;
    FSSpec          fileSpec;
    Boolean         hasFile;
    Boolean         changed;
    Boolean         hasGrow;
    ControlHandle   horizScroll;
    ControlHandle   vertScroll;

    short           docWidth;
    short           docHeight;

    long            moreProcs;
    long            windowData;
```

Each window you create gets its own set of these fields. The first field holds the Macintosh window pointer for the window associated with this data. EasyApp maintains a list of its own windows, and the links are in nextMacWindow and prevMacWindow.

Each window has an associated print job record. Printing is discussed in Chapter 16. Each window has an associated file type and may have an associated file. The File Manager is discussed in Chapter 15.

EasyApp keeps track of whether a window has changed so that it can warn you if you attempt to close a changed window. It also keeps track of whether the window has a grow box. Each window may have a horizontal and/or a vertical scroll bar. The EasyWindow record keeps handles to those items. Scroll bars are discussed in Chapter 9.

A window is simply a view of a document. EasyApp keeps the associated document's dimensions in docWidth and docHeight.

An EasyWindow also has a field titled moreProcs. Window procs are discussed a little later.

Finally, an Easy window has data associated with it. You store a reference to that data—usually a handle but it could be a pointer—in the windowData field. This is analogous to the Mac window's refCon field.

Each EasyWindow also has a long set of fields of type WindowProc. Here's a sampling.

```
WindowProc      DoActivate;
WindowProc      DoUpdate;
WindowProc      DoZoom;
WindowProc      DoDrag;
WindowProc      DoGrow;
WindowProc      DoResize;
```

There are about 45 of these fields. Look at the EasyWindow data structure to see what they are. Each begins with the word "Do." These are the messages that EasyApp can send to a window.

When you create an Easy window structure in memory, you initialize the structure so that each field contains a pointer to the function that responds to the message.

> For more information about function pointers, see the "Function Pointers" section of Appendix A.

What all this amounts to is quite simple. By filling in these fields with the appropriate function pointers, you are giving each window a unique set of behaviors. Each window has a set of functions that implements behavior like zooming, dragging, updating, resizing, and so forth. As a result, different kinds of windows can behave quite differently in response to the same message.

EasyApp might send a DoZoom message to a window, but exactly what that window does in response to the message depends entirely upon the function you attach to the DoZoom field of the EasyWindow record.

In the following steps, you implement this powerful, object-oriented strategy.

Step 2: Create a new window

Modify: EasyNew() in menus.c

When the user chooses the New item in the File menu, EasyApp calls NewHook(). That function calls EasyNew() by default. You have already dealt with menu and event parsing, so that code is provided for you.

In response to the user's request, you should ensure that there is adequate memory; then create the window, set its title, and position the window.

```
OSErr  EasyNew (WindowPtr *newWindow, OSType fileType)
{
  OSErr       error = 1;
  WindowPtr   macWindow;

  error = EasyCheckMemory(kWindowMemory);
  if (error)
  {
    return error;
  }

  error = MakeWindowHook(newWindow, fileType);
  if (error)
  {
    return error;
  }

  macWindow = *newWindow;

  EasySetWUntitled(macWindow);

  (GetEasyWindowPtr(macWindow))->DoPlaceNewWindow
                                (macWindow, nil);

  return error;
}
```

You preflight the request by calling EasyCheckMemory(). The constant kWindowMemory is declared in userDeclare.h.

If there is no error, you call MakeWindowHook() to create the window. You pass in newWindow—the address of a window pointer—and the file type for this window. MakeWindowHook() allows the application to provide its own window-making code. The default hook calls EasyMakeWindow(), a function you write in the next step. If there is no error, you set the macWindow variable to the new window pointer.

Next, you set the window's title by calling EasySetWUntitled(). This function is provided for you in windows.c. You can study it if you wish. It gets the string "untitled" from the EasyApp resources, adds a number to it, and then calls SetWTitle() to set the window's title.

Then you tell the window to position itself. You do this by sending the Easy window associated with the Mac window a DoPlaceNewWindow message.

> By default the DoPlaceNewWindow message does nothing, because EasyApp uses System 7's auto-positioning for windows. However, the message exists in case you want to provide a window behavior so that the window positions itself. How to supply a new behavior will become clear as you complete this lab exercise.

Step 3:   Make a window structure in memory

Modify: EasyMakeWindow() in windows.c

While the call to actually create the window is simple, there are several ancillary details you must attend to. The principle tasks are to allocate memory for the window, create the window, allocate memory for the associated EasyWindow structure, and initialize that structure. EasyApp allocates its own memory for windows to better manage the heap and avoid fragmentation.

Here's the rather lengthy code. The function receives the address of a window pointer in which to store the new window pointer, and the desired file type associated with the new window.

```
    short           windowID;

*newWindow = nil;
error = EasyAllocateHandle(sizeof(WindowRecord),
                            (Handle*)&windowHandle);
if (error)
{
  return error;
}
EasyLockHandle((Handle)windowHandle);

windowID = GetWindowResIDHook(fileType);

behind = EasyFindBehind();

/* create the window */
if (g.hasColorQD)
{
```

```
        macWindow = GetNewCWindow(windowID, *windowHandle, behind);
    }
    else
    {
        macWindow = GetNewWindow(windowID, *windowHandle, behind);
    }

    if (!macWindow)
    {
        error = memFullErr;
        EasyDisposeHandle((Handle*)&windowHandle);
        return error;
    }

    /* allocate memory for an EasyWindow */
    error = EasyAllocateHandle(sizeof(EasyWindow),
                                (Handle*)&easyHandle);
    if (error)
    {
        CloseWindow(macWindow);
        EasyDisposeHandle((Handle*)&windowHandle);
        return error;
    }

    EasyLockHandle((Handle)easyHandle);
    easyWindow = (EasyWindowPtr) *easyHandle;
    EasyAddWindowToList(macWindow, easyWindow);

    /* initialize EasyWindow fields */
    SetWindowInitHook(easyWindow, fileType);
    error = easyWindow->DoInitialize(macWindow, easyWindow);
    if (error)
    {
        easyWindow->DoClose(macWindow, nil);
        return error;
    }

    /* store results for caller */
    *newWindow = macWindow;

    return(error);
```

The first thing you do is set the data pointed to by newWindow to nil. In case of error, you want to return a nil window pointer. Then you allocate memory for a WindowRecord. If there is an error, you return. If not, you move the new block high in the heap and lock it permanently. You will never unlock this block because EasyApp relies on it remaining in one place. As a result you can ignore the return from EasyLockHandle().

Next you call GetWindowResIDHook(). The purpose of this hook is to allow applications to supply their own WIND resource. Different types of files may use different kinds of windows, so you pass the fileType to GetWindowResIDHook(). The default function returns the ID number of the WIND resource you created in the previous lab.

As you know, you must provide the pointer to the window behind which the new window should appear. The `EasyFindBehind()` function is provided for you to handle that detail. Typically, a new window goes in front of all other windows, but not always.

Next you create the window. If the environment has color, you call **GetNewCWindow()**. If not, you call **GetNewWindow()**. If that fails, you clean up and bail out, returning the error.

If all is well, you now have a Macintosh window. You must attach an `EasyWindow` structure to the Macintosh window to implement the EasyApp design. You allocate memory for an `EasyWindow`, and check for an error. If there is none, like the `WindowRecord`, you move it high in the heap and lock it permanently.

Next you dereference the handle to get an `EasyWindowPtr`—a pointer to the `EasyWindow` record. You then call `EasyAddWindowToList()` to attach the Easy window to the Macintosh window. You will complete this new function in the next step.

You now have an `EasyWindow` data structure in memory. You must initialize it. That means attaching the 45 or so functions to the various messages. Each kind of window will initialize itself a little differently. Different windows may have different functions for the same message.

You call `SetWindowInitHook()` to give the application the opportunity to set the `DoInitialize` field of the `EasyWindow` record with the correct function. The default behavior installs the `BaseInitialize()` function. After the initialize behavior is established, you send your first message to the window.

The code `easyWindow->DoInitialize()` calls the function whose pointer was placed in the `DoInitialize` field of the `EasyWindow` record. Each such message function receives two parameters, a Macintosh window pointer and a pointer to additional data—in this case the pointer to the `EasyWindow` structure. In the default EasyApp, `BaseInitialize()` installs all the other default window behaviors and sets some other fields in the `EasyWindow` record. Take a look at that function to see what it does.

If there is an error, you send the window a `DoClose` message. You implement the closing behavior in subsequent steps. If there is no error, you store the new Macintosh window pointer in the address pointed to by the `newWindow` parameter.

Step 4: Attach the EasyWindow to the Macintosh window
  Modify: `EasyAddWindowToList()` in windows.c

This function performs two principle tasks. It attaches the Easy window and the Macintosh window to each other, and it sets up a linked list of windows. A linked list is a list where each member points to the next and/or previous member of the list.

In this step you write the code to accomplish the first task. The code for the second task is provided for you. This function receives two parameters, a WindowPtr and an EasyWindowPtr.

```
void  EasyAddWindowToList (WindowPtr macWindow,
                                 EasyWindowPtr easyWindow)
{
  WindowPtr       thisWindow;
  EasyWindowPtr   oldLastWindow;

  SetWRefCon(macWindow, (long)easyWindow);

  easyWindow->itsMacWindow = macWindow;

  if (!g.windowList)  /* this is the first window */
```

You call **SetWRefCon()** to stuff the EasyWindowPtr into the Macintosh window's refCon field. Then you set the itsMacWindow field of easyWindow to the Macintosh window pointer that you received. Each data structure now has a pointer to the other, and the code throughout EasyApp uses this link to keep track of the two objects—Mac window and Easy window.

The rest of the code in this function maintains EasyApp's linked list of its own windows.

Step 5:   Get the Easy window pointer

Modify: GetEasyWindowPtr() in windows.c

On a regular basis, you will need to identify the Easy window record associated with a Mac window. This function serves that purpose.

```
EasyWindowPtr GetEasyWindowPtr (WindowPtr macWindow)
{
  EasyWindowPtr   easyWindow = nil;  /* assume failure */

  if (EasyIsMyWindow(macWindow))
  {
    easyWindow = (EasyWindowPtr)GetWRefCon(macWindow);
  }

  return easyWindow;
}
```

First, make sure that the Mac window has an Easy window. It might be a dialog, for example, in which case the Mac window is not an Easy window. Or it might be nil. Call EasyIsMyWindow(). This function is provided for you. It examines the Macintosh window record's windowKind field and compares it to the value expected for an Easy window.

If the window is indeed an Easy window, you can retrieve the Easy window pointer from the Mac window's refCon field. You stuffed the Easy window pointer into the refCon field in the previous step. Call **GetWRefCon()** to get it back. You typecast the return value as an EasyWindowPtr.

Now that you create a window, the other side of this process is to close a window when you are through with it. You accomplish that task in the next few steps.

Step 6: Close a window

Modify: EasyClose() in menus.c

When the user chooses the Close item in the File menu, EasyApp dispatches control to this function. Although in subsequent labs this task will become more complicated, at this juncture we can keep the process simple. Just send the window a DoClose message. The window is responsible for providing the correct closing behavior.

```
OSErr EasyClose (WindowPtr macWindow, short saveOptions)
{
  OSErr          error = noErr;
  EasyWindowPtr  easyWindow;

  easyWindow = GetEasyWindowPtr(macWindow);
  if (!easyWindow)
  {
    return noErr;
  }

  easyWindow->DoClose(macWindow, (void *)nil);

  return noErr;
}
```

First you make sure that the window is an Easy window. Only Easy windows have these behaviors. If it is not an Easy window, you just return.

If it is an Easy window, send it a DoClose message. Every such message has two parameters, the Mac window pointer and a pointer to additional data. In this case the additional data is unused.

Step 7: Implement the close behavior

Modify: BaseClose() in windowProc.c

Every Easy window "Do" message must have an associated function. You can find the default functions in the windowProc.c file. The name of each default window behavior begins with the word "Base" to reinforce the idea that these are simple default behaviors.

In this step you implement the BaseClose() behavior. The window receives a DoClose message whenever it is supposed to close. It must not only close the window, it must also dispose of any memory allocated for the window and its related structures.

```
OSErr BaseClose (WindowPtr macWindow, void *data)
{
  Handle macWindowHandle    = RecoverHandle((Ptr)macWindow);
  EasyWindowPtr easyWindow = GetEasyWindowPtr(macWindow);
  Handle easyWindowHandle  = RecoverHandle((Ptr)easyWindow);

  EasyRemoveWindowFromList (macWindow);

  CloseWindow(macWindow);

  EasyDisposeHandle (&macWindowHandle);

  EasyDisposeHandle (&easyWindowHandle);

  return noErr;
}
```

Recall that when you created a window in EasyMakeWindow(), you allocated handles for both the WindowRecord and the EasyWindow structures, locked them high in the heap, dereferenced them, and used pointers to the blocks throughout. You cannot simply dispose of the pointers because the memory was originally allocated as a handle. The calls to **RecoverHandle()** provide the original handles to the blocks. Now you have something to work with.

First, you remove the window from the EasyApp window list. You call EasyRemoveWindowFromList() to accomplish that goal. This function is provided for you. Study it at your leisure.

Then you call **CloseWindow()** to close the window. This removes the window from the screen but does not remove the structures from memory. Because you allocated them, you are responsible for disposing of them.

To do that, you call EasyDisposeHandle() for both the original WindowRecord and the EasyWindow structure.

Step 8:   Attach the close behavior to a window

Modify: `BaseInitialize()` in windowProc.c

That's all well and good, but none of this will work unless you actually attach the `BaseClose()` function as the `DoClose` behavior for the Easy window. The function that accomplishes this task is `BaseInitialize()`.

Most of this function is provided for you. However, in this step you attach the `BaseClose()` function to the `DoClose` behavior.

```
easyWindow->DoReadResource = (WindowProc)BaseReadResource;
easyWindow->DoClose        = (WindowProc)BaseClose;
easyWindow->DoSave         = (WindowProc)BaseSave;
```

Look at the existing code. Each "Do" field receives the address of the corresponding function, typecast as a `WindowProc`. Do the same for the `DoClose` field to stuff the address of the `BaseClose()` function into that field.

If you wanted a window to behave differently in some respect, you would identify the message you wanted to modify and substitute a different function for that message. You will do this when you work on the EasyPuzzle application in subsequent labs.

All right! That's plenty for one lab. This is not easy stuff, despite the "Easy" naming convention. You may be feeling confused right now, but don't worry about it. Eventually you will get your head around these concepts and they'll become second nature to you.

Just keep thinking of windows as objects with behaviors, and that you can substitute behaviors when you want to. The intricacy of the code that you have to write to attach the behavior is less important than the concept itself. If you master the concept, you will understand the code in due time.

Step 9:   Run the application

Modify: none

Save your work and run the project using the debugger. When the debugger window appears, launch EasyApp. Choose New from the file menu.

When you do, a window should appear. Congratulations!

Choose the New item again and another window appears! You can make as many windows as memory allows, if you want. The linked-list design means that there is no arbitrary limit to the number of windows. Feel free to walk through the code to study what happens as you create a window.

If you click a window, however, it doesn't behave properly. You cannot move, resize, zoom, or close the window by clicking in the close box. You cannot switch to another window. You can close a window by choosing the Close item in the File menu. Go ahead, try it.

When you are through observing, quit the application.

You're making real progress. You've accomplished the first two major goals of this chapter. You create and dispose of windows, and you know how to attach behaviors to window objects. You are just a few lines of code away from making a window behave like a real Macintosh window. In the rest of this chapter we discuss window behavior, and in the next lab exercise you implement standard window behaviors.

Events in Windows

In this section you learn how to implement basic window behavior: dragging, resizing, zooming, activating, and deactivating. The Mac OS handles most of the details for you.

Dragging a Window

When the user clicks and drags in the title bar of the window, you should respond by moving a dotted outline of the window along with the cursor (see Figure 8.7). When the user releases the mouse button, move the window to the new location. The Toolbox takes care of most of this for you.

Figure 8.7 Dragging a window

Remember from Chapter 7 on menus, that when you receive and parse a mouse-down event, you call `FindWindow()` to get the code for the part of the window that was hit. One possible return value is `inDrag`, meaning the user clicked in the title bar.

In that case, call `DragWindow()`. This call takes care of the entire process. You provide the window pointer, the starting point of the drag (the location of the mouse click from the `where` field of the event record), and a bounding rectangle within which the window must stay.

You want the window to stay on the Desktop, an area that could include several monitors. To get the entire area of the Desktop, call `GetGrayRgn()`. This returns a handle to the region that encompasses the Desktop. One field of a region is `rgnBBox`. This is the rectangle that encompasses the entire region. You pass this rectangle in the call to `DragWindow()`.

The window outline, the animation, tracking the cursor, and moving the window all happen automatically. Not bad for one or two Window Manager calls.

Resizing a Window

If the user clicks in the grow box, you should follow the cursor and draw a dotted line image that describes the new bounds of the window (see Figure 8.8). When the user releases the mouse button, you resize the window to match the new bounds. Once again, the Toolbox takes care of most of the process.

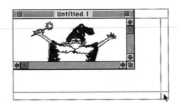

Figure 8.8 Resizing a window

When parsing a mouse-down event, one possible return value from `FindWindow()` is `inGrow`. If that's where the click is, call `GrowWindow()`. You provide the window pointer, the starting point, and the address of a `Rect` variable. A `Rect` is a rectangle. It has four fields, `top`, `left`, `bottom`, and `right`. In this case, the `top` and `left` fields in the rectangle are the minimum size of the window. The `bottom` and `right` fields are the maximum size of the window.

The call to `GrowWindow()` returns a long value. The top two bytes (the high word) are the new height, the bottom two bytes (the low word) are the new width. If the return value is zero, the window did not change size. If the window changed size, call `SizeWindow()`. You provide the window pointer, the new horizontal and vertical dimensions, and a Boolean value to tell the System whether the new area of the window needs updating. Typically you pass `true`.

Closing a Window

You have already written the function to close a window, but it works only in response to a menu selection. You want to respond to a click in the go away box, as well, but only if the user releases the mouse button while the cursor is inside the box. In addition, if the user presses the Option key and clicks in the go away box, all open windows should close.

To implement this behavior, you travel familiar territory—FindWindow(). One of the possible part codes returned from FindWindow() is inGoWay. You want to make sure the user releases the mouse button while inside the box, so call TrackGoAway(). You pass the window pointer and the location of the click. If the user releases the button while inside the box, the return value from TrackGoAway() is true.

If TrackGoAway() returns true, check to see whether the Option key was pressed. Examine the modifiers field of the event record. If it was pressed, close all the windows. If not, just close the front window. In EasyApp you can tell the window to close itself.

Zooming a Window

If the user clicks in the zoom box *and* releases the mouse button while still inside the zoom box, you should zoom the window to its maximum size, or shrink it back to its previous size.

A click in the zoom box generates one of two possible return values from FindWindow(): inZoomIn and inZoomOut. In truth, it doesn't matter which is which, because the System keeps track of two window states and labels one the "standard" state and the other the "user" state. Either one may be smaller or larger than the other.

If the return value from FindWindow() is either inZoomIn or inZoomOut, your first task is to ensure that the user releases the mouse in the zoom box. Call TrackBox(). You pass the window pointer, the location of the mouse click, and the part code for the box clicked—in this case, the return value from FindWindow(). If the user releases the button while inside the box, the return value from TrackBox() is true.

If the return value from TrackBox() is true, you could call ZoomWindow(). When you stop to think about it, though, truly cool zooming is a nontrivial task. ZoomWindow() is not very smart. It expands a window to fill the main monitor, even if the window starts out on a different monitor. The resulting window may be larger than the underlying document, and the window may hide items like your hard-drive icon, the trash, and other useful little things on the Desktop.

However, I have a present for you. EasyApp includes zooming code written by Dean Yu—a genuine Mac wizard. Dean's routine, `ZoomTheWindow()`, does zooming right. You get intelligent zooming for free. I have made minor modifications to `ZoomTheWindow()` so it fits into EasyApp a little more cleanly.

> Dean Yu's code first appeared in Apple's *develop* magazine in March of 1994. You can find the article and original code in the develop Articles folder on the CD. You can learn more about *develop* in Appendix D.

You do not have to reinvent the wheel for every feature of the Mac interface. Some of the rough spots in the road have been well-smoothed by the passage of programmers before you. Take advantage of their code when it is freely given, as is Dean Yu's zooming code.

Activating a Window

In a multiwindow environment, a click anywhere in a window, other than the active window, should activate the clicked window and deactivate the active window.

When a window is inactive, it has two parts: the title bar and the content area. All the other window elements are gone. When the click is in either of those locations—`inDrag` or `inContent`—determine whether the window clicked is the front window.

Call `FrontWindow()` to get the window pointer for the front window. The `FindWindow()` call provides the window pointer for the hit window. Compare the two window pointers. If the hit window is *not* the front window, call `SelectWindow()`. Pass the window pointer for the hit window.

When you call `SelectWindow()`, the System generates the necessary activate and deactivate events to make the hit window the active window. Shortly after you call `SelectWindow()` you will receive a deactivate event for the active window, followed immediately by an activate event for the new active window.

Handling Activate Events

When you activate a window you perform three tasks:

- Draw the grow box, if any
- Show controls, if any
- Highlight selected objects

When you deactivate a window, you do the opposite:

- Hide the grow box, if any

- Hide controls, if any

- Use background highlighting for selected objects

This section discusses activating and deactivating with respect to the grow box. Controls are discussed in the next chapter. Highlighting is discussed in Chapter 12.

If the window has a grow box, call `DrawGrowIcon()`. You provide the window pointer. This routine knows whether you are drawing in an active or inactive window. If you are drawing in an active window, `DrawGrowIcon()` draws the grow box and the lines along the right and bottom of the window that bound the scroll bars. If you are drawing in an inactive window, it erases the grow box.

Invalidating Areas

The Window Manager does a good job of keeping track of what parts of windows have been obliterated or changed and are therefore in need of updating. However, as you manage windows, you occasionally have to tell the system that certain additional portions of the window should be updated.

The Window Manager provides two routines for this purpose: `InvalRect()` and `InvalRgn()`. For the former, you provide the address of a rectangle that bounds the invalid area. For the latter, you provide a handle to the region that describes the invalid area. The System adds these to the window's update region. When a window's update region is no longer empty, the System generates an update event for that window at the next opportunity.

Conversely, you can specifically exclude areas from the update region with calls to `ValidRect()` and `ValidRgn()`.

Updating Windows

When parts of a window become invalid, the System generates an update event for the window. In response to the update event, you redraw the affected portion of the window.

You may receive update events while the window is not the active window. To ensure that you draw in the right port, you must set the current graphics port to the one associated with your window. Before changing the port, you must preserve the current port. Then you can restore the original port when you are through.

Call GetPort() to get the current graphics port so that you can preserve it. You provide the address of a GrafPtr variable to hold a pointer to the current graphics port. Then call SetPort(). You provide the pointer to your window as the new port.

You have one more task to perform before you draw. Call BeginUpdate(). You provide the window pointer for the window in question. This call restricts drawing to the intersection of the visible area of the window and the update region, so you draw only the visible invalid areas. It then clears the update region of the window.

After drawing the contents of your window, you must call EndUpdate(). You provide the window pointer for the window in question. This restores the normal visible region of the window.

Finally, you must restore the original graphics port. Call SetPort(), and pass in the port you retrieved with the original call to GetPort().

Lab 8.3 Managing Windows

You want your window to behave like a good window. It should move, grow, zoom, activate, deactivate, and close properly. In this lab you implement standard window behavior. You:

- Parse window-related events
- Implement window dragging
- Implement window growing
- Implement window resizing
- Implement window zooming
- Activate/deactivate a window

Use your code from the previous lab as the starting point for your work in this lab.

Step 1: Parse window-related events

Modify: EasyMouseDown() in events.c

All of this window behavior results from mouse clicks in various parts of the window. You have used **FindWindow()** to determine whether a click was in the menu bar. In this lab you extend the event parsing tree by responding to clicks on more parts of the window and Desktop.

In this step you simply parse the mouse-down event. In response to most clicks, you send the appropriate Easy window message to the window involved. In subsequent steps you implement the individual messages. Because you send messages, you need to know the Easy windows associated with the front window and the hit window.

```
frontWindow = FrontWindow();
windowPart = FindWindow(theEvent->where, &hitWindow);

easyFrontWindow = GetEasyWindowPtr(frontWindow);
easyHitWindow = GetEasyWindowPtr(hitWindow);

switch (windowPart)
```

The existing code gets the front window, hit window, and part hit. Before the exiting switch statement, get the pointers to the two Easy windows that might be involved. You will need both for the additional code you write in the rest of this step.

The rest of the code in this step goes inside the existing switch statement.

```
case inMenuBar:
  /* existing code */
  break;

case inDrag: /* in title bar */
  if (hitWindow != frontWindow)
  {
    SelectWindow(hitWindow);
  }
  else if (easyHitWindow)
  {
    easyHitWindow->DoDrag(hitWindow, (void*)theEvent);
  }
  else
  {
    dragRect = (**GetGrayRgn()).rgnBBox;
    DragWindow(hitWindow, theEvent->where, &dragRect);
  }
  break;

case inGrow: /* in resize box */
  if (easyHitWindow)
  {
    easyHitWindow->DoGrow(hitWindow, theEvent);
  }
  break;
```

```
      case inGoAway: /* in close box */
        if (TrackGoAway(hitWindow, theEvent->where))
        {
          if (theEvent->modifiers & optionKey)
          {
            error = EasyCloseAllWindows(kAskUser);
          }
          else
          {
            error = CloseHook(hitWindow, kAskUser);
          }
        }
        break;

      case inZoomIn: /* in zoom box */
      case inZoomOut:
        if (easyHitWindow)
        {
          if(TrackBox(hitWindow, theEvent->where,
                      windowPart))
          {
            short zoomDirection = windowPart;
            easyHitWindow->DoZoom(hitWindow,
                                  (void *)&zoomDirection);
          }
        }
        break;

      case inDesk:  /* do nothing */
        break;

      case inSysWindow: /* in desk accessory */
        SystemClick(theEvent, hitWindow);
        break;

      case inContent: /* in window content */
        if (hitWindow != frontWindow)
        {
          SelectWindow(hitWindow);
        }
        else if (easyHitWindow)
        {
          error = easyHitWindow->DoContentClick(hitWindow,
                                                theEvent);
        }
        break;
    } /* end switch on window part */
```

Existing code handles a click in the menu bar. The new code handles clicks in these new parts:

- inDrag—the title bar to move the window

- inGrow—the resize box

- `inGoAway`—the close box

- `inZoom`—the zoom box, either in or out

- `inDesk`—on the Desktop

- `inSysWindow`—in a desk accessory

- `inContent`—in the content area of a window

For a click in the title bar, there are three possibilities. If the hit window is not the front window, you call **SelectWindow()** to activate the hit window. Otherwise, if the hit window is an Easy window, you send the window a `DoDrag` message. If the hit window is not an Easy window, you call **GetGrayRgn()** to get the Desktop region, and then get the bounding rectangle of that region. This is the rectangle within which to drag. You then call **DragWindow()** to move the window along with the mouse.

For a click in the grow box, if the hit window is an Easy window, you send it a `DoGrow` message. Otherwise you do nothing.

If the click is in the close box, you call **TrackGoAway()** to ensure that the user releases the mouse button inside the box. If so, you check the state of the Option key. If the Option key is down, you call `EasyCloseAllWindows()`. Otherwise you call `CloseHook()`.

The `EasyCloseAllWindows()` function is provided for you. It simply calls `CloseHook()` for every open window. The default `CloseHook()` function calls `EasyClose()`, which sends a `DoClose` message to the window. You wrote the `EasyClose()` and `BaseClose()` functions in the previous lab. Figure 8.3.1 shows the calling chain.

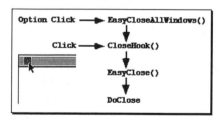

Figure 8.3.1 Closing a window

If the click is in the zoom box and the window is an Easy window, you call **TrackBox()** to ensure that the user releases the button inside the box. If so, you set the direction and send the window a `DoZoom` message.

If the click is on the Desktop and not in any window, you do nothing.

If the click is in a desk accessory (DA), you call SystemClick() to pass the event to the desk accessory.

Finally, if the click is in the content area of a window, and the hit window is not the front window, you call SelectWindow() to activate the hit window. Otherwise, if the window is an Easy window, you send the window a DoContentClick message.

Step 2: Implement window dragging

Modify: BaseDrag() in windowProc.c

The BaseInitialize() function sets BaseDrag() as the response to a DoDrag message. It receives two parameters, a Macintosh window pointer and a pointer to the event record. The existing code typecasts the void pointer to an EventRecord pointer.

```
OSErr BaseDrag (WindowPtr macWindow, void *data)
{
    EventRecord *theEvent = (EventRecord *)data;
    Rect     r;

    r = (**GetGrayRgn()).rgnBBox;
    DragWindow(macWindow, theEvent->where, &r);

    return noErr;
}
```

You call GetGrayRgn() to get the Desktop region, and then get the bounding rectangle of that region. This is the rectangle within which to drag. You then call DragWindow() to move the window along with the mouse. If you look back at the code in Step 1, you'll see that this is exactly the same thing you do for any other kind of window.

Why bother? You may want a window to drag in some unusual fashion. For example, you may want to align the window to a grid. By providing a window behavior, you can override the behavior and create your own dragging mechanism if you wish.

Step 3: Implement window growing

Modify: BaseGrow() in windowProc.c

The BaseInitialize() function sets BaseGrow() as the response to a DoGrow message. It receives two parameters, a Macintosh window pointer and a pointer to the event record. The existing code typecasts the void pointer to an EventRecord pointer. It also determines the maximum size of the document, allowing for scroll bars. This becomes the maximum limit for growing the window.

```
r.bottom = height;

result = GrowWindow(macWindow, theEvent->where, &r);
if (result)
{
  (GetEasyWindowPtr(macWindow))->DoResize(macWindow,
                                          &result);
}

return noErr;
```

You call **GrowWindow()** to track the mouse while the user grows or shrinks the window. The rectangle r contains the minimum and maximum size of the window. If the result is nonzero, you send the window a DoResize message.

Step 4: Implement window resizing

Modify: BaseResize() in windowProc.c

The BaseInitialize() function sets BaseResize() as the response to a DoResize message. It receives two parameters, a Macintosh window pointer and the address of a long value. The high word of the value has the window's new height, the low word of the value has the window's new width.

The existing code extracts the height and width. It preserves the existing graphics port, sets the current port to the window involved in the resizing, and invalidates the grow box area so that it is updated.

```
    InvalRect(&growBoxRect);
}

SizeWindow(macWindow, newWidth, newHeight, true);

easyWindow->DoSizeScrollBars(macWindow, nil);

SetPort(oldPort);
return noErr;
```

You call **SizeWindow()** to set the window's size. You then tell the window to resize its scroll bars. You work with scroll bars in the next chapter.

Existing code restores the graphics port and returns to the caller.

Step 5: Implement window zooming

Modify: BaseZoom() in windowProc.c

The BaseInitialize() function sets BaseZoom() as the response to a DoZoom message. It receives two parameters, a Macintosh window pointer and the address of the direction in which to zoom (in or out). The existing code typecasts the void pointer to zoomDirection. It also determines the ideal size of the document, allowing for scroll bars. This becomes the maximum limit for zooming the window.

```
if(easyWindow->horizScroll)
{
  idealSize.bottom += 16;
}

ZoomTheWindow((WindowPeek)macWindow, zoomDirection,
              &idealSize);

easyWindow->DoSizeScrollBars(macWindow, nil);

return noErr;
```

You call Dean Yu's ZoomTheWindow() function. You must typecast the Macintosh window pointer to the WindowPeek data type to match the prototype for ZoomTheWindow().

Because the window is changing sizes, you also send the window a DoSizeScrollBars message. You implement that behavior in the next chapter.

Step 6: Activate/deactivate a window

Modify: BaseActivate() in windowProc.c

In Lab 6.2 you wrote code to parse activate events. In EasyHandleEvent() you call EasyActivate(). You also call EasyActivate() in response to suspend or resume events. EasyActivate() is provided for you. It sends the window a DoActivate message.

The BaseInitialize() function sets BaseActivate() as the response to a DoActivate message. It receives two parameters, a Macintosh window pointer and the address of a Boolean value that indicates whether you are activating or deactivating the window. The existing code typecasts the void pointer to get the activate condition. It also preserves the existing graphics port, sets the port for the window involved, and sets the local hiliteCode variable appropriately.

```
else
{
  hiliteCode = 255;
}
```

```
if (easyWindow->hasGrow)
{
  EasyDrawGrowIcon(macWindow);
}

SetPort(oldPort);
```

If the window has a grow box, call EasyDrawGrowIcon(). This function is provided for you. Drawing the grow box also draws the lines that border scroll bars. However, you may have a grow box and not have both scroll bars. The EasyDrawGrowIcon() function makes sure that the scroll bar borders appear only when there is, in fact, a scroll bar. You work with scroll bars in the next chapter.

Step 7:   Run the application
Modify: none

Save your work and run the project using the debugger. When the debugger window appears, launch EasyApp and create a new window.

Play with the window. You should be able to drag, resize, and zoom the window. You will notice some unusual behavior with respect to the grow box. Sometimes it appears, sometimes it doesn't. You can click in the grow box area and resize the window even if the grow box is not there. EasyApp handles the grow box along with scroll bars. When you add scroll bars in the next chapter, this problem will disappear.

Create more windows and switch between them. The windows should activate and deactivate properly. Click in a close box to close a window. Option-click in a close box to close all windows.

When you are through observing, quit the application.

Things are really looking up. You now have functional windows that behave the way Macintosh windows should behave. In the next chapter you add scroll bars to the window. In Chapter 10 you start drawing in the window.

Window Manager Reference

This section summarizes the basic Window Manager calls that you use in a standard Macintosh application. For full details on all the Window Manager calls, consult Chapter 4 of *Inside Macintosh: Macintosh Toolbox Essentials.*

8

Control Manager calls can be found in the Reference section at the end of Chapter 9. Calls related to graphics ports can be found in the Reference section at the end of Chapter 10.

```
pascal void InitWindows(void)
```

Parameters	none
Returns	void
Description	Initialize the Window Manager for your app. Call at launch.

```
pascal WindowPtr GetNewCWindow(short windowID, void *wStorage, WindowPtr
                              behind)
```

Parameters	windowID	resource ID of WIND resource
	*wStorage	address where window record should be placed, nil means Window Manager allocates
	behind	window pointer to window in front of new window, −1 means new window is in front
Returns	window pointer to the new window (nil if it fails)	
Description	Create a window record in memory based on a WIND resource. Use this for color windows.	

```
pascal WindowPtr GetNewWindow(short windowID, void *wStorage, WindowPtr
                              behind)
```

Parameters	windowID	resource ID of WIND resource
	*wStorage	address where window record should be place, nil means Window Manager allocates
	behind	window pointer to window in front of new window, −1 means new window is in front
Returns	Window pointer to the new window, nil if it fails	
Description	Same as `GetNewCWindow()`. Use this for black and white windows.	

```
pascal void CloseWindow(WindowPtr theWindow)
```

Parameters	theWindow	pointer to window to close
Returns	void	

Description   Removes window from window list, removes window-related structures from memory. Does *not* release the memory allocated to the window record. Use this call to close a window when you allocate memory for the window record.

```pascal
pascal void DisposeWindow(WindowPtr theWindow)
```

Parameters   theWIndow   pointer to window in question

Returns   void

Description   Removes window-related structures from memory and releases the memory allocated to the window record. Use this call when the Window Manager allocates memory for the window record.

```pascal
pascal void SelectWindow(WindowPtr theWindow)
```

Parameters   theWindow   pointer to window in question

Returns   void

Description   Makes the window the active window.

```pascal
pascal void HideWindow(WindowPtr theWindow)
```

Parameters   theWindow   pointer to window in question

Returns   void

Description   Makes the window invisible, but the window still exists in memory and the window list.

```pascal
pascal void ShowWindow(WindowPtr theWindow)
```

Parameters   theWindow   pointer to window in question

Returns   void

Description   Makes the window visible.

```pascal
pascal void DrawGrowIcon(WindowPtr theWindow)
```

Parameters   theWindow   pointer to window in question

Returns   void

Description   In the active window, it draws the grow icon. In other windows, erases the grow icon.

```
pascal WindowPtr FrontWindow(void)
```

Parameters   none

Returns   window pointer for the front window

Description   Use this call to get the active window.

```
pascal short FindWindow(Point thePoint, WindowPtr *theWindow)
```

Parameters   thePoint   point you want to locate

    theWindow   address of a window pointer

Returns   part of a window the point is in

Description   Possible return values are inDesk (not in a window), inMenuBar, inSysWindow (in a desk accessory window), inContent, inDrag, inGrow, inGoAway, inZoomIn, inZoomOut. This call puts the window pointer to the hit window in theWindow. That value is nil if point is not in a window.

```
pascal void GetWTitle(WindowPtr theWindow, Str255 title)
```

Parameters   theWindow   pointer to window in question

    title   address of string to hold title

Returns   void

Description   This call puts the window's title into the string parameter.

```
pascal void SetWTitle(WindowPtr theWindow, ConstStr255Param title)
```

Parameters   theWindow   pointer to window in question

    title   address of string with new title

Returns   void

Description   This call gets the new title from the title parameter and sets the window's title to that value.

```
pascal long GetWRefCon(WindowPtr theWindow)
```

Parameters   theWindow   pointer to window in question

Returns   current value from the refCon field of the window record

Description   Typically, you typecast the return value to be the type you stored in the refCon in the first place.

```
pascal void SetWRefCon(WindowPtr theWindow, long data)
```

Parameters	theWindow	pointer to window in question
	data	value to stuff into refCon field
Returns	void	
Description	Typically you typecast some handle or pointer as a long vale to stuff into the refCon field. This connects the window to its content data.	

```
pascal RgnHandle GetGrayRgn(void);
```

Parameters	none
Returns	handle to the region defining the Desktop
Description	Use this call to get the Desktop region, usually used before calling **DragWindow()**.

```
pascal void DragWindow(WindowPtr theWindow, Point startPt, const Rect
                *boundsRect)
```

Parameters	theWindow	pointer to window in question
	startPt	point where drag starts, usually retrieved from a mouse-down event
	boundsRect	address of a Rect limiting the drag
Returns	void	
Description	Typically you set the boundsRect to the bounds of the Desktop region, usually obtained by calling **GetGrayRgn()**.	

```
pascal void MoveWindow(WindowPtr theWindow, short hGlobal, short vGlobal,
                Boolean front)
```

Parameters	theWindow	pointer to window in question
	hGlobal	new horizontal location in pixels, in global coordinates where (0,0) is the top left of the main monitor
	vGlobal	new vertical location in pixels, in global coordinates
	front	true => make this window the active window
Returns	void	

Description		Relocates the window on the Desktop to absolute coordinates provided. The top left corner of the content area of the window is placed at those coordinates, not the top left corner of the title bar.

```
pascal long GrowWindow(WindowPtr theWindow, Point startPt, const Rect
                *bBox)
```

Parameters	theWindow	pointer to window in question
	startPt	point where resize starts, usually retrieved from a mouse-down event
	bBox	address of `Rect`, top/left represents minimum size of window, bottom/right indicates maximum size of window
Returns		long value, height in high word, width in low word
Description		This routine manages the resize-window animation. It does not resize the window. Call **SizeWindow()** with the new dimensions. Return value of zero means window did not change.

```
pascal void SizeWindow(WindowPtr theWindow, short w, short h, Boolean
                fUpdate)
```

Parameters	theWindow	pointer to window in question
	w	new width of window, in pixels
	h	new height of window, in pixels
	fUpdate	whether to add newly created area of window to update region, typically `true`
Returns		void
Description		Sets the window to the size that is specified.

```
pascal void ZoomWindow(WindowPtr theWindow, short partCode, Boolean front)
```

Parameters	theWindow	pointer to window in question
	partCode	`inZoomIn` or `inZoomOut`
	front	`true =>` bring this window to front, typical value is `false`
Returns		void
Description		Switches dimensions of window between user state and standard state. Value `inZoomIn` switches to user state.

```
pascal Boolean TrackGoAway(WindowPtr theWindow, Point thePt)
```

Parameters	theWindow	pointer to window in question
	thePt	starting location of mouse, usually retrieved from a mouse-down event
Returns		Boolean value, true => mouse released in go away box
Description		Call this routine when the user clicks in the go away box.

```
pascal Boolean TrackBox(WindowPtr theWindow, Point thePt, short partCode)
```

Parameters	theWindow	pointer to window in question
	thePt	starting location of mouse, usually retrieved from a mouse-down event
Returns		Boolean value, true => mouse released inside box
Description		Call this routine when the user clicks in the zoom box.

```
pascal void InvalRect(const Rect *badRect)
```

Parameters	badRect	address of rectangle that bounds the area to add to the update region
Returns		void
Description		Adds area inside the badRect to the update region for the current window.

```
pascal void InvalRgn(RgnHandle badRgn)
```

Parameters	badRgn	handle to region describing area to add to the update region
Returns		void
Description		Adds area described by region to the update region for the current window.

```
pascal void ValidRect(const Rect *goodRect)
```

Parameters	goodRect	address of rectangle that bounds the area to remove from the update region
Returns		void
Description		Removes the area inside goodRect from the update region for the current window.

```
pascal void ValidRgn(RgnHandle goodRgn)
```

Parameters   goodRgn   handle to region describing area to remove from the update region

Returns   void

Description   Removes area described by region from the update region for the current window.

```
pascal void BeginUpdate(WindowPtr theWindow)
```

Parameters   theWindow   pointer to window in question

Returns   void

Description   Call before drawing in response to an update event. Limits drawing to intersection of visible and update regions, then clears the update region for the window. Must be matched with a call to `EndUpdate()`.

```
pascal void EndUpdate(WindowPtr theWindow)
```

Parameters   theWindow   pointer to window in question

Returns   void

Description   Call when you are finished redrawing your window contents. Restores the normal visible region of the window.

9

Control Freak: Controls In Windows

You're making real progress. You have multiple windows, you can switch between them at will, and they behave like good Macintosh windows. However, there is one common window feature still missing, the scroll bar.

A scroll bar is a control item. This chapter looks at controls in general, how the System stores control data in memory, and how to manage controls—particularly scroll bars. In the lab for this chapter, you use ResEdit to build a CNTL resource for a scroll bar, and then write the EasyApp code to add the scroll bar to a window and manage it correctly.

What Is a Control?

A control is an object inside a window that lets the user manipulate the window or a process controlled by the window. Controls are much more common in dialog boxes than they are in document windows. There is no real reason why this is so, except tradition. A control can appear in any window. The `controlList` field of the window record is the handle to the first control item in the window.

Standard controls include push buttons, radio buttons, checkboxes, popup menus, and scroll bars (see Figure 9.1). With a little work, you can create custom controls for sliders, dials, and other indicators. This book does not cover custom controls.

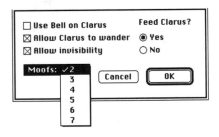

Figure 9.1 Dialog box with controls

A push button is a switch that activates or cancels some action—the classic OK or Cancel buttons, for example.

Radio buttons let the user choose from a set of mutually exclusive options. You organize the radio buttons into a group, and then ensure that one—and only one—radio button is selected. It is your responsibility to define and maintain the group in code.

Checkboxes let the user choose from a set of options that are *not* mutually exclusive. You can have several checkboxes selected simultaneously, or all may be off.

Popup menus give the user a simple way to select from a list of mutually exclusive options. You should be careful designing popup menus. They should list options, not actions. Think of popup menus as an alternative to radio buttons. Popup menus are especially effective when you have a list of five or more items.

Scroll bars (see Figure 9.2) control the view shown by a window. The scroll bar represents the entire document in one dimension. The position of the scroll box shows the position of the visible portion of the document relative to the entire document.

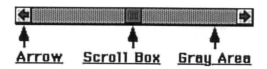

Figure 9.2 Scroll bar

The scroll bar is the only standard control that has parts. You interpret clicks in various parts differently. A click in an arrow moves the document one "line." What a line is depends upon the nature of your data. It might be one line of text, or 10 percent of the visible window.

A click in the gray area of a scroll bar moves the document almost one full page. Again, what a page is depends on the nature of your data. You should not move a full page because the users need some context from the previous view to make sense of what they are looking at in the new view.

A click in the scroll box—also known as the thumb—lets the user slide the view to any point in the document.

Controls may be active or inactive (see Figure 9.3). An active control appears normal and responds to clicks. An inactive control appears dim or gray, and does not respond to clicks.

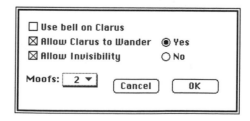

Figure 9.3 Inactive controls

Each control has a CDEF resource associated with it. A CDEF is a control definition resource—executable code that draws the control and may manage its behavior. For the standard controls, the CDEF resources are in the System file.

The same CDEF may draw several controls. For example, there is one CDEF that draws push buttons, checkboxes, and radio button controls. Each CDEF requires a control definition ID to distinguish among the controls it draws. When you create a CNTL resource, you specify the control definition ID for the type of control you want. Table 9.1 lists the values for the standard controls.

Table 9.1: Control Definition IDs

Control	ID
Push Button	0
Checkbox	1
Radio Button	2
Scroll Bar	16
Popup Menu	1008

The Control Record

Control information exists in memory as a ControlRecord. You usually reference a control with a handle to a ControlRecord, called a ControlHandle. Table 9.2 lists the more important fields of a ControlRecord and their purposes. One of them is a *UPP*. UPPs are discussed a little later in this chapter.

Table 9.2: Important ControlRecord Fields

Field	Data Type	Description
nextControl	ControlHandle	handle to next control in list
contrlOwner	WindowPtr	window containing this control
contrlRect	Rect	bounds of this control
contrlValue	short	current value

Field	Data Type	Description
contrlMin	short	minimum value
contrlMax	short	maximum value
contrlAction	ControlActionUPP	UPP for action routine
contrlTitl	Str255	control name

The nextControl field is the handle to the next control in the window. Like the nextWindow field in a window record, this field means that all controls in a window form a linked list. By starting at the front of the list (stored in the window record), you can find any control in the window. The nextControl field for the last control in the list is nil.

Each control knows the window to which it belongs and its bounds. Each control also has a value that exists within a certain range. For checkboxes and radio buttons, the minimum is zero and the maximum is one. The value 1 fills the control with an "x" or a dot, respectively, indicating that the control is selected. The value zero means that the control is not selected, in which case the checkbox or radio button is empty. For popup menus, the value is the item number of the currently selected item. For scroll bars, the value is the position of the scroll box. The minimum is typically zero, and the maximum varies depending on the size of the window and your document.

> There are additional fields in the ControlRecord of interest to advanced programmers. The ControlRecord has a handle that refers to the definition procedure for the control. You must provide a definition procedure for custom controls. A ControlRecord also has a refCon field that you can use to store information. You don't need to get into this level of detail if you stick to standard controls.

Using the Control Manager

Typically, you use a resource editor to create a CNTL resource to describe the control. To create the control in memory, you call **GetNewControl()**. You provide the resource ID and the window pointer to the window in which the control appears. This call returns a ControlHandle for the new control. Remember to check for a nil handle.

You can also make a control from scratch with NewControl(), but using a CNTL resource and GetNewControl() is more flexible, and much easier.

Of course, you must get rid of controls from time to time. To dispose of a single control, call DisposeControl(). You provide the handle. To get rid of all of the controls in a window, you can call KillControls(). You provide the window pointer. When you close or dispose a window, the Window Manager calls this routine automatically, so you don't have to use it unless you want to remove all controls from a window that you intend to keep.

To draw all controls in a window, you may call DrawControls(). You provide the window pointer. However, typically it is more efficient to call UpdateControls(). This draws controls that are in need of updating. You provide a window pointer for the window containing the controls, and a handle to the region within which you want controls updated. Usually, this is the visible region of the window. You can find the handle to this region in the visRgn field of the window record. To draw one control, call Draw1Control(). You provide the handle to the control.

You can manage the display of controls, as well. To make a control invisible, call HideControl(). To make it visible, call ShowControl(). You provide a handle to the control in either call.

HiliteControl() allows you to draw the control in an active or inactive state. You provide the handle and a value indicating how you want the control rendered. A value of 255 signifies that the control is inactive. A value of zero indicates it is active, but not highlighted. A value from 1 to 253 is a part code that tells the Control Manager to highlight (invert the pixels for) that part of the control. For radio buttons and push buttons, the value 1 highlights the control. The value 254 is reserved and should not be used.

You can relocate a control with MoveControl(). You provide the handle, and the new horizontal and vertical position. The position should be in pixels and in "window" coordinates, where the (0,0) point is the top left corner of the content area of the window.

You can change the size of a control with SizeControl(). You provide the handle, the new width and height in pixels.

To set the control's values, you use SetControlValue(), SetControlMinimum(), and SetControlMaximum(). In each case you provide the handle, and the value you want to use.

To get the existing values, call `GetControlValue()`, `GetControlMinimum`, and `GetControlMaximum()`.You provide the handle. Each function returns the value desired.

When there is a click in a control, you must respond. Controls are always in the content region of a window. As you parse a mouse-down event, if the click is in the content area of the window, call `FindControl()` to see whether the click was in a control. Of course, you have to do this only if the window has control items.

When you call `FindControl()`, you provide the point where the click occurred (in window coordinates), a pointer to the window, and an address where the function stores the handle. This routine returns a part number. If the click is not in an active and visible control, the handle is nil and the part number is zero. Otherwise the function fills in the handle, and returns the part hit.

To follow the cursor while it is in a control (for example, to allow the user to drag the scroll box), call `TrackControl()`. You provide the handle, the starting point, and the address of an action procedure. The action procedure determines what happens while the user drags the indicator in the control or continues to press the mouse button. `TrackControl()` returns when the user releases the mouse button.

Some controls don't have moving parts, and you can pass nil for an action procedure. If they do have moving parts, sometimes you don't do anything while the parts are moving. For example, if the click is in the scroll box of a scroll bar, you can pass nil.

However, in some cases you must provide an action function. If the click in a scroll bar is in an arrow or in the gray area of the scroll bar, you want to scroll the window as long as the user continues to press the mouse button. To do that, you pass a UPP for your application's scrolling function.

To create the UPP for a control action procedure, call `NewControlActionProc()` and pass the name of your application's scrolling function as the only parameter. This call allocates memory for the UPP, so it can fail. The UPP takes up memory, so when you're through with it call `DisposeRoutineDescriptor()` and pass the UPP as the only parameter.

{

All about UPPs

UPP is an acronym for *Universal Procedure Pointer*. A procedure pointer—function pointer—is the address of a function. However, in an environment that supports two completely different processors—the Motorola 68000 family and the Motorola PPC family—this is not enough information. A UPP contains the address of the function, and identifies whether the code in the function is 68K or PPC code. This allows the System to switch transparently between 68K and Power Mac native code.

continues

Use UPPs for procedure pointers in any circumstance where code compiled for one processor might call code compiled for the other processor. In this case, the Toolbox function might be in either 68K or Power Mac native code, and it in turn calls your function, which might be in either form. The UPP takes care of all the magic required to make sure the two kinds of code coexist peacefully.

When all the code has been compiled for the same processor, you do not need to use a UPP. When you use a function pointer internally in your own application (without using a System callback procedure), you can and should use a regular function pointer. In that case you know that your application's code is all for the same processor.

As a practical matter, you use UPPs as function pointers when dealing with the Toolbox. You use regular function pointers internally in your code.

You cannot simply typecast a procedure pointer to be a UPP. You must make a Toolbox call to allocate memory and set up the additional data inside the UPP. The Toolbox provides UPP-creating calls for all the common UPPs that you need to work with the Toolbox. You encounter several of them in subsequent chapters.

There is one more possible value for the action procedure parameter in the call to `TrackControl()`. You can pass the value –1. If you do, the System uses a UPP stored in the `contrlAction` field of the control record. For popup menu controls, use the value –1. The System handles everything else.

In the particular case of a scroll bar control, ultimately you want to scroll the window. QuickDraw provides a function for the purpose, `ScrollRect()`. You provide the address of a rectangle that describes the area to be scrolled, how far you want to scroll (in pixels) horizontally and vertically, and a region handle for an update region.

If all of this seems a trifle theoretical, it won't be for long.

Lab 9.1 Adding Scroll Bars

This lab focuses on scroll bars. Keep in mind that there is nothing to prevent you from using standard or custom controls for all sorts of purposes in any kind of window.

Because scroll bars are invariably attached to windows, in EasyApp, each window is responsible for creating, maintaining, and managing its own scroll bars. The `EasyWindow` record has two fields—`horizScroll` and `vertScroll`—to hold handles for each of the possible scroll bars. In addition, the window can receive three scroll-bar-related messages: `DoMakeScrollBar`, `DoSizeScrollBar`, and `DoScrollWindow`.

In this lab you:

- Create a CNTL resource
- Draw controls when activating
- Make a new scroll bar
- Adjust a scroll bar
- Resize a scroll bar
- Identify clicks in a scroll bar
- Scroll a window

Use your code from the previous lab as the starting point for your work in this lab.

Step 1: Create a CNTL resource

Modify: resources in EasyApp.µ.rsrc

Launch ResEdit and open the EasyApp resource file. In the Resource menu, choose the Create New Resource item (⌘-K). In the resulting dialog, choose or enter the CNTL resource type and click the OK button.

An empty CNTL template window appears in which you enter data describing the control. Figure 9.1.1 shows the CNTL template window and the values you should enter.

A scroll bar is 16 pixels wide. However, the values for BoundsRect are arbitrary because you resize the scroll bar when you place it in a window. For controls with an absolute size, the bounds are important.

In addition, set the Value to zero, Max to 100, and Min to zero. Set the ProcID to 16. This identifies the type of standard control—in this case a scroll bar. Set the RefCon to zero. Leave Title blank, scroll bars do not have titles. Set the Visible attribute to false.

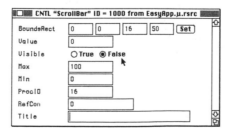

Figure 9.1.1 The CNTL template window

After you have set these values, choose the Get Resource Info item in the Resource menu (⌘-I). Set the resource ID for this CNTL resource to 1000. The code you write relies on this resource having the ID number 1000. You can name the control if you'd like. The name is not the same as the title. The System puts the title next to the control onscreen. The name just identifies the resource.

Save your changes. You may quit ResEdit; we're through with it for this chapter.

Step 2: Draw controls when activating

Modify: BaseActivate() in windowProc.c

As you learned in Chapter 8, the proper behavior is to show scroll bars when activating a window, and hide them when deactivating. For all other controls, you draw them normally when activating, and dim them when deactivating.

```
else
{
  hiliteCode = 255;
}

theControl = EasyGetControlList(macWindow);
while(theControl)
{
  if ((theControl == easyWindow->horizScroll) ||
      (theControl == easyWindow->vertScroll))
  {
    if (activate)
    {
      ShowControl(theControl);
    }
    else
    {
      HideControl(theControl);
    }
  }
  else
  {
    HiliteControl(theControl, hiliteCode);
  }
  theControl = (**theControl).nextControl;
}

if (easyWindow->hasGrow)
{
  EasyDrawGrowIcon(macWindow);
}
```

You call EasyGetControlList() to get the first control item in the window. Because all controls are linked together, this is the head of the control list. You step through all the controls using a while loop, taking advantage of the fact that the last control's nextControl is nil.

If the control is one of the scroll bars, you either **ShowControl()** or **HideControl()** depending upon whether you are activating or deactivating. If the control is not a scroll bar, you call **HiliteControl()** for that control. The existing code sets the variable hiliteCode to the correct value at the beginning of the function.

Then you get the next control and continue the loop until you run out of control items.

Step 3:   Make a new scroll bar

Modify: BaseMakeScrollBar() in windowProc.c

The BaseInitialize() function sets BaseMakeScrollBar() as the response to a DoMakeScrollBar message. It receives two parameters, a Macintosh window pointer and a pointer to a value that indicates which scroll bar to make—horizontal or vertical. The existing code typecasts the void pointer to indicate which to make.

```
short  which = *(short*)data;

theControl = GetNewControl(kBaseResourceID, macWindow);
if (!theControl)
{
  error = kNoResourceError;
  return error;
}

if (which == kVerticalBar)
{
  easyWindow->vertScroll = theControl;
}
else
{
  easyWindow->horizScroll = theControl;
}

EasyAdjustScrollBar(macWindow, theControl);

return error;
```

You call `GetNewControl()` to create a handle for a new scroll bar. You specify the ID number and the window in which the control should appear. If there is an error, you return immediately.

Otherwise, you set the appropriate field of the `EasyWindow` record. Then you call `EasyAdjustScrollBar()` to set the position, size, and maximum control value. You write that function in the next step.

Step 4: Adjust a scroll bar

Modify: `EasyAdjustScrollBar()` in windows.c

This is a utility function to set the position, size, and maximum control value for a scroll bar. It receives two parameters, the window involved, and the handle to the control. The existing code gets the top, right, bottom, and left edges of the window containing the scroll bar.

```
short        max;

if (theControl == easyWindow->vertScroll)
{
  MoveControl(theControl, right - 15, -1);
  SizeControl(theControl, 16, bottom - 13);
  max = easyWindow->docHeight - ((bottom - 15) - top);
}
else
{
  MoveControl(theControl, -1, bottom - 15);
  SizeControl(theControl, right - 13, 16);
  max = easyWindow->docWidth - ((right - 15) - left);
}

if (max < 0)
{
  max = 0;
}
SetControlMaximum (theControl, max);
```

You determine whether you are working with the horizontal or vertical scroll bar. Then you call `MoveControl()` and `SizeControl()` using appropriate parameters. Trust me, these put the scroll bar at the correct spot so that the edges of the scroll bar just overlap the edges of the window and the grow icon borders—assuming the scroll bar is 16 pixels wide.

Then you determine the maximum value for the scroll. This is based on the document size minus the part of the document visible in the window. These calculations assume the window has both scroll bars, and subtracts the area occupied by the scroll bar from the visible part of the window.

Finally, you call `SetControlMaximum()` to set the maximum value for the control.

Step 5: Resize a scroll bar

Modify: `BaseSizeScrollBars()` in windowProc.c

The `BaseInitialize()` function sets `BaseSizeScrollBars()` as the response to a `DoSizeScrollBar` message. This message arrives when a window has been resized. `BaseSizeScrollBar()` receives two parameters. The first is a Macintosh window pointer. The second is unused.

```
ControlHandle  theControl;

theControl = (easyWindow->horizScroll);
if (theControl)
{
  HideControl(theControl);
  EasyAdjustScrollBar(macWindow, theControl);
  ShowControl(theControl);
}

theControl = (easyWindow->vertScroll);
if (theControl)
{
  HideControl(theControl);
  EasyAdjustScrollBar(macWindow, theControl);
  ShowControl(theControl);
}

if (easyWindow->hasGrow)

{

  EasyDrawGrowIcon(macWindow);

}
```

You get each scroll bar in turn. If there is a scroll bar, you call `HideControl()` to make it invisible. Then you call `EasyAdjustScrollBar()` to reposition and resize the bar. Then you call `ShowControl()` to make the scroll bar visible again in its new location.

The existing code also draws the grow icon in its new position. This has nothing to do directly with scroll bars. However, including this task here means that this function takes care of the entire rim of the window.

Step 6: Identify clicks in a scroll bar

Modify: `BaseContentClick()` in windowProc.c

A scroll bar appears inside the content area of the window. You already identify clicks in the content area, and when one occurs, you send the window a `DoContentClick` message. You wrote that parsing code in Lab 8.3.

The `BaseContentClick()` function is a major branch of the event parsing tree. You will almost certainly override it in your own applications so that you can handle clicks in the content area of your window. However, here the code demonstrates how to identify and handle clicks on scroll bars. In the process you also identify what part of the control the user clicked.

If the click is in the "thumb," you handle the process one way. If the click is elsewhere in the scroll bar, you handle it another way.

```
EasyGlobalToLocal(macWindow, theEvent->where,
                  &localPoint);

controlPart = FindControl(localPoint, macWindow,
                          &theControl);

if (controlPart && theControl)  /* need both */
{
  if (theControl == easyWindow->horizScroll
      || theControl == easyWindow->vertScroll)
  {
    if (controlPart == inThumb)
    {
      short  startValue, endValue;
      Point  amountToScroll;

      /* get start and end values of scrolling */
      startValue = GetControlValue (theControl);
      TrackControl (theControl, localPoint, nil);
      endValue = GetControlValue (theControl);

      /* set amount to scroll */
      if (theControl == easyWindow->horizScroll)
      {
        amountToScroll.h = endValue - startValue;
        amountToScroll.v = 0;
      }
      else
      {
        amountToScroll.h = 0;
        amountToScroll.v = endValue - startValue;
      }
```

```
        /* do the scroll */
        easyWindow->DoScrollWindow (macWindow,
                                     &amountToScroll);
    }
    else  /* in arrows up/down or page up/down */
    {
        /* set up UPP */
        ControlActionUPP  myScrollAction =
                NewControlActionProc(EasyScrollAction);

        TrackControl (theControl, localPoint,
                       myScrollAction);
        DisposeRoutineDescriptor(myScrollAction);
    }

  }
  else  /* some other control */
  {
    easyWindow->DoControlHit((WindowPtr)theControl,
                             &localPoint);
  }
}  /* end of if we hit a control */

SetPort(oldPort);
```

The existing code converts the location of the click to local coordinates. You then call **FindControl()** to see whether the click is in a control, and if so, what part.

If it is, you determine whether the click is in a scroll bar. If it is in a scroll bar, you determine whether it is in the thumb or some other part of the scroll bar.

If it is in the thumb, you get the initial value of the control by calling **GetControlValue()**. Then you call **TrackControl()**. This allows users to drag the thumb wherever they want. When users release the mouse button, control returns to you. You call **GetControlValue()** again to get the new value of the control. The difference between them is the amount to scroll. You set amountToScroll based upon which scroll bar is involved, and then send the window a DoScrollWindow message.

If the users click elsewhere in the scroll bar, you proceed differently. You want the window to scroll continuously while the users hold the mouse button down in the arrow or grey area. You set up a universal procedure pointer (UPP) for the EasyScrollAction() function. Then you call **TrackControl()**, passing the UPP as the callback function to manage scrolling.

While the users hold the button down, the System calls EasyScrollAction() repeatedly. EasyScrollAction() is provided for you. It simply determines how much to scroll (similar to what you did with the thumb) and then sends the window a DoScrollWindow message. In both cases, the DoScrollWindow behavior does the real work. You write that code in the next step.

When the user releases the button, control returns to you. You call DisposeRoutineDescriptor() to dispose of the UPP.

If the click was in some control other than a scroll bar, send the window a DoControlHit message. Because EasyApp has no other controls, the corresponding BaseControlHit() function does nothing. However, this allows you to add controls to any EasyApp window and respond when they are clicked.

Step 7: Scroll a window

Modify: BaseScrollWindow() in windowProc.c

This function actually scrolls the pixels in the window. The BaseInitialize() function sets BaseScrollWindow() as the response to a DoScrollWindow message. It receives two parameters. The first is a Macintosh window pointer. The second is a pointer to data that contains the amount to scroll. The existing code typecasts the void pointer to extract the data. It also saves the current graphics port and sets the port for the window to be scrolled.

```
SetPort(macWindow);

easyWindow->DoGetContentRect (macWindow, &scrollRect);

updateRegion = NewRgn();

ScrollRect (&scrollRect, -amountToScroll.h,
            -amountToScroll.v, updateRegion);

InvalRgn (updateRegion);

easyWindow->DoUpdate(macWindow, nil);

DisposeRgn (updateRegion);

SetPort (oldPort);
```

First you tell the window to give you the content rectangle. The BaseGetContentRect() function is provided for you. It gets the content area of the window minus the scroll bars. This is the area that can be scrolled. You don't want to scroll the scroll bars!

You then call NewRgn() to create a region in memory. Regions are discussed in detail in the next chapter.

After that, you call ScrollRect(). This moves the pixels by the amount specified, leaving the former location blank.

You call `InvalRgn()` to mark the blank area for updating. The blank area should be filled in immediately. Do not wait for the System to generate an update event. You send the window a `DoUpdate` message. (The `DoUpdate` behavior should draw the part of the window in need of updating. At this stage of development, there is nothing to draw anyway.)

To clean up, call `DisposeRgn()` to dispose of the region you created.

Step 8:   Run the application

Modify: none

Save your work and run the project using the debugger. When the debugger window appears, launch EasyApp and create a new window.

It should have scroll bars! There isn't anything displayed in the window, but you can work with the scroll bars. Click in the various parts of a scroll bar to confirm that it is working correctly. Move, resize, and zoom the window—the scroll bars should follow right along with the window. If your monitor is large enough, when you zoom the window out to its maximum size, a scroll bar may become inactive. If you are looking at the full height or width of the document, there is nothing to scroll.

Create more windows and switch back and forth. As you do, the scroll bars should appear in the activating window and disappear in the deactivating window. Everything should behave exactly the way you expect a Macintosh application to behave.

When you are through observing, quit the application.

Coming Up for Air

You have reached the first major milestone on the road to becoming a Macintosh programmer. You know how the guts of the machine work—the low-level stuff like blocks in heaps, event records, and window pointers. You not only know what they are, you know how to use them. Absorbing all that knowledge is quite an accomplishment.

Look at what you have done with EasyApp so far. You have a menu bar with Apple, File, and Edit menus in place with the correct items in each menu. You have an event loop. You parse incoming events to identify their nature and content. Based on the events you receive, you dispatch control to the correct function to handle the events. Because you have been building an application shell, you typically dispatch control to a hook function or send a message to a window directly.

You can create multiple windows. Those windows are good Macintosh citizens and behave exactly the way windows should behave. They even have scroll bars! In the process you have also learned how to manage memory and resources in the Macintosh environment.

Well done! Take a moment to savor the accomplishment.

Now our focus shifts. The goal of the first nine chapters of *Programming Starter Kit for Macintosh* has been to teach you the fundamentals of Macintosh programming. Writing code for EasyApp has served that purpose.

However, there is more to a good Macintosh application than what you have done so far. For one thing, your windows have nothing in them. Fortunately, EasyApp is an application shell. In the rest of this book it forms the basis for writing a real application, EasyPuzzle. In the process you add some more features to EasyApp as the EasyPuzzle application demands them.

Along the way you learn how to draw in a Macintosh window, handle dialog boxes, play with sound and color, save and print files, share data, and much more. With that in mind, the next chapter jumps into some real application programming. It's time to put something in a window.

Control Manager Reference

This section summarizes the basic Control Manager calls you use in a standard Macintosh application. For full details on all the Window Manager calls, consult Chapter 5 of *Inside Macintosh: Macintosh Toolbox Essentials*.

In addition, this section contains the `ScrollRect()` Toolbox call, which is a QuickDraw call. The division of the Toolbox into managers is more or less arbitrary. There is a lot of overlap between them, and they call each other all the time.

```
pascal ControlHandle GetNewControl(short controlID, WindowPtr owner)
```

Parameters	controlID	resource ID of a CNTL resource
	owner	window pointer for window containing control
Returns	A handle to the control record	
Description	Creates a control record in memory and returns a handle to you. Remember to check for nil handles.	

```
pascal void DisposeControl(ControlHandle theControl)
```

Parameters   theControl   handle to the control in question

Returns   void

Description   Disposes of a single control record.

```
pascal void KillControls(WindowPtr theWindow)
```

Parameters   theWindow   pointer to the window involved

Returns   void

Description   Disposes of all controls in the window. You do not need to make this call when calling `CloseWindow()` or `DisposeWindow()`.

```
pascal void HideControl(ControlHandle theControl)
```

Parameters   theControl   handle to the control in question

Returns   void

Description   Make the control invisible.

```
pascal void ShowControl(ControlHandle theControl)
```

Parameters   theControl   handle to the control in question

Returns   void

Description   Make the control visible.

```
pascal void HiliteControl(ControlHandle theControl, short hiliteState)
```

Parameters   theControl   handle to the control in question

hiliteState   value 0 => draw normally, value 255 => draw dimmed, value 1-253 => highlight that part of control

Returns   void

Description   Call to dim controls when deactivating a window, or to draw them normally when activating a window. Pass the value 1 for the highlight state to highlight a button.

```
pascal void DrawControls(WindowPtr theWindow)
```

Parameters   theWindow   pointer to the window involved

Returns   void

Description   Draws all controls in the window. `UpdateControls()` is more efficient.

```
pascal void Draw1Control(ControlHandle theControl)
```

Parameters   theControl   handle to the control in question

Returns   void

Description   Draws specified control.

```
pascal void UpdateControls(WindowPtr theWindow, RgnHandle updateRgn)
```

Parameters   theWindow   pointer to the window involved

              updateRgn   region within which controls should be updated

Returns   void

Description   Draws any control that intersects the provided region. Make this call when updating any window that contains controls. Typically you call `BeginUpdate()` and then pass the visRgn of the window as the update region for controls.

```
pascal void MoveControl(ControlHandle theControl, short h, short v)
```

Parameters   theControl   handle to the control in question

              h   new horizontal position of the control, in pixels, in window coordinates

              v   new vertical position of the control, in pixels, in window coordinates

Returns   void

Description   Moves the control to the absolute position provided. Typically used to move scroll bars when resizing a window. If control is visible, this call first hides the control, then moves it, then draws it.

```
pascal void SizeControl(ControlHandle theControl, short w, short h)
```

Parameters	theControl	handle to the control in question
	w	new width of the control, in pixels
	h	new height of the control, in pixels
Returns	void	

Description   Changes the bounding rectangle of the control to match parameters passed in. If control is visible, this call first hides the control, then resizes it, then draws it.

```
pascal void SetControlValue(ControlHandle theControl, short theValue)
```

Parameters	theControl	handle to the control in question
	theValue	value to set
Returns	void	

Description   Changes the current value of the control and redraws it accordingly.

```
pascal short GetControlValue(ControlHandle theControl)
```

Parameters	theControl	handle to the control in question
Returns	The current value of the control	

Description   Retrieve the current value of a control. Useful for determining if a checkbox or radio button is selected, or the current item number in a popup menu.

```
pascal void SetControlMinimum(ControlHandle theControl, short minValue)
```

Parameters	theControl	handle to the control in question
	minValue	value to set
Returns	void	

Description   Set the minimum value of the control to the value provided.

```
pascal short GetControlMinimum(ControlHandle theControl)
```

Parameters	theControl	handle to the control in question
Returns	The current control minimum	

Description   Retrieve the current minimum value of a control.

```
pascal void SetControlMaximum(ControlHandle theControl, short maxValue)
```

Parameters   theControl   handle to the control in question

                    maxValue   value to set

Returns   void

Description   Set the maximum value of the control to the value provided.

```
pascal short GetControlMaximum(ControlHandle theControl)
```

Parameters   theControl   handle to the control in question

Returns   The current maximum value

Description   Retrieve the current maximum value of a control.

```
pascal short FindControl(Point thePoint, WindowPtr theWindow, ControlHandle
                  *theControl)
```

Parameters   thePoint   click location, usually retrieved from a mouse-down event

                    theWindow   pointer to window in which the click occurred

                    theControl   address of a ControlHandle, this call puts the handle to the hit control here

Returns   Part code for the hit part of the control. If the click does not hit a control, this value is zero and theControl is set to nil.

Description   Make this call when you receive a click inside the content region of a window, if the window has controls. If the click is in a control, respond accordingly.

```
pascal short TrackControl(ControlHandle theControl, Point thePoint,
                  ControlActionUPP actionProc)
```

Parameters   theControl   handle to the control in question

                    thePoint   starting point of track, usually retrieved from a mouse-down event

                    actionProc   a UPP pointing to the action to take while the user drags an indicator in the control

Returns   The part code for the part in which the mouse is released. Returns zero if mouse released outside of control, in which case the typical response is to do nothing.

Description   Typically called after calling `FindControl()` to determine if a mouse click occurred in a control. This call follows the user's cursor movement while dragging in a control. The `actionProc` parameter should be nil for buttons, checkboxes, radio buttons, and scroll bars. It should be –1 for popup menus. For custom controls you should provide a UPP for the function that implements your control's behavior.

```
pascal void ScrollRect(const Rect *r, short dh, short dv, RgnHandle
            updateRgn)
```

Parameters   r   address of a rectangle encompassing the scroll area, typically the content region of a window

   dh   distance in pixels to scroll horizontally

   dv   distance in pixels to scroll vertically

   updateRgn   handle to region to which to add scrolled area for update

Returns   void

Description   Moves the pixels in the provided rectangle by the amount in dh and dv. Positive values shift the pixels right and down. Pixels that scroll off the view disappear forever. You must preserve the underlying data. The empty area created by scrolling is filled with the port's background pattern, and that area is added to the update region provided. You must draw the data that should appear in the new area.

Quick on the Draw: Basic QuickDraw

QuickDraw is a set of routines that your application uses to render graphical information. Simply put, QuickDraw is how the Macintosh draws.

You have already used QuickDraw indirectly, although you may not have realized it. QuickDraw renders menus, windows, cursors, and much more. Essentially, if something shows up onscreen, QuickDraw put it there.

Previous chapters have alluded to some of these topics. Now we go into them in depth. The topics covered include:

- Graphics ports
- Coordinate systems
- The pen
- The clip region
- Drawing QuickDraw shapes
- Other QuickDraw shape operations
- Other QuickDraw utilities
- Pictures
- Working with color
- Drawing text

The lab exercise for this chapter focuses on pictures because that's what EasyPuzzle uses.

QuickDraw is like an elephant: very large, very wise, and difficult to consume in one bite. This chapter touches on the basic elements of QuickDraw—enough to give you a solid understanding of how to use it. As you gain expertise, you will want to explore some of the other tools available in this important Toolbox manager.

Graphics Ports

As you learned in Chapter 8, all drawing occurs in a graphics port. From now on I call it simply a port. In memory, it is a GrafPort record.

There are several kinds of ports. A basic port supports the eight colors of the original QuickDraw. A color port supports millions of colors. The Printing Manager uses a printing port to render an image for printing. (Printing is discussed in Chapter 16.) An offscreen graphics world contains a port that allows you to do all of your drawing in memory rather than onscreen; then you can transfer images directly to the screen.

> Using an offscreen graphics world—a GWorld—is a powerful technique used by advanced programmers for quality animation. Offscreen GWorlds are beyond the scope of this book. However, you can see them in use in the very cool EasyPuzzle About box.

Every port has a map of its contents. A basic port has a bitmap. Each bit represents the state of a corresponding pixel onscreen. A color port has a pixel map that represents the state of color pixels. The amount of data devoted to each pixel in a pixel map varies depending upon the color depth of the port—from one bit for black and white to 24 or even 32 bits for millions of colors.

Every window has its own port. The port encompasses the entire content region of the window, including the scroll bars. The title bar of the window is *not* in the port.

Although there may be several ports onscreen simultaneously, you can draw only into the current port. You get the current port with `GetPort()`. You provide an address where the call stores the resulting pointer to the port. You set the current port before drawing into it with `SetPort()`; and you provide the port that you want to use.

Coordinate Systems

If you want to draw something, you need to tell QuickDraw *where* to draw in the port. QuickDraw has two principle coordinate systems that allow you to specify points onscreen. These are the global and the local coordinate systems.

You have already encountered both systems. Each system measures in pixels from an origin or (0,0) point. The values in each system range from –32,768 to +32,767. At 72 pixels per inch, that's more than 900 inches in both the horizontal and vertical directions. That's a really big monitor!

The origin for global coordinates is the top-left corner of the monitor with the menu bar—called the main monitor. Imagine a grid of lines crossing the screen. The position of each pixel onscreen is defined by a coordinate consisting of its horizontal and vertical relationship with the top-left corner of the screen. The grid in Figure 10.1 is enlarged just a tad for easy viewing.

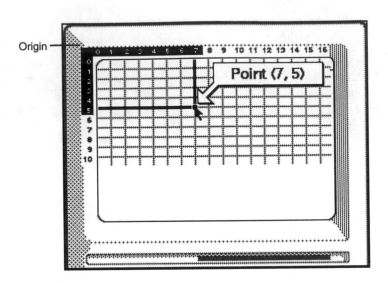

Figure 10.1 A point in global coordinates

In Figure 10.1, the coordinate appears with the horizontal coordinate first and the vertical coordinate second. This reflects an almost universal convention for displaying rectangular coordinates. However, QuickDraw declares the Point data type as:

```
struct Point {
    short   v;
    short   h;
};
```

Just to keep you confused, the structure of a Point has the field for the vertical dimension first and the horizontal dimension second. If you always use the names to refer to the Point fields, you'll have no problem with this little idiosyncrasy of QuickDraw.

A point is a mathematical concept and really has no dimension. A pixel, on the other hand, does have a horizontal and vertical extent. The pixel hangs down and to the right of the point, as shown in Figure 10.2.

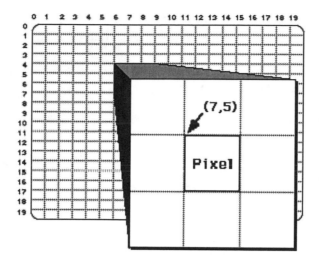

Figure 10.2 A pixel in global coordinates

There is only one global coordinate system, and all ports live within it. However, each port has its own coordinate system called the local coordinate system. The origin of each local system is the top-left corner of the respective port.

In Figure 10.3, notice that the top-left corner of the port has a coordinate in global space. A pixel inside the port has coordinates in both global and local space. The local coordinates are the same as the global coordinates minus the position of the port. In the figure, the point at (7,5) is in a port at (4,3) and the point's local coordinates are (3,2).

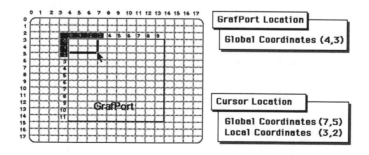

Figure 10.3 Local coordinates

To convert a global point to local coordinates, you call `GlobalToLocal()`. To convert a local point to global coordinates, call `LocalToGlobal()`. In each case you provide the address of a `Point`. The call puts the new values in the same variable, so the original values are lost. The conversion assumes the point is in the current port. You should set the port before calling either of these routines.

Coordinates may be negative as well as positive. In global space, negative coordinates are to the left and above the main monitor. For example, you might have a second monitor positioned to the left of your main monitor. In local space, negative coordinates are outside the display region of the port, but the coordinate is still valid. Your document may be scrolled, and part of it could extend either left of the port or above the port.

The Pen

Each port has its own pen. The pen draws all the QuickDraw shapes. You position the pen in the local coordinates of the port.

Pen information occupies five fields in the `GrafPort` record (see Table 10.1). These control the location, size, and visibility of the pen, as well as the pen's pattern and drawing mode.

Table 10.1: Pen-Related Fields of a GrafPort

Field	Data Type	Description
pnLoc	Point	pen location, local coordinates
pnSize	Point	dimensions of pen in pixels
pnMode	short	copy mode
pnPat	Pattern	pen pattern
pnVis	short	pen visibility

You set the pen location by calling `MoveTo()`. You provide the horizontal and vertical position in local coordinates. You can also move the pen a distance from its current position by calling the QuickDraw routine `Move()`. You provide the horizontal and vertical distance to move. You get the current location of the pen with `GetPen()`. You provide the address of a point, and the call fills in the current position of the pen.

The pen is a two-dimensional shape; it has height and width. Because the pen has size, you can use it to draw very thin or thick lines. The pen hangs down and to the right from its location, as illustrated in Figure 10.4.

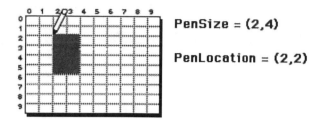

Figure 10.4 Pen size

Call PenSize() to set the pen's size. You provide the width and height. The values must be zero or greater. A pen of size (0,0) does not draw. When the pen draws, every pixel inside the pen is affected. Figure 10.5 illustrates what happens when you draw a line with a large pen.

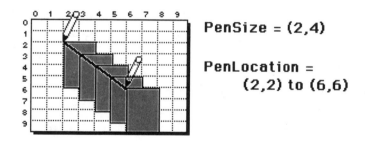

Figure 10.5 Drawing a line

Figure 10.5 shows a line drawn from (2,2) to (6,6). Each pen position is framed to show you the affected pixels, and the pen is gray. Although the pen moves from (2,2) to (6,6), the pixels affected extend from (2,2) to (8,10) because of the size of the pen. The pen extends two pixels horizontally and four pixels vertically from the end of the line.

The pen's mode is how the pixels in the pen interact with the pixels already onscreen. There are a variety of modes available. The most common is named patCopy, or copy mode. This overwrites whatever is already onscreen. Call PenMode() to set the pen's mode. Figure 10.6 shows the effects of various pen modes.

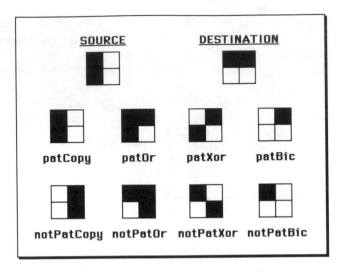

Figure 10.6 Pen modes

In Figure 10.6, the source and destination each have four pixels. When you overlay the source onto the destination, you get all possible combinations of pixels: both black, source black and destination white, source white and destination black, and both white. Table 10.2 lists the effects of each mode on the destination pixel.

Table 10.2: Result in Destination Pixel for Various Pen Modes

Mode	If Source is Black	If Source is White
patCopy	black	white
notPatCopy	white	black
patOr	black	unchanged
notPatOr	unchanged	black
patXor	invert	unchanged
notPatXor	unchanged	invert
patBic	white	unchanged
notPatBic	unchanged	white

The pen may be something other than solid black. The pen pattern is an 8×8 grid of pixels that describe the pen's pattern. System-defined patterns include white, black, gray, ltGray, and dkGray. You can create and use your own patterns if you wish. To set the pen's pattern, call PenPat(). You provide the address of a pattern.

Although not pen-related, a port also has a background pattern used to erase the insides of shapes. It is usually white. You can set this pattern with a call to BackPat(). You provide the address of the pattern you want to use.

> System patterns live in the QuickDraw globals. You access them using names like qd.white, qd.black, qd.gray, and so forth.

The PenNormal() call restores the pen to default conditions: a size of 1×1, a black pattern, and copy mode. This can be very useful when you want to adjust the pen and you have no idea what its current condition is. Of course, you should preserve the pen's state before changing it temporarily, and restore it when you're through. Call GetPenState() to get the state and SetPenState() to restore the state. In either call you provide the address of a PenState record. These calls save and restore the pen's location, size, pattern, and mode.

The final attribute of a pen is its visibility, which is stored in the penVis field of the GrafPort. The pen is visible if this value is zero or greater. Call HidePen() to decrement the penVis field by one. The ShowPen() call increments the penVis field by one. Neither call necessarily hides or shows the pen. They simply alter the value of the penVis field. If you start with penVis at zero, and then call HidePen() twice and ShowPen() once in that order, the pen remains invisible because the penVis field would be –1.

The Clip Region

Before a pixel can be drawn onscreen, it must clear three hurdles. The pixel must be within the port's boundaries as described in the portRect field of the GrafPort. The pixel must be in the visible area of the port, maintained in the visRgn field. Finally, it must be inside the clipping region, maintained in the clipRgn field of the GrafPort. Figure 10.7 illustrates the three areas of interest.

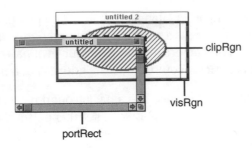

Figure 10.7 Window regions

Figure 10.7 shows an active window (artificially rendered transparent for this illustration) obscuring the "Untitled 2" window. Notice that the portRect is the entire window content region. The visRgn is the part of the "Untitled 2" window not covered by the active window. The "Untitled 2" window's clipping region is an ellipse. The hatched area in the illustration is the clipping region. During a drawing operation in "Untitled 2," only those pixels that appear within all three areas—portRect, visRgn, clipRgn—are actually drawn onscreen. Any pixel outside this area is unaffected.

Your application maintains the clipping region. Typically, you set it to the rectangle that encompasses the content region minus the scroll bars. In this way you do not draw on top of the scroll bars but can draw anywhere else in the visible part of the window. However, you are free to set the clipping region to any shape (even discontiguous shapes) and create all sorts of neat special effects.

QuickDraw provides two calls for setting the clip region. These calls permanently destroy whatever information is already in the clipping region. ClipRect() changes the existing clipping region to the rectangle that you provide. SetClip() changes the existing clipping region to match that of the region handle that you provide.

In many cases you want to change the clipping region temporarily. In that case you must preserve the existing clipping region and restore it when you are through. Call NewRgn() to create a new, empty region in memory. Then call GetClip(). You provide a handle to the new region. This call copies the current clip region to the new region, thus saving the clip region.

When you want to restore the original clipping region, just call SetClip() and pass your saved region. After you do that, you are typically through with the region used to save the clip. Call DisposeRgn() to release the memory occupied by the region.

Drawing QuickDraw Shapes

QuickDraw knows how to draw several different shapes (see Figure 10.8). You provide the appropriate data; QuickDraw does the rest.

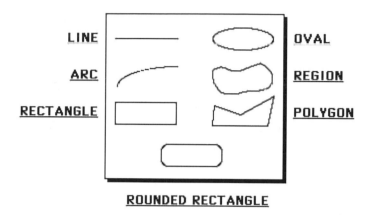

Figure 10.8 QuickDraw shapes

You create lines using one of two calls, Line() and LineTo(). In each case, you provide a horizontal and vertical pixel location—in local coordinates—to which the pen moves, drawing a line in its wake. The Line() call moves the pen from its current location by the amounts you provide. The LineTo() call moves the pen from its current location to the coordinates that you provide.

For all the other shapes, QuickDraw provides a series of operations that you can perform. You may frame, paint, fill, invert, or erase any of the shapes. Table 10.3 lists the QuickDraw calls that perform these operations. Information about these calls is available in the "QuickDraw Reference" section of this chapter.

Table 10.3: QuickDraw Calls

	Frame	*Paint*	*Fill*	*Invert*	*Erase*
Rectangle	FrameRect()	PaintRect()	FillRect()	InvertRect()	EraseRect()
Rounded Rectangle	FrameRoundRect()	PaintRoundRect()	FillRoundRect()	InvertRoundRect()	EraseRoundRect()
Oval	FrameOval()	PaintOval()	FillOval()	InvertOval()	EraseOval()
Arc	FrameArc()	PaintArc()	FillArc()	InvertArc()	EraseArc()

continues

Table 10.3: Continued

	Frame	Paint	Fill	Invert	Erase
Region	FrameRgn()	PaintRgn()	FillRgn()	InvertRgn()	EraseRgn()
Polygon	FramePoly()	PaintPoly()	FillPoly()	InvertPoly()	ErasePoly()

All operations use the current drawing mode. The frame command draws an outline of the shape using the current pen. The paint command fills the shape with the current pen pattern. The fill command fills the shape with whatever pattern you provide. The invert command reverses all the pixels in the shape. The Erase command fills the shape with the port's background pattern or color. Because the background pattern or color is usually white, this effectively erases the shape.

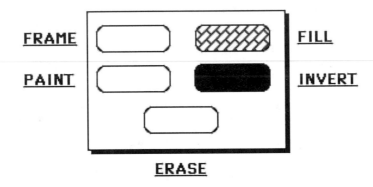

Figure 10.9 Basic QuickDraw operations

Each of these calls requires data on which to base the shape. Some require additional parameters. Rectangles, rounded rectangles, ovals, and arcs are all based on the Rect data structure. For each of the calls relating to these shapes, you pass the address of a Rect that defines the boundaries of the shape.

Regions are based on a region structure. You refer to region data with a RgnHandle. Polygons are based on a polygon structure. You refer to polygon data with a PolyHandle. Both of these shapes are discussed in just a bit.

In the following discussion I refer to each of these data types as a "reference to the shape." Keep in mind that if the shape is a region, that means a RgnHandle; if the shape is a polygon, it is a PolyHandle; and for the other shapes, it is the address of a Rect.

Regions are a patented feature unique to the Macintosh. You create a region structure by calling `NewRgn()`. This returns a region handle to you. You open a region by calling `OpenRgn()`. This call hides the pen and turns on recording. While the region is open, calls that create lines or framed shapes (except arcs) affect the outline of the region. Only the pen location matters. The size, pattern, and mode of the pen have no effect. You can create regions that contain two or more unconnected shapes.

When you are through drawing into the region, call `CloseRgn()` to close it and show the pen again. Because this is a data structure that occupies memory, when you are through with a region, you must dispose of it. Call `DisposeRgn()`. You provide the region handle.

You create a polygon data structure in much the same way. You call `OpenPoly()`. This call returns a handle to a polygon structure, a `PolyHandle`. It also hides the pen. While the polygon is open, all calls to `Line()` and `LineTo()` accumulate inside the polygon. Only the pen location matters. The size, pattern, and mode of the pen have no effect. When you are through, call `ClosePoly()`. Because this is a data structure that occupies memory, when you are through with it you must dispose of it. Call `KillPoly()`. You provide the `PolyHandle`.

Other QuickDraw Operations

QuickDraw has additional operations for some of the basic data shapes. You can use these calls to manipulate data very effectively.

These calls affect rectangles and regions:

- `EmptyRect()` and `EmptyRgn()`
- `EqualRect()` and `EqualRgn()`
- `InsetRect()` and `InsetRgn()`
- `OffsetRect()` and `OffsetRgn()`
- `SectRect()` and `SectRgn()`
- `UnionRect()` and `UnionRgn()`

Each call requires at least a reference to the shape. See the "QuickDraw Reference" section at the end of this chapter for details.

The "Empty" calls test whether the shape is empty. An empty shape is one with no bounds. If the shape is empty, the call returns a Boolean value of `true`. The "Equal" calls test whether two of the structures—rectangles or regions—are identical. If they are, the calls return `true`.

The "Inset" calls work to shrink or enlarge the shape. You provide the amount to move the bounds horizontally and vertically toward or away from the center. All sides move by the amounts provided, so the effect is to alter the size of the shape by twice the amount you pass in. If you pass negative values, the shape grows.

For the "Offset" calls, you provide the distance in pixels to move the shape horizontally and vertically. This moves the shape relative to its current position in the port.

The "Sect" calls require three shape references. QuickDraw looks for the intersection or overlap of the first two, and returns the shape that describes the overlap in the third parameter. If there is no overlap, this shape is empty (see Figure 10.10).

The "Union" calls also require three shape references. QuickDraw looks at the first two and returns the shape that describes them both in the third parameter (see Figure 10.10).

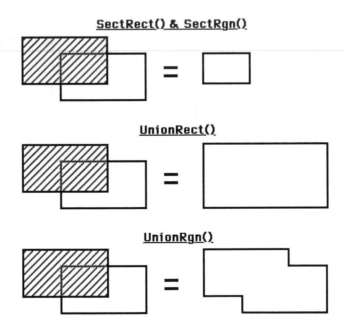

Figure 10.10 Sect and Union operations

Other QuickDraw Utilities

QuickDraw is a very large beast. In this section, you sample a few of dozens of other useful routines.

To determine whether a point (like a mouse click) is inside some shape, the calls `PtInRect()` and `PtInRgn()` help you. You provide a point in local coordinates and a reference to the shape. If the point is inside the shape, the call returns `true`.

You can make a copy of a region with `CopyRgn()`. You provide region handles for the source and destination regions. You can turn a rectangle into a region with `RectRgn()`. You provide a region handle and the address of the rectangle. You can set the region to be empty with `SetEmptyRgn()`.

In addition to the intersection and union functions for regions, you can get the difference between two regions. Call `DiffRgn()`. You pass in three region handles. This call subtracts the second region from the first, and returns the result in the third (see Figure 10.11).

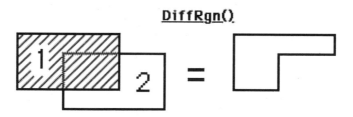

Figure 10.11 Effect of `DiffRgn()`

Pictures

With all of the shapes, all of the operations, and all of the patterns and colors that you can use, you'd think that QuickDraw was powerful and flexible. It is. It becomes even more powerful when you add pictures.

A picture is a sequence of saved QuickDraw commands. These commands are stored in a special format as a series of "opcodes." Opcodes are, in effect, the QuickDraw commands that result in drawing. In essence, a picture is a recording of drawing operations that you can replay any time you want.

Better still, pictures can contain pixel maps (and bitmaps). You can digitize almost any image and convert it into pixels. By including the pixel map in a picture, QuickDraw can render it quickly and painlessly.

Needless to say, we aren't going to cover everything there is to know about pictures on the Macintosh. However, in this section you'll learn how to add pictures to an application, and how to open and display them.

Programmers frequently store pictures as PICT resources in the resource fork of an application. PICT is a familiar inter-application data exchange format. If you have a PICT, you can copy and paste it into a PICT resource using a resource editor. That's how I got the pictures inside EasyPuzzle.

In addition to PICT resources, there are also PICT files. PICT files have a 512-byte header that applications can use for their own purpose. The real PICT data starts at the next byte after the header. In Chapter 15 you modify EasyPuzzle to import a PICT from a PICT file.

Like most Macintosh data structures, you access picture data through a handle of type `PicHandle`. The picture record has two fields followed by the picture opcodes. Of the two fields, the field of particular interest is the `picFrame` field. This is the bounding rectangle of the picture.

To get a picture from a resource, call `GetPicture()`. You provide the resource. This call returns a `PicHandle` to the resource. Because pictures can be very large, it is wise to preflight this call. You should always check for a nil handle. `GetPicture()` uses `GetResource()` so that the resulting handle is a resource handle and remains a resource, unless you detach it.

You may have picture handles that are resource handles, or that are ordinary handles. If the picture handle is a resource handle, call `ReleaseResource()` to dispose of it. If the picture handle is an ordinary handle, call `KillPicture()`. In either case, you provide the handle to the data.

To display a picture, call `DrawPicture()`. This call has two parameters, the handle to the picture and the address of a rectangle. The rectangle is the area where you want the picture to appear, in local coordinates for the current port. The `DrawPicture()` call automatically shrinks or enlarges the picture to fit the destination rectangle. This is a very handy way of scaling a picture. If you want to know the original size of the picture, read the rectangle stored in the `picFrame` field of the picture data.

On occasion, you need to create a picture—that is, record a series of QuickDraw calls into a picture record. To begin this process, call `OpenCPicture()`. You provide the address of an OpenCPicParams record. This structure contains information about the optimal size and resolution of the image. The call returns a new PicHandle to you.

> There is an older version of this call named OpenPicture(). OpenCPicture() is superior because it allows you to store additional information about the picture, such as its resolution. OpenCPicture() requires System 7. Do not call OpenCPicture() or OpenPicture() while a picture is already open. This is a certified Bad Thing. You may have one picture open at a time, no more.

The call to OpenCPicture() hides the pen. Every subsequent QuickDraw call accumulates inside the picture as long as the picture remains open. However, the settings of the current port—including the clipping region—affect the drawing. Keep this in mind. The process of storing QuickDraw opcodes in a picture is just like drawing onscreen, only it is invisible.

When you are through, call ClosePicture() to close the picture drawing. This also calls ShowPen() automatically so that drawing once again appears onscreen.

Working with Color

QuickDraw has had two incarnations with respect to color. The original QuickDraw included support for eight basic colors: white, black, yellow, magenta, red, cyan, green, and blue.

The reincarnation of QuickDraw is Color QuickDraw. Color QuickDraw is available on all Macintosh computers, except those that use the original Motorola 68000 chip—the Mac Plus, the Mac Classic, the Mac SE, and the PowerBook 100. If your application uses Color QuickDraw and you want it to work on those older machines, you must use alternative code that relies on the original QuickDraw when Color QuickDraw is not available.

With Color QuickDraw, you can manipulate and manage millions of colors in all kinds of deep and mysterious ways. However, this book sticks to the things that you need to know in order to use color simply and effectively.

The basic QuickDraw color model is the "RGB" model. RGB is an acronym for red, green, and blue, three primary colors out of which all other colors may be created. The RGBColor data structure represents a color. It has three fields, one for each color. Each field is a short value (16 bits), so each color value could range from zero to 65,535. That allows for literally trillions of colors (2.8×10^{14} for those who want to know).

As a practical matter, most applications use a maximum of 8 bits to represent each value in an RGB Color. That means you specify color with a total of 24 bits—more than 16 million colors. Plenty for every day use, don't you think? The System translates the numbers you provide into a color to display on the monitor.

There are two ways of translating color. An "indexed device" has up to 256 colors. The value for each pixel is really an index number into a color lookup table—a CLUT. Advanced graphics programmers like playing with CLUTs. In a "direct device" the color values for a pixel are sent directly to the monitor. This approach supports the display of millions of colors on the monitor. *Inside Macintosh: Imaging with QuickDraw* has more information on direct and indexed devices.

Color ports work like basic ports, except they have additional color-related information. There are RGB-based foreground and background colors. The fill pattern and background pattern are also color patterns rather than black and white bitmaps. Finally, instead of pointing to a bitmap that contains the image in the port, a color port points to a pixel map—a color bitmap.

All of the calls that work with a basic port also work with a color port. If you are using System 7 on a machine that has Color QuickDraw, *all the calls for Color QuickDraw also work with basic ports!* In other words, you can use all QuickDraw drawing commands in a color port, and all Color QuickDraw commands in a black and white port. They don't magically give you color in a black and white environment, but they work and behave reasonably. QuickDraw takes care of translating your RGB colors into the basic eight QuickDraw colors.

Remember two things. First, all nonwhite colors appear black on a black-and-white display, so things can get ugly very fast. Second, you can use Color QuickDraw only on 68020 or better Macintosh computers. As long as you stay with System 7, 68020 or better chip, and Color QuickDraw, you can forget all about the primitive color system.

We discussed how to create a color window in Chapter 8. You call `GetNewCWindow()`. This connects the window to a color port, and you're on your way.

To set the foreground color, call `RGBForeColor()`. To set the background color you call `RGBBackColor()`. In either call you provide the `RGBColor` you want to use. Remember, you can use these calls on a basic port, as well, *under System 7 only!* QuickDraw translates the color you provide into the best fit available.

You may want to preserve the current foreground or background color before changing it temporarily. Call `GetForeColor()` or `GetBackColor()`. You provide the address of an `RGBColor` record, and the call fills in the current values.

In many situations, good interface design dictates that you let the user choose a color. The Toolbox makes this simple. You call `GetColor()`. You do this in the lab exercise.

This call displays a standard dialog for picking a color. You provide the point at which you want the top-left corner of the dialog to appear, a string you want to appear in the dialog, and the addresses of two `RGBColor` records. The first color parameter is the initial or default color to use in the dialog. The call returns the user's color pick in the second `RGBColor` parameter that you provide. You don't have to do anything else, the System runs the entire dialog automatically.

If you specify a point with coordinates (–1, –1) the System puts the dialog in a standard position on the monitor with the most available colors. Very cool. A value of (0,0) causes the dialog to appear in a standard location on the main monitor (which might not be the monitor with the most colors).

Sometimes you want a color intermediate between two existing colors. This is especially useful when blending or creating color transitions. Color QuickDraw has a very nice tool to do the work for you, `GetGray()`. You provide a handle to the graphics device on which the colors appear, and the addresses of two `RGBColor` records. On input, these hold the two colors that you start with. On exit, this call returns the blended color in the second color you provide (wiping out the original).

> Don't let the name mislead you, `GetGray()` works in color. The System uses this call to determine the best gray to use when dimming objects, the color halfway between black and white—hence the name.

What's a graphics device you ask? It is a generic description of an output device—typically a monitor—used to manage the display of data on the device. You can get a handle to the current device by calling `GetGDevice()`. You can get a handle to the main screen (the one with the menu bar) by calling `GetMainDevice()`. Each call returns a handle to the device.

To set the pen to use a color pixel pattern, call `PenPixPat()`. To set the background pattern, call `BackPixPat()`. The color pixel pattern has a "best-fit" black-and-white bitmap built into it, and that information is used in a basic port.

Finally, recall from our discussion of basic QuickDraw shapes that when you fill a shape, it uses the bitmap pattern you provide. What do you do when you want to fill a shape with a color pixel pattern instead? Color QuickDraw provides these calls to accomplish that goal:

- `FillCRect()`
- `FillCRoundRect()`
- `FillCOval()`
- `FillCArc()`
- `FillCPoly()`
- `FillCRgn()`

In each case you provide a reference to the shape and a handle to the pixel pattern. The oval and arc calls require some additional information. Consult the "QuickDraw Reference" section at the end of this chapter for details.

Drawing Text

QuickDraw also has the capability to render text onscreen. QuickDraw does not manipulate the textual content of a string of characters, it simply draws the string. QuickDraw is a drawing engine, not a word processor. QuickDraw has some rather sophisticated typographic capabilities that we won't discuss. This section focuses on the simple task of drawing a series of characters at a location onscreen. For full information about QuickDraw's text capabilities, see Chapter 3 of *Inside Macintosh: Imaging With QuickDraw*.

To draw text onscreen, be it one character or a string of characters, you must perform the following tasks:

- Set the text-related fields of the port
- Determine the width of the text
- Set the pen location
- Draw the string

Setting Text-Related Fields

The text-related fields are the font, style, size, drawing mode, and spacing. You set each of these fields using QuickDraw calls. Do not set them directly. Table 10.4 lists each field and the Toolbox call that you use to set its value.

Table 10.4: Text-Related GrafPort Fields and Accessors

Field	Data Type	Toolbox Call	Description
txFont	short	`TextFont()`	font for text
txFace	Style	`TextFace()`	style for text (bold, outline, etc.)
txSize	short	`TextSize()`	size for text
txMode	short	`TextMode()`	drawing mode for text
spExtra	Fixed	`SpaceExtra()`	extra width for space character
chExtra	short	`CharExtra()`	extra width for non-space chars

To set the font, you provide a font number. You use `GetFNum()` to get the number. You provide a name for the font and the call provides the font number on the particular machine. Typically, you get the font name from a menu item in a font menu.

To set the style, you provide a declared constant, such as `bold`, `italic`, `underline`, `outline`, `shadow`, `condense`, or `extend`. You can add these together to create combinations.

For the size, you specify a size in points.

Text rendering has its own drawing mode separate from the pen mode, but it operates the same way. You specify the mode by providing the declared constant that represents the desired mode. There are also some special "arithmetic" modes that allow you to create transparent text or to blend text with a background.

`SpaceExtra()` and `CharExtra()` allow you to control the spacing between words and characters, respectively. You can use these fields to justify text, for example, or to give your letters a little more space for readability.

> `CharExtra()` is available only for color ports, and on Systems and machines that support Color QuickDraw. Don't use this call on a basic port.

Determining the Width of Text

You do not always need to know how wide the text you intend to draw will be, but this information is frequently useful. For example, if you want to draw right-justified text, you need to know the width of the string so that you can set the correct beginning point.

There are three calls: CharWidth(), StringWidth(), and TextWidth()—you provide a character, a string, or a pointer to any length of text, respectively. For the TextWidth() call, you also tell QuickDraw what character in the text to start at, and how many characters to use. Each call returns a value in pixels for the width of the provided text. The width takes into account the font, size, style, and spacing settings in the current port.

After you have the width of text that you are about to render, you can set your pen position properly.

Setting the Pen Location

You use the standard pen calls Move() and MoveTo() to set the pen's location to the point where you want the first character to appear.

How you figure out where this point is depends upon your application. For example, if you are drawing a series of right-justified strings, you need to have a right margin. Your horizontal position for the pen will be the right margin minus the width of the string. Your vertical position will be a certain number of pixels below the previous string.

Drawing Text

There are three calls for rendering text: DrawChar(), DrawString(), and DrawText(). You provide a character, a string, or a pointer to any length of text respectively. For the DrawText() call you also tell QuickDraw what character in the text to start at, and how many characters to use.

QuickDraw takes care of all the rest. It renders each character onscreen and advances the pen automatically to draw the next character at the right location—taking into account font, style, size, spacing, and text mode characteristics of the current port.

QuickDraw does not stop drawing at the edge of the window, it keeps right on going. It is your responsibility to keep things reasonable. You can draw text line by line, but you are responsible for determining where each line should break.

QuickDraw has several advanced calls to help you with these tasks, but they are beyond the scope of this book. Right now, it's time you put your new-found knowledge of QuickDraw to use.

Lab 10.1 Drawing a Picture

The goal of this lab is to display a picture in a window. In the process you start writing EasyPuzzle using the EasyApp shell.

In this lab you work primarily with pictures and regions. You can examine the code for the Hello World application you wrote in Chapter 2 to see some simple text display. Most of the geometric calls involving rectangles, ovals, and so forth do not play a central role in EasyPuzzle, although you will encounter them along the way. In this lab you:

- Create a new puzzle window
- Modify EasyApp to make a puzzle window
- Initialize a puzzle window
- Size a puzzle window
- Draw a puzzle window
- Draw a puzzle border
- Select a color for the puzzle border

Lab 10.1 has a new start code. Do not use your code from Lab 9.1 Make sure you have copied the start code for Lab 10.1 to your hard drive. Then double-click the project file (68K or Power Mac) in the new start code folder to launch the CodeWarrior project.

Step 0: Behind the scenes

Some important items have been provided for you in the start code. Let's take a quick look at what they are.

Within the EasyApp shell, additional support appears for dialog windows, drag-and-drop data exchange, and a few other details necessary to support the neat features you add to EasyPuzzle. This new code is added here because its presence in earlier labs would have needlessly complicated the code you wrote.

The CodeWarrior project has a new name, and it has a whole new section of files related to EasyPuzzle. You can find the files discussed in this step in the Puzzle Source folder in the start code. When you work on puzzle-specific code, you work in the puzzle files. In the remaining labs, you also work on EasyApp code as you add new features to the application shell.

The puzzle code has its own specific declarations and prototypes. In puzzle.h you can find some important data structures. Each puzzle has some associated data.

```
typedef struct
{
    PicHandle    thePicture;      /* the actual PICT */
    Rect         displayFrame;    /* scaled to fit */
    RGBColor     frameColor;      /* color around puzzle */
    PieceHandle  firstPiece;      /* handle of first piece */
    PieceHandle  lastPiece;       /* handle to last piece */
    WindowPtr    peekWindow;      /* see whole picture */
    WindowPtr    scrambleWindow;  /* a scramble dialog */
    RgnHandle    solutionRgn;     /* solved portion */
    RgnHandle    borderRgn;       /* frame around puzzle */

} PuzzleData, *PuzzlePtr;
```

The puzzle application also has some additional global variables.

```
typedef struct
{
    UserItemUPP  drawPeekProc;    /* draws solution peek */
    MenuHandle   puzzleMenu;      /* handle to puzzle menu */
    RGBColor     frameColor;      /* default color */
    Boolean      useSounds;       /* play sounds or not */
    Boolean      callSoundIdle;   /* for sound library */

} PuzzleGlobal;
```

You encounter these structures and their fields at various places in the lab exercises.

The original hooks.c file that is part of EasyApp is duplicated, replaced, and modified to become puzzleHooks.c. Some hook routines now call puzzle-specific functions. In this lab and in subsequent labs, you modify more hooks so you become familiar with this process.

The start code takes care of initializing the puzzle application, as well. The InitAppHook() routine in puzzleHooks.c calls EasyInitApp() and then calls InitPuzzleApp() in puzzleInit.c to set up the EasyPuzzle application.

Finally, the EasyPuzzle resources are in EasyPuzzle.µ.rsrc. This file replaces the YourApp.rsrc file in the plain vanilla EasyApp. The puzzle resources include a WIND for the puzzle window, and a PICT to display in the window. Feel free to explore both the resources and the code provided for you.

Step 1: Create a new window

Modify: NewHook() in puzzleHooks.c

Modify: NewPuzzle() in puzzleWindow.c

It is fitting that you modify a hook routine as the first step in building an application based on EasyApp. Each application built on EasyApp should replace the default file hooks.c with its own file of hooks. It starts life as an exact duplicate of hooks.c, and then you modify those hooks necessary to build your application.

Some hooks—such as InitAppHook()—have been modified for you in the start code for this lab. Others you modify yourself.

When the user chooses the New item in the File menu, EasyApp calls the NewHook(). You want to create a window different from the default EasyApp window, and this is the first place where you modify EasyApp behavior.

```
OSErr NewHook (WindowPtr *macWindow, OSType fileType)
{
/*
  return EasyNew (macWindow, fileType);
*/
  return NewPuzzle (macWindow, fileType);
}
```

In this case I have "commented out" the existing call to EasyNew() so that the compiler doesn't see it. You can simply delete it if you wish. You replace the call with a call to NewPuzzle(). When EasyApp calls the NewHook(), your routine gets called instead of EasyNew().

Here's the code for NewPuzzle().

```
Handle        thePicture;

error = EasyNew(newWindow, fileType);
if(error)
{
  return error;
}

thePicture = EasyGet1Resource(g.appResFile, kPictType,
                              kPuzzleBaseID);
if (thePicture == nil)
{
  error = kNoResourceError;
  return error;
}
```

```
DetachResource(thePicture);
HNoPurge(thePicture);

macWindow = *newWindow;
easyWindow = GetEasyWindowPtr(macWindow);

SetPuzzlePicture(easyWindow, (PicHandle)thePicture);
easyWindow->DoResize(macWindow, nil);

return error;
```

The first thing you do is call the original EasyNew() routine! It does a perfectly fine job of making a window. It checks memory, makes the window, sets the title, and so forth. You just want to add a few things to the window. (You must also modify the window-making behavior a little bit. You'll do that in the next few steps.)

The puzzle window contains a picture. The EasyPuzzle resources contain a PICT resource for the purpose. You call EasyGet1Resource() to get it for you, and check for error.

If there is no error, you call **DetachResource()** and **HNoPurge()**. Each puzzle should have its own independent data, and you don't want it to be purgeable.

Then you get the Macintosh window pointer and the Easy window pointer for the new window. You call SetPuzzlePicture() to attach the picture to the puzzle data. This routine is provided for you. It simply sets the thePicture field of the puzzle data.

Finally, you send the window a DoResize message. In EasyPuzzle, you use this message to adjust the size of the window, based on the size of the picture. You examine the resizing routine in a subsequent step.

Step 2: Modify EasyApp to make a puzzle window

Modify: GetWindowResIDHook() in puzzleHooks.c

Modify: SetWindowInitHook() in puzzleHooks.c

The EasyNew() routine calls EasyMakeWindow() to actually make the window. You wrote EasyMakeWindow() in Lab 8.2. You can modify how that routine makes a window by replacing two hooks. That routine calls GetWindowResIDHook() and SetWindowInitHook(). The first provides the WIND resource ID that EasyMakeWindow() uses. The second sets the initializing routine for the EasyWindow structure.

Here's the code for GetWindowResIDHook():

```
short GetWindowResIDHook (OSType fileType)
{
/*
  return kBaseResourceID;
*/

  return kPuzzleBaseID;
}
```

You return kPuzzleBaseID (declared in puzzle.h). This is the resource ID number that EasyMakeWindow() uses in a call to **GetNewCWindow()**. You don't have to rewrite EasyMakeWindow(), you just provide it with different information.

The other hook you modify is SetWindowInitHook():

```
void SetWindowInitHook (EasyWindowPtr easyWindow,
                        OSType fileType)
{
/*
  EasySetWindowInit (easyWindow, fileType);
*/
  SetPuzzleWindowInit (easyWindow, fileType);
}
```

Again, I commented out the existing code to emphasize that you are replacing existing behavior with a new behavior. This hook now calls SetPuzzleWindowInit(). The SetPuzzleWindowInit() routine is provided for you. It sets the window's DoInitialize behavior to point to InitPuzzleWindow(). You write that routine in the next step.

EasyApp still takes care of making the window at the right time. You modify the behavior by replacing a couple of hooks. Now EasyApp makes the right kind of window for the puzzle.

Step 3: Initialize a puzzle window

Modify: InitPuzzleWindow() in puzzleWindow.c

You already have a perfectly fine initializing routine, BaseInitialize(). All you really want to do is change a few things that it does. This code accomplishes that task.

```
PuzzlePtr     myPuzzle;

error = BaseInitialize(macWindow, data);
if(error)
{
  return error;  /* all done, problem */
}

easyWindow->hasGrow  = false;
```

```
DisposeControl(easyWindow->horizScroll);
DisposeControl(easyWindow->vertScroll);
easyWindow->horizScroll = 0;
easyWindow->vertScroll = 0;

easyWindow->DoReadResource = (WindowProc)ReadPuzzleResource;
easyWindow->DoClose       = (WindowProc)ClosePuzzleWindow;
easyWindow->DoWriteResource= (WindowProc)WritePuzzleResource;
easyWindow->DoRevert      = (WindowProc)PuzzleRevert;

easyWindow->DoContentClick = (WindowProc)ClickInPuzzle;
easyWindow->DoResize       = (WindowProc)SizePuzzleWindow;
easyWindow->DoDrawPage     = (WindowProc)DrawPuzzlePage;
easyWindow->DoDrawSelected = (WindowProc)DrawPuzzleSelected;
easyWindow->DoUpdateMenus  = (WindowProc)UpdatePuzzleMenus;
easyWindow->DoFlattenWindow= (WindowProc)FlattenPuzzleWindow;
easyWindow->DoUnflattenWindow =
                         (WindowProc)UnflattenPuzzleWindow;

easyWindow->DoAdjustCursor   = (WindowProc)EmptyProc;
easyWindow->DoMouseMoved     = (WindowProc)EmptyProc;
easyWindow->DoZoom           = (WindowProc)EmptyProc;
easyWindow->DoGrow           = (WindowProc)EmptyProc;
easyWindow->DoMakeScrollBar  = (WindowProc)EmptyProc;
easyWindow->DoSizeScrollBars = (WindowProc)EmptyProc;
easyWindow->DoScrollWindow   = (WindowProc)EmptyProc;

error = EasyAllocateHandle(sizeof(PuzzleData),
                         &myPuzzleHandle);
if (error)
{
  return error;
}

EasyLockHandle(myPuzzleHandle);
myPuzzle = (PuzzlePtr) *myPuzzleHandle;
easyWindow->windowData = (long)myPuzzle;

myPuzzle->frameColor = puzzleG.frameColor;

return error;
}
```

You start by calling BaseInitialize() to do a normal window setup. If there is an error, you bail out immediately. However, the puzzle window is a little different. If you are successful, you must change a few things in the basic window, and add a few things to it.

The puzzle window has no grow box, so you set the hasGrow field to false. It has no scroll bars, so you dispose of the controls created for the basic window, and set the corresponding fields to zero.

Then you replace several behaviors. (You replace more behaviors in subsequent labs.) When EasyApp sends one of these messages—like DoClose—the puzzle function is called instead of the base function.

Notice that several messages use the EmptyProc() routine. Every message must have an associated function, but some messages should have no effect. For example, the puzzle window has no zoom box. If it ever receives a DoZoom message it should do nothing. The EmptyProc() routine does nothing. So EmptyProc() is set as the response function.

A puzzle window has associated data. The remaining code allocates memory for that data, moves it high in the heap, locks it, dereferences it, and stuffs a pointer to that data in the windowData field. Finally, you set the default color for the puzzle frame from the puzzle's own global variables. All the other fields of the new puzzle data are zero to begin with. You know they are zero because the EasyApp memory allocation routine uses **NewHandleClear()** to allocate relocatable blocks.

Step 4:   Size a puzzle window

Modify: SizePuzzleWindow() in puzzleWindow.c

In this step you walk through the code instead of writing it. After making the puzzle window, initializing its data and behaviors, and attaching a picture to it, the NewPuzzle() routine sends a DoResize message to the window. The SizePuzzleWindow() function responds. Let's look at the code for that function.

First it sets the display frame for the picture. The frame is always 200 pixels high. The width varies depending upon the dimensions of the original picture. The code attempts to keep the same ratio of height to width, but if the frame gets too narrow or too wide the code uses minimum or maximum values for the display frame.

The picture has a border or margin around all four sides. The code sets the frame in the window's local coordinates, allowing for the margin.

```
displayFrame.top    = kPuzzleMargin;
displayFrame.left   = kPuzzleMargin;
displayFrame.bottom = kPuzzleMargin + newHeight;
displayFrame.right  = kPuzzleMargin + newWidth;
SetPuzzleFrame(easyWindow, &displayFrame);
```

Then the code sets the window's size to include the display frame and a margin around all four sides. It also sets the docWidth and docHeight fields of the Easy window to match.

```
newHeight += 2 * kPuzzleMargin;
newWidth  += 2 * kPuzzleMargin;

SizeWindow(macWindow, newWidth, newHeight, true);
easyWindow->docWidth  = newWidth;
easyWindow->docHeight = newHeight;
```

The puzzle application divides the window into two principle regions: the solution region and the border region. The remaining code disposes of any existing regions and builds new regions for the window. The solution region starts out as the display rectangle. The border region is the rest of the window (the entire window minus the display rectangle).

When you break the puzzle into pieces in subsequent labs, the solution region becomes that part of the display area that has been solved.

Step 5: Draw a puzzle window

Modify: `DrawPuzzlePage()` in puzzleWindow.c

When it is necessary to update a window, EasyApp sends the window a `DoUpdate` message. The `BaseUpdate()` function in windowProc.c works just fine for us, so we don't have to replace it. Take a look at that routine to see what it does. It sets the port and calls `BeginUpdate()`. Then it erases the drawing area (limited by the current clip region), updates any controls in the window, and sends the window a `DoDraw` message. When finished, it calls `EndUpdate()` and restores the original port.

The default `BaseDraw()` behavior simply sends a `DoDrawPage` message to the window. In Step 3, you set `DrawPuzzlePage()` as the response behavior for the `DoDrawPage` message. In a multipage document, the message specifies which page to draw. In the puzzle, you have a simple, one-page document.

```
RgnHandle    saveClip;

DrawPuzzleBorder(macWindow);

/* set the solution region as clip region */
if (solutionRgn)
{
  saveClip = NewRgn();
  GetClip(saveClip);
  SetClip(solutionRgn);
}

/* draw the picture */
GetPuzzleFrame(easyWindow, &theFrame);
DrawPicture(thePicture, &theFrame);
```

```
/* restore clip */
if (solutionRgn)
{
  SetClip(saveClip);
  DisposeRgn(saveClip);
}

return noErr;
```

First, you call DrawPuzzleBorder() to fill in the margins of the window. You complete that routine in the next step.

Then you preserve the current clip region by calling NewRgn() to create a region, and GetClip() to get the current clip region. You call SetClip() to set the clip to the current solution region. For now, this is the entire picture display area. Later on, this same code draws just those parts of the puzzle that have been solved.

To actually draw the picture, you first get the window's display frame. The frame contains the bounds of the picture as it is displayed in the window. The call to DrawPicture() automatically scales the picture to fit in the provided frame.

When finished, you restore the original clip and dispose of the region used to preserve it.

Step 6: Draw a puzzle border

Modify: DrawPuzzleBorder() in puzzleWindow.c

This is a utility routine that creates and draws the border around the puzzle picture. Most of the code is provided for you. The existing code preserves the window's clip region and tests to see whether the environment supports color. If it does, you must fill in the border with a color.

```
if (g.hasColorQD)
{
  GetForeColor(&saveColor);

  GetPuzzleColor(easyWindow, &thisColor);
  RGBForeColor(&thisColor);

  SetClip(borderRgn);
  PaintRect(&macWindow->portRect);

  GetPuzzleFrame(easyWindow, &puzzleFrame);
```

As you always do when being a good citizen, you preserve the existing state before altering it. You call GetForeColor() to get the current foreground color to preserve it.

Each puzzle has its own color. You call GetPuzzleColor() to retrieve the color for this puzzle from the puzzle's own data. In the next step, you allow the user to set the puzzle's color. Call RGBForeColor() to set the foreground color.

You already set up the border region when sizing the window, so you set the window's clip region to the border region. Then you call PaintRect() to fill the window with color. However, the clip region does not include the puzzle picture display, so nothing happens in there.

Why not just call PaintRgn() to fill the border region? In Chapter 16 you use this same code to print the puzzle on paper. PaintRgn() doesn't work when printing, but PaintRect() does. Printing hides the pen, and when the pen is hidden, no drawing happens when you fill or paint a region. That's life.

The remaining code makes things a little fancier. It sets up a narrow region between the picture and the rest of the border and outlines it as if it were a three-dimensional bevel. The code calls GetGray() to get a color halfway between the actual color and white or black, depending upon whether it is doing the shadowed part of the bevel or the light part of the bevel. Then it sets the color and paints the region. You'll see what this looks like in just a moment.

You must also close the puzzle window. The ClosePuzzleWindow() routine has been provided for you. It responds to a DoClose message. It disposes of puzzle-specific items in memory, and then calls BaseClose() to take care of the window.

Step 7:   Select a color for the puzzle border

Modify: ColorPuzzleDialog() in puzzleDialog.c

This routine displays the standard color dialog to allow the user to select a color. You need to provide an initial color, and you get back the new color.

```
Point      minus1;

if (easyWindow)
{
  GetPuzzleColor(easyWindow, &inColor);
}
else
{
  inColor = puzzleG.frameColor;
}
```

```
minus1.h = minus1.v = -1;

if (GetColor(minus1, "\p", &inColor, &outColor))
{
  if (easyWindow)
  {
    SetPuzzleColor(easyWindow, &outColor);
    EasyForceUpdate(macWindow);
    easyWindow->changed = true;
  }
  else
  {
    puzzleG.frameColor = outColor;
  }
}
```

If there is an EasyPuzzle window, you call GetPuzzleColor() to get the current color. Otherwise, you use the application's default color from puzzleG.frameColor. You set the location of the dialog to the point at (–1,–1) so it appears on the best screen.

After that, you call **GetColor()** to display and manage the dialog. That's all there is to it. The "\p" parameter says there is no prompt string. You also provide the addresses for both the original and the new colors. If this call returns true, the user approved the new color.

In that case, if there is an EasyPuzzle window, you set its color by calling SetPuzzleColor(). You then update the window and mark the window as changed. If there is no EasyPuzzle window, you change the default color.

Step 8: Run the application

Modify: none

Save your work and run the project using the debugger. When the debugger window appears, launch EasyPuzzle.

> EasyPuzzle is far from finished. There are some menu items and behaviors that are partially functional. You should avoid playing around with either the Page Setup item or the Open item in the File menu until you are specifically instructed to do so in the appropriate lab exercises. I don't think disaster will strike if you choose these items, but EasyPuzzle will not behave correctly.

With EasyPuzzle running, choose the Set Color item in the Puzzle menu. The standard color dialog should appear. Pick a new color. When you click the OK button, the dialog disappears. You have just set the default color for the border of new puzzles.

Now choose the New item from the File menu.

A puzzle window appears! It should look like Figure 10.1.1. Your border color should match the color you just selected.

Figure 10.1.1 The puzzle window

There should be no zoom box, no scroll bars, just the picture in the frame. Notice the beveled edges around the picture that give the window a sense of depth. That touch makes the difference between something that looks ordinary and something that looks more polished. Move the window around onscreen, make more windows and switch between them. Everything should work just fine. EasyApp provides all the standard window behavior.

If you would like to change the border color for an existing puzzle window, choose the Set Color item in the Puzzle menu when that window is active. The change you make applies to that window only.

When you are through observing, quit the application. You have just filled a window with color and a picture. That's a major enhancement to what you have accomplished so far. In the next chapter, we turn our attention to the various kinds of dialogs used to communicate with the user.

QuickDraw Reference

This section summarizes the basic QuickDraw calls you use in a standard Macintosh application. They are grouped by topic to make it easier to locate the call you want. For full details on all the QuickDraw calls, consult *Inside Macintosh: Imaging With QuickDraw*.

Initializing and Port Management

`pascal void InitGraf(void *globalPtr)`

Parameters	globalPtr	address of a global variable, thePort
Returns	void	
Description	Pass the address of qd.thePort. Initializes QuickDraw for your application. Call once when application launches. Initialize this manager first, before all others.	

`pascal void GetPort(GrafPtr *port)`

Parameters	port	address of a GrafPtr variable to hold current port
Returns	void	
Description	Retrieves the address of the current port. Call before changing ports so you can later restore original port.	

`pascal void SetPort(GrafPtr port)`

Parameters	port	the port you want to be the current port
Returns	void	
Description	Before drawing, make this call with your window's window pointer to ensure your window is the current port. Also used to restore the original port when you are through drawing.	

`pascal void ClipRect(const Rect *r)`

Parameters	r	address of Rect bounding desired clip area
Returns	void	
Description	Changes existing clip region to match the bounds of the Rect you pass in. Destroys original clip, so if it's a temporary change, you should save the existing clip first.	

321

```
pascal void GetClip(RgnHandle rgn)
```

Parameters	rgn	handle to an existing region
Returns	void	
Description	Copies the clip region into your existing region. Use this call to preserve the clip region when necessary.	

```
pascal void SetClip(RgnHandle rgn)
```

Parameters	rgn	handle to an existing region
Returns	void	
Description	Copies the existing region into the clip region.	

Pen- and Pattern-Related Calls

```
pascal void HidePen(void)
```

Parameters	none
Returns	void
Description	Decrements the penVis field of the port by 1. If penVis < 0, pen does not draw.

```
pascal void ShowPen(void)
```

Parameters	none
Returns	void
Description	Increments the penVis field of the port by 1. If penVis >= 0, pen draws.

```
pascal void GetPen(Point *pt)
```

Parameters	pt	address of a Point variable
Returns	void	
Description	Call puts the current position of pen (local coordinates) in pt.	

```
pascal void GetPenState(PenState *pnState)
```

Parameters	pnState	address of a PenState variable to hold current status of pen
Returns	void	
Description	Puts current pen position, size, pattern and mode in the variable provided.	

```
pascal void SetPenState(const PenState *pnState)
```

Parameters	pnState	address of a PenState variable used to set status of pen
Returns	void	
Description	Sets the pen position, size, pattern, and mode in the current port to the values in the variable provided.	

```
pascal void PenSize(short width, short height)
```

Parameters	width	desired width of pen, in pixels
	height	desired height of pen, in pixels
Returns	void	
Description	Sets the pnSize field of the current port.	

```
pascal void PenMode(short mode)
```

Parameters	mode	a number indication what bit transfer mode to use
Returns	void	
Description	Sets the pnMode field of the current port. The mode controls how bits in the pen interact with existing bits when drawing.	

```
pascal void PenPat(ConstPatternParam pat)
```

Parameters	pat	address of a bitmap pattern
Returns	void	
Description	Sets the pen's pattern to the pattern provided.	

```
pascal void PenNormal(void)
```

Parameters	none
Returns	void
Description	Sets the pen to size (1,1), copy mode, solid black.

```
pascal void MoveTo(short h, short v)
```

Parameters	h	desired horizontal position of pen, in local coordinates
	v	desired vertical position of pen, in local coordinates
Returns	void
Description	Moves pen to coordinates provided.

```
pascal void Move(short dh, short dv)
```

Parameters	dh	distance to move pen horizontally from current location, in pixels
	dv	distance to move pen vertically from current location, in pixels
Returns	void
Description	Moves pen amount desired from its current position. Positive values are to the right and down.

```
pascal void BackPat(ConstPatternParam pat)
```

Parameters	pat	address of a pattern
Returns	void
Description	Sets the background pattern of the current port to the value provided.

Point-Related Calls

```
pascal void GlobalToLocal(Point *pt)
```

Parameters	pt	address of a Point variable
Returns	void

Description		Converts the given Point from global to local coordinates based on the position of the current port.

```
pascal void LocalToGlobal(Point *pt)
```

Parameters	pt	address of a Point variable
Returns	void	
Description		Converts the given Point from local to global coordinates based on the position of the current port.

```
pascal Boolean PtInRect(Point pt, const Rect *r)
```

Parameters	pt	a Point to be tested
	r	address of a Rect
Returns		Boolean value; true if point is in or on the rectangle
Description		Both parameters should be in the same coordinate system.

```
pascal Boolean PtInRgn(Point pt, RgnHandle rgn)
```

Parameters	pt	a Point to be tested
	rgn	region handle
Returns		Boolean value; true if point is in or on the region
Description		Both parameters should be in the same coordinate system

Line-Related Calls

```
pascal void LineTo(short h, short v)
```

Parameters	h	desired horizontal position of end of line, in local coordinates
	v	desired vertical position of end of line, in local coordinates
Returns	void	
Description		Draws a line from pen's current location to location provided, using pen settings in current port.

```
pascal void Line(short dh, short dv)
```

Parameters   dh   distance to draw line horizontally from current pen position, in pixels

                      dv   distance to draw pen vertically from current pen position, in pixels

Returns   void

Description   Moves pen amount desired from its current position, drawing a line as it goes, using pen settings in the current port. Positive values are to the right and down.

Rect-Related Calls

```
pascal void FrameRect(const Rect *r)
```

Parameters   r   address of the rectangle describing the bounds of the shape

Returns   void

Description   Draws a rectangular frame, using pen settings in current port. Rectangle should be in local coordinates.

```
pascal void PaintRect(const Rect *r)
```

Parameters   r   address of the rectangle describing the bounds of the shape

Returns   void

Description   Fills the shape using the pen settings in the current port. Rectangle should be in local coordinates.

```
pascal void EraseRect(const Rect *r)
```

Parameters   r   address of the rectangle describing the bounds of the shape

Returns   void

Description   Fills the shape with the background pattern in the current port. Rectangle should be in local coordinates.

```
pascal void InvertRect(const Rect *r)
```

Parameters   r   address of the rectangle describing the bounds of the shape

Returns   void

Description   Inverts pixels in the shape (including contents). Rectangle should be in local coordinates.

```
pascal void FillRect(const Rect *r, ConstPatternParam pat)
```

Parameters   r   address of the rectangle describing the bounds of the shape

                      pat   address of a pattern

Returns   void

Description   Fills the shape with the pattern provided. Rectangle should be in local coordinates.

```
pascal void FillCRect(const Rect *r, PixPatHandle pp)
```

Parameters   r   address of the rectangle describing the bounds of the shape

                      pp   handle to a pixel pattern

Returns   void

Description   Fills the shape with the pixel pattern provided. Rectangle should be in local coordinates.

```
pascal void OffsetRect(Rect *r, short dh, short dv)
```

Parameters   r   address of the rectangle describing the bounds of the shape

Parameters   dh   distance to move horizontally from current position, in pixels

                      dv   distance to move vertically from current position, in pixels

Returns   void

Description   Changes values in rectangle provided.

327

```
pascal void InsetRect(Rect *r, short dh, short dv)
```

Parameters r   address of the rectangle describing the bounds of the shape

        dh   distance to move sides from current position, in pixels

        dv   distance to move top and bottom from current position, in pixels

Returns   void

Description Changes values in rectangle. Amount of change applied to all sides. Negative values cause the rectangle to grow, or be outset. Positive values shrink the rectangle.

```
pascal Boolean SectRect(const Rect *src1, const Rect *src2, Rect *dstRect)
```

Parameters src1   address of a rectangle

        src2   address of a rectangle

        dstRect   address to hold intersection of two rectangles

Returns   Boolean value; true if there is an intersection

Description Sets the values of dstRect to the rectangle describing the overlap between src1 and src2. The third parameter may be the same address as either of the first two rectangles if you wish, in which case the original contents of that rectangle are lost.

```
pascal void UnionRect(const Rect *src1, const Rect *src2, Rect *dstRect)
```

Parameters src1   address of a rectangle

        src2   address of a rectangle

        dstRect   address to hold union of two rectangles

Returns   void

Description Sets the values of dstRect to the rectangle enclosing both src1 and src2. The third parameter may be the same address as either of the first two rectangles if you wish, in which case the original contents of the rectangle are lost.

```
pascal Boolean EqualRect(const Rect *rect1, const Rect *rect2)
```

Parameters	rect1	address of a rectangle
	rect2	address of a rectangle

Returns Boolean value; `true` if rectangles have the same values

Description Compares coordinates in the two rectangles provided.

```
pascal Boolean EmptyRect(const Rect *r)
```

Parameters r address of a rectangle

Returns Boolean value; `true` if rectangle is empty

Description An empty rectangle is one where the bottom-right coordinates are the same as the top-left.

RoundRect-Related Calls

```
pascal void FrameRoundRect(const Rect *r, short ovalWidth, short
                          ovalHeight)
```

Parameters none

Returns void

Description Draws a rectangular frame with rounded corners, using pen settings in current port. Rectangle should be in local coordinates.

```
pascal void PaintRoundRect(const Rect *r, short ovalWidth, short
                          ovalHeight)
```

Parameters none

Returns void

Description Fills the shape using the pen settings in current port. Rectangle should be in local coordinates.

```
pascal void EraseRoundRect(const Rect *r, short ovalWidth, short
                          ovalHeight)
```

Parameters	r	address of the rectangle describing the bounds of the shape
	ovalWidth	width of oval describing corner
	ovalHeight	height of oval describing corner
Returns	void	
Description	Fills the shape with the background pattern in the current port. Rectangle should be in local coordinates.	

```
pascal void InvertRoundRect(const Rect *r, short ovalWidth, short
                           ovalHeight)
```

Parameters	r	address of the rectangle describing the bounds of the shape
	ovalWidth	width of oval describing corner
	ovalHeight	height of oval describing corner
Returns	void	
Description	Inverts pixels in the shape (including contents). Rectangle should be in local coordinates.	

```
pascal void FillRoundRect(const Rect *r, short ovalWidth, short ovalHeight,
                         ConstPatternParam pat)
```

Parameters	r	address of the rectangle describing the bounds of the shape
	ovalWidth	width of oval describing corner
	ovalHeight	height of oval describing corner
	pat	address of a pattern
Returns	void	
Description	Fills the shape with the pattern provided. Rectangle should be in local coordinates.	

```
pascal void FillCRoundRect(const Rect *r, short ovalWidth, short
                           ovalHeight, PixPatHandle pp)
```

Parameters	r	address of the rectangle describing the bounds of the shape
	ovalWidth	width of oval describing corner
	ovalHeight	height of oval describing corner
	pp	handle to a pixel pattern
Returns	void	
Description		Fills the shape with the pixel pattern provided. Rectangle should be in local coordinates.

Oval-Related Calls

```
pascal void FrameOval(const Rect *r)
```

Parameters	r	address of the rectangle describing the bounds of the shape
Returns	void	
Description		Draws an oval bounded by the rectangular frame, using pen settings in current port. Rectangle should be in local coordinates.

```
pascal void PaintOval(const Rect *r)
```

Parameters	r	address of the rectangle describing the bounds of the shape
Returns	void	
Description		Fills the shape using the pen settings in the current port. Rectangle should be in local coordinates.

```
pascal void EraseOval(const Rect *r)
```

Parameters	r	address of the rectangle describing the bounds of the shape
Returns	void	
Description		Fills the shape with the background pattern in the current port. Rectangle should be in local coordinates.

```
pascal void InvertOval(const Rect *r)
```

Parameters   r   address of the rectangle describing the bounds of the shape

Returns   void

Description   Inverts pixels in the shape (including contents). Rectangle should be in local coordinates.

```
pascal void FillOval(const Rect *r, ConstPatternParam pat)
```

Parameters   r   address of the rectangle describing the bounds of the shape

pat   address of a pattern

Returns   void

Description   Fills the shape with the pattern provided. Rectangle should be in local coordinates.

```
pascal void FillCOval(const Rect *r, PixPatHandle pp)
```

Parameters   r   address of the rectangle describing the bounds of the shape

pp   handle to a pixel pattern

Returns   void

Description   Fills the shape with the pixel pattern provided. Rectangle should be in local coordinates.

Arc-Related Calls

```
pascal void FrameArc(const Rect *r, short startAngle, short arcAngle)
```

Parameters   r   address of the rectangle describing the bounds of the shape

startAngle   angle to start arc, zero is the top center of bounding rectangle

arcAngle   number of degrees arc extends

Returns   void

Description   Draws an arc based on values provided, using pen settings in current port. Rectangle should be in local coordinates. Positive values for arcAngle are clockwise from startAngle.

```
pascal void PaintArc(const Rect *r, short startAngle, short arcAngle)
```

Parameters   r   address of the rectangle describing the bounds of the shape

startAngle   angle to start arc, zero is the top center of bounding rectangle

arcAngle   number of degrees arc extends

Returns   void

Description   Fills the shape using the pen settings in the current port. Rectangle should be in local coordinates.

```
pascal void EraseArc(const Rect *r, short startAngle, short arcAngle)
```

Parameters   r   address of the rectangle describing the bounds of the shape

startAngle   angle to start arc, zero is the top center of bounding rectangle

arcAngle   number of degrees arc extends

Returns   void

Description   Fills the shape with the background pattern in the current port. Rectangle should be in local coordinates.

```
pascal void InvertArc(const Rect *r, short startAngle, short arcAngle)
```

Parameters   r   address of the rectangle describing the bounds of the shape

startAngle   angle to start arc, zero is the top center of bounding rectangle

arcAngle   number of degrees arc extends

Returns   void

Description   Inverts pixels in the shape (including contents). Rectangle should be in local coordinates.

```
pascal void FillArc(const Rect *r, short startAngle, short arcAngle,
          ConstPatternParam pat)
```

Parameters	r	address of the rectangle describing the bounds of the shape
	startAngle	angle to start arc, zero is the top center of bounding rectangle
	arcAngle	number of degrees arc extends
	pat	address of a pattern
Returns	void	
Description	Fills the shape with the pattern provided. Rectangle should be in local coordinates.	

```
pascal void FillCArc(const Rect *r, short startAngle, short arcAngle,
          PixPatHandle pp)
```

Parameters	r	address of the rectangle describing the bounds of the shape
	startAngle	angle to start arc, zero is the top center of bounding rectangle
	arcAngle	number of degrees arc extends
	pp	handle to a pixel pattern
Returns	void	
Description	Fills the shape with the pixel pattern provided. Rectangle should be in local coordinates.	

Region-Related Calls

```
pascal RgnHandle NewRgn(void)
```

Parameters	none
Returns	Handle to the newly created region. Check for nil.
Description	Allocates memory for a new region. Region is empty.

```
pascal void OpenRgn(void)
```

Parameters   none

Returns   void

Description   Hides pen and opens recording. Bounds of all QuickDraw objects are
                     added to the region.

```
pascal void CloseRgn(RgnHandle dstRgn)
```

Parameters   dstRgn   region to close

Returns   void

Description   Shows the pen and closes recording. Recorded contours are added to
                     the region provided.

```
pascal void DisposeRgn(RgnHandle rgn)
```

Parameters   rgn   handle to the region in question

Returns   void

Description   Releases memory allocated to the region.

```
pascal void CopyRgn(RgnHandle srcRgn, RgnHandle dstRgn)
```

Parameters   srcRgn   handle to source region

                     dstRgn   handle to destination region

Returns   void

Description   Copies contents of source into destination, destroying original contents
                     of destination.

```
pascal void FrameRgn(RgnHandle rgn)
```

Parameters   rgn   handle to the region in question

Returns   void

Description   Draws outline of region provided, using pen settings in current port.
                     Region should be in local coordinates.

```
pascal void PaintRgn(RgnHandle rgn)
```

Parameters	rgn	handle to the region in question
Returns	void	
Description	Fills the shape using the pen settings in the current port. Region should be in local coordinates.	

```
pascal void EraseRgn(RgnHandle rgn)
```

Parameters	rgn	handle to the region in question
Returns	void	
Description	Fills the shape with the background pattern in the current port. Region should be in local coordinates.	

```
pascal void InvertRgn(RgnHandle rgn)
```

Parameters	rgn	handle to the region in question
Returns	void	
Description	Inverts pixels in the shape (including contents). Region should be in local coordinates.	

```
pascal void FillRgn(RgnHandle rgn, ConstPatternParam pat)
```

Parameters	rgn	handle to the region in question
	pat	address of a pattern
Returns	void	
Description	Fills the shape with the pattern provided. Region should be in local coordinates.	

```
pascal void FillCRgn(RgnHandle rgn, PixPatHandle pp)
```

Parameters	rgn	handle to the region in question
	pp	handle to a pixel pattern
Returns	void	
Description	Fills the shape with the pixel pattern provided. Region should be in local coordinates.	

```
pascal void SetEmptyRgn(RgnHandle rgn)
```

Parameters	rgn	handle to the region in question
Returns	void	
Description	Makes region provided an empty region. Destroys existing contents of region.	

```
pascal void RectRgn(RgnHandle rgn, const Rect *r)
```

Parameters	rgn	handle to the region in question
	r	address of rectangle
Returns	void	
Description	Makes region provided match the bounds of the rectangle provided. Destroys existing contents of region.	

```
pascal void OffsetRgn(RgnHandle rgn, short dh, short dv)
```

Parameters	rgn	handle to the region in question
Parameters	dh	distance to move horizontally from current position, in pixels
	dv	distance to move vertically from current position, in pixels
Returns	void	
Description	Changes location of region provided.	

```
pascal void InsetRgn(RgnHandle rgn, short dh, short dv)
```

Parameters	rgn	handle to the region in question
	dh	distance to move bounds horizontally from current position, in pixels
	dv	distance to move bounds vertically from current position, in pixels
Returns	void	
Description	Changes size of region. Amount of change applied to all sides. Negative values cause the region to grow, or be outset. Positive values shrink the region.	

```
pascal void SectRgn(RgnHandle srcRgnA, RgnHandle srcRgnB, RgnHandle dstRgn)
```

Parameters	srcRgnA	handle to a region
	srcRgnB	handle to a region
	dstRgn	handle to a region

Returns   void

Description   Sets the values of dstRgn to the region describing the overlap between srcRgnA and srcRgnB. The third parameter may be the same handle as either of the first two regions if you wish, in which case the original contents of that region are lost.

```
pascal void UnionRgn(RgnHandle srcRgnA, RgnHandle srcRgnB, RgnHandle
                     dstRgn)
```

Parameters	srcRgnA	handle to a region
	srcRgnB	handle to a region
	dstRgn	handle to a region

Returns   void

Description   Sets the values of dstRgn to the region describing the sum of srcRgnA and srcRgnB. The third parameter may be the same handle as either of the first two regions if you wish, in which case the original contents of that region are lost.

```
pascal void DiffRgn(RgnHandle srcRgnA, RgnHandle srcRgnB, RgnHandle dstRgn)
```

Parameters	srcRgnA	handle to a region
	srcRgnB	handle to a region
	dstRgn	handle to a region

Returns   void

Description   Sets the values of dstRgn to the region describing the difference of srcRgnA minus srcRgnB. The order is significant. The third parameter may be the same handle as either of the first two regions if you wish, in which case the original contents of that region are lost.

```
pascal Boolean RectInRgn(const Rect *r, RgnHandle rgn)
```

Parameters	r	address of rectangle to test
	rgn	handle to region to test
Returns		Boolean value; true if some part of the rectangle overlaps the region
Description		The rectangle does not have to be entirely within the region, just overlap it at least 1 pixel.

```
pascal Boolean EqualRgn(RgnHandle rgnA, RgnHandle rgnB)
```

Parameters	rgnA	handle to a region
	rgnB	handle to a region
Returns		Boolean value; true if they are identical in size, shape, and location
Description		Tests two regions for equality.

```
pascal Boolean EmptyRgn(RgnHandle rgn)
```

Parameters	rgn	handle to a region
Returns		Boolean value; true if the region is empty
Description		An empty region has no contents.

Polygon-Related Calls

```
pascal PolyHandle OpenPoly(void)
```

Parameters	none
Returns	Handle to a polygon record
Description	Hides the pen, all subsequent Line() and LineTo() calls added to the polygon. Pen data ignored, only pen location is significant. Only one polygon may be open for recording at a time.

```
pascal void ClosePoly(void)
```

Parameters	none
Returns	void
Description	Shows the pen, turns off polygon recording.

```
pascal void KillPoly(PolyHandle poly)
```

Parameters	poly	handle to a polygon
Returns	void	
Description	Dispose of the memory allocated for the polygon record.	

```
pascal void FramePoly(PolyHandle poly)
```

Parameters	poly	handle to a polygon
Returns	void	
Description	Draws the polygon, using pen settings in current port. Polygon should be in local coordinates.	

```
pascal void PaintPoly(PolyHandle poly)
```

Parameters	poly	handle to a polygon
Returns	void	
Description	Fills the shape using the pen settings in the current port. Polygon should be in local coordinates.	

```
pascal void ErasePoly(PolyHandle poly)
```

Parameters	poly	handle to a polygon
Returns	void	
Description	Fills the shape with the background pattern in the current port. Polygon should be in local coordinates.	

```
pascal void InvertPoly(PolyHandle poly)
```

Parameters	poly	handle to a polygon
Returns	void	
Description	Inverts pixels in the shape (including contents). Polygon should be in local coordinates.	

```
pascal void FillPoly(PolyHandle poly, ConstPatternParam pat)
```

Parameters	poly	handle to a polygon
	pat	address of a pattern

Returns	void
Description	Fills the shape with the pattern provided. Polygon should be in local coordinates.

```pascal
pascal void FillCPoly(PolyHandle poly, PixPatHandle pp)
```

Parameters	poly	handle to a polygon
	pp	handle to a pixel pattern
Returns	void	
Description	Fills the shape with the pixel pattern provided. Polygon should be in local coordinates.	

```pascal
pascal void OffsetPoly(PolyHandle poly, short dh, short dv)
```

Parameters	poly	handle to a polygon
Parameters	dh	distance to move horizontally from current position, in pixels
	dv	distance to move vertically from current position, in pixels
Returns	void	
Description	Changes location of polygon provided.	

Picture-Related Calls

```pascal
pascal PicHandle GetPicture(short pictureID)
```

Parameters	pictureID	resource ID of a PICT resource
Returns	Handle to the picture data, a `PicHandle`	
Description	Equivalent to calling `GetResource()` for type PICT. Handle returned is a resource handle, dispose with `ReleaseResource()` unless you detach it from the Resource Manager.	

```pascal
pascal void KillPicture(PicHandle myPicture)
```

Parameters	myPicture	handle to the picture data
Returns	void	
Description	Disposes of memory allocated to picture data. Use only for nonresource picture handles.	

```
pascal void DrawPicture(PicHandle myPicture, const Rect *dstRect)
```

| **Parameters** | myPicture | handle to the picture data |
| | dstRect | address of rectangle bounding picture, in local coordinates |

Returns   void

Description   Draws the picture, scales if necessary to fit destination rectangle.

```
pascal PicHandle OpenCPicture(const OpenCPicParams *newHeader)
```

Parameters   newHeader   address of a structure that contains information about the picture

Returns   Handle to the picture data

Description   Hides the pen. The handle is initially empty. All subsequent QuickDraw calls accumulate inside the picture.

```
pascal void ClosePicture(void)
```

Parameters   none

Returns   void

Description   Turns off QuickDraw recording in the picture and shows the pen again.

Color-Related Calls

```
pascal void RGBForeColor(const RGBColor *color)
```

Parameters   color   address of color data

Returns   void

Description   Sets the foreground color in the current port. For basic ports, the color data is translated into the closest fit from the eight basic QuickDraw colors (System 7 only).

```
pascal void RGBBackColor(const RGBColor *color)
```

Parameters   color   address of color data

Returns   void

Description   Sets the background color in the current port. For basic ports, the color data is translated into the closest fit from the eight basic QuickDraw colors (System 7 only).

```
pascal void GetForeColor(RGBColor *color)
```

Parameters	color	address of color data
Returns	void	
Description	Puts a copy of the current foreground color in the variable provided.	

```
pascal void GetBackColor(RGBColor *color)
```

Parameters	color	address of color data
Returns	void	
Description	Puts a copy of the current background color in the variable provided.	

```
pascal void PenPixPat(PixPatHandle pp)
```

Parameters	pp	handle to a pixel pattern
Returns	void	
Description	Sets the pen's pixel pattern in the current port to the value provided.	

```
pascal void BackPixPat(PixPatHandle pp)
```

Parameters	pp	handle to a pixel pattern
Returns	void	
Description	Sets the background pixel pattern in the current port to the pattern provided.	

```
pascal GDHandle GetGDevice(void)
```

Parameters	none
Returns	Handle to the current graphics device data
Description	Gets the current graphics device.

```
pascal GDHandle GetMainDevice(void)
```

Parameters	none
Returns	Handle to the main monitor graphic device data
Description	Gets the main screen's graphic device data.

343

```
pascal Boolean GetColor(Point where, ConstStr255Param prompt, const
                        RGBColor *inColor, RGBColor *outColor)
```

Parameters	where	point where top left corner of color dialog should appear
	prompt	string you want to appear in dialog
	inColor	starting or default color for dialog
	outColor	address for user's color selection
Returns	Boolean value; `true` means user accepted dialog (clicked OK)	
Description	For the where parameter, (–1,–1) puts dialog in standard position on deepest color device. Value (0,0) locates dialog in standard position on main monitor.	

```
pascal Boolean GetGray(GDHandle device, const RGBColor *backGround, RGBColor
                       *foreGround)
```

Parameters	device	handle to device data for monitor on which color will appear
	backGround	address of one of boundary colors
	foreGround	address of other boundary color
Returns	Boolean value; `true` means an intermediate color is available	
Description	Calculates the best color intermediate between the two colors provided. Calculated color returns in the `foreGround` parameter, wiping out whatever value was in there initially.	

Text-Related Calls

```
pascal void TextFont(short font)
```

Parameters	font	font number for desired font
Returns	void	
Description	Sets font for current port. Use **GetFNum()** to get the number when you have a font name.	

```
pascal void TextFace(short face)
```

Parameters	face	desired style (bold and so on)
Returns	void	
Description	Sets text style for current port.	

```
pascal void TextMode(short mode)
```

Parameters	none	
Returns	void	
Description	Sets text drawing mode for current port.	

```
pascal void TextSize(short size)
```

Parameters	size	size in points of text
Returns	void	
Description	Sets font size for current port.	

```
pascal void SpaceExtra(Fixed extra)
```

Parameters	extra	extra width for the space character
Returns	void	
Description	Sets extra width for space characters for current port. Typically this is zero unless you want to modify spacing.	

```
pascal void CharExtra(Fixed extra)
```

Parameters	extra	extra width for nonspace characters
Returns	void	
Description	Sets the extra width for nonspace characters for current port. Typically this is zero, unless you want to modify spacing. This feature available only in color ports.	

345

```
pascal short CharWidth(short ch)
```

Parameters ch   character to measure

Returns   Width in pixels of character

Description Measures width of character using current port settings. Use for one-byte script systems only.

```
pascal short StringWidth(ConstStr255Param s)
```

Parameters s   string to measure

Returns   Width in pixels of string

Description Measures width of string using current port settings. Works for all script systems.

```
pascal short TextWidth(const void *textBuf, short firstByte, short
                    byteCount)
```

Parameters textBuf   address where text is located

       firstByte   offset from first character where measurement starts

       byteCount   number of bytes to measure

Returns   Width in pixels of specified characters

Description Measures width of specified text using current port settings. Works with two-byte script systems, but you must specify number of *bytes*, not number of characters.

```
pascal void DrawChar(short ch)
```

Parameters ch   character to draw

Returns   void

Description Draws character using current port settings. Use for one-byte script systems only.

```
pascal void DrawString(ConstStr255Param s)
```

Parameters s   string to draw

Returns   void

Description Draws string using current port settings. Works for all script systems.

```
pascal void DrawText(const void *textBuf, short firstByte, byteCount)
```

Parameters   textBuf   address where text is located

                               firstByte   offset from first character where drawing starts

                               byteCount   number of bytes to draw

Returns   void

Description   Draws specified characters using current port settings. Works with two-byte script systems, but you must specify number of *bytes*, not number of characters.

Can We Talk?: All about Dialog Boxes

Things are getting good. You've got a picture in a window. The next thing you want EasyPuzzle to do is break the picture into pieces. How many pieces should you make?

The answer is easy. Let the user decide! It is a radical concept, but Clarus would approve. You cannot predict what the user will want. Different people will want different sized pieces. The same person may want the puzzle to be easy to solve on some occasions, and more challenging at other times.

Clearly you need to get some information from the user. How do you do that? There are several ways, but the most common technique is the dialog box.

I begin this chapter by introducing the four different kinds of dialogs available in the Mac OS, the resources you need to create a dialog, and the items you find inside dialogs. Then we discuss the different dialogs in detail. We talk about when to use each kind of dialog, how to use it, and some of the inside tips the wizards use to implement some very cool behavior. In three labs you create and manage each kind of dialog.

Dialogs and Dialog Items

You use a dialog to obtain information from the user, to alert the user to unusual circumstances, or to display information. There are four kinds of dialogs. Each type of dialog has special and unique functions and features. The different kinds of dialogs are

- Modal

- Movable modal

- Modeless

- Alert

A *modal dialog* cannot be moved. The dialog must be dismissed before switching to another window or application.

A *movable modal dialog* can be moved, but must be dismissed before switching to another window in the same application. Movable modal dialogs allow a user to switch applications.

A *modeless dialog* behaves like an ordinary window. The user can switch windows, move the dialog box, or switch applications while the modeless dialog remains open.

An *alert* is a modal dialog that warns the user of some problem.

The differences among these dialogs will become clear as you read this chapter. When you design an application, keep the alternatives in mind. Sometimes a modal dialog is just what you need. At other times, another kind of dialog serves the human interface better. Keep the end user in mind and give your design maximum flexibility and ease of use.

Creating a Dialog

Dialog boxes require two principal resources, a DLOG resource and a DITL resource. DITL is an acronym for dialog item list.

Alerts use an ALRT resource instead of a DLOG resource. Alerts are covered later in this chapter.

The DLOG resource is analogous to a WIND resource. It describes the location, size, and border of the dialog box. Figure 11.1 shows four possible borders you can use for modal and movable modal dialog boxes. Not all borders are appropriate for all dialog boxes.

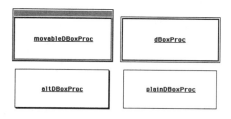

Figure 11.1 Modal dialog windows

Movable modal dialog boxes use the movableDBoxProc border. Modal dialog boxes and alerts use the dBoxProc border. Modal dialogs may also use the altDBoxProc and plainDBoxProc borders, although these are less common. Modeless dialogs typically use a document window with a close box, no zoom box, and no size box (see Figure 11.2).

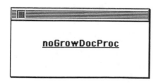

Figure 11.2 Modeless dialog window

A dialog box is a just a kind of window with all the features of a regular window, including a graphics port. The Dialog Manager builds on the Window Manager, so everything you learned in Chapter 8 applies to dialogs! You're already ahead of the game.

Creating a DLOG resource is very much like creating a WIND resource. When you create a DLOG resource, you set the window type, whether the dialog is visible, its location, size, and so forth. You can use System 7's automatic positioning features for dialogs just like you can for windows.

One difference between a DLOG resource and a WIND resource is that the DLOG resource contains the resource ID of the associated DITL resource. That's how the Dialog Manager knows what DITL to use for each dialog.

After you have created the resources, you use the Dialog Manager to display and manage dialogs. When your application launches, you must initialize the Dialog Manager for your application. Call `InitDialogs()`. Pass zero as the only parameter. The value is ignored.

Assuming that both the DLOG and DITL resources are in place, you create a dialog by calling `GetNewDialog()`. You provide the resource ID for the DLOG resource, the address in memory where you want the dialog record placed, and the window pointer for the window behind which the dialog appears (so the Window Manager can keep its window list in order). If you pass nil as the address for the dialog record, the Dialog Manager allocates memory for you. If you want the new dialog box to appear in front of all other windows (the usual case), pass the value –1 as the window behind which to appear. This works just like the call to `GetNewWindow()` discussed in Chapter 8.

You can make a dialog record from scratch with `NewDialog()` or `NewColorDialog()`. However, using DLOG and DITL resources and `GetNewDialog()` is more flexible, and easier. Dialogs created with `GetNewDialog()` use a color graphics port if there is a 'dctb' resource—dialog color table—with the same number as the DLOG resource.

The call to `GetNewDialog()` returns a pointer to a dialog record—a `DialogPtr`. You can treat a dialog pointer exactly like a window pointer. They are functionally identical. However, in order to use Window Manager calls, you may have to typecast the `DialogPtr` to tell the compiler to treat it as a `WindowPtr` from time to time.

You typically want the dialog to remain invisible while you create it. This allows you to do any setup work, initialize the controls, and so forth. Besides, something may go wrong while you are setting up the dialog. Generally, you display the dialog only when it is finished and ready to be seen. You set a dialog to be initially invisible in the DLOG resource. To display an invisible dialog, call ShowWindow(). To hide a visible dialog, call HideWindow(). In either case, you provide the window pointer—that is, the dialog pointer.

When you are through with a dialog, you must dispose of it. How you do that depends on how you created it. This process parallels how you dispose of windows.

If you allocated your own storage for the dialog record, call CloseDialog(). You provide the dialog pointer. You must then dispose of the memory you allocated yourself, using either DisposePtr() or DisposeHandle() as appropriate.

If, on the other hand, the Dialog Manager allocated the storage for you, call DisposeDialog(). You pass the dialog pointer. The Dialog Manager disposes of everything.

The System usually takes care of drawing and updating the dialog for you. If you need to explicitly draw a dialog, call DrawDialog() to draw the entire dialog and contents, or UpdateDialog() to draw the update area. You provide the dialog pointer.

Dialog Items

Dialog boxes have items inside them (see Figure 11.3). You may find one or more of the following items in a dialog box:

- Push button
- Radio button
- Checkbox
- Popup menu
- Static text
- Edit text
- Icon
- Picture
- User item
- Clarus

Figure 11.3 Dialog items

Figure 11.3 is a standard LaserWriter page setup dialog. It illustrates most of the common items that you find in a dialog box. You certainly recognize several of the items from our discussion of the Control Manager in Chapter 9—push buttons, radio buttons, checkboxes, and popup menus.

> Notice the absence of scroll bars from the list of controls you find in a dialog box. Scroll bars are almost never appropriate for a dialog box. A dialog box should have a limited number of choices, and most or all of them should be visible simultaneously. Check the human interface guidelines for lots of details about dialog box design.

In Figure 11.3, you can see that related dialog items are kept together visually, and that spacing is uniform. This is a fairly "busy" dialog box with several controls, yet the internal organization allows the user to understand clearly what each group of controls does. This is not accidental; it is the result of thoughtful design.

A static text item is simply a string of characters that the user cannot change. You use static text items to convey information to the user. The judicious use of static text can greatly enhance your application's ease of use. Simple, clear, informative language helps the user understand what is going on. Obscure messages do not. Figure 11.4 illustrates a very good use of static text.

Figure 11.4 A helpful dialog

A well-designed message mentions the precise nature of the difficulty, and offers possible solutions. A poorly designed message that covers the same problem might say "Required hardware not available."

An edit text item allows the user to enter letters or numbers by typing while that item is the active text item (the active text item in a dialog is the item with the blinking caret). Your program can read the contents of the edit text item while the dialog is open, and can act on the information it finds there.

The only items missing from Figure 11.3 are pictures and user items. Pictures are a PICT resource you include in the dialog box. You specify the PICT resource ID number when creating the DITL resource for the dialog.

A user item is anything you want it to be—a custom control, for example. The Dialog Manager reports to you when the user clicks the item. You can create an invisible user item to accomplish some neat magic, as you see in the labs.

Each item in a DITL resource has an item number. You identify items in Dialog Manager calls by item number. The numerical order is significant in certain respects, especially as it relates to the default button and tabbing through text fields.

The default button is the button that has an outline around it in the dialog. This is frequently the OK button. If the user presses Return, that is the equivalent of clicking the default button. You should set up your dialogs to have an OK button as the default button when that is the reasonable thing to do. Name it "OK" and not "Okay" to conform to the human interface guidelines. You should *not* use an OK button as the default button when confirming dangerous operations, such as erasing a disk or deleting a file.

By virtually universal convention, the default button should be item number one in the DITL. If there is a Cancel button, it should be item number two. Do not violate this convention without an extremely good cause. A good reason is that you have no default button! Although this is not common, you will encounter that very circumstance later in this chapter when you build a modeless dialog.

The second way in which the numerical order of items is significant concerns tabbing through text items. There can be only one active editable text item. If the user presses the Tab key, the Dialog Manager deactivates the current text item and makes the next text item the active field for data entry. The numerical order of editable text fields controls the tabbing order. The lowest numbered editable text item comes first.

No matter what type of item it is, every dialog item has the following properties:

- Type
- Bounding rectangle

- Handle to additional data

- Enabled/disabled state

The type of the item identifies it as a radio button, push button, checkbox, custom control, icon, and so forth. The bounding rectangle (in local coordinates for the dialog's port) defines the size and location of the item.

The handle to additional data refers to different kinds of data for different kinds of items. Table 11.1 summarizes the use of the item handle for the various kinds of items.

Table 11.1: Dialog Item Handle Usage

Item Type	Purpose of Item Handle
push button	control handle
radio button	control handle
checkbox	control handle
popup menu	control handle
static text	text handle
edit text	text handle
icon	handle to icon
picture	picture handle
user item	UPP for a drawing procedure

For the control items, the item handle is a handle to the control record for that item. You can use this value with all the Control Manager calls to change the item's title, set its value, dim or draw the item, and so forth. This is discussed in just a bit.

For a text item—static or editable—it is a handle to the string of text. There are special Dialog Manager calls for setting and getting the text.

For icons, it is a handle to the icon data. For a picture item, it is the handle to the picture data, which you can then manipulate in any way appropriate for a picture.

For a user item, the handle is a procedure pointer. Typically, this procedure draws the item. The System handles update events inside dialogs. Every time the System receives an update event for the dialog, it calls the user item procedure to draw the item. This procedure pointer should be a UPP—a universal procedure pointer—because the system calls your drawing function directly.

> To create the UPP, call `NewUserItemProc()` and pass the name of your handler function as the only parameter. When you're through with the UPP, call `DisposeRoutineDescriptor()`.

In the first lab, you take advantage of this feature to draw the outline around the default button in a dialog box. You accomplish this trick by creating a disabled user item in the dialog's DITL. When you open the dialog, your code sets a UPP to a drawing procedure for that item. However, rather than drawing the item, the procedure draws the outline around the default button! The user item remains invisible.

The last feature of a dialog item is that it may be enabled or disabled. In this context, being enabled means that if the user clicks the item, the Dialog Manager reports the click to you. Being disabled means that the Dialog Manager does not report if the user clicks the item. This status has nothing to do with the appearance of the item. Disabled dialog items are not grayed automatically. If the item is a control, you may use `HiliteControl()` to dim the item.

You use a resource editor to create a DITL. You choose the type of item you want, set its size and location, and determine whether it is enabled or disabled (clickable). If it is a text item, button, or checkbox, you set the initial text content or title.

You can use Dialog Manager calls to alter any of these properties—type, bounding rectangle, handle to data, or enabled state—while the program is running.

To get current information about an item, call `GetDialogItem()`. There are five parameters:

- The pointer for the dialog containing the item
- The item number
- Address of a `short` variable to store the item type
- Address of a `Handle` to store the item handle
- Address of a `Rect` to store the item's bounding rectangle

The call fills in the last three variables with the current information. The enabled state is stored inside the item type. You get all the information, but you may be interested in only one piece of it.

You may set the same information by calling SetDialogItem(). You provide:

1. The pointer for the dialog containing the item

2. The item number

3. The item type

4. The item handle

5. Address of a Rect with the item's new bounding rectangle

Again, you may want to change only one of the last three items, but you must provide all three—type, handle, and rectangle.

To retrieve the text from a text item, call GetDialogItemText(). You provide the dialog item handle—usually retrieved by a call to GetDialogItem(). You also provide an Str255 string variable. The call fills in the string with the contents of the text item. This works for both static and edit text items.

You can set text with SetDialogItemText(). You provide the dialog pointer and an Str255 variable containing the new text. This is useful for setting default values in edit text items, or for changing the content of a static text item if circumstances dictate a change.

You can hide or show a dialog item, although you shouldn't have to do this very often. Call HideDialogItem() or ShowDialogItem(). In either call you provide the dialog pointer and item number. These calls simply add or subtract 16,384 to or from the left and right coordinates of the item's rectangle. Essentially, HideDialogItem() sends the item off into outer space, and ShowDialogItem() brings it back. If the item is an active editable text item, the user can still tab to it and enter text in the hidden item.

You can add and remove dialog items, as well. This is frequently better than hiding or showing items. Use AppendDITL() or ShortenDITL().

You can determine what item occupies a point in the dialog box. Call FindDialogItem(). You pass the dialog pointer and a point in local coordinates. The call returns the item number to you. If more than one item overlaps the point, the call returns the lowest item number in the DITL. This call is particularly useful if you want to change the cursor while it is over a particular kind of item.

Modal Dialogs

Modal dialogs prevent the user from continuing with other activities until the modal dialog is dismissed, usually by clicking a button or pressing Return or Enter.

Running a Modal Dialog

A typical modal dialog has an OK and a Cancel button. The user clicks various items to make choices and set features. Or the user may type to enter text. If the user clicks OK, you should read the information from the dialog and act accordingly. If the user clicks Cancel, nothing should change.

After setting up a dialog box, to run a modal dialog you call `ModalDialog()`. This is the heart of modal dialog operation. This one call handles all the user interaction with the dialog. You provide a procedure pointer to an event filter and the address of a `short` variable (to hold the number of the item the user clicked). The event filter is discussed in just a bit.

When you call `ModalDialog()`, it goes into its own event loop. This loop intercepts all the events that occur while the dialog is open. If one of those events involves an enabled dialog item, `ModalDialog()` puts the number of the item (called the hit item) in the second parameter you pass when you make the call. You can get all the information you need about the state of the item starting with `GetDialogItem()`.

Using ModalDialog()

Because `ModalDialog()` has its own event loop, it controls the computer until the user dismisses the dialog. `ModalDialog()` is exceptionally versatile. It handles quite a few things for you, some better than others. `ModalDialog()` helps manage menus, the cursor, default dialog items, and events.

`ModalDialog()` handles menus especially well. When you call `ModalDialog()`, the System disables the Help menu (except for the Show/Hide Balloons item). It also disables the Application menu. If your application has an Apple menu, and the first item in the menu is enabled, `ModalDialog()` takes care of your application's menus as well. Talk about service! The System disables all the application menus. If the dialog contains a visible, enabled edit text item, the System enables the menu items that have the ⌘-X, ⌘-C, and ⌘-V equivalents. The user can then cut, copy, and paste text while in the dialog—assuming you followed the human interface guidelines for these key equivalents.

11

To support these features, you must call `DialogCut()`, `DialogCopy()`, and `DialogPaste()` in response to these Edit menu choices when the front window is a dialog. In each call, you provide the dialog pointer. The Dialog Manager takes care of the rest.

`ModalDialog()` provides cursor-management services. It turns the cursor from an arrow into an I-beam when it is over an editable text item (see Figure 11.5).

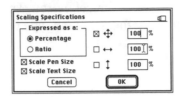

Figure 11.5 The I-beam

To get this service out of our friend, use a "hidden" Dialog Manager routine, `SetDialogTracksCursor()`. You provide the dialog pointer and a Boolean value, where `true` means you want it to track the cursor. You can turn off this service by passing `false` for the second parameter. This call is not documented anywhere in *Inside Macintosh*. It isn't really a secret—the routine is discussed in a technical note. You'll find information on this call in the "Dialog Manager Reference" section at the end of this chapter.

Remember that `ModalDialog()` runs its own event loop. While in the loop, `ModalDialog()` looks at key-down events. If the user presses either the Return or Enter key, and item one is a push button, `ModalDialog()` simulates a click.

You can enhance this behavior with two more "hidden" Dialog Manager calls. You can specify a default item other than item one by calling `SetDialogDefaultItem()`. You can also specify a cancel item with `SetDialogCancelItem()`. If the user presses ⌘-period, `ModalDialog()` reports that the cancel item was clicked. In each call, you provide the dialog pointer and the item number you want to use. These calls are not documented in *Inside Macintosh*. You'll find information on them in the "Dialog Manager Reference" section at the end of this chapter.

You might think that this is all pretty cool, and it is. The services described here are exceptional. However, in at least one respect, the event loop used by `ModalDialog()` is not very good.

Event Filters

`ModalDialog()` dates back to the era when one and only one application could be running at a time. In a multitasking environment, `ModalDialog()` has a serious short-coming.

Recall the discussion about update events from Chapter 6. When you receive an update event you *must* respond to it immediately. This is not an event you can ignore.

When you display a modal dialog, all events get handled directly in the dialog. If there is an update event *for the dialog window*, the Dialog Manager takes care of it for you. If there is an update event for any other window, *the Dialog Manager does nothing*. As a result, lots of bad things happen. The rest of the application doesn't get update events, idle tasks can't run, background applications don't get time, and so on. Essentially, the computer is locked up until the user dismisses the modal dialog. This is not good. Here's an excerpt from a technical note from Apple's Developer Technical Support:

> *"Under System 7 (and in System 6 under MultiFinder), if there is an update event pending for your application, no other applications, drivers, control panels, or anything else will get time. Updates pending for other applications do not cause the problem; they will be handled normally by the application in the background. But updates for the frontmost application must be serviced or the other applications will not get time. This is a potential Bad Thing. Many pieces of code need time to keep living, to maintain network connections, or just to look good."*

In other words, unless you do something about this problem, any time you display a modal dialog you seize control of the machine *completely*. Nothing can run in the background—network connections could be lost, background printing stops, time-related tasks can't find out what time it is. You get the idea. I would raise this to the level of a certifiable Very Bad Thing.

Solving this problem is easy. You provide a procedure pointer to an event filter when you call `ModalDialog()`. When `ModalDialog()` is running, every time there is an event *your event filter gets called first*. You can parse the event and do things with it. For example, if it is an update event for another window, you can update the window. You use the filter to maintain some control over the event stream.

The pointer to the event filter procedure must be a UPP to guarantee that it will work in both the 68K and Power Macintosh environments.

To create the UPP, call `NewModalFilterProc()` and pass the name of your handler function as the only parameter. Call `DisposeRoutineDescriptor()` to dispose of the UPP when you're through with it.

Although alerts are discussed later, you should provide an event filter for alerts, as well. The routines that display and manage alerts call `ModalDialog()` internally. This topic is revisited in the "Alerts" section of this chapter.

The event filter procedure must follow a particular prototype. The System calls your filter with a particular set of parameters. Your filter receives the dialog pointer, a pointer to the event record, and the address that contains the number of the item hit (if any). The filter must return a Boolean value. If your filter handles the event completely, it should return `true` to the System. If it does not handle the event completely, it should return `false`. This tells `ModalDialog()` whether it should process the event after you are through with it.

Using an event filter is very important. It not only saves you from potential disaster, it allows you to implement some very cool behavior when a modal dialog is open, as you see in the first lab.

You now have enough background on dialogs in general and modal dialogs in particular to get some significant work done on EasyPuzzle. Let's put these principles to good use.

Lab 11.1 Managing a Modal Dialog

In this lab you create and manage a modal dialog—the EasyApp about box. To do that you:

- Create a DLOG resource
- Examine `EasyGetDialog()`
- Outline the default button
- Set up default button drawing
- Create an event filter
- Display a modal dialog

Use your code from the previous lab as the starting point for your work in this lab.

Step 1: Create a DLOG resource

Modify: resources in EasyApp.µ.rsrc

In this step you create a DLOG resource with the ID number 1001. Launch ResEdit and open the EasyApp resource file. In the Resource menu, choose the Create New Resource item (⌘-K). In the resulting dialog, choose or enter the DLOG resource type and click the OK button.

A DLOG template window appears displaying default values. Change the settings so that they match those in Figure 11.1.1.

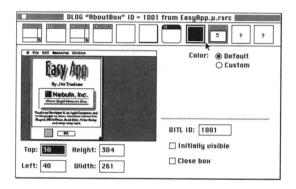

Figure 11.1.1 The DLOG template

Set the window type to the fourth icon from the right along the top of the template window. This is the dBoxProc type dialog. The top and left values are not critical. If your DLOG template displays the bottom and right coordinates of the window, choose the Show Height & Width item from the DLOG menu to convert the display. The height must be 304 pixels, and the width 261 pixels. Set both the "Initially visible" and "Close box" checkboxes to off. Set the DITL ID to 1001. The DITL resource already exists. This is discussed in a minute.

Now choose the Auto Position item from the DLOG menu. Set the dialog to appear centered on the parent window's screen. In a multiple-monitor environment, the about box will appear on whatever screen has the front window. That's most likely where the user is looking. Using the Auto Position feature of System 7, the window is placed automatically. The top-left value for the DLOG position is ignored.

Finally, choose the Get Resource Info item of the Resource menu and set this DLOG's resource ID to 1001. The code you write depends on that ID number. It also matches the associated DITL. The DITL ID number may be different from the DLOG, but it is usually wise to keep them consistent. Then it's easy to tell who belongs to whom.

Before continuing, take a quick look at the DITL that goes with this DLOG. Just double-click the miniature image of the dialog inside the DLOG template window. A DITL Template window opens, along with a tool palette (see Figure 11.1.2).

Figure 11.1.2 The About box DITL

There are three items in this DITL. Item 1 is the OK button. Item 2 is a PICT item. Item 3 is a user item. In Step 4 you attach a drawing procedure to this item. However, it doesn't draw the user item; it draws the outline around the OK button.

When you are through studying the DITL, save your changes. You may quit ResEdit if you wish. Most of the other DLOG and DITL resources required for this chapter have been provided for you so that you can concentrate on the code.

Step 2: Examine EasyGetDialog()

Modify: EasyGetDialog() in dialog.c

This step walks you through the code for this function. It has been in EasyApp all along because EasyApp uses it to set up the error dialog. This error dialog has been in place from the beginning, just in case.

This function preflights the memory request. Every dialog requires two resources, a DLOG and a DITL. Unfortunately, a quirk in the System causes the Mac to crash if the DITL is missing! So EasyGetDialog() first looks in the application resources to make sure each is present.

If they are, it calls **GetNewDialog()** to create a dialog record in memory based on the DLOG and DITL resources. Of course, it checks for error. If there are no errors, it returns the pointer to the dialog in theDialog.

Step 3: Outline the default button

Modify: EasyDrawDefaultButton() in dialog.c

The default button in a dialog should be outlined. That's the task of
EasyDrawDefaultButton(). In the next step, you attach a universal procedure pointer for
this function to a dialog user item. This function receives a pointer to the dialog, and
the item number of the user item to which this function is attached.

```
PenState   oldPen;

GetDialogItem(theDialog, ok, &itemType, &itemHandle,
             &itemRect);

if (itemType != ctrlItem + btnCtrl)
{
  return;
}

GetPenState(&oldPen);

PenNormal();
PenSize(3,3);

if (theDialog != FrontWindow())
{
  PenPat(&qd.gray);
}

InsetRect(&itemRect, -4, -4);
FrameRoundRect(&itemRect, 16, 16);

SetPenState(&oldPen);
```

First you call **GetDialogItem()** to get item one in the dialog. The constant ok is declared
in the Macintosh universal headers and represents the value 1. Then you make sure
that the item is a button control. If it is not, you bail out.

You preserve the state of the pen by calling **GetPenState()**. You call **PenNormal()** to set
the pen to a known condition, and change the size by calling **PenSize()**. If the dialog is
in the background, you set the pen pattern to gray.

You call **InsetRect()** to enlarge the bounds rectangle slightly, and **FrameRoundRect()** to
draw the outline around the button.

Then you restore the original pen.

365

Several dialogs use this function for the same purpose. EasyApp stores a UPP for this function in `g.drawDefaultButtonUPP`. The `InitErrorDialog()` function creates the UPP when the application launches by calling `NewUserItemProc()`.

Step 4: Set up default button drawing

Modify: `EasySetupDefaultButton()` in dialog.c

This step walks through the code for this function. It has been in EasyApp all along because EasyApp uses it to set up the error dialog. This error dialog has been in place from the beginning, just in case.

This function receives two parameters: a pointer to the dialog involved, and the number of an item to which you want to attach the default button drawing behavior. This is *not* the default button itself. It must be a "user item." Read the extensive comments for this function in the source code.

The function receives the dialog involved and the number of the user item to which to attach the drawing behavior. It gets the information about the item and ensures that it is indeed a user item. If it is not, the existing code sets an error value. Otherwise, it sets the drawing behavior for that user item.

```
else
{
  SetDialogItem(theDialog, defaultItem, itemType,
               (Handle) g.drawDefaultButtonUPP, &itemRect);
}
```

This code already exists; you don't have to type it. It calls **SetDialogItem()** to set the features of this item. The parameters specify the dialog pointer, the item number for the user item, the item type, the item handle, and the item bounds.

For user items, the item handle is a UPP to the function that draws the item. The `EasyInitErrorDialog()` function creates the UPP when the application launches. It is the UPP for `EasyDrawDefaultButton()`, the function you wrote in the previous step. In this case, the user item remains invisible and you use the procedure to draw the outline around the default button. Now that you have actually written the code for `EasyDrawDefaultButton()`, this will actually do something.

Step 5:   Create an event filter

Modify: `EasyModalFilter()` in dialog.c

In this step you create an event filter for modal dialogs. Rather than reinventing the entire main event loop, this filter determines that certain events should be handled normally. For those events, it calls `EasyHandleEvent()`. You get to reuse that code!

The existing code in the event filter gets the event record and switches based on the type of event.

```
switch(theEvent->what)
{
  case updateEvt:
  case activateEvt:
    if (EasyIsMyWindow((WindowPtr)theEvent->message))
    {
      callNormalHandler = true;
    }
    break;

  case mouseDown:
    if (theEvent->modifiers & cmdKey)
    {
      short      windowPart;
      WindowPtr  hitWindow;

      windowPart = FindWindow(theEvent->where, &hitWindow);
      if (windowPart == inDrag  && (hitWindow != theDialog))
      {
        callNormalHandler = true;
      }
    }
    break;

  case keyDown:
```

You add cases for update and activate events. In each of those events, the `message` field is a pointer to the window involved. If it is an application window, the regular event handler should take care of the event. `ModalDialog()` takes care of the dialog.

You also add a case for mouse-down events. This code implements a very neat trick. If there is a modal dialog present, you cannot move it. It may hide something the user wants to see. In this case, you determine whether the ⌘ key is pressed. If it is, you call `FindWindow()` to determine whether the click is in the title bar of a nondialog window. If it is, you pass the click to the regular event handler, which allows the user to ⌘-drag a window out from behind a modal dialog! This is a very nice feature.

The remaining code is provided for you. Keystrokes normally go to ModalDialog(). However, this code intercepts the Enter, Return, Escape, and ⌘-period keys. Examine the code for EasyFlashItem(). It rebuilds the event record and converts it from a keystroke to a click on the appropriate button!

All other events are passed to EasyHandleEvent() for normal processing.

Several different dialogs use this same event filter. EasyApp maintains a UPP for this function in g.modalEventFilterUPP. The InitErrorDialog() function creates the UPP when the application launches by calling NewModalFilterProc().

Step 6: Display a modal dialog

Modify: EasyAboutBox() in dialog.c

Let's put all this together and display the EasyApp about box.

When the user chooses the About item in the Apple menu, EasyApp calls AboutBoxHook(), which in turn calls EasyAboutBox(), which you write in this step.

```
OSErr    error;

error = EasyGetDialog(kAboutDialogID, nil, kInFront,
                         &theDialog);
if (error)
{
  ShowErrorHook(error);
  return;
}

EasySetupDefaultButton(theDialog, kAboutUserItem);

SelectWindow(theDialog);
ShowWindow(theDialog);

do
{
  ModalDialog(g.modalEventFilterUPP, &itemHit);

} while(itemHit != ok);

DisposeDialog(theDialog);
```

First you call EasyGetDialog(). This returns a dialog pointer to you in the local variable theDialog. If there is an error, you display the error and return. The DLOG resource sets the dialog to be invisible, so nothing appears on the screen yet.

Next you call `EasySetupDefaultButton()` so that the default button will be outlined. You pass the dialog pointer and item number for the user item in this dialog.

Then you call `SelectWindow()` to ensure that the dialog is the front window, and you call `ShowWindow()` to display the dialog.

In a `do` loop, you call `ModalDialog()`. You pass in the UPP for the event filter and the address of `itemHit`. `ModalDialog()` returns the item hit, if any. You continue the loop until the user clicks the OK button. When you are through, you call `DisposeDialog()` to close the dialog.

The about box has only one enabled item in it, the OK button. In a more complex dialog, you can respond to various items as `ModalDialog()` reports hits on the items.

Step 7: Run the application

Modify: none

Save your work and run the project using the debugger. When the debugger window appears, launch EasyPuzzle and create a new puzzle window.

Choose the About item from the Apple menu. The EasyApp about box appears. To confirm that your event filter is working, press the ⌘ key and click in the puzzle window's title bar to drag the window around.

Drag the window so that part of the window is obscured and then expose part of the window. Despite the fact that `ModalDialog()` is in control, the window should update properly. Your event filter is identifying update events and sending them to your regular event handler for processing.

Similarly, if you press the Return or Enter key, the OK button should flash and the about box dialog should disappear. The event filter is intercepting these keystrokes and processing them correctly.

When you are through observing, quit the application.

> If you want to see a really cool about box, make one small change and recompile EasyPuzzle. Change the `AboutBoxHook()` so that it calls `PuzzleAboutBox()` instead of `EasyAboutBox()`. Brad Mohr's code for the EasyPuzzle about box is provided for you in its entirety. This is an excellent demonstration of what you can do with advanced graphics techniques. When you write your own applications, you will want to create an eye-catching about box like this.

Movable Dialogs

The primary limitation of modal dialogs is that you can't move them. This can be a real problem because screen space is limited. The dialog may obscure something that the user needs to see.

A movable dialog is a lot more friendly. The user can reposition a movable dialog at any time. There are two kinds of movable dialogs, modal and modeless. They give different levels of flexibility to the user.

Movable Modal versus Modeless Dialogs

When there is a movable modal dialog open, the users cannot change windows or use most menu items. However, they can switch applications. This can be very helpful if they want to look at something in another application.

Modeless dialogs behave like normal document windows. These are the best kinds of dialogs. You should use them whenever possible in your application's human interface design. The user can move the dialog, make it active or inactive, switch windows, switch applications, and so forth.

Modeless dialogs are ideal for controlling actions that the user might like to perform often on various documents. For example, a Search dialog in a word processor could be a modeless dialog. A typical modeless dialog does not have a Cancel button, because it usually does not control the kinds of things you would want to cancel. However, it may have a Stop button if it runs a process like a search.

Finally, in most cases you want only one instance of a particular modeless dialog to exist. Typically, you set some global flag to indicate that the dialog is already open. If the dialog is already open, you don't allow the user to create another.

EasyPuzzle uses a modeless dialog to display a puzzle solution window. It allows one solution window per puzzle.

Handling Events in Movable Dialogs

Event handling for movable dialogs—movable modal or modeless—is quite different than event handling for modal dialogs.

There are two strategies you can follow with respect to events in movable dialogs. You can identify the event first, or identify the window first. There are advantages to either approach. EasyApp uses the window-first approach. Let's talk about both methods.

The event-first approach (see Figure 11.6) fits in quite well with a standard event-handling strategy. You retrieve an event. Your event handler parses the event. Based on the nature of the event, you respond.

When you add movable dialogs to the algorithm, this gets a little more complicated. You may have different responses based on the nature of the window involved. When you receive a key-down event, for example, you decide what to do based not only on the fact that it is a key-down event, but on the nature of the front window. If the front window is a dialog, you behave differently than if the front window is a regular document.

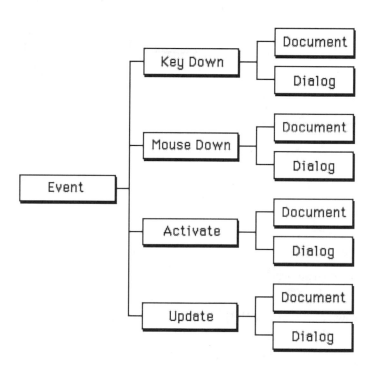

Figure 11.6 Event-first event handling

In the event-first approach, whenever the nature of the window makes a difference in how you handle an event, you test for the nature of the window. This means you test in several places throughout your event handling code.

The window-first strategy is a little easier to grasp, and that's the primary reason EasyApp uses this approach (see Figure 11.7). After you retrieve an event, but before parsing the event, you call `IsDialogEvent()`. You provide a pointer to the event record. If the event is related to a dialog, this call returns a Boolean value, `true`.

That doesn't mean the dialog is a *movable* dialog. It can be a modal dialog, because the modal event filter lets the regular event loop handle some events when a modal dialog is in front. So you must still test the nature of the window involved to make sure it is a movable dialog.

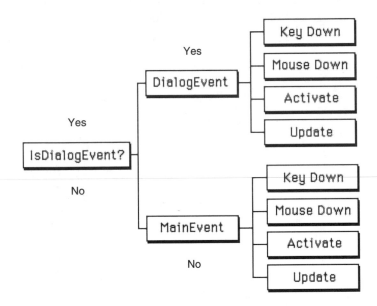

Figure 11.7 Window-first event handling

Whatever window is involved with the event, if that window is a movable dialog, you handle the event using separate event-handling code. If it is not a movable dialog, you let the main event handling function take care of it.

> Events that occur in the title bar of a movable dialog (clicks in the close box or title bar) are *not* dialog events! They are outside the grafPort of the dialog, so the main event handling loop will receive these events and should respond appropriately.

This means you have a separate set of event-parsing code to handle events in dialogs. This isn't as redundant as it seems.

The routine `DialogSelect()` takes care of most dialog events. You provide a pointer to the event record, an address where the call can store the dialog pointer to the dialog that contains the event, and the address of a `short` variable so the call can return the item hit (if there is one). This call returns a Boolean value; `true` if an enabled item is hit, `false` otherwise. `DialogSelect()` tells you two things: the item that was hit, and the dialog pointer to the dialog containing the item.

`DialogSelect()` takes care of activate events, update events, key-down events in editable text items, and mouse-down events.

In general, you should look for a few kinds of events before calling `DialogSelect()`. `DialogSelect()` does not recognize command-key combinations. A key-down event in a movable dialog might be a menu command because modeless dialogs allow the user full access to the application's menus. Look for command-key events by testing the `modifiers` field of the event record before passing a key event to `DialogSelect()`. You should also look for key events that should simulate a click on a button: Return and Enter key events for the default item, ⌘-period and the Escape key for the Cancel button.

Modeless dialogs move to the foreground and background like regular windows, so you may receive an activate or deactivate event for a modeless dialog. `DialogSelect()` takes care of this, but does not dim or draw controls. If you receive an activate event, you should walk through the control list to either dim controls or draw controls normally, depending upon whether the window is being activated or deactivated (just like you do for document windows). When you are through, you should still pass the activate or deactivate event to `DialogSelect()` so that it can take care of activating or deactivating the window properly.

If the user clicks an item in the dialog, `DialogSelect()` provides the item number for the hit item. In this respect it is like `ModalDialog()`. You get the information about the item starting with `GetDialogItem()`, and proceed from there to respond accordingly. All this comes together in the next lab.

Lab 11.2 Managing Movable Dialogs

In this lab you create and manage both kinds of movable dialogs—movable modal and modeless. As a result, this is really two labs in one. The movable modal dialog is the "scramble" dialog that breaks the puzzle picture into pieces. The modeless dialog allows the user to peek at the solution while the puzzle is scrambled.

So that you can concentrate on managing dialogs, the DLOG and DITL resources and nondialog code have been provided for you. The scramble dialog contains two popup menu control items. Although they have been provided for you, ResEdit is not the most intuitive tool for creating popup controls. A little explanation is in order here.

To create a popup CNTL resource in ResEdit, first create a new CNTL resource. This opens a CNTL template window. Set the ProcID Field to 1008. This value identifies the control as a popup menu. Set the Min field to the MENU resource ID for the popup menu. Set the Max field to the width of the menu. Set the Value field for the style and alignment you want to use for the menu. Table 11.2 lists the possibilities for the Value field. These are additive values, so you can add them up to create combinations of style features.

Table 11.2: Popup Control Styles

Value	Meaning
0	left alignment
1	center alignment
255	right alignment
256	bold
512	italic
1024	underlined
2028	outlined
4056	shadow

Even though a lot of material has been provided for you, there is still a lot to do. In this lab you:

- Open the scramble dialog
- Parse dialog events
- Handle dialog events
- Open the solution dialog
- Draw the solution picture
- Close the solution dialog

Use your code from the previous lab as the starting point for your work in this lab.

Step 1: Open the scramble dialog

Modify: `OpenPuzzleScramble()` in puzzleDialog.c

This dialog allows the user to choose the number of pieces for the puzzle. Figure 11.2.1 in Step 5 shows the dialog. There are two popup menus: one for rows and one for columns. As the user makes selections, lines appear on the picture to give the user feedback about the piece size.

Opening a movable modal dialog is very similar to creating a modal dialog:

```
if (!easyWindow)
{
  return error;
}

error = EasyGetDialog(kScrambleDialogID, nil, kInFront,
                      &theDialog);
if (error)
{
  return error;
}

EasySetupDefaultButton(theDialog, kScrambleUserItem);

SetPuzzleScramble(easyWindow, theDialog);
SetWRefCon(theDialog, (long) macWindow);

SelectWindow(theDialog);
ShowWindow(theDialog);

ForcePuzzleUpdate (macWindow);

return error;
```

The existing code (in italic) makes sure that the front window is an Easy window, and returns if it is not.

You call `EasyGetDialog()` to get the scramble dialog. If there is no error you call `EasySetupDefaultButton()` so the default button has an outline.

Then you call `SetPuzzleScramble()` and **SetWRefCon()**. The first call tells the puzzle what dialog holds its solution. The second call puts the Macintosh window pointer into the dialog record so that the dialog knows the window to which it belongs.

After that, you call **SelectWindow()** and **ShowWindow()** to display the dialog. Finally, `ForcePuzzleUpdate()` ensures that the puzzle is redrawn. This function is provided for you. In a subsequent step, you modify the drawing code so that when a scramble dialog is open for a window, you draw a grid on the puzzle to give the user feedback about the current size and number of pieces.

Step 2: Parse dialog events

Modify: `EasyHandleEvent()` in events.c

EasyApp separates events related to dialogs from those not related to dialogs. In this step you enhance the parsing tree for that purpose.

```
if (PreprocessEventHook(theEvent))
{
  return;
}

if (IsDialogEvent (theEvent))
{
  if (theEvent->what == updateEvt ||
      theEvent->what == activateEvt)
  {
    macWindow = (WindowPtr)theEvent->message;
  }
  else
  {
    macWindow = FrontWindow();
  }

  windowType = EasyIsDialog(macWindow);
  if (windowType == kMovableModal || windowType == kModeless)
  {
    MovableDialogHook((DialogPtr)macWindow, theEvent);
    return;
  }
}

switch(theEvent->what)
```

Before parsing the event, you call `IsDialogEvent()` to determine whether the event is related to a dialog. If it is, you get the window involved with the event. For update and activate events, that's the window in the `message` field of the event record. Otherwise you call `FrontWindow()` to get the front window.

Then you call `EasyIsDialog()` to find out what kind of dialog it is. This function is provided for you. If the dialog is movable or modeless, you call `MovableDialogHook()` and return. That hook leads to a function that handles all event parsing for movable dialogs. If the dialog is modal, you fall through and process the event with your normal event handler. Why? Because you might be receiving events from the modal event filter!

Step 3: Handle dialog events

Modify: `PuzzleMovableFilter()` in puzzleDialog.c

The `MovableDialogHook()` calls `PuzzleMovableFilter()` to handle events in movable dialogs. There are only two movable dialogs in EasyPuzzle, the scramble dialog and the modeless solution dialog. That simplifies things somewhat.

The existing code in this function performs processing similar to what you did with the modal event filter in the previous lab. It looks at key-down events for menu commands and keys that should be interpreted as button clicks. It looks at activate events and handles those properly, as well, because a modeless dialog can go into the background.

If this filtering does not handle the event, you go to work.

```
  } /* end switch(theEvent->what) */

if (!handled && DialogSelect(theEvent, &theDialog, &itemHit))
{
  WindowPtr  macWindow =
(WindowPtr)GetWRefCon(theDialog);
  EasyWindowPtr  easyWindow =
GetEasyWindowPtr(macWindow);

  switch (itemHit)  /* must be Scramble dialog */
  {
    case ok:     /* item 1 */
      if(ScramblePuzzle(theDialog))
      {
        SetPuzzleScramble(easyWindow, nil);
        DisposeDialog(theDialog);
        EasyForceUpdate(macWindow);
      }
      break;

    case cancel:  /* item 2 */
      SetPuzzleScramble(easyWindow, nil);
      DisposeDialog(theDialog);
      ForcePuzzleUpdate(macWindow);
      break;

    case kRowItem:
    case kColumnItem:
      ForcePuzzleUpdate(macWindow);
      break;

    default:
      break;
  }
}
```

If the event is not handled, you call `DialogSelect()`. If an enabled item in a dialog has been hit, this call returns true. Of the two movable dialogs, the only one that has enabled items is the scramble dialog; if `DialogSelect()` returns `true`, an item in the scramble dialog has been hit.

You need to know the identity of both the Macintosh window and the Easy window, so you extract those from where they are stored.

You then switch based on the item hit. If the OK button is hit, call `ScramblePuzzle()`. This function is provided for you because it has very little to do with dialogs or Macintosh Toolbox programming. Spending time writing all that code might distract you from your purpose. However, feel free to step through and examine the code that creates and manages pieces.

If `ScramblePuzzle()` returns `true`, there were no problems creating the pieces. In that case, you close the dialog. Break the connection with the puzzle window by calling `SetPuzzleScramble()` and setting it to nil. Call `DisposeDialog()` to dump the dialog. Then call `EasyForceUpdate()` to redraw the puzzle window. This removes the piece grid and draws the new pieces.

There are several other enabled items in the scramble dialog. If the user clicks the Cancel item, you break the connection with the puzzle window, dispose of the dialog, and update the puzzle. Notice that you call `ForcePuzzleUpdate()` rather than `EasyForceUpdate()`. The former just updates the puzzle display. The latter updates the entire window.

If the user clicks either the row or column popup menus, you call `ForcePuzzleUpdate()`. A click in these items means the user has changed the number of rows or columns. You update the window to redraw the piece grid. You accomplish that task in the next step.

Step 4: Modify puzzle drawing

Modify: `DrawPuzzlePage()` in puzzleWindow.c

Drawing a puzzle now involves two new tasks. If the scramble dialog is open, you want to display a grid to give the user feedback. If there are pieces, you must draw the pieces.

```
if (solutionRgn)
{
  SetClip(saveClip);
  DisposeRgn(saveClip);
}

if (scramble)
{
  DrawPuzzleGrid (macWindow, scramble);
}

if (thisPiece)
{
  ForEveryPiece(thisPiece, DrawPiece,
                (void *) macWindow->visRgn);
}

return noErr;
```

If the window you are drawing has a scramble dialog, you call `DrawPuzzleGrid()`. This function is provided for you. It gets the current number of rows and columns from the dialog, figures out where to draw the lines, and draws them.

If the puzzle has pieces, you call `ForEveryPiece()`. This is a function that steps through every piece and tells the piece to do something. In this case, you tell it to `DrawPiece`. In EasyApp, puzzle pieces are objects with certain behaviors. For example, a piece knows how to draw itself. The code to do all this is provided for you. Feel free to examine it at length.

Step 5: Run the application

Modify: none

Save your work and run the project using the debugger. When the debugger window appears, launch EasyPuzzle.

Create a puzzle window, and then choose the Scramble item from the Puzzle menu. The Scramble dialog appears and a grid shows up on the puzzle window that indicates the size of the pieces (see Figure 11.2.1). You should be able to drag the dialog around because it is a movable modal dialog.

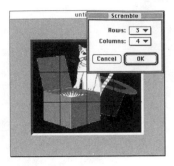

Figure 11.2.1 The Scramble dialog

Select an item in one of the popup menus. The window grid should update accordingly. The behavior of the popup menu itself is a gift from the System.

If you look in the EasyPuzzle menus, every item should be disabled. You cannot do anything in the application until you dismiss this dialog. However, you can switch applications.

With the puzzle set for just a few pieces, click the OK button in the scramble dialog. The puzzle should break into pieces scattered randomly around the window.

With a scrambled puzzle as the active window, look in the Puzzle menu again. The Scramble item is disabled! You can scramble a puzzle only once. Although the puzzle is in pieces, you cannot move the pieces around yet. That's coming in another chapter. However, the Solve item in the Puzzle menu has become active. If you choose this item, EasyPuzzle solves the puzzle automatically.

The code that solves the puzzle is provided for you. Here's how it works. For each piece in the puzzle, the code moves the piece incrementally toward its final destination. The code erases the original location, draws the frame and solved part of the puzzle, and then draws the piece in its new location. The code repeats this process until the piece reaches its final destination. Then the code sends a message to the piece to solve itself. The piece adds itself to the puzzle's overall solution, and then destroys itself. The code loops to the next piece, and continues until it runs out of pieces.

You can click to stop the automatic solution. Although you did not write the automatic solution code, you will work with it in the next lab exercise when you display an alert dialog.

When you are through observing, quit the application. Now let's work on the modeless dialog. All of the event parsing and handling code you just wrote for the movable modal dialog works for the modeless dialog as well! That's one task out of the way.

Step 6: Open the solution dialog

Modify: OpenPuzzlePeek() in *puzzleDialog.c*

This dialog allows the user to peek at the puzzle solution. It should simply display the picture, nothing more. The DITL for this dialog has one item in it. It is a user item to which you attach a function to draw the picture. The dialog varies in size depending upon the size of the picture.

```
if (!easyWindow)
{
  return error;  /* no error, just do nothing */
}

error = EasyGetDialog(kPuzzleBaseID, nil, kInFront,
                      &theDialog);
if (error)
{
  return error;
}

SetWRefCon(theDialog, (long)thePicture);

GetPuzzleFrame(easyWindow, &displayFrame);
OffsetRect(&displayFrame, -kPuzzleMargin, -kPuzzleMargin);
SizeWindow(theDialog, displayFrame.right,
           displayFrame.bottom, false);

GetDialogItem(theDialog, kPeekUserItem, &itemType,
              &itemHandle, &itemRect);
itemHandle = (Handle) puzzleG.drawPeekProc;
SetDialogItem(theDialog, kPeekUserItem, itemType,
              itemHandle, &itemRect);

SetPuzzlePeek(easyWindow, theDialog);

SelectWindow(theDialog);
ShowWindow(theDialog);

return error;
```

First you get the dialog by calling EasyGetDialog() and check for error. Then you stuff the picture handle into the dialog window's refCon. This is where the user item's drawing procedure looks for the picture to draw.

You then set the size of the dialog window. You get the picture frame for the current picture, call `OffsetRect()` to set the top left corner to (0,0), and then use the bottom right corner in a call to `SizeWindow()`.

Next you call `GetDialogItem()` to get the information on the dialog's one and only user item. You call `SetDialogItem()` to set the user item's "handle" to the universal procedure pointer stored in `puzzleG.drawPeekProc`. This UPP is for the drawing procedure to draw this item. You write the drawing procedure in the next step. The `InitPuzzleApp()` function calls `NewUserItemProc()` to create this UPP when the application launches.

The call to `SetPuzzlePeek()` tells the puzzle that it has a solution window open. Then you show the dialog.

Step 7: Draw the solution picture

Modify: `DrawPuzzlePeek()` in *puzzleDialog.c*

`DrawPuzzlePeek()` is a callback procedure used by the System to draw the user item in the solution dialog. In the previous step, you installed a UPP for this function as the drawing procedure for the user item. In this step you write the code that draws the solution so the user can peek at it while solving the puzzle. The dialog window has already been set to the correct size.

```
pascal void DrawPuzzlePeek(DialogPtr theDialog, short item)
{
  Rect      displayRect;
  PicHandle  thePicture;

  displayRect = theDialog->portRect;

  thePicture = (PicHandle)GetWRefCon(theDialog);

  DrawPicture(thePicture, &displayRect);
}
```

You use the size of the window as the picture's display rectangle. You get the picture handle by calling `GetWRefCon()` for the dialog. You stuffed the picture handle in here when you opened the dialog. To draw the picture, call `DrawPicture()`.

Step 8: Close a solution dialog

Modify: `CloseHook()` in *puzzleHooks.c*

Modify: `PuzzleClose()` in *puzzleMenu.c*

The user closes the solution dialog by clicking the close box. The event parsing mechanism calls CloseHook(), which in turn currently calls EasyClose(). EasyClose() handles modeless dialogs just fine. However, there is a connection between the puzzle window and the solution dialog. When you close a modeless dialog, you must break the connection so the puzzle knows that the solution is no longer open.

This is a perfect example of the benefits of flexibility in an application shell. You need to augment the behavior that occurs when you close a window.

First, modify CloseHook(). Here's the new code.

```
OSErr  CloseHook  (WindowPtr macWindow, short saveOptions)
{
/*
  return EasyClose(macWindow, saveOptions);
*/
    return PuzzleClose(macWindow, saveOptions);
}
```

You replace the existing call to EasyClose() with a call to a new routine, PuzzleClose(). Now, write PuzzleClose().

```
    EasyWindowPtr   easyWindow;

if (EasyIsDialog(macWindow) == kModeless)
{
  WindowPtr   thisWindow = g.windowList;

  while(thisWindow)
  {
    WindowPtr   thisDialog;

    easyWindow = GetEasyWindowPtr(thisWindow);
    thisDialog = GetPuzzlePeek(easyWindow);

    if (macWindow == thisDialog)
    {
      SetPuzzlePeek(easyWindow, nil);
      break;  /* all done */
    }
    thisWindow = easyWindow->nextMacWindow;
  }
}

error = EasyClose(macWindow, saveOptions);
return error;
```

You determine whether you are closing a modeless dialog. There is only one kind of modeless dialog in EasyPuzzle, so you know it's a solution dialog. If you are closing a solution dialog, you walk through the EasyApp window list. For each window, you get the solution dialog associated with the window (if any) by calling GetPuzzlePeek(). If it matches the modeless dialog you're closing, you call SetPuzzlePeek() with nil as a parameter to break the connection.

Then you call EasyClose() to finish the job of closing the dialog. You take full advantage of the shell's functionality, but you enhance it to suit your purpose.

Step 9: Run the application

Modify: none

Save your work and run the project using the debugger. When the debugger window appears, launch EasyPuzzle and create a new puzzle window.

When the puzzle window appears, choose the View Solution item in the Puzzle menu. When you do, the solution modeless dialog appears. You should be able to treat it like any other window. Move it around, deactivate it, activate it, switch applications, and so forth. The presence of the solution dialog does not interfere with your use of the application in any way. When it is active, appropriate menu choices remain enabled. For example, you cannot scramble a solution window, but you can create a new puzzle when a solution window is active.

When you have a solution open for a window, the View Solution item in the Puzzle menu becomes disabled. You can have only one solution open per puzzle. Close the solution window and the View Solution item becomes enabled once again.

Open two or more puzzles, and you can have a solution open for each. If you open more than one solution, notice that both solution windows have the same title. The title is set in the DLOG resource. It might be friendlier to have the title of the solution window match the window to which it is attached. For example, if the window title is "Cat Puzzle," the solution window might be titled "Cat Puzzle solution." Think about how you might do that, and where would be a good place to do that in the code.

When you are through observing, quit the application. Now it's time to take a look at the last kind of dialog, the alert.

Alerts

Alerts are a special form of modal dialog. The purpose of an alert is to notify the user of some unusual circumstance or problem. Alerts should be very simple, consisting of a brief, but clear message and one or two buttons. There are three kinds of alerts:

- Note alert
- Caution alert
- Stop alert

Note alerts provide the user with information that might be helpful in a given situation. Disaster does not strike if the user ignores a note alert. Note alerts should have an OK button. They may also contain a Cancel button if appropriate. On some occasions you may include a third button if necessary. For example, most applications use an alert to ask the user to confirm closing a file without saving changes. This alert typically has three buttons: Save, Discard, and Cancel.

Caution alerts tell the user that something unpleasant may happen. However, the user should be given the chance to continue. You may certainly be forceful in your use of language in the caution, but it is just a caution. A typical caution alert should have an OK button and a Cancel button. In caution alerts, the Cancel button is frequently the default button. Again, a third button is acceptable if the interface requires it.

A stop alert informs the user that some serious error has occurred that prevents the program from completing the operation in progress. There should be only one button, an OK button. The user has no alternative.

Alerts have an icon in the upper left corner that distinguishes them. In all other respects, they behave the same. Figure 11.8 illustrates the different icons.

Figure 11.8 Alert icons

Alert dialogs use an ALRT resource instead of a DLOG resource. It defines the size, shape, and location of the alert window. Unlike a DLOG, you don't get to choose the window type.

Like a DLOG, each ALRT has an associated DITL. The DITL contains the buttons and static text items for that alert. You do not include the icon in the DITL. The System takes care of the icon for you. You must allow room for the icon in the upper left corner of the alert.

There is a truly neat feature available for static text items in dialogs, including alerts. You see this trick used most commonly with alerts, because an alert should contain nothing but static text items and a button or two. However, this trick is useful for a static text item in *any* dialog.

When you create a static text item with a resource editor, you set the text for that item. If you use the magic character combination ^0, the System does a neat thing. It goes looking for a special string stored in low memory, called a parameter string. In fact there are four such strings, numbered zero through three. You can use those strings in any static text item by including the symbols ^0, ^1, ^2, and ^3 somewhere in the text of a static text item, as shown in Figure 11.9.

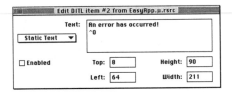

Figure 11.9 Using a parameter string

Figure 11.9 shows the editing window from ResEdit for a static text item. This item demonstrates a classic use of a parameter string. EasyApp uses the dialog that contains this item for all error messages. It puts the error message in parameter string zero and then displays the dialog. The System attempts to draw the static text item as part of the error dialog and encounters the ^0 characters. The System substitutes whatever text it finds at parameter string zero for the ^0 characters. As a result, EasyApp can use the same dialog to display all kinds of different messages.

You can use the same technique to display a document name in a dialog or alert. For example, if a user is about to close a document without saving it, you might display an alert that warns that the data is about to disappear forever. Using this trick, you can display the name of the document, thus helping the user understand exactly what is going on.

Because there are four parameter strings, you can have four variable strings inside a single dialog. In practice, you rarely use more than one or two in a dialog.

You set the parameter strings by calling the Dialog Manager routine `ParamText()`. You supply four `Str255` variables—one for each of the strings you want to use. Pass an empty string for any parameter string you don't need. You make this call just before displaying the dialog.

Parameter String Warnings!

DO NOT use parameter strings in modeless dialogs. If some other dialog appears that sets the parameter strings for itself, it affects the modeless dialog, as well. Oops.

Don't try to build a sentence out of two or more parameter strings. It may work for you in English but is almost sure to fail miserably in another language.

And don't use anything other than plain text. Don't put the ^0 symbol inside a parameter string, for example. This is a Bad Thing.

Displaying an alert dialog is simple. For a note alert, call `NoteAlert()`. For a caution alert, call `CautionAlert()`. And for a stop alert you call—that's right—`StopAlert()`. The only difference between these three Toolbox calls is the icon displayed in the alert. In each case you provide the resource ID of an ALRT resource and a UPP for an event filter.

Event filters are just as important for alerts as they are for modal dialogs. Each of these calls uses `ModalDialog()` internally to run the alert. The absence of an event filter can cause *serious* problems in a cooperative multitasking environment.

Each of the alert calls returns a `short` value—the item number of the item hit by the user to dismiss the dialog. You can use that value to respond accordingly, particularly for caution alerts where the user can continue the action or cancel it.

As you can see, alerts are pretty straightforward. A typical use for a caution alert is to ask the user to confirm an operation before continuing. In the next lab, you create an alert for that purpose.

Lab 11.3 Displaying an Alert

Alerts are like simple, automatic modal dialogs. The event filter you wrote in Lab 11.1 works just fine for alerts. As a result, implementing an alert is pretty easy. In this lab you:

- Examine alert resources
- Create an alert
- Display an alert

Use your code from the previous lab as the starting point for your work in this lab.

Step 1:   Examine alert resources

Modify: none in EasyApp.µ.rsrc

Launch ResEdit if it is not already running, and open the EasyApp resource file. When the list of resources appears, double-click the DITL resources. The DITL picker window should appear showing five DITL resources numbered from 1000 to 1004. Double-click the DITL resource with ID number 1004 to open the DITL template window. This particular DITL is named "Cancel/Confirm."

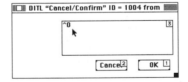

Figure 11.3.1 The Cancel/Confirm DITL

This DITL resource is associated with an ALRT resource that has the same ID number—1004. You can examine the ALRT resource if you wish. EasyApp uses this alert as a generic dialog for posting a message of the type, "Do you want to continue?"

There are three items in the DITL. Items 1 and 2 are the OK and Cancel buttons respectively. Item 3 is a static text item containing "^0" and nothing else. In the next step, you use **ParamText()** to display a string in this item.

Notice that there is no icon in the top left corner, although room is provided for one. The System provides the icon. EasyApp uses this alert as a caution alert.

If you're curious about what strings will ultimately appear in this alert, open the EasyPuzzle resources and examine the STR# resource with ID 2000. An STR# resource is a list of strings that you can retrieve using a one-based index number. That is, the first string is string number one, not zero.

There are three strings in this particular STR# resource. Each will appear at one time or another in this one alert.

You can quit ResEdit if you wish. You are through with it for this chapter.

Step 2: Create an alert

Modify: EasyConfirmDialog() in dialog.c

In this step you write EasyConfirmDialog(). This is an EasyApp utility function that allows you to display a dialog asking the user to confirm an operation before continuing. You provide the string to display in the dialog.

This function receives the resource ID for an STR# resource, and an index value for the string to retrieve from that resource.

```
short   EasyConfirmDialog (short resID, short index)
{
  Str255  message;

  GetIndString(message, resID, index);
  ParamText(message, "\p", "\p", "\p");

/* display alert, send item hit back to caller     */
  return CautionAlert(kConfirmDialogID,
                        g.modalEventFilterUPP);

  return 1; /* delete me */
}
```

Make sure you delete the existing return statement in this function and replace it with your new code.

You call GetIndString() to get an indexed string from an STR# resource with the specified ID. Then you call ParamText() to set up the string for use in the alert. This particular alert uses one string of the possible four, so the additional parameters in ParamText() are empty pascal strings.

Then you call CautionAlert(). You provide the resource ID number for an ALRT resource and an event filter. This uses the same modal event filter you wrote in Lab 11.1.

CautionAlert() returns the number of the item hit by the user—in this case either the OK or the Cancel button. You return that value to the caller so the caller knows how the user responded to the alert.

Step 3: Display an alert

Modify: SolvePuzzleDialog() in puzzleDialog.c

The user may choose to have the computer solve the puzzle automatically. Because any menu item might be chosen inadvertently, and because solving the puzzle automatically might take the fun out of everything, you should ask the user to confirm the operation.

```
if (!macWindow || !easyWindow || !thisPiece)
{
  return;
}
result = EasyConfirmDialog(kPuzzleBaseID, kSolveWarning);
if (result == cancel)
{
  return;
}
```

The existing code makes sure that this is a puzzle window and that it has pieces to solve. If it does, you call EasyConfirmDialog() to display an alert. You pass the resource ID for the STR# resource that contains the message, and the index number of the message you want to use.

Then you examine the return value. If the user canceled the request, you bail out. Otherwise, you fall through and continue with the function, which solves the puzzle automatically.

Step 4: Run the application

Modify: none

Save your work and run the project using the debugger. When the debugger window appears, launch EasyPuzzle and create a new puzzle window.

Scramble the puzzle. For efficiency, choose a low number of pieces. The automatic solution can take time if there are a lot of pieces. After the puzzle is broken into pieces, choose the Solve item from the Puzzle menu. The new alert should appear (see Figure 11.3.2). Notice the caution icon in the upper left corner of the dialog.

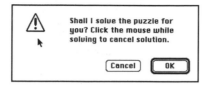

Figure 11.3.2 The Solve Puzzle alert

If you click the Cancel button the alert disappears and nothing happens. If you click the OK button, the puzzle should start solving itself. The pieces migrate to their original locations one by one and drop into the solution. Click the mouse to end the process if it takes too long.

When you are through observing, quit the application. You have now mastered the fundamentals of managing dialogs of all kinds on the Mac. However, the puzzle would be a lot more fun if you could drag individual pieces around. That's what you implement in the next chapter.

Dialog Manager Reference

```
pascal void InitDialogs(long ignored)
```

Parameters	ignored	a long value that is, well, ignored
Returns	void	
Description		Initializes the Dialog Manager for your application. Call once at launch. Pass zero as the parameter.

```
pascal DialogPtr GetNewDialog(short dialogID, void *dStorage, WindowPtr
                              behind)
```

Parameters	dialogID	resource ID of DLOG resource
	dStorage	address where dialog record should be placed, nil means Dialog Manager allocates
	behind	window pointer to window in front of new window, –1 means new window is in front
Returns		Pointer to the new dialog record
Description		Creates a dialog record in memory based on DLOG and DITL resources. Check for nil pointer because this may fail. If either the DLOG or DITL resource is missing, this call may crash the Macintosh.

```
pascal void CloseDialog(DialogPtr theDialog)
```

Parameters   theDialog   pointer to the dialog in question

Returns   void

Description   Removes the dialog from memory and disposes of dialog-related structures, but not the dialog record. Use this call to close a dialog if you provided storage when creating the dialog record. You must then dispose of that storage.

```
pascal void DisposeDialog(DialogPtr theDialog)
```

Parameters   theDialog   pointer to the dialog in question

Returns   void

Description   Removes the dialog from memory and disposes of all dialog-related structures, including the dialog record. Use this call to close a dialog if the Dialog Manager allocated memory when creating the dialog record.

```
pascal void ParamText(ConstStr255Param param0, ConstStr255Param param1,
                      ConstStr255Param param2, ConstStr255Param param3)
```

Parameters   param0   parameter string zero

                     param1   parameter string one

                     param2   parameter string two

                     param3   parameter string three

Returns   void

Description   Places the strings provided in low memory for use by Dialog Manager when it encounters ^0, ^1, ^2, or ^3 in a static text item. Typically you make this call just before showing the dialog.

```
pascal void ModalDialog(ModalFilterUPP modalFilter, short *itemHit)
```

Parameters   modalFilter   UPP for an event filter procedure

                     itemHit   address of a location to store item number if hit item, if any

Returns   void

Description   Runs the modal dialog. See description in text for full details.

```
pascal Boolean IsDialogEvent(const EventRecord *theEvent)
```

Parameters	theEvent	address of an event record for event in question

Returns   Boolean value, true => a dialog window is the front window

Description   Use this call before parsing an event in your main event handling function. If it is a dialog event, you can handle it separately. Note that events in the title bar of a movable dialog are not dialog events. Used for movable dialogs. **ModalDialog()** handles events for simple modal dialogs and alerts.

```
pascal Boolean DialogSelect(const EventRecord *theEvent, DialogPtr
                    *theDialog, short *itemHit)
```

Parameters	theEvent	address of an event record for event in question
	theDialog	address of a dialog pointer where call stores pointer to dialog where event occurred
	itemHit	address of a location to store item number if hit item, if any

Returns   Boolean value, true => an enabled item was hit in the dialog

Description   Use this call to handle update, activate, key-down, and mouse-down events in a movable dialog. See text for other events you should handle yourself.

```
pascal void DrawDialog(DialogPtr theDialog)
```

Parameters	theDialog	pointer to the dialog in question

Returns   void

Description   Draws the dialog window and its contents. Necessary only when the System does not draw the dialog for you.

```
pascal void UpdateDialog(DialogPtr theDialog, RgnHandle updateRgn)
```

Parameters	theDialog	pointer to the dialog in question
	updateRgn	handle to the region to be updated

Returns   void

Description   Draws the update region of the dialog window. Rarely necessary; the System takes care of this for you.

```
pascal short NoteAlert(short alertID, ModalFilterUPP modalFilter)
```

Parameters	alertID	resource ID for an ALRT resource
	modalFilter	UPP for an event filter procedure
Returns	Item number hit to dismiss dialog	
Description	Displays and manages a note alert.	

```
pascal short CautionAlert(short alertID, ModalFilterUPP modalFilter)
```

Parameters	alertID	resource ID for an ALRT resource
	modalFilter	UPP for an event filter procedure
Returns	Item number hit to dismiss dialog	
Description	Displays and manages a caution alert.	

```
pascal short StopAlert(short alertID, ModalFilterUPP modalFilter)
```

Parameters	alertID	resource ID for an ALRT resource
	modalFilter	UPP for an event filter procedure
Returns	Item number hit to dismiss dialog. Usually it's item one, the OK button, as that should be the only enabled item in a stop alert.	
Description	Displays and manages a stop alert.	

```
pascal void GetDialogItem(DialogPtr theDialog, short itemNo, short
                    *itemType, Handle *item, Rect *box)
```

Parameters	theDialog	pointer to the dialog in question
	itemNo	number of item in DITL list
	itemType	address of variable to hold the item type
	itemHandle	address of variable to hold the item handle
	box	address of variable to hold the item's bounding rectangle
Returns	void	
Description	Provides the item type, handle, and bounds for the requested item in the dialog.	

```
pascal void SetDialogItem(DialogPtr theDialog, short itemNo, short
                    itemType, Handle item, const Rect *box)
```

Parameters	theDialog	pointer to the dialog in question
	itemNo	number of item in DITL list
	itemType	the new item type
	itemHandle	the new item handle
	box	address of the item's new bounding rectangle
Returns	void	
Description	Sets the item type, handle, and bounding rectangle to the values provided.	

```
pascal void HideDialogItem(DialogPtr theDialog, short itemNo)
```

Parameters	theDialog	pointer to the dialog in question
	itemNo	number of item in DITL list
Returns	void	
Description	Moves specified item out of view by adding 16,384 to the bounding rectangle's left and right coordinates.	

```
pascal void ShowDialogItem(DialogPtr theDialog, short itemNo)
```

Parameters	theDialog	pointer to the dialog in question
	itemNo	number of item in DITL list
Returns	void	
Description	Shows a specified item by subtracting 16,384 from the bounding rectangle's left and right coordinates.	

```
pascal void AppendDITL(DialogPtr theDialog, Handle theHandle, DITLMethod
                    method);
```

Parameters	theDialog	pointer to the dialog in question
	theHandle	handle to a DITL list to add to the dialog
	method	how to locate the new items
Returns	void	

Description		Adds the items in the provided DITL to the existing dialog. Each item in a DITL has a bounding rectangle. The method parameter controls how the new items are located in the dialog. It may use constants. overlayDITL => relative to top-left corner of dialog appendDITLRight => relative to top-right corner appendDITLBottom => relative to lower-left corner negative of item number => relative to specified item Item; numbers of new items go after existing items.

```
pascal short CountDITL(DialogPtr theDialog);
```

Parameters	theDialog	pointer to the dialog in question
Returns	Number of items in the DITL	
Description	Determines how many items are in a dialog.	

```
pascal void ShortenDITL(DialogPtr theDialog, short numberItems);
```

Parameters	theDialog	pointer to the dialog in question
	numberItems	number of item to remove from DITL list
Returns	void	
Description	Removes the requested number of items from the end of the DITL list.	

```
pascal void GetDialogItemText(Handle item, Str255 text)
```

Parameters	item	item handle, obtained from **GetDialogItem()**
	text	variable to hold item's text content
Returns	void	
Description	Retrieves the text from the specified item handle. The item parameter must be an item handle from a text item, static or editable.	

```
pascal void SetDialogItemText(Handle item, ConstStr255Param text)
```

Parameters	item	item handle, obtained from **GetDialogItem()**
	text	variable to hold item's new text content
Returns	void	

Description   Sets the text for the specified item handle to match that provided in the `text` parameter. The `item` parameter must be an item handle from a text item, static or editable.

```
pascal void SelectDialogItemText(DialogPtr theDialog, short itemNo, short
                                 strtSel, short endSel)
```

Parameters   theDialog   pointer to the dialog in question

itemNo   number of item in DITL list

strtSel   character number at start of selection

endSel   character number at end of selection

Returns   void

Description   Selects text in an editable text item. Selection range includes characters specified.

```
pascal short FindDialogItem(DialogPtr theDialog, Point thePt)
```

Parameters   theDialog   pointer to the dialog in question

thePt   a point in local coordinates

Returns   The item number of the hit item, if any. Returns –1 if the point is not inside any item.

Description   Use to locate an item at a point in the dialog. Useful for cursor management.

```
pascal void DialogCut(DialogPtr theDialog);
```

Parameters   theDialog   pointer to the dialog in question

Returns   void

Description   Cuts text from an editable text item.

```
pascal void DialogCopy(DialogPtr theDialog);
```

Parameters   theDialog   pointer to the dialog in question

Returns   void

Description   Copies selected text from an editable text item.

```
pascal void DialogPaste(DialogPtr theDialog);
```

Parameters   theDialog   pointer to the dialog in question

Returns   void

Description   Pastes text into an editable text item at current insertion point. Replaces any existing selected text.

```
pascal void DialogDelete(DialogPtr theDialog);
```

Parameters   theDialog   pointer to the dialog in question

Returns   void

Description   Deletes selected text from an editable text item.

```
pascal OSErr SetDialogDefaultItem(DialogPtr theDialog, short newItem)
```

Parameters   theDialog   pointer to the dialog in question

                newItem   item number for item you want to be default item

Returns   An error value if the call fails

Description   Specifies the default item in a dialog, which ModalDialog() will hit if the user presses Return or Enter.

```
pascal OSErr SetDialogCancelItem(DialogPtr theDialog, short newItem)
```

Parameters   theDialog   pointer to the dialog in question

                newItem   item number for item you want to be default item

Returns   void

Returns   An error value if the call fails

Description   Specifies the cancel item in a dialog, which ModalDialog() will hit if the user presses ⌘-period.

```
pascal OSErr SetDialogTracksCursor(DialogPtr theDialog, Boolean tracks)
```

Parameters   theDialog   pointer to the dialog in question

                tracks   true => will adjust cursor

Returns   An error value if the call fails

Description   If this feature is on, the Dialog Manager turns the cursor to an I-beam when over an editable text item.

12

What's Happening?: Providing Feedback to the User

Macintosh applications should be consistent and easy to use. That's what the people who use Macintosh software have come to expect, and rightfully so.

Throughout this book I have reminded you that most visible features of Macintosh software—menu arrangement, window behavior, dialog design, and so forth—are user-centered. The design and operation of these elements of your program should match the standard Macintosh *human* interface.

This is not a programmer's interface, or a computer-wizard's interface. It is an interface designed for people who use computers. The Macintosh human interface guidelines have grown out of years of research and experimentation. They are filled with simple, common sense. Following them guarantees that your program will be easy to use. Appendix D has information about where to find the guidelines.

One part of the human interface is feedback to the user. Feedback is what your program does to let the user know what's happening. You have already encountered several forms of feedback.

In this chapter, we review and expand on the standard behavior of menus, windows, controls, and dialogs. Then we'll discuss managing selection feedback and dragging items in a window. The fun stuff comes next when we talk about time-consuming operations and how to let the user know that the computer is hard at work. You learn how to use an animated cursor and display a progress window.

In the lab at the end of the chapter, you implement animated dragging of puzzle pieces. You also create an animated cursor and implement a simple progress window.

Menus

The System provides most of the visual feedback related to menus—pulling down a menu, following the cursor, item highlighting, and so forth. However, there are additional design considerations you should keep in mind.

The titles for pull-down menus appear in the title bar. Make sure that your menu bar fits on the smallest screen on which it might appear. Remember to allow room for the application, help, and keyboard menus on the right side of the menu bar.

Individual menu titles should remain constant. Titles should not change names, and you should avoid adding or removing menus from the menu bar. Changing the contents of the menu bar can confuse a user, because menu bars typically change only when you switch applications. ResEdit changes its menu titles regularly, and it is confusing.

You should dim a menu title when all of the items in the menu are disabled. The user can still pull down a dim menu to see the items. Whenever you dim or enable a menu title, you should update the menu bar so that the System draws it correctly. You can use `InvalMenuBar()` or `DrawMenuBar()`, as discussed in Chapter 7.

The items in a pull-down menu may be verbs or adjectives. Verbs relate to *actions* that the user wants to perform on selected objects. Adjectives relate to *attributes* the user wants to change for selected objects. Because verbs represent actions, the menu item text should fit comfortably into a sentence like "<verb> the selected objects." Adjectives should fit into a sentence like "set the attribute of the selected objects to <adjective>."

Keep related items together in the menu, and separate groups of items with separator bars. You should put frequently used items near the top of the menu. Use a check mark to the left of an item that applies to all currently selected objects. Use a dash to the left of an item that applies to some, but not all, of the selected objects. Figure 12.1 shows an example of a menu interface.

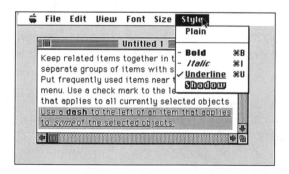

Figure 12.1 Menu interface

You may change the text in a menu item (see Figure 12.2). This allows the user to toggle between two states, so you have two alternative versions of text for a single item. Each version of the item should be worded in such a way that the user clearly understands what the choices are.

The sound-related items in the EasyPuzzle menu clearly indicate both the action and its opposite. The menu item "Turn Sounds Off" clearly implies that sounds are currently on and that choosing this item turns sound off. An alternative interface design might use a single item, perhaps "Use Sounds," and put a check mark before the item when sounds are active. This isn't quite as clear as using alternative text, but it does work.

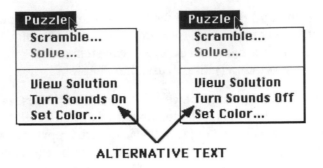

ALTERNATIVE TEXT

Figure 12.2 Changing menu items

The ellipsis character at the end of a menu item indicates that the operation will not proceed until the user provides more information, usually through a dialog. This is an important human interface convention. You should follow it closely.

Submenus from hierarchical menus should consist of adjectives, not verbs. Hiding commands in a submenu is bad design because the user must hunt for the commands. If possible, you should avoid submenus completely. If you do use submenus (and they are quite common), you should never have a submenu appear off another submenu. This type of design really hides the user's options. It is also physically difficult for some people to navigate through more than one layer of submenus.

A popup menu should be a list of mutually exclusive attributes—adjectives, not verbs—and can be thought of as a replacement for a set of radio buttons. The choices in a popup menu should be exclusive because you can display only one choice when the menu is "unpopped" or closed. The item displayed must be the currently active item in the menu. Otherwise, it is too easy for the user to click the menu and unintentionally change the setting when the mouse button is released.

Windows

You are familiar with the standard behavior of windows, including zooming. However, you must pay attention to some finer points to conform to the human interface.

When you create a new window, it should be named "untitled n", where n is a unique number indicating how many untitled windows have been created. If it's the first window, just call it "untitled."

When the user closes a window, a very friendly program remembers where the window was onscreen and saves that information along with the contents of the window. If you do, remember that when you open the document again the position might be offscreen. For example, the user might be opening the document on a PowerBook after creating the document on a 21-inch monitor at the office. You should check the document's position against the available Desktop real estate to make sure it is visible.

When activating or deactivating a window, you must handle the contents of the window. The click that activates a window should not alter the selection state of the contents of the window. You are also responsible for drawing (or dimming) control items in the window.

When you move a window to the foreground, you are responsible for highlighting selected objects. Highlighting might take the form of selection handles on graphic items, inverse video or a color behind selected text, and so on.

When you prepare a window for a move to the background, you should use some form of background selection that indicates what items would be selected if the window were in the foreground. This might be an outline around the selected items.

Displaying a background selection is a new feature of the human interface, designed primarily to support drag and drop (see Figure 12.3). Drag and drop is discussed in Chapter 19. If your application does not support drag and drop, you might not need to display background selections.

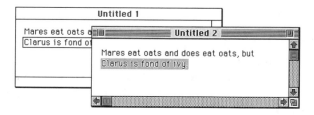

Figure 12.3 Background and foreground selections

Controls

Recall that there are five standard controls: push buttons, radio buttons, checkboxes, popup menus, and scroll bars. Buttons and checkboxes deserve some extra attention because they are critical elements in interface design—particularly in dialogs.

Push Buttons

Buttons should be actions. The text inside a button should be a simple verb clearly describing the action. Sometimes you need two words to convey the action performed when the user clicks the button.

The System provides most of the immediate feedback behavior for push buttons. When the user clicks a push button, it should be highlighted (drawn using inverse video). On occasion, you have to provide that behavior yourself.

The default button has an outline. When the user presses the Return or Enter key and there is a default button present, you should treat the key event as a click in the default button. Similarly, if there is a Cancel button and the user presses either the Escape key or ⌘-period, you should treat the key event as a click on the Cancel button.

> **note** The EasyApp function `EasyDrawDefaultButton()` shows you how to draw an outline around a button. `EasyFlashItem()` shows you how to flash a button and mimic a click on the default or Cancel buttons.

Radio Buttons

Radio buttons reflect a grouped set of mutually exclusive choices. Your application is responsible for managing the group. Only one radio button in a group may be "on." If the user clicks a radio button, you must turn it on, and make sure all the others in the group are off.

You do this using `GetDialogItem()` to get the item's handle. Because a radio button is a control, the item handle is a control handle. You can then use `GetControlValue()` or `SetControlValue()` to get or set the value of the radio button. For radio buttons, a value of 0 is off and a value of 1 is on.

For the human interface design, organize the buttons in visually distinct groups. You can put space between two groups, put a line between groups, put a box around a group, or even label the groups. Figure 12.4 shows an excellent method for grouping radio buttons. You can implement the box and label as a user item or picture.

Figure 12.4 Well-grouped radio buttons

Checkboxes

Checkboxes are radio buttons that aren't exclusive. If the user clicks the control, it toggles the state of the control between on and off. You do not change the state of any other checkbox, they are independent of each other.

Group checkboxes logically, using the same techniques you use for radio buttons.

Dialogs

Dialogs are a major part of your application's human interface. Enhance your application's friendliness with the right kind of dialog in the right spot. Use a good event filter to implement behaviors that users have come to expect.

Modal dialogs are good when your application *must* get information before continuing. Make them movable if possible. Modeless dialogs are good for situations where the user may want to use the dialog for several documents, or use the options frequently on the same document.

You can take advantage of System 7's automatic window positioning features for dialogs. You may center, stagger, or use the alert position on the main screen, on the front document's screen, or on the document.

If the dialog relates to a particular document, position it relative to the document. This clearly identifies the relationship between the dialog and the document. Otherwise, it is usually best to locate the dialog on the front document's screen, which is where the user is working. For some dialogs you may prefer to locate them on the main screen—where the menus are—or on a monitor that has some desirable feature like lots of colors or a large size.

Finally, you can enhance the user's interactions with the dialog through your event filter. For example, if the user presses the Tab key, the next edit text field becomes active. You can implement "Shift-Tab" functionality in your event filter. If the Shift key is down when the user presses the Tab key, go to the previous edit field. You can also look for up and down arrow keys to move through a list in the dialog.

> Do not use the left and right arrow keys to change edit fields. These keys move the text caret from character to character within a single edit field.

To help ensure the accuracy of data, check the validity of the data immediately. If the user tabs to a different field, check the contents of the previous field immediately. If it isn't valid, let the user know right away with a helpful alert or note.

Selecting and Dragging

The user clicks an item in your window to select it, and drags an item to move it. You are responsible for managing both operations.

You indicate selection by drawing the item differently. For text, highlight the selected text. For other kinds of items, you get to decide how to provide visual feedback so the user can identify selected items. However, there are guidelines.

Many programs use selection "handles" for graphic items. Little squares appear at the corners of the item. Some programs use a dotted outline around a shape. Still other programs use both techniques at different times or circumstances.

When the user drags items, you can draw a simple dashed outline that encompasses all the selected items. You move that rectangle around as you follow the cursor. You move the rectangle by implementing some simple animation. As the mouse moves, you erase the old position and draw the rectangle in the new position.

A better approach is to create a region that consists of the outline of each *individual* selected item. You can then draw the outline of the region (which therefore draws the outline of each selected item), and move the region around.

The best approach is to move the actual image of the selected items around, not just an outline. Then the user can see exactly what is happening. This is a great help when it comes time to drop the item at its new location. You use this technique to drag puzzle pieces.

Time-Consuming Operations

If your application is about to embark on a process that will take a substantial amount of time, you should let the user know that you are working. Otherwise, it looks like the computer has crashed or frozen. In this context, a "substantial period of time" is anything longer than one or two seconds.

There are three ways you can provide this feedback to the user: set the watch cursor, use an animated cursor, or use a progress window.

Setting the Watch Cursor

Setting the watch cursor tells the user that the computer is busy, but functioning properly, and will be done in just a second or two.

Use SetCursor() to set the cursor in use. You pass the address of a cursor record. This is such a common technique that most applications get the watch cursor at startup and store it in a global variable for easy use. You can do this by calling GetCursor(). You provide the resource ID for a CURS resource. The call returns a handle to the cursor data, a CursHandle. EasyApp uses this technique.

When you are through, you can return to the standard arrow cursor by calling InitCursor(). It sets the cursor to the arrow automatically. Use SetCursor() for other cursors.

There are corresponding calls for color cursors: GetCCursor() and SetCCursor(). You get and use a handle to a color cursor record, a CCrsrHandle.

You can hide and show the cursor, as well. This is helpful during animation to get the cursor out of the way. HideCursor() hides the cursor. ShowCursor() displays the cursor again. Actually, these calls decrement and increment the cursor "level." This is analogous to pen visibility. If the cursor level is less than zero, the cursor is not drawn. However, the ShowCursor() call does not increment the cursor level above zero. As a result, a HideCursor() call always hides the cursor.

> Wizards like ObscureCursor(). This call hides the mouse until the next time the user moves it! ObscureCursor() has no effect on the cursor's level.

Using an Animated Cursor

If the time involved is more than one or two seconds, you can use an animated cursor. You provide an 'acur' resource in your application with an ID number of zero. This lists the cursors to use in the animation. You also provide a series of CURS resources, each a separate frame in the animation. You can use a resource editor to create these resources.

When your application launches, call InitCursorCtl(). This call loads the resources necessary to display an animated cursor. You need to make this call only once, and only if you use an animated cursor. You do *not* need to make this call to initialize cursors generally, the way you do with several Toolbox managers. InitCursorCtl() initializes only the animated cursor.

To display the spinning cursor, call RotateCursor() or SpinCursor(). If you use RotateCursor(), you provide an index value. If the value is a multiple of 32, the System advances to the next cursor in the animated sequence. Typically, you pass the value returned by TickCount(). In effect, by passing the number of ticks the call to RotateCursor() changes the cursor every 32 ticks—about twice a second. However, this is reliable only if you can make the call at least once per tick. If you cannot call TickCount() that often, you must provide your own index value that animates the cursor at a good speed.

Alternatively, you can call SpinCursor(). You provide a value of zero, and the System advances to the next cursor in the animated sequence. You must make the call repeatedly at appropriate intervals for smooth animation.

Displaying a Progress Window

If the time involved is more than a few seconds, you should use a progress window. The typical progress window is a dialog that contains a bar. As your process runs, it updates the bar to indicate how far along you are. This tells the user that everything is working, and provides an idea of how much time the entire operation requires. Perhaps it's enough time to go get a cup of coffee or have a snack! Now that's friendly.

A progress dialog (see Figure 12.5) should also give the user an opportunity to cancel, pause, or stop a long operation if that's appropriate. This allows the user to perform some other task and continue the long operation when it is more convenient to do so. Cancel means that you restore the state of the program to exactly what it was before the user started the operation. Pause means you temporarily stop the operation, but you allow the user to resume where the operation left off. Stop means to terminate the operation without restoring the program's state, as you do with the Cancel option.

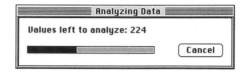

Figure 12.5 A progress dialog

Let's put this theory into practice and drag some puzzle pieces around.

Lab 12.1 Providing Feedback

In this lab you implement three different feedback mechanisms. First, you allow the user to drag a piece around. Second, you implement an animated cursor. Third, you display a progress dialog when solving the puzzle.

In this lab you:

- Identify a click in a puzzle piece
- Drag a puzzle piece
- Set up an animated cursor
- Use an animated cursor
- Set up a progress dialog
- Run a progress dialog

Use your code from the previous lab as the starting point for your work in this lab.

Step 1: Identify a click in a puzzle piece

Modify: `ClickInPuzzle()` in puzzleWindow.c

When the user clicks in the puzzle window, EasyApp sends the window a `DoContentClick` message. For EasyPuzzle, the function that responds to that message is `ClickInPuzzle()`. It should get the location of the click in local coordinates and determine whether a piece is at that location. If the click is inside a piece, drag the piece.

```
DragPiece        dragData;

EasyGlobalToLocal(macWindow, theEvent->where, &localPoint);

while(thisPiece && !done)
{
  done = ClickInPiece (thisPiece, &localPoint);
  if (!done)
  {
    thisPiece = (PieceHandle)(**thisPiece).previousPiece;
  }
}

if (thisPiece)  /* this is the clicked piece */
{
  /*   handle piece dragging   */
  dragData.theEvent  = theEvent;
  dragData.thisPiece = thisPiece;

  error = DragPuzzlePiece(macWindow, &dragData);
}
return error;
```

First you get the mouse click in local coordinates by calling `EasyGlobalToLocal()`.

Then you walk through the window's list of pieces to see whether the click is in any one of them. For each piece you call `ClickInPiece()`. This simple function is provided for you in puzzlePiece.c. It returns `true` if the click is inside the piece. At the end of the walk-through, the variable `thisPiece` is either nil (because you went through the whole list without finding a piece) or is the piece that the user clicked.

> If pieces are piled on top of each other, how do you know which one the user clicked? You start with the last piece and work backwards through the list because the last piece is drawn last in the window, and hence is the "top" piece of the pile. If there are two overlapping pieces, you interpret the click as being in the top piece.

If the user clicked a piece, you put the event record pointer and the piece handle together in a single data structure and call `DragPuzzlePiece()`. You write this function in the next step.

Step 2:   Drag a puzzle piece

Modify: `DragPuzzlePiece()` in puzzleDrag.c

This function performs some simple animation with puzzle pieces. You determine how far the mouse moved, move the piece by that much, clean up its old location, draw it at its new location, and repeat until the mouse button is released.

The existing code does some setup work. It preserves the port and clip. It sets a rectangle to the size of the window less four pixels on every side. You keep the mouse pinned inside this rectangle to prevent the user from dragging a piece out of the window and losing it. The existing code also gets the distance (the offset) from the top left corner of the piece to the click location. This allows you to draw the piece in the proper location relative to the mouse as it moves. If the piece clicked is not the last (topmost) piece, it makes the piece the last piece. This is equivalent to bringing the piece to the front.

```
HideCursor();

while (WaitMouseUp())
{
  GetMouse(&newPoint);
  if (DeltaPoint(oldPoint, newPoint)) /* if it is changed */
  {
    Point  delta;  /* distance piece moved */

    /* pin the new point to the window's contents rect  */
    pinnedPoint = PinRect(&contentRect, newPoint);
    newPoint.v = (pinnedPoint >> 16);
    newPoint.h = (pinnedPoint & 0x0000FFFF);

    /* move the piece */
    delta.h = newPoint.h - oldPoint.h;
    delta.v = newPoint.v - oldPoint.v;
    MovePiece(thisPiece, &delta); /* invalid old location */

    /*  draw the piece at it's new location  */
    SetClip((**thisPiece).shape);
    theFrame = (**thisPiece).frame;
    OffsetRect(&theFrame,
            (**thisPiece).where.h - (**thisPiece).offset.h,
            (**thisPiece).where.v - (**thisPiece).offset.v);
    DrawPicture((**thisPiece).picture, &theFrame);

    /* we just drew it, so this area is valid */
    ValidRgn((**thisPiece).shape);

    /* frame the picture  */
    FrameRgn((**thisPiece).shape);

    SetClip(saveClip);
    easyWindow->DoUpdate(macWindow, nil);

    /* save the current point for the next time through  */
    oldPoint = newPoint;
  }
}
/* done moving, show the cursor again  */
ShowCursor();
```

```
/* see whether the piece is near its final resting place. */
if (HomePiece(thisPiece))
{
  SolvePiece(thisPiece, easyWindow);
}

SetClip(saveClip);
```

The existing code calls HideCursor() to avoid flicker. Then you call WaitMouseUp() to see whether the button has been released. This call returns true as long as the mouse button is down. You put this call in a while loop, and the dragging code repeats indefinitely as long as the mouse button remains down.

You call GetMouse() to get the current location of the mouse, and DeltaPoint() to see whether the mouse moved from its former location. If it has, you must move the piece.

To move the piece, you first call PinRect() to keep the mouse position inside the shrunken content rectangle. Then you extract the vertical and horizontal coordinates for the mouse location from the return value out of PinRect(). You determine how far the new point is from the old point, and call MovePiece() to move the piece. MovePiece() invalidates the original location of the piece.

Then you draw the piece. You set the clip to match the shape of the piece, offset the piece's frame, and draw the picture. The only part of the picture that actually appears is what appears inside the piece's shape, because that's what you set the clip to be.

Because you just drew the region, you call ValidRgn() to validate that region. You draw a frame around the piece with FrameRgn().

You restore the original clip and send the window a DoUpdate message. This updates the old location of the piece.

Your new point is now your old point, and you repeat the loop to get the latest mouse position.

When you are all done, call ShowCursor() to restore the cursor. You call HomePiece() to determine whether the piece was dropped close enough to its final resting place to count. If it is, the call returns true and you call SolvePiece() to drop the piece into the final solution and destroy the piece.

Step 3: Set up an animated cursor

Modify: `LoadCursorsHook()` in puzzleHooks.c

Modify: `InitPuzzleCursor()` in puzzleInit.c

Although EasyApp has no direct support for animated cursors, it is flexible! Adding an animated cursor to your application is trivial. At startup, EasyApp calls the `LoadCursorsHook()`. Simply add a call to your own function.

```
error = EasyLoadCursors();
if (error)
{
  return error;
}

InitPuzzleCursor();

return error;
```

If an error happens setting up the EasyApp cursors, bail out. Otherwise, call `InitPuzzleCursor()`. Here's the code for that function:

```
void  InitPuzzleCursor (void)
{
  InitCursorCtl(nil);
}
```

You just call **InitCursorCtl()**. It doesn't get much easier than that. The animated cursor resources have been provided for you. Use ResEdit to explore the EasyPuzzle acur and CURS resources if you want to see them.

Step 4: Use an animated cursor

Modify: `SolvePuzzleDialog()` in puzzleDialog.c

The automatic puzzle solution takes some time. This a good place to demonstrate how easy it is to use an animated cursor.

```
if(Button())
{
  canceled = true;
  break;
}
SpinCursor(0);
```

413

After the existing code checks for a click, call **SpinCursor()**. This advances the cursor animation one frame. The alternative call—**RotateCursor()**—is not reliable here because the code requires more than one tick to go through the loop.

Step 5:   Set up a progress dialog

Modify: SolvePuzzleDialog() in puzzleDialog.c

The automatic puzzle solution really requires too much time for just a simple spinning cursor. In this step you display a progress dialog as well. The code that creates the dialog has been provided for you.

Before starting the solution loop, set up the progress dialog.

```
result = EasyConfirmDialog(kPuzzleBaseID, kSolveWarning);
if (result == cancel)
{
  return;
}

error = GetProgressDialog(&progressDialog);
if(error)
{
  return;
}
UpdateProgressDialog(progressDialog, 0);

GetPuzzleFrame(easyWindow, &puzzleFrame);
```

After the user confirms the operation, call GetProgressDialog() to create and display the dialog. Then call UpdateProgressDialog() to set it up. The second parameter is the percent of progress that has been made. Zero indicates that no progress has been made yet.

Step 6:   Run a progress dialog

Modify: SolvePuzzleDialog() in puzzleDialog.c

While in the solution loop, update the progress dialog after each piece is solved. This is easy.

```
if(!canceled)
{
  SolvePiece(thisPiece, easyWindow);
  thisPiece = nextPiece;   /* go do the next one */

  UpdateProgressDialog(progressDialog,
      (short)((100 * ++completedPieces)/(totalPieces)));
}
```

You calculate what percentage has been solved, and update the dialog accordingly. The `++completedPieces` code adds one to the number of completed pieces before each calculation. Feel free to examine the `UpdateProgressDialog()` code.

Step 7: Run the application

Modify: none

Save your work and run the project using the debugger. When the debugger window appears, launch EasyPuzzle and create a new puzzle window.

Scramble the puzzle. Click and drag a piece. It should follow the mouse around the screen. The animation may be less than smooth, and we'll talk about that problem in a bit.

Try to drag a piece out of the window. There is always some part of the piece left visible in the window so you can grab it and pull it back in. If you click a piece, it comes to the foreground and becomes the topmost piece. Drop the piece near its solution position, and the piece should drop right into the puzzle solution (behind all the other pieces). You can no longer drag that piece, it has ceased to exist.

Now choose the Solve item from the Puzzle menu. Click the OK button in the confirming alert, and watch what happens. The cursor displays the phases of the moon, and a progress dialog appears. As pieces drop into place, the progress dialog updates. The cursor should change each time a piece moves.

If you click the mouse, the solution process stops, the progress dialog disappears, and you return to the puzzle in its current state.

When you are through observing, quit the application.

Let's talk about a couple of shortcomings of EasyPuzzle. The progress dialog is not the slickest thing in the world. It has no buttons and it takes over the screen. It's really a modal dialog placed on top of the puzzle. A movable modal or modeless dialog would be much slicker. It would also be cool if it had a cancel button. These are the kinds of design issues you face when designing a commercial-quality application.

Of greater significance is the smoothness of the dragging animation. The EasyPuzzle approach is simple, but primitive. There are much better methods for animating images in a window. Check out the EasyPuzzle about box and watch the image of the astronaut floating behind the puzzle piece. That animation is far superior to the technique we used for dragging a puzzle piece. You can also examine the Glypha source code on the CD in the Glypha III folder to see how a high-quality game uses animation.

Advanced animation uses a data structure called a GWorld. In a nutshell, a GWorld is an offscreen image in memory of the pictures you work with. You can blast the pictures—or parts of pictures—onto the screen wherever and whenever you need them. This process is extremely fast, smooth, and powerful. You can learn more about GWorlds in *Inside Macintosh: Imaging With QuickDraw*.

Cursor Utilities Reference

`pascal void InitCursor(void)`

Parameters   none

Returns   void

Description   Sets the current cursor to the arrow cursor and makes it visible. Equivalent to calling `SetCursor()` with address of the arrow cursor data.

`pascal void InitCursorCtl(acurHandle newCursors);`

Parameters   newCursors   handle to acur data, usually obtained from call to `GetResource()`

Returns   void

Description   Initialize animated cursor control. Loads cursor resources into memory. If you have only one animated cursor, use acur resource ID zero and pass nil to this routine. Call once at startup. If you have more than one animated cursor, use acur resource IDs > 127, get a handle to the acur data using `GetResource()`, and call this routine to set your animated cursor. Call it before every time you use a different animated cursor.

`pascal CursHandle GetCursor(short cursorID)`

Parameters   cursorID   resource ID of a CURS resource

Returns   Handle to the cursor data

Description   Use defined constants `iBeamCursor`, `crossCursor`, `plusCursor`, and `watchCursor` to get system cursors.

```
pascal void SetCursor(const Cursor *crsr)
```

Parameters	crsr	address of cursor data
Returns	void	
Description	Sets current black and white cursor.	

```
pascal CCrsrHandle GetCCursor(short crsrID)
```

Parameters	crsrID	resource ID of a crsr resource
Returns	Handle to the color cursor data. This is a resource handle.	
Description	Call once to get handle to data.	

```
pascal void SetCCursor(CCrsrHandle cCrsr)
```

Parameters	cCrsr	handle to color cursor data
Returns	void	
Description	Sets current color cursor.	

```
pascal void DisposeCCursor(CCrsrHandle cCrsr)
```

Parameters	cCrsr	handle to color cursor data
Returns	void	
Description	Disposes of memory allocated to color cursor. This is a resource handle. Call when you are through with the cursor.	

```
pascal void HideCursor(void)
```

Parameters	none
Returns	void
Description	Decrements the cursor level by one, guaranteed to hide the cursor. If level < 0, System does not draw the cursor.

```
pascal void ShowCursor(void)
```

Parameters	none
Returns	void
Description	Increments cursor level, but does not increment beyond zero.

```
pascal void ObscureCursor(void)
```

Parameters   none

Returns   void

Description   Hides the cursor until the user moves it. Has no effect on cursor level.

```
pascal void RotateCursor(long counter);
```

Parameters   counter   index value

Returns   void

Description   The System advances to the next frame in the animation if `counter` is a multiple of 32. Typically you call `TickCount()` to get number of ticks, and the cursor animates at about two frames/second. Negative value causes cursor to spin backward.

```
pascal void SpinCursor(short increment);
```

Parameters   increment   value indicating direction to animate

Returns   void

Description   Value zero advances cursor to next frame. Negative value causes cursor to spin backward.

```
pascal long PinRect(const Rect *theRect, Point thePt);
```

Parameters   theRect   rectangle within which to keep a point

                thePt   point to keep in rectangle

Returns   long value with vertical coordinate in high byte, horizontal coordinate in low byte

Description   Returns a coordinate inside the rectangle provided that is closest to the point provided.

Bundling Up: Icons, Bundles, and Looking Cool

Real Macintosh programmers want their programs to have the neatest, coolest icons in the solar system. I suspect that more than one bright programmer has said, "Hey, I've got a great icon. All I have to do is write a program for it."

An icon is what the user sees of your application on the Desktop. It is the package that the user opens to get at the toys inside. Like a present, you want the wrapping to look good. From the human interface perspective, distinctive icons for your application and its documents help the user easily locate and identify the files.

> The complete development cycle is: design T-shirt, design icons, start writing code, set project schedule, decide what the program does, get someone to write something that looks like documentation, change all features at the last minute, finish code, have a party.

In this chapter, we talk about the magic tricks you must perform to create custom icons and have them show up on the Desktop.

Creating Icons

The most important ingredient in creating an icon is an idea. After you have the idea, creating the icon isn't that hard. You can use almost any drawing program because ResEdit supports copy and paste. You can draw in your favorite environment, and then copy and paste the results into ResEdit's icon editor for further work.

That's right. ResEdit has its own icon editor (see Figure 13.1).

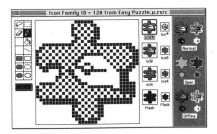

Figure 13.1 ResEdit icon family editor

The icon family window appears when you open any of several types of icon resources, or when you create a new icon. The left side of the window has simple drawing tools. The main part of the window is a "fatbits" view of the icon. To the right of the fatbits view is a display of all the icons in the icon "family." The right side of the window shows what the icons look like on a Desktop.

Kinds of Icons

As you can see from Figure 13.1, there are six members of an icon family: three large and three small. Large icons are 32 pixels square. Small icons are 16 pixels square. Icons may be in 1-bit, 4-bit, or 8-bit color—that is, black and white, 16 colors, or 256 colors. In addition, there are two "masks." The masks affect the appearance of the icon when the file that the icon represents is open or offline.

A typical mask is simply the icon in solid black. There is one for large icons and one for small icons. Each mask must be the exact shape as the icons of the same size. When the Finder draws the icon, it uses the mask to clip the icon. The mask is also the shape that the Finder uses to determine if you clicked the icon. As a result, if your icon and its mask have a hole in the middle, the Finder does not recognize a click on the hole. The only clickable spots on the icon are the pixels covered by the mask.

There are two more standard icon resources, the ICON and cicn. Each is 32 pixels square. ICON resources are black and white, cicn resources use color. The Finder does not use these two types of icons. Your application may use them to display icons—in either color or black and white—in its own dialogs and windows. Table 13.1 shows the icon resources.

Table 13.1: Icon Resources

Type	Size	Colors	Used by Finder
ICN#	32×32	b/w	yes
ics#	16×16	b/w	yes
icl4	32×32	16	yes
ics4	16×16	16	yes
icl8	32×32	256	yes
ics8	16×16	256	yes
ICON	32×32	b/w	no
cicn	32×32	millions	no

The Finder uses all members of an icon family to display icons on the Desktop and in the menu bar. Therefore you should supply resources for each member of the family. For example, if you do not provide small icons, the Finder scales large icons to fit into a 16×16 square. The result of scaling large icons is almost universally ugly. Similarly, if you do not provide color icons, you lose the advantage of presenting a colorful, more recognizable image to the user. You can use color to immediately convey significant information. Besides, black and white icons tend to look drab on a color Desktop.

> You can omit the 8-bit color icons if your 4-bit icons give you all the color you need.

Designing Icons

Creating an icon is an artistic process involving important decisions. Every art uses design principles, and icon creation is no different.

Your first step should be to create some kind of graphical element that all of your icons can share. This provides a unity and repetition among application and document icons so that the user quickly learns to recognize files related to your program. EasyPuzzle uses the outline of a puzzle piece for its icons.

When you start to draw, usually it is a good idea to start with a black-and-white icon. It is easier to add color highlights to a black-and-white icon than it is to reproduce color effects in black and white. The principle outlines of your icon should be in black in all members of an icon family, however colorful. This provides sharp contrast and should always work well in any color environment.

You might want to start with the Finder's generic icons as a basis for further design (see Figure 13.2). The hand in the generic application icon is a clear indication that the icon represents an application. The dog-eared rectangle is a common and powerful symbol commonly used in document icons. Although these make good starting suggestions, you are certainly free to come up with your own icon designs.

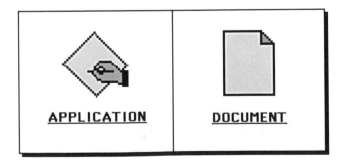

Figure 13.2 Generic icons

Before setting colors for your color icons, choose the Apple Icon Colors item from the ResEdit Color menu. This limits your color options to 36 recommended colors in the System's color palette (see Figure 13.3). These colors are optimized for Desktop display. Why is this important? Remember that the user can change the Desktop pattern and color at will. Other applications may change the color palette as well. Limiting yourself to the recommended colors helps keep your icon looking good at all times.

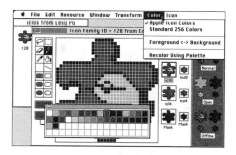

Figure 13.3 Apple icon color palette

> All of the icon resources in the same family share the same resource ID number, although they are different resource types. If you use the ResEdit icon family editor to create your icons, ResEdit handles this important detail for you.

After you have all your icon resources lined up in the application's resources, the next task is to let the Finder know where they are.

Talking with the Finder

The Finder keeps a record of what icons to display for which applications—including document icons—in the Finder's private Desktop database. It originally gets this information from your application. If it doesn't have or can't find the right icon, the Finder displays generic icons.

For your application to get along with the Finder, it should provide several items in places where the Finder can locate them—specific resources with specific ID numbers inside your application or its documents. For icons you must provide:

- A bundle resource
- A signature resource
- One or more file reference resources
- One or more families of icon resources

For general System management and behavior, you must supply:

- A size resource

In addition, to be a very good citizen you should also supply:

- A version resource
- A missing-application name string resource

Let's discuss each of these three groups.

The Bundle and Related Resources

The resource type for a bundle resource is BNDL. The BNDL gathers necessary icon-related information into one place so the Finder can locate it.

The BNDL includes references to an application's signature and file reference (FREF) resources. If you create the BNDL with ResEdit, ResEdit will set up these resources for you, based on the information you provide in the bundle.

An application typically has one BNDL resource, one signature resource, and two file reference resources (see Figure 13.4). Each FREF resource in turn refers to the resources for one icon family.

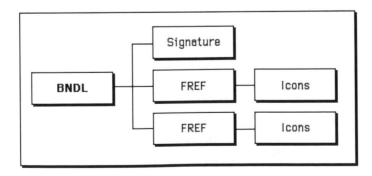

Figure 13.4 The relationship of icon-related resources

The application's signature resource contains the copyright string for the application. An FREF resource identifies the file type that an icon family is associated with, and specifies the resource ID number for the family.

When you create a new BNDL resource in ResEdit, the BNDL template appears. Don't stop there. When the BNDL template window opens, choose Extended view in the BNDL menu (see Figure 13.5). The window extends so that you can see and set all the information in the BNDL resource.

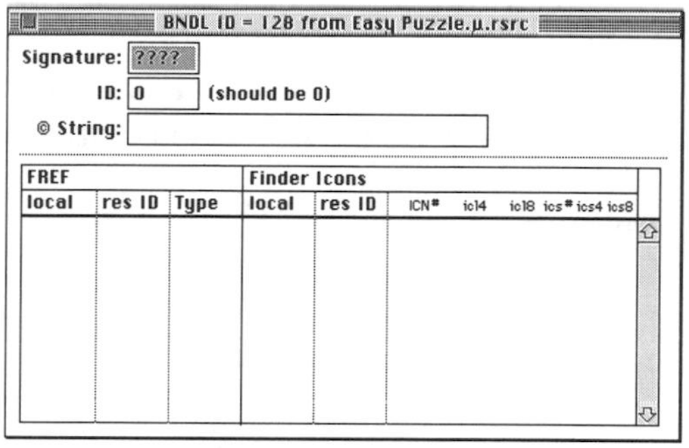

Figure 13.5 Bundle template—Extended view

The initial value in the Signature field is a series of question marks. Set the Signature field to your application's signature. This is a four-character code that identifies your particular application. For example, the EasyPuzzle signature is "Puzl." The signature is case sensitive.

Your application's signature is very important. The Finder uses it to identify your application and the documents it creates. It is your application's fingerprint, and it should be unique. You should register your application's signature with Apple's Developer Technical Support to ensure that no one else uses your signature. Registering is free, easy, and the right thing to do. The tools you need are included in the C/F Registration Requests folder in the Tools You Need folder on the CD.

The ID number of the signature resource should be zero. The resource type is the same as your application's signature. To complete the signature resource, type your copyright string into the appropriate field. ResEdit creates your application's signature resource for you based on this information.

Next, you need to create the FREF resources. While the BNDL window is open, choose the Create New File Type item from the Resource menu, or type ⌘-K. This creates an entry in the bundle resource for a file type. Each file type has its own FREF and icons. In a typical application, you have two FREF resources, one for the application icons, and one for the document icons.

For each FREF resource, provide the local ID, resource ID, and file type for the FREF. The local ID and resource ID can be any unique number. The values supplied by ResEdit are fine. The file type for the FREF is either APPL (for the application icons) or the document type created by your application (for document icons).

You also provide the local ID and resource ID for the icons. The local ID can be any number. The value provided by ResEdit will do just fine. The resource ID is the resource ID number for that family's icons. When you enter the number, the related icons appear so you can see which icons are associated with each file type.

If all this seems a little confusing, take a look at Figure 13.6.

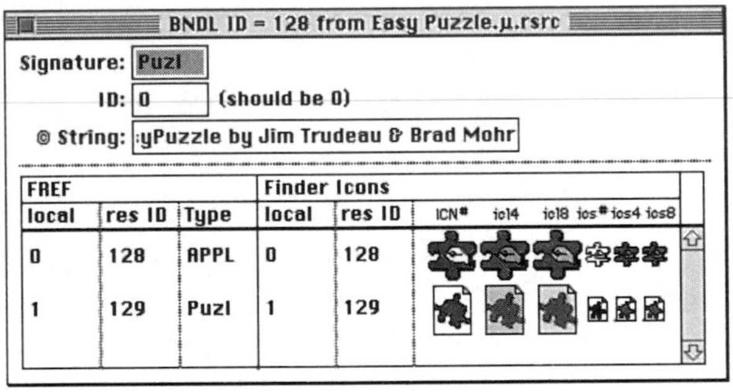

Figure 13.6 EasyPuzzle bundle resource

This is the EasyPuzzle BNDL resource. It has the signature information and two FREF resources.

The application FREF has a local ID of zero, a resource ID of 128, and specifies that this FREF is for files of type APPL—the EasyPuzzle application. It says that the icons to use for that type of file have a local ID of zero and a resource ID of 128.

The document FREF has a local ID of one, a resource ID of 129, and specifies that this FREF is for files of type Puzl. (The EasyPuzzle document type is the same as the application's signature. This is simply coincidence and is not required.) The icons for an EasyPuzzle document have a local ID of one, and a resource ID of 129.

When you close the bundle window, ResEdit creates the signature and FREF resources automatically.

What is the purpose of the local ID for icons? Your application's icons might have a resource number of 128. That might conflict with the ID number for some other application. The Finder uses the local ID number to keep track of icons and avoid potential conflicts.

If you have more than one kind of document and want each to have its own icons, create an Icon family for each document type, and then add an FREF resource to the application's BNDL for each kind of document.

There's one more step. Now that you have all the information in all the right places, and you've left a trail for the Finder in the BNDL resource, you must tell the Finder to go looking for the information.

After you build the application, choose the GetFile/Folder Info item from the ResEdit File menu. A standard "Get File" dialog appears. Navigate to your new application, and select it. A dialog window appears in ResEdit giving you all sorts of information about the file (see Figure 13.7). Of particular interest in this context are the Finder Flags listed at the bottom of the dialog.

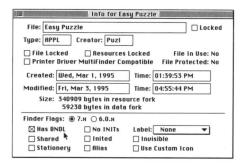

Figure 13.7 File Info for Easy Puzzle

You should set the "Has BNDL" flag so the Finder knows the file has a BNDL resource. You should also clear the "Inited" flag. This tells the Finder that it should go look in the file for the information and put it in the Desktop database. Once it has done so, the Finder sets this flag so it doesn't go looking again.

Even after jumping through all these hoops, the icon doesn't always appear on the Desktop immediately. You may need to restart, or even rebuild the Desktop to force the Finder to retrieve the icons for the application and add them to the Desktop database. When it does, you'll feel a glow of pride as your icon appears as if by magic on the Desktop. Indeed, it is a form of magic, and you are the magician who makes it happen.

To rebuild your Desktop, restart your computer while holding down the ⌘ and Option keys. Continue to hold these down until a dialog box appears asking you if you're sure you want to rebuild your Desktop. Click OK (you can release the ⌘ and Option keys now) and your Mac will rebuild its Desktop file.

The SIZE Resource

The System uses the SIZE resource to know how to communicate with your application. Every development environment worth its salt creates the SIZE resource for you when you build and link the application. In CodeWarrior you use the Project preferences to provide the information that CodeWarrior uses to build the SIZE resource for you.

The SIZE resource tells the System how much memory the application wants and needs (not necessarily the same number). In the CodeWarrior Project preferences, you specify the preferred heap size (how much memory you want) and the minimum heap size (how much memory you need).

In addition, you set a series of flags in the SIZE resource that tell the System how to deal with your application (see Figure 13.8). As discussed in Chapter 2, you specify what kinds of events the application recognizes, and what features of the system it knows about. A good, modern Macintosh application can accept suspend/resume events, is 32-bit compatible, can run in the background, is high-level event aware, and activates/deactivates its own windows when switched into the foreground or background.

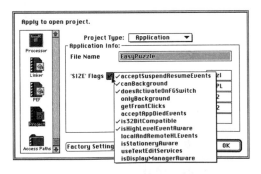

Figure 13.8 The SIZE flags

Setting the suspend/resume flag means the System sends your application the suspend/resume operating system events discussed in Chapter 6. This flag works with the "does activate on foreground switch" flag. They should either both be set, or both be clear. The "does activate on switch" flag means that your application takes responsibility for activating or deactivating windows when you receive a suspend or resume event.

The 32-bit compatible flag means your application can run with the 32-bit Memory Manager. If you follow the instructions in this book, your application will be 32-bit compatible.

The "can background" flag tells the System to send your application null events when it is in the background. If you have nothing to do in the background, clear this flag. You still get background update events.

The high-level event aware flag tells the System to send you Apple events. We discuss Apple events in Chapter 17.

The Version and Missing-Application Resources

The version resource—type vers—specifies the version of the application. If you use ResEdit to create a vers resource, you can specify the version number, the stage of development (alpha, beta, and so forth), and an informational string (see Figure 13.9). This information appears in the Finder's Get Info dialog that displays file-related information.

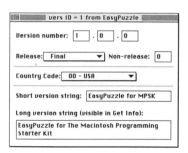

Figure 13.9 EasyPuzzle vers resource

When you create this resource for the first time, ResEdit assigns it the default re-source ID of 128. Change it to resource ID 1. That's the resource ID that the Finder looks for when displaying version information. If the Finder does not find a vers resource with ID 1, it uses the information you put into the application's signature resource.

The special "application-missing" resource does not belong in your application! Your application should put this string inside each openable document it creates.

One of the most frustrating events for Macintosh users occurs when they double-click a document and the application that created the document cannot be found. Before System 7, the Finder displayed a less-than-helpful message that left many users in the dark about what was going on. In System 7, the Finder has been much improved in this respect, but it needs your cooperation.

When you save a document, you add a special resource to the resource fork of the document. This is an 'STR ' resource (note the trailing space in the resource type) with the ID number –16396. This should be a string that has your application's name in it, and nothing more. The Finder is responsible for the message. The message includes the name of your application. The Finder just wants to know the name of the creating application.

If this special resource is available *in the document*, when the Finder cannot find the application that created the document, it displays a helpful message identifying your application as the creator, and letting the user know that the specific application is not available.

We discuss how to save resources to disk in Chapter 15.

The Pause that Refreshes

Time to take a look around and see what's going on.

EasyPuzzle is in good shape. From the user's perspective, the application seems fairly complete. The user can break up the puzzle into any number of pieces, drag the pieces around, drop them where they belong, take a peek at the solution, and even have the program solve the puzzle automatically. And it all works in color!

From the programming perspective, you have met the principle Toolbox managers, and learned how to use them, including:

- Memory Manager
- Resource Manager
- Event Manager
- Menu Manager
- Window Manager
- Control Manager
- Dialog Manager

Along the way you have learned a little about animation, and a lot about good human interface design.

Congratulations! You have reached the second major milestone on the road to becoming a Macintosh programmer. You have learned the core principles of Macintosh programming. You can implement a real application, complete with icons on the Desktop.

Perhaps your greatest accomplishment so far, however, is that you have opened the door to the universe of Macintosh programming. In the rest of *Programming Starter Kit for Macintosh*, you explore some of that universe.

There are quite a few features that are very common in Macintosh programs that are still missing from EasyPuzzle. For example, there is no sound. You cannot save or open a file. You cannot print the puzzle. Perhaps worst of all, you cannot bring any other picture into the puzzle! You are stuck with whatever resource you build into the program. What happened to copy and paste?

How much better would EasyPuzzle be if it had some of these features? You're about to find out as you continue your journey. You're going to add all of them to EasyPuzzle!

14

Make a Joyful Noise: Playing Sounds on the Mac

Programmers frequently use the term "API" to refer to the calls in a Toolbox manager. "API" is an acronym for application programming interface. That's exactly what each of the Toolbox managers is—the programming interface you use to write applications or other software.

The Sound Manager is a marvelous API. With a few very simple calls, you can play all kinds of sounds with remarkable fidelity. On the other hand, you can get deep into the Sound Manager to perform amazing magic if you want.

In this chapter we discuss:

- How sound works on the Mac
- Sound resources
- How to play sounds synchronously
- How to play sounds asynchronously

Synchronous sounds must finish playing before control of the computer returns to your application. Asynchronous sounds play in the background, so control returns to your application immediately.

In the lab accompanying this chapter, you add sounds to EasyPuzzle. The sound resources have been provided for you. You'll write the code that plays them.

Sound on the Mac

Sound on the Macintosh started out at a fairly primitive level. You had to talk to sound "drivers" almost at the hardware level. The pain involved in that process fostered the invention of the Sound Manager, an API that matured along with System 7.

The Sound Manager lets you play and record sound without knowing anything about the hardware. From the application programmer's perspective, you never look deeper than the Sound Manager. As a result, you get to ignore all the nitty-gritty hardware details.

The Sound Manager works by sending *sound commands* to other pieces of software called *sound components*. The components, in turn, deal with sound-related hardware to produce or modify a sound in response to the command (see Figure 14.1). A string of such commands—together with the data on which they operate—make up the sounds that you hear from your Macintosh. Although you can work directly with sound commands, you don't do so in this book. This book sticks to high-level Sound Manager routines that make your programming task much simpler.

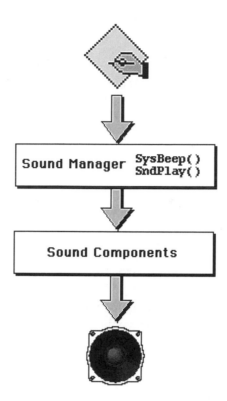

Figure 14.1 Sound chain of command

A *sound channel* is a string of sound commands treated as a first-in, first-out queue. The Sound Manager also has a declared data type, SndChannel, that it uses to manage the channel. Because you work at a high level in this chapter, you don't have to worry about allocating or managing this data structure.

> If you work directly with the Sound Manager to create asynchronous sounds, you do have to worry about some of these details that are being glossed over. However, in EasyPuzzle you use a small code library named SoundHelper. This library makes playing asynchronous sounds simple. SoundHelper is discussed a little later in this chapter.

The Sound Manager may have several sound channels open simultaneously. These channels may all be from one application, or from several applications. The quality of the sound produced and the number of possible channels is limited by hardware. The more powerful your machine, the more simultaneous high-quality sounds you can play without significantly degrading performance.

Sound Resources

The Sound Manager stores sampled—digitized—sound as resources of type 'snd ' (note the trailing space in the resource type), or in files that follow the audio interchange file format (AIFF). Compressed sound files are known as AIFF-C. The Sound Manager can play sounds directly from these files on disk.

In this book you work with 'snd ' resources. Most applications that play sounds use sound resources. The resource approach for sounds is so popular because it is so easy to use.

Sound resources contain sound commands and (usually) the data associated with the commands. Sound resources are just like any other resource. You can use all the Resource Manager calls on them.

You can not only play sounds, you can probably also use your Macintosh to digitize sound. Many Macintosh computers come with a microphone. Digitizing a sound on these machines is no more complex than opening the Sound control panel, clicking a few buttons, and speaking into the microphone (see Figure 14.2).

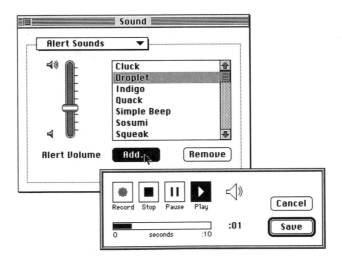

Figure 14.2 Recording a sound

This sound recording and playback interface is simple and effective. However, it is not a professional sound studio. There are many sound creation and management packages available on the market, ranging from simple shareware to high-end commercial sound samplers.

The EasyPuzzle application does not record sound. However, if you wanted to record a sound resource in an application, you can use the same interface as that shown in Figure 14.2. Simply call `SndRecord()`. This call displays the sound-recording dialog built into the System. You provide a procedure pointer (a UPP, as always) to an event filter as the first parameter. This filter is the functional equivalent of the modal dialog event filter discussed in Chapter 11.

In addition, you provide three other parameters: the point where the dialog should appear, the quality of the sound recording you want, and the address of a handle where the Sound Manager stores the resulting digitized sound data. This is a handle of data type `SndListHandle`.

The Sound Manager stores the digitized data in 'snd ' resource format. You can use Resource Manager calls to save it to disk. You can use other Sound Manager calls to play the sound or do other tricks.

You can record the digitized sample directly to a file. First, you must create and open a file. (The File Manager is discussed in the next chapter.) After you have an open file, call `SndRecordToFile()`. This call opens the same sound-recording dialog as `SndRecord()`. You provide the UPP for an event filter procedure, the point where the dialog should appear, the quality desired, and a reference number to the open file. The call writes the data to disk for you. You must close the sound file yourself when you are through recording.

Synchronous Sounds

Playing a sound synchronously means that the Sound Manager retains control of the computer until the sound is finished. Your application "freezes" while the sound is playing and cannot do work.

Clearly this is appropriate only for very short sounds, no more than a second or two. Playing synchronous sounds is simple.

To play the current System alert sound, call `SysBeep()`. You pass a short value that is the duration of the sound in ticks. This value is ignored except on older machines like the Mac Classic. On those machines, 30 ticks is a good value, so the beep sound plays for about 1/2 second.

To play a sound stored in a sound resource, call `SndPlay()`. There are three parameters. You provide a pointer to a sound channel, a handle to the sound data, and a Boolean value indicating whether to play the sound synchronously or asynchronously. You have some options here.

You can pass nil for the pointer to the sound channel. In that case, the Sound Manager creates the channel for you and plays the sound synchronously (regardless of the Boolean value). To play the sound asynchronously, you must allocate and manage a sound channel yourself. This topic is discussed in more detail in just a bit.

You get the handle to the sound data by calling `GetResource()` or `Get1Resource()`. You specify the resource type 'snd ' and the resource ID of the sound you desire.

> The `SndPlay()` call moves memory, so it may relocate the sound data or purge it (if it is purgeable). Either event would be a disaster. You must lock the sound before calling `SndPlay()`.

Typically, you write a little function to take care of the housekeeping details for you. The code snippet here is what you used in the Hello World program back in Chapter 2 when you played sounds. Now that you understand a lot more about programming the Macintosh, this code will probably seem pretty clear to you:

```
OSErr MyPlaySound(short soundResID)
{
    Handle   soundHandle;
    OSErr    error = noErr;

    soundHandle = Get1Resource('snd ', soundResID);
    if (soundHandle)
    {
            HLock(soundHandle);
            error = SndPlay(nil, (SndListHandle)soundHandle,
false);
            ReleaseResource(soundHandle);
    }
    else
    {
            error = ResError();
    }

    return error;
}
```

This function requires the resource ID of the desired sound. It assumes that the current resource file is the one you want to use. It gets the sound data from the Resource Manager, locks it, and calls `SndPlay()` to play the sound synchronously. When through, it releases the sound data. Even though it is locked, you can still dispose of the data. The locked state refers only to whether the data moves in memory.

You may also play a sound from an AIFF or AIFF-C file by calling `SndStartFilePlay()`. For details on this call, see the "Sound Manager Reference" section at the end of this chapter.

Asynchronous Sounds

Playing asynchronous sounds is a nontrivial task. This is not a topic normally found in an introductory book on Macintosh programming.

However, I have a gift for you. Like Dean Yu's zooming code, Bryan K. Ressler (a.k.a. Beaker) has smoothed out the rough spots in the asynchronous highway. His efforts have made asynchronous sounds as easy to play as synchronous sounds.

The Toolbox is not always the simplest or easiest interface to master. Some parts of the Toolbox are downright intimidating. In situations like this, some bright programmer usually writes a little library of code to make things simpler. After mastering the technical details, the programmer pounds out all the rough spots and produces a simplified mechanism for accomplishing your goal.

The SoundHelper library is a perfect example of this process. This library of code appeared in Apple's *develop* magazine in August 1992 as part of Bryan's article "The Asynchronous Sound Helper." He has succeeded in turning an otherwise complex task, fraught with the possibilities of error, into a simple programming interface with a few function calls. Since that time, the Power Macintosh has come along. Brad Mohr updated the SoundHelper code for this book so that it uses UPPs for procedure pointers. SoundHelper now works in the mixed 68K/Power Mac universe.

The modified code is already included in the EasyPuzzle project. For future reference you can find the original code and Bryan's article in the develop Articles folder on the CD. In the Async Sound Helper folder you'll also find Rapmaster, a neat asynchronous sound application.

The SoundHelper code is actually very flexible. You can use it at an expert level to help manage complex Sound Manager tasks. It also has a simple, high-level interface that you can use to play sounds asynchronously with very little effort.

Here's how it works. You tell SoundHelper to play a sound. This is just like making a Toolbox call, except the function you're calling is not in the Toolbox—it's in the SoundHelper library. When you make the call, SoundHelper uses the Sound Manager to create a sound channel and start the sound playing asynchronously. SoundHelper also tells the Sound Manager to let it know when the sound is finished. In the meantime, your application goes on its merry way, while the Sound Manager continues to play the sound in the background. Your aural landscape is enhanced while you continue to work.

Figure 14.3 Playing a tune

When the sound finishes, the Sound Manager tells SoundHelper that it is all done. SoundHelper sets a flag to tell your application it needs some attention so it can clean up the sound channel. You check the attention flag every time through your main event loop. If the flag is set, you call SoundHelper to give it a chance to clean up.

You can do all this with four function calls. After you include the source file in your development project, here's what you have to do to use this little library to play sounds asynchronously.

When the application launches, call SHInitSoundHelper(). You pass the address of a Boolean flag that the SoundHelper library sets when it needs attention. You also pass the number of sound channels you want pre-allocated. If you pass zero, the library sets up a default number of channels.

After you have initialized the library, you call SHPlayByID() to play a sound. You pass the resource ID number and the address of a variable to get the SoundHelper's reference number for the sound channel. You can pass nil as the address of the reference number variable if you don't want the information. The SoundHelper takes care of all the details.

EasyPuzzle checks the attention flag every time through the event loop, and on a couple of other occasions when the program is especially busy (and might take some time before it gets back to the event loop). If the attention flag is set, you know that SoundHelper needs to clean up after playing a sound. Call SHIdle().

When you are all through playing sounds—typically when the application quits—call SHKillSoundHelper() to close the library.

The SoundHelper also has sound recording functions and advanced functions for asynchronous playback and recording. These will not be discussed. Examine the soundHelper.h and soundHelper.c files if you'd like to explore the inner workings of the Sound Manager.

With SoundHelper you can play asynchronous sounds with very little effort. Let's do that right now.

Lab 14.1 Playing Asynchronous Sounds

Using Bryan Ressler's SoundHelper, playing sounds is easy and fun. All of the necessary sound resources are included in the EasyPuzzle resource file.

In this lab you:

- Initialize the SoundHelper library
- Close the SoundHelper library
- Clean up sound channels
- Play a sound asynchronously
- Play some tunes

Use your code from the previous lab as the starting point for your work in this lab.

Step 1: Initialize the sound library
Modify: `InitPuzzleApp()` in puzzleInit.c

Like many code libraries, the SoundHelper library has some internal data that it must initialize before you use it. The right time to do this is usually when your application launches. Typically libraries provide a simple call that handles this task, and the SoundHelper is no exception.

```
GetDateTime( (unsigned long *) &qd.randSeed);

error = SHInitSoundHelper(&puzzleG.callSoundIdle, 0);

return error;
```

Call `SHInitSoundHelper()`. You provide the address of a `Boolean` variable. When a sound is finished playing, the SoundHelper library sets this value so you know it is time to clean up.

Step 2: Close the SoundHelper library

Modify: `ShutdownHook ()` in **puzzleHooks.c**

Keeping things symmetrical, most code libraries also have a function to close or kill the library when you are through with it. The library is responsible for disposing of any data structures or memory that it has allocated. Again, the SoundHelper library follows the standard. For our purposes, the right time to close the library is when the application is shutting down. At that time, EasyApp calls `ShutdownHook()`.

```
OSErr ShutdownHook (void)
{
  SHKillSoundHelper();

  return EasyShutdown();
}
```

Simply call `SHKillSoundHelper()`. Job done. The existing code then continues the shutdown process.

Step 3: Clean up sound channels

Modify: `PreprocessEventHook()` in **puzzleHooks.c**

Modify: `SolvePuzzleDialog()` in **puzzleDialog.c**

Modify: `IdlePuzzleSounds()` in **puzzleSounds.c**

You should clean up the memory used for playing the sound when it stops playing. However, once a sound starts playing, you never know when it will finish. The only reasonable solution is to check every time through the main event loop. Happily, the EasyApp shell provides a handy mechanism for modifying the main event loop without having to mess directly with the EasyApp code. EasyApp calls `PreprocessEventHook()` every time through the loop.

```
Boolean  PreprocessEventHook (EventRecord *theEvent)
{
  Boolean handled = false;  /* assume not handled */

  IdlePuzzleSounds();

  return handled;
}
```

You simply call `IdlePuzzleSounds()`. You write that function in just a bit. Notice that you do not change the value of the `handled` variable. You really aren't handling an event here at all. You are just taking advantage of the architecture to get something else done at the right time.

A second problem occurs in `SolvePuzzleDialog()` when solving the puzzle. You will play sounds while the puzzle is solving automatically, and it will be a long time before you get back to the main event loop. You have to clean up sounds at this time, as well. This new code goes near the end of the function.

```
if(!canceled)
{
  SolvePiece(thisPiece, easyWindow);
  thisPiece = nextPiece;  /* go do the next one */

  UpdateProgressDialog…

}

if (puzzleG.useSounds)
{
  IdlePuzzleSounds();
}
```

If sounds are active, you call `IdlePuzzleSounds()`, just like you do from `PreprocessEventHook()`.

The `IdlePuzzleSounds()` function in *puzzleSounds.c* is also very simple.

```
void  IdlePuzzleSounds(void)
{
  if (puzzleG.callSoundIdle)
  {
    SHIdle();
  }
}
```

You check the flag that the SoundHelper library sets when it needs time. If the flag is set, call `SHIdle()`. The library takes care of the work. It even clears the flag. That's service.

Step 4:   Play a sound asynchronously

Modify: `PlayPuzzleSndAsync()` in *puzzleSounds.c*

Let me tell you, it doesn't get much easier than this. Here's the code to play a sound asynchronously, with the SoundHelper library.

```
OSErr   PlayPuzzleSndAsync(short soundID)
{
  OSErr error  = noErr;

  error = SHPlayByID(soundID, nil);
  return error;
}
```

That's right, one simple call to SHPlayByID().

Step 5:   Play some tunes

Modify: CreatePieces() in puzzlePiece.c

Modify: SolvePiece() in puzzlePiece.c

Now that you've done all that hard work, it's time to play some tunes. Let's play sounds when the user scrambles the puzzle, drops a piece where it belongs, and when the puzzle is completely solved. The puzzle menu also allows the user to turn off sounds. EasyPuzzle keeps track of that setting in puzzleG.useSounds. The menu management code has been provided for you because you have already dealt with menus extensively.

Without further ado, let's boogie.

EasyPuzzle calls CreatePieces() to create the pieces when the user scrambles the puzzle. That's when it's time to play our scrambling tune, right at the start of the function.

```
PieceHandle  nextPiece  = nil;

if (puzzleG.useSounds)
{
   PlayPuzzleSndAsync(kScrambleSound);
}
```

In SolvePiece(), just before the end of the function, you can play a sound after dumping a piece because it has been solved. This is also a good place to check whether that happened to be the final piece in the puzzle.

```
DisposePiece(thisPiece, easyWindow);

if (puzzleG.useSounds)
{
  PlayPuzzleSndAsync(kDropPieceSound);

  if (!GetPuzzleFirstPiece(easyWindow))
```

```
   {
     PlayPuzzleSndAsync(kSolveSound);
   }
 }
```

return false;

You play the piece-solution sound. When you've done that, see if there are any more pieces left. If there aren't any pieces, the puzzle is completely solved! Play another tune.

And with that, you have fully implemented sound in EasyPuzzle.

Step 6:   Run the application
Modify: none

Save your work and run the project using the debugger. When the debugger window appears, launch EasyPuzzle and create a new puzzle window.

Look in the Puzzle menu to make sure sounds are on. They are on when the menu has a Turn Sound Off item. Sounds are off when the menu has a Turn Sounds On item. The text in this menu item changes depending upon the state of the application.

In any application that uses sound, it is polite to allow the user to turn sound off entirely. You never know when the program will be running at 3 AM with someone sleeping nearby. As a matter of fact, if it's 3 AM where you are, you may want to wait until morning or turn the volume down!

When you're ready to go, choose the Scramble item from the Puzzle menu. Prepare to be shattered when you click the OK button in the scramble dialog.

Drag a piece to its solution position and drop it there to hear the second sound, a brief click. Solve the entire puzzle to hear the final sound, a slow chord.

This next test depends upon how fast you are. Try to do something before the sound stops playing. You might use the Return key to approve the scramble dialog while you prepare to click the mouse on a menu. As soon as you hit the Return key, pull down the menu. It should appear and be ready for service, even while the sound is playing. You should see no hesitation or delay. That's the beauty of asynchronous sounds.

When you are through listening, quit the application.

Sound Manager Reference

```
pascal void SysBeep(short duration)
```

Parameters duration length of beep sound in ticks

Returns void

Description The duration value is ignored except on older Macs, including the Classic, SE, and Mac Plus. Recommended value of duration on those machines is 30. Use that as the standard value whenever you call SysBeep().

```
pascal OSErr SndPlay(SndChannelPtr chan, Handle sndHdl, Boolean async)
```

Parameters chan pointer to a SndChannel record

sndHdl handle to data in 'snd' resource format

async true => play asynchronously

Returns Operating system error if call fails

Description You must already have the handle to the sound data. Lock the handle before playing the sound. If you pass nil for the chan parameter, the Sound Manager allocates the channel and plays the sound synchronously.

```
pascal OSErr SndStartFilePlay(SndChannelPtr chan, short fRefNum, short
       resNum, long bufferSize, void *theBuffer, AudioSelectionPtr
       theSelection, FilePlayCompletionUPP theCompletion, Boolean async)
```

Parameters chan pointer to a SndChannel record

fRefNum reference number for the file; to play a sound resource this should be zero

resNum should be zero to play a file; otherwise is resource ID of desired 'snd' resource

bufferSize size of buffer to use for inputting data from file; zero allocates default buffer

theBuffer pointer to buffer (of size bufferSize) to hold data as it is read from file; nil tells Sound Manager to allocate itself

theSelection pointer to audio selection record; nil plays the entire sound

	theCompletion	a UPP to a completion routine called when the Sound Manager is through playing the sound asynchronously
	async	true => play asynchronously

Returns   Operating system error if call fails

Description   If you pass nil for the chan parameter, and true for the async parameter, the Sound Manager returns an error. You may also pass zero for bufferSize, nil for theBuffer, and nil for theSelection to play an entire sound and let the Sound Manager handle memory allocation.

```
pascal OSErr SndRecord(ModalFilterUPP filterProc, Point corner, OSType
                quality, Handle *sndHandle)
```

Parameters

	filterProc	UPP to an event filter procedure
	corner	point in local coordinates for the top-left corner of the sound input dialog
	quality	good, better, or best
	sndHandle	address of a handle to hold resulting digitized sound data

Returns   Operating system error if call fails

Description   This call displays and manages the standard sound input dialog. For the quality parameter, use declared constants siBestQuality, siBetterQuality, or siGoodQuality.

```
pascal OSErr SndRecordToFile(ModalFilterUPP filterProc, Point corner,
                OSType quality, short fRefNum)
```

Parameters

	filterProc	UPP to an event filter procedure
	corner	point in local coordinates for the top-left corner of the sound input dialog
	quality	good, better, or best
	fRefNum	file reference number for file in which to store data

Returns   Operating system error if call fails

Description   This call displays and manages the standard sound input dialog. For the quality parameter, use declared constants siBestQuality, siBetterQuality, or siGoodQuality. The file must already exist and be open before making this call. You must also close the file after this call returns.

447

You're on File: Saving and Opening Files

Most applications need to save data in one form or another for extended periods of time. The storage medium of choice is magnetic—your hard drive. The Toolbox routines you use to work with the Macintosh file system are collectively called the File Manager.

This chapter explains how to write data to disk for long-term storage, and how to read that data back into memory when you need it. In this chapter we discuss:

- Data streams
- The Macintosh file system
- Working with data forks
- Working with resource forks
- Miscellaneous File Manager tasks

At the end of this chapter, two lab exercises give you real-world experience working with files.

Data Streams

A file is a named, ordered sequence of bytes. It is the principle means by which you store data on the Macintosh. The usual location of a file is a hard drive, but the data may also exist on a tape drive, an optical device like a CD-ROM disk, a floppy disk, or any of a number of other alternative storage media.

If you broaden your perspective, a file can exist on all sorts of devices. In a very real sense, if you use a modem to fetch a file from a remote location, the file exists *in your modem!* That's where the Macintosh gets the file. If your Macintosh is connected to a network, the file may be a stream of bytes coming to you over the wires (see Figure 15.1).

In this book you work with files on disk. However, the concept that data is a stream—an ordered sequence—of bytes is fundamental to good software design. When your application wants to export data, it should make no assumptions about the nature of the destination. The program should gather up the necessary bytes, and send them to whatever function manages the export. You have one function to gather the data, and several functions to export it. You might have one for saving to disk, one for sending information out over the network, one for communicating via modem, and so forth.

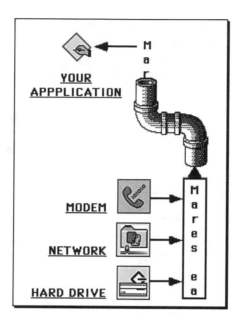

Figure 15.1 The data stream

The process of gathering your data and converting it into a single block or stream ready for transmission to any destination is called "flattening." The reverse process of converting a stream into a form your application recognizes is called "unflattening."

In the labs for this chapter you implement a flattening/unflattening strategy in EasyPuzzle. For now, however, you'll focus once again on a particular use of the data stream—accessing files on disk—and how the Macintosh manages files.

The Macintosh File System

The largest unit of storage with which the File Manager concerns itself is a volume. A volume is a *portion* of a storage device formatted to store files. It may be an entire disk, or just part of a disk. The File Manager knows nothing about disks as such.

When a volume appears on the Desktop, it is said to be mounted. The File Manager gives each mounted volume a reference number. This number remains constant as long as the disk remains mounted. You use this number to identify a volume because mounted volumes may have the same name.

Volumes are subdivided into directories. Each directory appears to the user as a folder. A directory may contain files and/or other directories. It may also be empty. The File Manager assigns each directory an ID number to keep track of it. Because directories may contain other directories, we call this a hierarchical file system (see Figure 15.2).

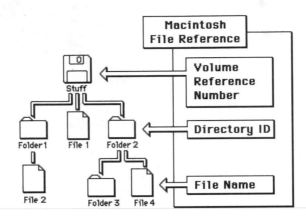

Figure 15.2 The hierarchical file system

The low-level details of how the File Manager stores information on disk are not of direct interest to an application programmer, with a few exceptions.

Bytes in a file are tracked using a zero-based count, so the first byte in a file is byte zero. The logical end-of-file—known as the logical EOF—is the actual number of bytes of data in the file—one greater than the index number of the last byte of data. If a file had one byte of data, that byte is byte zero and the logical EOF is one.

When you open a file, the File Manager creates a data structure called a file control block and opens an access path to that file. Each path gets a file reference number. The file reference number is frequently called the file ID number. A file may have multiple access paths, so a single file may have several file ID numbers.

Each file path has a file mark. The mark is the position at which a byte of data is about to be accessed. For example, if the mark is at 10, the 11th byte of data will be the next byte affected by a read or write operation (because bytes start counting at zero).

Finally, each time you read or write to a file, you must give the File Manager the address of a place to put the data it reads, or get the data you want to write. This is the data buffer.

In summary, the important numbers to remember are

- Each volume has a volume ID
- Each directory has a directory ID
- Each access path to a file has a file ID
- Each access path has a file mark

File Specifications

The File Manager keeps most of the information you need to identify a file in a single, neat package—the file system specification or FSSpec. For easy reference, we will refer to this data structure as a file spec. Table 15.1 lists the members of a file spec and their use.

Table 15.1: Fields in a File System Specification

Field	Data Type	Description
vRefNum	short	volume reference number
parID	long	directory ID of parent directory
name	Str63	name of the file or directory

Before the advent of System 7, using the File Manager was a lot more complicated. The file spec—and new Toolbox calls that use the file spec—eliminated the complications.

The file spec contains the location of the file: volume, directory, and name. It does not contain the actual access path to the file because a single file may have multiple access paths. You use a file ID to specify a particular access path. The File Manager gives you the file ID when you provide the file spec and tell it to open a file.

Data and Resource Forks

As you know from our discussions as far back as Chapter 1, a Macintosh file consists of a data fork and a resource fork.

In one respect, this makes file management a little more complicated. You use separate functions to create, open, read, write, and close files for each fork. You work with each fork independently. The reason for this is simple. The data storage structures of the two forks are very different (see Figure 15.3).

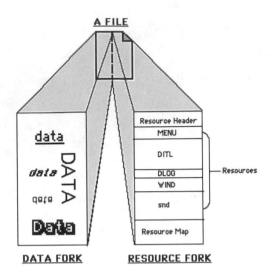

Figure 15.3 The data and resource forks

The data fork is sequential in nature and unstructured. Data in the data fork is a continuous stream of bytes. If you want a piece of it, you have to keep track of the precise byte count where the piece starts and stops.

The resource fork, on the other hand, is a random-access database of blocks of data of known size. By providing type and ID number, the Resource Manager can go to the right spot and pull out exactly the right amount of data. The many advantages of the Resource Manager far outweigh the disadvantages of having to work with two separate forks.

Working with the Data Fork

The data fork is a series of bytes that starts at byte number zero and goes to the last byte in the file. The File Manager makes no divisions within the data fork. You may read any number of bytes from any position in the fork.

Your principal tasks when working with the data fork are to:

- Make a file spec—`StandardPutFile()`
- Get a file spec—`StandardGetFile()`
- Create a file—`FSpCreate()`

- Open the data fork—`FSpOpenDF()`

- Set the file mark—`SetFPos()`

- Write data to a file—`FSWrite()`

- Read data from a file—`FSRead()`

- Close a file—`FSClose()` and `FlushVol()`

- Swap files—`FSpExchangeFiles()`

The data you want to save is almost always associated with a window in some way. You must save whatever data is necessary so that later on, when you read the data, you can recreate the contents of the window exactly.

This task will be much easier if you store all the necessary data in a single structure of some kind. You can then easily locate what needs to be saved, and pass that information to the File Manager in one lump.

This unified organization is not mandatory, but it is a good idea. Alternatively, you might have data scattered around in various structures. Then, when it is time to save a file, you must gather all that data into a single block before saving it. Or you must make a series of calls to the File Manager to write each chunk separately to disk in a defined order. It is generally faster and more reliable to write data in a large block rather than to write lots of little blocks.

Either way, the process begins when the user chooses the Save or Save As item in the application's File menu.

Make a File Spec

Assume for the moment that the data in a window has never been saved. When the user chooses to save the data, you must get the name for a new file and the directory in which to put the file. Then you can create the file in the correct spot with the correct name.

The File Manager provides a function to manage this interaction with the user—`StandardPutFile()`. You pass a string with a prompt for the dialog, a string with the default file name to put in the dialog, and the address of a `StandardFileReply` structure. The File Manager fills in the data in the reply structure based on the user's choices in the standard put-file dialog (see Figure 15.4).

Table 15.2 lists the important fields of a `StandardFileReply` structure. The File Manager uses this same structure for the standard get-file dialog as well.

Figure 15.4 Standard put-file dialog

Table 15.2: Important Fields in a StandardFileReply

Field	Data Type	Description
sfGood	Boolean	true if the user clicked Save
sfFile	FSSpec	file specification for the file
sfScript	ScriptCode	script system for name

After calling `StandardPutFile()`, you check the `sfGood` field to make sure the user clicked OK. If so, the file spec you need is in the `sfFile` field. The File Manager builds the file spec for you based on the user's actions in the dialog. Pretty good service.

> If a document has already been saved once, you should store that document's file spec with the document data. Then when the user chooses to save the file, you don't need to display the standard put-file dialog. You just use the file spec that you already have. Of course, if the user chooses the Save As item from the File menu, then the person wants to specify a new name. You must use the standard put-file dialog and create a new file in that case.

The call to `StandardPutFile()` does not create a file! It just gives you a file spec for a hypothetical file. You must create the file yourself. How to do that is discussed after the next section about how to get a file spec when the user wants to open a file.

Get a File Spec

Like saving a file, if the user is opening a file for the first time, you must get the information about what file to open from the user. Once again, the File Manager comes to the rescue with `StandardGetFile()`. This call displays a standard dialog in which the user selects a file (see Figure 15.5). The File Manager takes care of all the interaction with the user.

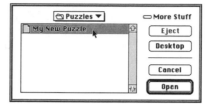

Figure 15.5 Standard get-file dialog

There are four parameters. You pass a UPP for a file filter procedure, a short value indicating the number of different file types to display in the dialog, a list of the file types, and the address of a `StandardFileReply` structure.

The standard dialog lists files for the user. The File Manager displays files of the types you specify, and no others. You can specify the types of files to list in two ways. The optional file filter procedure can identify which files to list. Writing a file filter is an advanced topic that we won't discuss further.

The simple way to specify what types of files should appear in the get-file dialog is to provide a list of types. You can specify up to four types. You must provide the number of types and a list of types in the call to `StandardGetFile()`. If you specify –1 as the number of types, the File Manager displays files of all types. If you specify one file type and say it must be the PICT file type, only PICT files appear in the dialog.

The File Manager returns information in the `StandardFileReply` structure. The `sfGood` and `sfFile` fields have the same meaning as they did for the standard put-file dialog. In addition, the `sfType` field returns the file type of the selected file. This can be very important if your application supports multiple file types.

Table 15.3: Important Fields in a StandardFileReply

Field	Data Type	Description
sfGood	Boolean	true if the user clicked Open
sfFile	FSSpec	file specification for the file
sfScript	ScriptCode	script system for name
sfType	OSType	file type of selected file

If you already have a file spec, you don't need to display the standard get-file dialog. For example, let's say the user has opened a file, made some changes, and then wants to revert to the file's original contents. You should already have the file spec for that file, so you can just get the data directly.

Now that the two standard dialogs are out of the way, the following section goes a little deeper into the File Manager to teach you how to manipulate real files.

Creating a File

To create the file, call `FSpCreate()`. You pass the address of the file spec for the new file, the application's creator code, the file type code, and the script system in which the file name should be established. You typically get the file spec from the `StandardPutFile()` call. The standard file reply structure has the script system for the new file name. Lacking that, you can use the constant `smSystemScript`.

This call returns a value indicating whether there was an error, as do most File Manager routines. You should *always* make sure the return value from a File Manager call is the constant `noErr`, declared to be zero. I won't mention this for all the routines, but keep it in mind.

When creating a file, it is possible that the file already exists. This is a duplicate file error. This isn't really an error as much as it is a warning that the user is replacing an existing file.

If the user is replacing the contents of an existing file, the best thing to do is to create a temporary file with a random name, write the data to the temporary file and then swap files when you're through. With this strategy, if some problem arises during the saving process the original file is not destroyed. We revisit this topic when we discuss swapping files a little later.

Creating a file does not open it. You must do that explicitly.

Opening the Data Fork

You must open the data fork before you can either read or write data in the fork. By the time you get here, you have a file spec—from a standard dialog or a file spec that you saved with the document.

To open the data fork, call `FSpOpenDF()`. You provide the address of the file spec for the file that you want to open. You also specify the read/write permission status of this access path to the file. Table 15.4 lists the possible values. You also provide the address of a short variable. The call fills this variable with the file reference number—the file ID—for the new access path to the data fork. Check for error before attempting to read or write data.

Table 15.4: Read/Write Permission Modes

Constant	Description
fsCurPerm	use current permission
fsRdPerm	read only permission
fsWrPerm	write only permission
fsRdWrPerm	exclusive read/write permission
fsRdWrShPerm	shared read/write permission

Typically you use fsRdPerm for reading data, and either fsWrPerm or fsRdWrPerm for writing data. Using shared permission is hazardous to your data integrity (see Figure 15.6).

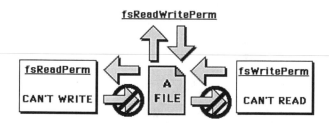

Figure 15.6 Read/write permissions

Setting the Mark

To read data you call FSRead(). To write data, you call FSWrite(). Before we discuss these calls, however, you need to know a little bit about how they work.

FSRead() and FSWrite() either read or write the number of bytes you specify *starting at the current mark in the file*. You must make sure that the mark is in the correct spot. To get the current position of the mark in the file, call GetFPos(). You pass two parameters. The first is the file ID number. Typically you get the file ID number from the call to FSpOpenDF(). The second parameter is the address of a long value. The File Manager puts the current position of the mark in the second parameter.

The SetFPos() call moves the mark to a new position. You typically do this before reading or writing data to ensure that the mark is at the correct position. You provide the file ID number, a mode, and an offset.

Table 15.5 lists the possible modes. The offset value specifies how many bytes to move. For example, to set the mark to the beginning of the data fork, you use the fsFromStart mode with an offset of zero. The offset may be positive or negative. If you are positioning from the end of the file, the offset must be zero or negative.

Table 15.5: Positioning the Mark Modes

Constant	Description
fsAtMark	don't move the mark at all
fsFromStart	move offset bytes from start of fork
fsFromLEOF	move offset bytes from logical end of fork
fsFromMark	move offset bytes from current mark

To get the current logical end-of-file, call GetEOF(). You provide the file ID number and the address of a long variable to hold the result. Typically you make this call to find out how many bytes of data there are in a data fork so that you can allocate memory before reading them all.

Writing Data

After ensuring that the mark is in the correct location, it is time to actually write data. To write data, call FSWrite(). You must provide three pieces of information.

First, you pass the file ID number for the access path to the file.

Second, you pass the address of a byte count. When you call the routine, this is the precise number of bytes you want to write. When the call returns, this variable contains the number of bytes actually written. Typically you can ignore that value, but it may have some significance if an error occurs. You can use it to figure out how much data was actually written.

Third, you pass the address of the data you want the File Manager to write to disk. Because you are passing an address and the call may move memory, make sure that the data is locked or nonrelocatable.

Reading Data

Reading data is the converse of writing. You must ensure that the mark is at the correct location. Then you call `FSRead()`. You pass the same three parameters: file ID number, address of a byte count, and address of a data buffer.

In this case, the data buffer is where the File Manager puts the data that it reads from the file. It must be locked. You'd better make sure you don't have anything there that you care about, because the File Manager will stomp on it.

Closing a File

To close a file, call `FSClose()`. You pass the file ID number, typically obtained from a call to `FSpOpenDF()`. The File Manager does the rest. However, there are two points to consider:

- First, you should close the file even if the read or write operations failed. It is a bad idea to leave open files hanging around.

- Second, *do not close a closed file*. Attempting to close an already closed file is a certified Very Bad Thing. It can cause permanent loss of data on the volume. So if the call to `FSpOpenDF()` failed, don't close the file.

> You might want to set the file ID number to zero right away if `FSpOpenDF()` fails. That way if you inadvertently call `FSClose()`, the call will fail. A valid reference number to a file path is always greater than zero.

What you do after calling `FSClose()` depends upon how much success you have had and what operation you are closing down.

If you have *successfully written* data to a file, you should call `FlushVol()` to update the catalog information for the file. You should pass nil for the name string (volume names may be identical), and use the volume reference number from the file spec for the file you just closed.

If you have *unsuccessfully written* data to a file, do not call `FlushVol()`. You should just close the file.

If you have *read* data from a file, do not call `FlushVol()`. Reading a file does not change the volume or catalog information.

The call to `FSClose()` also returns an error value. If you had an earlier error writing or reading data, you might want to preserve that error, or ignore any possible error return from `FSClose()`.

Swapping Files

Consider this scenario. The user wants to save changes to an existing file. You open the file and start writing data. Then an error occurs. You bail out of the operation and return an error to the user. Friendly? Not really.

You started writing data into the original file. Because an error occurred, the integrity of the original file has been destroyed. Data is lost forever! That's not very friendly. In fact, it's a Bad Thing.

There is an easy way to avoid this problem. Instead of overwriting the original file, save the new data in a temporary file. If no error occurs while creating the temporary file, you call `FSpExchangeFiles()`. You provide two file specs. The first is the new temporary file you just created. The second is the original file you want to replace (see Figure 15.7)

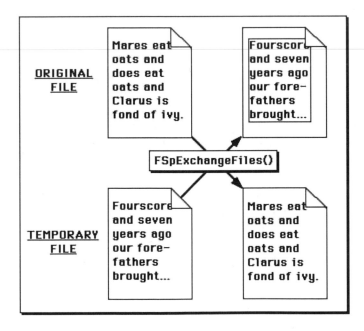

Figure 15.7 Swapping files

This call performs a little sleight of hand. It swaps the catalog information for the two files. After you make the call, the catalog information for the original file points to the new data. The temporary file points to the old data. You then delete the temporary file. Pretty slick.

Don't replace the original data until the new data is complete and secure. `FSpExchangeFiles()` swaps both the data and resource forks, so make the exchange after you have written all the data for the file in both forks.

The only limitation is that both the temporary and the original files must be on the same volume. You can make sure they are on the same volume by creating the temporary file in the temporary items folder of the volume with the original file. How to do that is discussed a little later in this chapter.

To delete a file, call `FSpDelete()`. You provide the file spec. The file must be closed before you can delete it.

Although it takes a long time to explain all the details, using the File Manager to manipulate a data fork is really quite straightforward. You get the file spec, create the file if necessary (perhaps a temporary file if you are replacing an original), open the data fork, make sure the mark is at the correct position, read or write the data, and close the file. If you write data successfully, you also write the volume information to disk. If you created a temporary file, you swap it with the original file. Check for errors each step of the way and you'll be safe.

Working with the Resource Fork

Reading and writing to the resource fork is both simpler and more restrictive than working with the data fork.

It is simpler because you don't have to worry about byte counts, or where in the fork to look for data. The Resource Manager takes care of that for you when you specify the resource by type and ID number.

When writing data to the resource fork you need to perform the following tasks:

- Create a resource fork
- Open the resource fork
- Write data to the fork
- Close the resource fork

These tasks—and how to read data from the resource fork—will be discussed in just a bit. But before that, there is an important question to answer. "What do I put in the resource fork?"

What to Save in the Resource Fork

Think about the nature of the data you are saving. Is it a resource? A resource is typically a block of data of known size with a definable structure.

For example, you may want to save the position of a window. That's clearly a definable amount of data (a single point) that will be the same size for every window. This data is a good candidate to store in the resource fork.

The data may vary in size, but can still be structured in such a way that it makes sense to treat it as a resource. For example, a communications software package might store a list of phone numbers in a resource. The list may vary in size as the user adds or removes elements, but the elements in the list are consistent.

By contrast, the content of a text document is not a resource. The text is an amorphous block of data of varying length created by the user. Typically, if the user creates the data, it goes in the data fork.

There are no absolute rules about what kind of data goes in which fork. Use your common sense, and do what fits best in your application. Keep in mind, however, that for all its flexibility and ease of use, the Resource Manager was not designed as a data storage engine. There are some limitations.

A resource fork may have no more than about 2700 resources in it. In addition, to find the requested resource, the Resource Manager searches from front to back. In other words, the Resource Manager accesses resources in linear fashion (see Figure 15.8). That means the more resources you have in a file, the slower data access becomes. After you have more than a few hundred resources, performance may no longer be acceptable.

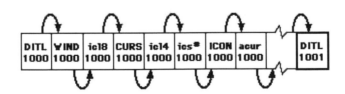

GetResource('DITL', 1001);

Figure 15.8 Linear search

Writing to the Resource Fork

Before you write, make sure the fork exists. You should already have a file spec—typically from the standard put-file dialog. Call `FSpCreateResFile()`. You pass the address of the file spec for the new file, the application's creator code, the file type code, and the script system in which the file name should be established. You typically get the file spec from the `StandardPutFile()` call. The standard file reply structure has the script system for the new file name. Lacking that, you can use the constant `smSystemScript`. These parameters should match those used in any call to `FSpCreate()` that might have already created this file.

This is a Resource Manager call. You must call `ResError()` to determine whether an error occurred. If the error is a duplicate file error, you can ignore it. The purpose of this call is to create a resource fork if it does not already exist. If it already exists, you're all set. Do not ignore any errors other than the duplicate file error.

Once you know the resource fork exists, call `FSpOpenResFile()`. Like the call to open the data fork, you provide the file spec and the read/write permission. This call returns the file ID for the access path to the resource fork.

This is a Resource Manager call. You must call `ResError()` to determine whether an error occurred.

After you have the fork open, you can add data to it. Refer to Chapter 4 for the details. Typically you call `AddResource()` to add data to the file's resource map in memory, and then call `UpdateResFile()` to write the resource map and resource data to disk. You can also write a specific changed resource to disk with `WriteResource()`. Remember to call `ResError()` each step of the way. Don't let minor problems mature into major disasters.

When you are through with the resource fork, call `CloseResFile()`. You specify the file ID number, typically obtained from a call to `FSpOpenResFile()`. This call updates the resource fork of the file if you have changed any resources.

Reading from the Resource Fork

Reading from the resource fork is simple. You may need to open the fork. The Resource Manager takes care of your application's resource fork, but you may want to read resources from your document files. Call `FSpOpenResFile()` as detailed previously.

To get the data, call `GetResource()` or `Get1Resource()`. You provide the resource type and ID number, and either call returns a handle to the data. Refer to Chapter 4 for more details if you need a refresher on this topic.

If you opened the resource fork yourself, you should close it by calling `CloseResFile()`. You provide the file ID number.

> Don't close your application's resource fork! Your program will die a horrible death if you do. If you call `CloseResFile()` with a zero—the System resource fork—the Toolbox simply ignores your request. You cannot close the System resource fork.

Other File Manager Tasks

When you work with the File Manager, there are two other tasks that you are likely to perform. You will work with various standard folders maintained by the File Manager, and you will need to get information about files.

Using System Directories

Under System 7 the File Manager maintains a series of directories—folders—for specific purposes. Table 15.6 lists the various kinds of folders. You may need to put a file inside one of these folders, especially the temporary items or preferences folders. How do you find the folder?

Call `FindFolder()`. You provide several parameters. The first is the volume reference number for the volume on which to look. If you want to look on the startup volume, pass the constant `kOnSystemDisk`. The second parameter is the folder type. The possible types are listed in Table 15.6.

The third parameter tells the File Manager whether to create the folder if it doesn't exist. The possible values are `kCreateFolder` and `kDontCreateFolder`.

The fourth and fifth parameters are the addresses where the File Manager puts the volume reference and directory ID of the desired folder (after it finds or creates the folder for you). Don't rely on the information if an error occurs.

Table 15.6: Folder Types

Constant	Value	Description
kPreferencesFolderType	'pref'	preferences
kTemporaryFolderType	'temp'	temporary items
kSystemFolderType	'macs'	System folder
kDesktopFolderType	'desk'	Desktop folder

Constant	Value	Description
kTrashFolderType	'trsh'	trash
kPrintMonitorDocsFolderType	'prnt'	spooled print files
kStartupFolderType	'strt'	startup items
kAppleMenuFolderType	'amnu'	Apple menu items
kControlPanelFolderType	'ctrl'	control panels
kExtensionFolderType	'extn'	extensions
kFontsFolderType	'font'	fonts

To work with files you use file specs. To create a file spec based on the information from `FindFolder()`, call `FSMakeFSSpec()`. You pass the volume reference number and directory ID that you get from `FindFolder()`. You also specify the name of the new file. The fourth parameter is the address of a file spec to receive the results of the call.

You should always call `FSMakeFSSpec()` to build a file specification. Don't fill in the fields yourself. Whenever the Toolbox provides a function like this, use it. You never know when things might change. If you use the Toolbox call, your code is far less likely to break in the future.

After you have the file spec, you are on your way.

Getting File Info

To get information about a file, call `FSpGetFInfo()`. You provide the file spec and the address of a Finder information record. Table 15.7 lists all the fields of an `FInfo` record and their purposes.

Table 15.7: FInfo Record Fields

Field	Data Type	Description
fdType	OSType	the type of the file
fdCreator	OSType	file's creator
fdFlags	unsigned short	has bundle, invisible, and so on
fdLocation	Point	file icon's location in folder
fdFldr	short	folder containing file

Most often, you want to examine a file's type to see if it is appropriate for your program.

Lab 15.1 Saving a File

Saving a file frequently requires that you write data to the data fork and resources to the resource fork. The approach you follow in this lab gathers all the data into one block and writes it as a single unit to the data fork. You write resources one at a time to the resource fork. This strategy conforms to the different approaches used by the File Manager and Resource Manager. However, it is possible to write data to the data fork in separate blocks, as long as you keep track of the precise bytes where everything belongs. For the resource fork, the Resource Manager takes care of that for you.

The menu dispatch code for saving files has been provided. Let's take a quick look at it so you know what's happening. When the user chooses the Save item in the File menu, control passes from `EasyMenuDispatch()` through `FileMenuHook()` to `EasyHandleFileMenu()` to `EasySave()`. Examine that code.

In `EasySave()` the EasyApp shell determines whether there is already a file associated with the window. If there is, it sends the window a `DoSave` message. Otherwise it sends a `DoSaveAs` message. In response to the `DoSave` message, the window should save all necessary data and resources. In response to the `DoSaveAs` message, the window should use the standard put-file dialog to get a file specification from the user, and *then* save all the necessary data and resources.

In this lab I make a distinction between "saving" and "writing" information. Saving implies managing the process of gathering the data and preparing it for writing. Writing means actually sending the data to disk.

In this lab you:

- Display the put-file dialog
- Save data and resources to a file
- Save data to the data fork
- Flatten data for the data fork
- Write data to the data fork
- Save resources to the resource fork

- Write resources to the resource fork

- Ask the user to save changes

Use your code from the previous lab as the starting point for your work in this lab.

Step 1: Display the put-file dialog

Modify: EasyPutFile() in file.c

This is an EasyApp utility function to display and manage the standard put-file dialog. It receives the window pointer for the window involved, and the address of a file spec where the function can store the user-selected file specification.

```
StandardFileReply reply;

error = EasyCheckMemory(kDialogMemory);
if (error)
{
    return error;
}

EasyGetIndString(kSaveDocStringID, 1, prompt);

GetWTitle(macWindow, defaultName);

StandardPutFile(prompt, defaultName, &reply);
if (!reply.sfGood)
{
    error = userCanceledErr;
    return error;
}

/* store result for caller */
*theFile = reply.sfFile;

return error;
```

You preflight the operation by calling EasyCheckMemory(). You also provide a prompt string for the dialog and a default name for the file. You call EasyGetIndString() to get the prompt. In the EasyApp resources, this string is "Save document as:". You call **GetWTitle()** to get the window title to use as the default file name.

Then you call **StandardPutFile()** and provide the prompt, the default name, and the address of a StandardFileReply structure. On return, you check the sfGood field to see whether the user canceled the dialog. If so, you bail out. Otherwise you copy the file spec from reply and store the result for the caller.

Step 2: Save data and resources to a file

Modify: BaseSave() in windowProc.c

This function responds to the DoSave message. This is the default EasyApp behavior, but it serves just fine for EasyPuzzle. It has several tasks. This function creates a new or temporary file, writes data to the data fork, writes data to the resource fork, swaps files if using a temporary file, and cleans up. It delegates most of these responsibilities to other functions, most of which you write in subsequent steps in this lab. Therefore, BaseSave() is really a handler that manages the saving process.

```
FSSpec      newFile;

/* create a new file, or find out if file already exists */
error = FSpCreate(theFile, g.creator, easyWindow->fileType,
                  smSystemScript);
if (error == dupFNErr)  /* file exists, make temp file */
{
  /* make a file spec for it */
  error = EasyCreateTempFileSpec(theFile, &newFile);
  if (error)
  {
    return error;
  }

  /* create the temporary file */
  error = FSpCreate(&newFile, g.creator,
                    easyWindow->fileType, smSystemScript);
  if (error)
  {
    return error;
  }
  replacing = true;   /* swap when done */
}

else if (error)  /* error other than duplicate file */
{   /* we're outta here */
  return error;
}
else  /* no temporary file, we created new file already */
{
  newFile = *theFile;
}

/* newFile may be new or temporary file, doesn't matter */

/* write the data fork */
error = easyWindow->DoWriteData(macWindow, &newFile);
if (error)
{
  FSpDelete(&newFile);  /* delete file */
  return error;
}
```

```
/* make a resource fork */
FSpCreateResFile(&newFile, g.creator, easyWindow->fileType,
                 smSystemScript);
error = ResError();
if (error && error != dupFNErr)  /* if exists, no problem */
{
  FSpDelete(&newFile);
  return error;
}

/* write the resource fork */
error = easyWindow->DoWriteResource(macWindow, &newFile);
if (error)
{
  FSpDelete(&newFile);
  return error;
}

/* if replacing an old file, swap "newFile" for original */
if (replacing)
{
  /* exchange, if no error, newFile becomes the old file */
  error = FSpExchangeFiles(&newFile, theFile);

  FSpDelete(&newFile);  /* delete file, error or not */
  if (error)
  {
    return error;
  }
}

/* if not replacing, newFile is original, don't delete */

/* all okay, set this window's title, spec, and hasFile */
SetWTitle(macWindow, theFile->name);
easyWindow->fileSpec = *theFile;
easyWindow->hasFile = true;

/* this is now a clean window */
easyWindow->changed = false;

return error;
```

First you create a file by calling **FSpCreate()**. If the file already exists, you get a dupFNErr. In that case you create a temporary file. You call EasyCreateTempFileSpec() to make a file spec. That function is provided for you. Then you create the temporary file with **FSpCreate()** and set the replacing flag to true.

If you get any error besides a duplicate file, you bail out.

If there is no error at all, you set newFile to match theFile. From here on, newFile is either a new file or the temporary file you created, it doesn't matter which. What is important is that newFile is not an existing file.

You then send the window a DoWriteData message to write the data fork. If that fails, you call FSpDelete() to delete the new file and bail out.

Next you create the resource fork and check for errors. If there is no problem, you send the window a DoWriteResource message. If that fails you delete the new file and return.

If you are using a temporary file, you call FSpExchangeFiles() to swap the temporary and the existing files. Then you delete the temporary file. If you are not replacing, you don't delete anything because newFile is the only file around, it is the final data.

Finally, you do some clean up. You set the window title to the new file name, attach the window to the file, set the hasFile flag to true, and mark the window as unchanged.

Step 3: Save data to the data fork

Modify: BaseWriteData() in windowProc.c

This function manages sending the necessary data to the data fork of the file. It gathers the data together and sends it to disk. It receives the window pointer and the file spec for the file.

```
long       numberBytes;

error = easyWindow->DoFlattenWindow(macWindow, &buffer);
if (error)
{
  return error;
}

EasyLockHandle(buffer);
numberBytes = GetHandleSize(buffer);

error = FSpOpenDF(theFile, fsRdWrPerm, &fileID);
if (error)
{
  EasyDisposeHandle(&buffer);
  return error;
}

error = EasyWriteFile(fileID, 0, numberBytes, *buffer);
if(error)
{
```

```
    FSClose(fileID);
  }
  else
  {
    error = FSClose(fileID);
    if(!error)
    {
      error = FlushVol(nil, theFile->vRefNum);
    }
  }

  EasyDisposeHandle(&buffer);
  return error;
```

The first thing you do is get the data to write. You send the window a DoFlattenWindow message. This call returns a handle to all the data in a single block in a local variable named buffer. You then lock the handle and get its size.

You call FSpOpenDF() to open the data fork. If there is no problem, you call EasyWriteFile() to write the data. You provide the file path ID, where to start writing, how many bytes to write, and where the data is located in memory.

If there is an error, you call FSClose() and ignore any potential error because you want to return the original error to the user.

If there is no error, you call FSClose() and check for error. If there is no error, you call FlushVol() to write the directory data to disk.

When you are all through, you dispose of the data buffer.

Step 4: Flatten data for the data fork

Modify: FlattenPuzzleWindow() in puzzleWindow.c

This function responds to the DoFlattenWindow message. Its task is to convert data associated with the window into a single block, nothing more. If the data is already in a single block, the task is easy. This function has no idea where the data is going, and doesn't care.

The BaseFlattenWindow() behavior does nothing because a generic EasyApp window has no contents. The puzzle window has data, and that's what you need to flatten to save to disk. Make sure you modify FlattenPuzzleWindow() and not BaseFlattenWindow().

```
OSErr       error;
*result = RecoverHandle((Ptr)easyWindow->windowData);

error = HandToHand(result);
if (error)
```

```
{
    *result = nil;
}

return error;
```

First, you call RecoverHandle() and store the handle in the address pointed to by result. The puzzle data associated with the window was originally allocated as a handle. You moved it high in the heap, locked it permanently, dereferenced it to get a pointer to the data, and stuffed the pointer into the windowData field. That pointer still has a handle, but you don't have that information any more because you didn't preserve it. You can call RecoverHandle() to get the handle back.

After you get the handle, you call HandToHand() to make a copy of the data. This call is a trifle dicey, so pay attention. You provide the address of a handle to an *existing* relocatable block—in this case the puzzle data. The Memory Manager makes a new block, copies the data, and returns the handle to the new block *in the same address you passed in*, overwriting and destroying your original handle—not the original data, just the original handle.

When you're all through, you return to the caller. It now has a *copy* of the window data in the address pointed to by result. The caller is responsible for disposing of this new block. You did that in the previous step when you disposed of the data buffer.

Step 5: Write data to the data fork

Modify: EasyWriteFile() in file.c

After all that work setting things up, actually writing the data is anticlimactic and easy. This EasyApp utility function receives the file path, the number of bytes from the start of the file to write, the number of bytes to write, and the address of the data.

```
OSErr       error;

error = SetFPos(fileID, fsFromStart, offset);
if (error)
{
    return error;
}

error = FSWrite(fileID, &numBytes, buffer);

return(error);
```

You call SetFPos() to set the file mark to the correct location. Then you call FSWrite() to write the data.

Now that you have taken care of the data fork, it's time to turn your attention to the resource fork.

Step 6: Save resources to the resource fork

Modify: `WritePuzzleResource()` in puzzleWindow.c

In addition to the puzzle data, each puzzle has a picture attached to it. When you save the file, you save the picture as a resource.

This function responds to the `DoWriteResource` message for EasyPuzzle. It is analogous to `BaseWriteData()` that you wrote in Step 3, but simpler because the Resource Manager handles most of the details (like how many bytes are in the resource). The existing code calls `BaseWriteResource()`, which at this point does nothing.

```
error = BaseWriteResource(macWindow, data);
if (error == kNoResourceError)
{
    error = noErr;
}

fileID = FSpOpenResFile(theFile, fsRdWrPerm);
error = ResError();
if (error)  /* failed to open */
{
  return error;
}

error = EasyAddResource(fileID, (Handle)thePicture,
            kPictType, kPuzzleBaseID);
if (error)
{
    CloseResFile(fileID);
    return error;
}

CloseResFile(fileID);
error = ResError();

return error;
```

First you open the resource fork by calling **FSpOpenResFile()** with the correct permission. If there is no error, you call `EasyAddResource()` specifying the file, the data, the resource type, and the resource ID that you want to use. If there is an error, you call **CloseResFile()** and ignore any potential error because you want to return the original error to the user.

If there is no error, you still call **CloseResFile()** to close the file, but be sure to check for error.

475

Step 7:   Write resources to the resource fork

Modify: `EasyAddResource()` in file.c

This is an EasyApp utility function to add a specified resource to the resource fork of a file. To accomplish this task, you must use the correct file, delete any duplicate resource, add the new resource to the file's resource map, and then write the resource to disk.

This function receives four parameters: the file ID specifying the file to use, a handle to the data for the resource, the resource type you want it to be, and the resource ID number you want to use. The existing code ensures that the handle is a valid, nonresource handle. It gets the handle's state and then makes it nonpurgeable. Then you go to work.

```c
HNoPurge(resHandle);

/* save the current resource file and use the one we want */
saveResFile = CurResFile();
UseResFile(fileID);
error = ResError();
if (error)
{
  HSetState(resHandle, state);
  UseResFile(saveResFile);
  return error;
}

/* does the resource already exist */
SetResLoad(false);
oldHandle = EasyGet1Resource(fileID, resType, resID);
SetResLoad(true);

/* if it does, dump it */
if (oldHandle)
{
  RemoveResource(oldHandle);
  error = ResError();
  if (error)
  {
    HSetState(resHandle, state);
    UseResFile(saveResFile);
    return error;
  }
  DisposeHandle(oldHandle);
}

/* add the resource to the file's resource map */
AddResource(resHandle, resType, resID, "\p");
error = ResError();
if (error)
```

```
{
  HSetState(resHandle, state);
  UseResFile(saveResFile);
  return error;
}

/* make sure everything is updated to disk */
UpdateResFile(fileID);
error = ResError();

/* restore state */
DetachResource(resHandle);
UseResFile(saveResFile);
HSetState(resHandle, state);
return error;
```

First, you call `CurResFile()` to save the existing resource file, followed by a call to `UseResFile()` to specify the file you want to use. Then you check for error. If there is an error, you restore the state to what it was before the function was called.

You then check to see if this resource already exists in this file. If it does, you remove it. You don't really want to load the old resource into memory, you just want to see if it is there. You call `SetResLoad()` with `false` as a parameter to prevent the resource from loading into memory needlessly. Then you call `EasyGet1Resource()` to get the resource handle. Next you call `SetResLoad()` with `true` as a parameter to turn resource loading back on. This is vital because the System relies on it being on.

If the resource already exists, you call `RemoveResource()` to remove the handle from the resource map. This does not dispose of the memory. To release the memory, call `DisposeHandle()`. Do not call `ReleaseResource()` because the handle is not a resource handle after a call to `RemoveResource()`.

Next, you add the new resource to the file's resource map. You call `AddResource()` to do that, and check for error. This call makes the handle a resource handle.

To write everything to disk, you call `UpdateResFile()` and check for error.

Finally, you restore things to what they were before any of this happened. You call `DetachResource()` to restore the original handle to being a nonresource handle—which was its state on entry—and `UseResFile()` to restore the original resource file. The existing code calls `HSetState()` to restore the handle's purgeable condition.

Step 8: Ask the user to save changes

Modify: EasyClose() in menus.c

When the user closes a window, the window may have unsaved changes. This may be intentional or unintentional. Now that you can save a file, the polite thing to do is to alert the user to the fact that they are discarding changes.

EasyApp keeps track of whether a file has changed in the Easy window changed field. This function receives a parameter named saveOptions that tells the function how to behave. It should save changes always, never save changes, or ask the user whether to save changes.

```
if (!easyWindow->changed)
{
  easyWindow->DoClose(macWindow, (void *)nil);
  return noErr;
}

switch(saveOptions)
{
  case kAlwaysSave:
    error = EasySave(macWindow);
    if (error)
    {
      return error;
    }
    break;

  case kNeverSave:
    break;

  default: /* ask user */
    response = EasyAskUser(macWindow);
    switch(response)
    {
      case ok:
        error = EasySave(macWindow);
        if (error)
        {
          return error;
        }
        break;

      case cancel:
        error = userCanceledErr;
        return error;
        break;
    }
}

easyWindow->DoClose(macWindow, (void *)nil);
```

You switch based on the saveOptions value. If it is kAlwaysSave, you do that. If there is an error, you return without closing the file. If it is kNeverSave, you close the file without warning.

Otherwise the option is to ask the user. In that case, you call EasyAskUser(), a function provided for you that displays an alert asking the user whether to save, cancel, or discard the changes. You switch on the response.

If the user clicks the Save button, you save the changes. If there is a problem, you return without closing the file. If the user clicks the Cancel button, you return userCanceledErr. This terminates the close operation but does not cause an error alert to appear.

There is no case for the Discard button, because in that case you simply close the file. The existing code closes the file by sending the window a DoClose message.

Step 9: Run the application
Modify: none

Save your work and run the project using the debugger. When the debugger window appears, launch EasyPuzzle and create a new puzzle window.

EasyPuzzle does not save the pieces or their positions, although you could add that feature if you wanted to. EasyPuzzle just saves the puzzle picture and its color. Change the color of the puzzle border, and choose the Save item in the File menu.

Because there is no file attached to this untitled document, the standard put-file dialog appears. Notice the folder where you are saving the file, change it if you wish. Enter a file name and click the Save button. The put-file dialog disappears, and EasyApp saves the file to disk.

Now change the color of the puzzle border, and then choose the Save item again. This time, the put-file dialog does not appear because this window is connected to an existing file. EasyPuzzle just saves the changes.

Finally, change the color one more time, and then try to close the window. When you do, an alert appears asking you whether you want to save the changes. EasyPuzzle reminds you that you have unsaved changes and protects you from inadvertently throwing them away. Save the changes or not as you wish, and quit the application.

You cannot open the file just yet. You write the code to open a file in the next lab. However, you can go to the Finder and see the file you saved. If you're really curious, use ResEdit to open the new file. There should be a PICT resource with ID number 2000—the puzzle picture.

Now that you have a file, let's write the code to open the file.

Lab 15.2 Opening a File

This lab is the converse of Lab 15.1. In Lab 15.1 you gathered up the data and resources and sent them to disk. In this lab you read the data and resources from disk, and display them in a window.

There is a twist, however. We want to add a significant feature to EasyPuzzle, the ability to open *any* PICT file and read the picture inside it. That's going to complicate matters slightly, as you'll see when we get into the code.

Like Lab 15.1, the menu dispatch code is provided for you. The process starts when the user chooses the Open item from the File menu. Control passes from `EasyMenuDispatch()` through `FileMenuHook()` to `EasyHandleFileMenu()` to `OpenHook()`. Examine that code. The `OpenHook()` function gives you the opportunity to override the file opening process, which is what you're going to do in this lab.

In the default EasyApp, `OpenHook()` calls `EasyOpen()`. For EasyPuzzle it calls `OpenPuzzleFile()`. That's where you begin the lab. You override the file-opening process because EasyPuzzle opens more than one kind of file—its own puzzle files and PICT files.

In this lab we make a distinction between "opening" and "reading" information. Opening implies managing the process of gathering the data and converting it into a form the application can use. Reading means actually getting the data from disk.

In this lab you:

- Open a puzzle or a PICT file
- Open a puzzle file
- Open the data fork of a file
- Read data from the data fork
- Unflatten data into a window

- Add a new message to an Easy window

- Import a PICT file

Use your code from the previous lab as the starting point for your work in this lab.

Step 1:   Open a puzzle or PICT file

Modify: OpenPuzzleFile() In *puzzleFile.c*

Because EasyPuzzle supports more than one file type, you cannot rely on the EasyOpen() function inside EasyApp. However, you don't have to completely reinvent the wheel. You just want to give it a different spin. Therefore, when you first look at the OpenPuzzleFile() function, it is an exact duplicate of EasyOpen(). In this step you make some minor modifications to accommodate EasyPuzzle's particular needs.

There are two places where you make changes. The first is in the acceptable file types to display in the get-file dialog.

```
if (theFile->name[0] == 0)   /* no file specified yet */
{
  theTypes[0] = g.defaultType;
/*
  numberTypes = 1;
*/

  theTypes[1] = kPictType;
  numberTypes = 2;

  error = EasyGetFile(theTypes, numberTypes, theFile);
  {
    return error;
  }
}
```

The g.defaultType variable is set in InitPuzzleApp() to be kPuzzleType. That code is fine. You comment out the line of code that sets numberTypes. You specify a second file type as acceptable—kPictType—and set numberTypes to 2.

The existing code then calls EasyGetFile(). This function is provided for you. It is similar to the EasyPutFile() function you wrote in the previous lab. EasyGetFile() displays and manages the standard get-file dialog. The get-file dialog will display both puzzle files and PICT files. The user may select either type of file to open.

The existing code then determines if the file is already open. The EasyAlreadyOpen() function is provided for you. If the file is open, it just brings that window to the front. Otherwise, the code calls EasyGetFileType() to get the file type for the file the user selected. This function is also provided for you. The user may have selected a puzzle file or a PICT file. Then the code calls EasyNew() to make a new window of the correct type. You have already written that code. Then the existing code gets the window pointer and Easy window pointer for the new window.

The second place where you modify the original EasyOpen() code has to do with actually opening the file after the user has selected it. You must identify the kind of file being opened.

```
/* tell the window to open this file and read data */
if (thisType == kPuzzleType)
{
  error = easyWindow->DoOpen(macWindow, theFile);
}
else  /* importing from a PICT file */
{
  MoreProcsPtr  moreProcs =
                  (MoreProcsPtr)easyWindow->moreProcs;

  error = moreProcs->DoImport(macWindow, theFile);
}

if (error)
{
  *newWindow = nil;
  easyWindow->DoClose(macWindow, nil);
  return error;
}

/* size the new window */
easyWindow->DoResize(macWindow, nil);

return error;
```

If it is a puzzle file, you send a DoOpen message to the window. If it is a PICT file, you send a DoImport message to the window. DoImport is not a standard EasyApp message. This is a new message created as part of the puzzle window initializing process, and is assigned to the moreProcs field of the Easy window structure. You will set this up in a subsequent step in this lab.

Either way, after the existing code checks for errors, you then send the window a DoResize message to adjust the size of the window to fit the picture.

Step 2: Open a puzzle file

Modify: BaseOpen() in windowProcs.c

In this step you write BaseOpen(), the default EasyApp function for opening a file. It serves just fine for EasyPuzzle. This function's tasks are to read data from the data fork, read resources from the resource fork, set the window's title and handle other details. This function receives the window pointer for the new window, and a pointer to the file spec for the file to be opened.

```
OSErr       error       = noErr;

/* read the data fork */
error = easyWindow->DoReadData(macWindow, theFile);
if (error)
{
  return error;
}

/* read the resource fork */
error = easyWindow->DoReadResource(macWindow, theFile);
if (error)
{
  return error;
}

/* set this window's title, spec, and hasFile */
SetWTitle(macWindow, theFile->name);
easyWindow->fileSpec = *theFile;
easyWindow->hasFile = true;
easyWindow->changed = false;

return error;
```

This code is straightforward. You send a DoReadData message to the window and check for error. You send a DoReadResource message to the window and check for error. If all is well, you set the window's title to the name of the file, attach the window to the file, and mark it as an unchanged window.

Step 3: Open the data fork of a file

Modify: BaseReadData() in windowProcs.c

Once again, the default EasyApp behavior serves EasyPuzzle just fine. The tasks for this function are to open the data fork, determine how many bytes to read, read them all, close the file, and unflatten the data.

```
Handle      buffer      = nil;

error = FSpOpenDF(theFile, fsRdPerm, &fileID);
if (error)
{
  return error;
}

error = GetEOF(fileID, &fileSize);
```

```
  if (error)
  {
    FSClose(fileID);
    return error;
  }

  error = EasyAllocateHandle(fileSize, &buffer);
  if (error)
  {
    FSClose(fileID);
    return error;
  }

  EasyLockHandle(buffer);

  error = EasyReadFile(fileID, 0, fileSize, *buffer);

  FSClose(fileID);
  if (error)
  {
    EasyDisposeHandle(&buffer);
    return error;
  }

  error = easyWindow->DoUnflattenWindow(macWindow, buffer);

  EasyDisposeHandle(&buffer);

  return error;
```

You call **FSpOpenDF()** to open the data fork, and check for error. Then you call **GetEOF()** to determine how many bytes are in the file, and check for error.

After you have this information, you call EasyAllocateHandle() to allocate memory to hold the data you are about to read. You also lock the handle.

Then you call EasyReadFile() to read the data. You write this function in the next step. Then you close the file by calling **FSClose()**, and check for error.

If you have successfully retrieved data, you send the window a DoUnflattenWindow message, and dispose of the data buffer. The function that responds to the DoUnflattenWindow message is responsible for making a copy of the data for the window. You write this function in Step 5.

Step 4: Read data from the data fork

Modify: EasyReadFile() in file.c

Like writing the data, actually reading the data from disk is simple. This function receives the file path ID, the starting position, the number of bytes, and the address of the data buffer.

```
OSErr   error = noErr;

error = SetFPos(fileID, fsFromStart, offset);
if (error)
{
  return error;
}

error = FSRead(fileID, &numBytes, buffer);

return(error);
```

You call **SetFPos()** to set the file mark to the correct location. Then you call **FSRead()** to read the data into the buffer.

Step 5: Unflatten data into a window

Modify: UnflattenPuzzleWindow() in puzzleWindow.c

This is where the real work happens. You receive the data in one lump. You make no assumptions about where the data comes from. In addition, you can make no assumptions about the current state of the window. You may be putting data in a new window, or replacing data in an existing window—for example, if the user chooses the Revert item in the File menu.

The BaseUnflattenWindow() behavior does nothing because a generic EasyApp window has no contents. The puzzle window has data, and that's what you need to unflatten to display in the window.

```
Handle       newData, oldData;

newData = buffer;
error = HandToHand(&newData);
if (error)
{
  return error;
}

DisposePuzzleContents(macWindow);
oldData = RecoverHandle ((Ptr) easyWindow->windowData);
EasyDisposeHandle (&oldData);

EasyLockHandle(newData);

easyWindow->windowData = (long) *newData;

SetPuzzlePicture(easyWindow, nil);
SetPuzzleFirstPiece(easyWindow, nil);
SetPuzzleLastPiece(easyWindow, nil);
SetPuzzlePeek(easyWindow, nil);
```

485

```
SetPuzzleScramble(easyWindow, nil);
SetPuzzleSolutionRgn(easyWindow, nil);
SetPuzzleBorderRgn(easyWindow, nil);

return error;
```

Remember, you must make no assumptions about where the data came from, or what's going to happen to it. So, the first thing you do is make a copy of the data for yourself by calling `HandToHand()`. Remember the warning about `HandToHand()` in the previous lab. You don't want to trash the existing `buffer` handle, so you make a copy of it and use that when you call `HandToHand()`.

You then dump any existing window contents. You call `DisposePuzzleContents()` to take care of that, get the existing puzzle data structure, and release that memory.

Then you move the new data high in memory and lock it permanently. You put a pointer to this data in the `windowData` field of the Easy window structure.

However, all is not finished. When you write the data, much of it contains various handles and pointers that refer to locations in memory. None of that information is accurate any more. The next lines of code call puzzle data accessors to clean out all those invalid handles and pointers. You recreate the necessary information when you get the picture from the resource fork and resize the window.

As for the resource fork, that code is provided for you. You have already worked extensively with the Resource Manager. Examine `ReadPuzzleResource()`, the function that responds to the `DoReadResource` message for EasyPuzzle.

This completes the process of opening a puzzle file. What about opening a PICT file?

Step 6: Add a new message to an Easy window

Modify: `InitPuzzleWindow()` in puzzleWindow.c

We would like to allow the user to import data from a PICT file. Recall from Step 1 that there are two file types supported, puzzle and PICT. If the user opens a PICT file, `OpenPuzzleFile()` sends a `DoImport` message to the window. In this step you add that message to the Easy window vocabulary.

A puzzle version of an Easy window has one additional `windowProc`. The `MoreProcs` structure is declared in puzzle.h.

```
typedef struct
{
  WindowProc     DoImport;  /* for importing PICT files */

} MoreProcs, *MoreProcsPtr;
```

When you create a puzzle window, you allocate memory for this structure and put a pointer to the structure in the moreProcs field of the EasyWindow record. Then you can retrieve that pointer and send the new message, like you did in Step 1.

Here's the code that sets up the new message.

```
easyWindow->DoScrollWindow     = (WindowProc)EmptyProc;

error = EasyAllocateHandle( sizeof(MoreProcs),
                            &myProcsHandle);
if (error)
{
  return error;
}

EasyLockHandle(myProcsHandle);

myProcs = (MoreProcsPtr)*myProcsHandle;
easyWindow->moreProcs = (long) myProcs;

myProcs->DoImport = (WindowProc)ImportPuzzlePICT;

error = EasyAllocateHandle( sizeof(PuzzleData), &myPuzzleHandle);
```

You allocate memory for the MoreProcs structure, move it high in the heap, and lock it permanently. Then you dereference it and keep the pointer in the local variable myProcs. You save that pointer in the moreProcs field of the Easy window. Then you initialize the DoImport message so that it contains the function pointer for ImportPuzzlePICT(). This is the function that responds to the DoImport message sent by OpenPuzzleFile() when the user opens a PICT file.

You have just added a new message to the window's vocabulary. You could have added several, if that was necessary. Although the EasyApp vocabulary is fairly comprehensive, this is a good example of how to extend it further.

Step 7: Import a PICT file

Study: ImportPuzzlePICT() in puzzleWindow.c

You have already written BaseReadData(). ImportPuzzlePICT() is so much like BaseReadData() that we're just going to walk through it rather than write it.

In a PICT file, the picture is stored in the data fork of the file. However, the defined file format for a PICT file requires that the first 512 bytes of the file be reserved for application data.

Look at the code for ImportPuzzlePICT(). When it gets the file size, it subtracts kPictFileHeaderSize bytes (512 bytes) from the size of the file. When it calls EasyReadFile() to read the data, it tells the function to start reading at the kPictFileHeaderSize byte, so EasyReadFile() skips the first 512 bytes and reads the actual picture data.

Finally, ImportPuzzlePICT() does not send the window a DoUnflattenWindow message. That message is intended for puzzle data, not pictures. It calls SetPuzzlePicture() to set this puzzle's picture to the data just read.

That's all you have to do to import PICT data. The carefully designed window-creation code does all the rest—setting up the various puzzle data structures, resizing the window, and so forth.

Step 8: Run the application
  Modify: none

Save your work and run the project using the debugger. When the debugger window appears, launch EasyApp.

Choose the Open item in the File menu and open the puzzle file that you saved at the end of the previous lab. It should be the same color as it was when you saved it. Experiment with saving and opening puzzle files to confirm that it all works as expected. If you attempt to open a file for which a window is already open, that window should come to the front.

Choose the Open item again to open a PICT file. If you do not have a PICT file handy, there are several on the CD in the Extra PICTs folder. Open one of those files and the picture should appear in the puzzle. Save the file as a puzzle file, and then open it again. When it opens, the same picture should appear in the puzzle window because you saved it in the file's resources.

If you choose New from the File menu, you still get our friendly cat. That's the default PICT installed in the EasyPuzzle resources. To change the default picture, use ResEdit to replace the PICT with resource ID number 2000.

When you are through observing, quit the application. You are making real progress with EasyPuzzle. However, the average user is not familiar with ResEdit. One feature you might want to add is to allow the user to save a picture as the puzzle's default picture. Think about how you might do that. Where would you put the menu item? Where would you store the picture?

Ideally, a careful design considers all options ahead of time and plans for them before you start writing code. However, no design is ever perfect. As you develop an application, sometimes you get good ideas about design while you're writing code. One of the principle benefits of maintaining a flexible software architecture is that you can implement new ideas with a minimum of fuss.

At the same time, you should beware of creeping featuritis. This disease afflicts all software. It results in all sorts of new options being added to software for no particular purpose. The user's need should drive the design. Before you start adding features, always ask yourself, "Does the user need this feature?"

In the next chapter you add printing to EasyPuzzle. I think it's safe to say that's a useful feature in most applications.

File Manager Reference

This section summarizes the basic File Manager calls you use in a standard Macintosh application. For full details on all the File Manager calls, consult *Inside Macintosh: Files*.

For information about Resource Manager calls related to the resource fork, refer to the Resource Manager Reference at the end of Chapter 4.

```
pascal void StandardPutFile(ConstStr255Param prompt, ConstStr255Param
                            defaultName, StandardFileReply *reply)
```

Parameters	prompt	string for prompt in dialog
	defaultName	string for default file name
	reply	address of a standard reply record
Returns	void	
Description	Displays and manages the standard put-file dialog. On return, check the sfGood field of reply to ensure the user clicked Save. If not, the other data is invalid. If so, the file spec for the destination file is in the sfFile field of reply.

```
pascal void StandardGetFile(FileFilterUPP fileFilter, short numTypes,
                     SFTypeList typeList, StandardFileReply *reply)
```

Parameters   fileFilter   UPP to file filtering procedure

                     numTypes   number of file types to display

                     typeList   array of four file types

                     reply   address of a standard reply record

Returns   void

Description   Displays and manages the standard get-file dialog. On return, check the sfGood field of reply to ensure the user clicked Open. If not, the other data is invalid. If so, the file spec for the source file is in the sfFile field of reply. The file type is in the sfType field.

```
pascal OSErr FSpCreate(const FSSpec *spec, OSType creator, OSType fileType,
                     ScriptCode scriptTag)
```

Parameters   spec   file spec for file to create

                     creator   your app's creator code

                     fileType   file type code for this file

                     scriptTag   script system to use for name

Returns   Error value if call fails for any reason

Description   Creates a file according to data provided (both forks). Does not open the file. File is empty and unlocked.

```
pascal OSErr FSpOpenDF(const FSSpec *spec, char permission, short *refNum)
```

Parameters   spec   file spec for file in question

                     permission   read/write permission for this operation

                     refNum   address of variable to return file ID

Returns   Error value if call fails for any reason

Description   Opens the data fork of the file. Provides reference number for this access path in the refNum parameter. This is the file ID number. A file may have more than one such ID number if there are multiple access paths open simultaneously.

```
pascal OSErr FSClose(short refNum);
```

Parameters	refNum	file ID for access path being closed

Returns   Error value if call fails for any reason

Description   Closes the access path and the file. *Do not close an already closed file.* If writing data, call **FlushVol()** after calling **FSClose()** to update the file's catalog entry on the volume.

```
pascal OSErr GetFPos(short refNum, long *filePos);
```

Parameters	refNum	file ID for access path
	filePos	address of value to store position

Returns   Error value if call fails for any reason

Description   Puts the current position of the mark in filePos.

```
pascal OSErr SetFPos(short refNum, short posMode, long posOff);
```

Parameters	refNum	file ID for access path
	posMode	whether to work from start, end, or current position of mark
	posOff	number of bytes to move the mark

Returns   Error value if call fails for any reason

Description   Moves the mark by posOff bytes from start of file, logical end of file, or current position of mark.

```
pascal OSErr GetEOF(short refNum, long *logEOF);
```

Parameters	refNum	file ID for access path
	logEOF	address of value to store end of file

Returns   Error value if call fails for any reason

Description   Puts the number of bytes of actual data in the logEOF parameter.

```
pascal OSErr FSRead(short refNum, long *count, void *buffPtr);
```

Parameters	refNum	file ID for access path
	count	address containing number of bytes to read
	buffPtr	address where data should be placed

Returns   Error value if call fails for any reason

Description   Reads count bytes from current mark into location buffPtr. On return, count contains the number of bytes actually read. The block at buffPtr must be locked or nonrelocatable.

```
pascal OSErr FSWrite(short refNum, long *count, const void *buffPtr);
```

Parameters   refNum   file ID for access path

                 count   address containing number of bytes to write

                 buffPtr   address where data should be obtained

Returns   Error value if call fails for any reason

Description   Writes count bytes from location buffPtr into file starting at current mark. On return, count contains the number of bytes actually written. The block at buffPtr must be locked or nonrelocatable.

```
pascal OSErr FlushVol(StringPtr volName, short vRefNum);
```

Parameters   volName   name of volume to flush, pass nil

                 vRefNum   volume ID of volume to flush

Returns   Error value if call fails for any reason

Description   Use nil as the address for volName to ensure that the call uses the vRefNum parameter. Volume names are not guaranteed to be unique. This call writes contents of volume buffer to disk. This updates catalog info for any changed files.

```
pascal OSErr FSpExchangeFiles(const FSSpec *source, const FSSpec *dest)
```

Parameters   source   address of source file spec

                 dest   address of destination file spec

Returns   Error value if call fails for any reason

Description   Swaps information for the two files specified. On successful return, dest points to the data that was in source, and source points to the data that was in dest. Swaps both data and resource forks. Both files must be on the same volume.

```
pascal OSErr FSpDelete(const FSSpec *spec)
```

Parameters   spec   file spec for file in question

Returns   Error value if call fails for any reason

Description   Deletes file from disk. File must be closed before this call.

```
pascal OSErr FindFolder(short vRefNum, OSType folderType, Boolean
                  createFolder, short *foundVRefNum, long
                  *foundDirID)
```

Parameters   vRefNum   volume on which to look

                      folderType   type of folder to search for

                      createFolder   true => create if not found

                      foundVRefNum   volume ID found by File Manager

                      foundDirID   directory ID found by File Manager

Returns   Error value if call fails for any reason

Description   You specify the kind of folder you're looking for, where to look, and
                      whether to create it if not found. Call returns actual volume ID and
                      directory ID where folder is located.

```
pascal OSErr FSMakeFSSpec(short vRefNum, long dirID, ConstStr255Param
                  fileName, FSSpecPtr spec)
```

Parameters   vRefNum   volume ID where file is located

                      dirID   parent directory ID where file is located

                      fileName   name of file

                      spec   address of file spec to store results

Returns   Error value if call fails for any reason

Description   Creates a file spec based on information provided. Results returned in
                      spec parameter.

```
pascal OSErr FSpGetFInfo(const FSSpec *spec, FInfo *fndrInfo)
```

Parameters   spec   address of file spec for file in question

                      fndrInfo   address of an FInfo structure to store results

Returns   Error value if call fails for any reason

Description   Returns Finder's information about this file, including type, creator, and
                      other data.

493

Gutenberg's Dream: Printing on the Mac

The Macintosh completely revolutionized the printed page in a way that has not been seen since the invention of movable type. What the Macintosh did is the logical extension of Gutenberg's brilliant insight. Gutenberg realized that letters could be made into interchangeable blocks, reorganized on a single plate, clamped together, inked, and pressed onto paper. The shock waves from that simple idea transformed the world.

The Macintosh took modern printing one step further. Letters are not metal castings, but electrons that can be molded into virtually any shape. The traditional printing plate has been transformed into a phosphor screen where flexibility is queen, and innovation king. Add into the mix a host of graphic elements and you have power beyond anything Gutenberg ever imagined.

What made the Macintosh so unique is that not only could you do this on a computer monitor, you could print the result on paper! What you see is what you get at the Macintosh printing shop.

In this chapter, you learn how the designers of the Macintosh implemented this power. The feat is both brilliant and elegant in its simplicity. In this chapter, we cover these topics:

- An overview of printing
- Managing the Page Setup dialog
- Managing the Print dialog
- Printing a document
- Printing one copy of a document

In the lab exercise for this chapter, you use what you learn to print the puzzle window.

The Macintosh is a machine in constant transition. The art of printing a document on the Macintosh is currently undergoing a significant revision. After the lab exercise, we take a brief look at what's in your future—QuickDraw GX printing.

Printing Overview

You have learned about QuickDraw and how the Macintosh puts an image onscreen. Now consider this problem: how do you get that onto paper? The Macintosh designers had a brilliant solution. Use QuickDraw to print a page! The very same code that draws your document onscreen draws your page for the printer.

QuickDraw is a graphics engine that manipulates pixels. It doesn't matter to QuickDraw whether the pixel is a phosphor on a monitor or a spot on a page. The task of converting QuickDraw commands into something the printer understands is not your responsibility. That magic resides in printer drivers.

The graphics environment within which the Printing Manager does its work is our old friend, the graphics port. You create a printing graphics port in which to render your printed image. Whether the port is color depends upon the printer's capabilities and whether you have color QuickDraw on your computer.

If your drawing code manipulates the graphics port in typical ways—perhaps to modify the clip region or to set a color—that same code works with a printing graphics port. That is true elegance in design.

However, there are still some significant tasks you must handle to get from the monitor to the printed page.

The TPrint Record

The basic data structure for printing is a TPrint record. Table 16.1 lists the important fields of the TPrint record. A THPrint is the handle to the TPrint record.

Table 16.1: Important TPrint Record Fields

Field	Data Type	Description
rPaper	Rect	size of the paper
prStl	TPrStl	print request's style record
prInfo	TPrInfo	PrInfo data for this print record
prJob	TPrJob	print job request

The rPaper field is the size of the paper, not the size of the printable area on the paper.

The prStl field of the TPrint record is a TPrStl record. The TPrStl record contains data relating to the Page Setup dialog (also known as the Print Style or PrStl dialog). Typically, you do not manipulate the information in this record directly. The Printing Manager takes care of it for you through the Page Setup dialog.

The other two items of importance in the TPrint record are also records, the TPrInfo record and a TPrJob record. Both of these contain important data to which you refer when printing.

For ease of reading, we will call the TPrint record a print record, the TPrInfo record a print info record, and a TPrJob record a print job record. Figure 16.1 shows the TPrint record.

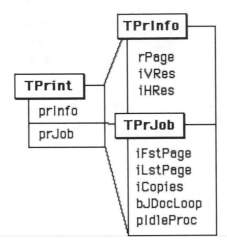

Figure 16.1 Inside a TPrint Record

The prInfo field of the print record is a TPrInfo record. This record has three fields of interest listed in Table 16.2.

Table 16.2: Important TPrInfo Record Fields

Field	Data Type	Description
rPage	Rect	the printable rectangle
iVRes	short	vertical resolution of printer
iHRes	short	horizontal resolution of printer

The rPage field of the print info record is the size of the printable area on the page, in pixels. This is a vital bit of data that you use to calculate the number of pages in your document. The other two fields don't usually affect how you print the page.

The prJob field of the print record is a TPrJob record. The print job record contains several important items, as listed in Table 16.3.

Table 16.3: Important TPrJob Record Fields

Field	Data Type	Description
iFstPage	short	number of first page to print
iLstPage	short	number of last page to print
iCopies	short	number of copies
bJDocLoop	char	draft or deferred printing
pIdleProc	PrIdleUPP	printing idle procedure pointer

You use the iFstPage, iLstPage, and iCopies fields to determine what pages to print and how many copies of them to print.

The bJDocLoop field is a relic from the ImageWriter printer, but you should still support it. If this is set for deferred printing, you have to take an extra step to print a document. We revisit this topic when we talk about the printing loop.

The pIdleProc field is a universal procedure pointer to a function you provide. You can use the procedure to display messages to the user while printing is in progress.

Creating a TPrint Record

Unfortunately, there is no Printing Manager call to allocate a print record. There is no equivalent to GetNewWindow() or GetNewControl(). As a result you have to do a little more work, but it is really very simple.

The first thing you do is call NewHandle() to allocate a block of memory the size of a TPrint record. You now have the necessary memory available.

Before making any Printing Manager calls, you must call PrOpen(). This opens the current printer driver so the Printing Manager can communicate with it.

> PrOpen() is not a routine to initialize the Printing Manager. Do not call it once at launch, like you do for InitWindows() or InitGraf(). Because the user can change printers at any time, you typically call PrOpen() just before you need the printer driver, and PrClose() as soon as you're done. Every call to PrOpen() must be balanced with a call to PrClose().

After opening the current driver, call PrintDefault(). You provide the handle to the TPrint record you just allocated. This call sets the print record to the default values for the current printer driver. After this call, use PrClose() to close the printer driver.

Your application is now snug and secure with a default print record in hand that matches the current printer.

note Like the Resource Manager and the Memory Manager, the Printing Manager does not report errors directly. After most Printing Manager calls, call `PrError()` to look for errors.

A Printing Strategy

Your program must be well designed if you want it to be useful. It isn't enough to know how to write code. You must think about the structure of your code—how the pieces work together to accomplish the ultimate goal of the software. Developing a strategy for the user's interaction with printing is a good example of how intelligent design can greatly enhance a program's friendliness.

Everything that happens with respect to printing relies on the print record. Of course, the user may want different documents to print differently. How do you handle this? Clearly, each printable document should have its own print record. When the user interacts with the printing dialogs, you use the print record associated with the active document. When you save a document, you save the print record as a resource along with the document. When the user opens a document, you read the print record from the resources so that the document's printing attributes remain unchanged.

So far so good, but it could be better. Let's take this approach a step further.

You should also have a print record that is *not* attached to any window. Call this the application's print record as distinguished from an individual window's print record. Why do you want to have an application-level print record? Because it helps you create a very friendly human interface.

When the user chooses Page Setup and there are no windows open, you modify the *application's* print record. This allows the user to set up how new documents are printed. Perhaps the user likes to print *everything* in landscape mode (broadside) instead of the more common portrait mode. No problem if you have an application-level print record. With this approach, when the user creates a new document, you as the programmer give the document a copy of the *application* print record. As a result, all the user's current default choices apply to every new document automatically.

That is much better than the alternative. If you don't have an application-level print record, the user must go to the Page Setup dialog for *every* new document and modify the settings. What a pain.

An application-level print record enhances the user's experience in yet another way. You can save the application's print record as part of the application's preferences. Every time the application launches, you read the preferred print record and set it up accordingly. Users don't have to go to the Page Setup dialog and reset the printing to landscape mode when the program launches. You remember it for them! That's service.

You can provide two approaches to setting preferences: a formal dialog approach, or the automatic "make a choice while no window is open, and the program remembers how you like things set up." These approaches are not mutually exclusive. You can use both!

You can extend this idea beyond printing. Create application-level default structures for the various options available to the user in your program. Save those structures as part of your application's preferences. Use this idea in your applications and users will think your software is both cool and smart.

Now that you have some background on the necessary data structures—and some ideas about an overall printing design—let's look at how to use the data.

Running the Page Setup Dialog

A modern File menu should have at least three items: Page Setup, Print One, and Print. In the typical printing process, the first thing the user does is choose the Page Setup item from the File menu.

In response to this choice, you present the standard Page Setup dialog. You call `PrOpen()` to open the current print driver. Then call `PrStlDialog()`. You provide one parameter, a handle to the appropriate print record. This call returns a `Boolean` value. If the user confirms the dialog box, the function returns `true`. When you make the call, the dialog appears (see Figure 16.2).

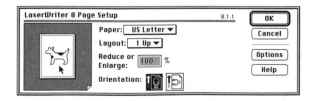

Figure 16.2 The LaserWriter Page Setup and Options dialogs

The actual Page Setup dialog that appears varies depending on the current printer driver. Different printers have different options. Your application doesn't have to worry about this. One call does it all.

The Printing Manager handles the entire interaction for you. It modifies the print record's TPrStl record automatically if the user confirms the dialog.

When you're done, call **PrClose()**. That's it. The Page Setup dialog is a Toolbox freebie.

Running the Print Dialog

The user chooses the Print item in the File menu to print a document. Your program should display the standard Print dialog at that time. Like the Page Setup dialog, this is a freebie.

Call **PrOpen()** to open the current printer driver. Then call **PrJobDialog()**. You provide one parameter, a handle to the appropriate print record. This call returns a Boolean value. If the user confirms the dialog, the function returns true. When you make the call, the dialog appears (see Figure 16.3).

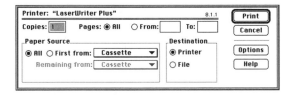

Figure 16.3 The LaserWriter Print dialog

Like Page Setup, the actual Print dialog that appears varies depending on the current printer driver. You use the same call for all Print dialogs.

If the user confirms the dialog, the Printing Manager modifies the values in the print record's TPrJob record automatically. It sets the page range and the number of copies. When you are through, call **PrClose()** to close the printer driver.

If the user confirms the dialog, you should print the document according to the settings in the print job record. You can reopen the printer driver at that time.

Why not just leave the printer driver open? Because you want to keep interface code separate from content. Running the Print dialog is an interface task. Printing a document is a content task. There may be many occasions when the user prints a document without seeing the Print dialog, as you'll see in the next chapter when we discuss Apple events. Therefore, the printing code must open and close the current print driver independently of the dialog code. Besides, the user might switch printers at any time.

The Printing Loop

Printing a document is straightforward, although there are several steps you must follow. A good design in your application can make things much easier. To send your document to the printer, perform the following tasks:

- Open the printer driver—`PrOpen()`
- Validate your print record—`PrValidate()`
- Determine the first and last pages to print
- Open the document—`PrOpenDoc()`
- Print each page
- Close the document—`PrCloseDoc()`
- Send any deferred image to the printer—`PrPicFile()`
- Close the printer driver—`PrClose()`

To print each page, you perform three tasks:

- Open the page—`PrOpenPage()`
- Draw the page
- Close the page—`PrClosePage()`

Printing is page-based. If you have designed your document so that your window's drawing functions are also page-based, printing is as simple as drawing your document page by page. If your document is one-page in size, this becomes almost trivial.

If your window-drawing functions are not page-based, you have to determine what objects appear on what printed page and draw them when it is time to print the page.

Handling Errors

Remember, you should call PrError() each step of the way to check for possible printing errors. If you detect an error, you must retrace your steps to exit gracefully. If you have opened the printer driver, close the printer driver. If you have opened the document, close the document. If you have opened a page, close the page. Keep everything balanced and you will have no problems. Do not display any error dialogs until after you have exited the entire printing operation and the printer driver is closed.

Let's look at the Printing Manager calls in detail to see how this all flows together.

Validating the Print Record

After opening the printer driver with PrOpen() (and checking for an error), you call PrValidate() to ensure that the data in the print record is compatible with the current driver. The user may have switched printers with the Chooser desk accessory without going to the Page Setup dialog afterwards. You provide the handle to the print record in the call to PrValidate(). The call returns a Boolean value. If the return value is false, everything is OK and the call made no change to the print record. If the return value is true, the original data was not compatible and it has been replaced with the driver's default values.

If the call replaced the original values, you can print using the driver's default values. Or you can tell the user to go to the Page Setup dialog and update the settings. Which strategy you should follow depends on the needs of your application.

Regardless of the return value, true or false, check for a printing error. If a printing error occurs, you must not continue printing.

Determining the Page Range

To determine which pages to print, extract the user's settings from the prJob field of the print record. Typical code might look like this if the handle to the print record is in a variable named printJob:

```
firstPage  = (**printJob).prJob.iFstPage;
lastPage   = (**printJob).prJob.iLstPage;
```

However, the user may have set the page range outside the actual available pages in a document. If the first page is outside the range of the document, you shouldn't print anything. If the last page is outside the range of the document, you should set the last page to equal the actual last page of the document.

To do that you must know how many pages your document has. That determination is application specific—that means, it's up to you. The Toolbox can't help you with that task. The number of pages depends not only on the data in your document, but on the printable page size of the current print record. You can get the printable area from the rPage field of the prInfo field of the print record.

Opening the Document for Printing

To print a document, you need a printing graphics port. Call PrOpenDoc(). You provide three parameters. The first is our old friend, the handle to the print record. Typically you pass nil for the other two parameters. The second parameter is a pointer to a printing graphics port. If you pass nil, the Printing Manager makes one for you. The third parameter is a pointer to an input-output buffer used by the Printing Manager during printing. If you pass nil, the Printing Manager takes care of it for you.

The call to PrOpenDoc() returns a pointer to a printing graphics port, a data type TPPrPort. You use this value in subsequent calls to open and close pages, and to close the document. This call also makes the current port the printing graphics port. You are now on your way to printing the document.

Printing a Page

Here's where the loop comes into play. You must perform these steps individually and in sequence for each page of the document that is in the user-specified page range.

First, you open a page by calling PrOpenPage(). You provide the pointer to the printing graphics port and the address of a rectangle. Pass nil for the second parameter. This tells the Printing Manager to use the printable area rectangle from the print record.

PrOpenPage() reinitializes the graphics port. If you want to set any features of the port in advance of drawing, you must set those features after each call to PrOpenPage(). Also, PrOpenPage() uses the QuickDraw call OpenPicture() to preserve all your drawing into an image for the printer. Because you can have only one picture open at a time, you cannot call OpenPicture() to record a picture while a page is open for printing.

To actually print the page, you draw the contents of the page just like you do when you draw in a window. That process is application specific. If your window drawing is page-based, it should be pretty simple.

When you are finished with the page, call PrClosePage(). You provide the pointer to the printing graphics port. This tells the Printing Manager that you are done with one page. The Printing Manager in turn tells the printer driver, and the driver does whatever is necessary to close out the page.

You then loop back to do the next page in the document and repeat the process until you have printed all the pages.

Notice that you do not have to be concerned with the number of copies. The printer driver takes care of that. You draw the page once. The printer driver takes care of the copies.

Closing the Document

When you have completed all of the pages, call `PrCloseDoc()`. You provide the pointer to the printing graphics port. This closes and disposes of the port. In response to this call, most printer drivers start printing the document on the destination printer.

Handling Deferred Printing

The ImageWriter printer may use something called deferred printing. This is not background printing or spooling a document to disk for printing at a later time. It was designed so that the ImageWriter could print documents in low memory conditions on the 128K Mac. If deferred printing is going on, the `bJDocLoop` field of the `prJob` field of the print record is a value declared as `bSpoolLoop`. Have your eyes glazed over yet?

Don't worry about what it means. Just check for that value. If the value of that particular field is `bSpoolLoop`, deferred printing is going on. Call `PrPicFile()` to complete deferred printing. For details on the parameters, see the "Printing Manager Reference" section at the end of this chapter.

Printing One Copy

A nice feature to provide for the user is the ability to print one copy of the current document using current printer settings. The user doesn't see any dialogs at all. With the advent of QuickDraw GX, this feature is now part of the Macintosh human interface guidelines. You should support it. Doing so is fairly simple.

You preserve the current values for first page, last page, and number of copies that you find in the active document's print job record. Then you set the `iFstPage` field to one, the `iLstPage` field to some ridiculously high number to ensure that you get all the pages, and the `iCopies` field to one.

Then you print the document just as if the user had clicked the Print button in the Print dialog box.

When you are all through, restore the original values to the print job record and you're all done.

Lab 16.1 Printing the Document

In this lab you write code to manage the standard Page Setup and Print dialogs and create a printing loop to print a multipage document. Because printing uses the same calls as drawing onscreen, you can use the DoDrawPage behavior to print a document one page at a time.

In this lab you:

- Give EasyPuzzle a default print job

- Give each window its own print job

- Read and write print job resources

- Manage the Page Setup dialog

- Manage the Print dialog

- Print a multipage document

- Print one copy of a document

Use your code from the previous lab as the starting point for your work in this lab.

Step 1: Initialize the default print job

Modify: EasyInitApp() in init.c

In this step you set the default values in a print job record. You allocated memory for a default print job way back in Chapter 3. It has been sitting there unused ever since. Now it's time to use it.

```
error = EasyAllocateHandle(sizeof(TPrint),
                           (Handle*)&printJob);
if (error)
{
  return error;
}

PrOpen();
error = PrError();
if (error)
{
  error = kNoPrinterError;
```

```
}

/* try anyway, best we can do */
PrintDefault (printJob);
g.defaultPrintJob = printJob;
PrClose();

return error;
```

The existing code allocates memory for a TPrint record. You then call PrOpen() to open the current printer driver, and check for error. The most likely cause of error is that no printer driver could be found. If there is an error, you set the error to kNoPrinterError. This will display a helpful alert that tells the user to go to the Chooser to select a printer. You do not return, you continue anyway so that you can get the best result possible.

You call PrintDefault() to set default values for the print job. If a printer driver is open, it uses values from the printer. You then store the handle to the print job in g.defaultPrintJob.

Finally, you call PrClose() to close the printer driver.

Step 2: Give each window its own print job

Modify: BaseInitialize() in windowProc.c

When you create a window, make a copy of the current default print job for the window.

```
easyWindow->DoUnflattenWindow =
                    (WindowProc)BaseUnflattenWindow;

newPrintJob = g.defaultPrintJob;
error = HandToHand((Handle*)&newPrintJob);
if (error)
{
  return error;
}
easyWindow->printJob = newPrintJob;

easyWindow->docWidth  = kDocumentWidth;
```

First you make a copy of the handle to the default print job. Then you call HandToHand() to allocate memory for a new block and copy the data into it. As always, check for error. If there is no error, you set the window's printJob field to the new copy of the print job.

Because the EasyPuzzle window-initializing function calls BaseInitialize() first, you have made this change for both EasyApp and EasyPuzzle with this one piece of code.

Step 3: Read and write print job resources

Modify: BaseWriteResource() in windowProc.c

Modify: BaseReadResource() in windowProc.c

EasyApp and EasyPuzzle store the print job as a resource with each file. You must write the resource when saving the file, and read it when opening a file. The code provided for you in WritePuzzleResource() and ReadPuzzleResource() calls the equivalent "base" function to write the print job resource, so this code works for EasyPuzzle.

In BaseWriteResource() you take care of writing the print job data as a resource. The existing code opens the file:

```
error = EasyAddResource(fileID, (Handle)easyWindow->printJob,
                        kPrintJobType, kBaseResourceID);
if (error)
{
  CloseResFile(fileID);
  return error;
}
CloseResFile(fileID);
```

You call EasyAddResource() to handle the task. You save the resource as type kPrintJobType—an application-defined constant.

Reading the resource is the converse operation:

```
thisResource = EasyGet1Resource(fileID, kPrintJobType,
                                kBaseResourceID);
if (thisResource == nil)
{
  CloseResFile(fileID);
  error = kNoResourceError;
  return error;
}

DetachResource(thisResource);
error = ResError();

CloseResFile(fileID);
```

You use EasyGet1Resource() to fetch the required resource and then do some error checking. After that you call DetachResource() to convert the resource handle into a regular handle so you can do with it as you please. The existing code disposes of the print job already attached to this window and replaces it with the new print job.

Now that you have a default print job and each window has its own print job, you can manage printing properly.

Step 4: Manage the Page Setup dialog

Modify: BasePageSetup() in windowProc.c

When the user chooses the Page Setup item from the File menu, EasyApp calls the PageSetupHook(). You can override behavior at that point if you wish. The default hook calls EasyPageSetup(), which in turn sends the front window a DoPageSetup message. BasePageSetup() is the default function that responds. It should open the printer driver, run the dialog, and close the printer driver.

```
Boolean        result;

PrOpen();
error = PrError();
if (error)
{
  error = kPrintingError;
  return error;
}

result = PrStlDialog(printJob);

if (result)
{
  easyWindow->changed = true;
}

PrClose();
return error;
```

First you call **PrOpen()** and check for error. If there is no error, you call **PrStlDialog()** to display and manage the Page Setup dialog.

If result is true, the user approved the dialog. In that case, you should mark the window as changed. If your window is sensitive to page breaks and the user changes settings in the Page Setup dialog, you should update your window at this point because all sorts of things might change, such as page size, orientation, and so forth. EasyPuzzle is not sensitive, so it does not bother.

Then you call **PrClose()** to close the printer driver.

What if there is no window open? EasyPageSetup() does pretty much the same thing as BasePageSetup(), but it uses the default print job instead of the window's print job. Check it out.

Step 5: Manage the Print dialog

Modify: BasePrintDialog() in windowProc.c

When the user chooses the Print item in the file menu, EasyApp sends the window a DoPrintDialog message. BasePrintDialog() is the default behavior, and it serves fine for EasyPuzzle.

```
Boolean        result;

PrOpen();
error = PrError();
if (error)
{
  return error;
}

printJob = easyWindow->printJob;

result = PrJobDialog(printJob);

PrClose();
error = PrError();
if (error)
{
  return error;
}

if (result == true)   /* user OK */
{
  error = easyWindow->DoPrint(macWindow, nil);
}

return error;
```

First you open the printer driver with PrOpen() and check for error. Then you get the print job for the window and call PrJobDialog() to display and manage the Print dialog.

Then you call PrClose() to close the printer driver and check for error. If there is none, you examine the result variable to determine whether the user approved the Print dialog. If approved, send the window a DoPrint message.

Step 6:   Print a multipage document

Modify: `BasePrint()` in windowProc.c

This is where all the work happens. `BasePrint()` is the default EasyApp function that responds to a `DoPrint` message. A window may receive this message from the Print dialog when the user chooses the Print One item in the File menu, or as a result of a print-document Apple event. We discuss Apple events in the next chapter.

There is a lot of code in this step, but most of it is simple error checking. The steps are very logical. The existing code opens the printer driver:

```
PrOpen();
error = PrError();
if (error)
{
  PrClose();
  return error;
}

/* validate print job */
printJob = easyWindow->printJob;
PrValidate(printJob);
error = PrError();
if(error)
{
  PrClose();
  return error;
}

/* get max number of pages for document */
totalPages = EasyGetTotalPages(easyWindow,
                        &(**printJob).prInfo.rPage);

/* get the desired page range */
firstPage = (**printJob).prJob.iFstPage;
lastPage  = (**printJob).prJob.iLstPage;

if (lastPage > totalPages)
{
  lastPage = totalPages;
}

/* create a GrafPort for printing document */
printPort = PrOpenDoc(printJob, nil, nil);
error = PrError();
if (error)
{
  PrCloseDoc(printPort);
  PrClose();
  return error;
}
```

```
/* print the pages the user wants */
for (thisPage = firstPage; thisPage <=lastPage; thisPage++)
{
  PrOpenPage(printPort, nil);
  error = PrError ();
  if(error)
  {
    PrClosePage(printPort);
    PrCloseDoc(printPort);
    PrClose();
    return error;
  }

  easyWindow->DoDrawPage(macWindow, &thisPage);

  PrClosePage(printPort);
}

/* close the document */
PrCloseDoc(printPort);
error = PrError();
if(error)
{
  PrClose();
  return error;
}

/* check to see if printing was deferred */
if ((**printJob).prJob.bJDocLoop == bSpoolLoop)
```

You start out by getting the print job and calling PrValidate() to make sure it is OK. Then you call EasyGetTotalPages() to get the actual number of pages in the document. This function is provided for you, and is likely to be application specific.

Next, you get the page range the user set in the Print dialog. If the last page is greater than the total pages, you use the total page number as your last page.

You call PrOpenDoc() to create a printing graphics port. And of course you check for error. Notice that the error code when you bail out reverses every printing call. In this case, for example, because you called PrOpenDoc() you call PrCloseDoc() if an error happens.

Then you loop through the pages the user wants to print. For each page you call PrOpenPage() and check for error. Then you send a DoDrawPage message to the window, identifying what page it should draw. The same code that draws the screen prints the page. Then you call PrClosePage() to close the page.

When printing is complete, call PrCloseDoc() to close the graphics port and check for error.

The existing code handles the `bSpoolLoop` problem discussed in this chapter, closes the printer driver, and returns.

Step 7: Print one copy of a document

Modify: BasePrintOne() in windowProc.c

When the user chooses the Print One item in the File menu, EasyApp sends a `DoPrintOne` message to the window. Printing one copy of a document without interference from a dialog is very simple.

```
short       saveFirst, saveLast, saveCopies;

saveFirst  = (**printJob).prJob.iFstPage;
saveLast   = (**printJob).prJob.iLstPage;
saveCopies = (**printJob).prJob.iCopies;

(**printJob).prJob.iFstPage = 1;
(**printJob).prJob.iLstPage = 10000;
(**printJob).prJob.iCopies  = 1;

error = easyWindow->DoPrint(macWindow, nil);

(**printJob).prJob.iFstPage = saveFirst;
(**printJob).prJob.iLstPage = saveLast;
(**printJob).prJob.iCopies  = saveCopies;

return error;
```

You get the page range and number of copies from the existing print job information and save them.

> This a pretty obscure set of field names and structures. Just in case you're wondering, not even a wizard can remember all the field names for all the structures in the Toolbox. This is what reference materials are for. When you program, you spend a significant percentage of your time looking things up in reference works like *Inside Macintosh*.

After you save the existing values, you set the page range and use one as the number of copies. In EasyApp, I picked 10,000 pages as the upper limit. That should take care of most printing projects. The maximum number of pages is 32,767 because `iLstPage` is a short variable.

Then you send the window a `DoPrint` message. When finished, you restore the original values and return.

Step 8:   Run the application

Modify: none

Save your work and run the project using the debugger. When the debugger window appears, launch EasyApp.

Before opening a puzzle window, choose the Page Setup item in the File menu. Change some settings and click the OK button. This changes the application's default print job. Then create a new puzzle. Choose the Page Setup item again while that window is active. The settings should match those you set when no window was open.

Change the Page Setup settings for the window, and then save the file. Open the file, and the settings should be the same as they were when you closed the file.

> By the way, don't try to open any puzzle file you saved in Chapter 15. They did not have a valid print job resource saved in their resources. Because you have been practicing defensive coding all along by checking for errors, disaster will not strike. But you may get an error alert if you try to open them.
>
> *note*

Now choose the Print item and play with that dialog. You should be able to print as many copies of a puzzle window as you'd like. Break the puzzle into pieces and print a scrambled puzzle if you wish. Have a good time, but try not to kill too many trees. When you are through observing, quit the application.

Now that you have implemented QuickDraw printing, it's time to learn about an entirely new approach to printing in the Mac OS.

QuickDraw GX Printing

QuickDraw GX introduces a new printing architecture to the Macintosh. The greatest changes are to the human interface and to the underlying engine that drives printing.

From the programmer's perspective, QuickDraw GX doesn't change that much. QuickDraw GX uses a different print record with many different features. However, the application code you use for QuickDraw GX printing takes a very similar approach to the code in this chapter.

There is one major change to the programming architecture. A QuickDraw GX print job may have more than one set of styles. As a result, the same document may have some pages that use landscape orientation and others that use portrait orientation. Some pages may use one size of paper, and others print on a different size paper.

If you support this feature in your applications, you must add a Custom Page Setup item in the File menu to allow the user to select and format individual pages. I don't go into the details here, but that is perhaps the most radical programming change to an application's printing architecture.

The biggest visible change in QuickDraw GX printing is to the human interface. QuickDraw GX has desktop printer icons, drag-and-drop printing, a new Printing menu in the Finder, new print-related features in the File menu, new Page Setup and Print dialogs, printer extensions, and portable digital documents. It is an amazing list of features.

A desktop printer icon allows the user to control the printing process, much like the Print Monitor that it replaces. You "open" the printer just like a hard drive—you double-click the printer's icon. When you do, a window opens allowing you to control when and how documents print. You can drag new documents into the printer queue, remove them, rearrange them, or pause the printing. It is as easy as moving files around on the Desktop.

The user can print documents in the traditional way—by selecting Print from a File menu. However, when users want to direct a document to a particular printer, they can select the printer from the Print dialog (see Figure 16.4)! There is no need to go to the Chooser. Or they can simply drag a document and drop it on the icon of the desired printer.

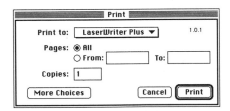

Figure 16.4 The QuickDraw GX Print dialog

Printing extensions allow the user to modify the printed output. For example, the user might have a printing extension that puts the date on every page, or prints the word "draft" as a light grey background on the document. Printing extensions require no support from your application, yet they enhance your application's capability to produce a document that is exactly what the user wants.

Finally, the user can create a portable digital document. A PDD includes everything necessary to print the document, including font information. You can send the document to anyone who has QuickDraw GX without concern as to whether they have the same application or fonts. If they have GX, they can print the document.

Gone are the days when the document looked good on your machine, but lousy when it reached its destination. Once again, from the application programmer's perspective, this is a gift from QuickDraw GX.

You can learn the technical details in *Inside Macintosh: QuickDraw GX Printing.* The ease of use, flexibility, and power of the new printing interface makes QuickDraw GX printing a highly desirable feature in any application. It is already here as part of System 7.5. If it hasn't reached you yet, it will be coming soon to a Macintosh near you.

Another Milestone

You have reached the third milestone on your road to becoming a Macintosh programmer. You can now implement all of the critical features that a program needs: you can create windows, draw in them, save and open files, print documents, and much more. Well done! Take a breather and enjoy your accomplishments. And while you do, let's take a quick peek at what lies ahead in *Programming Starter Kit for Macintosh.*

The single biggest feature missing from EasyPuzzle is the capability to communicate with other applications.

Applications should communicate with other applications. In a multitasking environment, several applications may be running at once. If they can communicate with each other, significantly more work can get done because the applications can use each other's services. This is the future of computing. Applications must share their data.

Chapter 17 teaches you what high-level events are, and what to do with one when your application receives it. In Chapter 18, you implement cut, copy, and paste between EasyPuzzle windows, and between EasyPuzzle and other applications. And in Chapter 19, you have the opportunity to implement drag-and-drop technology in EasyPuzzle. You'll watch the boundaries between applications start to fade away as data becomes instantly and transparently portable from one application to another. You'll be impressed.

All three chapters share a single theme—interapplication communication. In a very real sense these chapters are the first steps you take into the future of Macintosh programming. It's waiting for you just ahead.

Printing Manager Reference

This section summarizes the basic Printing Manager calls you use in a standard Macintosh application. For full details on all the Printing Manager calls, consult Chapter 9 of *Inside Macintosh: Imaging With QuickDraw*.

`pascal void PrOpen(void)`

Parameters	none
Returns	void
Description	Opens the current printer driver. User chooses the current printer in the Chooser desk accessory.

`pascal void PrClose(void)`

Parameters	none
Returns	void
Description	Closes the current printer driver.

`pascal void PrintDefault(THPrint hPrint)`

Parameters	hPrint handle to the print record in question
Returns	void
Description	Initializes the values in a `TPrint` record to the default values for the current printer driver. Driver must be open.

`pascal Boolean PrValidate(THPrint hPrint)`

Parameters	hPrint handle to the print record in question
Returns	Boolean value, `true =>` changed contents of `TPrint` record
Description	Checks values in print record for internal consistency and for consistency with the current driver. Sets values to default values for printer driver if they are inconsistent.

```
pascal Boolean PrStlDialog(THPrint hPrint)
```

Parameters	hPrint	handle to the print record in question
Returns	Boolean value, true => user confirmed dialog	
Description	Displays and manages the Page Setup dialog. Modifies contents of the TPrStl part of the print record if the user confirms the dialog.	

```
pascal Boolean PrJobDialog(THPrint hPrint)
```

Parameters	hPrint	handle to the print record in question
Returns	Boolean value, true => user confirmed dialog	
Description	Displays and manages the Print dialog. Modifies contents of the TPrJob part of the print record if the user confirms the dialog.	

```
pascal TPPrPort PrOpenDoc(THPrint hPrint, TPPrPort pPrPort, Ptr pIOBuf)
```

Parameters	hPrint	handle to the print record in question
	pPrPort	pointer to storage for a printing graphics port; nil => Printing Manager allocates
	pIOBuf	pointer to a 522-byte storage for the Printing Manager's input/output; nil => Printing Manager allocates
Returns	Pointer to the printing graphics port	
Description	Creates the printing graphics port for a print job. Call once before printing any pages.	

```
pascal void PrCloseDoc(TPPrPort pPrPort)
```

Parameters	pPrPort	pointer to a printing graphics port
Returns	void	
Description	Disposes of the port. Call when printing is complete.	

```
pascal void PrOpenPage(TPPrPort pPrPort, TPRect pPageFrame)
```

Parameters	pPrPort	pointer to a printing graphics port
	pPageFrame	rectangle to scale image; nil => use the printable area of the page

519

Returns	void	
Description	Call before drawing page to be printed. Calls `OpenPicture()` to store your QuickDraw commands for the page before sending them to the printer driver.	

```
pascal void PrClosePage(TPPrPort pPrPort)
```

Parameters	pPrPort	pointer to a printing graphics port
Returns	void	
Description	Call when page drawing is complete. Closes the accumulating picture and tells printer driver page is complete.	

```
pascal void PrPicFile(THPrint hPrint, TPPrPort pPrPort, Ptr pIOBuf, Ptr
                    pDevBuf, TPrStatus *prStatus)
```

Parameters	hPrint	handle to the print record in question
	pPrPort	pointer to storage for a printing graphics port; nil => Printing Manager allocates
	pIOBuf	pointer to a 522-byte storage for the Printing Manager's input/output; nil => Printing Manager allocates
	pDevBuf	pointer to a device buffer; nil => Printing Manager allocates
	prStatus	pointer to a TPrStatus record
Returns	void	
Description	Call if deferred printing is in use. Check the `bJDocLoop` field of `prJob` field of the print record. If the value is `bSpoolLoop`, deferred printing is in progress. This call prints the accumulated picture file that has been saved to disk as part of the deferred printing process.	

```
pascal short PrError(void)
```

Parameters	none	
Returns	Error value for most recent printing error	
Description	Call after every Printing Manager call in which any error may cause problems. Make absolutely sure you check for errors after `PrOpen()`, `PrOpenDoc()`, and `PrOpenPage()`.	

17

Play Well with Others: Working with Apple Events

Until now, EasyPuzzle has been an isolated application. This is very much the traditional model of a computer program. It stands alone, it does its work. End of story.

This is not how things should be. Interapplication communication opens up a world of possibilities that Macintosh software is only beginning to explore. You can be on the leading edge of that exploration by supporting Apple events in your programs.

An Apple event is a high-level event. We discussed high-level events briefly back in Chapter 6. In this chapter, we cover the subject in detail as we discuss:

- An overview of Apple events
- Receiving an Apple event
- Handling an Apple event
- Extracting data from an Apple event

In the lab exercise for this chapter, you put all this knowledge to good use as you bring EasyApp into the Apple event world.

Finally, we take a look at the real power of Apple events and where they can take you in the Macintosh programming universe.

Overview of Apple Events

An Apple event is a message that your application receives from an application. That message usually has some data attached to it.

Whenever two applications share data, they must use a common protocol so that each can understand the data. An Apple event follows the Apple Event Interprocess Messaging Protocol defined by Apple Computer. You do not need to know the gory details. You just need to know what an Apple event is, where it keeps its data, and how to get it. That's what this chapter is all about.

An Apple event tells your application to do something, or provides information your application needs to get work done. Each Apple event is a kind of message. Different messages have very different purposes. Clearly, you need some way to identify the kind of message you receive.

Each Apple event has an event class and an event ID. These are analogous to a file's creator and type. The event class and ID uniquely identify each kind of Apple event.

Apple events are organized into "suites" of related Apple events. There are suites of events devoted to text manipulation, spreadsheets, core application behavior, and so forth. One of the suites is the "required" suite of Apple events. These are the events that *all* applications should support and that you implement in the coding lab for this chapter.

The four required Apple events are:

- Open application
- Quit application
- Open document
- Print document

The System and the Finder rely on these events to control your application in a multitasking environment.

If your program does not support Apple events, the System can still work around the problem some of the time. But Apple events are the future, and the future is now. You absolutely should support the four required Apple events if no others.

Table 17.1 lists the specific class and ID for each of the required Apple events.

Table 17.1: Required Apple Events

Event Class	Event ID	Function
aevt	oapp	Perform setup functions on launch
aevt	quit	Quit the application
aevt	odoc	Open one or more documents
aevt	pdoc	Print one or more documents

Notice that all four messages have the same class. That's not a problem because you use both class *and* ID to identify the message.

> **The Open Application Event**
>
> The open application event does not launch the application. The application must already be running to receive the event! The open application event allows your application to do setup work *after* the System launches it. For example, you may want to open a default window of some kind.
>
> When your application launches, the Finder sends one and only one of three possible events: open application, open document, or print document. For example, if you are opening documents from the Finder, you get the open document event but *not* the open application event.

Most Apple events have data attached to them. Precisely what data is attached depends on the nature of the event. After you determine what the class and ID of an event is, you know what kind of data is attached because Apple events are standardized. Apple Computer maintains an official registry of these events that specifies the class, ID, and parameters for each event (see Figure 17.1).

```
┌─────────────────┐
│ Open Application │
├─────────────────┴──────────────────────────────┐
│                                                 │
│       Event Class   kCoreEventClass ('aevt')    │
│          Event ID   kAeOpenApplication ('oapp') │
│        Parameters   none                        │
│   Reply Parameters  none                        │
│                                                 │
└─────────────────────────────────────────────────┘
```

Figure 17.1 Some information from the event registry

In the terminology of the Apple Event Manager, each separate piece of attached data is a "parameter." This is not the same thing as the parameter in a function call. Unfortunately, the reuse of the term does cause confusion. I'll try to be very clear.

Different kinds of messages have different kinds of data—"parameters"—attached. For example, the open application Apple event has no such "parameter." The open document Apple event has one "parameter"—a list of documents. We talk about how to get the data from the "parameter" when we discuss how to handle the event after you receive it.

When you receive an Apple event, you may have the opportunity to reply to the sender. That's the purpose of the reply parameter information shown in Figure 17.1. None of the required Apple events requires a reply.

Receiving an Apple Event

Just tell the System you're willing to receive Apple events, and the System gives them to you. In the application's SIZE flags, you set the flag that tells the System that your application is aware of high-level events (see Figure 17.2).

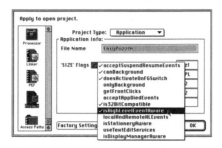

Figure 17.2 Setting the SIZE flag

If this flag is set, the System creates a high-level event queue for your application. When you call `WaitNextEvent()` in your main event loop, the event retrieved may be a high-level event. Your event-parsing code should have a case to handle a high-level event.

If you receive a high-level event, call `AEProcessAppleEvent()`. You pass the address of the event record. The Apple Event Manager determines the class and ID of the event for you, and then calls *a function you provide* to handle that particular kind of Apple event.

You must provide a function to handle each kind of Apple event that your application receives. You must also tell the Apple Event Manager what event each function is meant to handle. The Apple Event Manager puts all this information into an Apple event dispatch table. The dispatch table puts each kind of event—identified by class and ID—together with a function to handle that event. Conceptually, it looks something like the information in Table 17.2.

Table 17.2: Apple Event Dispatch Table

Event Class	Event ID	Function
aevt	oapp	EasyHandleOAppAE()
aevt	quit	EasyHandleQuitAE()

continues

Table 17.2: Continued

Event Class	Event ID	Function
aevt	odoc	EasyHandleODocAE()
aevt	pdoc	EasyHandlePDocAE()

When you call `AEProcessAppleEvent()`, the Apple Event Manager gets the class and ID of the event, looks up the corresponding handler function in the dispatch table, and calls it.

Handling an Apple Event

The Apple Event Manager relies on you for the basic information it needs to parse the Apple event successfully. You handle an event by providing this information to the Apple Event Manager. To successfully handle Apple events you must do two things:

- Build the dispatch table
- Write the handler functions

Building a Dispatch Table

Building the dispatch table is straightforward. The Apple Event Manager does most of the work. Call `AEInstallEventHandler()`. You provide the necessary information. This call has five parameters, and returns an error value. If the call fails, the error value is non-zero.

You call `AEInstallEventHandler()` once for each Apple event for which you have a handler function. The first two parameters in the call identify the event class and the event ID for the event to which the handler will respond.

The third parameter is a universal procedure pointer—a UPP—for the function that responds to that particular kind of event. To create the UPP, call `NewAEEventHandlerProc()` and pass the name of your handler function as the only parameter.

The fourth parameter is a refCon value you want passed to your handler function. This can be any value you find useful. Pass zero if you don't use it.

The fifth parameter is a Boolean value indicating whether this handler should be added to the System's dispatch table or the application's dispatch table. Pass `false` to add the function to the application's dispatch table. Typically, you want to avoid messing around with the System's dispatch table.

Writing a Handler Function

The Apple Event Manager calls handlers directly. That means each handler is a System callback function, and as such it must exactly match the function prototype the System expects to encounter. This code listing shows the prototype that your handler must follow.

```
pascal OSErr MyHandler (const AppleEvent *theAppleEvent,
                        AppleEvent *reply,
                        long handlerRefcon);
```

Notice that you must tell the compiler that your handler is a "pascal" function. This just means that the compiler orders the parameters differently. It does not mean you have to write it in Pascal.

Your function must return an OSErr value—zero if there is no error or a non-zero number if there is an error during your handling of the event.

Your handler receives three parameters. The first is a pointer to an Apple event record that contains the Apple event information. The second is also a pointer to an Apple event record in which you can place any reply information.

The third parameter is the refCon value you provided for yourself when you build the dispatch table.

> If the reply pointer is nil, there is no reply expected. Do not assume there is a reply and write to it. You'll be writing to a nil pointer! Always check the value of the reply parameter before writing to it. None of the required Apple events uses a reply.

You need a handler for each kind of Apple event to which you respond. However, the same handler can handle more than one kind of Apple event. In that case, you install the same handler more than once in the dispatch table, each time identifying the class and ID you want to use the handler for. Typically, however, each of your handlers takes care of one kind of Apple event.

If your application receives an Apple event for which you have not installed a handler, nothing awful happens. The Apple Event Manager looks at the System's Apple event dispatch table to see whether there is a System-level handler for that kind of event. If there is, that's what gets called.

If there is not a System-level handler, the Apple Event Manager either does nothing or responds to the sender that the event was not handled.

Extracting Data from an Apple Event

So far, so good. You tell the System you can handle high-level events. Your event loop gets them and your event parser dispatches them to the Apple Event Manager for identification. You have created an application dispatch table for your event handlers, and the Apple Event Manager calls the appropriate handler when you receive an event. Now what do you do with the event?

If there is data, you pull it out of the event and act on it. Easier said than done, but the task is manageable. You look for the right kind of data, and you use Apple Event Manager calls to get it.

First, you have to know what kind of data is attached to the event. You look in the Apple event registry for that information when dealing with events. Table 17.3 provides the information for the required Apple events that you work with in this book.

An Apple event may have several different kinds of data attached to it, not just one. The Apple Event Manager identifies different kinds of data by keyword. The keyword is analogous to the event class used to identify the kind of event in the first place. See Table 17.3.

Table 17.3: Data Keywords and Types for Required Apple Events

Event	Keyword	Type
oapp	none	none
quit	none	none
odoc	keyDirectObject	typeAEList
pdoc	keyDirectObject	typeAEList

The `keyDirectObject` keyword represents the primary repository for the most important piece of data attached to an Apple event. It is frequently the *only* data attached to the event.

The Apple event registry tells you that for an open document or print document event, you should look in the direct object "parameter" for data with the type known as `typeAEList`.

To actually retrieve data, you tell the Apple Event Manager the keyword for the data you want. You also provide the type for the data you're looking for (more on the data type in a bit).

There are two Apple Event Manager calls you can use to retrieve the attached data or "parameter." You may use either `AEGetParamPtr()` or `AEGetParamDesc()`. The first call is good if the data type is a single unit of a known, fixed length. The second call is good if the data type is of variable length, like a list. `AEGetParamPtr()` gets you a pointer to your own copy of the raw data. You must allocate memory to hold the data. `AEGetParamDesc()` gets you a descriptor record for the data.

What is a descriptor record? A *descriptor record* is the basic data structure used by the Apple Event Manager (see Table 17.4). It is very simple, and very generic. It is a data structure declared as type `AEDesc`. There are two fields in this structure. The first field is a four-character type, and the second field is a handle to the data.

Table 17.4: A Descriptor Record, an AEDesc

Field	Data Type	Description
descriptorType	DescType	type of data
dataHandle	Handle	handle to the data

The `dataHandle` field refers to data of the type described in the `descriptorType` field. The type tells you what to look for; the handle tells you where to look. However, *don't use the raw handle*. Use Apple Event Manager calls to extract data from the event and the handle—either `AEGetParamPtr()` or `AEGetParamDesc()`.

For example, let's look at what happens when you receive an open document event. The attached data is of type `typeAEList`. This is a list of `AEDesc` records. Figure 17.3 shows the logical arrangement of the data associated with an `AEDescList`.

note
The actual structure of the data in memory may be very different from Figure 17.3. The data in an Apple event is private. That's why you should use the Apple Event Manager calls to extract the data.

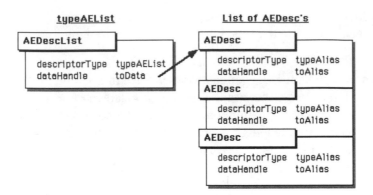

Figure 17.3 Logical view of AEDescList

Because this is a list, its length is unknown. Therefore, use **AEGetParamDesc()** to get the descriptor record. In this case, the descriptor record is the AEDescList on the left of Figure 17.3.

After you have the descriptor record for the list, you must find out how many items are in the list. Call **AECountItems()**. You provide the address of the AEDescList, and the address of a variable where the Apple Event Manager stores the number of items. In the current example, you get the number of AEDesc records in the list (three in Figure 17.3).

Each member of the list is an alias to a file. You have to get each item and convert the file alias into a file specification before you can open the file. Believe it or not, you can do all that with one call—**AEGetNthPtr()**.

The Apple Event Manager allows you to convert data of one type into data of another type. This is a form of automatic type coercion designed to make your life a lot easier. In this case, you are asking the Apple Event Manager for alias data, but you specify that you want the data returned to you as a file specification. The Apple Event Manager does all the work for you.

The call to **AEGetNthPtr()** retrieves the data, converts it, and gives you a pointer to the data. You can then do what you need to do with the data.

That's exactly what you will do in the lab exercise in just a bit. Apple events are not the easiest topic to understand. If this all seems confusing, it should become more clear when you actually get your hands on some real code.

Interacting with the User

All of the Apple Event Manager calls return an error value to notify you if a problem arises. You should, of course, check for problems. However, you should not always notify the user right away. Your application can receive Apple events while it is in the background. If your application is in the background, you should not put up a dialog box. It might interfere with the foreground application. Even more startling, if your program works over a network, the user might be on a completely different machine! Displaying a dialog on the machine running the application is then pretty useless.

Instead, call `AEInteractWithUser()` for permission. If the error value returned by this call is zero (no error), your application is in the foreground. This call may actually bring your application to the foreground if that is allowed by the application sending the Apple event. If you are in the foreground, you can display your error.

Lab 17.1 The Joy of Factored Code

In this lab, you write all the code necessary to parse and handle Apple events. This is a manageable task because EasyPuzzle has been factored. If you're not clear on what well-factored code is, you find out as you work on this lab. You:

- Install Apple event handlers
- Parse Apple events
- Handle an open application Apple event
- Handle a quit application Apple event
- Handle an open document Apple event

Use your code from the previous lab as the starting point for your work in this lab.

Step 1:   Install Apple event handlers

Modify: `main()` in main.c

Modify: `EasyInstallAEHandlers()` in init.c

Typically, you install event handlers at launch for the entire application. You start the process in `main()`.

```
error = InstallAEHandlersHook();
if (error)
```

```
{
    ShowErrorHook(error);
    return;
}

EasyEventLoop();    /* where all the real fun happens */
```

Just before calling the main event loop, call `InstallAEHandlersHook()` and check for error. Because EasyApp relies on the presence of Apple events, an error is fatal and the application quits after displaying an error statement.

`InstallAEHandlersHook()` is provided for you. It simply calls `EasyInstallAEHandlers()`. You can override it to install different or additional handlers.

In `EasyInstallAEHandlers()` you perform the actual installation. This is really the same call repeated four times, once for each event.

```
OSErr  error = noErr;

error = AEInstallEventHandler(kCoreEventClass,
                kAEOpenApplication,
                NewAEEventHandlerProc(EasyHandleOAppAE),
                0, false);
if (error)
{
  return error;
}

error = AEInstallEventHandler(kCoreEventClass,
                kAEQuitApplication,
                NewAEEventHandlerProc(EasyHandleQuitAE),
                0, false);
if (error)
{
  return error;
}

error = AEInstallEventHandler(kCoreEventClass,
                kAEOpenDocuments,
                NewAEEventHandlerProc(EasyHandleODocAE),
                0, false);
if (error)
{
  return error;
}

error = AEInstallEventHandler(kCoreEventClass,
                kAEPrintDocuments,
                NewAEEventHandlerProc(EasyHandlePDocAE),
                0, false);
return error;
```

You call **AEInstallEventHandler()** for each of the four events to which EasyApp responds. You provide the event class, the event ID, a UPP for the event handler, a refCon (zero in this case because EasyPuzzle doesn't use it), and the Boolean value false to install the handler in the application's dispatch table. To create the UPP, you call **NewAEEventHandlerProc()** for each of the four handlers. You write three of these four handlers in subsequent steps.

Step 2: Parse Apple events

Modify: EasyAppleEvent() in events.c

In Lab 6.2, you wrote event-parsing in EasyHandleEvent(). At that time you identified a high-level event and called EasyAppleEvent(). In this step you complete EasyAppleEvent() which has done nothing so far.

```
OSErr  error;

error = AEProcessAppleEvent(theEvent);

if (error)
{
  if (AEInteractWithUser(kNoTimeOut, nil, nil) == noErr)
  {
    ShowErrorHook(error);
  }
}
```

You call **AEProcessAppleEvent()**. The System identifies the class and ID of the event and calls the event handler you specified when you installed the handlers in Step 1. Then you check for error.

Each handler returns an error if a problem occurs. If there is an error, call **AEInteractWithUser()** to confirm that it is OK to display an alert. If it is, call ShowErrorHook().

Step 3: Handle an open application Apple event

Modify: EasyHandleOAppAE() in AppleEvents.c

In Step 1 you installed this function as the handler for an open application event. This function should perform any setup work necessary after the application launches. A typical task is to open a default window.

```
OSErr     error = noErr;

if (g.newOnLaunch)
{
  WindowPtr  newWindow;

  error = NewHook(&newWindow, g.defaultType);
  if (!error)
  {
    ShowWindow(newWindow);
  }
}

return error;
```

In EasyApp, the g.newOnLaunch flag controls whether you create a window automatically at launch. You check that flag. If it is true, call NewHook(). If there is no error, call **ShowWindow()** to display the new window.

The fact that this code is simple is the result of design, not coincidence. A request for a new document may come from more than one source. For example, this is the same thing that happens when the user chooses New from the File menu.

All of the code required to create a new window has been factored (separated) into a cohesive unit. Therefore you can access that code with a single call to NewHook() whenever you need a new document. That keeps the code simple.

There is a significant additional benefit as well. If you modify behavior from NewHook() on down, any change you make in the process of creating a new window is automatically reflected any place you call NewHook(). If you want to change behavior, you change only one set of code. If there's a problem, you fix it once and it is fixed everywhere.

Step 4: Handle a quit application Apple event

Modify: EasyHandleQuitAE() in AppleEvents.c

In Step 1 you installed this function as the handler for a quit application event. It should do any work necessary to properly shut down the application. As with opening, the quitting code in EasyApp is factored.

```
OSErr     error = noErr;

error = QuitHook(kAskUser);
if (error == noErr)
{
  g.done = true;
```

```
}
else
{
  error = errAEEventNotHandled;
}

return error;
```

You simply call QuitHook() specifying that you ask the user whether to save any changed documents. If successful, you set the global done flag to true. This is the same thing that happens when the user chooses the Quit item from the File menu.

Step 5: Handle an open document Apple event

Modify: EasyHandleODocAE() in AppleEvents.c

In Step 1 you installed this function as the handler for an open document event. This event requires some additional processing before you can call the factored code for opening a document. The processing is necessary to extract the Apple event parameter that contains the list of documents to open. You then walk through the list opening each document.

```
long    numFiles, fileCount;

/* the direct object parameter is the list of aliases */
error = AEGetParamDesc(theAEvent, keyDirectObject,
                       typeAEList, &theList);
if (error)
{
  return(error);
}

/* that should be all, but in case something is screwy... */
error = EasyHasUnusedParameters(theAEvent);
if (error)
{
  return(error);
}

/* get number of files in list */
error = AECountItems(&theList, &numFiles);
if (error)
{
  return(error);
}

/* open each file - keep track of errors    */
for (fileCount = 1; fileCount <= numFiles; fileCount++)
{
  FSSpec    fileToOpen;
```

```
long     actualSize;
AEKeyword  dummyKeyword;
DescType  dummyType;
WindowPtr  newWindow;

/* get the alias for the nth file, convert to an FSSpec */
error = AEGetNthPtr(&theList, fileCount, typeFSS,
                    &dummyKeyword, &dummyType,
                    (Ptr) &fileToOpen, sizeof(FSSpec),
                    &actualSize);
if (error)
{
  return(error);
}

/* open the file (also creates window) */
error = OpenHook(&newWindow, &fileToOpen);
if (error == kAlreadyOpenError)
```

First, you call **AEGetParamDesc()** to get the descriptor for the direct object. For this type of event, that's a list of aliases. As usual you check for error. In addition, you call EasyHasUnusedParameters() to make sure that there isn't additional information. There shouldn't be. If there is, something funny is going on and you should bail out. The code for EasyHasUnusedParameters() is provided for you.

Call **AECountItems()** to get the number of items in the list. Existing code then sets up a loop to step through the list of items.

The key to the entire process is the call to **AEGetNthPtr()**. With these parameters, you tell the System which item in the list you want, and that you want the data returned to you as a file spec. If no error occurs, you now have a file specification for the *n*th item in the list of files.

With that precious bit of data in hand, you can call OpenHook(). The code to open a file is factored, so all you have to do is check for error. The rest of the code in this function is provided for you. It is simply error checking.

As for the print document Apple event, examine EasyHandlePDocAE() if you wish. It is almost identical to the code for opening a document, except that it prints the document without showing a window.

Step 6:   Run the application
Modify: none

Save your work and run the project using the debugger. When the debugger window opens, launch EasyPuzzle.

When you do, a puzzle window appears automatically! The open application event handler has done its work. The code in `EasyInitApp()` sets the `g.newOnLaunch` flag to `true`, so the open application event handler responds by creating a new window. Until now this event handler did nothing. Now it works!

Save two puzzle files and close all your puzzle windows. Then go to the Finder, locate the puzzle files, and drag and drop them onto the EasyPuzzle icon. EasyPuzzle should open the files and display the puzzle windows. This works whether EasyPuzzle is running or not. If EasyPuzzle is not running, the Finder launches the application before sending the open document event. In this case, the Finder does *not* send an open application event; it sends the open document event. No untitled window should appear.

Now test the print document and quit handlers. Quit EasyPuzzle. Select a puzzle file in the Finder and choose the Print item (not the Print Window item) from the Finder's File menu. The Finder launches EasyPuzzle, sends it a print document event, and then sends it a quit application event. In response, EasyPuzzle launches, prints the document, and quits. In a few moments, your printer should print the document you selected.

When you are through observing, quit the application.

Interapplication Communication

This chapter provides just a hint of the real power of interapplication communication. It would be unfair to you to leave it at that. There is a lot more to Apple events than what you have seen so far.

In this chapter you have opened a path that gives the Finder rudimentary control over EasyPuzzle. A full implementation of the Apple event architecture turns that path into a superhighway.

For example, the core suite of Apple events is designed to control typical application behavior. If you implemented the core suite, you would allow another application to open, close, count, copy, get, make, move, set, or delete objects in your application. Depending on how you define your application's behavior and the objects within the application, those objects might be windows, items within a window, items inside other items, groups of items, or parts of an items, all the way down to individual characters of text.

And that's not all! There are other events within the core suite, and there are other suites of events that you might implement if they were appropriate for your kind of application.

An Apple-event-savvy application can be a server to other applications. You might write a spelling-checker program that has no public interface at all! Other Apple-event-aware word processing applications could send Apple events to your spell checker and use it to do work. You could write a list sorter or a database engine. Properly designed and structured—a nontrivial but attainable goal—almost any application can be fully controlled by Apple events from an outside source.

If you fully implement Apple event support into your application, your program becomes "scriptable." A scriptable application is one that can act in response to Apple events received from a scripting environment—like AppleScript. In a scripting environment, nonprogrammers can write simple scripts that make your application do work, typically in conjunction with some other application. This allows the adept user to combine the functionality of two or more applications into a single, custom-designed package that gets work done that neither application could do alone.

Finally, you can design your application so that it gets work done by sending Apple events to itself! For example, when the user chooses an item in a menu you don't jump directly into the code that implements the behavior. Instead, you build an Apple event and send it to yourself. In response to the Apple event, your handler for that kind of event gets called. The same functionality is implemented, but by a slightly indirect route.

> Building an Apple event and sending it to yourself doesn't slow things down very much. The System is smart enough to know that the target application for the event is the same as the sending application. So the Apple Event Manager short circuits the usual process and puts the event directly into your queue. The performance hit is minimal. The only time required is the time it takes to build the Apple event to send to yourself, and to extract the data once you receive it.

This approach requires well-factored code. Your application's functionality must be carefully broken down into pieces that can be controlled by Apple events. The benefit of this approach is two-fold.

First, you get to reuse code. You saw this in the lab exercise. When you received a quit application Apple event in the exercise, you were able to call the same function that implements the Quit item in the File menu. Although the source of the commands was completely different—one from the Finder, one from the user selecting a menu item—you can use the same code over again. This saves you programming time and effort. It also reduces the possibility of mistakes creeping into your code because you don't have two or three versions of code to implement the identical behavior.

Second, if you send Apple events to yourself your application becomes recordable. This means that a scripting environment—like AppleScript—can record the events that occur inside your application and automatically build a script to duplicate those events. The user can then play back the script at any time. This is ideal for preserving a complex series of steps. You do it right, you do it once, and then you let the machine take care of the rest.

This power and flexibility does not come for free. It requires careful thought and hard work writing code to support what Apple calls the Open Scripting Architecture—of which Apple events are an important part.

If you are intrigued by an operating system where smaller is better and applications communicate with each other to get significant work done, you are not alone. This kind of cross-application freedom may lead to the death of monolithic software that attempts to be all things to all users. It also means that small companies and individual programmers can carve out a niche in a market place dominated by software giants.

Apple Event Manager Reference

This section summarizes some of the basic Apple Event Manager calls you use in a standard Macintosh application. For full details on all the Apple Event Manager calls, consult Chapter 4 of *Inside Macintosh: Interapplication Communication*.

```
pascal OSErr AEProcessAppleEvent(const EventRecord *theEventRecord)
```

Parameters	theEventRecord	address of event record
Returns	Error value if call fails	
Description	When you receive a high-level event, use this routine to parse the event and call the appropriate handler.	

```
pascal OSErr AEInstallEventHandler(AEEventClass theAEEventClass, AEEventID
                    theAEEventID, AEEventHandlerUPP handler,
                    long handlerRefcon, Boolean
                    isSysHandler)
```

Parameters	theAEEventClass	class of event to be handled

	theAEEventID	ID of event to be handled
	handler	UPP for the event handler function
	handlerRefcon	application-provided value
	isSysHandler	true => install handler in system dispatch table, false => install handler in application dispatch table

Returns   Error value if call fails

Description   Creates entry in Apple event dispatch table for that particular class and ID of event.

```
pascal OSErr AEGetParamPtr(const AppleEvent *theAppleEvent, AEKeyword
                    theAEKeyword, DescType desiredType, DescType
                    *typeCode, void *dataPtr, Size maximumSize,
                    Size *actualSize)
```

Parameters

	theAppleEvent	pointer to Apple event record involved
	theAEKeyword	keyword for kind of data you want
	desiredType	how you want the data returned
	typeCode	address to store actual type of returned data
	dataPtr	address where returned data should be placed
	maximumSize	maximum number of bytes you want
	actualSize	address to store actual size of data returned

Returns   Error value if call fails

Description   The dataPtr parameter must point to enough memory to store the returned data, at least the size of maximumSize. You are responsible for allocating the memory. Therefore, this call is useful when you know the size of the data you are requesting.

```
pascal OSErr AEGetParamDesc(const AppleEvent *theAppleEvent, AEKeyword
                    theAEKeyword, DescType desiredType, AEDesc
                    *result)
```

Parameters

	theAppleEvent	pointer to Apple event record involved
	theAEKeyword	keyword for kind of data you want
	desiredType	how you want the data returned
	result	address of an AEDesc to store result

Returns	Error value if call fails	
Description	This call returns the requested descriptor record in the `result` parameter. The returned value is coerced into the desired type.	

```
pascal OSErr AECountItems(const AEDescList *theAEDescList, long *theCount)
```

Parameters	theAEDescList	address of a descriptor record that contains a reference to a list of other descriptor records
	theCount	address of a long value to store result
Returns	Error value if call fails	
Description	This call returns the number of items in the supplied list.	

```
pascal OSErr AEGetNthPtr(const AEDescList *theAEDescList, long index,
                DescType desiredType, AEKeyword *theAEKeyword,
                DescType *typeCode, void *dataPtr, Size
                maximumSize, Size *actualSize)
```

Parameters	theAEDescList	address of a descriptor record that contains a reference to a list of other descriptor records
	index	which item in the list to retrieve
	desiredType	how you want the data returned
	theAEKeyword	address to store keyword for kind of data returned
	typeCode	address to store actual type of returned data
	dataPtr	address where returned data should be placed
	maximumSize	maximum number of bytes you want
	actualSize	address to store actual size of data returned
Returns	Error value if call fails	
Description	Retrieves the data from the specified member of the list provided.	

```
pascal OSErr AEInteractWithUser(long timeOutInTicks, NMRecPtr nmReqPtr,
                AEIdleUPP idleProc)
```

Parameters	timeOutInTicks	amount of time you are willing to wait for user reply; kAEDefaultTimeOut => Apple Event Manager decides; kNoTimeOut => wait forever

nmReqPtr	pointer to a notification record so Notification Manager will alert user if your app is in the background
idleProc	UPP to a procedure to run while waiting, typically to handle events while waiting for the Apple Event Manager to return control to you

Returns   Error value if call fails

Description   Call before displaying alert to the user. The Apple Event Manager switches your app to the foreground if possible. If you pass nil for the second parameter, Apple Event Manager looks for a SICN with the same ID as the app icons specified in FREF resource. If it finds one, it flashes the icon in the menu bar to alert the user.

Share Your Toys: Cut, Copy, and Paste

One of the radical ideas introduced with the Macintosh was that sharing data between applications should be simple. When data flows freely, the user can mix and match letters, numbers, sounds, and pictures from a wide variety of sources to create whole new ideas.

In this chapter, we talk about what you as a programmer must do to implement cut, copy, and paste—the original data sharing model for the Macintosh. By supporting the cut, copy, and paste model, your program fosters the spirit of creativity that made the Macintosh famous.

You'll see how as we discuss:

- Data formats
- The Clipboard
- Putting data on the Scrap
- Getting data from the Scrap
- Supporting editing operations in dialogs

In the lab for this chapter, you implement copy and paste between EasyPuzzle windows and between EasyPuzzle and other applications that understand pictures.

Data Formats

When data exchange occurs within a single application (such as between windows), there isn't a problem. Clearly an application should understand its own data format. When data exchange occurs between different applications, you have a problem. Every program stores its data in some unique and usually proprietary format.

To solve the problem, the two applications must each understand a common data format. This principle is fundamental to all data sharing. Both the sender and receiver of the data must speak the same language, as it were. Privately, an application can continue to speak its own language. When dealing with other applications, however, it must convert its proprietary data into a public and standard format. Any other program that subscribes to the format can then understand and use the data.

There are several standard formats on the Macintosh. Each of these formats is given a type—analogous to a document type or a resource type. The type is a case-sensitive four-character symbol that uniquely identifies the data format. Some of the standard formats are illustrated in Figure 18.1. There are other standard formats as well.

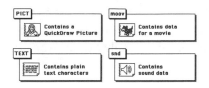

Figure 18.1 Some standard Scrap data types

The Clipboard

Using common data formats solves one problem. There's a second problem that arises when you want to exchange data between applications. Where do you find the other application's data?

In addition to a standard format, to implement data exchange between applications you also need a standard location to store data. On the Macintosh, this is the "Scrap," also known as the "Clipboard." These terms are interchangeable.

On the Macintosh, the System allocates memory to hold the Scrap *inside each application's heap*. As a result there are several blocks of memory devoted to the Scrap—one per application (see Figure 18.2). However, only one is current and in use. The current foreground application has the up-to-date Scrap. If that application puts data on the Scrap, its Scrap is the only Scrap that changes right away.

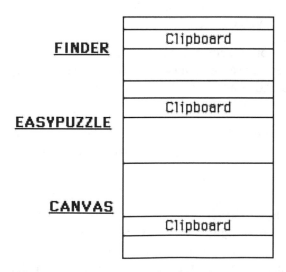

Figure 18.2 Location of the Clipboard

When an application switches to the foreground, the System copies the Scrap data from the suspending application to the resuming application's Scrap. As a result, when your application becomes active it always has the current Scrap data stored in its Scrap.

In addition, if the Scrap has changed since the last time your application was in the foreground, the convertClipboardFlag is set in the event record for the resume event you receive. If your application maintains a private Scrap for data exchange among your own windows, this flag tells you that you should convert the contents of the public Scrap into your private Scrap, so that your private Scrap remains current as well.

Conversely, if your application uses a private Scrap and receives a suspend event, before suspending you should move your private Scrap data onto the regular Scrap. Then other applications can access the latest data.

You are not restricted to standard formats. You can put proprietary data formats on the public Scrap for your own use. All you have to do is specify a four-character type. The Scrap Manager treats all types as if they were simply streams of data. It is the application's responsibility to ensure that the data is formatted correctly before placing it on the Scrap.

The same data can be on the Clipboard in more than one format at the same time. For example, you may have a graphics application that has a proprietary data format it calls 'DraW.' Assume that this drawing program also supports text. If you copy a text object, should you put that on the Scrap as text, as a picture, or in your proprietary format? The answer is, you can do all three.

The same data can be on the Scrap in several formats at the same time. In Figure 18.3, the application placed the same data three times: once in its proprietary format, a second time as type 'PICT,' and a third time as type 'TEXT.' The text might be the picture caption, or a comment or note attached to the picture.

Although the Scrap supports multiple data formats, all the data in all the formats should be consistent. If you have multiple formats, each one should contain data representing the same items.

Similarly, when you retrieve data from the Scrap, you ask for it by type. Typically you look first for the "richest" data format you understand—the format that holds the most information for your application. When our hypothetical drawing program reads data from the Scrap, it looks first for its own private data type. If it doesn't find any data of that type, it looks next for 'PICT' data, and then 'TEXT.'

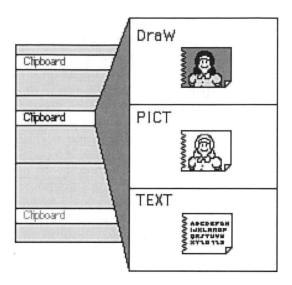

Figure 18.3 Multiple simultaneous data types

> There is no Scrap Manager call to get the names for all the types available on the Scrap at any moment. You have to look for them one by one.

Putting Data on the Scrap

The following discussion applies to your application's document windows. We discuss what to do for dialog windows a little later in this chapter.

When the user chooses either Cut or Copy from the Edit menu, your responsibility is to put the currently selected items on the Scrap in one or more appropriate standard data formats. You may also put the data on the Scrap in one or more proprietary formats used by your own application.

To do this you must clear out anything already on the Scrap before you start loading your data. Call `ZeroScrap()` to empty the Scrap. This call returns a `long` value. If it is non-zero, the call failed.

> If you don't clear the Scrap and put new data on it that has the same type as some existing data, you lose your new data. The Scrap Manager puts the new data after the original data. But you can't ever get the new data because calls to `GetScrap()` always get the first instance of a requested data type. So you get the original and never get the new!

After the Scrap is empty, you can copy data onto the Scrap. Call PutScrap(). You specify the number of bytes, the data type, and the address of the data. It is your responsibility to put all of the data into a single block formatted correctly for the data type. (This is analogous to flattening window data when you save a file. In this case, you are flattening selected objects rather than all the data in the window.)

If you want to put the same data onto the Scrap in more than one format, create a block containing the data in the appropriate format, and call PutScrap() again. Do not call ZeroScrap() again; doing so would wipe out the first data you put on the Scrap.

From a human interface perspective, the cut and copy operations are identical with one exception. When the user chooses the Cut item from the Edit menu, you should put the items on the Scrap and then delete them from the window. If the user chooses Copy, put a copy of the data on the Scrap and leave the contents of the window unchanged.

Getting Data from the Scrap

When the user chooses the Paste item, you use GetScrap() to do two things: determine whether the Scrap contains data your application understands, and retrieve the data. GetScrap() has three parameters: a handle to a location where the data should be stored, the type of data you want, and the address of a variable where the Scrap Manager puts the byte offset to where the data is located in the Scrap.

This last value is of little use. GetScrap() returns a long value. If data of the requested type is available, the return value is the size of the data. If the requested data type is not available the return value is a declared constant, noTypeErr. If an error occurs, the value is negative.

The first time you call GetScrap(), you don't want to read the data. You don't know whether the data is available, or how many bytes the data occupies. Pass nil for the handle to storage. If the storage handle is nil, the Scrap Manager doesn't copy the data, it simply returns the length of the data. If the return value is valid, you can allocate a handle of the correct size to hold the data.

Then call GetScrap() again. This time pass the handle to the storage you just allocated. The Scrap Manager puts the requested data into your storage. After that, do whatever is appropriate for your application with that data.

From the human interface perspective, when you paste data into a window, the data should replace any currently selected objects. It is your responsibility to determine whether there are any selected objects, and if so to delete them before completing the paste operation. You should also make sure that at least one of the newly pasted objects actually appears in the window. That way the user receives immediate visual feedback that the paste operation was successful.

Finally, you may want to inspect the Scrap to determine whether to enable or disable the Paste item in the Edit menu. If the Scrap does not contain any data that your application can understand, the Paste item can be disabled.

Supporting Editing Operations in Dialogs

Everything we have covered so far applies to your application's document windows and not to dialog windows. Dialogs frequently have editable text fields, and a user should be able to cut, copy, paste, or clear text in those fields.

To support this functionality, when the user chooses an Edit menu command, you must identify the type of window involved. If the window is a dialog window, the Dialog Manager provides special calls to support editing operations. You should call `DialogCut()`, `DialogCopy()`, `DialogPaste()`, or `DialogDelete()` as appropriate. In each case you provide a pointer to the dialog. It doesn't get much easier than that.

Now let's implement cut, copy, and paste with some real code—for documents and dialogs in EasyApp and EasyPuzzle.

Lab 18.1 Implementing Cut, Copy, and Paste

Menu dispatch code for the Edit menu has been provided for you. Let's take a quick look at it so you know how control passes through EasyApp.

In response to a choice in the Edit menu, EasyApp calls `EditMenuHook()`, which in turn passes control to `EasyHandleEditMenu()`. You can override all Edit menu dispatch by overriding `EditMenuHook()`; however, `EasyHandleEditMenu()` should suffice for most applications. `EasyHandleEditMenu()` calls a corresponding EasyApp function for each item in the menu—`EasyCut()`, `EasyCopy()`, and so forth. You write most of those functions in this lab.

In those functions, if the window is an Easy window, you send a message to the window to take care of the operation. If the window is a dialog, you use the Dialog Manager to handle the operation.

In this lab you:

- Handle cut operations
- Handle copy operations
- Handle paste operations
- Handle clear operations
- Cut data from a window
- Copy data from a window
- Paste data in a puzzle window

Use your code from the previous lab as the starting point for your work in this lab.

Step 1:   Handle cut operations

Modify: EasyCut() in menus.c

When the user chooses the Cut item in the Edit menu, the EasyApp dispatch code ultimately calls here. You identify what type of window is involved and respond accordingly. The algorithm in this function forms the pattern for each of the next three steps as you manage copy, paste, and clear operations.

```
EasyWindowPtr easyWindow = GetEasyWindowPtr(macWindow);

if (easyWindow)
{
  error = easyWindow->DoCut(macWindow, nil);
  easyWindow->changed = true;
}
else if (EasyIsDialog(macWindow))
{
  DialogCut((DialogPtr)macWindow);
}

return error;
```

If the window is an Easy window, you send it a DoCut message. You write BaseCut() in a subsequent step. You also mark the window as changed. Cutting removes something from a window, therefore changing its contents.

Otherwise, you call EasyIsDialog() to determine whether the window is a dialog window. If it is, call DialogCut().

Step 2: Handle copy operations

Modify: `EasyCopy()` in menus.c

This follows the same algorithm as cutting.

```
EasyWindowPtr easyWindow = GetEasyWindowPtr(macWindow);

if (easyWindow)
{
  error = easyWindow->DoCopy(macWindow, nil);
}

else if (EasyIsDialog(macWindow))
{
  DialogCopy((DialogPtr)macWindow);
}

return error;
```

If the window is an Easy window, you send it a DoCopy message. The window then responds accordingly. You write BaseCopy() in a subsequent step.

Otherwise, call EasyIsDialog() to determine whether the window is a dialog window. If it is, call **DialogCopy()**.

Step 3: Handle paste operations

Modify: `EasyPaste()` in menus.c

This should look very familiar to you:

```
EasyWindowPtr easyWindow = GetEasyWindowPtr(macWindow);

if (easyWindow)
{
  error = easyWindow->DoPaste(macWindow, nil);
  easyWindow->changed = true;
}
else if (EasyIsDialog(macWindow))
{
  DialogPaste((DialogPtr)macWindow);
}

return error;
```

If the window is an Easy window, you send it a DoPaste message. You write PuzzlePaste() in a subsequent step. You also mark the window as changed. Pasting adds or replaces something in a window, therefore changing its contents.

Otherwise, call EasyIsDialog() to determine whether the window is a dialog window. If it is, call **DialogPaste()**.

Step 4:   Handle clear operations

Modify: EasyClear() in menus.c

You can probably guess what this code looks like:

```
EasyWindowPtr easyWindow = GetEasyWindowPtr(macWindow);

if (easyWindow)
{
  error = easyWindow->DoClear(macWindow, nil);
  easyWindow->changed = true;
}

else if (EasyIsDialog(macWindow))
{
  DialogDelete((DialogPtr)macWindow);
}

return error;
```

If the window is an Easy window, send it a DoClear message. You also mark the window as changed. Clearing removes something from a window, therefore changing its contents.

Otherwise, call EasyIsDialog() to determine whether the window is a dialog window. If it is, call **DialogDelete()**.

The code for EasySelectAll() is provided for you. It sends a DoSelectAll message to an EasyWindow. There is no corresponding Dialog Manager routine for select all, so it ignores dialog windows.

Step 5:   Cut data from a window

Modify: BaseCut() in menus.c

Cutting is the same as copying, only you delete items from the window after you copy them:

```
OSErr      error = noErr;

error = easyWindow->DoCopy(macWindow, nil);
if (error)
{
```

```
        return error;
    }

    error = easyWindow->DoClear(macWindow, nil);

    return error;
```

You send the window a DoCopy message. If there is no error, you send the window a DoClear message. Job done.

Exactly how to respond to the DoClear message is completely dependent upon the data structures in your application. As a result, in EasyApp this function is empty. It is also empty in EasyPuzzle because EasyPuzzle does not allow the user to clear the contents of a puzzle window. A typical implementation is to step through each object in your window. If it is selected, delete it.

Step 6: Copy data from a window

Modify: BaseCopy() in windowProc.c

This function responds to a DoCopy message. This default implementation simply puts a PICT of all selected items on the Scrap. It relies on the window to provide the picture. In EasyPuzzle the contents of the window are already a PICT, so this works just fine for EasyPuzzle.

```
    Size        size;

    error = easyWindow->DoDrawSelected(macWindow, &thePicture);
    if (error || thePicture == nil)
    {
      return error;
    }

    EasyLockHandle (thePicture);

    error = (OSErr)ZeroScrap();
    if (error)
    {
      KillPicture((PicHandle)thePicture);
      return error;
    }

    size  = GetHandleSize(thePicture);
    error = PutScrap(size,'PICT', *thePicture);

    KillPicture((PicHandle)thePicture);

    return error;
```

You send the window a DoDrawSelected message. In response to that message, the window identifies selected items, makes a PICT of those items, and returns a handle to the new picture in the variable thePicture. You then lock the handle.

You call ZeroScrap() to empty the Scrap. If there is an error, call KillPicture() to release memory and return.

Otherwise, you get the size of the picture with GetHandleSize() and put it on the Scrap by calling PutScrap(). This puts a copy of the data on the Scrap. You then dispose of the picture and return.

Depending on the contents of your application's windows, you may want to substitute a more powerful function that also puts data on the Scrap as plain text, styled text, or in some proprietary format for copying among your own windows.

Step 7: Paste data in a puzzle window

Modify: InitPuzzleWindow() in *puzzleWindow.c*

Modify: PuzzlePaste() in *puzzleWindow.c*

The default BasePaste() behavior does nothing significant in response to a DoPaste message, because an EasyApp window has no contents. In this step, you override the default behavior by substituting PuzzlePaste() as the function that responds to a DoPaste message. You also write PuzzlePaste().

In the InitPuzzleWindow() function, add this line of code:

```
easyWindow->DoRevert    = (WindowProc)PuzzleRevert;
easyWindow->DoPaste     = (WindowProc)PuzzlePaste;
easyWindow->DoDragItems = (WindowProc)DragPuzzleItems;
```

This sets the Easy window's DoPaste field to be the function pointer for the PuzzlePaste() function.

PuzzlePaste() should determine whether there is a PICT on the Scrap. If there is, fetch it and replace the existing picture with the new picture. Easier said than done, but here's the code:

```
long        scrapOffset;

/* first, see if there is a PICT */
size = GetScrap(nil, 'PICT', &scrapOffset);
if (size == noTypeErr)
```

```
  {
    return error;
  }
  else if (size < 0)
  {
    error = (OSErr)size;
    return error;
  }

  /* Confirm operation */
  if (GetPuzzleFirstPiece(easyWindow))
  {
    short  result;
    result = EasyConfirmDialog(kPuzzleBaseID, kPasteWarning);

    if (result == cancel)
    {
      return noErr;
    }
  }

  /* allocate memory to hold the data */
  error = EasyAllocateHandle(size, &thePicture);
  if (error)
  {
    return error;
  }

  /* get the data from the Scrap */
  size = GetScrap(thePicture, 'PICT', &scrapOffset);
  if (size < 0)
  {
    EasyDisposeHandle(&thePicture);
    error = (OSErr)size;
    return error;
  }

  /* wipe out any existing structures */
  DisposePuzzleContents(macWindow);

  /* install new picture */
  SetPuzzlePicture(easyWindow, (PicHandle)thePicture);

  /* resize the window */
  easyWindow->DoResize(macWindow, nil);

  /* force an update */
  EasyForceUpdate(macWindow);

  return error;
```

First, call `GetScrap()` with a nil handle to look for a PICT. The return value contains either an error or the size of the data. You handle the error if any occurs.

If the current puzzle is already in pieces, pasting a new picture destroys the puzzle. It is polite to ask the user to confirm that. You call GetPuzzleFirstPiece() to see whether there are pieces. If there are, you call EasyConfirmDialog() to post an alert to the user. If the user cancels the operation, you bail out.

Next, you allocate memory to hold the PICT data, based on the size you got from the first call to **GetScrap()**. You call **GetScrap()** again to actually retrieve a copy of the data. Once again you check for error.

If everything is successful, only then do you replace the original picture. You call DisposePuzzleContents() to wipe out the existing data. You call SetPuzzlePicture() to attach the new picture to the puzzle data. You send the window a DoResize message. This sets up all the associated puzzle data and adjusts the window to the size of the new picture. Then you force an update so the window is completely redrawn.

Notice that you do not dispose of the picture! You have just attached it to the window and it is in use. You have transferred "ownership" of the picture to the window. It is now the window's responsibility to take care of the picture.

Step 8: Run the application

Modify: none

Save your work and run the project using the debugger. When the debugger window appears, launch EasyPuzzle.

An untitled window appears with the default picture. Open a saved puzzle file that has a different picture in it, or import a PICT, so you have two windows with different pictures. Don't scramble either. While one is active, choose Copy from the Edit menu. Switch windows and choose Paste. The new picture appears in the destination window, and the window resizes to accommodate it.

Repeat this process, but scramble the destination window before pasting. When you choose Paste, an alert appears asking you to confirm the operation. Click OK and the paste continues. Click Cancel and the operation terminates leaving the destination window unchanged.

Try copy and paste between EasyPuzzle and a drawing application of some kind. It should work just fine, as long as the drawing program supports PICT.

When you are through observing, quit the application.

You have crossed a significant threshold into the world of data sharing. Applications should share data as painlessly and transparently as possible. In the next chapter, you explore the latest software technology for achieving this goal—drag and drop.

Scrap Manager Reference

This section summarizes the basic Scrap Manager calls you use in a standard Macintosh application. For full details on all the Scrap Manager calls, consult Chapter 2 of *Inside Macintosh: More Macintosh Toolbox*.

The related Dialog Manager calls for editing in a dialog appear in the "Dialog Manager Reference" section at the end of Chapter 11.

`pascal long ZeroScrap(void)`

Parameters   none

Returns   An error value, non-zero indicates error

Description   Empties the Scrap in preparation for adding data to it. Call once before adding data. Do not call before adding additional types.

`pascal long PutScrap(long length, ResType theType, Ptr source)`

Parameters

length	number of bytes of data
theType	type to store it as
source	address where data is located

Returns   An error value, non-zero indicates error

Description   Add data of specified size and type to the current Scrap. It is your responsibility to make sure data is formatted correctly for the type specified.

`pascal long GetScrap(Handle hDest, ResType theType, long *offset)`

Parameters

hDest	handle to storage where data should be placed, nil => don't copy data
theType	type of data you want
offset	address where call puts byte offset to start of data in Scrap

Returns   A value, positive is the length of the data, negative is an error. Value −102 is `noTypeErr`.

Description   Use nil for `hDest` to determine whether a type is available and how many bytes it occupies. Allocate storage and call again, passing your storage as destination for the data.

Really Share Your Toys: Drag and Drop

Drag and drop is the latest data exchange model from Apple Computer. It is a descendant of cut, copy, and paste. Unlike some other developments in System software, drag and drop does not replace its ancestor. Cut, copy, and paste remain vital and important tools in the Macintosh human interface.

Drag and drop is copy and paste on steroids. To exchange data, all the user has to do is select one or more items and drag them to a destination, wherever that might be. Drag and drop allows single-gesture copy and paste operations across windows, either within the same application or from one application to another. The Drag Manager also supports moving items within a single window as well as dropping items on the Finder's Desktop.

Drag and drop is an integral part of System 7.5, and is available as an extension for earlier versions of System 7. Programming for drag and drop is a more advanced topic than most in this book. However, the functionality is so cool and so intuitive to the user that every program should support the drag and drop model for data exchange.

How to accomplish that goal becomes clear as we discuss:

- An overview of drag and drop
- The drag and drop human interface
- Programming for drag and drop

In the lab exercise, you implement drag and drop for EasyPuzzle.

Drag and Drop Overview

Drag and drop allows the user to manipulate data directly in simple and intuitive ways. Ideally, the user should be able to drag any data from any window to any other window that accepts that data type. The user can even drop the data on the Desktop to create special "clipping" files that contain data for later use. It's just like being able to save a Clipboard for future reference.

Drag and drop is a significant benefit to every Macintosh user. The ability to drag data and drop it where you want it is simple, intuitive, and leaves the average person wondering why things haven't always worked this way. There is no question that your users will enjoy and appreciate drag and drop functionality.

Even better—from the programmer's perspective—if you support copy and paste, adding drag and drop is straightforward.

> In fact, if you design your application to *require* drag and drop, the Drag Manager relieves you of writing separate code to manage dragging within your own application. You can use the Drag Manager to move data within your window (although to drag an actual image such as you do for puzzle pieces you have to override the Drag Manager's default dragging routines, a topic beyond the scope of this chapter). You may not want to require drag and drop in your programs right away, however. It is a new feature of System 7.5 and not everyone has it yet.

Because drag and drop is a technology that is highly visible to the user, human interface issues are very important. We discuss them in depth before we discuss the Drag Manager API.

Drag and Drop Human Interface

This section gives you an overview of the drag and drop feedback mechanisms. It also covers the Finder's clipping files, and the distinction between moving data and copying data as it affects the human interface.

Feedback

As the user selects, drags, and ultimately drops an object or group of objects, you provide feedback every step of the way. Figure 19.1 illustrates the various phases and outcomes of a drag operation using the Drag Manager—from the user's perspective. They are: selection feedback, drag feedback, destination feedback, and drop feedback.

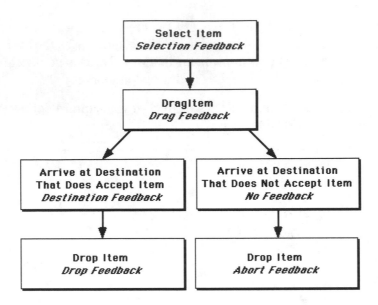

Figure 19.1 Drag and drop feedback steps

Selection Feedback

Selection feedback is not a new concept. It's the same thing you do to let your user know that some object or group of objects are the subject of the next operation. When an item is selected, use your normal selection feedback: highlight text, outline shapes, display selection handles, and so forth.

The user should be able to select and drag an item with one click. This is called *single-gesture dragging*. The Drag Manager provides a routine named `WaitMouseMoved()` for detecting the beginning of a drag.

Background selection is important to drag and drop. We discussed this briefly in Chapter 12. With drag and drop, the user should be able to drag items from an inactive window into an active window without the background window becoming active. Therefore the user should be able to see what is selected, even when the window is inactive. Text and graphic items can have a single pixel outline, for example. Of course, when an inactive window becomes active, the selection becomes highlighted as a normal selection.

Drag Feedback

When the user begins a drag, the Drag Manager (with your help) provides feedback in the form of a dotted outline of the items being dragged. This outline follows the cursor around the screen.

You specify a drag region to the Drag Manager. The Drag Manager displays this region at the current mouse position and tracks the mouse until the user releases the mouse button and drops the items.

Typically, drag feedback consists of a dotted outline framing each selected item. Figure 19.2 shows a simple outline for a text item. For a compound object or multiple selections, you can substitute a dotted rectangle encompassing all the selected items, but this is not as helpful to the user in placing the drop. An outline framing each individual item is superior. Figure 19.5 later in this chapter illustrates a drag with multiple items.

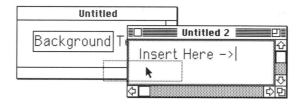

Figure 19.2 Drag feedback

You can provide different behavior, such as moving the actual picture along with the drag. The Drag Manager allows you to override the default drawing behavior for the drag region.

Destination Feedback

When the cursor crosses an acceptable destination—say the content portion of a window—you let the user know by providing destination feedback. Typically this takes the form of highlighting the destination's boundaries. If the destination is not acceptable—perhaps a scroll bar or window title—there is no feedback. The absence of feedback conveys a message as clearly as the presence of feedback.

Destination feedback should occur only when the destination can accept the type of data contained in the dragged items. For example, an editable text box should only accept a drop of a text item, not a picture or sound item.

A drag may have multiple items. These items may be a cohesive unit of some kind. You should accept the drop only if your destination can accept all items in the drag.

The Drag Manager has routines to highlight any region. Typically this is the content area of a window that can accept a drag. It might be some part of a window, and not the entire content area.

Drop Feedback

If the item is dropped at an acceptable location, the dragged items appear at the destination. This provides clear visual feedback whether you are moving or copying.

A copy operation creates an issue with respect to item selection. Assume you are copying items within a single window. The new copies should be selected, and the originals deselected. The user can then reposition the items without having to select them all over again.

If a drop is "unrecoverable," you can post a confirming dialog asking the user to ensure that they wish to drop the item there. For example, dropping a picture onto a scrambled puzzle in EasyPuzzle destroys the puzzle in progress. Allow the user to confirm the drop before allowing it to occur.

Abort Feedback

Dropping outside an acceptable destination is considered an "abort." If the destination is not acceptable, the Drag Manager uses zooming rectangles moving back to the origin of the drag to indicate what happened. This is called a zoomback (see Figure 19.3).

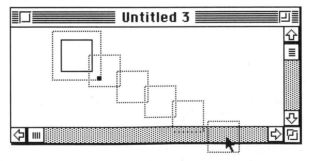

Figure 19.3 A zoomback

You should also use the zoomback if the drop fails for other reasons, such as a lack of memory to create the dropped items in your destination.

Clipping Files

In a copy operation using the Clipboard, you put data on the Clipboard in a variety of formats so that other applications can use the data. In drag and drop, these data types are called "flavors."

When an item is dragged from an application to the Desktop, the Finder creates a clipping file that contains the data in the dragged item. Figure 19.4 shows the different Finder icons for text, sound, picture, and generic clipping files.

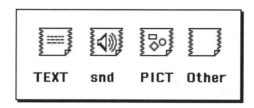

Figure 19.4 Clipping file icons

Your application should present a number of flavors to ensure flexibility with different destinations. Likewise, when you return a clipping file to the original application, round-trip data integrity should be preserved. When the user drags a clipping file and drops it onto your window, you extract the richest flavor of data that your application understands.

Move versus Copy

Any drag between windows or applications should be considered a copy operation. A drag *within a single window* should become a copy operation if the user holds down the Option key. If the Option key is down at the start of the drag, it's a copy operation.

If the Option key is not down at the start of the drag, you can (optionally) check again at the end of the drag. If the Option key was not down at the beginning, but is down at the end, you can make the drag a copy operation. This allows the user to decide to copy after the drag begins.

Of course, sometimes even a move across windows may not be a copy operation. You might have two windows showing different views of the same data. A drag and drop across two such windows is a move, not a copy. You have to apply this principle to your particular application. If you are dragging to a new container, copy. If you are dragging to the same container (in whatever form), move—or copy if the Option key is pressed.

For more details on the human interface, consult the *Drag and Drop Human Interface Guidelines*. You can find a copy in the Macintosh Drag and Drop folder, inside the Tools You Need folder on the CD.

Programming for Drag and Drop

You use the Drag Manager to set up necessary data structures for the drag. While the drag is in progress, the Drag Manager repeatedly calls a tracking handler. This handler manages the user feedback and performs other functions. When the drag is complete—the user drops the item—the Drag Manager calls a receive handler to extract the data. You provide both the tracking and receive handlers. They are System callback functions—like the Apple event handlers you installed in Chapter 17.

The tracking and receive handlers are the core of your drag and drop functionality, so we look at them first. Then we look at a series of tasks that you must perform to implement drag and drop. The specific tasks are

- Registering handlers
- Identifying a drag
- Creating a drag
- Creating a drag region
- Attaching data to a drag
- Tracking and disposing a drag
- Providing destination feedback
- Extracting data from a drag

Notice that your application does not need to initialize the Drag Manager. For details on the Drag Manager calls, see the "Drag Manager Reference" at the end of this chapter.

Drag Handlers

The Drag Manager relies on handlers in your application. There are two kinds of handlers, and both must be present in your application: the tracking handler and the receive handler.

The Drag Manager calls the tracking handler repeatedly while the drag is in progress. It sends a series of messages to the handler. Your application responds to those messages. When the user drops an item, the Drag Manager calls the receive handler. We discuss the programming details of the handlers a little later.

Each window may have its own tracking and receive handlers. Because a window can have its own handlers, dragging behavior can vary from window to window within an application. Windows may have more than one of each handler as well. If there is more than one handler for a window, the Drag Manager calls them all sequentially.

You may also install default handlers. The Drag Manager uses the default handlers for any window that does not have a special handler.

Registering Handlers

Typically you register default handlers at application startup, and specific handlers for individual windows when you create the window. Call InstallTrackingHandler() and InstallReceiveHandler() to install each kind of handler. You pass a UPP for the handler, a pointer to the window, and a refCon parameter for your own use. If the window pointer parameter is nil, the System treats the handler as a default handler. You can use the refCon to provide additional information to your handler, such as a pointer to a data structure used by the handler.

To create a UPP for a tracking handler, call NewDragTrackingHandlerProc(). To create a UPP for a receive handler, call NewDragReceiveHandlerProc(). In each case you provide the name of the function you want to be the handler.

You may also remove handlers using complementary routines, RemoveTrackingHandler() and RemoveReceiveHandler(). If you do, you must dispose of the associated UPP structures as well or you will have a small memory leak.

Identifying a Drag

To determine whether a drag is starting, call WaitMouseMoved(). You typically do this somewhere in the event-parsing section of your application that handles and identifies mouse clicks. If the user clicks on some data in a context that implies selection or dragging, make this call. The call returns true if the mouse has moved and a drag is beginning.

For the call to WaitMouseMoved() you provide a point that represents the starting position of the mouse. It must be in *global* coordinates. The Drag Manager operates on the global level, drawing across applications and windows.

You also want to ensure that you allow for single-gesture dragging. If an object is unselected and clicked, you must check for a drag so that the user can select and drag with a single click.

Creating a Drag

Creating a drag record is trivial. Call `NewDrag()`. You provide the address of a `DragReference` variable. The System allocates memory and puts the new reference to the drag record in your variable. The drag record is a private data structure. You do not need to access its contents. You use the reference to the drag record in several Drag Manager calls. This call allocates memory, so make sure you check for errors.

There's something significant going on here. Notice that you aren't getting anything called a pointer or a handle, but a "reference." Because the drag data structure is private, the System takes care of all dereferencing. You don't have to worry about whether to access the data via pointer or handle. Using references for private data structures is the latest trend in system software design. Window pointers and control handles will turn into references soon. Using references makes programming much easier, because you don't have to worry about the distinctions between handles and pointers.

Creating a Drag Region

Unless you override the process, the Drag Manager is responsible for drawing the outline of selected shapes that follows the mouse as it moves around the screen. This outline should be a region that is the 1-pixel-wide frame of each selected object. For text, it is the bounds of the text.

You are responsible for creating this region. After you have created the region, you pass a handle to the region to the Drag Manager for its use. The Drag Manager then draws the region in a 50% gray pattern (a dotted outline). The region follows the mouse around the screen without any additional effort on your part.

Figure 19.5 shows three selected items in the window of a hypothetical drawing program. The contours of the drag region to the lower right of the illustration show how the drag can escape the source window.

Creating the drag region is your application's responsibility. You can use Toolbox calls that you already know about. A typical algorithm might look like the code here:

```
/* for each selected item */
{
    /* get item region, then do the following… */
    CopyRgn(originalRgn, copyRgn);
    InsetRgn(copyRgn, 1,1);
    DiffRgn(originalRgn, copyRgn, copyRgn);
```

```
    UnionRgn(copyRgn, dragRgn, dragRgn);
}
OffsetRgn(dragRgn, toGlobal.h, toGlobal.v);
```

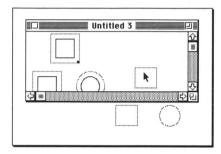

Figure 19.5 Typical drag region

This algorithm makes a copy of each selected item's region, and then insets the region by one pixel. It gets the difference between the original and the copy, resulting in a 1-pixel wide border region. It adds that region to the accumulating drag region.

Note especially that when completed, the drag region is converted to global coordinates. It must be in global coordinates because the Drag Manager operates at the global level, drawing across applications and windows.

Attaching Data to a Drag

Ultimately some destination will receive the items being dragged. The drag record must contain the relevant data so that the destination can rebuild the items. The destination may be your own application, another application, or even the Desktop.

To allow for interapplication portability, the data must be in a format understood by both applications. Like cut, copy, and paste, you can attach data to the drag record in various formats—called flavors in the Drag Manager. For example, you may create a proprietary format for use within your own application, and then attach PICT or TEXT flavors of the data as well.

To attach data, call `AddDragItemFlavor()`. You provide a drag reference, the item number, the data type (flavor), the address of the data to attach, the number of bytes, and some flags.

You make this call for each flavor of data being added to the drag. Unlike a copy and paste operation, a drag may have more than one item, although typically you attach one item to a drag in a variety of flavors.

If creating the data involves a lot of work, you can use advanced Drag Manager techniques to supply data on demand rather than actually attaching the data. You might want to do this to avoid wasting time if the drag is ultimately aborted.

The flags you pass restrict use of the data in some way. For example, the flavorSenderOnly flag indicates to any receiver that this data should be used only by the sender. If that flag is set, the Finder will not store that flavor in a clipping file on the Desktop.

When receiving a drop, your application can look for the "richest" flavor—the flavor it understands best—and rebuild the objects based on that flavor.

Tracking and Disposing a Drag

After you have the drag set up—you have a drag reference, a drag region, and attached all data in all flavors—you call TrackDrag().

You pass a reference to the drag record, a pointer to the event record containing the mouse click that started the drag, and a handle to the drag region. Note that the coordinates for the mouse click in the EventRecord must be *global*. They normally are unless you convert them.

While the drag is in progress, the Drag Manager uses your drag tracking handler. When the user drops the items, the Drag Manager calls your drag receive handler. After that the drag is complete. The Drag Manager returns to the line of code after your call to TrackDrag(). At that point you are through with the drag record and you should dispose of it. Call DisposeDrag(). You provide the drag reference.

Providing Destination Feedback

After you call TrackDrag() and while the drag is in progress, the Drag Manager calls your tracking handler repeatedly. The primary function of the tracking handler is to provide feedback to the user as the drag progresses across that handler's scope of responsibility—a window or several windows.

Because the tracking handler is a System callback function, it must conform to the declared prototype for a tracking handler.

```
pascal OSErr DragTrackingHandler
                (DragTrackingMessage message,
                 WindowPtr theWindow,
                 void *handlerRefCon,
                 DragReference theDragRef);
```

There are five possible messages that the handler may receive:

- dragTrackingEnterHandler
- dragTrackingEnterWindow
- dragTrackingInWindow
- dragTrackingLeaveWindow
- dragTrackingLeaveHandler

The Drag Manager sends a dragTrackingEnterHandler message when the focus of a drag enters the handler for the first time. The drag may move between windows that have the same handler without generating a dragTrackingEnterHandler message.

When the drag enters a new window, the Drag Manager sends a dragTrackingEnterWindow message. When leaving, it sends "leave window" and "leave handler" messages as appropriate.

While the drag continues within a window, the Drag Manager repeatedly sends a dragTrackingInWindow message.

This gives you the context within which you are operating. When you enter the window, you can do any setup work. When you are in the window, you can check for mouse location and examine other attributes of the drag.

To get the mouse location, call **GetDragMouse()**. You provide a drag reference, and the addresses of two point variables. The call returns the current position of the mouse and the "pinned" position of the mouse. The pinned mouse location is the mouse location used to draw the drag region onscreen. Unless your tracking handler is constraining cursor movement, the two points are the same.

> You might want to constrain cursor movement for a variety of reasons. For example, we did this when dragging pieces around the puzzle in Chapter 12 to make sure the user didn't drag the piece right out of the window.

Each drag has attributes that you can retrieve from the drag record. They are declared as:

- dragHasLeftSenderWindow
- dragInsideSenderApplication
- dragInsideSenderWindow

To get the attributes for a drag, call **GetDragAttributes()**. You provide the drag reference, and the address of a DragAttributes variable.

Based on the attributes, the mouse location, and the nature of the message, you can provide the correct feedback to the user. The typical feedback is to highlight a region—usually the content region of the window, but it can be any appropriate region. To do this, call ShowDragHilite(). You provide the drag reference, the region to highlight, and a Boolean value indicating whether you want the highlighting frame to be inside or outside the region bounds. Call HideDragHilite() to turn off highlighting.

You see how this works in the lab exercise when you write a tracking handler.

> The default ShowDragHilite() routine works well only if you're highlighting something with a white background. After you implement this feature in EasyPuzzle, you'll notice that the highlighting doesn't show up because the puzzle border is usually in color. If you set the color to white, the highlighting appears. You can override the default function with a highlighting function you provide, but that's a topic beyond the scope of this chapter.

Extracting Data from a Drag

When the user drops a drag in one of your windows, the Drag Manager calls that window's receive handler. Your receive handler is responsible for extracting the data from the drag record, assuming the data is a flavor your application understands.

The Drag Manager has a variety of routines that help you reach your goal. These routines perform the following tasks:

- Determine how many items are in the drag record
  CountDragItems()

- Get each item's reference number
  GetDragItemReferenceNumber()

- Get the number of flavors for each item
  CountDragItemFlavors()

- Get the type for a particular item flavor
  GetFlavorType()

- Get the size of each flavor's data
  GetFlavorDataSize()

- Get the data
  GetFlavorData()

You can find details for the parameters for these calls in the reference section at the end of this chapter. Precisely how you use these routines depends on your application. However, the lab exercise for this chapter gives you hands-on practice using them to extract a picture from a drag record.

Remember, the drag may be from any application, not just your own. Typically you extract the richest data format your application understands from among the available flavors. You ignore the others.

You should also accept the drop if and only if your application can extract some form of data for *all* items in the drag. The items in the drag may be part of a cohesive unit, and accepting some but missing others may render the group useless.

Is Drag and Drop Available?

Before we get to the lab exercise, however, there is a significant task that applies to all aspects of Macintosh programming that we haven't discussed yet. Drag and Drop is integral to System 7.5, but may or may not be present on machines using earlier versions of System 7. How can your software determine whether drag and drop is available on any given machine?

This is critical, because if you make a Drag Manager call on a machine that doesn't have drag and drop, your program will crash.

This problem extends far beyond drag and drop and is a critical aspect of Macintosh application programming. How do you determine whether any particular feature—hardware or software—is available on a machine? How do you find out if System 7 is available, or if the machine is color-capable?

One Toolbox call does it all, `Gestalt()`. With `Gestalt()` you can psych-out your Mac. It is a simple call with remarkable power. You provide two parameters. The first is a selector value that specifies the feature you want to know about. The second is the address of a `long` value for `Gestalt()` to fill in with some results. This is the response value.

There is a very long list of selector values described in *Inside Macintosh*. Table 17.1 has a small sampling of the selectors available.

Table 17.1: Gestalt() Selector Values

gestaltSystemVersion	gestaltDragMgrAttr
gestaltAppleEventsAttr	gestaltQuickdrawVersion

continues

Table 17.1: Continued

gestaltAliasMgrAttr	gestaltFindFolderAttr
gestaltFontMgrAttr	gestaltFPUType
gestaltFSAttr	gestaltHardwareAttr
gestaltKeyboardType	gestaltLogicalRAMSize
gestaltNotificationMgrAttr	gestaltProcessorType
gestaltQuickdrawFeatures	gestaltPhysicalRAMSize
gestaltResourceMgrAttr	gestaltScrapMgrAttr
gestaltSoundAttr	gestaltSpeechAttr
gestaltTextEditVersion	gestaltQuickTime
gestaltMachineType	gestaltROMVersion

When you call `Gestalt()`, the System puts a response value in the second parameter. The interpretation of the response varies with the selector you use. Table 17.2 lists the typical interpretation of the response value based on the name of the selector.

Table 17.2 Interpreting `Gestalt()` Response

Selector Suffix	Response
Attr	bits of response used as flags to determine what related features are available
Count	the number of items that exist
Size	the actual size of the item
Table	the address of the specified table
Type	an index value indicating the type of feature
Version	version number (ROM, System, and so forth)

The precise meaning of individual bits in an attribute response, the meaning of an index value in a type response, or how to interpret the response to other kinds of selectors are all described in great detail in *Inside Macintosh*.

For all its apparent simplicity, `Gestalt()` has the occasional "gotcha." For example, the `gestaltQuickDrawFeatures` selector has a bit to determine whether color is available. It's not reliable. You should check the QuickDraw version number. The only way to find out about this kind of problem is to check the Tech Notes, read *Inside Macintosh*, and keep abreast of the literature in the Macintosh programming universe.

In the case of drag and drop, you want to find out if support is available in the System before using it. So you call `Gestalt()` with a selector of `gestaltDragMgrAttr`. The drag and drop documentation tells you that—for this selector only—if bit zero of the response is `true`, the Drag Manager is available. You test that bit of the response value and act accordingly.

For a 68K Macintosh, that's all you have to do. For a Power Mac you may have to take two other steps:

- Check for a shared library
- Check that you have access to the shared library

In the Power Mac architecture, certain parts of System software exist as "shared libraries." Much like you used the zooming library and the sound helper library in previous chapters, parts of the System now exist as libraries of code. They are called shared libraries because more than one application may use the library at the same time.

Drag and drop is implemented as a shared library on the Power Mac. For a Power Mac native application. you must make sure that the shared library is present and that you are connected to the shared library.

For drag and drop, the same response you got from your original call to `Gestalt()` also has a bit to indicate whether the shared library is present. You test that bit. If it is `true`, the library is present.

Actually, it tells you that the library was present when the computer started up. If the user moved it after the fact, you might be in trouble. That's why you need to take the next step. There is no sure way of telling whether a shared library is present other than to follow the next step.

Even if the library is present, your application may not be connected to it. You can connect to a library in one of two ways: strong or weak. A strong connection is the default connection. Each connection has certain advantages.

If you absolutely *must* have the library present to run your application, you want to use the strong connection. If you have a strong connection, the System makes sure you are connected to the library before running your application. If you are not connected, the System displays a dialog informing you that the application cannot run because of the absence of a shared library.

If the library is optional, you should use a weak connection. The advantage of a weak connection is that if the features supported by that library are optional, your program can run without the library. Figure 19.6 shows how to set up a weak connection in the CodeWarrior project window. You click the popup box to the right of the library and choose the Import "weak" item from the menu.

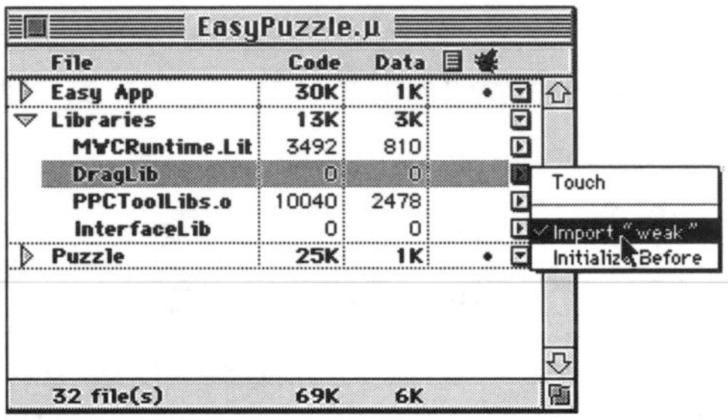

Figure 19.6 Setting a weak connection

If you have a weak connection, the System does not ensure that you are connected to the library. You are telling the System that you will take care of this yourself.

To take care of the connection, look for one of the Toolbox calls in that library to see whether its address is the same as a constant—kUnresolvedSymbolAddress. If they *are* the same, the call is not available, which means that you do not have access to the shared library and you cannot use the calls included in that library.

If they are *not* the same, you are connected. The System does have an address it can call for that Toolbox routine. You will make such a check in the lab exercise, because drag and drop is an optional feature of EasyPuzzle.

You use the same general technique to test for every hardware or software feature that is of significance to your application. If your application requires color, you should make sure it is available on the machine before getting too far into the program. If the feature is part of a shared library in the Power Mac environment, check for both the presence of the library and your connection to it.

Typically, you check the operating environment at launch. If a critical feature is not available, you politely inform the user why the application can't run, and then quit. If you can work without a feature, set flags for yourself so you know what's available.

Let's see how to write code to test for the presence of drag and drop, and to use drag and drop to move a picture from the Puzzle to the Desktop and back again.

Lab 19.1 Implementing Drag and Drop

In this lab, you implement drag and drop for puzzle pictures, but not for puzzle pieces. After you finish, the user can simply click and drag to drop a picture into a puzzle.

To accomplish this goal you:

- Check for drag and drop availability
- Install drag handlers
- Track a drag
- Receive a drag
- Identify the start of a drag
- Drag a picture

The code you write in this lab makes a difference in the performance of EasyPuzzle only if drag and drop is available in your environment. To use drag and drop with the Finder, you must have the Clipping Extension installed. If you are using System 7.5, that's the only requirement. If you are using an earlier version of System 7, you must also have the Macintosh Drag and Drop and Dragging Enabler extensions installed in your system.

Use your code from the previous lab as the starting point for your work in this lab.

Step 0: Connect to a shared library

In this step you look at how to control the manner in which you connect to a shared library. If you are using the 68K version of CodeWarrior, you can skip this step entirely. These instructions apply to the Power Macintosh only.

In the EasyApp and EasyPuzzle design, drag and drop is not mandatory. If you are using the Power Macintosh version of EasyPuzzle, the project file includes a library named DragLib. This is a shared library that implements drag and drop.

As discussed in this chapter, you can connect to this library in a "strong" or "weak" manner. The default connection is "strong," but that means the presence of the library is mandatory for the application to run. This is not what we want to do.

Click the popup menu beside the DragLib name in the project window and look at the Import Weak item. Notice that it has a check mark beside the item indicating that this feature is enabled. This means that the library can be absent and EasyPuzzle will still run. You check for the presence of the library in the next step.

Step 1: Check for drag and drop availability

Modify: EasyCheckEnvironment() in init.c

As part of the launch process, EasyApp calls CheckEnvironmentHook(), which calls EasyCheckEnvironment(). The existing code in this function ensures that certain critical features of the operating environment are available. It checks that the Gestalt() call is available, that System 7 or better is operating, that Apple events are available, and determines whether color QuickDraw is supported.

In this step, you add a check for drag and drop. Drag and drop is not mandatory, but the features you implement in this lab work only if drag and drop is present. You set a flag so the application knows whether it has drag and drop. The new code goes at the end of the function.

```
g.hasColorQD = (response >= gestalt8BitQD);

error = Gestalt(gestaltDragMgrAttr, &response);
if (!error)
{
  if (response & (1 << gestaltDragMgrPresent))
  {
    g.hasDragAndDrop = true;

    #ifdef  powerc

    if ( (response & (1 << gestaltPPCDragLibPresent)) == 0)
    {
      g.hasDragAndDrop = false;
    }
    else if  ((Ptr)NewDrag == (Ptr)kUnresolvedSymbolAddress)
    {
      g.hasDragAndDrop = false;
    }

    #endif
  }
}

return error;
```

You call `Gestalt()` to look for the presence of the Drag Manager, and check for error. If there is no error in the call, examine the `gestaltDragMgrPresent` bit of `response` to see whether it is set. You take the value 1, shift it to the correct bit position, and perform a bitwise AND with `response`.

If the answer is `true`, the corresponding bit in `response` is set and the Drag Manager is present. For a 68K Mac, that's the only test you must perform.

For a Power Macintosh, you must also check for the presence of the shared library and make sure that you have access to the library. The code to accomplish this task occurs after a compiler directive—`#ifdef powerc`.

> For more information about compiler directives, see the "Compiler Statements" section of Appendix A.

The directive tells the compiler to compile the code between it and the `#endif` only if the term "powerc" has been declared. The development environment declares this term if you are compiling code for a Power Mac. If you compile this same source file for a 68K Mac, the code bracketed by the compiler directives is not compiled.

> The directive tells the compiler to compile the code between it and the `#endif` only if the term "powerc" has been declared. This is called a conditional compile. Heavy use of conditional compiles can interfere with the legibility of code, so you haven't seen them until now. However, conditional compiles are powerful tools. They allow you to tailor your code for a variety of conditions or environments without having to create separate source files for each possibility.

To check for the library, examine the `gestaltPPCDragLibPresent` bit of `response`. If it is set, the library was present at startup. You then check the address of a function in the Drag Manager library to see if it really exists. `NewDrag()` is a good choice. You compare the result against the declared constant `kUnresolvedSymbolAddress`. If they are the same, that means the System is unable to "resolve" the address for `NewDrag()`. In other words, the System does not have access to that call. Ergo, you better not use it!

Step 2: Install drag handlers

Modify: `InitPuzzleWindow()` in puzzleWindow.c

In the EasyApp design, drag and drop is a window's responsibility. The window knows the kind of data it contains, the kind of data it can receive, and what to do with it. Therefore, you install handlers on a window-by-window basis. Each window gets its own handler.

EasyApp tries to make installing the handlers as easy as possible. When you initialize a window, you specify what function you want to be the drag handler, and what function you want to be the receive handler. For the puzzle window, that happens in InitPuzzleWindow().

```
myPuzzle->frameColor = puzzleG.frameColor;

easyWindow->dragRoutine    = (ProcPtr)EasyDragTrackHandler;
easyWindow->receiveRoutine = (ProcPtr)PuzzleReceiveHandler;

return error;
```

You use the standard EasyApp-supplied tracking handler, and a special receive handler for the puzzle. After you have done that, EasyApp takes care of everything else. Here's how it works.

In EasyMakeWindow(), EasyApp tells the window to install its own handlers. You do not have to enter this code, it is part of EasyApp.

```
error = easyWindow->DoInstallDragHandlers(macWindow,
                                         (void*) nil);
```

It sends the window a DoInstallDragHandlers message. If there is an error, it closes the window and bails out.

The BaseInstallDragHandlers() function should work for all applications that use window-based drag and drop handlers. Examine the code for that function as well. It makes sure that the environment supports drag and drop, and that you have specified a drag handler and a receive handler.

If everything is all right, it creates a UPP for each handler and stores those in the Easy window record. It calls **InstallTrackingHandler()** to install the UPP for the tracking handler, and **InstallReceiveHandler()** for the receive handler. If all goes well, it sets a flag that tells EasyApp that this window supports drag and drop.

You get all of this for free. All you have to do is specify which functions you want to use as handlers.

Similarly, when you close a window, EasyApp removes the handlers and disposes of the UPPs. When closing a window, the BaseClose() function sends the window a DoRemoveDragHandlers message, and BaseRemoveDragHandlers() responds.

Step 3: Track a drag

Modify: EasyDragTrackHandler() in drag.c

A tracking handler receives five messages. You respond as necessary based on the message and what's happening. This is a lot of code, but what it does is straightforward.

```
case  dragTrackingEnterHandler:
  break;

/* first time in window, assume not in content */
case  dragTrackingEnterWindow:
  easyWindow->inContent = false;
  if (easyWindow->DoCanReceiveDrop(macWindow,(void *)theDrag)
      == noErr)
  {
    easyWindow->canReceive = true;
  }
  else
  {
    easyWindow->canReceive = false;
  }
  break;

/* while we're in this window - get this repeatedly */
case  dragTrackingInWindow:
  if (!easyWindow->canReceive)
  {
    break;  /* no */
  }

  /* get attributes for this drag */
  GetDragAttributes(theDrag, &attributes);

  /* if we've left the sender window */
  if (attributes & dragHasLeftSenderWindow)
  {
    /* get content area of window and mouse point */
    easyWindow->DoGetContentRect(macWindow,
                                (void*)&contentRect);
    GetDragMouse(theDrag, &mousePt, 0L);
    EasyGlobalToLocal(macWindow, mousePt, &mousePt);

    /* if the drag point is in the content area */
    if (PtInRect(mousePt, &contentRect))
    {
      if (!easyWindow->inContent)  /* first time in */
      {
        /* hilite the window */
        easyWindow->inContent = true;
        hiliteRegion = NewRgn();
        RectRgn(hiliteRegion, &contentRect);
        ShowDragHilite(theDrag, hiliteRegion, true);
        DisposeRgn(hiliteRegion);
      }
    }
```

```
      else  /* not in content area of window */
      {
        if (easyWindow->inContent) /* we're not any more */
        {
          /* unhilite the window */
          easyWindow->inContent = false;
          HideDragHilite(theDrag);
        }
      }
    }
    break;

  case  dragTrackingLeaveWindow:
    /* if we hilited the window */
    if (easyWindow->canReceive && easyWindow->inContent)
    {
      HideDragHilite(theDrag);  /* unhilite it */
    }

    /* no longer can receive, no longer in content */
    easyWindow->canReceive = false;
    easyWindow->inContent = false;
    break;

  case  dragTrackingLeaveHandler:
```

This handler has no response to the dragTrackingEnterHandler or dragTrackingLeaveHandler messages.

You receive a dragTrackingEnterWindow message the first time into a window. You assume you are not in the content area, and you send the window a DoCanReceiveDrop message to find out if you can receive the contents of this drag. The BaseCanReceiveDrop() function is provided for you. It determines whether there is a PICT flavor available in the drag.

You receive the dragTrackingInWindow message repeatedly while the drag is in the window. If the window cannot receive the drag you do nothing. If it can, you call **GetDragAttributes()** to see whether the drag has left the sender window. If it has, you provide feedback to the user. If it has not, you do nothing.

To provide feedback, determine whether the mouse is in the content area of the window. You get the content area by sending the window a DoGetContentRect message. You call **GetDragMouse()** to get the position of the mouse. You convert that to local coordinates with a call to EasyGlobalToLocal().

If the mouse is in the content area and this is the first time this has happened, highlight the content region to indicate that you can accept the drag. You call **ShowDragHilite()**.

If the mouse is not now in the content area but it has been in the past, the drag has moved outside the content area. Turn off the highlighting. You call **HideDragHilite()**.

You receive a dragTrackingLeaveWindow message once when the drag leaves the window. If the content area is still highlighted, you call **HideDragHilite()**.

Step 4: Receive a drag

Modify: PuzzleReceiveHandler() in puzzleDrag.c

When the user drops something in your window, the Drag Manager calls this function. The existing code makes sure the drop is actually in the content area of the window. If not, it bails out.

```
if (!PtInRect(mousePt, &contentRect))
{
  return dragNotAcceptedErr;
}

GetDragItemReferenceNumber(theDrag, 1, &theItem);

error = EasyGetDragData(theDrag, theItem, kPictType,
                        &thePicture);
if (error)
{
  return error;
}

GetDragAttributes(theDrag, &attributes);

if (!(attributes & dragHasLeftSenderWindow))
{
  return dragNotAcceptedErr;
}

if (thePicture)
```

You call **GetDragItemReferenceNumber()** to get the first item in the drop. EasyPuzzle takes only one item. Then you call EasyGetDragData() to get the actual data. You specify the drag record, the item reference number, the data type, and you provide a place to store the handle to the resulting data. EasyGetDragData() is a utility function provided for you in drag.c. Examine it if you like. It calls **GetFlavorDataSize()** to find out how much data there is, allocates the necessary memory, and calls **GetFlavorData()** to get the data. This is similar to the process you follow for pasting—get the size of the data, and then get the data.

You then call `GetDragAttributes()` so that you can determine whether the drag has left the sender window. If not, you are receiving the same picture as the one already in the window, a clear waste of time. So you bail out.

If this drag *has* left the sender window, the existing code does exactly the same thing you did when pasting a new picture into the window. It warns the user and replaces the contents of the puzzle.

Step 5:   Identify the start of a drag

Modify: `ClickInPuzzle()` in puzzleWindow.c

In this step, you further parse a click in the content area of a puzzle window. If the click is in the solved area of the puzzle and the application supports drag and drop, you start a drag.

The code you have already written identifies and handles clicks in a piece. If the click is not in a piece, you do further processing:

```
if (thisPiece)
{
  dragData.theEvent  = theEvent;
  dragData.thisPiece = thisPiece;

  error = DragPuzzlePiece(macWindow, &dragData);
}
else if (easyWindow->hasDragAndDrop)
{
  solved = GetPuzzleSolutionRgn(easyWindow);
  if (PtInRgn(localPoint, solved) &&
    WaitMouseMoved(theEvent->where) )
  {
    error = easyWindow->DoDragItems(macWindow, theEvent);
  }
}

return error;
```

First, determine whether the window supports drag and drop. If it does, you get the solution region for the puzzle. You call `PtInRgn()` to determine whether the click is in the region, and `WaitMouseMoved()` to see whether this is the beginning of a drag.

If both conditions are true, send the window a `DoDragItems` message. In EasyPuzzle, this means drag the picture, not the pieces.

Step 6: Drag a picture

Modify: `InitPuzzleWindow()` in puzzleWindow.c

Modify: `DragPuzzleItems()` in puzzleWindow.c

You must override the default `BaseDragItems()` in EasyApp. The EasyApp window has no contents, and no items to drag.

In this step you override that behavior by substituting `DragPuzzleItems()` as the function that responds to a `DoDragItems` message. You also write `DragPuzzleItems()`.

In the `InitPuzzleWindow()` function, add this line of code.

```
easyWindow->DoPaste        = (WindowProc)PuzzlePaste;
easyWindow->DoDragItems    = (WindowProc)DragPuzzleItems;
easyWindow->DoContentClick = (WindowProc)ClickInPuzzle;
```

You set the field of the Easy window record so that it contains a function pointer to `DragPuzzleItems()`.

Here's the code for `DragPuzzleItems()`. Once again there is a lot of code, but the steps are quite logical:

```
    Rect        frame;

/* create a drag record */
error = NewDrag(&theDrag);
if (error)
{
  return error;
}

/* get the data to be copied */
error = easyWindow->DoDrawSelected(macWindow, &thePicture);
if (error)
{
  DisposeDrag(theDrag);
  return error;
}

/* get drag region */
GetPuzzleFrame(easyWindow, &frame);
dragRegion = NewRgn();
EasyGetDragRect (macWindow, dragRegion, &frame);

/* set drag item dimensions */
SetDragItemBounds(theDrag, 1, &(**dragRegion).rgnBBox);
```

```
    /* lock data in memory */
    state = EasyLockHandle(thePicture);

    /* add a picture item to the drag */
    error = AddDragItemFlavor(theDrag, (ItemReference)1,
                              kPictType, *thePicture,
                              GetHandleSize(thePicture), 0);
    if (error)
    {
      EasyDisposeHandle(&thePicture);
      DisposeDrag(theDrag);
      DisposeRgn(dragRegion);
      return error;
    }

    /* we don't care about option key, no copying here */
    g.dragMoving = true;

    /* track the drag  */
    error = TrackDrag(theDrag, theEvent, dragRegion);

    /* clean up */
    g.dragMoving = false;
    EasyDisposeHandle(&thePicture);
    DisposeDrag(theDrag);
    DisposeRgn(dragRegion);

    return error;
```

You call **NewDrag()** to create a drag record. Then you send the window a DoDrawSelected message. For EasyPuzzle, this gives you a copy of the picture attached to the puzzle.

Next you create the drag region. This is the one-pixel outline of the dragged object. In this case, you call GetPuzzleFrame() to get the puzzle size. You call **NewRgn()** to create a region, and EasyGetDragRect() to set the region based on the Rect. EasyGetDragRect() is provided for you. It sets the region up properly in global coordinates.

You call **SetDragItemBounds()** to pass the bounds information into the drag record.

Then you lock the picture in memory and add it to the drag item. The parameters for the call to **AddDragItemFlavor()** say that you are adding a flavor to item one, it is a PICT flavor, point to the data, tell the size of the data, set a flavorFlags value of zero—meaning that there are no limitations on the destination.

You set g.dragMoving to true because you are not making a copy of the picture in the same window. That's not allowed in EasyPuzzle. You are moving the picture elsewhere.

Then you call `TrackDrag()` so the Drag Manager can do its magic. When this call returns, everything has happened. The handlers have been called, highlighting and feedback has taken place, and the drag has been received—or not.

You clean up by disposing of all the memory you allocated, and you're done.

Step 7:   Run the application
Modify: none

Save your work and run the project using the debugger. When the debugger window appears, launch EasyPuzzle. These instructions assume you have the Clipping Extension installed. This gives the Finder the capability to support Desktop clipping files.

A puzzle window appears when you launch the application. Click and drag the puzzle picture. Notice the dotted outline appear and follow your mouse. Drag the picture to the Desktop and drop it there. A picture clipping file appears. It was a lot of work in code, but to the user it's as simple as that.

Open a second puzzle window that has a different picture in it. Drag the picture clipping file to the new window and drop it. The picture from the original window appears in the second window. It really is that easy.

Experiment with all kinds of combinations. Drag pictures from one window to another, from Desktop to window and window to Desktop, with puzzles scrambled and not scrambled. Try it with the scramble dialog open, or with the solution dialog open. If you have other drag-and-drop-savvy applications, put them in the loop and have fun dragging stuff around.

When you are through observing, quit the application.

Enhancing EasyPuzzle

There is one way in which EasyPuzzle does not meet the drag and drop human interface guidelines. If you have two puzzle windows open, and you attempt to drag the background window into the active window, EasyPuzzle activates the background window! It doesn't start a drag.

If you want to work on this, the solution is fairly straightforward. This gives you good practice in solving programming problems. I left this little problem in EasyPuzzle for just this purpose.

EasyApp has a DoBackgroundClick message that it sends when there is a click in a background window. To solve the problem, you must override the default BaseBackgroundClick() function and replace it with a function designed for the puzzle. That function should check whether the click is in the solution region, and call WaitMouseMoved() to see whether a drag has commenced. If both conditions are true, send the window a DoDragItems message. Otherwise, activate the window. The code in the EasyPuzzle Complete folder has a solution. That version of EasyPuzzle behaves properly.

In an earlier chapter, you worked with puzzle pieces to allow the user to move them from place to place in a window. Drag and drop can do that for you as well, but in this chapter we focused on using drag and drop to smash the barriers between applications.

Although this is an introductory book, implementing drag and drop puts you ahead of many experts. There's no question that it is a fair amount of work to implement. But the end result to the user is so smooth, clean, and intuitive that it is worth the trouble.

Drag and drop is more than just cool, however. In Chapter 21, we discuss the future of Macintosh programming, and you'll learn how drag and drop is going to become a fundamental attribute of all things Macintosh.

Drag Manager Reference

This section summarizes the basic Drag Manager calls you use in a standard Macintosh application. At the time of this printing, the Drag Manager had not made it into a volume of *Inside Macintosh*. For full details on all the Drag Manager calls, consult the *Drag Manager Programmer's Guide*.

```
pascal OSErr InstallTrackingHandler(DragTrackingHandler trackingHandler,
         WindowPtr theWindow, void *handlerRefCon)
```

Parameters	trackingHandler	a UPP to handler function
	theWindow	use handler for this window, nil => default handler
	handlerRecCon	value for your use
Returns	Error value, zero => no error	
Description	Installs tracking handler function either for particular window or as default handler.	

```
pascal OSErr InstallReceiveHandler(DragReceiveHandler receiveHandler,
                                    WindowPtr theWindow, void
                                    *handlerRefCon)
```

Parameters	receiveHandler	a UPP to handler function
	theWindow	use handler for this window, nil => default handler
	handlerRecCon	value for your use
Returns	Error value, zero => no error	
Description	Installs receive handler function either for particular window or as default handler.	

```
pascal OSErr RemoveTrackingHandler(DragTrackingHandler trackingHandler,
                                    WindowPtr theWindow)
```

Parameters	trackingHandler	a UPP to handler function
	theWindow	remove handler for this window, nil => default handler
Returns	Error value, zero => no error	
Description	Removes tracking handler function either for particular window or as default handler.	

```
pascal OSErr RemoveReceiveHandler(DragReceiveHandler receiveHandler,
                                   WindowPtr theWindow)
```

Parameters	receiveHandler	a UPP to handler function
	theWindow	remove handler for this window, nil => default handler
Returns	Error value, zero => no error	
Description	Removes receive handler function either for particular window or as default handler.	

```
pascal OSErr NewDrag(DragReference *theDragRef)
```

Parameters	theDragRef	address where call stores reference to a newly allocated drag record
Returns	Error value, zero => no error	
Description	This call allocates memory, so make sure you check for errors.	

```
pascal OSErr DisposeDrag(DragReference theDragRef)
```

Parameters　　theDragRef　　　　reference to the drag in question

Returns　　　　Error value, zero => no error

Description　　Disposes of the drag record.

```
pascal OSErr AddDragItemFlavor(DragReference theDragRef, ItemReference
     theItemRef, FlavorType theType, void *dataPtr, Size dataSize,
     FlavorFlags theFlags)
```

Parameters　　theDragRef　　　　reference to the drag in question

　　　　　　　　theItemRef　　　　a reference to the item, usually an index
　　　　　　　　　　　　　　　　number, could be a handle or pointer to the
　　　　　　　　　　　　　　　　item

　　　　　　　　theType　　　　　data type (flavor)

　　　　　　　　dataPtr　　　　　address of data

　　　　　　　　dataSize　　　　　number of bytes in data

　　　　　　　　theFlags　　　　　attributes for this flavor

Returns　　　　Error value, zero => no error

Description　　Copies data provided to drag record as flavor specified.

```
pascal OSErr TrackDrag(DragReference theDragRef, const EventRecord
     *theEvent, RgnHandle theRegion)
```

Parameters　　theDragRef　　　　reference to the drag in question

　　　　　　　　theEvent　　　　　event record for click that starts the drag,
　　　　　　　　　　　　　　　　the where field must be in global coordinates

　　　　　　　　theRegion　　　　handle to the drag region (outline of selected
　　　　　　　　　　　　　　　　shapes)

Returns　　　　Error value, zero => no error

Description　　Performs the drag. The Drag Manager tracks the mouse, calls tracking
　　　　　　　　handler, calls receive handler when the drag ends. If user drops in bad
　　　　　　　　location, returns a user-canceled error and does an automatic
　　　　　　　　zoomback.

```
pascal OSErr CountDragItems(DragReference theDragRef, unsigned short
                            *numItems)
```

Parameters   theDragRef   reference to the drag in question

                      numItems   address to store result

Returns   Error value, zero => no error

Description   Provides number of items in the drag in variable provided.

```
pascal OSErr GetDragItemReferenceNumber(DragReference theDragRef, unsigned
                            short index, ItemReference
                            *theItemRef)
```

Parameters   theDragRef   reference to the drag in question

                      index   index number for desired item reference

                      theItemRef   address to store item reference value

Returns   Error value, zero => no error

Description   Gets the item's reference value.

```
pascal OSErr CountDragItemFlavors(DragReference theDragRef, ItemReference
                            theItemRef, unsigned short *numFlavors)
```

Parameters   theDragRef   reference to the drag in question

                      theItemRef   reference number to item

                      numFlavors   address to store number of available flavors attached to this item

Returns   Error value, zero => no error

Description   Returns number of available flavors for the specified item in the drag record.

```
pascal OSErr GetFlavorType(DragReference theDragRef, ItemReference
                            theItemRef, unsigned short index, FlavorType
                            *theType)
```

Parameters   theDragRef   reference to the drag in question

                      theItemRef   reference value to item

                      index   index number of desired flavor (each item may have more than one)

                      theType   address to store the flavor type for this item

Returns   Error value, zero => no error

591

19

Description   Get the data type (PICT, TEXT, and so on) for the specified flavor for the specified item in a drag record.

```
pascal OSErr GetFlavorFlags(DragReference theDragRef, ItemReference
        theItemRef, FlavorType theType, FlavorFlags *theFlags)
```

Parameters   theDragRef   reference to the drag in question

                    theItemRef   reference value to item

                    theType   the desired flavor type

                    theFlags   address to store the attribute flags

Returns   Error value, zero => no error

Description   Gets the flags for this particular flavor of this item. The flag of most interest in a typical application is `flavorSenderOnly`, meaning that a particular flavor is intended for use by the sending application. This is appropriate for proprietary data types.

```
pascal OSErr GetFlavorDataSize(DragReference theDragRef, ItemReference
      theItemRef, FlavorType theType, Size *dataSize)
```

Parameters   theDragRef   reference to the drag in question

                    theItemRef   reference value to item

                    theType   the desired flavor type

                    dataSize   address to store the number of bytes of data for this flavor

Returns   Error value, zero => no error

Description   Get the size of the requested data, typically use this before allocating memory to hold the data.

```
pascal OSErr GetFlavorData(DragReference theDragRef, ItemReference
        theItemRef, FlavorType theType, void *dataPtr, Size *dataSize,
        unsigned long dataOffset)
```

Parameters   theDragRef   reference to the drag in question

                    theItemRef   reference value to item

                    theType   the desired flavor type

                    dataPtr   address where data should be stored

                    dataSize   address for number of bytes, on entry is number of bytes you want, on exit is the number of bytes of data returned

	dataOffset	where in the flavor data to start reading data, typically zero to get all the data
Returns		Error value, zero => no error
Description		Use to get all or part of the data in a particular flavor. You must allocate memory pointed to by `dataPtr` before calling this function.

```
pascal OSErr GetDragItemBounds(DragReference theDragRef, ItemReference
                              theItemRef, Rect *itemBounds)
```

Parameters	theDragRef	reference to the drag in question
	theItemRef	reference value to item
	itemBounds	address of `Rect` to store bounds of item
Returns		Error value, zero => no error
Description		Get bounds of the drag item. Bounds are in global coordinates.

```
pascal OSErr SetDragItemBounds(DragReference theDragRef, ItemReference
                              theItemRef, const Rect *itemBounds)
```

Parameters	theDragRef	reference to the drag in question
	theItemRef	reference value to item
	itemBounds	address of `Rect` containing bounds of item in global coordinates
Returns		Error value, zero => no error
Description		Sets the bounds of the item; you must use global coordinates.

```
pascal OSErr GetDragAttributes(DragReference theDragRef, DragAttributes
                              *flags)
```

Parameters	theDragRef	reference to the drag in question
	flags	address to store current flags
Returns		Error value, zero => no error
Description		Get the current state of the drag attribute flags. The possible values are `dragHasLeftSenderWindow`, `dragInsideSenderApplication`, and `dragInsideSenderWindow`.

```
pascal OSErr ShowDragHilite(DragReference theDragRef, RgnHandle
                           hiliteFrame, Boolean inside)
```

Parameters	theDragRef	reference to the drag in question

593

	hiliteFrame	handle to region defining shape to be high-lighted
	inside	true => draw frame inside region shape
Returns	Error value, zero => no error	
Description	Draws highlighting frame, used to provide destination feedback to user. Note, the highlight frame should be in *local* coordinates for the window in which the frame appears.	

```
pascal OSErr HideDragHilite(DragReference theDragRef)
```

Parameters	theDragRef	reference to the drag in question
Returns	Error value, zero => no error	
Description	Hides the current highlighting. The drag reference should be to the drag showing a highlight. This call assumes the window in which you are hiding the highlight is the current graphics port.	

```
pascal Boolean WaitMouseMoved(Point initialMouse)
```

Parameters	initialMouse	mouse location at start of drag, in global coordinates
Returns	Boolean value, true => mouse has moved	
Description	Waits for either the mouse button to be released, or for the mouse to move. Returns false if button released without moving (a click). Returns true if mouse moves before button released (a drag).	

```
pascal OSErr GetDragMouse(DragReference theDragRef, Point *mouse, Point
                      *pinnedMouse)
```

Parameters	theDragRef	reference to the drag in question
	mouse	address to put current location of mouse
	pinnedMouse	address to put current pinned location of mouse
Returns	Error value, zero => no error	
Description	Values returned are in global coordinates. The drag region is drawn at pinnedMouse, which is the same as mouse unless the tracking handler restricts movement.	

20

The Write Way: Fonts and Text on the Mac

The Macintosh was the first desktop computer to treat text the way it should be treated: as a graphical object with special lexical properties. Letters are just symbols that have special meaning. On the Macintosh you can manipulate letters in the same way as other graphical objects.

The treatment of text on the Macintosh is a very complex subject. This chapter introduces you to some of the basic principles of text management and shows you how to display and manipulate text using a single font, style, and size.

In Chapter 10, we talked briefly about QuickDraw's basic text capabilities. At that time, I limited the discussion to the display of individual characters, strings of characters, and blocks of text drawn directly into a graphics port.

In this chapter, you learn about TextEdit—the text-handling Toolbox manager. This chapter covers the following topics:

- Fonts

- Text-related menus

- The TERec structure

- Working with TextEdit

In the lab exercise, you create a window devoted to text entry. In fact you will be creating your own simple, TextEdit-based word processor!

I close out the chapter with a brief look at two more powerful features of the Mac OS devoted to managing text: styled TextEdit and QuickDraw GX.

Font Overview

The first thing we're going to do is define some terms. The definitions here may not be what classical typographers use for the same terms, but this is how the terms are used in the Macintosh world today. Although typography has an extensive vocabulary all its own, definitions of these five terms are sufficient for this discussion:

- Glyph

- Font

- Style

- Font family

- Script system

Typically, a *glyph* is the symbol for a letter in an alphabet. More precisely, a glyph is the distinct visual representation of one or more characters or pieces of characters. See Figure 20.1.

A *font* is a group of stylistically related glyphs that typically represents a complete alphabet or a set of symbols.

A *style* is a visual attribute—other than size—applied to a font to modify its appearance in a consistent way. The styles available in TextEdit are plain, bold, italic, underline, outline, shadow, condense, and extend. Figure 20.1 shows some examples.

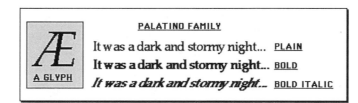

Figure 20.1 Glyphs, fonts, and styles

A *font family* is a group of stylistically related fonts. For example, a series of fonts may all use the same underlying design, but apply different variations on the design to create a unique look—such as bold, italic, heavy, and so forth.

A *script system* is the software used to manage and display a specific writing system (like Chinese, Roman, Arabic, and so forth). This system usually includes keyboard resources, fonts, and other resources necessary to display the characters properly.

Font Metrics

Typographic measurements are made in *points*. A typographic point is a unit of measurement equal to approximately 1/72nd of an inch. The classic Macintosh screen resolution is 72 pixels/inch. Because one pixel equals one typographic point, what you see on the screen is what you get from the printer. This correspondence is not a coincidence. It helped make the Macintosh a powerful desktop publishing machine.

Each glyph has a certain size and shape. The spatial relationships between and among glyphs requires a second set of terms. Figure 20.2 illustrates the principle concepts required to work with TextEdit.

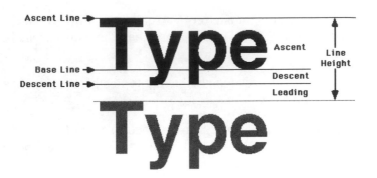

Figure 20.2 Font metrics

The *baseline* is the line along which the main body of the glyphs aligns. The *ascent line* is the line that just touches the tops of the tallest glyphs in a font. The *descent line* is the line that just touches the bottom of the glyphs that extend the furthest below the baseline.

A font's *ascent* is the distance from the baseline to the ascent line. A font's *descent* is the distance from the baseline to the descent line. *Leading* (pronounced "ledding") is the distance from the descent line of one line of text to the ascent line of the next line of text.

The *line height* is the distance from the ascent line to the descent line, plus the leading—in other words, the distance from the top of one line of text to the top of the next line of text.

A font file stores all of this information in a form that the Mac OS can understand. It also includes all the glyphs used to render the font. There are several font formats that have developed over the years as the Mac OS has become typographically more powerful. Happily, as an application programmer you can ignore most of the details of font formats. However, there is one detail you must attend to: whether the font is a bitmap or an outline font.

Bitmap and Outline Fonts

In a bitmap font, each glyph has its own little bitmap that tells the operating system, "These pixels are on and these pixels are off." Bitmaps are designed for a particular font size. The Mac OS can scale bitmaps to generate a glyph for any point size, but the end result can look very ugly.

Figure 20.3 shows the uppercase letter "A" from a Palatino bitmap font. The particular bitmap in the illustration is designed for 18-point type. On the left side of the illustration is the actual bitmap, magnified so that you can see its pixel-by-pixel arrangement clearly. At its normal size, the letter "A" looks rather nice. Scaled to a much larger size, however, the true nature of the bitmap is revealed. This is what you see onscreen; it isn't very attractive.

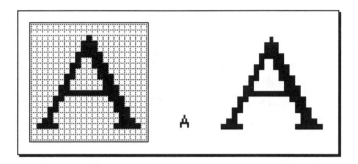

Figure 20.3 Scaling a bitmap font

Dissatisfaction with scaled bitmaps led to the development of *outline fonts*. Each glyph in an outline font is described as a set of mathematical curves. The curves can be scaled to any size; the Mac OS then generates a corresponding bitmap from the curve data. Because the curves are scaled first, no detail is lost in the scaling process. As a result, the rendered image looks good at any size (see Figure 20.4).

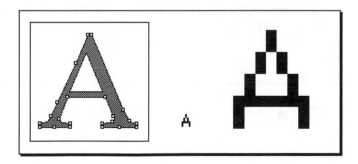

Figure 20.4 Scaling an outline font

Outline fonts are used throughout the typographic world. TrueType™ is the standard outline font format for the Mac OS. The Mac OS also handles PostScript™ fonts very well. However, to get a good appearance for scaled PostScript fonts, you must have a system extension named Adobe Type Manager installed.

When you work with fonts you generally do not have to know whether the font in question is a bitmap font or an outline font, except when displaying some text-related menus. These menus—and the text-related human interface in general—are very important to you as a programmer.

Text-Related Menus

An application that uses text should provide three menus. In left to right order in the menu bar they are the Font, Style, and Size menus. If at all possible, these should be separate menus. If you do not have enough space in the menu bar, you can make Style and Size appear as submenus from hierarchical items at the top of the Font menu.

You provide resources for these menus in your application's resources. You add the menus to the menu bar like any other menu, as discussed in Chapter 7.

The standard Font menu should list all fonts available on the machine. You cannot know what fonts will be available on any particular machine, so for the Font menu you simply provide a title. When the application launches, you add items to the menu by calling `AppendResMenu()`. You provide a handle to the Font menu data (obtained from `GetMenu()` or `GetMenuHandle()`). And you pass a constant 'FONT' to add all the available fonts.

Table 20.1 lists the standard Style menu items for a QuickDraw application (as distinguished from QuickDraw GX).

Table 20.1: Standard Style Menu

Command	Key	Purpose
Plain		remove all styles from selected text
Bold	⌘+B	set selected text to bold
Italic	⌘+I	set selected text to italic
Underline	⌘+U	underline selected text
Outline		set selected text to outline
Shadow		set selected text to shadow

You may also include Condense and Extend as items if that is appropriate for your application. The keyboard equivalents for the Style menu items listed here are not part of the official human interface guidelines. They are common keys widely used in text-related applications. There are many variations on this theme.

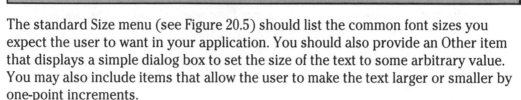

Many applications use Shift-⌘ key equivalents for font styles. The display of a Shift symbol as part of a key equivalent in a menu item is not part of the standard menu definition procedure. To display multiple characters for command key equivalents, you must provide a custom MDEF resource.

The standard Size menu (see Figure 20.5) should list the common font sizes you expect the user to want in your application. You should also provide an Other item that displays a simple dialog box to set the size of the text to some arbitrary value. You may also include items that allow the user to make the text larger or smaller by one-point increments.

```
Size
   6
   9
  10
✓ 12
  14
  18
  24
 ─────────────
  Other...
  Reduce      ⌘ <
  Increase    ⌘ >
```

Figure 20.5 The Size menu

If a bitmap is available in a given size, you should display the item in the Size menu in outline style. If a bitmap is not available, display the item in plain style. This tells the user exactly what sizes of the font look best.

To find out whether a bitmap is available in a given size, call **RealFont()**. You pass the font ID, and the desired size. If a bitmap is available in that font and size, the call returns true. If it is not available, it returns false. The call always returns true for outline fonts.

The TERec Structure

TextEdit is a text-handling system for small pieces of text that you need in your application. It works best when the number of characters in a single TextEdit object is fewer than 4,000. However, it can handle up to 32,767 characters. TextEdit contains all the functionality you need to create the text component of your application, unless your application is extremely intensive in its use of text.

The primary TextEdit data structure is the TERec—the TextEdit record. TextEdit uses this record to store all the information about a text object. The structure is fairly complex. However, some members of the record are relevant only for assembly language programming or are used internally by TextEdit.

Table 20.2 lists the fields of a TextEdit record of interest to application programmers.

Table 20.2: Important TERec Fields

Field	Data Type	Description
destRect	Rect	text margins
viewRect	Rect	bounds of visible area of text
lineHeight	short	top of one line to top of next line
fontAscent	short	height of highlighting and caret
selStart	short	index of first selected character
selEnd	short	index of last selected character + 1
just	short	alignment: left, center, or right
teLength	short	number of characters in the object
hText	Handle	handle to the actual text
crOnly	short	word wrap or not
txFont	short	font ID number
txFace	Style	style
txMode	short	drawing mode
txSize	short	size of text in points
nLines	short	number of lines of text
lineStarts[]	short	index of character at start of each line

TextEdit provides accessors for some of these fields. If there is an accessor for a field, I describe it as I describe the field. If there is not an accessor, you must access the field directly.

The destRect defines the actual margins of the text: top and bottom, left and right, in local coordinates for the port in which the text appears. The top of the rectangle is the top of the top line of text. The left and right sides of the rectangle are the margins of the text. They determine where TextEdit breaks lines of text if you have word-wrap on. The bottom of the rectangle is flexible. TextEdit changes it as necessary to allow for more text. You can think of the rectangle as being bottomless. The size of the destRect does not have to match the size of the port, nor does it control the text that you see.

The viewRect defines the visible part of the text in a TextEdit object. You can think of the viewRect as a clipping region of sorts. The bounds of the rectangle are in local coordinates for the port in which the text appears. The relative positions of the destRect and viewRect determine what text is actually visible in the TextEdit object. Figure 20.6 shows the destRect and viewRect fields.

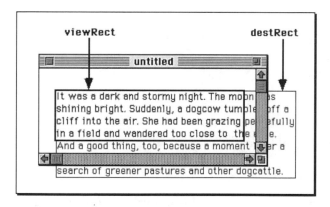

Figure 20.6 The destRect and viewRect fields

The lineHeight field is the distance between the top of one line and the top of the succeeding line.

The fontAscent field defines the height of the insertion caret and the height of the highlighting over the selected text. When you change the lineHeight, you should also change the fontAscent so the highlighting and insertion caret are drawn correctly. TextEdit does not automatically update the fontAscent member for you.

The selStart and selEnd fields contain the index numbers for the characters at the start and end of the current selection range. The character index is zero-based, so the first character has an index number of zero. The selEnd field is one greater than the index number of the last selected character (to include that character in the selection range). When selStart equals selEnd, there is no selection range and TextEdit displays the text entry caret. In general, the user defines the selection region. However, if your code needs to set the values of selStart and selEnd, call **TESetSelect()**. You provide the start and end values and the handle to the TextEdit record.

The just field is badly named. It really controls alignment, not justification. The four possible alignments are teCenter, teFlushLeft, teFlushRight, and teFlushDefault. The default value aligns the text according to the primary direction of the script system. To set this value, call **TESetAlignment()**. You provide the value and the handle to the TextEdit record.

The teLength field contains the actual number of characters in the text associated with the TextEdit object. If there is one character, this field has a value of one. Normally you don't need to set the contents of this field, as it is maintained by TextEdit. You may need to get the contents to find out how many characters are in the TextEdit object.

The hText member of the TextEdit record contains a handle to the text associated with the TextEdit object. Use **TESetText()** to associate text with a TextEdit object. Use **TEGetText()** to get the current handle.

The crOnly field controls word wrapping. If the value of the crOnly member is less than zero, TextEdit starts a new line when it sees a carriage return. Otherwise TextEdit starts a new line when the text reaches the right edge of the destRect. Remember that the viewRect does not influence where TextEdit creates line breaks. The viewRect only determines which part of the text is drawn onscreen.

The txFont, txFace, txMode, and txSize fields of the TextEdit record override the same fields in the grafPort structure. These fields control the font, style, size, and drawing mode for text in the text object. In this book, all of the text in a text object must have one font, style, and size. We'll discuss text objects with multiple fonts, styles, and sizes later in this chapter.

The txFont field contains the font ID number. Typically, when the user chooses an item in the Font menu, you get the text for that item, call **GetFNum()** to get the corresponding font ID number, and then set the txFont field.

The txSize field contains the size of the text in points. Remember: when you change the value of the txSize member, you must also change the values of the lineHeight member and the fontAscent member. TextEdit does not do this for you.

The nLines member of the TextEdit record contains the number of lines of text in the text object. TextEdit calculates this for you. This is also the number of valid entries in the lineStarts array.

Each element of the lineStarts array contains the index of the character that starts a new line. The first entry in the lineStarts array is always zero, because the first line always starts with the first character in the TextEdit object. You should never need to set the values in the lineStarts array (see Figure 20.7). TextEdit maintains this array for you.

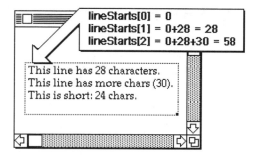

Figure 20.7 The lineStarts array

This discussion gives you some hints about the services provided by TextEdit. As the user enters text, TextEdit automatically breaks lines, wraps the text, and keeps the related fields current. It also handles text selection when the user clicks. Exactly how to avail yourself of these services is the topic of the next section.

Working with TextEdit

To use TextEdit in your application, you must perform four tasks:

- Initialize the environment
- Create a text object
- Modify the text object
- Support data exchange for the text object

In case you're wondering about the "use TextEdit Services" flag in the application's SIZE resource, *you do not have to set this flag to use TextEdit.* This flag relates to two-byte script systems—used for some languages like Japanese—and a feature known as "inline input." Inline input converts two-byte representations of a character to a corresponding ideograph. See *Inside Macintosh: Text* for more information on advanced TextEdit services.

Initializing TextEdit

When your application launches, call `TEInit()` when you initialize the other Toolbox managers. You should always call `TEInit()` even if your application does not explicitly use TextEdit calls. Dialogs and alerts use TextEdit, so TextEdit must be initialized.

Before calling `TEInit()` you must call `InitGraf()` to initialize QuickDraw; `InitFonts()` to initialize the Font Manager; and `InitWindows()` to initialize the Window Manager.

As part of setting up the environment, you should also create the Font menu as discussed previously.

If you are using System 7 or later, support for outline fonts is always available. You may want to call `SetOutlinePreferred()`. Pass a Boolean value `true` as the only parameter. This tells the System that if *both* a bitmap and an outline version of a font are available, you want to use the outline version. By default the System uses the bitmap font.

Using outline fonts does not always result in the neatest screen appearance! If you have a 12-point bitmap available for an outline font, the bitmap is likely to be sharper looking. Why? Because it has been designed pixel by pixel for legibility and aesthetic appeal.

Creating a Text Object

To accomplish this task you perform a series of steps. You must:

- Create a TextEdit record
- Set the text-related fields of the record
- Put some text in the object
- Activate the object

- Calculate line breaks
- Display the object

Creating and Disposing of a TextEdit Record

You may have more than one text object in a window. For each object you create a TextEdit record.

Creating the record is as easy as calling `TENew()`. You provide the destination and view rectangles for the new object. The call returns a handle to the new TextEdit record. If the call fails, the handle is nil. This type of text object may have one font, style, and size.

To dispose of the record when you are through, call `TEDispose()`. This disposes of all subsidiary structures as well, including the text attached to the TextEdit object.

Setting Text-Related Fields

After you create a TextEdit record, initialize the font, style, size, line height, and font ascent. There are no TextEdit calls to set these values. Set the fields directly by dereferencing the handle to the TextEdit record. You can set the font, style, and size to whatever the current default values for your application are. The line height and font ascent are a little trickier.

To get the information you need, call `GetFontInfo()`. You provide the address of a `FontInfo` data structure. Table 20.3 lists the fields of this structure and their purposes. This Font Manager call calculates the necessary information for you.

Table 20.3: The FontInfo Structure

Field	Data Type	Description
ascent	short	font ascent
descent	short	font descent
widMax	short	width of widest character
leading	short	leading

You need the ascent and line height. The font ascent is available directly from the `FontInfo` record. The line height is the ascent plus the descent plus the leading.

There is a complication here. The `GetFontInfo()` call returns values based on the font, size, and style set for the current *port*, not for the TextEdit record. So you must preserve the existing port values, set them temporarily to match those in your TextEdit record, make the call, get the information you need, and then restore the original values that were in the port to begin with. Strange, but true.

Attaching Text

If you are creating a new, empty text object, TextEdit creates an empty text handle for you. This might be the case if you were opening a new text document, for example.

If you want to attach existing text to a TextEdit record, call `TESetText()`. You provide the address of an existing block of text, the number of bytes, and the handle to the TextEdit record. This call allocates a new handle, and then copies the text from your original block into that handle.

If the TextEdit record already has attached text, you must dispose of the existing text yourself. Call `TEGetText()` to get the current handle before calling `TESetText()`. Then you can dispose of the current handle and replace it with a new handle.

Activating/Deactivating a Text Object

The active text object is the object with the insertion caret or in which a selection range is displayed. TextEdit takes care of displaying or hiding the highlighting of the selected text and the insertion caret.

If you want to make an object the active text object, call `TEActivate()`. You provide the handle to the TextEdit record. You must make this call whenever you want to activate an inactive text object—for example, when activating a window that contains the text.

Similarly, if you want to deactivate the object, call `TEDeactivate()`. You make this call when deactivating a window containing the object, for example, or if you want to deactivate the text object even though the window remains active.

TextEdit will also take care of background highlighting for you! Call `TEFeatureFlag()`. Pass the constant `teFOutlineText` as the feature you want to set, and `teBitSet` to enable the feature. You also provide the handle to the TextEdit record. *The text object must be deactivated before you make this call.*

It is possible to have more than one active text object, but you should avoid this situation. If there are two active text objects in a window, both will have insertion carets and the user will have no idea in which object text will appear.

Calculating Line Breaks

If you change the dimensions, appearance, or content of a text object, you should call TECalText() to recalculate line breaks. You provide the handle to the TextEdit record. This tells TextEdit to recalculate the line breaks.

You must rebreak lines when you change: the destination rectangle; the font, size, or style of the text; add or remove text; or change the crOnly field (word wrapping). Remember that if you change font size, the font ascent or the line height for the TextEdit record does not change. You update those to match the new font and size before calling TECalText(), or leave them if you want to force a particular line spacing.

Strictly speaking, a call to TECalText() isn't necessary immediately after calling TESetText() because that call calculates the line starts itself.

Displaying the Text Object

TextEdit also takes care of drawing the text. Call TEUpdate() whenever you need to redraw the text. You provide a rectangle and the handle to the TextEdit record. The rectangle specifies the bounds of the area that should be updated.

Among the many things TextEdit handles for you is the blinking text insertion caret. However, you must give TextEdit time to do so. Every time through your event loop you should call TEIdle(). You provide the handle to the active text object. TextEdit blinks the caret at whatever interval the user sets for the caret blinking time. If you want to find out what that interval is, call GetCaretTime(). We discussed this call in Chapter 6.

Modifying a Text Object

There are really three general ways in which a user can change a text object. They can change the settings for the text object (the font, size, and so forth). They can change the contents of the object by entering or deleting text. They can scroll the object. Let's look at how to handle each situation.

If you have multiple text objects, the user must select the text object—typically with a text tool of some sort—before making changes. This allows you to activate the individual text object. If you have a window with nothing but a single text object, selecting the object prior to making changes is not an issue.

Changing Settings

Typically this happens in response to a menu choice. The user chooses a font, size, style, or other feature for which you provide a choice. For example, you might allow the user to turn word wrapping on and off, change alignment, and so forth.

You determine what setting the user wants to modify, and what the new value should be based on the menu item they choose. Then you set the appropriate field in the TextEdit data record. For example, if the user chooses 14 point type, you set the txSize field of the TextEdit record (not the window) to 14. Don't forget to reset the font ascent and line height fields. This typically involves a call to GetFontInfo() as discussed previously.

Then you must recalculate line breaks. Call TECalText().

Finally, you must redraw the text. You can invalidate the view rectangle with a call to InvalRect(). This will force the System to generate an update event, and your update handling code can take care of drawing the window.

You can also call TEUpdate() directly as soon as you make the change, but the InvalRect() approach is usually safer. Why? Because it keeps your window drawing code all together in one place. This keeps your content-related code (changing the contents of the TextEdit record) separate from your interface code (drawing the window).

Changing Text

This is what you've been waiting for. When the user types a key, how do you put it in the TextEdit record? TextEdit does almost all the work. You'll love it.

You must handle two kinds of events: clicks and key presses. The user sets the insertion point or selects text with the mouse. The user types keys to enter or delete text (or move the insertion point).

To handle a click in an active text object, call `TEClick()`. TextEdit takes care of the rest. You provide the point clicked (in local coordinates for the graphics port), a flag denoting the state of the Shift key (so TextEdit can extend an existing selection if the Shift key is down), and the handle to the TextEdit record.

Everything that happens as a result of a click is a gift from the makers of TextEdit. TextEdit removes any selection highlighting if that's appropriate, displays newly selected text, moves the caret, even selects a word if the user double-clicks the word. Very cool.

Handling a key event is not much harder.

You must do a little event filtering before passing the key to TextEdit. TextEdit dutifully puts every key you send it into the text record. You should filter out command-key equivalents, special keys, and certain nonprinting characters.

You can and should pass TextEdit the arrow keys (they move the caret), the Backspace or Delete keys, the Return key, and—of course—any actual text character.

Exactly how you handle some other keys is up to your design. For example, you might convert the Enter key into a Return key, or you might use the Enter key for some special purpose. TextEdit does not support tabbing, so you might convert a Tab into a series of spaces.

How do you pass the key to TextEdit? Call `TEKey()`. You provide the key, and the handle to the TextEdit record. After you pass in the key, TextEdit takes care of the rest—with one exception. TextEdit has a limit of 32K characters. You must test the length of the existing text before passing a character in, to make sure it fits.

Of course, entering or removing a character may change line breaks. You should call `TECalText()` and update the text after every keypress.

Scrolling Text

If the user clicks the scroll bar for a text object, TextEdit comes to the rescue again. You call `TEScroll()` or `TEPinScroll()`. In either case you provide the distance in pixels to scroll horizontally or vertically, and the handle to the TextEdit record. Positive values move the text to the right or down. Negative values move the text left or up.

For vertical scrolling, you pass one line height when the click is in the arrow. To scroll a page, pass the height of the view rectangle minus one line height, so one line remains onscreen. This gives the user a context to understand how the newly displayed text relates to the previous text.

For horizontal scrolling, pass a percentage of the view rectangle—perhaps 10 percent for the arrows, 90 percent for a page.

Either call scrolls the text in the view rectangle by the amount specified and updates the view rectangle immediately. The only difference between the two calls is that `TEPinScroll()` stops scrolling when the last line of text is in view.

Cut, Copy, and Paste for TextEdit

If there is an active text object, the standard Edit menu commands should apply to it. TextEdit maintains a private scrap and gives you simple calls to use when appropriate.

In response to the user's command key or menu choice, you should call `TECut()`, `TECopy()`, `TEPaste()`, or `TEDelete()`. In each case you provide the handle to the TextEdit record. TextEdit performs the appropriate operation with the text using its private Clipboard. Use `TEDelete()` for the Edit menu's Clear command. You can implement the Select All command very simply. Call `TESetSelect()` with a range of zero to 32K.

`TEPaste()` is not the only way to insert text into a text object. You can call `TEInsert()`. You provide the address of the text to insert, the number of bytes, and the handle to the TextEdit record. The new text appears at the insertion point or before any currently selected text. This call does not replace currently selected text, nor does it check the 32K limit.

Because TextEdit uses a private Scrap, when your application moves from the background into the foreground it should call `TEFromScrap()` to put the text contents of the public Scrap into the TextEdit private Scrap. Then any text that might be on the public Scrap appears in the private Scrap for your use with the TextEdit copy and paste commands.

Similarly, when your application moves from the foreground to the background you *may* want to call `TEToScrap()` to put the TextEdit private Scrap onto the public Scrap for use in other applications. You should also call `ZeroScrap()` before making this call, and that may cause you pause.

If your program uses both the public Scrap (perhaps for a graphic object of some kind) and TextEdit, the user may have data on both Scraps simultaneously. Putting the TextEdit Scrap onto the public Scrap wipes out whatever was there!

One way to manage this problem is with a global flag that tells you which Scrap was used most recently. If it is the TextEdit Scrap, put it on the public Scrap when going into the background.

Now it's time to put all that theoretical knowledge to practical use.

Lab 20.1 A TextEdit Word Processor

In this lab you add a text window to EasyPuzzle. In fact, the text window is patched on top of EasyPuzzle and doesn't have much of practical connection to a puzzle program. However adding a text window serves two purposes. It gives us an opportunity to discuss TextEdit, and it gives you another example of how to extend the EasyApp shell.

You are about to graduate into the world of real Macintosh programmers. As a programmer, you regularly encounter new software technologies. Some of them will be of little interest. Some will be crucial to your work. You will have to master those that intrigue you.

Previous labs have included step-by-step instructions detailing what code you should write and what it all means. This lab takes a different approach to solving programming problems—one that is a lot more like the real world.

When some new and whizzy software technology comes along, like drag and drop or QuickDraw GX, you can get your hands on documentation that details the new API, some example source code, and sample applications demonstrating the new technology. You get this material on the national networks, or by subscribing to various developer services like those listed in Appendix D, "Resources for Macintosh Programmers."

What do you do with all the background material? You read the overview and documentation, you look at the code, you play with the sample applications, and then you start writing your own code. With the API documentation by your side, you implement the new technology in your own way in your own project. Usually you work on a pet project—something you have fun playing with. This gives you two advantages. First, you start from a base of code that you understand intimately. Second—and more importantly—it's fun. That takes a lot of the pain out of implementing alien technology.

So, in this lab we take a look at TextEdit. This chapter is your overview. The TextEdit reference section at the end of this chapter is your guide to the TextEdit API. You have the solution code for this lab as example code. EasyPuzzle is your example application.

There are no steps in this lab, and there are no code excerpts. Instead we talk about the tasks you must accomplish to implement text in an application. It is up to you to write the code.

Lab 20.1 has a new start code. Make sure you have copied the start code for this lab to your hard drive. The only thing new in the start code is that the project includes the textPuzzle.c file.

Let me warn you right now, what lies ahead in this lab is a nontrivial task. This isn't easy. Don't try to do this in one sitting. Stop regularly at reasonable spots, build the application, and test your new code as it develops. You will certainly have bugs. Hunt them down and kill them.

First, you need some new resources. The text window needs a WIND resource. In the EasyPuzzle design, we have added a New Note Window item to the Puzzle menu. The user chooses this item to open a new text window. We also added three new menus: Font, Style, and Size. In addition, you might want to modify the bundle resources to include icons for the new type of file the puzzle now supports. This includes an icon family, a new FREF, and modifying the existing BNDL resource. You can use ResEdit to add these to the start code. Use the solution code resources as your guide.

You should declare new constants and structures in the application's header file to support the new menus, their items, and other text-related tasks. You'll find these in puzzle.h. Examine the solution code for menu constants, the PuzzleGlobal structure, and the new PuzzleTextData structure used to save text style information as a resource.

There are two classes of changes you must make to the source code: application-level and window-level. You must modify the EasyPuzzle application so that it supports the new text features. This includes menu installation and updating, as well as creating a new text window and opening existing text files. At the window level, you must create and establish a text window and its behaviors. You should make no changes to the EasyApp files.

At launch you add the new menus to the application. EasyApp calls the SetupAppMenusHook() function, and that in turn calls PuzzleMenuInstall(). You must build the Font menu on the fly, the same way you do the Apple menu.

You must also update menus properly. The three new menus—Font, Style, and Size— have no meaning to any other window but a text window, so they should be disabled by default. When a text window is active, it can activate the menus it needs. Examine

PuzzleMenuUpdate() to see what the solution code does for default purposes. Because the menus are active only when a text window is active, the window can handle all the menu dispatching.

You must create a new text window when the user chooses the New Note Window item. You must add some dispatch code to PuzzleMenuDispatch() to handle this new item. The solution code calls EasyNew(), and ultimately passes through the EasyMakeWindow() function. You must modify GetWindowResIDHook() to provide the correct WIND resource ID, and SetWindowInitHook() to specify the correct window initializing function.

You should also allow the user to open any plain text file. The OpenPuzzleFile() function in puzzleFile.c handles the task of opening a file. Modify the function so that it recognizes files of type 'TEXT' as acceptable.

As part of implementing cut, copy, and paste, consider converting the TextEdit private Scrap to the public Scrap and vice versa. EasyApp calls application-level hooks when appropriate, PrivateToClipHook() and ClipToPrivateHook().

Implementing window-level support is a lot more involved, because you must identify and write code for every unique behavior of a text window.

> All of the necessary text-related window behaviors are in the puzzleText.c file in the solution code. As you write your own code, feel free to refer to the functions in the solution code. Study them, and even copy them into your own code in whole or in part after you're sure you understand them. It's what a wizard would do with sample code.

Text windows require a window initializing function. Examine InitTextWindow() in puzzleText.c to see what it does. The EasyPuzzle text window has a vertical scroll bar and no horizontal scroll bar. It overrides a series of window behaviors. You can replace the default behaviors as you write each function. Notice that you can completely alter how a window behaves by substituting different functions. Text windows don't behave at all like the puzzle window, yet the same shell drives them both.

The initializing function for a text window calls TENew() to create the TextEdit record. It stores the handle in the Easy window's windowData field for future reference. This is the only data in the window. It also initializes the TextEdit record and updates the menus. When a text window is open, you must give the window a chance to activate the text menus.

The text window must update and handle menus appropriately. For example, it should enable the text-related menus. What should the window do if the user chooses an item in the Font menu? Think about how the window should behave, and write the code to implement that behavior. Substitute the function you write for the default functions. Examine the `TextUpdateMenus()` and `TextHandleMenu()` functions in the solution code.

The rest of the task of implementing a text window boils down to deciding how the window should behave and what messages you must override to implement the behavior. For example, when closing a text window you must dispose of the TextEdit record. So you write `TextClose()` and substitute that function to respond to the `DoClose` message. The EasyApp shell sends the `DoClose` message at the right time to whatever window is involved. EasyApp doesn't care what kind of window, it just sends the message. *It is the window that is ultimately responsible for its own behavior.*

Look at the solution code for `InitTextWindow()` and examine the list of messages it overrides. Each begins with the word "Text." Think about why each message should be overridden, and think about what behavior a text window should exhibit in response to that message. Then implement that behavior or study the solution code to see how it works. The solution code is full of comments outlining the specific tasks that each bit of code accomplishes. It is a great learning tool.

Some of the functions are very simple, like `TextClose()`, `TextOpen()`, `TextCut()` and many others. Some are complete and complicated replacements of the default EasyApp behavior, such as `TextPrint()`.

Of particular interest are the `TextFlattenWindow()` and `TextUnflattenWindow()` behaviors. Because EasyApp follows the stream approach to reading and writing data, these functions are pretty much all you need to implement reading and writing files. You'll do more work with `TextReadResource()` and `TextWriteResource()` to save the necessary resources along with the data, but this is a good example of the kind of functionality an application framework provides.

Implementing drag and drop is a nontrivial task. Most of the difficulty arises from keeping track of where the insertion caret should appear in the destination window, and making sure the behavior corresponds to the drag and drop human interface.

The solution code implements dragging text across windows and within the same window. Play with the finished EasyPuzzle application. Create a note window and type some text, or open a text file. Then start dragging text around. You can see the power and flexibility that drag and drop provides.

At the end of the puzzleText.c file there are about a dozen utility functions for manipulating menus and performing other services. Pay particular attention to `AdjustTextWindow()`. This function keeps the text formatted properly with a call to **TECalText()** and keeps the scroll bar current. The `TextScrollAction()` function determines how much to scroll. The `TextScrollWindow()` function actually scrolls the text with **TEPinScroll()**.

As you implement features of the text window, you are certain to forget some things and have bugs, crashes, problems, inconsistencies, and unexpected behavior. Computers are very literal. They do exactly what we tell them.

The solution code you're looking at did not arise whole and complete in one session. It took a long time to write and debug. That's the reality of writing software. As you find and fix the problems, you learn. Good luck!

Advanced Text Features

We can finish the discussion of text with a look at some advanced text-handling tools available on the Macintosh right now.

The text support you add to EasyPuzzle is cool, but limited. In a more text-intensive application, you want many more features, chief among them the capability to use multiple fonts, styles, and sizes in a single text object. In this section, we discuss briefly two avenues you can follow if text is important to your programs: Styled TextEdit and QuickDraw GX.

Styled TextEdit

Most of what you have learned about TextEdit applies to Styled TextEdit as well. There are a couple of different calls, and several new calls you use to implement multiple fonts, styles, and sizes in a single text object. For example, to create a Styled TextEdit record, you call **TEStyleNew()** rather than **TENew()**. To paste styled text, you call **TEStylePaste()** rather than **TEPaste()**. New calls like **TEContinuousStyle()** help manage the new features.

In its latest incarnation, TextEdit keeps track of style runs in the object and maintains a style record for each run. The style record specifies all the text-related information you are familiar with: font, style, size, and so forth. This makes modifying text styles slightly more complicated. You must determine the number of styles within the selection range and then modify each individual style. Styled TextEdit provides very helpful calls to simplify the process. You can learn all about these features of Styled TextEdit in *Inside Macintosh: Text*.

QuickDraw GX

You should also keep QuickDraw GX in mind. If your interests run toward truly sophisticated typography, there is no better avenue to follow than GX. QuickDraw GX is the first typographically aware operating system for desktop computers. I can't begin to cover all the features that GX provides to support the advanced manipulation of text and fonts. They are absolutely remarkable. In an attempt to give you a concept of what QuickDraw GX can do, let's look at one tiny feature.

In traditional typography, typesetters manipulated real pieces of metal type. They could shave an edge here or pad a little there to adjust spacing and make things look really good. One technique that typesetters developed is called "optical alignment." Optical alignment says that it is more important for things to *look* aligned than actually *be* aligned. If you apply a perfect edge to an optically aligned page, you discover that the elements are slightly out of line even though they look perfectly straight.

One part of optical alignment concerns the right margin of a page of text. Some punctuation marks—like commas—may be allowed to extend beyond the right margin. These marks are so small that they do not interfere with the "look" of a straight line. However, if you forced a letter to stop just short of the margin to provide room for the comma within a perfectly straight edge, there is a tiny gap at the end of the line between the right edge of the letter and the perfectly straight right margin. That gap does break the flow of the visual edge and imparts a slightly ragged appearance to the text.

Where is all this taking us? To this simple fact: QuickDraw GX lets you control the placement of a trailing comma at the end of a line so that you can implement optical alignment. If QuickDraw GX encompasses typographic details that tiny, imagine what it does for the big things! QuickDraw GX is available right now as part of System 7.5. It is the latest realization of Gutenberg's brilliant invention.

That idea leads us into the next and final chapter of *Programming Starter Kit for Macintosh*. What does the future hold in store for this amazing machine?

TextEdit Reference

This section summarizes the basic TextEdit calls you use in a standard Macintosh application. For full details on all the TextEdit calls, consult *Inside Macintosh: Text*. There are a few Font Manager calls listed at the end of the reference.

TextEdit Calls

```
pascal void TEInit(void)
```

Parameters	none
Returns	void
Description	Initializes TextEdit for your application. Make this call once at launch, even if you do not use TextEdit explicitly.

```
pascal TEHandle TENew(const Rect *destRect, const Rect *viewRect)
```

Parameters	destRect	address of rectangle describing the bounds of the text object
	viewRect	address of rectangle describing the visible portion of the text object
Returns	Handle to the new TextEdit record	
Description	This call allocates memory, the handle is nil if the call fails. The coordinates of the rectangles should be local to the graphics port containing the object.	

```
pascal void TEDispose(TEHandle hTE)
```

Parameters	hTE	handle to a TextEdit record
Returns	void	
Description	Disposes of the TextEdit record and all memory associated with it, including the text in the object.	

```
pascal void TESetText(const void *text, long length, TEHandle hTE)
```

Parameters	text	address of new text
	length	number of bytes in the text
	hTE	handle to the TextEdit record

Returns	void
Description	Allocates a new handle, copies the specified text into the handle, and puts that handle in the hText field of the TextEdit record. If a handle is already there, it is not disposed. You must get the original handle and dispose of it yourself.

`pascal CharsHandle TEGetText(TEHandle hTE)`

Parameters	hTE	handle to the TextEdit record
Returns	Handle to the block of text associated with the TextEdit record	
Description	Retrieve the handle to the text.	

`pascal void TESetAlignment(short just, TEHandle hTE)`

Parameters	just	how you want the text aligned
	hTE	handle to the TextEdit record
Returns	void	
Description	Sets the just field of the TextEdit record to the value provided. Possible values are teCenter, teFlushLeft, teFlushRight, and teFlushDefault.	

`pascal void TESetSelect(long selStart, long selEnd, TEHandle hTE)`

Parameters	selStart	index value of first character in selection range
	selEnd	index value of last character in selection range plus one
	hTE	handle to the TextEdit record
Returns	void	
Description	Sets the selStart and selEnd fields of the TextEdit record to values provided. If they are equal, the text caret is displayed. Otherwise the selected text is highlighted. The selStart must be less than selEnd.	

`pascal void TEActivate(TEHandle hTE)`

Parameters	hTE	handle to a TextEdit record
Returns	void	
Description	Makes the TextEdit record active so caret or foreground highlighting is displayed.	

```
pascal void TEDeactivate(TEHandle hTE)
```

Parameters   hTE   handle to a TextEdit record

Returns   void

Description   Makes the TextEdit record inactive, so caret or foreground highlighting is hidden.

```
pascal void TEIdle(TEHandle hTE)
```

Parameters   hTE   handle to the active TextEdit record

Returns   void

Description   Gives time for TextEdit to flash text insertion caret. Call once every time through event loop.

```
pascal void TEClick(Point pt, Boolean fExtend, TEHandle h)
```

Parameters   pt   point clicked, in local coordinates

                     fExtend   state of shift key, true => pressed

                     hTE   handle to a TextEdit record

Returns   void

Description   This routine handles clicks in a text object. It will modify the selection range, update highlighting, and/or move the text insertion caret as appropriate.

```
pascal void TEKey(short key, TEHandle hTE)
```

Parameters   key   character to insert in the text

                     hTE   handle to a TextEdit record

Returns   void

Description   Places character at current insertion point. If there is a selection range, deletes selected text. You must ensure that the character is appropriate, and that placing the character in the TextEdit record does not exceed the 32K limit.

```
pascal void TECalText(TEHandle hTE)
```

Parameters   hTE   handle to a TextEdit record

Returns   void

Description   Tells TextEdit to recalculate line breaks.

```
pascal void TEUpdate(const Rect *rUpdate, TEHandle hTE)
```

Parameters   rUpdate   area to be updated

    hTE   handle to a TextEdit record

Returns   void

Description   Draws the text in the specified text object that appears in the update area.

```
pascal void TEScroll(short dh, short dv, TEHandle hTE)
```

Parameters   dh   horizontal distance to scroll, in pixels

    dv   vertical distance to scroll, in pixels

    hTE   handle to a TextEdit record

Returns   void

Description   Scrolls text by amount provided, and updates text display.

```
pascal void TEPinScroll(short dh, short dv, TEHandle hTE)
```

Parameters   dh   horizontal distance to scroll, in pixels

    dv   vertical distance to scroll, in pixels

    hTE   handle to a TextEdit record

Returns   void

Description   Same as TEScroll(), but scrolling stops when the last line appears in the view rectangle.

```
pascal void TECut(TEHandle hTE)
```

Parameters   hTE   handle to a TextEdit record

Returns   void

Description   Copies selected text to the TextEdit private Scrap, and then deletes selected text from the text object.

```
pascal void TECopy(TEHandle hTE)
```

Parameters   hTE   handle to a TextEdit record

Returns   void

Description   Copies selected text to the TextEdit private Scrap.

```
pascal void TEPaste(TEHandle hTE)
```

Parameters   hTE   handle to a TextEdit record

Returns   void

Description   Copies text from the TextEdit private Scrap to the specified text object. New text replaces any existing selection or appears at the insertion point.

```
pascal void TEDelete(TEHandle hTE)
```

Parameters   hTE   handle to a TextEdit record

Returns   void

Description   Deletes text in the selection range. Also recalculates line starts.

```
pascal void TEInsert(const void *text, long length, TEHandle hTE)
```

Parameters   text   address of text to insert

                     length   number of bytes in the text

                     hTE   handle to the TextEdit record

Returns   void

Description   Places specified text at the insertion point or before existing selected text. Does not replace selected text, change selection range, or check to see whether total amount of text remains within the 32K limit. Also recalculates line starts.

```
pascal OSErr TEFromScrap(void);
```

Parameters   none

Returns   Error value, non-zero if call fails

Description   Copies any text on the Clipboard into the TextEdit private Scrap. Do this when your application comes to the foreground.

```
pascal OSErr TEToScrap(void);
```

Parameters   none

Returns   Error value, non-zero if call fails

Description   Copies any text on the TextEdit private Scrap into the public Clipboard. Call `ZeroScrap()` before making this call. You *may* do this when your application goes to the background, depending upon the circumstances of your application.

```
pascal short TEFeatureFlag(short feature, short action, TEHandle hTE)
```

Parameters

feature	feature to change
action	what you want to do to the feature
hTE	handle to a TextEdit record

Returns   If testing current settings, a value of one means the feature is on, a value of zero means the feature is off

Description   Possible features are `teFAutoScroll`, `teFTextBuffering`, `teFOutlineHilite`, `teFInlineInput`, and `teFUseTextServices`. Possible actions include `tebitClear`, `teBitSet`, and `teBitTest`. The last returns the current value of the bit.

```
extern pascal OSErr TEGetHiliteRgn(RgnHandle region, TEHandle hTE)
```

Parameters

region	handle to region to hold drag region
hTE	handle to a TextEdit record

Returns   Error value, non-zero if call fails

Description   For drag and drop support. TextEdit calculates the outline of selected text for your use as the drag region outline. You must create the region first with a call to `NewRgn()`.

Font Manager Calls

```
extern pascal void SetOutlinePreferred(Boolean outlinePreferred)
```

| **Parameters** | outlinePreferred | `true` => prefer outline font |

Returns   void

Description   If both a bitmap and an outline font are available, the System chooses the bitmap by default unless you call this routine with `true` as the only parameter.

```
extern pascal void GetFontInfo(FontInfo *info)
```

Parameters   info   address of a `FontInfo` record to store results

Returns   void

Description   Fills in the contents of the `FontInfo` record: font ascent, descent, leading, and width of widest character in the font. Uses the font, size, and style settings *from the current graphics port*, not any text object.

```
extern pascal Boolean RealFont(short fontNum, short size)
```

Parameters   fontNum   ID number of font in question

size   desired type size

Returns   Boolean value, `true` => this size bitmap is available for the specified font

Description   Determines whether a bitmap is available for the specified font and size. This call always returns `true` for outline fonts.

21

The Once and Future Mac: A Peek Over the Horizon

Congratulations! You have reached the next milestone on the road to becoming a Macintosh programmer. You know how to do *everything* a basic Macintosh application is required to do, and more. Think back to what you knew when you started this book, and then consider what you know now. You have done well.

It has been a long road, but one that I hope has been worth the effort. The first steps on your journey to becoming a Macintosh programmer are complete. You stand now at a crossroads. This chapter points out some of the directions you can take as you head out from here. This is the gee-whiz chapter. And there are a lot of gee-whizzy things about the Macintosh.

Other Languages

A decade ago Pascal was *the* programming language. The original Macintosh operating system was written largely in Pascal. You will run across this heritage every time you look at *Inside Macintosh*. The code examples for most of *Inside Macintosh* are in— that's right—Pascal.

C is now the most widespread language. Each volume of *Inside Macintosh* now has a C-language summary for each manager. The code in the newest volumes of *Inside Macintosh* is written completely in C.

A decade from now it is likely that some other language will be *the* language to use. I don't know what language that will be. But I'll venture an educated guess that whatever language replaces C, it will be an object-oriented language.

An Object-Oriented Future

This is not a book about object-oriented concepts and principles, but I do want to leave you with one thought. The future of Macintosh programming lies in object-oriented languages. The hottest new toys arriving on our desktops are written in object-oriented languages. The best application frameworks are all object-based.

There's a reason for that. Object-based code has significant and measurable advantages over the kind of procedural code you have written in this book. By now you should be familiar with function pointers and how to use them to attach behaviors to windows. That's a very cool trick. As neat as this piece of magic is, compared to a powerful object-oriented language it is a clumsy technique. The best example is to take a look at the BaseInitialize() function in EasyApp. This function initializes an Easy window and attaches behaviors to the window. In C++, that function disappears completely because objects are automatically initialized and behaviors are automatically part of the window—not something you have to attach like a trailer to a hitch.

There are several object-oriented languages to choose from, including C++, Object Pascal, SmallTalk, and Common LISP. Soon to come is Dylan, a new dynamic language currently under development at Apple Computer that promises to have some very cool development tools.

Object-oriented programming is more than a language, however. It is a frame of mind. You need to learn some basic principles of object oriented analysis and design along with the language. Unfortunately, most books on the topic concentrate on the language alone and neglect to instruct you on how to use the language wisely.

As you become familiar with programming in general, and the Macintosh in particular, keep the idea of object-oriented programming in mind. When you're ready to pursue this avenue, check out Appendix D, "Resources for Macintosh Programmers," for some good suggestions.

Other Directions

Whatever language you use, you're going to want to do something with your programming skills. You have had a taste of graphics and animation, text processing, sound manipulation, and interapplication communication. Each of these areas has great potential for futher development.

Graphics and Animation

Graphics are the core of what makes the Macintosh the powerful and popular machine that it is. If you're interested in fast, smooth animation, games, virtual reality, and other programming areas that depend on manipulation of images on the monitor, you should definitely learn about GWorlds, QuickTime, and QuickDraw GX.

A GWorld is an offscreen graphics environment. If you want to see the difference between the simple animation techniques used in EasyPuzzle and GWorlds, run the About box for EasyPuzzle. The code that makes the astronaut float smoothly in space uses a GWorld.

QuickTime is Apple's marvelous system-level multimedia engine. Multimedia applications—games, educational packages, simulations and such—are very hot right now. In addition, QuickTime VR adds powerful virtual reality features that allow you to walk through a scene and view it from all perspectives. The possibilities are amazing.

QuickDraw GX is a new graphics engine destined to replace QuickDraw. The power and potential of QuickDraw GX is unlike anything ever seen on a desktop computer. GX completely reinvents the drawing environment. All graphical objects are shapes—including typographic text. All shapes may be modified, rotated, scaled, skewed, inked, and transformed in marvelous and magical ways. This kind of flexibility and power takes graphics rendering to a new plane. By comparison, QuickDraw seems primitive and limited.

Text Processing

If you want to write the coolest word processor in the solar system, QuickDraw GX may do it for you. At the end of the last chapter, we talked about the amazing typographic power of QuickDraw GX. I have discussed GX with programmers who are at the leading (some say bleeding) edge of development as they struggle to design powerful GX-savvy software. And why are they struggling? One of the big problems is that QuickDraw GX gives the user so *many* choices that no one has figured out a good human interface. There is a lot of territory to explore with QuickDraw GX.

Sound

We merely touched upon what you can do with sound on the Macintosh. The Speech Manager can speak any text in a human voice that you can easily understand. You can give the user a choice of voices. And we're not talking tinny, mechanical voices from bad science fiction movies. You can generate rich, digital-quality stereo sound with your Macintosh.

Before long your Macintosh will not only speak to you, it will listen. The Macintosh stands at the threshold of a true voice-activated interface. The development in voice command and control is ongoing. There are programmers out there today writing the code that will move this idea from the virtual to the real.

Interapplication Communication

Much of this work depends upon Apple's Open Collaboration Environment—AOCE. Everything I talked about with respect to Apple events and interapplication communication provides a hint of the power of AOCE. AOCE provides system-level support for database management and access, scripting languages, electronic mail with digital signatures and much more. If you are interested in writing powerful tools that allow users to access huge amounts of data easily, or working with networks, or writing scriptable applications, AOCE is one way to go.

This book deals primarily with application programming. There are other kinds of programming as well: printer drivers, control panels, system extensions, neural networks, and more. Everything we've discussed so far is right here, right now, at the leading edge of software development. Macintosh programming is a boundless and expanding universe. There is more to come tomorrow.

The Future

The Macintosh has had quite a journey from 1984, when most of the industry laughed at the little toy machine. Apple's success over the past decade has rested in no small part on innovation, and on its willingness to improve both the hardware and system-level software for the Macintosh. Realizing the narrowness of its original vision, Apple added more memory, opened up the box for third-party cards, added color, and the list goes on. Now the Macintosh has an entirely new processor!

At all levels, from the very small to the very large, innovation has been the driving force. Innovation is likely to be the touchstone for the future as well. Hot new ideas develop and appear as extensions to system software. The successful ideas are ultimately folded into the core of system software to become part of the Toolbox. A perfect example of that is QuickDraw 3D.

Developers have struggled to create powerful 3D rendering programs using sophisticated mathematical techniques to map and model light and surfaces. Driven by the need for an easier way, Apple began work on QuickDraw 3D to provide system-level support for the kinds of things graphics wizards do in 3D imaging software. Soon, the kind of power that only the masters could wield will be available in calls as simple and straightforward as `GetNewWindow()`. Having this power at your fingertips will open up a whole new realm of programming possibilities.

Sometime down the road the very nature of the entire System will change. All Macintosh programs live in a cooperative multitasking environment where things go right only if everyone is well-behaved. If one application fouls up, the entire house of cards comes tumbling down. One reason is that this architecture is pasted onto a design intended to run one application at a time.

Perhaps not in version 8, but somewhere down the road the System will implement preemptive multitasking and protected memory. Your application will never totally control the computer. The System will parcel out time, events, and memory as needed. You will not be able to write data outside of your allocated space. Your application might be interrupted at any moment—in mid-calculation even—and control returned at the System's whim. The nature of `WaitNextEvent()` will change radically. It will be a great improvement.

As radical as this might seem, Apple's long history of striving for backwards compatibility means your programs should still work as long as you follow the programming principles we've talked about in this book.

There is one more major innovation just over the horizon. This is not only a software advancement, it is a new concept of how a desktop computer should work. This idea has the potential to completely change how we all think about computers. It's called OpenDoc.

OpenDoc

As I write, the latest version of OpenDoc development software is arriving on the desks of Macintosh programmers. My copy of the CD is patiently sitting in its envelope waiting for me to finish this book so we can go out and play. The real magic inside that envelope, encoded in the invisible optical pits of the CD, is potential.

OpenDoc is the culmination of what this book is about: the potential to do great things. It is fitting that we end our discussion not with a conclusion, but an introduction into a whole new world of Macintosh programming.

How does the Desktop work today? You open applications that create documents. To move data around, you copy it from one document to another. You hope it fits, and you hope your favorite application accepts data in the form you want to use. Everything centers on the *programs* that create the documents. The data is almost secondary. The programs force us to use their techniques and obey their limits.

This is not how we like to work. You don't tell people what brand of pen you use to write a note! Imagine the acknowledgment: "This note was written using the latest PenTastic Industries gold-plated whizzy-pen, version 5.2." Why should the application you use to create a document be so important?

Now imagine a model that is a lot more like the way we work intuitively. Imagine a blank piece of paper waiting to be filled. You want a picture on part of it. You want some words on part of it. You want a chart on part of it that reflects the numbers in the text.

You choose the tools necessary to render the data. You don't really care what "applications" create the data, you want them all to work transparently so that you can get your ideas on paper. When you save the document, you save the product of all these different parts of the document, not a chart file, a picture file, and a word processing file—just a single document.

OpenDoc brings this model to your desktop. It's fair to say that OpenDoc turns the desktop on its head, inside out, and upside down. Applications are pushed into the background where they belong. The document is the center of the action, and the data is the star. The applications are mere servers that come when you call and disappear when you dismiss them. In fact, in OpenDoc we no longer call them applications. We call them "part editors" and "part viewers." Why? Because they serve parts of a compound document, nothing more.

A part editor allows the user to change data on that part of the document served by the editor. A part viewer allows the user to view but not change data. The distinction between the "part" of the document and its server is quickly lost if the part editor or viewer is well-designed. Editor or viewer functionality should be absolutely transparent to the user. So we find ourselves calling the editors and views "parts" just like the document.

For this to work, data exchange between parts of a document must be seamless—no more complex than dragging the data where you want it to be and dropping it there. Sound familiar? Drag and drop is the beginning of OpenDoc. That's why drag and drop is included in this book.

As you develop your skills as a Macintosh programmer, you will probably write OpenDoc parts. Programming for OpenDoc is a lot like writing an object-oriented application. Your "part" responds to messages in much the same way that an EasyApp window does. OpenDoc—the System—sends your part messages telling it of events occurring. Based on the nature of the message, your part responds.

Your entire part is an OpenDoc object. Like EasyApp window objects with their attached behaviors, your OpenDoc part has and must implement a series of behaviors. To build an OpenDoc part you must handle and respond to about 50 different messages (fewer for simple parts). These tend to match fairly closely the kinds of things an application does—like draw the contents of a window. For a part, you receive a message to update your designated part of the document.

The biggest difference between OpenDoc and the current desktop model is that your part editor doesn't own the document. The document owns your part editor. Your part—or more precisely instances of your part—may appear on several documents simultaneously. Your part editor exists as a shared library—remember them from the drag and drop chapter? Various documents can share your part. This imposes certain restrictions, but provides substantial benefits as well. In a very real sense, your part never "runs" the way an application runs. It is and always will be subsidiary to the document that uses its services.

It's a radical concept, but the Macintosh has always been a radical machine. Apple's huge research effort provides this power to you, the programmer. Even better, the OpenDoc Parts Framework (currently under development) will give programmers the core of a part in the same way that EasyApp gives you the core of an application.

With the OpenDoc Parts Framework, the Mac OS, and the other tools available to you, you can concentrate your creative efforts where they do the most good: developing new ideas and turning them into software. Whatever comes down the highway, as a Macintosh programmer you will have the power in your hands to program *the* machine that leads the world in desktop innovation.

Your ultimate task as a programmer is to make creative tools and toys that people can use to do whatever interests them. As people pursue their interests, who knows what ideas will appear or what inventions will follow?

Programmers are the tool makers of the 21st century. If you have good tools, there is no limit to your potential. The Macintosh is a *great* tool. Welcome to tomorrow, and the world of Macintosh programming.

A

Guide to C

A

Contents

This appendix introduces the important and central features of the C programming language. A few obscure or little-used features of C are not explained in this appendix. However, those features are not used in the code accompanying this book.

The "Guide to C" is a reference for the C language, not a tutorial. You can sit down and read the "Guide to C" from beginning to end—a truly mind-numbing exercise—and you would certainly learn something about the language depending upon your tolerance for tedium. However, you will not master the concepts in this guide until you actually use them in the code that you write.

That's why you find "C Notes" throughout this book. As explained earlier, when you encounter some feature of the language for the first time, a C Note refers you to the "Guide to C." If you ever encounter something you don't understand, look it up in this appendix. If you are new to C, you can come here to learn more about that particular feature of the language. You can read about the concept, and then use it right away. There's no better way to learn a programming language.

However, the "Guide to C" is not a comprehensive explanation of C. There are several good books available on the C language. If you would like to learn more about C, consult the "Resources for Macintosh Programmers" appendix.

Introduction

This appendix discusses the important features of C. The discussion covers the following concepts:

- Keywords—special symbols and words that represent commands in the C language. For every specific concept or keyword that you encounter, the guide provides an explanation of its purpose, a clear statement of its syntax, and one or more examples of how to use it. When necessary, the typical uses or common pitfalls associated with that particular aspect of the language are discussed.

- Data—constants and variables—and how to use them in C. Also discussed are the various types of data, how they differ, and how to switch between them at will.

- Pointers—a critical feature of C—are discussed. This appendix describes what pointers are, why you use them, and how to use them in C.

- Operators—commands that do things to data: add it, subtract it, compare it to other data, and so forth.

There are a lot of operators in C, including:

Arithmetic

Assignment

Relational

Logical

Bitwise

- The order of precedence for operators.

- Program flow—how to control it in C with loop and branching statements. These are the statements that allow you to get work done. For all of its power, there are surprisingly few flow-control statements in C.

- Functions—the routines that make up a program. You learn what functions are, how to declare them, how to pass parameters to them, and how to get data back from them. This section also covers an advanced and powerful programming technique—function pointers.

- Preprocessor directives—common statements used to control a compiler. The code you write in C must be converted into a form the computer understands. That task is the responsibility of a compiler. You can't accomplish much in C programming without them. Most environments support a common set of compiler directives.

- Header files—what they are and why you use them.

- Standard libraries are briefly discussed. These libraries are not used in *Programming Starter Kit for Macintosh*, but they are a common feature of any good C development environment. You should be aware of what the standard libraries are, and why they exist.

Conventions

The "Guide to C" presents syntax information in a standard format that looks like this:

Keyword:	`#define`
Syntax:	`#define` *name* *value*
Example:	`#define pi 3.141592654`

The keyword (or other language feature) is specified on the first line. In the text, language keywords usually appear in bold face.

The second line presents the formal syntax. The explanatory text following each citation tells you when an item in the syntax is optional. Items in bold face are precise syntax. That is, they must exist in the exact form shown.

Items in plain italic are placeholders. You substitute appropriate names or values when you write an actual statement. For example, in the previous citation the syntax requires the exact word **#define** followed by a name that you supply, followed by a value that you supply.

The example illustrates how to use the syntax. In this example, note that the precise word #define appears, followed by the name "pi" that you provide, followed by a value—in this case 3.141592654. We discuss how to use this kind of statement later in this appendix.

Data in C

As in most computer languages, data in C may be constant or variable. Constants are typically numbers, single characters, or strings of characters that cannot be changed. Variables have names, and the data represented by the name may change.

This section discusses:

- Basic data types
- Constants
- Variables—including arrays and typecasting
- Strings
- Structs and typedefs
- Data scope

Basic Data Types

Data—either constant or variable—can be any of a wide variety of data types. The term *data type* means a particular kind of data. For example, in C there are several different kinds of numbers—integers, floating point, and so forth. You may also have characters, strings of characters, and arrays of characters or numbers. A character is, for all practical purposes, a letter of text. Technically, it is a byte of data with a value in the range 0–255. The value usually represents a letter in the alphabet or a key on a keyboard. You may even declare your own data types. This is discussed a little later.

The particular data types covered in this section include:

- **char**—one-byte value, typically a character
- **int**, **short int**, **long int**—integer value
- **float**, **double**, **long double**—floating-point value

Some other data types are also discussed—strings, for example—a little later.

Char Values

A **char** (usually pronounced like the first syllable in "charcoal") is typically one byte in size. The value of a **char** data type ranges from 0 to 255 (unsigned) or from –128 to 127 (signed). Often a **char** represents a letter in the standard ASCII character set. Depending upon the compiler, the actual amount of memory allotted to store a **char** may be more than one byte.

Integer Values

Integers are whole numbers—that is, numbers with no fractional or decimal part. For example, the numbers, 1, –9, 195, and 42 are all integers. The number of bytes of memory occupied by a generic integer—a number of data type **int**—is not defined in the official ANSI C standard. Unless specified, the compiler assumes that you intend to use a generic integer. On most platforms, an **int** is the same size as a **short** integer. However, the number of bytes allocated to an **int** may vary from compiler to compiler, and this can cause problems.

To avoid problems, you should explicitly declare integers as **short** or **long**. A **short int** occupies two bytes of memory, and can range from –32768 to 32767. A **long int** typically occupies four bytes of memory, and can range from –2,147,483,648 to 2,147,483,647. In C, the term **short** is a synonym **short int**, and the term **long** is a synonym for **long int**.

Integers may be **signed** or **unsigned**. A **signed** number may have a negative value. Unless specified, the compiler assumes that you are using **signed** values. An **unsigned** value is positive. If you are using **unsigned** values, a **short** ranges from 0 to 65,535; and a **long** ranges from 0 to 4,294,967,296.

note When you specify a value in actual code, you do not use commas to separate numbers.

Floating-Point Values

Floating-point values are numbers with a fractional part. For example, the value 23.147 is a floating-point number. The term *floating-point* refers to the position of the decimal point in the number. It can be anywhere in the number, so its position "floats." For example, if you multiplied 23.147 by 10 the new number would be 231.47.

There are three standard floating-point data types, **float**, **double**, and **long double**. Unless you specify, the compiler assumes that you intend to use a **float**. Like an **int**, the actual number of bytes used for a **float** is not specified in the ANSI C standard. On most platforms it is a four-byte value. The size of a **double** varies among compilers, and even within a single compiler depending upon the settings you choose. A **double** may be 8, 10, or 12 bytes in a typical compiler. Most compilers treat a **long double** the same as a **double**. Most compilers also recognize a **short double** data type. The details are summarized in Table A.1. The various types of floating-point values allow you to perform math operations to varying degrees of precision.

The maximum value of the various floating-point data types varies depending on the compiler and the number of bytes assigned to the value. Because the internal representation of a floating-point number uses exponents, the value in that number can be very large or very small.

Each of these three kinds of data—single byte, integer, floating-point—can be either a constant or a variable. C requires that you use a different syntax for constants than you do for variables, but it's not that complex. The next sections detail the syntax.

Table A.1 summarizes the basic data types in C. The bit size for some can vary from the values shown in the table, depending upon the compiler. The sizes listed are common and typical in most compilers.

Table A.1: Basic Data Types

Type	Size	Range
char	8 bits	–128 to 127
unsigned char	8 bits	0 to 255
int	16/32 bits	–32768 to 32767 or –2147483648 to 2147483647
unsigned int	16/32 bits	0 to 65535 or 0 to 4294967296

Type	Size	Range
short	16 bits	–32768 to 32767
unsigned short	16 bits	0 to 65535
long	32 bits	–2147483648 to 2147483647
unsigned long	32 bits	0 to 4294967295
float	32 bits	floating point number
short double	64 bits	floating point number
double	64/80/96 bits	floating point number
long double	64/80/96 bits	floating point number

Most compilers have settings that allow you to select the number of bits to use for **double** and **long double** values. The compiler converts source code into object code—the data the computer understands—based on your instructions. In general, a greater number of bits means your calculations are accurate to more decimal places. Strangely, using a bigger size may also result in code that runs faster. You have to read the documentation for a particular compiler to learn more about how it handles such matters. Some sizes may not be available on some compilers.

Constants

You may use byte values, integers, and floating-point values as constants. This section discusses each in turn. Then it talks about two ways to name constants so that they are easy to use.

Char Constants

A **char** constant is a one-byte value. You can specify the value of the constant using a letter, a value, or a character combination used to represent common special characters. In each case, you put the value (however specified) inside *single quote marks*.

Data type:	`char` (specified by letter)
Syntax:	`'letter'`
Example:	`'G'` specifies an uppercase G (decimal 71)

To specify by letter, you simply put the letter inside the single quote marks. This is clearly the simplest way to specify a letter, because you do not have to remember the corresponding numerical value for the letter. However, you can specify the constant by value. The values for characters in the English alphabet are standardized in the ASCII character set that dates back to teletype technology.

Data type:	`char` (specified by value)
Syntax:	`'\value'`
Example:	`'\x74'` specify G using hexadecimal
	`'\107'` specify G using octal
	`71` specify G using decimal

To specify by value, you precede the value with a backslash. If the first character after the backslash is the letter x, the number is hexadecimal. If the first character after the backslash is a digit, the value is interpreted as octal (base 8). You may specify decimal values by using numbers, without any quote marks or a backslash.

There are some "characters" for which there are no corresponding symbols in the English alphabet. Other symbols (like the quotation mark) have special purposes in C. You can specify such characters by using special built-in values, again preceding the value by a backslash. In C-speak, these are called *escape sequences*.

Data type:	`char` (specified by special character)
Syntax:	`'\letter'`
Example:	`'\n'` specifies the newline character

There are several such escape sequences; they are defined in Table A.2.

Table A.2: Character Constant Escape Sequences

Value	Definition
`'\a'`	alert (bell)
`'\b'`	backspace

Value	Definition
'\f'	formfeed
'\n'	newline
'\r'	return
'\t'	horizontal tab
'\v'	vertical tab
'\\'	backslash
'\?'	question mark
'\''	single quote
'\"'	double quote

When programming for the Macintosh, you won't use these values very often.

Integer Constants

The value of an integer constant may be specified in decimal, octal, or hexadecimal. Octal isn't used very much. When using an integer as a constant, you may use an **int** value or a **long int**. Either may be signed or unsigned. You do not use commas when entering the literal value of any number.

Data type:	`signed int` (specified by decimal)
Syntax:	*value*
Example:	`-1296`
Data type:	`unsigned int` (specified by decimal)
Syntax:	*value*U no space, upper- or lowercase
Example:	`1342U`

continues

Data type:	`signed long` (specified by decimal)
Syntax:	*value*L no space, upper- or lowercase
Example:	-143546L
Data type:	`unsigned long` (specified by decimal)
Syntax:	*value*UL no space, upper- or lowercase
Example:	1217345713UL

For hexadecimal constants, you begin the constant with 0x and then enter hexadecimal digits. *Two* hexadecimal digits define *one* byte in memory. The byte-size in memory of the constant depends upon the number of characters you specify. For example, if you specify 0x12AE, the resulting constant is two bytes long. Some compilers may actually allot an even number of bytes in memory no matter how many hexadecimal digits you provide.

You may use the same U and L suffixes as you do with decimal constants. They are, of course, optional.

Data type:	`hexadecimal constant`
Syntax:	`0x`*value*`UL`
Example:	`0xFF` specifies a 1-byte value = decimal -1
	`0xFFu` specifies a 1-byte value = decimal 255
	`0x00FFl` specifies a 4-byte value = decimal 255

Floating-Point Constants

Floating-point constants default to a data type **double**. To be interpreted correctly as a floating-point value, the constant must be defined with either a decimal point, an exponent, or both in the value. You may use the letter F to specify a float data type, or the letter L to specify a **long double** data type. The **long double** data type isn't used very often. On most compilers, the **double** and **long double** types are the same.

Data type:	`double`
Syntax:	*value* (must include a decimal point or exponent)

Example:	`1.2`
	`-75.  note decimal point is present`
	`3e2`
	`3.14159e2`

Data type:	`float`
Syntax:	*value*`F` no space, upper- or lowercase
Example:	`-3.14159e3F`
Data type:	`long double`
Syntax:	*value*`L` no space, upper- or lowercase
Example:	`1.2L`

Defined Constants

It is frequently useful to have a name represent a constant value because it is easier to remember names, and you are less likely to make a mistake using names. For example, let's say you have a program that uses the value of   regularly. Every time you want to use it, you could type 3.14159 and hope you don't make a typo. If you later want to change that number (to be more precise for example), you have to find every location in the code where you use the number, and then change it.

Now imagine doing that to a few thousand lines of code.

Using a special compiler statement, you can make writing and editing your program easier and more efficient by using a name for that constant.

C compilers support special statements called *preprocessor directives*. Although other compiler directives as a group are discussed later in the "Guide to C," there is one compiler command that clearly belongs as part of this discussion of constants: `#define`.

This statement (usually pronounced "pound define" or simply "define") declares a name that you can use in place of a constant.

Keyword:	`#define`
Syntax:	`#define` *name* *value*
Example:	`#define pi 3.14159`
	`#define lucky 7`
	`#define bell '\7'`

Follow the `#define` keyword with the name of the constant, and then the value. There is no semicolon at the end. Constants named in this way can be any standard data type: integer, floating point, or **char**.

Typically you put `#define` statements in header files. You then `#include` the header file in the source files that use the constant. Header files and `#include` are discussed later in this guide.

After you have defined and included a constant, every time you want to use the constant in the source code, use the name. When it compiles the code, the compiler substitutes the value for the name.

A `#define` statement does not allocate memory to hold this value. It simply gives the compiler some text to substitute for the defined term when necessary.

This can cause some confusion with the correct use of the terms "define" and "declare." These terms have particular and precise meanings in C:

- In proper C-speak, the term *define* means to allocate memory for something. For example, when you define a variable you are allocating memory to hold the value. You aren't setting the value of the variable, just allocating memory.

- The term *declare* means you are telling the compiler (declaring) what a term means, and not allocating memory. So, in proper C-speak the `#define` statement is a declaration, not a definition.

No wonder programmers get confused.

A

Enumerated Constants

It is fairly typical in programming to have a series of named constants. For example, you might want constants to represent the months of the year.

You can enter a series of **#define** statements, but there is an easier way. You can create a series of named constants using the **enum** keyword (short for *enumerate*).

Keyword   **enum**

Syntax: **enum** { name1, name2, name3, etc. };

Example: enum {jan = 1, feb, mar, apr, may, jun, jul,
         aug, sep, oct, nov, dec };

After the keyword, use braces—the { and } keys—to hold the list of constants. Follow the close brace with a semicolon.

Inside the braces, enter a name for each item, separated by a comma. Do not put a comma after the last item in the list. By default, the value of the first item in the list is zero and each subsequent item increments by one. You may assign any integer value to any item you wish.

In the previous example, the constant jan has a value of 1, and each subsequent constant has a value one greater than the preceding constant. The assignment of a value to the constant jan is explicit. The assignment of values to the other constants is automatic. If you had not assigned the value 1 to jan, by default jan is assigned the value 0.

You can assign any value anywhere in the list at any time. Here's a silly example:

```
enum { twostep = 2, sixpence = 6, fourscore = 4, five };
```

In this example, the first three constants have values explicitly assigned to them. The constant five has a value of 5, one more than 4 (the preceding assigned value).

If you wish, you can declare the list of items to be a unique data type. Simply name the data type before the opening brace or after the closing brace. You can then use that data type as you do any other data type in C.

```
Keyword:        enum (declaring data type)

Syntax:         enum typeName { name1, name2, name3 };
                enum { name1, name 2, name3 } typeName;

Example:        enum  myMonth { jan = 1, feb, mar, apr, may,
                          jun, jul, aug, sep, oct, nov, dec };

                enum { jan = 1, feb, mar, apr, may, jun, jul,
                          aug, sep, oct, nov, dec } myMonth;
```

These examples both declare a data type named myMonth and enumerate several constants, one for each month. Although both methods are legal, the standard language guides usually include the type name before the actual enumeration.

Variables

Variables are similar to named constants. The only significant difference is that the value of a variable can change. The value of a named constant cannot.

Naming Variables

You may name a constant or variable using any combination of characters and numbers (including the underscore character if you wish). C is a case-sensitive language, so the names March, march, and MARCH refer to different variables. You cannot use a *reserved word* in C as a variable name. There is a list of these reserved words at the end of this guide.

Most programmers follow naming conventions for constants, variables, and functions. See Appendix C, "A Brief C Style Guide," for information on some naming conventions.

Defining Simple Variables

When you define a variable in C, you allocate room in memory to hold the value referred to by the name you choose.

<table>
<tr><td>Concept:</td><td>defining a variable</td></tr>
<tr><td>Syntax:</td><td>type name;</td></tr>
</table>

```
Concept:        defining a variable

Syntax:         type  name;

Example:        char             myChar;
                short            xValue;
                long             yValue;
                unsigned double  reallyBigNumber;
                float            yetAnotherValue;
```

The syntax is simple. You declare the data type and name the variable. End the definition with a semicolon. The same syntax applies to all data types: you specify the data type, provide a name for the variable, and end the statement with a semicolon.

You are not required to assign a value to the variable when you define it. That is, you do not have to initialize the value of the variable, as you can see in the previous syntax examples. If you do not assign an initial value to a variable, the value of the variable is unpredictable.

Unfortunately, there is nothing in C that prevents you from using such an uninitialized variable. If you forget to set a proper value before you use the variable, you create a bug that can be difficult to track down. To avoid this problem, you may assign an initial value to a variable by specifying a value when you define the variable.

```
Concept:        initializing variables

Syntax:         type  name = value;

Example:        char    myChar = 'f';
                short   xValue = -23;
                long    yValue = 0x3E4B;
                double  reallyBigNumber = 9e102;
                float   yetAnotherValue = 3.14;
```

You may define more than one variable *of the same data type* in a single statement. Separate each item with a comma.

Concept:	defining multiple variables
Syntax:	`type   name1, name2, name3;`
Example:	`short  x, y, zelda;`
	`short  x = 23, y = 32, z = 45;`

note

You may have noticed that none of the examples use the **int** data type. Using **int** as a data type is not a good practice because the byte size of an **int** is undefined in the ANSI C standard. As a result, using the **int** data type can cause compatibility problems if you change compilers.

Defining Arrays

An array is an indexed set of variables of the same type. You can set up arrays of data of *any* type: **char**, **short**, **long**, **double**, and so forth. Let's look at an example to see what an array is, and why it is useful.

Let's say you have 10 students, and you want to track a test grade you assigned to each student. You can define 10 variables like student1Grade, student2Grade, and so forth. However, that's a clumsy approach that requires a lot of redundant code. You have to write 10 lines of code—one for each variable—every time you want to do something with the students. Furthermore, your code would be good for only 10 students.

You can use an array of values instead. An array allows you to create an index into a set of values of the same data type.

Concept:	defining an array
Syntax:	`type   name [ number of elements ];`
Example:	`short   studentGrade [10];`

To create an array, you define a variable. Follow the variable name with open and close brackets—the [and] keys—and then a semicolon. Inside the brackets, you put the number of items in the array. In the present example, the code sets the size of the array to 10 items. When the compiler encounters this code, it allocates room for 10 **short** values.

In C, the first element in the array is element zero. C uses a zero-based counting system for arrays. Therefore, a ten-element array has elements from zero to nine. The alternative would be to number the elements from one to ten. While counting from one to ten might seem to be a lot more reasonable, that's not how C works.

The contents of the array are unpredictable; therefore, you must set the values appropriately. You may initialize the contents of an array *when you define it* by providing a list of initial values of the appropriate type. This technique works only at the moment the array is defined. You cannot use this syntax to set the values in an array at any other time.

Concept: initializing an array when defined

Syntax: `type name [elements] = { value 1, value 2, value3 };`

Example:
```
short  myArray[3] = { 3, 2, 1 };
short  myArray[ ] = { 3, 2, 1 };
```

Use braces—{ and }—to indicate the items in the list. List items are separated by commas. There is no comma after the last item. A semicolon terminates the entire statement.

If you provide initial values for an array, you do not have to specify the number of elements in the array. The compiler reads the list of initializers, determines how many elements there are, and sizes the array accordingly. Precisely how the compiler sizes the array depends on the compiler, but it will be at least big enough to hold your initial data. If you plan on *adding* elements to the array after you set the initial values, you had better be sure the array is large enough to hold all the data. The wisest approach in such a situation is to size the array explicitly and not rely on the automatic sizing.

Both of the examples here accomplish the same thing. The code creates an array of three elements, numbered 0, 1, and 2. The first element of the array is assigned the value 3, the next element has the value 2, the last element has the value 1. To refer to these values at a later time, you specify the index number of the element you wish. To get the value in the first element, you refer to `myArray[0]`, *not* `myArray[1]`.

Array Gotchas

Remember, in C *the first element in an array is element zero.* This fact is critical to the proper use of arrays in C. All array-counting is zero-based. You must remember this, or you're going to run into serious problems.

There are two common problems that occur, because programmers forget that the numbering of array elements starts at zero: they assign values to the wrong element, and they overrun the array. Let's talk about both problems.

In the student example, the code creates an array for 10 students like this:

```
short    studentGrade[10];
```

This line allocates memory for 10 **short** values, with index numbers from zero to nine. Let's say you want to save the grade for the first student. You say, "This is the first student, so I'll put the student's grade in studentGrade[1]." You have made the first mistake. You put the first student's data into the second element of the array. Remember, element zero is the first element, element one is the second element.

Continue on through all the students until you reach number 10. You then try to put that student's grade into studentGrade[10]. You have made the second mistake. No memory has been allocated for studentGrade[10]. You are in fact trying to put this student's grade in the *11th* element of a 10-element array! You have overrun the bounds of the array.

There are no array bounds checks in C, so the compiler happily lets you put the value in a nonexistent array element. Whatever was at that place in memory gets stomped, and the results are unpredictable. You have a bug that is extremely difficult to locate, and one that may cause all sorts of strange problems ranging from an instantaneous crash of the entire computer to general weirdness.

The best way to avoid this problem is to always remember to count from zero when working with arrays. You can carry this over to all of your numerical thinking when you write programs. Don't think of your first student as student one, but as student zero. Then you avoid the problem of a set of numbers that start at one, and another set of numbers that start at zero. This sort of zero-based numbering is very common in programming situations, not just in arrays.

The second solution is to make your array one element larger than you need, and never use element zero. For 10 students you create an array of 11 elements like this:

```
short    studentGrade[11];
```

This code creates an array of **short** values with index numbers from zero to 10 (a total of 11 elements). Then you have slots for students 1 through 10. You put your first student in element 1, your second student in element 2, and so forth. Because you have allocated room for 11 elements (zero through 10), the tenth student ends up in element 10 with no problem. With this approach, you never use element zero and the space allocated for it is wasted.

In my opinion this approach is inferior to counting from zero. You must remember to allocate extra memory (11 slots for 10 students in our example). You waste space. And when it comes time to write code, starting from zero has significant advantages.

Typecasting

C is a "strongly typed" language. What this means is that a C compiler makes sure that data is of the right type before converting the source code into object code. C is also a "static" language. In this context, the term "static" means that data of one type cannot change to become data of another type.

This might seem to create a problem. There are many occasions when you want to mix data of different types. For example, you may want to multiply a **long** value by a **short** value. How can you do this in C?

The solution is *type conversion* (also called *type coercion*). You may implicitly or explicitly tell the compiler that on a particular occasion you want the compiler to treat data of one type as if it were data of another type. If that's possible, the compiler gladly complies.

Type conversion may be automatic or explicit. In C-speak, explicit type conversion is called typecasting.

For mathematical operations using standard C data types (**char**, **int**, **short**, **long**, **float**, **double**, **long double**), the conversion is automatic. For example, if you multiply a **long** value by a **short** value, the compiler *automatically* treats the **short** value as if it were a **long** value, and performs the multiplication. The result is a **long** value.

Automatic typecasting causes the shorter type (the type occupying fewer bytes of memory) to be promoted to the longer type. This promotion is temporary. It does not permanently convert the shorter type to the longer type. The result of any such operation is a value of the longer type.

Most of the time you can forget all about this process. However, there are times when what you want to accomplish does not happen automatically. In that case, you have to explicitly typecast your variables as necessary.

Concept:	typecasting
Syntax:	*(desired type)* *variable*
Example:	(short) myVariable

To tell the compiler that you are typecasting, you put the name of the desired data type in parentheses before the name of the variable you want to typecast.

Let's look at a practical example. For example, let's say you want to get the fractional part of a **double** value. The following code won't work.

```
double aDouble = 6.236;
double fractionalPart;
fractionalPart = aDouble - aDouble;
```

The result of this code is zero. No type conversion occurs automatically, because all the values are the same type: **double**.

You have to explicitly tell the compiler how you want the data treated. In other words, you must perform a typecast. In this case, rather than promoting a value, you want to "demote" it to a shorter type. The following code gets the job done:

```
double aDouble = 6.236;
double fractionalPart;
fractionalPart =  aDouble - (short) aDouble;
```

In this code, you explicitly tell the compiler to subtract the **short** value of the variable aDouble from the normal aDouble. The **short** value of 6.236 is 6. You then subtract that **short** value from the full value of aDouble.

Later on, this guide discusses other data types that you create yourself. Casting those types (or more precisely, the pointers to data of those types) is a common and regular feature of C code.

Now that the common numerical data types are covered, you can turn your attention to strings.

Strings

In C, a string is—for all practical purposes—a specialized array of **unsigned char** values. Each element in the array is a character in the string. After the last character in the string there is a "null terminator," the value zero. C strings are called null-terminated strings because of this feature. A C string can be any length. Table A.3 shows the structure of a C string.

Table A.3: Structure of a C String

Element	0	1	2	3	4	5
Data	H	e	l	l	o	0

Element zero contains the first character in the string. The zero in element 5 is the null terminator and indicates the end of the string. See Appendix B for a discussion of how C and Pascal differ with respect to strings.

String Constants

You define a string constant using double quotation marks. There is no need to specify the terminating zero, that's handled for you automatically by the compiler.

Data Type:	`char[ ]` (a string, an array of type `char`)
Syntax:	`"text of string"`
Example:	`"Mac programmers are cool."`

You don't see string constants very often in Macintosh programming.

String Variables

You can assign a name to a string, making it a variable. You can then manipulate the contents of the string as you wish. To do this, you define an array of type **char**. You set the initial value of the array equal to your text, in quotation marks. Terminate the entire statement with a semicolon.

Data Type:	`char[ ]` (a string, an array of type `char`)
Syntax:	`char name[] = "text of string";`
Example:	`char myString[] = "Mac programmers are cool.";`

What's happening here is that you are defining (allocating memory for) an array of type **char**. You are initializing that array with some text. Like arrays of other types, this works only when you are defining the array for the first time. You cannot use this syntax to set the contents of a string after it already exists. There are two other items you should note with respect to this syntax.

First, like other arrays, you do not have to specify the size of the array when you provide a list of initial values—in this case the initial text between quotes.

Second, rather than putting the list of initial values in braces and separating each element by a comma, you can put the text between quotation marks for strings. This is a special form of initializer list for arrays of type **char**.

Working with Strings

Strings are very common and very useful. You will use strings extensively in your C code. You will want to copy strings, compare strings, put two strings together (*concatenate* them), get the length of strings, and so forth.

However, working with strings is inherently tedious. For example, say you want to make one string equal to another string. You cannot just write code such as:

```
destinationString = sourceString;
```

Remember that in C, strings are really arrays of type **char**, and you cannot set the contents of one array equal to another array by a simple statement. You must set each element in an array individually. You must treat strings exactly as you do an array of any other data type.

In this example, you have to go through each element of the source string and copy it into the corresponding element in the destination string. If the source is longer than the destination, you can exceed the bounds of the destination string array. This is a Bad Thing.

Other kinds of string-related tasks—such as concatenating, determining if two strings are the same, and so forth—have similar problems. You must manipulate the elements of the array.

The bad news is—no surprise—this is boring.

The good news is, this has already been done for you. Every good C development environment comes with libraries of routines that conform to the ANSI C standard. One of those libraries is devoted to string manipulation. You can use standard library routines to manipulate strings easily and reliably. See the "Standard Libraries" section of this appendix for more information about the standard string functions. The Macintosh Toolbox also has some string manipulation routines.

Structs and Typedefs

One of the most powerful features of C is the **struct**. The keyword **struct** is short for "structure." A structure is a formal way of organizing a group of variables. Each variable has a name, and typically you assign each variable a value. When collected into a **struct**, you can then treat all of those variables as a single unit. Of course, you can still access individual variables within the structure at any time.

In correct C-speak, each variable in a structure is called a *field*. The word *member* is a widely used synonym for field. The fields in a structure can be of any data type, including other structures. The naming rules for ordinary variables also apply to fields in a structure. However, even though you have a **struct** with fields named xAxis and yAxis, you can still use those same names elsewhere in your program; for example, as local variables or as fields in some other struct. The compiler never gets confused because you always refer to the field as a member of the **struct**, not as an independent entity. Therefore there is never a name collision.

Keyword:	`struct`

Syntax:	`struct`
	`{`
	    `type   name;`
	    `type   name;`
	`} structname;`

Example:	`struct`
	`{`
	  `short xAxis;`
	  `short yAxis;`
	`} Coordinate;`

The syntax is straightforward. You use the keyword **struct**, followed by braces. Inside the braces you declare the fields just as you do a variable. A structure may have any number of fields. You simply add more of them between the braces. The only requirement is that each field have a unique name within the **struct**. After the closing brace, you name the **struct**. End the statement with a semicolon.

note
Technically, the name of the **struct** is optional. However, not naming a **struct** defeats the purpose of the **struct** because the name gives you a handy way to refer to a group of related variables.

A name is fine, but to make structures really useful, another concept must be introduced, the **typedef**. The **typedef** keyword is short for "type definition." (Actually it is a declaration, not a definition, but we pick nits here.) In C, you declare your own data types using the **typedef** keyword. You can do this with any data type. Typically you do this with the **structs** you declare, because then you can treat the **struct** like other data types. You can allocate memory for them, pass them as parameters to functions, and so forth. By declaring the **struct** to be its own data type, you give yourself tremendous flexibility and power.

Keyword:	`typedef`
Syntax:	`typedef  originalType   newName;`
Example:	`typedef  unsigned long   uLong;`

	`typedef struct`
	`{`
	`  short xAxis;`
	`  short yAxis;`
	`} Coordinate;`

In the first example, the code declares a new data type named uLong. You might want to declare uLong to save yourself some typing every time you want to define an **unsigned long** variable. Once declared, the compiler treats the symbol uLong as an **unsigned long**.

The second example is more apt for this discussion of **structs**. The code declares the structure of the **struct**—that is, it specifies the structure's fields using the appropriate syntax. Then the code names the **struct**. Because it uses the **typedef** keyword, Coordinate is now a formal data type recognized by the compiler.

Typically, you make **struct** and **typedef** declarations in header files. The nature and role of header files are discussed later in this guide. Once declared, however, you're free to use the new data type as you would any other. For example, once you have declared the Coordinate data type, you can define (allocate memory for) a **struct** of type Coordinate, like so:

```
Coordinate  thisCoordinate;
```

This is the exact same syntax you use for a **short**, **double**, or other simple data types. This statement allocates all the memory necessary to hold a **struct** of type Coordinate, and names the local variable thisCoordinate.

Once you have a **struct** variable, you will want to access the contents of its fields.

Concept:	accessing a field in a local struct
Syntax:	`variableName.fieldName;`
Example:	`thisCoordinate.xAxis = 6;`

To access a field in a **struct**, you use a period between the name of the **struct** variable and the name of the field. Note that you use the name of the *variable*, not the name of the data type.

In this example, you set the value of the xAxis field of the variable named thisCoordinate to a value of six. You use a different syntax to access fields using a pointer to a **struct**. Pointers (and pointer syntax) are discussed a little later in this appendix.

That covers the basic C data types, and how to use them. However, one more important issue concerning data must be discussed.

Data Scope

The concept of "scope" is critical to understanding C code. A variable's scope is that part of the code from which you can access the variable. That may seem a trifle obscure. Let's start with the concept of a local variable, and discuss its scope. Then you can move on to more difficult concepts relating to scope: **static** variables, **extern** variables, and global variables.

Listed next is a simple C function. Don't worry about the first line of the example. Function syntax is discussed a little later. The part relevant to this discussion is the code between the braces.

```
short AddOneToNumber (short number)
{
  short  newNumber;

  newNumber = number + 1;
  return newNumber;
}
```

In this example, the code defines a *local variable* named newNumber. This is a local variable because its scope is limited to this function. The variable comes into existence when this function executes, and disappears when this function terminates. You cannot access the variable newNumber from anywhere else in the code. Because the variable's scope is limited to the function, however, you can use the same variable name in any other function.

In C, this kind of variable is an *automatic variable*. All automatic variables are valid only within their scope. Their scope is defined by the braces on either side of their definition. If you are outside those braces, the variable does not exist. That's neat, clean, and simple.

What if you don't want the contents of the variable to disappear? You can identify this variable as belonging to a special storage class called **static**. A **static** variable retains its value even when its scope ends.

Keyword:	`static`
Syntax:	`static` *type* *name*;
Example:	`static long counter = 0L;`

To identify a variable as **static**, simply put the keyword before the regular variable definition.

To better illustrate what a static variable is and how it works, let's expand the example slightly so you have a complete function to look at.

```
void KeepCount (void)
{
  static long  counter = 0L;
  counter = counter + 1;
}
```

In this function, the code defines a **long** variable named counter as **static**. The scope of this variable is the function. Because this is a **static** variable, the compiler allocates memory for it in a special place and sets the contents to zero *before you ever call this function*. The compiler is very smart. Now that it has created and initialized counter, it ignores the first line of code when you call the function. Every time you call the function, the value of counter goes up by one. It is never reset to zero. When the function ends the first time, counter has a value of 1. You call the function again. The variable counter is not set to zero. Because it is **static** it still has the value 1, and it goes up to 2. The next time it has the value 2 and goes up to 3, and so forth.

The *value* of a **static** variable persists beyond the scope of the variable. You still cannot access the variable outside of its scope, but next time it comes into scope it has the same value it had the last time it went out of scope. In C-speak, **static** is a storage class specifier, because the compiler stores the data separate from normal local variables so that the value can persist. There are times when this advanced technique is extremely useful, because it allows you to keep persistent data private to a particular function. It's as if the function can keep track of things, even when the function disappears out of scope.

However, sometimes you want to access data that lives elsewhere in a program. To do this, you must expand the scope of the variable that holds the data. In C, you can control the scope of a variable with a couple of techniques. Before those are discussed, you need to learn about the typical structure of C code in a development project.

In a typical programming project, you spread your source code across several files. Some of this information is in header files (usually declarations like **structs**, **typedefs**, **#defines**, and function prototypes) and some is in source files (the variables and functions that make up your program).

You can expand the scope of a variable to include every function in an individual source file by defining it outside the scope of any function in that file. The scope of such a variable is then the entire source file in which it is defined. Typically you see this kind of variable definition at the start of a source file. Before you define any function, you define the variables for which you want every function *in that file* to have access.

What if you want to use that same variable from within a function that is in some other source file?

To do this, you must tell the compiler that the variable is defined in another source file. You use the keyword **extern** to tell the compiler that the variable is external to the file.

Keyword:	`extern`	
Syntax:	`extern` *type*	*name*`;`
Example:	`extern short myGlobalVariable;`	

You follow the keyword with the data type of the external variable, and its name. You terminate the statement with a semicolon. This example assumes you have defined a **short** variable named myGlobalVariable in another source file in your code. Typically you find **extern** statements like this at the beginning of a source file.

The **extern** statement must use the identical data type and variable name as the variable to which you wish to refer. You do not need to specify the source file in which you defined the original variable.

An **extern** statement does not allocate memory or create a new variable. It simply tells the compiler where an existing variable is located. The keyword **extern** is also a storage class specifier.

For a variable to be truly global—that is, for you to be able to refer to it from anywhere in your code—you must include an **extern** reference to it in every source file except the one in which you originally define the variable.

Pointers

A pointer is the address in memory of a piece of data. That's all there is to it. It is a simple concept, but one whose importance in C cannot be overstated. Pointers cause new programmers no end of trouble. In this section, I try to take the mystery out of pointers. Pointers are easy to use, and they are a powerful and vital tool in the C programmer's tool kit.

This discussion of pointers covers the following topics:

- What is a pointer?
- Why use pointers?
- Pointer syntax
- A simple example
- Pointers to structs
- Void pointers

Of necessity, this discussion is somewhat theoretical. You're reading about pointers. You probably will not become comfortable with pointers until after you actually use them for a while. It's rather like riding a bicycle. You can read all the books you want about how to ride a bicycle, but until you get up on the seat and start pedaling, you really aren't going to master the skill.

What Is a Pointer?

Although pointers have already been defined, it bears repeating. A pointer is the address in computer memory of a piece of data. In Figure A.1, the left column shows the address of some locations in memory. These are pointers to the memory. The right column shows the contents of memory at each address, in hexadecimal values.

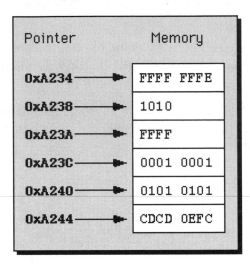

Figure A.1 Pointers

A common drop box may help you understand what pointers are. Let's say you would like a friend to work on a document that you have. To match how a programming language works, assume that you can do this in only two ways.

First, you can make a *copy* of the document and give your friend the copy. Your friend makes changes to the copy, and ultimately returns the copy to you. All the while, your original document sits on your desk unchanged. After the copy comes back, you have two versions of the document—the original and the copy. This method is called "passing by value."

Or, you can simply tell your friend where the document is in a drop box. Essentially, you give the friend the address of the document. This allows your friend to go to the document and make some changes. The next time you look at the document, your original has been changed. This second method is called "passing by reference." In programming terms, the address is a reference to the document, hence the term "passing by reference."

A pointer is simply the address of a variable. When you use a pointer, you are using the variable's "drop box." However, it is a drop box with a particular size and shape. If you know the address, you can change the contents of the drop box as long as the data fits into the box—that is, the data must be of the correct data type.

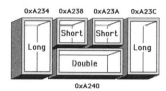

Figure A.2 Pointers to types

Why Use Pointers?

Why are pointers important? There are several reasons. We are going to talk about two reasons concerning how and why you pass data as parameters into a function. Some programmers prefer the term *argument* as a synonym for parameter. In this guide, the term *parameter* is primarily used. Parameter passing is discussed again in the "Functions" section of this guide.

For now, you should realize that when you call a function, you can pass data to the function in one or more parameters. You can pass data by value, or by reference. Let's be a little more specific about what they mean in a programming environment:

- *Passing data by value* means that you pass the actual value to the called function. This gives the function you call a *copy* of the data to work on. The original data back in the calling function remains untouched.

- *Passing data by reference* means you pass the address of the data rather than its actual value. This means that you are letting the called function have direct access to the original data back in the calling function.

You want to pass data by reference—that is, use a pointer—in two cases.

First, you use a pointer when you want the function that you call to change the original data for you. Because you pass the address of the data, the called function can change the data at that address—the original data.

Assume the boxes in Figure A.3 represent variables in a calling function. You call another function and pass the address of one of your short variables, 0xA238, to that other function. That function then changes the contents of the box from the value 39 to the value 42. When control returns to you, your short variable now has a 42 inside.

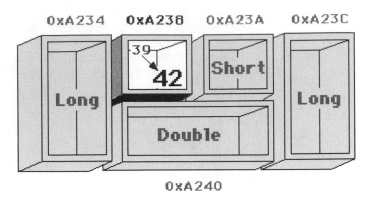

Figure A.3 Changing the contents of an address

Second, you use a pointer to the data when the data is so large that you prefer not to pass the actual data. Why is this a problem? Read on.

When you pass data from one function to another, that data resides in memory in a place called the "stack" or the "function stack." This is where every function's local variables and parameters that are passed between functions reside. Passing large amounts of data across the stack can cause problems because the stack has a limited amount of memory allocated for its use. In addition, copying all that data onto the stack can slow down a program.

To avoid these problems, it is wise to pass data by reference whenever the data occupies more than a few bytes of memory.

Pointer Syntax

In C-speak, creating a pointer to a variable is called *referencing* the variable because you are creating a reference to the data in the named variable.

Concept:	referencing a variable
Syntax:	`&variableName`
Example:	`&myNumber`

When you want to use the address of a variable for any reason, you use the ampersand before the variable name. There must be no space between the ampersand and the variable name. The example assumes that you have a local variable named `myNumber`. When you see this syntax, translate it as "the address of..." and you will have an easier time grasping what is really going on. So "`&myNumber`" means the address of `myNumber`.

You cannot have any space between the ampersand and the variable name. C uses the ampersand for other purposes. If you put a space between it and the variable name, the ampersand will be misinterpreted. We discuss the other uses of the ampersand when we discuss logical operators.

Perhaps the most common situation where you see this syntax is as a parameter in a function call, as in this code example.

```
ChangeMyNumber(&myNumber);
```

In this example, the code calls a function named `ChangeMyNumber()`. It passes the *address* of a local variable, `myNumber`. `ChangeMyNumber()` does something with or to the data at that address.

Of course, to do something with the data the function must access the data referred to by the pointer. In other words, the called function must look inside the drop box. This is called *dereferencing* a pointer.

Concept:	dereferencing a pointer
Syntax:	`*variableName`
Example:	`*myPtr`

The syntax for dereferencing a simple pointer is to use the asterisk symbol before the variable. Like the ampersand character, the asterisk has other uses. There can be no white space between the asterisk and the name of the variable.

To help you grasp what this syntax means, it helps to have an English translation. You can translate the asterisk character in this syntax as:

- "the data pointed to by..."
- "the data at the address referred to by..."
- "the contents of..."

In this example, you are looking at the data pointed to by `myPtr`. For this to work correctly, `myPtr` must in fact be a pointer—that is, an address of a variable.

A

A Simple Example

The code in these two functions works together to create, pass, receive, and dereference a pointer. Take a quick look, and then I'll walk you through the code.

```
void SetMyNumber(void)
{
  double  myNumber = 3.14159;
  ChangeMyNumber(&myNumber);
}

void ChangeMyNumber (double *myNumberPointer)
{
  *myNumberPointer = 1.0;
}
```

Let's translate this code into English. In the SetMyNumber() routine, the code defines a local **double** variable named myNumber and initializes its value to 3.14159. Then it calls another function, ChangeMyNumber(). That call passes a single parameter, &myNumber—the address of myNumber. At this point, the *contents* of that address are the value 3.14159. The address points to some location in memory. It doesn't matter precisely where.

Control flows to the ChangeMyNumber() routine. The title of that routine specifies that it receives one parameter. The syntax is, double *myNumberPointer. Translated into English, that means that this function receives a parameter named myNumberPointer, and that myNumberPointer must be a pointer to a **double** value.

The body of the function has this code:

```
*myNumberPointer = 1.0;
```

This code translates into "Set the data pointed to by myNumberPointer to the value 1.0." In other words, it sets the *value* of myNumber—the variable back in the original routine SetMyNumber(). Why? Because myNumberPointer is the address of myNumber.

Control then returns to SetMyNumber(). At the moment control returns, the value inside the local variable myNumber is 1.0. It is no longer 3.14159.

Pointers to Structs

Remember that when you have a **struct** as a local variable, you use the period operator between the name of the **struct** variable and the name of the field.

However, in C you frequently have the *address* of a **struct**—that is, a pointer to a **struct**—rather than the **struct**. The syntax required to access a field of a **struct** when you have a pointer is a little different.

Concept:	dereferencing a pointer to a struct
Syntax:	`structName->fieldName`
Example:	`myStructPointer->firstField`

To access the field of a **struct** when you have a pointer to the **struct**, use the -> operator between the name of the pointer to the **struct** and the name of the field. This symbol consists of the hyphen and the greater-than symbol. It looks like an arrow, further reinforcing the concept that this is a pointer to something.

As an example, let's use the `Coordinate` **struct** from the "Data in C" section earlier in this guide. The declaration of a `Coordinate` follows.

```
struct { short   xAxis;
         short   yAxis;
       } Coordinate;
```

Let's say you want a routine to initialize these values to 0, and that you pass this routine the address of a `Coordinate` **struct**. It might look like this:

```
void InitCoordinate (Coordinate *thisCoordinate)
{
  thisCoordinate->xAxis = 0;
  thisCoordinate->yAxis = 0;
}
```

The -> operator handles all the dereferencing for you. You do not need to use the asterisk operator anywhere to access the individual fields in the `Coordinate` **struct**. In English, this syntax translates into "Set the contents of the `xAxis` field of `thisCoordinate` to zero."

Void Pointers

You may have noticed that in each case in which you pass a pointer to a function, that function definition requires that the pointer point to a particular data type. This is required because C is a strongly typed language. You must specify data types at all times, and if the actual data does not match the expected type, the compiler will complain.

This approach has the advantage of catching a lot of mistakes at compile time when you do things like try to pass a **double** value to a routine that wants a pointer to a **double** value. Strong type checking can save you untold grief.

However, there are times when you do not want to specify the data type. You want to be able to pass pointers to a variety of data types to a single routine. Of course, the routine receiving the pointer must be able to handle data of various types.

Assuming that you have written such a routine, there is a way to free yourself from the rigors of strong type checking. You define the routine to receive a **void** pointer, meaning a pointer to data of any type. In place of the usual data type, you use the keyword **void**.

Concept:	void pointers
Syntax:	`void *variableName`
Example:	`void *dataPointer`

This is identical to defining a pointer to an ordinary data type, except that you specify **void** as the data type. The danger inherent in this technique is that you lose the benefits of strong type checking. When you pass a **void** pointer, you must make sure that the pointer points to data that the routine can handle. The compiler does not check the type of **void** pointers.

The various data types, how to use them in variables, the scope of variables, and how to extend the scope of variables has been discussed. Pointers to data have also been covered. The next step is to do something with the data, and for that you need operators.

Operators

Operators are symbols that represent some operation you perform on data—either constants or variables. There are several classes of operators discussed in this section:

- Arithmetic   perform math operations
- Assignment   make one item equal another
- Relational   compare two items
- Logical   perform true/false analysis on items
- Bitwise   manipulate bits in an item
- Increment/Decrement   increase/decrease a value by one

This section also talks about the order of precedence followed in C for various operations. Finally, a special operator for determining the number of bytes in a piece of data is covered.

Before discussion begins, I should clarify the terms used to describe operations and operators. *Operators* are symbols that represent operations. *Operations* are performed on values. In this context, the values are called *operands*. Operands may be constants or variables.

Operators are classified as binary or unary operators, depending upon the number of operands required in the operation. Binary operators require two operands. Most operators are binary. For example, the addition operator requires two numbers to add. Unary operators require one operand. For example, the increment operator is a unary operator because it requires just one variable.

There is also a ternary operator that requires three operands, but this won't be discussed. It is too obscure, never necessary, and not used anywhere in the code for this book.

In the following sections, the term *value* means either a constant or a variable. The code examples illustrating syntax are minimal. Typically you see the example code in a more complete statement that does something with the result of the operation.

Now that the terms have been defined, let's discuss each of the various operators and how to use them.

Arithmetic Operators

Arithmetic operators perform simple math operations on numbers—constants, variables, or one of each. Most arithmetic operators are binary. For the binary arithmetic operators, the syntax is to type the appropriate symbol between the two numbers. Spaces are not required, but help the readability of code.

The binary arithmetic operators are:

+	Addition
–	Subtraction
*	Multiplication
/	Division
%	Modulo division

For all binary arithmetic operators, both operands must be numerical. You cannot add arrays, strings, or **structs**.

Operator:	+ (addition)
Syntax:	*value + value*
Example:	6 + x

The example code adds the value of x to the constant 6.

Operator:	– (subtraction)
Syntax:	*value - value*
Example:	x - y

The example subtracts the value of y from the value of x.

Operator:	* (multiplication)
Syntax:	*value * value*
Example:	6 * x

The example multiplies 6 by the value of x. Note that the symbol for the multiplication operator is the same as the symbol for dereferencing a pointer. This can lead to some confusion when reading C code. The use of the same symbol for two purposes doesn't cause significant problems after you become familiar with how the two operators are used. The multiplication operator is binary. The pointer dereference operator is unary.

Operator:	/ (division)
Syntax:	*value / value*
Example:	6 / x

The example statement divides the value 6 by the value of x. In other words, the value preceding the operator is the dividend, the value following the operator is the divisor.

Operator:	% (modulo division)
Syntax:	`value % value`
Example:	`x % 6`

The symbol is the percent sign. Values must be *integers*. You cannot use modulo division with floating point values, arrays, strings, or **structs**. The value preceding the modulo operator is the dividend. The value after the operator is the divisor.

Modulo division is a little peculiar. It is also called "remainder division" because the result of modulo division is the remainder of normal division. For example, assume you divide the value 11 by the value 3 with normal division. The answer is 3 with a remainder of 2. The result of 11 % 3 is 2—the remainder of the normal division. So 15 % 3 is zero because there is no remainder, and 23 % 4 would be 3.

There is no operator to raise a number to a power. The standard libraries include several useful math functions, one of which fills this need. Standard libraries are discussed later in this appendix.

There are two unary arithmetic operators, the unary + and the unary – (minus). Both of these are discussed in the interest of completeness, but the unary + is, for all practical purposes, useless.

Operator:	+ (unary plus)
Syntax:	`+value`
Example:	`+x`

In this case, the + symbol does not mean to add two values. It says to take a value at its actual value, positive or negative. This is a unary operator, and as such it has one operand. The operand may be a constant or variable with any numerical value.

You won't see the unary + very often, because it is redundant. It tells the compiler to use the value as is. That's what the compiler does anyway, so the statement is meaningless. *Putting a unary + in front of a negative value does not convert that value to a positive value.* Here's some sample code to show you what happens.

```
short x = -35;
short y;
y = +x;
```

This code sets the value in y to –35, not 35.

Operator:	– (unary minus or negation)
Syntax:	*-value*
Example:	-x

In this case, the – symbol does not mean to subtract two values. It says to use the *negative* of a value. This is a unary operator, and as such it has one operand. The operand may be a constant or variable with any numerical value.

Unlike the unary plus operator, the unary minus operator is extremely useful. *Putting a unary minus in front of a value converts that value to its negative.* Here's some sample code to show you what happens.

```
short x = 35;
short y;
y = -x;
```

This code sets the value in y to –35—the negative of 35. Note that the value in x remains 35! The negation operator does not change the contents of a variable. It is an instruction to the compiler that says "Use the negative of this value." C programmers use the negation operator so often it is almost unconscious. Every time you have a variable and set its contents to a negative number, you use the negation operator. For example, this code:

```
x = -9;
```

uses the negation operator to set the value of x to the negative of 9.

Take care to distinguish the unary minus from the binary minus. Although the symbol is the same, they are both common and familiar operators that perform very distinct operations.

Assignment Operators

Assignment operators are binary operators that make one value equal to another. In each case, the value to the left of the assignment operator becomes equal to the operand on the right side of the operator. Once again the examples are minimal.

For all the assignment operators, the left operand must be a variable. The right operand can be any constant, variable, function, operation, or group of operations that resolves to a single value. Everything on the right of the operator is resolved first, and then the result is applied to the value in the variable on the left side of the operator. For example, the statement x = y + 9 * z - 5 % 3 is perfectly valid.

The classic assignment operator is the equal sign.

Operator:	= (assignment)
Syntax:	`variable = value`
Example:	`x = 6`

You can also use the assignment operator to set one **struct** equal to another **struct**, if both are the same type. Assuming you had two Coordinate **structs**, this code is legal.

```
thisCoordinate = thatCoordinate;
```

You can perform any assignment with this operator. However, C has other assignment operators that provide very useful shortcuts. You may want to perform some operation on a variable and save the result in the same variable. For example, you may want to add a value to a variable x, and keep that value in x. You can do this with the classical assignment operator by writing code like so.

```
x = x + 6;
```

However, combined assignment operators let you write such a statement more succinctly.

Operator:	+= (addition with assignment)
Syntax:	`variable += value`
Example:	`x += y - 1`

677

Although there are two characters representing the operator, this is a single operator—the += operator. There can be no space between the + and = symbols or the compiler will misinterpret the operator. In the example, assume the value of y is 4. The y – 1 operation goes first, generating a result of 3. The value 3 is added to the value of x. This final result remains in x.

Operator:	– = (subtraction with assignment)
Syntax:	`variable -= value`
Example:	`x -= y - 1`

In the example, if the value of y is 4, 3 is subtracted from the value of x. This final result remains in x.

Operator:	*= (multiplication with assignment)
Syntax:	`variable *= value`
Example:	`x *= y - 1`

In the example, if the value of y is 4, x is multiplied by 3. This final result remains in x.

Operator:	/= (division with assignment)
Syntax:	`variable /= value`
Example:	`x /= y - 1`

In the example, if the value of y is 4, the value in x is divided by 3. This final result remains in x.

Operator:	%= (modulo division with assignment)
Syntax:	`variable %= value`
Example:	`x %= y - 1`

In the example, if the value of y is 4, the value in x will be the result of x % 3.

There are a few other assignment operators that result from combining the bitwise operators with the assignment operator in exactly the same way as the arithmetic operators. The bitwise operators are discussed in a little while, but the bitwise assignment operators are not discussed any further.

Relational Operators

Relational operators are binary operators that compare two values. The result of the comparison is either true or false. It is true if the relational statement is true, false if the relational statement is false. For example, the > symbol is the "greater than" operator. If you wrote 6 > 4, that would resolve to true. If you wrote 4 > 6, that would resolve to false. Such a true or false value is called a Boolean value.

Typically, you find such relational operators inside `if` and `while` statements. Those statements are discussed in the "Flow Control" section of this guide. Typically, you use a relational statement as a conditional test in the form of "if (or while) something is true, do something."

There are six relational operators:

- < Less than
- > Greater than
- <= Less than or equal to
- >= Greater than or equal to
- != Not identity (not equal to)
- == Identity (the same as)

For relational operators, either operand may be anything that resolves to a value. You cannot use arrays, strings, or **structs**.

Operator:	< (less than)
Syntax:	`value < value`
Example:	`x < y`

If the left operand has a numerical value less than the right operand, the statement resolves to true. Otherwise the statement resolves to false.

Operator:	> (greater than)
Syntax:	`value > value`
Example:	`x > y`

If the left operand has a numerical value greater than the right operand, the statement resolves to true. Otherwise the statement resolves to false.

Operator:	<= (less than or equal to)
Syntax:	`value <= value`
Example:	`x <= y`

If the left operand has a numerical value less than or equal to the right operand, the statement resolves to true. Otherwise the statement resolves to false.

Operator:	>= (greater than or equal to)
Syntax:	`value >= value`
Example:	`x >= y`

If the left operand has a numerical value greater than or equal to the right operand, the statement resolves to true. Otherwise the statement resolves to false.

Operator:	!= (not identity)
Syntax:	`value != value`
Example:	`x != y`

This operator compares two values to determine whether they are the same. If the left operand has a different numerical value than the right operand, the statement resolves to true. Otherwise the statement resolves to false. In other words, if the values are *not* the same, the statement is true. If the values are the same, the statement is false.

Operator: == (identity)

Syntax: `value -- value`

Example: `x == y`

This operator compares two values to determine whether they are the same. If the left operand has the same numerical value as the right operand, the statement resolves to true. Otherwise the statement resolves to false.

Problems with the Identity Relational Operator

The identity operator causes C programmers no end of problems. Here's why: take the previous example, x == y, and translate it into simple English. You might say, "If x equals y." That makes semantic sense in English, but you have ignored a very important distinction in C. In C, the term "equals" means assignment, not identity. If you translate that English back into C, you get x = y, and that's *wrong*! That is not the same thing as x == y.

The statement x = y sets the value of x to the value in y. The statement x == y compares the values in x and y to see whether they are the same. In the latter case, the value of x does not change.

Typically you find the correct statement in code like this:

```
if (x == y)
```

And if you make a mistake it comes out as:

```
if (x = y)
```

The problem is that when you mean to type x == y, you forget the second equal sign and type x = y.

The result of this mistake is that you inadvertently change the value of x to y, with unpredictable results. The statement inside the parentheses is resolved first. So after you set the value of x equal to y, what you're really saying is

```
if (x)
```

If y has a non-zero value, x will have a non-zero value, and the statement resolves to true regardless of whether the *original* value of x was the same as the value of y.

This kind of bug can be extremely difficult to find. There is no defense against this problem except eternal vigilance and a really good compiler. Your vigilance should take the form of a mental discipline. Every time you want to compare values, always think to yourself "if x is the same as y." Do not use the word "equals" in your head. Using the phrase helps you remember that the == operator means "is the same as" and the = operator means "equal."

If you're fortunate enough to have a really friendly compiler, it will look for the assignment operator (=) inside `if` and `while` statements. If it finds one, the compiler will warn you. Most compilers do not warn you of this common mistake because making an assignment inside an `if` or `while` statement is perfectly legal, although uncommon and usually a bug.

Logical Operators

Relational operators allow you to test for a single condition: the relationship between two values. Logical operators allow you to test for two conditions simultaneously. You can test whether two conditions are both true, or if one or the other is true. By combining these operators into a series, you can test for multiple conditions.

There are three logical operators: **logical and**, **logical or**, and **logical not**. These operators are called "logical" because they perform a Boolean logic operation. This also distinguishes them from the "bitwise" operators of the same name that are discussed a little later. A Boolean logic operation does a true/false analysis of two operands.

You typically encounter the logical operators in `if` or `while` statements that test for multiple conditions.

Operator:	**&&** (logical and)
Syntax:	`condition && condition`
Example:	`x != y && y < 10`

The syntax for the **logical and** is a conditional statement of some kind, a double ampersand, and a second conditional statement. If *both* operands—the statements on either side of the operator—resolve to true, the entire statement resolves to true. If either operand is false, the statement as a whole resolves to false.

You can test for multiple conditions by adding more operators. For example,

```
x != y && y < 10 && r == 9
```

is a valid statement that tests three conditions. The conditions are tested left to right. If any one is false, the statement resolves to false.

Operator:	‖ (logical or)
Syntax:	*condition* ¦¦ *condition*
Example:	x != y ¦¦ y < 10

The symbol for the **logical or** operator is double vertical lines. If *either* of the operands resolves to true, the entire statement resolves to true. Only if *both* operands are false does the statement as a whole resolve to false.

You can combine both types of logical operators in a single statement. For example,

```
x != y && y < 10 ¦¦ r == 9
```

is a valid statement that tests three conditions. The tests are evaluated left to right. However, it can be very confusing trying to figure out which statement is being tested against which other statement. Usually such compound tests use parentheses to explicitly control what happens, like this:

```
(x != y && y < 10) ¦¦ r == 9
```

In this example, the statement as a whole resolves to true if either of two conditions is true. Either (x != y && y < 10) is true, *or* r == 9. That's not the same as the following code:

```
x != y && (y < 10 ¦¦ r == 9)
```

Operator:	! (logical not)
Syntax:	*!condition*
Example:	!(x == 10)

The symbol for the **logical not** is the exclamation point. Among C programmers, the ! symbol is pronounced either "bang" or "not." The **logical not** operator is a unary operator that tests whether a single condition is false. If the condition is false, the statement resolves to true. Normally, there is a more straightforward syntax you can use that is more intuitive and easier to read. For example, you could accomplish the same thing as the example if you write code like this:

```
if (x != 10)
```

Most people find this style easier to understand than !(x == 10).

However, the **logical not** operator does provide a simple shorthand to test whether a variable is zero. For example,

```
if (!x)
```

tests whether the variable x is zero. If it is zero, the condition resolves to true. Strange, but true. If x has a value, !x is false. If x has no value (that is, its value is 0), !x is true. This is the same as writing:

```
if (x == 0)
```

However, in this case the ! operator makes things simpler to write, and you avoid a possible assignment/identity operator error.

Bitwise Operators

Bitwise operators perform bit-level testing and manipulation of values. They use Boolean logic at the bit level in a value.

You can use these operators to test whether the same bits in two different values are both true, if one or the other is true but not both, if one or the other or both are true, or if both bits are false. A true bit has a binary value of 1 or on, a false bit has a binary value of 0 or off. Typically you use these tests to "mask" or test bits in a variable against those in a constant.

Operator:	**&** (bitwise and)
Syntax:	`value & value`
Example:	`x & 1`

The symbol for the **bitwise and** operator is a single ampersand. Either value may be the right or left operand, they are interchangeable. (In other words, the **bitwise and** operation is commutative, like addition or multiplication.) Either operand must be a numerical value, or a statement that resolves to a value. The bits in each value are compared. If *both* bits in a given position are true, the corresponding bit in the result is set to true. Otherwise, the bit in the result is set to false. Table A.4 illustrates the potential bit combinations for each bit of the operands, and the value of the bit in the result after the operation.

Table A.4: Bitwise And (&)

operand	1	1	0	0
operand	1	0	1	0
result	1	0	0	0

In a classic example of the use of this operator, you would **&** a variable against the constant value 1. The rightmost digit of any odd number is true. If the final result of the operation is one, the rightmost digit of the value in the variable was true, hence the variable is an odd number. In other words, if (x & 1), x is odd.

Operator:		(bitwise or)
Syntax:	*value	value*
Example:	x	1

The symbol for the **bitwise or** operation is a single vertical line. Either value may be the right or left operand; they are interchangeable. Either operand must be a numerical value, or a statement that resolves to a value. The bits in each value are compared. If *either or both* bits in a given position are true, the corresponding bit in the result is set to true. Otherwise, the bit in the result is set to false. Table A.5 illustrates the potential bit combinations for each bit of the operands, and the value of the bit in the result after the operation.

Table A.5: Bitwise Or (|)

operand	1	1	0	0
operand	1	0	1	0
result	1	1	1	0

Operator:	~ (bitwise not)
Syntax:	~value
Example:	~x

The ~ symbol is the tilde (pronounced "till-dah"). The **bitwise not**, like the **logical not**, is a unary operator. The operand must be a numerical value, either constant or variable. The bits in the value are inverted in the result. If the bit in the operand is true, the bit in the result is false. If the bit in the operand is false, the bit in the result is true. Table A.6 illustrates the potential bit combinations for each bit of the operand, and the value of the bit in the result after the operation.

Table A.6: Bitwise Not (~)

operand	1	0
result	0	1

Operator:	^ (bitwise exclusive or)
Syntax:	value ^ value
Example:	x ^ 1

Either value may be the right or left operand, they are interchangeable. Either operand must be a numerical value, or a statement that resolves to a value. The bits in each value are compared. If *either* bit in a given position is true, the corresponding bit in the result is set to true. If neither bit is true, or if both bits are true, the bit in the result is set to false. Table A.7 illustrates the potential bit combinations for each bit of the operands and the value of the bit in the result.

Table A.7: Bitwise Exclusive Or (^)

operand	1	1	0	0
operand	1	0	1	0
result	0	1	1	0

note Many programming languages use the ^ symbol to raise a number to a power. C is not one of them.

The remaining bitwise operators are for bit shifting. You can shift bits left or right in a value. You can use these operators to perform multiplication or division by factors of two on integer values.

Operator:	>> (bitwise shift right)
Syntax:	`value >> value`
Example:	`x >> 1`

The left operand is the number to be shifted. The right operand is the number of positions to shift. Either operand must be a numerical value, or a statement that resolves to a value. The bits in the left operand are shifted by the number of positions in the right operand. Table A.8 shows such a shift for one position to the right for an 8-bit number. The rightmost bit disappears, the leftmost bit is set to zero.

Table A.8: Bitwise Shift Right

>> by 1	Value	Bits							
operand	219	1	1	0	1	1	0	1	1
result	109	0	1	1	0	1	1	0	1

This has the same effect as dividing the original value by two using integer division, with no remainder. Notice that although the original value is 219, the result is not 109.5, but 109. If the original value is an integer and you don't care about the remainder, you can use this for very quick division.

Operator:	<< (bitwise shift left)
Syntax:	`value << value`
Example:	`x << 1`

The left operand is the number to be shifted. The right operand is the number of positions to shift. Either operand must be a numerical value, or a statement that resolves to a value. The bits in the left operand are shifted by the number of positions in the right operand. Table A.9 shows such a shift for one position to the left for an 8-bit number. The leftmost bit disappears, the rightmost bit is set to zero.

Table A.9: Bitwise Shift Left (Multiply)

<< by 1	Value	Bits							
operand	27	0	0	0	1	1	0	1	1
result	54	0	0	1	1	0	1	1	0

If the original value is an integer, and you have enough bits to hold everything, you can use this for very quick multiplication. Shifting left usually (but not always) has the same mathematical effect as multiplying the original value by a power of two for each bit you shift. So shifting one bit left is multiplying by two, shifting two bits is multiplying by four, and so forth.

However, if shifting left pushes a true bit off the left side of the number, the final result is not a true multiplication, as shown in Table A.10.

Table A.10: Bitwise Shift Left (Not Multiplying)

<< by 1	Value	Bits							
operand	219	1	1	0	1	1	0	1	1
result	182	1	0	1	1	0	1	1	0

Increment/Decrement Operators

Increasing or decreasing the value of a variable by one is a common task in programming. For example, in a loop you may want to increment a loop-index variable. C has special operators for incrementing and decrementing.

Operator:	++ (increment)
Syntax:	`++variable` pre-increment
	`variable++` post-increment
Example:	`++x`
	`x++`

The symbol for the increment operator is a double plus sign. The increment operator is a shorthand way of saying x = x + 1. The increment operator is a unary operator. It has a single operand that must be a numerical variable. You cannot increment an array, string, or **struct**. You can increment an index into an array, and you can increment an element in an array (if it is a numerical value). Similarly, you can increment a field in a **struct** if that field contains a numerical value.

If the increment operator precedes the name of a variable, the variable is incremented before use. If it follows the name of a variable, the variable is incremented after use. In C-speak, the former is called pre-increment, and the latter post-increment. This can be a critical distinction.

For example, assume that you are using a variable as an index into elements of an array. Call this variable index, and assume it has a starting value of 2. This code:

```
result = myArray[index++];
```

puts the value of element two (the third element) into the variable result, and then increments index to the value of 3. On the other hand, this code:

```
result = myArray[++index];
```

increments the value of index to 3, and then puts the value of element three (the fourth element) into result.

You will probably see the post-increment operator more frequently than the pre-increment operator, but both are useful tools.

Operator:	-- (decrement)	
Syntax:	--variable	pre-decrement
	variable--	post-decrement
Example:	--x	
	x--	

The symbol for the decrement operator is a double minus sign. The decrement operator is a shorthand way of saying x = x – 1. The decrement operator behaves exactly like the increment operator, except that it reduces the value of the variable by one instead of increasing it by one. The decrement operator is a unary operator. It has a single operand that must be a numerical variable. You cannot decrement an array, string, or **struct**. You can decrement an index into an array, and you can decrement an element in an array (if it is a numerical value). Similarly, you can decrement a field in a **struct** if that field contains a numerical value.

If the decrement operator precedes the name of a variable, the variable is decremented before use. If it follows the name of a variable, the variable is decremented after use. In C-speak, the former is called pre-decrement, and the latter post-decrement. You should be aware that, like the increment operator, the decrement operator has this distinction. Read about the previously mentioned increment operator for an example of the difference between pre-incrementing and post-incrementing.

Operator Precedence

Quite a variety of operators that you can use to manipulate data have been discussed. You can mix and match these operators in a single statement almost at will.

However, you should realize that all operators are not created equal. Some operators are more important than others. The compiler sets up the final code so that the operations that take precedence are performed first. There is a rigid and formal pecking order among operators that resolves any ambiguity that might arise when a single statement includes more than one operator. This is necessary so that the compiler always knows what to do.

Here's a fairly simple example of C code that uses more than one arithmetic operator.

```
answer = 6 + 3 * 9;
```

Do you mean to add three to six and multiply the result by nine? In that case the answer is 81. Or do you mean to multiply three by nine, and add the result to six? In that case the answer is 33.

This is a simple example where all the operators are arithmetic. The rules of precedence in this case are that multiplication comes before addition, so the result is 33. If you want the addition performed before the multiplication, you have to surround that part of the statement with parentheses, like this:

```
answer = (6 + 3) * 9;
```

In this case the result is 81.

For arithmetic operators, C follows the rules of standard algebra. Operations in parentheses come first. Multiplication and division come before addition and subtraction, and the statement is interpreted left to right.

Things get a lot more complicated when you have arithmetic, dereferencing, bitwise, logical, and other operators all mixed into a single statement.

Table A.11 summarizes all the rules of precedence for operators in C. The rows are ordered from top to bottom, with rows towards the top taking precedence over rows toward the bottom. All operators in the same numbered row are of the same precedence. The compiler interprets them in the order of appearance, either left to right, or right to left as indicated in the table. In all cases, parentheses supersede. If there are nested parentheses, the compiler evaluates statements in the innermost parentheses first.

Table A.11: Operator Precedence

	Type	*Operator*	*Order*
1	precedence	( )	inside to outside
2	dereference	->, .	left to right
3	dereference arithmetic logical bitwise increment decrement size	*, & +, – (unary) ! (not) ~ (not) ++ -- sizeof( )	right to left
4	arithmetic	*, /, %	left to right
5	arithmetic	+, – (binary)	left to right
6	bitwise	>>, <<	left to right
7	relational	<, >, <=, >=	left to right
8	relational	==, !=	left to right
9	bitwise	& (AND)	left to right
10	bitwise	^ (XOR)	left to right
11	bitwise		(OR)	left to right
12	logical	&& (and)	left to right
13	logical	|| (or)	left to right
14	relational	?:	right to left
15	assignment	=, +=, –=, *=, /=, %=, &=, |=, ^=, >>=, <<=	right to left

A

The "Guide to C" does not discuss the ?: operator in row 14 of the table. That's the obscure ternary operator mentioned earlier in the guide. The bitwise assignment operators in row 15 are equally obscure. They are included here in the interest of completeness.

The sizeof( ) Operator

This discussion of C operators cannot be completed without mentioning a special operator, `sizeof( )`. Sometimes you need to know the number of bytes that some data occupies. You may need to allocate memory to hold a **struct**, for example. Or you may want to make sure that something fits in available space.

Operator:	`sizeof( )`
Syntax:	`sizeof (dataType)`
Example:	`sizeof (long)`

The `sizeof( )` operator is a unary operator. It has one operand, typically a data type. You may use a variable or constant, as well. If you use a value rather than a data type, the compiler substitutes the type of data that the variable or constant represents, and returns the size in bytes for that type of data.

The data type can be any type, including your own **structs** or other defined types.

This concludes our discussion of C operators. You now have learned about two important elements of the C language: data, and the operators that manipulate the data. These are the foundation of the language.

However, as you write code, you frequently need to control what happens and when it happens. C has several statements for controlling program flow.

Flow Control

For all of its power, C has only eight statements that control program flow. These statements can be classified as conditionals, loops, breaks, and switches. Conditionals branch based on conditions. Loops repeat sections of code. Breaks stop what's happening and go elsewhere. Switches branch to one of several possible destinations.

The **if** statement is purely conditional. However, it has a variety of forms that allow you tremendous flexibility. The **while** statement is both a conditional and a loop control statement. The **do...while** statement is very similar to the **while** statement. There is one other kind of loop, the **for** loop. There are two ways of breaking out of a block of code or loop, **break** and **continue**. Finally, there are two kinds of switches, the **switch/case** combination, and the much maligned **goto** statement.

This section examines the required syntax for each of these flow control statements, and provides examples of how to use them properly.

The if Statement

Keywords: `if/else if/else`

Syntax:
```
if (conditional statement)
{
  statements
}
else if (conditional statement)
{
  statements
}
else
{
  statements
}
```

Example:
```
if (x > y)        /* no semicolon */
{
  x = 1;
}
else if (x == y)  /* note identity operator */
{
  x = 0;
}
else
{
  x = -1;
}
```

Notice that there is no semicolon after the conditional statements. The previous syntax and example include a complete **if/else if/else** series of statements. You have many options for manipulating this syntax.

Options with if/else if/else

The **if** keyword is required. The **else if** or **else** keywords are *not* required. In other words, you can have a simple **if** statement all by itself.

```
if (x == y)
{
   /* do something */
}
```

You may have an **if** followed by an **else**, with no **else if** statement.

```
if ( x == y)
{
   /* do something */
}
else
{
   /* do something else */
}
```

You may have an **if** followed by **else if**, and no else statement.

```
if ( x == y)
{
   /* do something */
}
else if (x < y)
{
   /* do something else */
}
```

Of course you can use all three keywords in a series, as shown in the original syntax example.

In addition, an **if** may be followed by any number of **else if** statements. Each **else if** statement tests for another condition. You can create a chain of conditions. This is called the **if** chain.

Conditionals in if Statements

The conditional statement in parentheses can be *any* statement, however complex, that ultimately resolves to a numerical value. The conditional test is Boolean—that is, true or false. If the resulting numerical value is zero or false, the condition is false. Otherwise the condition is true.

The code controlled by a condition executes when the condition resolves to true. You locate code controlled by the condition between braces after the **if**, **else if**, or **else** statement. If the condition resolves to false, this code does not execute.

If you have an **if** chain, you have a *series* of conditions. You test for each condition in turn. When a condition resolves to true, the code controlled by that conditional executes. After that, *no subsequent condition in the chain will be tested, and no other code controlled by any other condition in the chain will execute*. The following code example illustrates what happens.

```
x = 5;
y = 0;

if (x < 6)
{
   y = 1;
}

else if (x < 7)
{
   y = 2;
}

else
{
   y = 3;
}
```

Because the first condition resolves to true—5 is less than 6—the code controlled by that condition executes and the value of the variable y is set to 1. That's it. Even though, in principle, the second condition in the **else if** statement is also true—5 is in fact also less than 7—that condition is never tested and the code controlled by that condition does not execute. In simple terms, once a condition is met in the **if** chain, that's it. That's the code that executes. No other conditions are tested, and no other code controlled by any other condition in the **if** chain executes.

Although you may have any number of **else if** statements with conditions, there can be only one **else** statement. If you use an **else** statement, it must come last. It is the catch-all that executes when all conditions in the **if** chain resolve to false.

A

The **else** statement does not have a conditional. If there is an **else** statement, the code it controls executes whenever none of the preceding conditions is met. If any condition is met, the **else** code does not execute.

Coding Conventions with if Statements

In the syntax and examples you have seen so far, the code controlled by any condition has always been surrounded by braces. The syntax *requires* braces only if there are two or more statements controlled. If there is only one statement, the braces are technically optional.

Even if there is only one statement, the braces are useful for two reasons:

- They clearly and visually delineate the code controlled by the condition. This is very helpful when reading the code.

- If you decide to modify your code in such a way that you add a second statement, you might forget to put in the braces. If there are no braces, the condition controls only the first statement. The second statement executes every time, regardless of whether the condition is met. This kind of bug is difficult to locate.

It is a good idea to use braces all the time, regardless of the number of lines of code controlled by the condition.

You have also seen that statements inside the braces are indented. This is a coding convention, and not a requirement of syntax. Indenting code helps you comprehend the relationship between various elements in the code. For example, you can see at a glance precisely what's controlled by a condition simply by how much the code is indented.

The location of the braces in the code is also optional. Many programmers prefer the style shown here, with the opening brace on the same line as the condition:

```
Jif (x < y) {
    /* statements */
}
```

For simple situations, programmers sometimes put everything on one line, like the following example that does not even use braces:

```
if (x < y) y = 0;
```

Other programmers, myself included, prefer putting the braces on their own lines. This helps identify the controlled code and makes it easy to locate missing braces.

What's important here is not that you adopt the style used in this book. You should adopt a style that you are comfortable with, and be consistent. A consistent style can help you avoid mistakes, and help you find them if you make them.

Speaking of mistakes…

The if Gotcha

There is a very sneaky, very hard to find, and very common bug that is easy to spawn when typing an **if** statement. It's in the code example that follows. See if you can spot it.

```
if (y > 0);
{
   y = 0;
}
```

This code is supposed to set the variable y to zero if and only if its original value is greater than zero. If y is negative, it is supposed to stay negative. Unfortunately, this code doesn't work. If you run this code, the variable y always ends up as zero, regardless of its initial value. Why?

The bug is the semicolon at the end of the **if** statement. Most C statements end in a semicolon. As a result, C programmers get in the habit of ending a line with a semicolon. However, you do *not* terminate the **if** statement (or the **else if** or **else** statements) with a semicolon.

Remember the rule that says if you have only one line of code after an **if** statement, the braces are optional? The compiler sees the semicolon and thinks that *the semicolon* terminates the statement that you intend to control with the condition! The fact that the semicolon terminates an empty statement is irrelevant to the compiler. It is perfectly legal to have an empty statement.

In the previous example, if the variable y is negative, the *semicolon* doesn't execute. Wow! That's the end of the **if** statement—one empty line of code, no braces! The next line of code, y = 0, is *not* controlled by the **if** statement, even though it is in braces. It executes every time. In this case, the compiler treats the braces as limiting the scope of any variable you might define between the braces. Because of the spurious semicolon, the braces do not define the code controlled by the **if** statement.

And all that because of a measly little semicolon you inadvertently typed at the end of an **if** statement. The worst part about it is, when you go looking for the bug, the semicolon is virtually invisible to both the mind and the eye.

If you're aware of the nature of the problem, you can do your best to avoid it in the first place; and keep it in mind as a possibility when you step through your code trying to locate the problem. One of the greatest benefits of a consistent coding style is that it minimizes this kind of problem.

> **note** One of the great benefits of a good compiler is that it will warn you of this problem! The CodeWarrior compiler will warn you if you turn on the "Possible Errors" option in the Warnings preferences.

The while Statement

<table>
<tr><td>Keyword:</td><td><code>while</code> (the while loop)</td></tr>
<tr><td>Syntax:</td><td>

```
while (conditional statement)
{
    statements
}
```
</td></tr>
<tr><td>Example:</td><td>

```
while (x > y)    /* no semicolon */
{
    x--;
}
```
</td></tr>
</table>

Like an **if** statement, **while** includes a conditional. The conditional statement in parentheses can be *any* statement, however complex, that ultimately resolves to a numerical value. The conditional test is Boolean—that is, true or false. If the resulting numerical value is zero or false, the condition is false. Otherwise the condition is true.

> **note** There is no semicolon after the conditional statement. Like the **if** statement, adding a semicolon causes flow control problems. See the previous discussion of the **if** gotcha.

If the condition resolves to true, the code between the braces executes. When that code terminates, however, *the condition is evaluated again*. If it is true, the code between the braces executes again. The code between the braces executes repeatedly until the condition evaluates to false. In other words, the code loops. The loop terminates when the conditional statement becomes false. In the previous example, the value of x decrements repeatedly until it is no longer greater than y. At that point the condition fails and the loop terminates.

Clearly, you must do something inside the loop that ultimately results in the condition evaluating to false. Otherwise you end up in an infinite loop because the conditional breaks the loop. If it never turns false, you spin electrons forever.

Like the **if** statement, the braces are optional if the **while** statement controls one line of code. However, it is good coding style to always use braces even when you have only one line of code in the loop.

In the **while** statement, the condition is evaluated first. If it is true, only then does the code execute. Contrast that behavior with the **do...while** statement.

The do...while Statement

Keywords:	`do`/`while` (the `do` loop)
Syntax:	```do```

```
do
{
    statements
} while ( conditional statement);
```

Example:

```
do
{
    x--;
} while (x > y);
```

This syntax is a little unusual. The keyword **do** begins the syntax. The keyword **while** appears after some intervening code. The **while** is followed by a conditional statement in parentheses. Then, just to be perverse, *the conditional is followed by a semicolon.* In all other cases, conditional statements are not followed by a semicolon. This one is.

The **do...while** statement is identical to the **while** statement, except that the condition is evaluated *after* the loop executes for the first time. As a result, the code in the **do** loop always executes at least once—before the first time the condition is evaluated.

If the condition resolves to true, the code between the braces repeats. The code between the braces executes repeatedly until the condition evaluates to false. You must do something inside the loop to ensure that the condition ultimately resolves to false. Otherwise, you get caught in an infinite loop. In the example, the value of x decrements until, ultimately, x is no longer greater than y. The condition resolves to false, and the loop terminates.

Like the **if** and **while** statements, the braces are optional if the **do** statement controls one line of code. However, it is good coding style to always use braces regardless of whether you have one or more lines of code in the loop.

The for Statement

Keyword:	`for`

Syntax:	`for (initialValue; conditional; step)`
	`{`
	  `statements`
	`}`

Example:	`for ( index = 0; index < 10; index++)`
	`{`
	  `y[index] = x * index;`
	`}`

The syntax for the **for** loop is fairly complex. It begins with the keyword **for**, followed by parentheses. Inside the parentheses are three elements: the initial value of the variable you use to index the loop, a conditional test that ends the loop, and a step value by which the index is increased. Each element is separated from the next by a semicolon. There is no semicolon at the end of the **for** statement. Braces define the code in the loop. Like other loops, if there is only one line of code, the braces are optional.

The loop executes repeatedly until the condition in the **for** statement fails. If the condition fails at the outset, the loop never executes.

In the previous example, the code uses a local variable named `index` and sets its initial value to zero. The code sets up the condition so that this loop repeats as long as `index` is less than the value 10. Each time through the loop, the code increments `index` by one. Because the loop starts at zero, the loop repeats 10 times. In the loop itself, the code sets the first 10 elements of an array (elements zero to nine) to a value. Note that because `index` uses the post-increment operator, it has a value of zero the entire first time through the loop. It increments *after* the loop completes. If you used the pre-increment operator to control the step, `index` would increment to the value one *before* the loop begins.

Although this is a typical simple example, you have a lot of flexibility with a **for** statement. Let's discuss the three elements in the **for** statement: initial value, condition, and step.

Initial Value

In a typical **for** statement, you have one initial value. You are not limited to only one initial value. You may have several or none if you wish. If you have more than one, separate them with commas. The values you initialize (if any) need have nothing to do with the loop index. The values you initialize must be numerical, but they are not limited to integers. Each of these examples is legal code:

```
for (x = 1.9, y = -23; n < limit; n++)

for ( ; n > limit; n -= 1.2) /* initial semicolon */
```

In the first example, the code sets initial values for both x and y. The condition (n < limit) and the step (n++) have nothing to do with either value. In the second example, the code doesn't initialize anything. In both cases, the variables n and limit must be set before you start the loop, or unpredictable results occur. That's why, in a typical **for** statement, the initializing element usually sets the value of whatever variable represents the loop index.

note
> You must have the semicolon between each of the three sections of a **for** statement, even if the section is empty. The minimum syntax is for (; ;).

Condition

You may have zero, one, or more conditions. Each condition must resolve to a numerical value, and is evaluated for true or false. The conditions do not need to have anything to do with any loop index. They can test for anything.

If you have no conditions, the loop runs forever (because the condition can never be false). This is not common or wise, but is legal. There are other ways out of a loop, as you'll see when **break** and **continue** are discussed.

If you have two or more conditions, they are separated by a comma. The loop runs until any condition evaluates to false. In other words, all conditions must be true for the loop to execute.

The list of conditions, whether empty or not, always ends with a semicolon.

These examples are all legal code:

```
for (x = 0; ; y = y * 3)
for (x = 0; y < limit, limit < max; x++)
for (x = 0, y = 5; x < 10, y < 10; x++)
```

In the first example, there is no condition. Some code inside the **for** loop would have to exit the loop, because the condition can never fail. In the second example there are two conditions. The variables y, limit, and max must all have proper values. They are not initialized in the **for** statement, and they have nothing to do with the step increment. In the third and somewhat more typical example, the code initializes values for x and y, and the two conditions test those values. If either condition fails, the loop terminates.

Step

The step changes some value, increasing it or decreasing it by a set amount each time through the loop. The step does not have to modify a loop index, although it usually does. Like the initial values and conditions, you may have zero, one, or more steps. If you have more than one, separate them by commas. There is no semicolon terminating the list of steps. You can step forward or backward by any increment or decrement, integer or floating-point. In fact, the step doesn't have to be a step at all.

These examples are all legal code:

```
for (x = 0; x < y; )
for (x = 0; x < limit; x++, y += 2.3)
for (x = 0, y = 5; x < 10, y < 10; z = 12)
```

In the first example, there is no step increment. Some code in the loop would have to cause the test to fail at some point. In the second example, there are two steps, one of which is related to the loop index. In the third example there is a "step" but all it does is initialize the value of the variable z. This value would be re-initialized each time through the loop—probably a waste of time but perfectly legal.

Although you have lots of freedom with respect to **for** statements, most of the time you use them in typical fashion: initialize a loop index, test the index, step the index.

One problem that was discussed with respect to **for** statements was that you could get yourself caught in an infinite loop. This would be a good time to discuss a way to break out of a loop arbitrarily rather than testing for conditions.

The break Statement

Keyword:	`break`
Syntax:	`break;`
Example:	`break;`

The syntax is trivial. You simply type the keyword and follow it with a semicolon.

The **break** statement breaks you out of the current loop or switch. The loop could be a **for**, **while**, or **do...while** loop. You don't encounter **break** statements inside loops very often, but sometimes they are very helpful. You may want to terminate the loop before the condition that controls the loop fails. In that situation you can use a **break**. Here's an example.

```
for (x = 0; x < r; x += 5)
{
  y = x/5;
  if (y < 0 || y > 5)
  {
    break;
  }
  myArray[y] = x;
}
```

In this example, the code calculates the value of y. Assume you intend to use that value as an index into an array. Before you use it, you test the value of y to ensure it is a valid array element (assuming the array has six elements numbered zero to five). If it is a bad index into the array, you use **break** to exit the loop before disaster strikes.

When **break** is encountered, the loop ends. You typically use conditionals to ensure that the **break** executes only when it is appropriate.

You find the **break** keyword used most commonly in **switch** statements. **Switch** statements are discussed in just a bit.

The continue Statement

Keyword:	`continue`
Syntax:	`continue;`
Example:	`continue;`

The syntax is trivial. You simply type the keyword and follow it with a semicolon.

The **continue** statement terminates a *particular iteration* of a loop. However, the loop (**for**, **while**, or **do...while**) continues to iterate. More precisely, the conditional that controls the loop will be tested again. If the test passes, the loop iterates again.

Here's an example similar to the one we used in the **break** section.

```
for (x = 0; x < r; x += 5)
{
  y = x/5;
  if (y == 2)
  {
    continue;
  }
  myArray[y] = x;
}
```

Here you want to make sure that the third element in the array (`myArray[2]`) remains unchanged, but you want the loop to change all the other parts of the array. So, when the value of y is 2, you **continue**. That means you skip the rest of the loop but return to the **for** statement to advance a step, test the conditional, and perhaps go through the loop again.

The **break** statement terminates a loop completely. The **continue** statement terminates one iteration of the loop.

The switch/case Statements

A **switch** statement allows you to channel program flow into one block of code that you want to execute from among several possibilities. Depending on some value, you jump to a particular place in the code. For example, in a given situation, assume there are five things that might happen. You can **switch** to the code you want to execute in each of the five **cases**.

Keywords:	`switch/case/default`
Syntax:	```switch (variable)```

```
switch (variable)
{
  case integer constant:
    statements
    break;

  default:
}
```

continues

Example:
```
switch (x)
{
    case 1:
        y = 1;
        break;

    case 2:
        z = 1;
        brcak;

    default:
        y = 0;
        z = 0;
        break;
}
```

The syntax is somewhat complex. You begin with the **switch** keyword, followed by parentheses. In the parentheses is a value. This value may be an integer variable (**int**, **short**, or **long**) or any statement that resolves to an integer value. There is no semicolon after the parentheses.

After the parentheses there are braces defining all the code controlled by the switch. Inside the braces is a series of one or more **case** statements, and perhaps a **default** statement. The **default** statement is optional. The **break** statement listed in the syntax is also optional.

Each **case** keyword is followed by an integer *constant*, and that constant is followed by a colon. The constant may be literal (a number) or the name of a defined constant.

The **case** statements are *labels* that indicate the places to which the code branches depending upon the value in the original **switch** variable. A practical example should help make this clear.

Assume you switch on a variable, X. X has a value of 2. The code would branch to the code immediately after the **case** 2: label inside the **switch**.

You can have as many **case** statements inside a **switch** as you like. However, each must have a unique value. You cannot have two **case** 2: labels inside a **switch**.

The **default** statement is a special kind of label. The code branches here when no other **case** is met. This is similar to the use of the **else** statement after a series of **if** and **else if** statements. The **default** statement inside a **switch** is optional. Let's see what it does.

For example, assume you have **case** statements to handle the values 1 and 2. What happens if the variable has some other value? If there is a **default**, the code branches there. If there is no **default**, no code inside the switch is executed.

After you branch to a particular **case**, the code that begins at that spot executes. The **case** statements are not conditional tests. They are labels that mark entry points into the code inside the **switch** statement. Wherever you enter, you execute all the code from there to the end of the **switch**, unless you run into a **break**.

In the previous example, each **case** terminates with a **break** statement. The **break** is optional, but almost always used. The **break** statement takes you out of the **switch** so that no other **case** executes.

To illustrate the point, here's an example of a series of **case** statements without **breaks**.

```
switch(x)
{
  case 1:
     y = 0;

  case 2:
     y = 1;

  case 3:
     y = 2;
}
```

In this example, if x has a value of 1, 2, or 3, the variable y is set to the value 2. If the value of x is 1, the code branches to **case** 1. The variable y is set to 0. Because there is no **break**, the next line of code executes. The next line of code is y = 1; and not case 2:. The case 2: statement does not test the value of x, nor does it execute. It is merely a label. So the value of y is set to 1. Then y is set to 2.

There are circumstances in which you would like such a cascade to happen, but this example is not one of them. Most of the time, each individual **case** is a separate entity, and you want to make sure that it and it alone executes, so you terminate it with a **break**.

Although all of the examples so far have done so, the list of **case** statements does not have to be organized in numerical order. You can have them in any order you want.

Finally, you may have multiple **cases** controlling entry to the same point in the code. Here's an example. It assumes that you have declared constants named kMarch, kApril, and kMay.

```
switch(x)
{
  case kMay:
  case kMarch:
  case kApril:
    spring = true;
    break;

  default:
    spring = false;
}
```

The goto Statement

The **goto** statement allows you to jump to another labeled location in your code. The **goto** statement is the black sheep of C. Before the advent of structured languages like Pascal and C, about the only way you could move around easily or break out of a loop was to use something like a **goto** statement. However, programmers often used **goto** loosely and indiscriminately. This allowed program logic and structure to be convoluted, to put it politely. As a result, the command has a very bad reputation.

However, it is a legal C command, and one that has utility when used sparingly.

Keyword:	**goto**
Syntax:	**goto** *label*;
Example:	goto DONE;

The syntax is trivial. You type the keyword **goto**, and follow that with the label of the place to which you wish to jump. The label must be for a location somewhere in your code. This label is functionally identical to the **case** labels used inside **switch** statements.

The syntax for a label is equally simple. Type the name you want to use, and follow it with a colon (just like **case** statements). The name must follow the same naming rules as variables. Here's an example that demonstrates the use of a **goto** and how to create a label:

```
if (error)
{
  goto DONE;
}
```

```
  x = 1;


DONE:
```

This code tests a variable named `error`. If there is an error, program flow jumps directly to the `DONE:` label. The intervening code is not executed. There is no actual code at that label in this example. In a real program, you would handle the error in whatever way was appropriate. Note that the label does not have to be in all capital letters.

As a general rule, you should use the **goto** statement sparingly, if at all. The code in this book never uses **goto**.

Nesting Flow Control Statements

The flow control part of the "Guide to C" is almost finished. But there is one important point that hasn't been covered, and that's nesting.

If, **while**, **for**, and **switch** statements in isolation have been discussed. These are tools that you frequently use together. You can nest any one of these statements inside any other, nest another statement inside that, and so on. You can see practical examples of such nesting throughout this book. You can have **if** statements inside other **if** statements, **switch** statements inside **while** loops, and so forth. There is no practical limit to how you can nest, or how deep you can nest. Your development environment may impose some limits, but it is unlikely that you will ever run into them.

If you find yourself writing code with several layers of nesting, however, that's usually an indication that you should rethink your program logic. Deep nesting is a sign that you should break up your code into smaller pieces so that each piece is simpler and easier to understand. In other words, if you are deeply nested, you may need to create new functions.

Here's a good example of nesting:

```
if(hasCandy == 0)
{
  hasCandy = BuyCandy();
}
else
{
  while(hasCandy)
  {
```

```
        EatCandy();
        hasCandy--;
    }
}
```

Here we test if a variable named hasCandy is zero. If it is, we call a function to buy candy. If we have candy, we go to a **while** loop nested inside the **else** condition. While we have candy, we eat it. What's all this about calling functions? Read on.

Functions

Functions are what make your program manageable. While it is theoretically possible to write a significant C program with only one function, you wouldn't want to do so.

This section discusses why that is true. This discussion of functions covers the following topics:

- Understanding functions
- Declaring a function
- Defining a function
- Calling a function
- Passing parameters
- Returning a value
- Function design
- Function pointers

What Is a Function?

Functions are the atoms out of which you build a program. Extending the metaphor, C keywords, variables, and data are the subatomic particles with which you build functions. A function is the smallest functional unit in a program. There are several synonyms for the word "function" that are derived from many different programming languages, including method, procedure, subroutine, and routine.

In the ideal program, each function performs one simple task. It receives the data on which it must operate, performs its task, returns any information required of it, and disappears. In other words, a function should be, well, functional. The responsibilities of the function should be based on the task it performs. That task should be defined as narrowly and clearly as possible.

Make sure that the function has everything it needs to accomplish its task, that it does what you want it to do, and that it doesn't mess up anything else in the process. If you keep your functions small and simple, this task becomes easier.

Deciding what functions you need and what they should do is not a linear process. A computer program typically performs a wide variety of tasks on several levels. As you identify the basic goals of the software, you get your first clues about what your functions should do.

After you identify general tasks, you look at each general task more closely. What subtasks must you perform to accomplish each general task? You continue this process at finer levels of detail until you have every single task—however minor—identified and placed in a function.

You can summarize the software development process as one where you identify the tasks that must be accomplished, write the functions that accomplish the tasks, and hook the functions together into a cohesive unit.

All C programs begin with a function called `main()`. When a C program launches, the operating system calls the program's `main()` function. You can pass parameters to `main()`, but that particular topic is not discussed in the "Guide to C."

Once inside `main()`, you may do a variety of things, such as call other functions. When you call another function, you create a caller/called relationship between the function that does the calling and the function that is being called. How to call a function is discussed a little later.

You have already seen some functions in earlier code examples. Here's the code for an example function.

```
short MovePicture (MyPicture *thePicture,
                   short deltaX, short deltaY)
{
  short result;

  thePicture->x += deltaX;
  thePicture->y += deltaY;

  result = (short) sqrt(x * x + y * y);

  return result;
}
```

A function has a return type, a name, a parameter list, and a body. The first three items are collectively referred to as the function title. The parameter list contains the data the function receives from the caller. The function body contains the code that defines what the function does. The return value is the single piece of information that the function may return directly to its caller.

The following sections discuss each of the four parts of a function.

Return Type

A C function may or may not have a return value. You identify the type of return value as the very first thing in the function title. All you do is put the name of the returned data type before the name of the function. In Figure A.4, the return type is a **short** value.

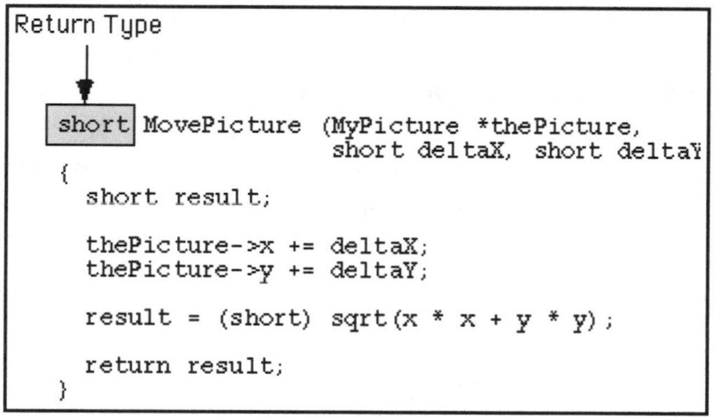

```
Return Type

     │
     ▼
 ┌───────┐
 │ short │ MovePicture  (MyPicture *thePicture,
 └───────┘                short deltaX,  short deltaY
 {
   short result;

   thePicture->x += deltaX;
   thePicture->y += deltaY;

   result = (short) sqrt(x * x + y * y);

   return result;
 }
```

Figure A.4 Return type

The returned data may be of any type, including types that you have defined. You may also return a pointer if you wish. If there is no return value, you must use the keyword **void**.

A C function may return one item, and only one item. You do this with the keyword **return**. The syntax details are discussed a little later in this guide.

Function Name

You can name a function just about anything you want. The name follows the return type in the function title. In Figure A.5, the function name is MyPicture.

```
        Function Name

short MovePicture (MyPicture *thePicture,
                    short deltaX,  short deltaY
{
  short result;

  thePicture->x += deltaX;
  thePicture->y += deltaY;

  result = (short) sqrt(x * x + y * y);

  return result;
}
```

Figure A.5 Function name

The rules for naming a function are the same as they are for naming variables. The name consists of letters, numbers, and the underscore character. No spaces are allowed. The name is case-sensitive. Two functions with the same name cannot share the same scope. In other words, each name must be unique so that the compiler does not get confused.

Although you have great freedom naming functions, there are widely recognized naming conventions that you should follow. See Appendix C, "A Brief C Style Guide," for a discussion of naming conventions.

Parameter List

The third part of a function is the parameter list. Typically, for a function to do something it must have something to work on. Usually you pass that information to the function in the parameter list.

The parameter list specifies the type of data for each parameter, and provides a name for the parameter. You may pass data of any type to a function, including data types that you have defined. You may pass actual values, or pass references to values. Parameter passing is discussed in detail a little later in this section.

Parameters are separated by commas. Enclose the list in parentheses. In Figure A.6, the first parameter is a pointer to an application-defined type named MyPicture. The second and third parameters are **short** values.

```
                          Data Type    Variable Name


short MovePicture    (MyPicture *thePicture,
                         short deltaX, short deltaY)
{
  short result;

  thePicture->x += deltaX;
  thePicture->y += deltaY;

  result = (short) sqrt(x * x + y * y);

  return result;
}
```

Figure A.6 Parameter list

Parameters are optional, however. You can design, build, and call a function that has no parameters. Such functions are, in fact, fairly common in C. You can either leave the parameter list empty, or specify **void** in the parameter list.

Function Body

After the function title, braces define the function body. Inside the braces you put the code that makes the function work. These are the local variables and C statements that accomplish the task of the function. In Figure A.7, the function adds the "delta"—the distance you want to move—to the picture's current position. It then calculates how far you actually moved the picture and returns the distance moved to whatever function called this function.

```
short MovePicture (MyPicture *thePicture,
                      short deltaX, short deltaY)

{
  short result;                              Function
                                             Body
  thePicture->x += deltaX;
  thePicture->y += deltaY;

  result = (short) sqrt(x * x + y * y);

  return result;
}
```

Figure A.7 Function body

713

A

Declaring a Function

As it converts your source code into object code, the compiler must interpret your function calls. To do that, it must know three things about your function: return type, name, and parameter list. These are the three items in the function title.

To tell the compiler about your function, you declare a function prototype.

Concept:	function prototype
Syntax:	type FunctionName (parameter list);
Example:	short MovePicture (MyPicture *thePicture, short deltaX, short deltaY);

The prototype is the function title with a semicolon at the end. This tells the compiler everything it needs to know about the function. The return type comes first, and then the function name, and then the parameter list. In this example, the parameter list assumes you have defined a data type named MyPicture.

In the parameter list, you must specify data types. Parameter *names* are optional in a function prototype. This prototype is legal, even though the parameters have no names.

```
short MovePicture (MyPicture*, short, short);
```

However, using parameter names in the prototype is a big help when figuring out what the function's parameters actually do. In the previous example, if you specify the names deltaX and deltaY for the parameters, it becomes clear that you pass the horizontal and vertical movement of the picture in that order. If you do not provide names, all you know is that you pass two **short** values. You have no idea what they are supposed to be, or in what order they must be.

The parameter names you use in the actual function definition do not have to match the names in the prototype. Once again, however, it is usually a good idea if they do. It makes keeping track of things easier.

Function prototypes typically appear in header files along with other declarations such as defined constants and **typedef** statements. In a typical C project, each source file has a corresponding header file that includes prototypes for the functions in the source file.

Having said all that about function prototypes, the C language in fact does not *require* them. You should ignore that fact. Always use prototypes for your functions. They help make your code a lot safer and bug-free.

Defining a Function

A function definition is the function title (return type, name, parameter list) and the function body. This is the information that the compiler turns into object code.

Concept:	function definition

Syntax:	`type FunctionName (parameter list)`
	`{`
	
	`}`

Example:	`short MovePicture (MyPicture *thePicture,`
	`                              short deltaX, short deltaY)`
	`{`
	`  C statements`
	`}`

The syntax is very similar to the function prototype. You begin with the data type of the return value, followed by the function name and parameter list. There is *no* semicolon at the end of the parameter list. The parameter list must specify the data type of each parameter and provide a variable name for the parameter. Unlike prototypes, parameter names are not optional. Parameter names are required.

Underneath the function title, braces enclose the body of the function. This is the C code that makes the function do what you want it to do.

Calling a Function

Calling a function is as simple as typing in the function name, passing required parameters, and receiving any return value in an appropriate variable. If there is no return value, you don't have to receive the return.

<table>
<tr><td>Concept:</td><td>calling a function</td></tr>
</table>

Concept:	calling a function
Syntax:	*variable = FunctionName (parameter list);* *FunctionName (parameter list);*
Example:	distance = MovePicture(&thePicture, xMove, 10); MovePicture (&thePicture, xMove, 10);

The syntax is straightforward. The first example assumes that you have defined a local **short** variable named distance. You assign the return value from MovePicture() to distance. The second example ignores the return value.

To call MovePicture() successfully, you type the name of the function and provide the necessary parameters in the parameter list. Separate each item in the parameter list with a comma. In the example, the code passes the address of thePicture and two **short** values: xMove and the constant value 10.

You do not have to specify the data type when you pass a parameter. The compiler already knows what type it is. However, the *actual* data type of the variable or constant must match the function definition for that parameter. If it does not, you must typecast the parameter to match the required data type. For example, the MovePicture() function as defined in the examples requires two **short** parameters for deltaX and deltaY. Assume you have **double** variables that you would like to pass. You would write code like this:

```
MovePicture (&thePicture, (short)doubleX, (short)doubleY);
```

This code typecasts the **double** variables as **short** variables so the compiler can pass them to the function that expects to receive **short** values.

The names of the variables you pass do not have to match those in the function definition. You may pass constants as well as variables.

Finally, you do not have to receive the return value. If you call a function that returns a value, but you are not interested in the return value, you can call the function as if it returned a **void** and ignore the return value. The previous example code ignores the return value from MovePicture() completely.

Passing Parameters

It is important that you understand exactly what happens when you call a function and pass parameters to the function. You can pass a parameter in two ways: by value and by reference. The difference between these two concepts is significant.

Passing by Value

Passing data by value means that you pass the actual data across the stack. The *stack* is a location in memory where functions store parameters and local variables. It is like a cup. It has a limited size and if you put too much into it, it overflows. The term in C-speak for this condition is stack overflow. It is a Bad Thing. When the stack overflows, the data that doesn't fit stomps all over other things in memory, causing anything from occasional weirdness to disaster.

When passing data by value, the calling function makes a copy of the data and puts it on the stack. The called function gets the data from the stack. This gives the function you call its own copy of the data on which to work. The original data in the calling function remains untouched. Here's a code example with two functions that demonstrate that point.

```
void Caller (void)
{
  short x = 42;
  short y;

  y = PassByValue(x);
}

short PassByValue(short theValue)
{
  theValue = 54;
  return theValue;
}
```

The first function is the caller. It calls a second function named PassByValue() and passes the *value* of x, which is 42. The second function receives a **short** value (42) in a parameter named theValue. It changes theValue to 54. It then returns theValue to the caller. Caller() puts the returned value (54) in a local variable y. The value in x remains 42. The *variable* x was not passed to PassByValue(). The *value* in x was passed. The variable x remains unchanged.

When passing by value, you pass a copy of the original data. Now you can look at passing by reference to see how it differs.

Passing by Reference

Passing by reference means you pass the *address* of the data rather than its actual value. This means that you are giving the called function direct access to the data in the calling function. Here's a code example to show you how this works.

```
void Caller (void)
{
  short x = 42;

  PassByReference(&x);  /* passes the address of x */
}

void PassByReference(short *theValue)
{
  *theValue = 54;
}
```

As before, the first function is the caller. It calls a second function named PassByReference() and passes the *address* of the **short** variable x in memory. The second function receives a *pointer* to a **short** value, in this case it is the address of x from the Caller() function. PassByReference() changes the value at that address to the value 54. The syntax *theValue = 54; translates as "the data pointed to by theValue equals 54."

The function then returns automatically to Caller(). On return to Caller(), the value in x is 54. Because the code passed the parameter by reference, the called function was able to change the contents of a variable in the calling function.

Using a pointer as a parameter—passing data by reference—is a powerful technique widely used in C. You will use it often. Sometimes you will pass by reference more than you pass by value. In other code, passing by value is more common. Both are useful tools.

Passing structs

Usually you pass **structs** and other large amounts of data by reference because you don't want to overload the function stack with large amounts of data. Passing the address of the data (passing by reference) is more efficient than passing the actual data.

Passing Arrays

Earlier on, it was mentioned that you can pass data of any type as a parameter, including arrays. However, there is a subtlety in the way that C handles an array parameter that can cause problems.

When you pass an array, C always passes a *pointer* to the array, whether or not you tell it to. You cannot pass an entire array by value. You can, however, pass the value of a single element of an array.

Because arrays are unbounded in C, the compiler really has no way of knowing how much data it should pass! C has no hidden record of the size of your array. Therefore, when passing an array, C always uses the address of the array, not the contents of the array. This code example demonstrates the difference between passing an array and an array value.

```
void ArrayPassing (void)
{
  short  myArray[20];

  PassAnArray(myArray); /* pass address automatically */
  PassAnArray(&myArray); /* specify address of array */
  PassAnArray(&myArray[0]); /* address of 1st element */

  PassAnArrayValue(myArray[2]); /* pass value in 3rd element */
}

void PassAnArray(short thisArray[])  /* one way */
{
}

void PassAnArray2(short *thisArray)  /* another way */
{
}

void PassAnArrayValue (short thisValue)
{
}
```

The first function, named ArrayPassing(), defines an array of **short** values. It then calls a function named PassAnArray() three times. The precise syntax for the parameter varies each time. However, the effect is identical. In each case, the address of the first element of myArray is passed to the called function.

The PassAnArray() function is defined to receive a short array. C always passes arrays by reference, so the compiler knows this means a pointer to an array of shorts. There is an alternative way of defining the function, as illustrated in the function PassAnArray2(). PassAnArray() receives an array of **short** values. PassAnArray2() receives a pointer to a **short** value. When you pass an array, you always pass the address of the array. Because this is an array of **short** values, the address of the array is, in fact, a pointer to the first element in the array, hence a pointer to a **short** value.

Sometimes, however, you want to pass the actual value of a single element in an array. The call to PassAnArrayValue() demonstrates how to do so.

A

Returning a Value

Now that you know how to get data into a function, how do you get data out of a function? You return a value from a called function to the calling function with the **return** keyword.

Keyword:	`return`
Syntax:	`return value;`
Example:	`return success;`

The syntax is trivial. You use the keyword, and then the value you want to return. The returned value must be a constant, variable, or expression that resolves to the return data type specified in the function title. You can return only one value.

If the return type is **void**, you do not have to include a **return** statement in the body of the function because there is nothing to return. The function returns automatically. You may use a **return** statement if you wish and include no value, but such a statement is redundant and unnecessary.

If you want to return two or more items, you're not entirely out of luck. You can defeat the one-item return limit if you use pointers as parameters. The calling function can provide the addresses of whatever data it wants changed. The called function can then change the contents of the data, in effect returning any number of new values to the caller. The "Passing Parameters" section has example code that illustrates how to do this. Here's another:

```
SetDate (&month, &day, &year);


void SetDate (short *mn, short *day, short *yr)
{
    *mn= 9;
    *day= 13;
    *yr= 95
}
```

Here a line of code calls the function `SetDate()`. We assume it has defined three **short** variables named `month`, `day`, and `year`. It passes pointers to all three. `SetDate()` sets the values for each variable, in effect returning three values to the original caller.

This technique is widely used in well-designed code. The principle behind it is simple. The *calling* function "owns" the data that it wants manipulated. It is the "client" that wants to use the services of the called function. As a "server," the *called* function does not own the data and is not responsible for creating or maintaining data. It simply changes it. Therefore, it should not create or return values. It should receive pointers to existing data, manipulate it appropriately, and disappear.

A function may have multiple **return** statements. You can return from a variety of locations inside a single function.

Function Design

Volumes have been written on the subject of software design. This topic is not covered very deeply. However, there are a few simple rules that you should follow as you write functions.

As a basic principle, a function should do as little as possible and as much as necessary. Well-designed procedural software has a hierarchy of functions. High-level functions usually set things up and then call lower-level functions to get work done. They in turn call even lower functions to perform specific services, and so on. At the lowest level, functions provide very generic services for data manipulation. These low-level functions are those that should be simplest in concept, performing one simple task.

The "ideal" function has only one entry and only one exit. That means every time you call a function, you start at the same spot in the code. You leave the function in the same place as well. You may have several alternative paths through the function, but you always start and end at the same spot.

However, functions may have more than one exit. For example, in the code exercises, many functions return whenever an error occurs. This is one common method of handling error conditions. There are other techniques for handling errors.

Of necessity, functions change things. Otherwise, nothing would ever get done. However, you must be careful to keep the changes to a minimum. When you enter a function, the program and the computer are in a particular state. Before you change the state, you preserve it, and then do your work, and then restore the state to its original value before returning. Change whatever data you need to change, but leave everything else exactly as you found it.

For example, in the Macintosh environment, the pen size might be set to a particular value. If your function must change the pen size for its own purposes, it should save the current state of the pen before changing it. When finished, the function should restore the original state of the pen before exiting. The code might look like this:

```
GetPenState(&savedState)
PenSize(4,4);
/* do your drawing with the pen, when done… */
SetPenState(&savedState);
```

This code first preserves the state of the pen in a local variable named savedState. It changes the pen's size, does its work, and then restores the original pen to what it was before anything happened.

In general, a function should be simple, have one entry and exit, and preserve whatever state is necessary. It should be an ideal conspirator: it comes and goes at need, and leaves no tracks.

Function Pointers

As you know, a pointer is the address in memory of some data. A function pointer is simply the address of a function. Function pointers are an extremely powerful and elegant programming technique.

Why would you want to use the address of a function instead of calling the function directly? Well, there are several kinds of programming problems where a function pointer provides an elegant solution, but here's one that's fairly obvious.

Assume you have a window in your application, and that window has various shapes inside it that may or may not be selected. You can do a variety of things to selected shapes. You can move them, draw them, change their color, rotate them, and so forth. You might have dozens of actions the user can perform.

For each action, you need a function to modify the selected shape appropriately. Without function pointers, each function must search through the window contents, identify selected shapes, and then perform a unique action every time it finds a selected shape. The only different aspect of these functions is the action. The search code is identical. That's a lot of redundant code.

Using a function pointer makes this more elegant and more flexible. If you use function pointers, you can write one function to do the search for selected shapes. Every time you want to perform an action, you tell *the search function* what action to perform. The search function takes care of the rest.

The following search function is called a "dispatch" routine, and the function that really does something to the shape is an "action" routine.

Concept:	function pointer
Syntax:	`typedef` *type* `(*`*typeName*`) (`*parameter list*`);`
Example:	`typedef void (*ActionProc) (MyShape *theShape,` `void *params);`

The next example constitutes the basis for furthering the discussion of function pointers.

The example code looks like a regular function prototype with two exceptions. First, note the **typedef** keyword at the beginning of the line. This code declares a data type. The data type declared here is `ActionProc`. Second, note that the syntax `(*ActionProc)` takes the place of a normal function name. This syntax says that the name for this kind of function—that is, a function that has these parameters and return type—is an `ActionProc`. In other words, an `ActionProc` is a pointer to a function with these parameters and return type.

The declaration says that an `ActionProc` type of function must receive two parameters. The first is a pointer to a data type called `MyShape`. That parameter points to the shape you want changed. The second parameter is a void pointer to a variable named `params`. By making this parameter a void pointer, you can pass a pointer to any kind of data, depending upon the needs of the action routine. You can even pass a pointer to a structure, so the possibilities for passing data are virtually unlimited.

For example, if you were rotating a shape, you might point to a **short** variable that contained the number of degrees by which to rotate the shape. If you were moving the shape, you might point to a **struct** with two fields containing the changes in the x and y coordinates for the shape. You get the idea. Different kinds of actions need to know different kinds of things, so you have a void pointer that lets you pass any kind of data. In this example, an `ActionProc` function returns void.

When you write the code for your action routines, you design them so that each receives these and only these parameters, and returns void. Each function knows what kind of data it needs, so it treats the void pointer parameter as a pointer to the right kind of data. It's up to you to ensure that you pass the right data.

Now look at the prototype for a hypothetical ForSelectedShapesDo() dispatch routine. This function's responsibilities are to search through a window and identify selected shapes. When it finds a selected shape, it calls an action routine:

```
void ForSelectedShapesDo (ActionProc doToShape,
                          void *params);
```

This function receives two parameters. The first parameter is an ActionProc—the function pointer that points to the action routine the caller wants to use. The second is a void pointer for the data that the action routine needs. The dispatch routine receives the void pointer parameter but merely passes it on to the action routine.

You can look at a more practical example to see how function pointers work. Say you want to rotate each selected shape 45°. Assume you have a Rotate() action routine. You might write code like this:

```
short angle = 45;
ForSelectedShapesDo ((ActionProc)Rotate, (void*)&angle);
```

You call the dispatch routine. For the first parameter, you use the name of the action routine you want to call. You typecast the name as an ActionProc to match the required data type in the function declaration. You also pass the address of the local variable, angle, typecast as a void pointer.

The ForSelectedShapesDo() function loops through each shape in the window to determine if the shape is selected. If the shape is selected, it calls the action routine to operate on the particular shape. The code might look like this:

```
void ForSelectedShapesDo (ActionProc doToShape, void *params)
{
  short  shapeIsSelected = false;
  MyShape  *thisShape;

/*
   Assume we have code here to loop through shapes,
   and identify and get a selected shape. When we find
   one, thisShape points to the selected shape.
*/

  shapeIsSelected = true;

  if (shapeIsSelected)
  {
    doToShape(thisShape, params);
  }
}
```

The dispatch routine does not need to "know" what action routine it calls. If it finds a selected shape it calls doToShape(). In this example, the doToShape variable holds the address of the Rotate() action routine. When you type the name of a function in source code, the compiler translates the name into the address of the function. The fact that in this case the name is a variable makes no difference to the compiler.

The dispatch routine also passes params through to the action routine. In this case, the dispatch routine calls the Rotate() function. The Rotate() function does what it is supposed to do, and rotates the shape by 45°.

You can pass the name of any ActionProc to the dispatch routine. The only restriction is that all ActionProc functions must have the same parameter list, which are the parameters in the function pointer declaration. Any function that uses these and only these parameters can be an ActionProc function.

In *Programming Starter Kit for Macintosh*, you'll see this technique used to manipulate puzzle pieces.

Comments in C Source Code

As you write code, you should add comments. Comments assist you in remembering why you did things a certain way. They also assist other programmers in understanding your code. The examples in the "Guide to C" have already used comments without explanation. This section discusses what comments are and how to use them. This is a fairly simple topic.

There is one official method in C for adding comments to source code.

Concept:	Comment
Syntax:	`/* your comment */`
Example:	`/* C is a neat language */`

The syntax requires a slash followed by an asterisk to begin the comment, and an asterisk followed by a slash to end the comment. You can put a comment just about anywhere, even in the middle of a statement. A comment can extend across multiple lines. The compiler ignores everything between the comment markers.

The C++ language introduced a second technique for commenting C files, the double slash. Although it is not part of standard ANSI C, most C compilers now support this comment as well. It is very popular with programmers.

Concept:	Comment
Syntax:	`//  your comment`
Example:	`// This is a neat way to comment`

Everything after the double slash *on the same line* is a comment. This technique has some advantages and disadvantages over the traditional technique. It is easier to type, for one. Best of all, you don't have to remember to terminate your comments because there is no terminating syntax. However, your comment cannot extend across multiple lines. If you have a multiline comment and you want to use the // syntax, each new comment line must begin with //.

Compiler Statements

Ultimately, a compiler translates the source code you write into object code. Object code is what your computer understands. Most of what the compiler does is automatic. However, in some circumstances you must give the compiler instructions.

The compiler supports special commands called *preprocessor directives*. You put these commands inside your code. When the compiler encounters the command, it responds accordingly.

One compiler command, the **#define** statement for creating defined constants, has been discussed. You can refer to the "Defined Constants" section of this appendix for details. This section discusses several more preprocessor directives, including:

- `#include`
- `#ifdef`
- `#ifndef`
- `#undef`

#include

Command:	`#include`
Syntax:	`#include  "filename"` `#include  <filename>`
Example:	`#include "myHeader.h"` `#include <Traps.h>`

The syntax is simple. You use the keyword followed by a file name. The name is either between quotation marks or between the <> symbols. Typically, you would put an **#include** statement near the beginning of a source file when that file uses some term or function prototype declared in another file, usually a header file. This statement tells the compiler to read the contents of the named file and to include them in the declarations used for the source file. You also see **#include** statements in header files to include additional headers.

If the file name is in quotations, that tells the compiler to look for the file in the current default folder (directory), usually the folder with the current development project. If the file name is between the <> symbols, that tells the compiler to look for the file in some other folder, usually the folder with the development environment. In some development environments, the compiler looks in both places if it cannot find the file where you asked it to look.

#ifdef

Command:	`#ifdef/#else/#endif`

Syntax:	`#ifdef term`
	 `...`
	 `#else`
	 `...`
	 `#endif`

Example:	`#ifdef GENERATINGPOWERPC`
	 `  // any statements for Power Mac`
	 `#else`
	 `  // any statements for 68K Mac`
	 `#endif`

This command translates as "if this term is defined…" It must be terminated with a corresponding **#endif** statement. The **#else** is optional. Note that there are no braces and no semicolons. In between the **#ifdef** and **#endif** statements can be anything— declarations, definitions, C statements, other compiler directives, and so on. When you use this command, you're telling the compiler that if the particular term has been declared, do everything between the **#ifdef** and the **#else**. Otherwise, do everything between the **#else** and the **#endif**. If there is no **#else** statement, you do everything between the **#ifdef** and the **#endif**; otherwise ignore that code.

You can use these commands inside source code to do conditional compiles. For example, you might want to write one kind of code for a Power Mac, and another for an older Macintosh. You use **#ifdef** to test for the term GENERATINGPOWERPC. This is the term that Apple's universal headers use to distinguish between code for the two processors. The compiler declares this term for you, based upon your compiler settings.

#ifndef

Command:	`#ifndef/#else/#endif`
Syntax:	`#ifndef term`
	`...`
	`#endif`
Example:	`#ifndef __MYHEADER__`
	`  #define __MYHEADER__`
	`  // rest of my header file`
	`#endif`

This command is the opposite of **#ifdef**. It translates as "if this term is *not* defined…" It must be terminated with a corresponding **#endif** statement. You may also include the **#else** directive if you wish. You can include anything in between these statements. When you use this command you're telling the compiler that if the term is *not* defined, do everything between the **#ifndef** and the **#else** (if it is used) or the **#endif**; otherwise, ignore it completely.

The example demonstrates the most common use of this term. You cannot include a header file more than once, because the compiler will complain about multiple declared items if it reads the same file twice. In a project with many source files, it is almost impossible to keep track of what files include what header files. Instead, programmers have adopted a convention using **#ifndef** that solves the problem.

Inside each header file, use **#define** to declare a term unique to that header file. In the example, the code declares a term __MYHEADER__ . Then it puts all the other declarations in the header file inside an **#ifndef** statement that tests for that term.

Assume the example code is at the beginning of a header file. The first time that this file is included, the term __MYHEADER__ is undeclared. As a result, the compiler reads the entire header file. In the process, the term __MYHEADER__ is declared, the compiler gets all the other necessary declared terms and prototypes, and proceeds happily on its way. But if the same header file is subsequently included in any other file in the project, when the compiler looks at this file, the first line it sees is the **#ifndef** statement. However, this time the term __MYHEADER__ has been declared, so the compiler skips the rest of the file.

The naming convention for this **#ifndef** trick is to use the name of the header file (or something very similar) in all caps, with one or more underscore characters before and after the name. The purpose of the naming convention is simply to ensure that the declared term is unique.

#undef

Command:	#undef
Syntax:	#undef *term*
Example:	#undef ForgetMe

The **#undef** term tells the compiler to forget some term that you have already declared. You probably won't use this compiler directive very often, but it might prove useful.

Header Files and Source Files

The "Guide to C" has regularly made references to header and source files and what you find in them. By now, you probably have a pretty good idea what they are and why they exist.

The primary distinction between a header file and a source file is that—in general—a header file contains declarations, and a source file contains definitions. Typically, the code inside a header file does not allocate any memory, create variables, define functions, and so forth. When a compiler reads a header file, it usually does not create any object code.

The opposite is true for source files. When the compiler reads a source file, it usually creates object code. You may make declarations inside source files, and you certainly will in many cases. However, source files primarily contain the statements that the compiler turns into object code.

Programmers also refer to header files as "interface" files. Headers typically contain declared terms and function prototypes used in a variety of source files. These declarations control how you call functions, what functions you can call, and what terms you can use. Taken together, these declarations are the programmer's interface into the code in your program.

In a typical header file, you may see one or more of the following elements of the C language that have been discussed:

- Compiler directives (**#include** and others)
- Constant declarations (**#define**)
- Enumerated constants (**enum**)
- New data types (**typedef**)
- **struct** declarations
- Function prototypes

You do not usually see variables or function *definitions* in header files. You typically find those only in source files. In a source file you are likely to encounter these elements of C:

- Compiler directives
- Variable definitions (including **static** and global variables)
- Function definitions

You may also encounter:

- Constant declarations (**#define**)
- Enumerated constants (**enum**)
- Function prototypes

You might put these last three items in a source file to declare items that you use only in that file. No other source file needs these items, so you can "hide" them inside the source file that uses them. Because no other source file can use these items, they become a "private" interface into that part of the code in that single source file. Sometimes there are good design reasons for doing this.

note
There are important naming conventions for source and header files. Header files end with a .h extension. Source files for the C language end with .c. Some development environments rely on these extensions to determine which compiler to use on the code in that file.

Whenever you make a change in a header file, all source files that include that header must be recompiled. A good development environment keeps track of this for you and updates the dependent source files automatically.

In a typical C project, each source file has an associated header file. That header contains the declarations and prototypes required for the source file. One advantage of this arrangement is that when you change such a header file, it is likely to affect very few source files. The time required to recompile the code is correspondingly reduced.

However, this is not a required or universal arrangement by any means. You may decide to create a generic header that includes most of the widely used declarations and prototypes in our code. For example, in the projects accompanying *Programming Starter Kit for Macintosh*, most of the function prototypes are in one file so that you can find them easily when you need to refer to them.

Feel free to organize your programming interface into your code in whatever way best suits your needs.

Standard Libraries

The official ANSI C guidelines require that a standard implementation of the C language provides a variety of utility functions. These functions allow you to perform simple string handling, input/output, math operations, memory allocation, error trapping, and more.

note
A class library is an analogous feature of object-oriented languages. Class libraries tend to be cohesive collections of routines designed to accomplish some general purpose. Because of the nature of an object-oriented language, class libraries are easily extensible. A good class library can be a framework on which you hang your code. By contrast, the standard libraries are a collection of essentially unrelated utility routines that you can use at will. They are not easily modifiable or extensible.

There are perhaps 150 different functions in the standard libraries. Because they are a part of the official ANSI C standard, they are, for all practical purposes, universal

731

extensions of the C language. If you write software using only the standard C libraries, that software is likely to be platform independent.

Unfortunately, the Macintosh interface is far richer and more powerful than the simple routines in the standard libraries. However, there are some very useful utilities in the standard libraries. Consult your development environment's documentation for detailed information about the standard libraries.

For example, there are several functions devoted to strings. Table A.12 lists some of the string-manipulation routines and their purposes.

Table A.12: Standard Library String Functions

Function	Purpose
strcpy( )	Copies one string to another
strncpy( )	Copies n characters of one string to another
strcat( )	Appends one string to the end of another
strncat( )	Appends n characters of one string to another
strcmp( )	Compares two strings for identity
strncmp( )	Compares the first n characters of two strings
strlen( )	Returns the length of the string

The Macintosh operating system uses Pascal-language strings, and they have a different structure than C strings. See Appendix B, "Strings in C and Pascal."

The standard library also includes a rich set of math functions. Table A.13 lists several of these.

Table A.13: Standard Library Math Functions

Function	Purpose
fabs( )	Gets absolute value of a floating-point number
log( )	Gets the natural log of a number
log10( )	Gets the base-10 log of a number
sqrt( )	Gets the square root of a number

continues

Table A.13: Continued

Function	Purpose
pow( )	Raises a number to a power
sin( )	Gets the sine of an angle
asin( )	Gets the angle from a sine
tan( )	Gets the tangent of an angle
atan( )	Gets the angle from a tangent
atan2( )	Gets the angle from a tangent, correct quadrant
cos( )	Gets the cosine of an angle
acos( )	Gets an angle from a cosine

Macintosh development environments usually provide full-featured math libraries that are substantially faster than those in the ANSI standard libraries.

The standard libraries (see Table A.14) also include generic memory management functions.

Table A.14: Standard Library Memory Functions

Function	Purpose
calloc( )	Allocates a block of memory for array
free( )	Releases a block of memory
malloc( )	Allocates block of memory
realloc( )	Changes size of a block of memory
memcpy( )	Copies a range of memory
memcmp( )	Compares two blocks of memory
memchr	Looks for a character in a block of memory
memmove( )	Moves a block of memory

On the Macintosh, you usually use Memory Manager calls in the Toolbox.

There are file handling functions in the standard libraries, listed in Table A.15.

Table A.15: Standard Library File Functions

Function	Purpose
fclose( )	Closes a file
fopen( )	Opens a file
fread( )	Reads data from a file
fwrite( )	Writes data to a file
rename( )	Renames a file
setbuf( )	Sets a file buffer
fgetpos( )	Gets current position in file
fsetpos( )	Sets current position in file
fseek( )	Sets file position by seeking

On the Macintosh, you usually use File Manager calls in the Toolbox.

The standard library contains a useful set of string/number conversion routines (see Table A.16).

Table A.16: Standard Library Conversion Functions

Function	Purpose
atof( )	Converts string to double
atoi( )	Converts string to integer
atol( )	Converts string to long integer
strtod( )	Converts string to a double
strtol( )	Converts string to long integer, base 8/10/16
strtoul( )	Converts string to unsigned long, base 8/10/16

Some similar routines exist in the Macintosh Toolbox, but you may find the standard library routines very useful.

There are many more routines defined in the standard libraries, including character manipulation (changing text from uppercase to lowercase, and so forth), time management, simple error handling, array searching and sorting, and much more. Consult the standard library documentation that comes with your development environment.

Reserved Words

C keywords are the commands that make up the language. You cannot use these words as the name of any variable, function, data type, or label. In other words, they are reserved by C. Table A.17 lists all of C's reserved words.

Table A.17: Reserved Words in C

asm	double	long	struct
auto	else	operator	switch
break	enum	register	typedef
case	extern	return	union
char	float	short	unsigned
const	for	signed	void
continue	goto	sizeof	volatile
default	if	static	while
do	int		

This "Guide to C" does not explain the programming concepts and syntax for every one of these reserved words. For example, this guide does not discuss **volatile**, **register**, or **auto** variables. If you want more information about C, consult the bibliography for suggestions on further study.

B

Strings in C and Pascal

B

Data comes in many flavors. One common flavor you use when writing code is the "string." A string is a series of characters. The characters usually make up a word, phrase, or sentence, but in fact the string can be any sequence of characters.

C and Pascal are both programming languages. Programming languages usually differ in their approach to manipulating string data, and C and Pascal are no exception. They have very different ways of determining where a string starts, how long it is, and where it ends.

Because the Macintosh Toolbox was originally written in Pascal, most of the routines require Pascal-style strings. If you program in C, you must allow for the differences in how C and Pascal handle strings. In this appendix, I discuss:

- The difference between Pascal and C strings

- How the Toolbox uses Pascal strings

- How to convert a string from one type to the other

C and Pascal String Storage

Although each language defines a string the same way—as an array of characters—C and Pascal use different methods for storing information and determining the length of a string.

In Pascal, the first byte of the string (element zero of the array) is the length byte. In the byte zero location, the compiler puts the total number of characters in the string. A Toolbox routine that expects a Pascal string will always look here to figure out how long the string is, and act accordingly. Because the string length value is stored in a byte, the maximum length of a Pascal string is 255 characters—the highest value you can store in one byte.

In C, there is no length byte. Byte zero of the string contains the first actual character. The string continues until you encounter the "null terminator." This is the value zero—not the ASCII code for the number zero, but the actual value zero. When a C-based string routine encounters a zero, it knows it has reached the end of the string. Because there is no length byte, a C string may be any length.

If you want to figure out how long a string is for yourself and it is a Pascal string, you simply look at byte zero. For C strings, you can use a standard library routine—strlen()—that walks through the string looking for the null terminator.

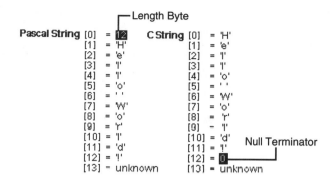

Figure B.1 Pascal and C strings

The Toolbox and Pascal Strings

The Toolbox uses Pascal strings almost exclusively. The difference in the structure of C and Pascal strings is significant.

Because the Toolbox assumes that the string you provide is a Pascal string, if you pass a C string to a Toolbox routine, it reads the value of the first byte and assumes the string is that long. If you passed the C version of the string illustrated in Figure B.1, the Toolbox would think that the string was 72 characters long—the ASCII value for an uppercase H. If you called **DrawString()**, for example, it would dutifully draw 72 characters beginning with "ello World!" and continue with whatever unknown values come after the actual text. The first character of the string would not appear, because the Toolbox interpreted that character as a length byte.

The Toolbox declares several data types for use as Pascal strings. In C these are arrays of unsigned chars. Each has a corresponding data type that the Toolbox uses when passing the string as a parameter. In raw C these are pointers to an unsigned char, that is, the address of the first char in the data—the length byte. Table B.1 summarizes the available data types.

B

Table B.1: Pascal-Based String Data Types

Toolbox Data Type	C Equivalent
Str255	unsigned char[256]
ConstStr255Param	unsigned char*
Str63	unsigned char[64]
ConstStr63Param	unsigned char*
Str32	unsigned char[33]
ConstStr32Param	unsigned char*
Str31	unsigned char[32]
ConstStr31Param	unsigned char*
Str27	unsigned char[28]
ConstStr27Param	unsigned char*
Str15	unsigned char[16]
ConstStr15Param	unsigned char*

The data types provide for strings of different lengths so that you can manage your memory usage. The Toolbox uses Str255 primarily, but you will see the other data types as well. Note that each array is one byte larger than implied by the name of the corresponding data type. This allows for the length byte at the beginning of the Pascal string.

Each of the "param" data types is the address of a constant unsigned byte. Because it is constant, the data cannot change. Therefore you see the "param" data types used only to pass information into the Toolbox, not to get strings back out of the Toolbox.

For example, here's the prototype for SetControlTitle(). You pass the control handle and a ConstStr255Param. You are passing a string *to* the Toolbox, so the contents of the string do not change (therefore they can be constant).

```
pascal void SetControlTitle(ControlHandle theControl,
    ConstStr255Param title)
```

In contrast, here's the call to GetControlTitle(). You pass the control handle and a Str255. In this case, you are getting a string *from* the Toolbox. The string parameter is not constant so that the Toolbox can modify the contents of the string storage that you provide.

```
pascal void GetControlTitle(ControlHandle theControl,
   Str255 title)
```

Remember that because the str255 is really an array, the address of the array is passed to the Toolbox, not the actual array. You do *not* need to explicitly tell the compiler you are passing an address by using the ampersand (&) operator. C always passes arrays by reference.

Converting Strings

When programming for the Macintosh, you can limit yourself to Pascal strings exclusively. This makes working with the Toolbox simple. However, you may find yourself in a situation where you prefer to work with C strings.

For example, the ANSI standard string library included with C development environments provides some very useful C string manipulation routines. The "Standard Libraries" section of Appendix A has a list of some of the more common C string manipulation routines. You may want to use C strings to take advantage of these routines.

If you use C strings, you must convert them to Pascal before making Toolbox calls. The Toolbox provides string conversion routines for both directions: C to Pascal or Pascal to C. They are **c2pStr()** and **p2cStr()**. The details for each call are listed in the "String Reference" section that follows.

Each of these calls converts the string "in place." That means that when you pass in a string, the actual contents of the string are rearranged to convert the data from one form to the other.

String Reference

The Toolbox has some useful string-manipulation routines. Those listed here provide for comparing strings, making a string uppercase, converting numbers and strings, and converting Pascal and C strings.

Some of the calls listed here assume the string is in English. The Toolbox contains many more string-related utilities for managing "localizable" strings—strings in other languages—and for working with text in general (as opposed to particular strings). You can find information on various string routines in *Inside Macintosh: Operating System Utilities*, and in other volumes of *Inside Macintosh*.

```
pascal Boolean EqualString(ConstStr255Param str1,
                    ConstStr255Param str2, Boolean
                    caseSens, Boolean diacSens);
```

Parameters   str1   address of a Pascal string

                  str2   address of another Pascal string

                  caseSens   true => consider case (A != a)

                  diacSens   true => consider diacritical marks

Returns   Boolean value, true => the strings are identical

Description   Determine whether two strings are identical within specified limits for case or diacritical mark sensitivity. A diacritical mark is typically an accent mark over a letter.

```
pascal short RelString(ConstStr255Param str1,
                ConstStr255Param str2, Boolean
                caseSens, Boolean diacSens);
```

Parameters   str1   address of a Pascal string

                  str2   address of another Pascal string

                  caseSens   true => consider case (A != a)

                  diacSens   true => consider diacritical marks

Returns   Value indicating alphabetical relationship of two strings: –1 = str1 < str2; 0 = identical; 1 = str1 > str2

Description   Useful for sorting strings.

```
pascal void UpperString(Str255 theString, Boolean diacSens);
```

Parameters   theString   address of a Pascal string

                  diacSens   true => strip diacritical marks

Returns   void

Description   Converts string to uppercase.

```
pascal void StringToNum(ConstStr255Param theString, long *theNum);
```

Parameters   theString   address of a Pascal string of numbers

                  theNum   address of a long value to store result

Returns	void
Description	Converts string provided into a `long` value. String may contain a leading plus or minus sign, and up to 10 numerical characters, no commas or periods.

```
pascal void NumToString(long theNum, Str255 theString);
```

Parameters	theNum	long value to convert to a string
	theString	address of a Pascal string to store result
Returns	void	
Description	Converts number provided into a Pascal string. If number is < 0, string starts with a minus sign.	

```
pascal StringPtr C2PStr(Ptr cString)
```

Parameters	cString	address of a C string
Returns	The address of the resulting Pascal string	
Description	Converts provided string "in place." The actual memory occupied by the original C string is converted into the equivalent Pascal string. C string must be no more than 255 bytes long.	

```
pascal Ptr P2CStr(StringPtr pString)
```

Parameters	pString	address of a Pascal string
Returns	Address of the first character of the resulting C string	
Description	Converts provided string "in place." The actual memory occupied by the original Pascal string is converted into the equivalent C string.	

A Brief C Style Guide

There are very few rules in C: you can write legal code using all sorts of odd constructions; you can put multiple commands on a single line, use braces or not, and generally be extremely obscure if you choose to be.

Benefits of Consistent Style

As a programmer, you will be required to read and understand code written by other programmers. Likewise, other programmers will read and attempt to understand your code. You may work on a team developing a project, you may inherit code from a predecessor, or—horror of horrors—you may even have to go back and look at your own code to figure out what you did.

When looking at strange code, it takes a fair amount of effort to figure out what's going on. Understanding is a lot easier when the code follows a particular style. If there is a consistent style, you don't have to waste energy trying to decipher the hieroglyphics. If the style is clear, you can quickly see what the code intends to accomplish. You are also far more likely to detect any introductory problems because the coding style doesn't get in the way of seeing what's going on.

Over years of experience, C programmers have developed conventions to make code more clear. These conventions are not universal, but they are widespread. Studying them serves two purposes:

- You become familiar with the style used by many programmers. This increases your level of understanding when you see code that follows the same or a similar style.

- If you adopt a consistent style and your code is much more readable—not only to yourself, but to others.

This appendix discusses conventions relating to:

- Header files
- Names
- Comments
- C syntax

These conventions are most widespread in the Macintosh programming community. Other programming communities—UNIX programmers, for example—may have different conventional styles.

Header Files

Put type declarations and prototypes in header files. Use the ".h" extension at the end of your header files to clearly identify them.

Organize the contents of the header files logically. In many cases, each source file has a header file on which it is dependent. You may include declarations relating to several source files in a single header file if that is more convenient. *The Macintosh Programming Starter Kit for Macintosh* does that so you can find things, such as function prototypes, more easily.

Make it easy to include header files without causing multiple includes. Including a header file more than once terminally confuses the compiler because the compiler ends up with multiple declarations for the same names. Trying to keep track of which source files include which header files is not only a pain, it's needless. Use the following style for each of your header files:

```
#ifndef __MYHEADER__
#define __MYHEADER__

#include "whatever.h"

/* rest of declarations for this header */

#endif
```

For the term __MYHEADER__ in the example, substitute a name unique to your header file. The double-underscore before and after the name, and the use of all capital letters, are naming conventions designed to ensure that this declaration is unique.

If you follow this convention, your header will be included only once no matter how many source files try to include it. The compiler reads the declarations if the term __MYHEADER__ is undeclared. After the first time the file is read, that term *is* declared and the declarations in the file are never read again. No pain, great gain.

Always use function prototypes. In case you missed that, I'll repeat it. *Always use function prototypes.*

Name the parameters in function prototypes. Parameter types are required in a function prototype, but parameter *names* are not. Here's the difference.

```
void BadSetPoint(short, short); /* it's bad, bad... */

void GoodSetPoint(short h, short v);
```

Both of these are legal prototypes. One is obscure, the other helpful. In the prototype for BadSetPoint(), you haven't a clue as to the significance of the two parameters. To find out what the significance is, you have to locate the actual source code for the function. In the prototype for GoodSetPoint(), the parameter names clearly indicate the purpose of each parameter. This is much better.

In the actual function, use the same parameter names as those used in the prototype. It is legal to use different names. However, if at all possible you should use the same names, because consistency aids understanding. If the function has the same parameter names as the prototype, you can see the relationships more clearly.

For example, given the previous prototype, here are two alternative function definitions for GoodSetPoint().

```
GoodSetPoint(short x, short y)
{

}

GoodSetPoint(short h, short v)
{

}
```

Each is legal. The second is preferred because it uses the same names as the prototype.

Use consistent parameter names. For functions that use the same kind of parameters, settle on a single name to use in all functions. For example, look at the use of the macWindow parameter name in EasyApp. Every window pointer parameter is named macWindow, and every macWindow is a window pointer.

Naming Conventions

All names—structures, types, fields, global variables, local variables, constants, functions, and parameters—must be a single string of characters. This is not a convention; it is a requirement of C.

The first character in the name is upper- or lowercase depending upon the type of variable. I discuss which is which in this section.

Second and subsequent natural words in a name begin with capital letters. All other characters are lowercase. Examples: thisVariable, MyFunction, gHasCoolFeature. This enhances readability. Do not use the underscore character to separate words in a name.

The names for structures and data types that you declare should begin with a capital letter. The Boolean data type is a good example. It is not a C data type; it is declared as part of the Toolbox. (The Toolbox frequently violates this rule, but it is still a good rule.)

The names for fields in a structure should begin with a lowercase letter. Many programmers like to use the letter "f" as the first character to emphasize that the variable is a field. For example, you might have fields named fVisible or fSize. This is a strong convention in C++, and not used very often in C.

Global variable names should begin with a lowercase "g" before the rest of the name. Examples: gHasColor, gHasDragAndDrop. In EasyApp you extend this convention further by declaring a structure whose members are the global variables for EasyApp. You define a single instance of the structure, name it "g" and dereference it to get individual members of the structure. This makes it easy to declare an external reference to all the globals you need. You declare a single external reference to "g" and you're done with it.

Local variables should begin with a lowercase letter. Examples: savePort, theRegion, bounds.

Constants should begin with a lowercase "k" before the rest of the name. Examples: kErrorDialogID, kPictType, kFileNotFoundError. Once again, for consistency you should develop a style for different kinds of constants and stick to it. For example, the names for all DLOG resource ID number constants might end with "DialogID." Some programmers prefer to use all uppercase letters to denote constants, and use the underscore character to separate words. You'll see this often in older code. This style has gone out of favor because text that is all uppercase is more difficult to read. In addition, underscores are not preferred because they are a bother to type.

Function names should begin with a capital letter. The name is typically a verb and reflects as succinctly as possible what the function accomplishes. Examples: DrawWindow, MovePiece. Don't be afraid to use long function names if this is necessary to be descriptive, but don't go overboard. The EasyRemoveWindowFromList() routine in EasyApp is a good example. I wanted "easy" in all the EasyApp-specific routines so you could identify them. To adequately describe the nature of the function, I needed four additional words.

Function parameters follow the naming conventions for local variables. In all respects, function parameters *are* local variables, so there is no need to distinguish them.

Comments

Comment everything. That should take care of that.

Comment anything left over. This should cover those rare cases when the first guideline fails you.

Seriously and most especially, comment anything subtle that's going on in the code. If you have paid attention to guidelines one and two, this should follow naturally. For example, sometimes a function call has invisible side effects. If those are significant, remind yourself and others about those effects.

```
/* this makes the handle a resource handle */
AddResource(resHandle, resType, resID, "\p");
```

Here the person reading the code is reminded that a call to the Macintosh Toolbox routine `AddResource()` changes the nature of the handle involved. That little reminder just might save someone an entire day while bug hunting.

You should write comments as you write the code. There is no time when you will better understand what you are doing and why you are doing it. Not only that, if your understanding is less than perfect, the fact that you have commented how and why you did things can help you find the problem!

You can use commenting as a design tool. When you are about to write a function, write the comment that describes the function first. Detail the logical steps that the algorithm takes and the tasks it must accomplish. This can help organize your thinking. After you have a decent outline, fill in the code. As you write code, you may modify the comments. There is a synergistic feedback between the two processes: comment begets code begets comment.

As a practical matter, in most development environments you can use either the `/*… */` traditional syntax or the C++ `//` syntax for comments. However, if you want to conform to the ANSI standard, you cannot use the `//` comment syntax in C code.

Syntax Conventions

If you don't follow any of the following guidelines, remember one: **be clear and consistent**. More specific advice is sure to raise howls of protest from more experienced programmers who follow different conventions.

The following guidelines, then, are suggestions for new programmers. It is not imperative that you follow each of these guidelines to the letter, but rather that you pick conventions that make sense and be consistent.

Avoid obscure syntax. Using C shorthand tricks to save a line or two of code will not enhance the final performance of your program, but will damage the readability of your code. Here's a good example. These two methods for solving a problem are functionally identical.

```
/* method one */
x = (a < b) ? a : b;

/* method two */
if (a < b)
{
  x = a;
}
else
{
  x = b;
}
```

In all likelihood, when encountered by the compiler, each will generate the identical object code and run identically. The first method does *not* generate faster code. In addition, unless you are familiar with the intricacies of C, the first method is pure gobbledygook.

The second method is much easier to understand because it requires no special knowledge of C. The people reading your code may not be C wizards. In fact, they may not even know C! Perhaps a Pascal programmer wants to look at one of your algorithms to see how you accomplished some magic. When you have an alternative, use a simple construction. If you try to impress people with your C vocabulary, you may lose them entirely.

Several style issues arise concerning the use of braces (the { and } punctuation marks) after conditional statements.

Use braces even if there is only one statement controlled by a conditional. C syntax *requires* braces only when there are two or more statements controlled. If there is only one statement, the braces are technically optional. Use them anyway. There are two good reasons for doing so:

- First, braces clearly and visually delineate the code controlled by the condition. This is very helpful when reading the code.

- Second, if you decide to modify your code in such a way that you add a second statement, you might forget to put in the braces. If there are no braces, the condition controls only the first statement. The second statement executes every time, regardless of whether the condition is met. If you indent your code as detailed in the next guideline, it looks like the condition controls everything it is supposed to control, but it doesn't.

This kind of bug is difficult to locate, and compilers don't flag one-line conditionals as possible errors. It is a good idea to use braces all the time, regardless of the number of lines of code controlled by the condition.

Indent your code inside braces. This is a coding convention, and not a requirement of syntax. Indenting code helps you comprehend the relationship between various elements in the code. For example, you can see at a glance precisely what's controlled by a condition simply by how much the code is indented.

Locate braces consistently. Some programmers, myself included, prefer putting each brace on its own line. This helps identify the controlled code and makes it easy to locate missing braces.

```
if (x < y)
{
   /* statements */
}
```

Other programmers prefer the style shown here, with the opening brace on the same line as the condition:

```
if (x < y) {
   /* statements */
}
```

Have one statement per line of code. For simple situations, programmers sometimes put everything on one line, like this:

```
if (x < y) {y = 0; x = 10;}
```

This is not a recommended style. When perusing code it is easy to miss additional statements on a line because C programmers quickly become accustomed to one statement per line. Second, you can only set one breakpoint per line on your source code. If you have multiple statements on a single line, you may not be able to stop precisely where you'd like when you are debugging your code. If you write perfect code every time, this will not be a consideration for you.

Be generous with white space. It's free after all. You might use up a few extra pieces of paper if you print your code, but that's a small price. Even within a single function, you should group various segments of the algorithm into logical units. Identify them with a comment, leave a line or two between these units so you can clearly see which code does what and when. There is nothing harder to fathom than endless lines of code without a break. Breaking your code up into segments serves the same purpose as paragraphs in text. Imagine a book without paragraphs and you get some idea of how difficult it is to read solid blocks of code.

Conclusion

You should adopt a style that you are comfortable with. What's important here is not that you adopt the style used in *The Macintosh Programming Starter Kit for Macintosh*, or even that you follow the style guidelines outlined in this appendix religiously. Feel free to embellish, augment, or modify as *need* demands.

However, it will help you—and everyone else who ever looks at your code—if your style is similar to the general style outlined in this appendix, particularly with respect to names.

After you settle on a style, be consistent. A consistent style helps you avoid mistakes, helps you find them after you make them, and helps other people understand your code more easily.

D

Resources for Macintosh Programmers

D

This appendix includes annotated references for software, books, magazines, online resources, and education available for programmers. You can think of it as an informal bibliography.

This list is not intended to be comprehensive. In fact, it is really a cross-section of the tools and titles I have run across as a programmer. There are certainly many good resources of which I am unaware. However, this appendix is an excellent starting point for further explorations in the area of Macintosh programming.

The presence of any item in these listings is not a recommendation or endorsement of the product by Hayden Books. Likewise the absence of any item should not be construed as a judgment about the product or a criticism of its value. Any prices specified are approximate and may change.

Software

Commercial programming software may be available from the customary mail-order houses. The market for this software is smaller than for most commercial software, so some resellers do not carry programming products. You can obtain most of these items from APDA—The Apple Programmers and Developers Association—at 1-800-282-2732 in the U.S. or 1-800-637-0029 in Canada. Call them and request a catalog for the current prices.

The software is divided into four categories:

- Development environments
- Debuggers
- Reference software
- Other tools

Development Environments

Environments are available in a variety of languages: BASIC, C, C++, FORTRAN, Pascal, Smalltalk, and others.

Title:	**CodeWarrior**–$399
Publisher:	Metrowerks
Description:	Includes Pascal, C, and C++ compilers for both 68K and Power Mac code, source-level debugger, and the PowerPlant application framework. Price includes one year of free updates. The "bronze" version of

CodeWarrior does not have the Power Mac compilers, and costs $99. CodeWarrior Platinum (not released at the time of this writing) will include a cross-compiler for Intel processors.

Title:	**THINK C–$199**
Publisher:	Symantec
Description:	Includes a C compiler for 68K and Power Mac code, source-level debugger, and the THINK Class Library application framework.

Title:	**Symantec C++–$499**
Publisher:	Symantec
Description:	Includes C and C++ compilers for 68K and Power Macs. Also includes a Visual Architect interface designer, THINK Class Library, and more.

Title:	**MPW Pro–$495**
Publisher:	Apple Computer, Inc.
Description:	Complex programming environment; supports compilers in many languages, includes C and C++ compilers for 68K and Power Mac. Has many other tools. Includes MacApp, the original—and much enhanced—Macintosh application framework.

Title:	**Essentials, Tools, and Objects–$1,095**
Publisher:	Apple Computer, Inc.
Description:	The works: MPW, MacApp framework, Symantec C++, Virtual User testing tool, Macintosh Debugger, ResEdit, MacsBug, pre-release versions of the hottest new toys, and lots of other stuff. Updated regularly; price includes a 3-issue subscription. Renewals are $400.

Title:	**THINK Pascal–$165**
Publisher:	Symantec
Description:	The original version was one of the first integrated development environments on the Mac. Includes a 68K compiler and the THINK Class Library.

Title:	**Prograph CPX–$1,495**
Publisher:	Pictorius
Description:	Fully pictorial object-oriented programming environment, with source-level debugging and a class library for application programming.

Title: VIP C–$395

Publisher: Mainstay

Description: C compiler; environment automatically creates flow charts of your code for easy design and access. Excellent interface into Toolbox routines.

Title: VIP BASIC–$295

Publisher: Mainstay

Description: Similar to VIP C only in BASIC. Has the same excellent visual design and application-building aid.

Title: Think Pascal–$165

Publisher: Symantec

Description: Includes compiler for 68K code and an excellent debugger.

Title: MacFortran II–$550

Publisher: Absoft

Description: Includes a FORTRAN77 compiler for 68K Mac; runs under MPW (included). Includes the Macintosh Runtime Windows Environment application framework.

Title: FORTRAN77 SDK for Power Macintosh–$699

Publisher: Absoft

Description: Includes a FORTRAN77 compiler for Power Mac; runs under MPW (included).

Title: FORTRAN v 3.3–$495

Publisher: Language Systems

Description: Includes a FORTRAN77 compiler for 68K code that runs under MPW. Available with MPW for $595.

Title: Smalltalk/V Mac–$395

Publisher: Digitalk

Description: Includes a Smalltalk compiler and a collection of sample applications.

Title: SmalltalkAgents–$695

Publisher: Quasar Knowledge Systems

Description: Includes a Smalltalk compiler for 68K and Power Mac, an extensive class library for Macintosh programming, and an interactive interface builder.

Debuggers and Debugging Tools

Title: **Macintosh Debugger**–n/a

Publisher: Apple Computer

Description: A source and assembly level debugger for Power Mac native code. Works with code from any compiler that generates standard SYM files, including CodeWarrior and the latest version of Symantec C++. Available only with purchase of other Apple products (such as MPW, ETO, and so forth).

Title: **MacsBug**–$35

Publisher: Apple Computer

Description: A strictly low-level debugger for 68K code; has some limited functionality with Power Mac code. Cannot view or trace source code. Powerful, but hard to use. Included free of charge with many products, including *develop* magazine CDs. If you pay money for this, I have a bridge that you might be interested in.

Title: **The Debugger**–$350

Publisher: Jasik Designs

Description: Very powerful source and low-level debugger for both 68K and Power Mac code. Does it all, but has an idiosyncratic interface. Some swear by it, some hate it.

Title: **QC**–$99

Publisher: Onyx Technology

Description: A memory-related system extension for stress-testing code under development. Checks integrity of heap, scrambles and purges heap, invalid pointer and handle usage, writes to zero, block bounds checking, free memory invalidation, and more.

Title: **MemoryMine**–$99

Publisher: Adianta

Description: Memory-use debugger and viewer; checks integrity of heap, memory leaks, scrambles the heap to look for dangling pointers, and more.

Title: **EvenBetterBusError**–free

Author: Greg Marriott

Description: System extension that checks for attempts to reference address zero. A great utility.

Title:	**DisposeResource**–free
Author:	Greg Marriott, ©Apple Computer
Description:	System extension that checks for disposing a resource handle as a regular handle.

Title:	**DoubleTrouble**–free
Author:	Greg Marriott, ©Apple Computer
Description:	System extension that checks for double-disposing a handle.

Reference Software

Title:	**Macintosh Toolbox Assistant**–$89
Publisher:	Apple Computer
Description:	Electronic cross-reference to all of *Inside Macintosh*, current and up to date. This is an invaluable tool for the professional programmer.

Title:	**THINK Reference**–$89
Publisher:	Symantec
Description:	Electronic cross-reference that contains all the information in *Inside Macintosh* up through the introduction of System 7. Does not include latest Toolbox APIs, so somewhat outdated.

Other Tools

Title:	**ResEdit**–$30
Publisher:	Apple Computer
Description:	A resource editor. Widely included free of charge with other products. Like MacsBug, if you actually pay money for this, see me about that bridge.

Title:	**Resorcerer**–$256
Publisher:	Mathemaesthetics
Description:	A full-featured resource editor. Has all the bells and whistles, and can handle some resource types that ResEdit can't. Particularly useful for creating resources used for scriptable/recordable applications.

Title:	**SoftPolish**–$169
Publisher:	Language Systems
Description:	Proofreader for software developers. Looks for typos in resources, incorrect or incompatible resources, and other problems. Puts the final polish on a product.

Title:	**BBEdit–$89**
Publisher:	Bare Bones Software
Description:	Source code editor with extensive and excellent feature list. Can be fully integrated with THINK to replace built-in source code editor. Also supports effective (but not complete) integration with CodeWarrior.

Title:	**QUED/M–$69**
Publisher:	Nisus Software
Description:	Source code editor with extensive feature list. Can be integrated with THINK to replace built-in source code editor.

Title:	**ObjectMaster Universal Edition–$289**
Publisher:	ACIUS
Description:	Source code editor and browser that understands C, C++, Pascal, and other languages and all major development environments.

Title:	**Mac OS Software Developer's Kit–$299**
Publisher:	Apple Computer
Description:	Contains 32 individual SDKs covering the entire Mac OS. Price is a one-year subscription with automatic updates as necessary. The SDKs include documentation, software, system extensions, sample code, and many other goodies.

Title:	**Apple Developer Mailing–$250/year**
Publisher:	Apple Computer
Description:	Monthly mailing, includes the Developer CD. There are three CDs in the Developer series: Worldwide System Software, the Tool Chest, and the Reference Library. You get one of the three each month, so each is updated quarterly. Includes all the latest and greatest stuff.

Books

There are many titles available on various aspects of Macintosh programming. The listings here just touch on the resources available. Books on four topics have been included: reference books, programming the Macintosh, the C language, and object-oriented programming with C++. All of the titles (except the pure language references) have a decidedly Macintosh flavor.

Reference Books

Title: *Inside Macintosh* (25 titles in the series)

Author: Apple Computer—actually, some real people wrote it

Publisher: Addison-Wesley (1992-1995)

Description: The definitive work with everything you ever wanted to know about the details of the Toolbox. All 25 volumes are also available as *Inside Macintosh CD-ROM* for $90. You should also consider the Macintosh Toolbox Assistant listed with the software reference materials.

Title: *Macintosh Human Interface Guidelines*

Author: Apple Computer

Publisher: Addison-Wesley

Description: Authoritative information on what makes a Macintosh application look and behave like a Macintosh application. Also available on CD as *Electronic Guide to Macintosh Human Interface Design*.

Title: *ResEdit Reference*

Author: Apple Computer

Publisher: Addison-Wesley (1990)

Description: The ResEdit manual.

Title: *MacsBug Reference*

Author: Apple Computer

Publisher: Addison-Wesley (1990)

Description: The MacsBug manual.

Programming the Macintosh

Title: *How to Write Macintosh Software, 3rd Edition*

Author: Scott Knaster and Keith Rollin

Publisher: Addison-Wesley (1992)

Description: Aimed at gaining a deep understanding of the guts of the machine for help with debugging software (and avoiding bugs in the first place). Not an introductory text.

Title: *Macintosh Programming Secrets, 2nd Edition*

Author: Scott Knaster

Publisher:	Addison Wesley (1992)
Description:	Tips from one of the masters. I'd say more, but I loaned this one and it never came back.
Title:	*Debugging Macintosh Software with MacsBug*
Author:	Konstantin Othmer and Jim Straus
Publisher:	Addison-Wesley (1991)
Description:	Everything you ever wanted to know about MacsBug, and in the process learn some deep internal dirt on how things work in the Toolbox.
Title:	*Power Macintosh Programming Starter Kit*
Author:	Tom Thompson
Publisher:	Hayden Books
Description:	Brief overview of Macintosh programming in general, and an in-depth look at the guts of the Power Macintosh.

The C Language

Title:	*The C Programming Language, 2nd Edition*
Author:	Brian W. Kernighan and Dennis M. Ritchie
Publisher:	Prentice Hall (1988)
Description:	This is the official C handbook by the people who invented the language. Dry and dense, but it has the answers.
Title:	*Learn C on the Mac*
Author:	Dave Mark
Publisher:	Addison-Wesley
Description:	Introduction to C, not Macintosh programming. A whole lot more fun than *The C Programming Language*.

Object-Oriented Programming and C++

Title:	*The C++ Programming Language, 2nd Edition*
Author:	Bjarne Stroustrup
Publisher:	Addison-Wesley (1991)
Description:	This is the official C++ handbook by the person who invented the language. Not a fun read, but a necessary reference.

Title:	*The Annotated C++ Reference Manual*
Author:	Margaret Ellis and Bjarne Stroustrup
Publisher:	Addison-Wesley (1990)
Description:	Widely known as "The ARM," it should be on the desk of every C++ programmer. This is the answer book.
Title:	*Learn C++ on the Macintosh*
Author:	Dave Mark
Publisher:	Addison-Wesley (1993)
Description:	Introduction to the basics of the C++ language, not object-oriented design or Macintosh programming. Assumes knowledge of C.
Title:	*Effective C++*
Author:	Scott Meyers
Publisher:	Addison-Wesley (1992)
Description:	Specific ideas for improving design and code in object-oriented programs.
Title:	*Symantec C++ Programming for the Macintosh*
Author:	Neil Rhodes and Julie McKeehan
Publisher	Brady (1993)
Description:	Covers three topics: the Symantec C++ environment, C++, and object-oriented programming.
Title:	*Developing Object-Oriented Software for the Macintosh*
Author:	Neal Goldstein and Jeff Alger
Publisher:	Addison-Wesley
Description:	Primarily about analysis and design and the development process, not programming. Introduces the Solution Based Modeling approach to object-oriented design.

Magazines

Title:	*develop*–$27/year, quarterly
Publisher:	Apple Computer
Description:	Apple's quarterly technical journal, provides an in-depth look at code and techniques that have been reviewed for robustness by Apple engineers. Each issue comes with a CD that contains the source code for

that issue, as well as all back issues, Technical Notes, sample code, and other useful software and documentation. Subscriptions to *develop* are available through APDA (1-800-282-2732), AppleLink DEV.SUBS, or Internet dev.subs@applelink.apple.com. This is a real bargain! It is aimed at professional programmers, but don't let that scare you. The CD has some great resources on it.

Title: *MacTech*–$47/year, monthly

Publisher: Xplain

Description: Aimed at all Macintosh programmers, beginner and expert, covering all facets of Macintosh programming. For subscriptions, contact custservice@xplain.com on the Internet, 71333,1063 on CompuServe, MTCUSTSVC on AppleLink, MT CUSTSVC on AOL, and MACTECHMAG on GEnie. Voice, call 310-575-4343, or write Xplain Corporation, 1617 Pontius Ave. 2nd floor, Los Angeles, CA 90025-9555. See the coupon in the back of this book for a discount.

Online Resources

The information available electronically is overwhelming. Most of the national networks have active Macintosh programming areas where developers meet, chat, exchange ideas, and share code. You can find solutions to problems and employment opportunities on the nets.

Network: **America Online**

Contact: 1-800-827-6364

Description: Has an active development area supporting programming in a variety of languages. Software vendors also present.

Network: **AppleLink**

Contact: 1-408-974-3309

Description: Electronic access to Apple employees, the latest developer-related information. Access to Developer Technical Support for Partner developers. Lots of information, most of it available elsewhere for less money. AppleLink is expensive.

Network: **CompuServe**

Contact: 1-800-881-8961

Description: Has a variety of forums for developers, programming languages, and software vendors.

Network:	**Delphi**
Contact:	1-800-695-4005
Description:	National network with active areas for programmers. Also provides full Internet access.
Network:	**eWorld**
Contact:	1-800-775-4556
Description:	Apple's own national network. Will eventually replace AppleLink.
Network:	**GEnie**
Contact:	1-800-638-9636
Description:	Has an active development area for Macintosh and other platforms, supporting a variety of languages. Fewer software vendors.
Network:	**Internet**
Contact:	A local Internet service provider
Description:	Resources on the Internet for programmers include active message areas on many topics in the Usenet, gigabytes of Macintosh software at various ftp (file transfer protocol) sites around the globe, and the online presence of many companies that cater to developers, both via ftp site and the World Wide Web. Among places of interest for developers are

World Wide Web:

- http://www.info.apple.com/dev
- http://ftp.support.apple.com
- http://www.iquest.com/~fairgate/cw/cw.html (CodeWarrior support)
- http://www.info.apple.com/dev/dts/dogcow.html

ftp sites:

- ftp.info.apple.com
- seeding.apple.com
- mac.archive.umich.edu or a mirror site
- ftcp.cc.umanitoba.ca

newsgroups:

- comp.sys.mac.programmer.codewarrior
- comp.sys.mac.programmer.help
- comp.sys.mac.programmer.misc
- comp.sys.mac.programmer.tools

Education

There are programming courses available at universities and other educational institutions nationwide. If you are interested in taking a course in programming, contact your local college or university. It might have something for you. It may even be on a Macintosh!

There are companies devoted to training Macintosh programmers. They primarily teach small groups of programmers during intense one- or two-week sessions, usually at the site of some business involved with Macintosh programming. If you are a programmer for such an organization, contact your training department. It may have information for you.

In addition, Developer University (DU) at Apple Computer offers self-paced, interactive CD-ROM versions of their most popular courses. Among the titles available through APDA and some other software sources are:

- Macintosh Programming Fundamentals (MPF)–$595

- Intermediate Macintosh Application Programming (IMAP)–$495

- Object-Oriented Fundamentals (OOF)–$350

These courses have been very successful at training programmers all over the world. They are frequently available at a discount. Check for package deals and the latest prices. At the time of this writing, some parts of MPF are outdated (it dates from System 6 days) but the fundamentals don't change much. IMAP covers several topics not covered in this book: some advanced memory management strategies, QuickTime, and Publish and Subscribe, to name a few. OOF covers object-oriented analysis, design, and programming in C++.

DU also has an active, year-round curriculum with instructor-led courses in all aspects of Macintosh programming—from Macintosh Programming Fundamentals to OpenDoc. At the present time, courses are taught either in Cupertino, CA, or Portsmouth, NH. The courses are expensive, running about $300 per day. Courses range from two to five days. DU will send an instructor onsite.

For more information about Developer University courses and schedules, contact the registrar at devuniv@applelink.apple.com on the Internet. Voice is 408-974-4897, or write to Developer University, 5 Infinite Loop M/S 305 1TU, Cupertino, CA 95014.

E

A Guide to EasyApp

E

This appendix gives you an overview of the EasyApp application shell: its design, its functionality, and how to use it.

Although you have written much of the code for EasyApp during the lab exercises in this book, at no point have you created a stand-alone application shell. You can find the complete, stand-alone EasyApp on the CD in the MPSK Code folder, in the EasyApp Complete folder.

EasyApp is a small but very useful little application shell. Designed and created in 1995 by the author especially for *Programming Starter Kit for Macintosh*, EasyApp takes advantage of some of the latest features available in System 7.5, including Drag and Drop. EasyApp is designed to meet three principle goals:

- Run on any Macintosh
- Be an extensible application shell
- Demonstrate basic Macintosh programming techniques

The first goal means that EasyApp works on any Macintosh—from the Mac Plus on up. However, it requires System 7. EasyApp does not work with earlier releases of System software. That is the only significant limitation. EasyApp does not require color or the presence of any other feature of System software. It can compile and run in Power Macintosh native code and 68K code.

The second goal means you can use EasyApp in your own programming projects. In this book you use the shell as the basis for EasyPuzzle.

The third goal means that you can learn a lot about Macintosh programming by looking at the EasyApp code. All of the code is heavily and clearly commented. The code is written in a consistent style throughout. Functions have been kept as short and simple as possible to ease understanding.

However clear the details, a big-picture view of the structure of EasyApp and what it does can help you use the shell more easily and more effectively.

Overall Design

When you open the EasyApp project file (either 68K or Power Mac), you see that it has three sections labeled EasyApp, Libraries, and Your App (see Figure E.1).

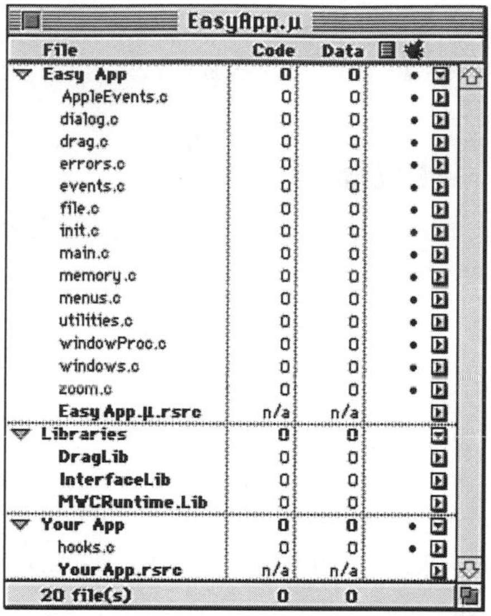

Figure E.1 EasyApp project file

Files specific to EasyApp are in the EasyApp section. You should never change any of these files. You *may* change them if you wish, but that defeats the purpose of an application shell. The original files are in the Easy Source folder inside the EasyApp Complete folder.

The Libraries section contains libraries appropriate for the Macintosh that are intended to run the final code. For 68K Macs, that's MacOS.lib. For Power Macs, that's DragLib, InterfaceLib, and MWCRuntime.Lib. The original library files are part of the Metrowerks CodeWarrior package.

Files specific to your application appear in the Your App section and any other sections you might add to the project. There are two files in this section already; they are hooks.c and YourApp.rsrc. The nature of the hooks file will become clear in a bit. The .rsrc file should contain your application resources. It already contains MENU resources for the Apple, File, and Edit menus. The original files are in the Your Source folder inside the EasyApp Complete folder.

The CD contains a pristine and unmodified version of the EasyApp package. When starting a new project, use a copy of the original EasyApp.

The operating principle behind EasyApp and any application shell is that a substantial percentage of basic application behavior can be described by some simple default functions. With careful design, even those default functions can be easily replaced if you have unique or unusual needs.

771

E

EasyApp identifies two classes of services that it performs for an application: application-level services and window-level services.

Application-Level Services

Application-level services are those things that an *application* should do. This includes:

- Startup and quit
- Manage memory
- Retrieve and parse events
- Create windows
- Update menus
- Dispatch menu choices
- Provide application-level utilities

EasyApp supports these services through "hook" functions. EasyApp's naming convention is that each hook ends with the word "Hook." For example, the hook to check the operating environment is CheckEnvironmentHook(). In EasyApp, all the hooks are in the hooks.c file. There are about 40 hook functions.

The idea behind a hook function is simple. The shell identifies certain kinds of situations when something should happen. For example, an error occurs and the application should display a message. Every time such a situation arises, the shell calls a hook function—in our example, it would be ShowErrorHook().

If you look at the hook functions, you see that most of them are one or two lines long. The default hooks call corresponding "Easy" functions that implement default behavior for EasyApp. For example, the error hook calls EasyShowError(). In many cases, the default behavior does quite nicely in your application and you don't have to replace it.

There will be times when you want to replace the default behavior. There may be a half-dozen different places inside EasyApp that call a particular hook, but you don't have to worry about that. Because control *always* passes through these gateways at the right time, you have a "choke point" where, if necessary, you can interrupt the flow of control and direct it to a destination better suited to your application.

Overriding behavior is discussed in just a bit. Before that, you need to know about the other class of service provided by EasyApp, window-level services.

Window-Level Services

Window-level services support window-related behaviors. Because the content and behavior of a window in any arbitrary application is essentially unpredictable, this imposes a serious design constraint. How can EasyApp provide support for undefined operations?

The solution is to borrow from object-oriented design principles and make the window responsible for its own behavior. EasyApp causes the behavior to happen, but the precise nature of the behavior remains undefined until you provide it.

Although the actual response may vary substantially, there are several clearly defined moments when all windows must respond to identical events. When such a moment arrives, EasyApp sends a message to the window identifying the nature of the event and provides any data necessary to respond to the event. It is then up to the window to respond appropriately.

Whenever you see a line of code that looks like this:

```
error = easyWindow->DoWriteData(macWindow, &newFile);
```

EasyApp is sending a message to the window. In this case it is telling the window that it is time to write data to a file, and provides information about the file.

There are about 45 such window messages in EasyApp. These are categorized as messages that pertain to:

- File operations
- Edit menu operations
- Event handling
- General window behavior
- Window content behavior
- Menu management at the window level
- Miscellaneous window behavior

EasyApp follows some naming conventions that can help you identify what's going on. All window messages begin with the word "Do," like DoWriteData. This is not a function; it's the name of a variable that holds the address of a function. The distinction is important.

Each message *must* have a corresponding function that responds to the message, even if that function does nothing. You put the address of the function in the "Do" variable. These variables are fields in the `EasyWindow` data structure declared in EasyApp.h.

EasyApp provides default response functions for many messages. The name of each of these functions replaces the "Do" of the message with the word "Base." The default function that responds to the `DoWriteData` message is `BaseWriteData()`. The "Base" functions are all located in the file `windowProc.c`. The word "Base" emphasizes the default nature of the function.

In many cases, the default response function serves your application just fine. In other cases, you must replace the default behavior with behavior specific to your application.

Changing Default Behavior

In EasyApp there are about 85 hooks or window messages that you can override. It might seem like you would have to write a tremendous amount of code to override 85 functions, and that's true. The good news is, you do not have to replace them all.

EasyApp provides default behavior for most of the hooks and messages. You will find that the default behavior will be perfectly acceptable for your application in many cases.

The question remains, how do you modify default behavior? In fact, there are two questions to answer, one practical and one strategic.

The strategic question is, "What techniques do I use when modifying default behavior?" In general, you have two strategies you can follow: You can augment the default behavior or you can replace it entirely. Sometimes one strategy is better, sometimes the other. It depends upon how different your desired behavior is from the default behavior. That will be discussed in just a bit.

But first, you need to ask and answer the practical question, "How do I call my own functions?"

Calling Your Own Functions from EasyApp

The method for calling your own functions differs for hooks and messages.

For hooks, you simply call your own function in addition to or in place of the default EasyApp function. For example, here is the default code for the hook to initialize the Toolbox. It calls the default function `EasyInitToolbox()` to initialize the Mac OS.

```
void    InitToolboxHook (void)
{
    EasyInitToolbox();

/* call your own routine for additional initializing */


}
```

As you develop your own application, you may take a look at `EasyInitToolbox()` and decide that it doesn't do everything you need it to do. You don't have to replace it. After the existing call, you can simply call your own function. (Notice how the comment tells you the same thing.) You have just modified the default EasyApp behavior for initializing the Toolbox by augmenting the default behavior.

For window messages, the process is a bit more complicated.

In the `EasyWindow` data structure declared in EasyApp.h, there is a long series of fields—the names of which are the window messages. For example, an EasyWindow has fields such as `DoActivate`, `DoUpdate`, `DoDraw`, `DoWriteData`, and so forth. Like all fields, these fields are variables. They are declared as variables of type `WindowProc`. A `WindowProc` is a pointer to a function that responds to a window message. Each of the "Base" window functions is a `WindowProc`.

When you create a new window, you must fill in each and every one of these fields with a good value. For example, for the `DoActivate` field, you provide the address of the function that you want to handle that message. In the default EasyApp, that's `BaseActivate()`.

If you want to replace that with your own behavior, you install the address *for your own function* in the `DoActivate` field, perhaps named `MyActivate()`. Then, every time EasyApp sends a `DoActivate` message to your window, the `MyActivate()` function is called instead of the `BaseActivate()` function. You have replaced the default EasyApp response to the message with your own response.

In fact, you can change the behavior at any time, not just when you create the window. If you want the window's behavior to change after it has been created, just put a pointer to a different function in the appropriate "Do" field. This feature makes EasyApp a "dynamic" shell because you can modify behavior while the application is running, and you can modify a window's behavior while it is open.

E

Different types of windows can respond differently to the same message. Simply install the pointer to the desired response function for each window. They do not have to be the same. EasyApp sends the same message to each window, but the windows respond differently because each window "knows" how it is supposed to respond to the message.

> In object-oriented terminology, this kind of varying response to a common message is called polymorphism.

In summary, for hooks you simply call your own function in addition to or in place of the existing code in the hook function. For windows, you install a pointer to your function in the appropriate "Do" field of the EasyWindow record.

Now let's take a look at the strategies you can use: augmenting behavior or replacing behavior. This discussion applies to both hooks and window messages.

Augmenting Behavior

In some cases EasyApp will do most of what you want, but it won't do everything you want. The LoadCursorsHook() is a perfect example—it calls EasyLoadCursors(). You take a look at this function and see that it puts the basic cursors in the EasyApp global structure. However, you want to use additional cursors.

In the hook function, after the existing call to EasyLoadCursors(), you call your own function. The EasyPuzzle application does this by calling InitPuzzleCursor().

With this approach you don't reinvent the wheel, you simply put a new spin on it. You take advantage of all the functionality provided for you in EasyApp, and just add a little more for yourself. This is the best way to modify behavior because you know that EasyApp's default behavior still exists unchanged.

You can call your function before the default behavior or after, depending upon what is appropriate under the given circumstances. Most of the time you'll call your function after using the EasyApp default services.

You can augment window behaviors, as well. You must substitute your own function, but your new function calls the original base function in addition to performing its additional tasks.

The UpdatePuzzleMenus() function does just that. When EasyApp sends a DoUpdateMenus message to an EasyPuzzle window, UpdatePuzzleMenus() is the response function. However, the puzzle doesn't want to completely replace menu updating behavior, it just wants to augment it. So the first thing it does is call BaseUpdateMenus() to duplicate the default behavior. Then it makes a few changes.

If the changes were extensive, it might be more efficient to replace the default behavior completely. You must use your judgment as to when it is better to augment, and when it is better to replace a behavior entirely.

Replacing Behavior

When you decide to replace default behavior entirely—either a hook or a message—you must exercise a little care. The default functions frequently perform some critical service without which the behavior will fail utterly. If your replacement function does not perform the same service, you could be in big trouble.

You must ensure that any critical functionality implemented in the default function—or in any function it calls—is duplicated in your own function. In fact, a reasonable approach for implementing a complete replacement of a default function is to make a copy of the default function, rename it, and then make modifications to it.

For hooks, you remove the existing call to the "Easy" default function and substitute a call to your own function. For window behaviors, you create a replacement function and substitute it for the default function in the appropriate EasyWindow "Do" field.

> If you're worried about having unused code waste space, don't. Smart linkers can tell when code is never called, and do not include that code in the final build. If you don't believe it, while in the CodeWarrior debugger try to set a break point in an unused function. You can't. Although you can see the source code in the SYM window, there is no corresponding object code on which to set the break.

Doing Nothing

Sometimes you don't want to respond to a message. EasyPuzzle has some good examples of that. There is no zoom box in an EasyPuzzle window. Therefore it does not want to respond to a DoZoom message, should one arrive. However, *every message must have a handler!*

The solution is simple. You install a do-nothing function as the response function. There is one provided for you in EasyApp, in the file **windowProc.c**. Its name is EmptyProc(). Use this function as the response function for any message to which you do not wish to respond.

E

If there is no zoom box in a window, EasyApp never generates a DoZoom message for that window. You could get away with not replacing the default behavior. However, you should never be that trusting. Always assume the worst and be prepared to handle any eventuality.

Hooks versus Messages

In some cases you can jump into the flow of control by replacing a hook or by replacing a window behavior. Usually, there is a significant difference in the net effect, and one option is better for you. Keep the distinction between application-level and window-level services in mind to help you decide which is the better way to modify default behavior.

Let's use a mouse-click event as an example. This is a critical event in the operation of almost any application. How you handle a mouse click in many ways defines your application.

EasyApp detects the mouse click for you and calls MouseDownEventHook() right away. This is your first opportunity to modify default behavior. The default hook function calls EasyMouseDown().

EasyMouseDown() is a relatively complex function that takes care of a lot of the mouse-down event parsing. This function identifies the front window and the hit window, determines whether the click is in the menu bar, title bar, grow box, close box, zoom box, desktop, DA, or in the content area of your window. In response to all the possibilities, it calls a wide variety of hook functions or sends messages to the window involved.

EasyMouseDown() is carefully designed to be as generic as possible and to handle all eventualities intelligently. However, it might not be right for your application as a whole. In that case you can replace the call to EasyMouseDown() in the MouseDownEventHook() function with a call to your replacement function. That function then becomes responsible for *all* mouse-down event parsing.

However, it is far more likely that what is really different about your application is how you handle a click in the content area of your window. If this is all that's different, you don't need to replace EasyMouseDown(). If the click is in the content area of a window, EasyMouseDown() sends a DoContentClick message to the window. All you need to do is replace the window behavior, not the entire event-handling mechanism.

The same kind of potential overlap between hooks and window messages occurs in several places: key-down events, menu updating and so forth. Whenever faced with the choice, perform an analysis similar to the mouse-down example. Ask yourself, "Am I changing the application's behavior, or the window behavior?" Most often it will be a window behavior that you modify. Sometimes it will be the application behavior. Occasionally you may want to do both.

EasyApp and Menus

Menus are one area where you are certain to add to the default capabilities of EasyApp. Why? Because EasyApp has no way of knowing what menus you will create or use.

EasyApp provides complete support for three standard menus: Apple, File, and Edit. To do this it uses the resources you provide for your application. The default YourApp.rsrc file contains resources for the three standard menus. If you want to add any other menus—or change the three standard menus—you must modify EasyApp's default behavior in some way.

Let's look at how EasyApp handles menu creation, updating, and dispatch to see how you can modify menus in EasyApp.

Menu Creation

When it launches, EasyApp calls EasySetupMenus() directly, not through a hook. You cannot override this function. This function is responsible for adding the three standard menus to the application using the resources you provide. It also builds the Apple menu and inserts the menus in the menu bar.

If you want different items in the standard menus, modify the resources. For example, you should change the About item in the Apple menu to reflect the name of your application.

After installing the three standard menus, EasyApp calls SetupAppMenusHook(). This gives you an opportunity to build your own menus and add them to the menu bar. You do not need to draw the menu bar, EasyApp takes care of that for you.

E

Menu Updating

EasyApp calls UpdateMenusHook() whenever menus should be updated. This occurs when the user clicks the menu bar, when the user types a command-key equivalent, and when a window activates (because different menus may be appropriate for different kinds of windows).

The calls to UpdateMenusHook() occur inside default EasyApp code, some of which you may override. Remember, if you override default behavior, you are responsible for making sure that critical functionality is duplicated in your own code. For example, if you replace the EasyApp default function EasyKeyDown(), you must ensure that menus are updated before responding to a keyboard equivalent.

You can modify the menu updating process for all menus, for individual menus, or for individual windows.

UpdateMenusHook() calls EasyUpdateMenus(). You can replace this call if you want to replace all menu updating behavior.

However, EasyUpdateMenus() is very generic. It is unlikely that you need to replace it. It calls four hooks and sends a message to the front window. The hooks are UpdateAppleMenuHook(), UpdateFileMenuHook(), UpdateEditMenuHook(), and UpdateAppMenusHook(). EasyUpdateMenus() then sends a DoUpdateMenus message to the front window, if there is one.

The window comes last because it should have the last say as to what menu items are enabled or disabled. EasyApp does application-level menu updating first, and window-level menu updating last because the menus should ultimately be window-dependent.

You may override the individual menu updating hooks. The default Apple, File, and Edit menu updating functions may be all that your application needs, in which case you can leave them unchanged. The only one you are certainly going to override is the UpdateAppMenusHook(). This should call your function to update all the menus specific to your application.

You may also override the default BaseUpdateMenus() response function for the DoUpdateMenus window message. The default behavior disables the Close item if the window does not have a close box, and the Revert item if the window has no changes or no file to which it is attached. It is fairly likely that your windows will require somewhat more sophisticated menu updating. For example, an EasyPuzzle text window enables the text-related menus when it comes to the foreground.

> If you ever disable an entire menu, remember to invalidate the menu bar immediately! Do not wait for the menu update function to be called. If you do, you might have the unfortunate occurrence of the user clicking a menu thinking it is active, and watching it become inactive just as they click. Update the menu bar right away, because it is always visible. Update menus before you show them.

Menu Dispatch

When the user selects an item in a menu, the application must dispatch control to the correct function. The EasyApp menu dispatch model follows a pattern similar to the menu updating model.

For every circumstance in which menu dispatch is required, EasyApp calls MenuDispatchHook(). This function calls EasyMenuDispatch() to see whether EasyApp handles the menu command. The default EasyMenuDispatch() should handle things quite well for most applications.

You can replace all dispatch behavior by overriding this hook entirely, but it is unlikely that you will do so. It is more likely that you will augment it. After calling EasyMenuDispatch(), if the choice is not handled, call your own dispatch function to handle the choice.

EasyMenuDispatch() first sends a DoHandleMenu message to the front window, if there is one. If the window does not handle the item, it calls the appropriate hook: AppleMenuHook(), FileMenuHook(), or EditMenuHook() for the menu that contains the choice. If the choice is in your menu, the item is not handled. Control returns to MenuDispatchHook() where you can call your own function.

> When responding to a menu choice, the window comes first, not last. The choice is primarily window-dependent, and handled at the application level only if the window does not handle the menu choice.

You can override the individual menu dispatch hooks, if necessary. Each calls a related default function, EasyHandleAppleMenu(), EasyHandleFileMenu(), and EasyHandleEditMenu().

Study these functions to see what they do before replacing them. They are likely to do everything you need them to do. Each of these functions either calls a hook or sends a message that you can override to get the behavior you want (without having to replace all the dispatch code).

For example, if the user chooses the Page Setup item in the File menu, EasyApp ultimately calls the `PageSetupHook()` function. If the user chooses the Cut item from the Edit menu, EasyApp sends a `DoCut` message to the front window. You can augment or replace this default behavior, if necessary, rather than replacing all the dispatch code.

Before dumping dispatch code wholesale, look at the hooks and messages to see whether you can implement your behavior most efficiently at that level. The only time you should start replacing dispatch code is if you change the contents of the menus: adding items, moving them around, and so forth. This is a good argument for leaving the standard menus exactly as EasyApp sets them up, if this is acceptable for your application.

If it is not acceptable, make sure you duplicate the functionality provided by the default EasyApp menu dispatch code.

Utilities

EasyApp also provides some low-level utility functions. You can call them directly from your code. These relate to memory management, file access, string manipulation, and other miscellaneous application tasks. The following table lists each file and the types of utilities it contains.

memory.c	Contains memory-related utilities
file.c	Contains file access utilities
utilities.c	Contains string and other utilities

Open those files and study the available functions.

You may also want to avail yourself of the error-reporting function in errors.c. You can augment it through the `ShowErrorHook()` function.

Conclusion

For all its simplicity, EasyApp can be deep and powerful. When you're trying to figure out what's going on, study the source code and the comments carefully. The comments detail the circumstances under which a window message is received or a hook function called.

Study how EasyPuzzle modifies the shell's behavior to see how it is done. EasyPuzzle intentionally performs every kind of modification discussed in this appendix.

Finally, there is one more feature of EasyApp that should be mentioned. If the window messages don't cover what you want them to do, you can create more! Of course, EasyApp won't call them directly, but you can call them yourself.

If you'd like to see how, study EasyPuzzle. It performs this little trick so it can open a PICT file as well as a PICT resource. Look in the function that initializes an EasyPuzzle window. EasyPuzzle adds a DoImport message to the window's vocabulary. Start exploring, and have a good time discovering! It's the best way to learn.

Glossary

Numbers

24-bit addressing—Only the low 24 bits of an address are significant.

32-bit addressing—All 32 bits of an address are significant.

32-bit clean—Code that works with the 32-bit Memory Manager. The code makes no assumptions about an address's size, nor does it modify any values in a master block directly. Put another way, it locks, unlocks, or releases blocks using Memory Manager calls exclusively.

68K Mac—A Macintosh computer that uses a Motorola 68000 family processor: 68000, 68020, 68030, or 68040.

A

A-trap—Processor instructions that begin with hexadecimal value "A" cause an exception—thus they are trapped. When such an exception occurs, control passes to the A-trap dispatch table that provides the entry points into the Mac Toolbox.

A5 world—The part of the application's run-time environment that is accessed as an offset from the address pointed to by register A5 on 68K Macs. An application's globals, QuickDraw globals, and jump table are all part of the A5 world.

access path—Route the File Manager uses to read/write data in a file. Each path receives a reference number.

activate event—Generated when a window is brought to the foreground.

active window—The front window, it has stripes in the title bar and active controls. The active window is owned by the foreground application, and is the focus of most user events.

address—A location in memory.

AIFF—Audio Interchange File Format, data storage format for sound.

AIFF-C—Compressed sound data storage format.

alert box—A type of modal dialog box that informs or warns the user. There are three kinds: note, caution, and stop.

alias—A file or data structure that represents another file, directory, or volume.

allocate—To assign a memory block of arbitrary size in the heap.

allocation block—The smallest unit of space on a volume that can be allocated to a file. Typically consists of a number of logical blocks. The larger the volume, the larger the number of logical blocks in the allocation block. See also *logical block*.

ALRT—Resource type that defines an alert dialog box.

ANSI—American National Standards Institute; establishes baseline standards for all kinds of technical and engineering fields, including computer languages.

API—Application Programming Interface—a collection of related function calls.

Apple event—A high-level event used in interapplication communication.

AppleScript—A high-level scripting language used to control applications.

application heap—The memory available to your program for dynamic memory allocation. Does not include the A5 world or the stack.

application partition—All the memory allocated to your application, including the stack, A5 world, and application heap.

application shell—Code necessary to create a generic, empty application. See also *framework*.

argument—See *parameter*.

array—In C, an indexed list of variables of the same data type.

ascender—Part of a character that extends above the x-height.

ascent line—The line that just touches the top of the tallest ascenders in a font.

ASCII—American Standard Code for Information Exchange. Standard numerical values for the roman alphabet.

asynchronous sound—Sound that plays in the background.

auto-key event—Generated when the user presses a key continuously.

B

background color—The default color used where no drawing takes place, typically white.

background highlighting—Alternative method of highlighting selected objects when a window is in the background.

background pattern—The default pattern used when an area is erased.

background printing—The printer driver creates a file on-disk and printing occurs while your application resumes work.

Bad Thing—Writing code in such a way that things do not go exactly as you planned, or as they should. For Clarus, a lawn mower.

baseline—The line on which characters in a font rest.

bit pattern—See *pattern*.

bitmap—A data structure in which (typically) one bit represents one pixel's state, either on or off. Also used in basic QuickDraw for eight colors.

bitmap font—A font whose individual characters are represented by a bitmap.

block—An area of contiguous memory in the heap.

BNDL—Resource type in your application used by the Finder to locate icons and version information.

Boolean value—A true or false value. With respect to numbers, zero means false, and any non-zero value means true.

breakpoint—Location in source code where a debugger should stop running the code so you can look around. These are set by the programmer in the debugging environment before running code.

bug—A mistake in code. Can be either a mistake in logic or a mistake in the actual code syntax. Occasionally the cause of a Bad Thing. See also *Bad Thing*.

bundle bit—Bit in the Finder information for a file that tells the Finder whether it has already retrieved icons for that file.

bundle—The information that allows the Finder to locate your application and document icons.

bus error—What happens when the processor is told to access a nonexistent address. It cannot use the data bus for that purpose, hence a bus error results.

button—A control item that consists of a rounded rectangle with a title centered inside. Buttons are used to present a limited choice of actions.

C

callback routine—An application-provided routine used by the System. Examples include event filters, file filters, drag tracking handlers, and so forth.

caret—The insertion point in text, usually a blinking solid line. Not a cursor. See also *cursor*.

cast—See *type coercion*.

CDEF—Resource type for a control definition function.

checkbox—A control item, a small square with an adjacent title. An "X" appears inside the square if the control is active.

Clipboard—See *Scrap*.

clipping region—Area in a graphics port where drawing may occur.

close box—Item at the left side of the title bar in some windows. Clicking the close box closes the window.

closed file—A file with no access path.

code fragment—A piece of executable code in the Power Macintosh environment. It can be any size. Typically an entire application or a shared library exists in a single code fragment.

code segment—A section of executable code in the 68K environment, usually limited to 32K in size. 68K applications typically have more than one segment. Segments may be swapped in and out of memory as needed, a topic not covered in this book.

CodeWarrior—A very cool development environment for the Macintosh from Metrowerks.

coercion—See *type coercion*.

color lookup table (CLUT)—A table that relates index values to individual colors. Used to choose display colors on an indexed device.

command-key equivalent—Allows the user to choose a menu item by pressing the command key and another character simultaneously. For example, ⌘-N for "New."

compacting—See *heap compacting*.

compiler—A magical piece of software that turns source code into object code.

constant—A value that does not change.

content region—The area of a window within which drawing may occur.

control—An item in a window with which the user controls behavior or sets options for future behavior.

control definition function—A code resource that defines the appearance and behavior of a control and its parts.

control list—The window record contains the first control. Each control points to the next control in the window. Taken together, this interconnection is the control list.

cooperative multitasking—An environment where multiple processes run concurrently by explicitly surrendering time to the operating system, which mediates control.

creator type—A four-character code assigned to each file indicating which application created it.

current resource file—The default resource file for the Resource Manager. A search for a resource begins with this file.

cursor level—Determines whether the cursor is visible.

cursor—The onscreen icon that tracks the mouse. Standard cursors include the arrow, watch, I-beam, and crosshairs. See also *caret*.

D

dangling pointer—A nasty beast. Occurs when you dereference a handle to a relocatable block, and the block moves. The pointer now points to the wrong location, and is left "dangling." This is a Bad Thing.

data fork—An amorphous data store accessed using the File Manager. See also *resource fork*.

data stream—An ordered series of bytes.

data type—Identifies the nature of the data to a compiler. For example, `short`, `long`, `Boolean`, and so forth.

deactivate event—An activate event generated when a window is sent to the background.

debugger—Software to control program execution so you can see what's happening and identify problems.

declare—Inform the compiler of a name you intend to use and its meaning. Does not allocate memory. With respect to a function, to specify a function prototype. See also *define*.

default button—In a dialog box, the button with a bold outline. Pressing the Return or Enter keys should result in the same action as if the button were clicked.

define—Allocate memory to hold a variable or data. With respect to a function, to write the actual code that implements the function. See also *declare.*

dereference—To look directly at the contents of data referred to by a pointer or handle. For example, dereferencing a handle gets you the master pointer (the thing pointed to by the handle). Dereferencing a pointer gets you the data pointed to by the pointer.

descent line—The line just touched by a font's longest descenders.

descender—Part of a character that extends below the baseline.

Desktop—Metaphor for the Finder's working area. Also, the extent of all monitors attached to the computer.

dialog box—A specialized window for interacting with the user. Classified by window design and behavior.

dialog item—A control or other item that appears in a dialog.

direct device—A monitor capable of supporting millions of colors. See also *indexed device, color lookup table.*

directory ID—Number assigned to each directory by the File Manager.

directory—In the hierarchical file system, a subdivision of a volume. It may contain other directories (also called subdirectories) or files.

disabled item—An item that does not respond to user actions like clicks or key presses. Typically displayed dimmed—in gray outlines of text.

disk—A data storage device. Not to be confused with a volume.

disk-inserted event—Generated when the user puts a disk into a disk drive.

disposed handle—A handle whose block has been released back to the Memory Manager.

dithering—Using patterns of pixels to create the illusion of additional colors or gray levels.

DITL—Resource type for a dialog item list.

DLOG—Resource type for a dialog window.

document window—An application window, typically containing a data display.

double dereference—What you do to a handle to get at the data to which it refers. When working with a handle, a single dereference gets you a copy of the master pointer. A double deference gets you the data pointed to by the master pointer. Also called *double indirection.*

drag region—The outline of individual items being dragged using the Drag Manager. Also, the area of a window's title bar used to initiate moving the window.

E

empty handle—A handle whose master pointer is nil. This can happen if the block has been purged. Also, a handle to a block of zero bytes logical size (that is, a block of no length).

enabled item—An item that responds to user clicks and actions.

end-of-file—See *logical end-of-file* and *physical end-of-file*.

event filter function—An application-defined function to handle events outside of the main event loop. Typically attached to modal dialog boxes.

event—Generated by the System to inform applications of user actions and other significant incidents.

event loop—Code that continuously retrieves and parses events in an application.

F

feedback—Providing information to the user about the state of affairs in an application.

FIFO—A queue that uses first-in, first-out order. The event queue is a FIFO queue most of the time. See also *LIFO*.

file—An ordered group of bytes preserved in some storage medium.

file filter function—An application-provided function to control what types of files appear in the standard get-file dialog.

file ID—Two meanings. First, the number for the access path to a file (the file reference number). Also, the number assigned to this file on a volume, analogous to the directory ID and having nothing whatsoever to do with access paths.

file mark—The position in a file where the next data access occurs (either reading or writing).

file name—The name of the file. In the Mac OS, limited to 31 characters. The name cannot include a colon.

file reference number—See *file ID*.

file spec—See *file system specification*.

file system specification—A data structure that includes all the information necessary to locate a file on a volume.

file type—A four-character code that identifies the nature of the file.

Finder—The application that manages the Desktop and keeps track of files.

flush—To write data to a volume.

font—A group of stylistically related characters that typically represents a complete alphabet or a set of symbols.

font family—A group of stylistically related fonts.

font ID—The number on a particular machine used by the System to identify a particular font. The same named font may have different ID numbers on different machines.

font name—The name of a font. For example, Palatino. Typically consistent across machines, unlike font ID numbers.

foreground color—The color used for drawing; the default color is black.

fragmentation—See *heap fragmentation*.

framework—A cohesive group of functions designed to work together to accomplish some task and form the basis for further programming. Application frameworks are the typical example and provide a generic application that you can modify and extend.

free block—A block of memory available to the Memory Manager for allocation.

FREF—Resource type in your application used by the Finder to locate icons.

FSSpec—See *file system specification*.

function pointer—The address of a function.

function—The smallest functional unit in a program. A section of code with a return type, name, parameter list, and statements that accomplish the task of the function.

function stack—See *stack*.

G

global coordinate system—A pixel-based description of the entire QuickDraw drawing space. The origin (0,0) is the top-left corner of the main monitor and the space extends 32K pixels in all directions in the drawing plane. See also *local coordinate system*.

glyph—The distinct visual representation of one or more characters or pieces of characters.

go away box—See *close box*.

graphics device—A device in which QuickDraw can draw. Typically a monitor, printer, or offscreen GWorld.

graphics port—A separate drawing environment in which QuickDraw works. Every window has a graphics port.

gray region—The area occupied by the entire Desktop.

grow box—Item in the bottom-right corner of the content region of some windows that allows the user to interactively resize a window by clicking and dragging the box.

grow-zone function—An application-provided callback function used by the operating system when it runs out of memory.

GWorld—See *offscreen GWorld*.

H

handle—A pointer to a master pointer that ultimately refers to a relocatable block in memory. The handle itself refers to a master pointer, which never moves. The *content* of the master pointer changes as the relocatable block moves.

header file—A source file that includes declarations using code that includes the header file, such as constant declarations, enumerations, function prototypes, and so on.

heap—A section of RAM. Also, the area available for your application to do work, that is, the application heap.

heap compacting—The process of reordering relocatable blocks in a heap to create a larger contiguous block of free memory.

heap fragmentation—The condition where free memory is broken into discontiguous blocks separated by locked or nonrelocatable blocks.

hierarchical file system (HFS)—The organization of files on a volume in the Mac OS, where volumes contain directories or files, directories contain other directories and files, and so on.

hierarchical menu—A menu item that has a submenu attached.

high-level event—Generated when an Apple event is pending for your application. See also *low-level event* and *operating-system event*.

high-level event queue—List of high-level events for your application, maintained by the Event Manager.

highlighting—The visual indication that an object or group of objects is selected. This may be inverse video to display the object, outlining the object, and so forth.

hook—In an application shell, a routine through which all control passes at the appropriate time. This is the "public" surface of the shell. By overriding a hook routine, you modify the behavior of the underlying shell.

I-K

icon—A graphical representation of an idea or object. Also, data structures that describe icons of 16×16 or 32×32 pixels, in black and white or color.

icon family—A group of related icons in the various sizes and color options available.

IDE—Integrated Development Environment. An application that hosts the editor, compiler, and linker. These parts all function as one unit, making for fast development work. For example, CodeWarrior.

idle function—A function called when the application receives null events.

inactive window—A window in the background. The title bar has no stripes, control items are dim, and selected items are displayed with background highlighting or no highlighting.

indexed device—A device capable of displaying up to 256 colors. The actual color values are determined by using an index into a color lookup table.

initialize—To set the beginning value for a variable. Also, to perform necessary setup work when an application launches.

insertion point—Where the next character(s) will appear in text.

integer—A whole number, that is, one without a fractional part.

invalidate—To tell the operating system that an area needs updating.

jump table—A list of addresses for a group of functions. The A-trap dispatch table is a jump table. Each application also has a jump table.

keyword—A reserved word in a programming language.

key-down event—Generated when the user presses a key.

key-up event—Generated when the user releases a key.

keyboard equivalent—A combination of a modifier key or keys, and any other key used to choose a menu item. See also *command-key equivalent*.

L

leading—Pronounced "ledding." The vertical space between lines of text.

length byte—In a Pascal string, the first byte of storage. It contains the number of characters in the string (up to 255).

library—A code module you can access. Can be compiled and linked to your project, or the source code can be included and compiled directly in the project.

LIFO—A queue that uses last-in, first-out order. The stack is a LIFO queue. See also *FIFO*.

line height—In TextEdit, the distance from the ascent line for a line of text to the ascent line for the next line of text.

linker—Puts all the pieces of code together when building an application. Creates jump tables and performs all sorts of other magic.

local coordinate system—A pixel-based description of the drawing space in a graphics port. The origin (0,0) is the top-left corner of the graphics port, and the space extends 32K pixels in all directions in the drawing plane. See also *global coordinate system*.

localize—To adapt software to work in other countries and languages.

lock—To prevent a relocatable block from moving.

logical block—Unit of space on a volume, typically 512 bytes. See also *allocation block*.

logical end-of-file—The last byte of actual data in a file. See also *physical end-of-file*.

logical size—The number of bytes available for data storage in a memory block. See also *physical size*.

low-level event—Events that report hardware related occurrences, such as mouse clicks and key presses. See also *high-level event* and *operating-system event*.

low-memory globals—Addresses low in RAM used by the System for system-level services to applications.

M

Mac OS—Apple Computer's multitasking operating system for Macintosh and Macintosh-clone computers.

main screen—In a multimonitor environment, the monitor with the menu bar.

mark—See *file mark*.

master pointer—A location in memory whose contents point to a relocatable block. The Memory Manager updates the contents of the master pointer whenever it moves the relocatable block.

master pointer block—A nonrelocatable block of 64 master pointers.

MDEF—Resource type for a menu definition function.

memory block—See *block*. Also, what happens to your brain when you've been writing too much code.

memory reserve—A block of memory held for emergency release in low-memory conditions.

MENU—Resource type for menu data.

menu—A list of items from which the user may choose. See also *hierarchical menu, pull-down menu, popup menu,* and *submenu*.

menu bar—The menu titles for pull-down menus available in an application. Appears at the top of the main monitor.

menu definition function—A code resource that defines the appearance and behavior of a menu.

menu ID—The resource ID for a MENU resource.

menu item—An individual option or choice listed in a menu.

menu title—The word that appears in the menu bar or in a dialog indicating the position of the menu.

modal dialog box—Dialog box that must be dismissed before the user can perform other work in the application or switch to another application. It cannot be moved by the user.

modeless dialog box—Dialog box that acts like a regular window. The user can perform other work or switch applications without dismissing the dialog.

modifier key—The ⌘, Option, Control, Shift, and Caps-lock keys.

mouse-down event—Generated when the user presses the mouse button.

mouse-moved event—Generated when the mouse moves outside of an application-defined region.

mouse-up event—Generated when the user releases the mouse button.

movable modal dialog box—A modal dialog that can be moved by the user. The user must dismiss the dialog before performing other work in the application, but may switch to other applications.

N-Q

native code—Code compiled to run on the Power Macintosh only.

nonrelocatable block—A block of memory that cannot be moved.

null event—Generated when there are no other events waiting.

null terminator—Marks the end of a C string; the value zero.

object code—This is the code that the computer's central processor understands. Produced by the compiler and linker after interpreting source code. See also *source code*.

offscreen GWorld—A data structure and graphics environment for preparing image data. Used by advanced graphics applications for rendering images before displaying them onscreen.

opcode—A value indicating a QuickDraw operation.

open file—A file that has an access path.

OpenDoc—A document-centric desktop metaphor where applications are servers that display data on parts of compound documents.

operand—A value (constant or variable) operated on by an operator.

operating-system event—Events concerning the application's active status and movement of the mouse. See also *low-level event* and *high-level event*.

operator—A symbol that represents an operation.

optimize—Modify code to run more quickly and/or occupy less space.

order of precedence—The order of priority in which a series of operations (usually mathematical) occur.

outline font—A font whose glyphs are stored as a series of mathematical curves.

parameter—Data passed to a function when called. It may be an actual value or a reference to data.

pathname—The names of the volume and all directories leading to a file.

pattern—A bitmap or pixelmap used as a repeating tile to fill a space or draw lines.

pen—The QuickDraw drawing implement.

physical end-of-file—The actual size of a file on a volume, including any "empty" space not used for actual data storage. See also *logical end-of-file.*

physical size—The actual size of a memory block. Includes the block header used by the Memory Manager. See also *logical size.*

picture—A saved series of QuickDraw opcodes that define the ultimate appearance of a drawing.

pixel—A picture element. On a monitor, a phosphor dot (or group of dots for color monitors). In QuickDraw, the smallest dot QuickDraw can make.

pixel pattern—See *pattern.*

pixelmap—A color bitmap.

point—In QuickDraw, a horizontal and vertical coordinate.

pointer—The address of an item in memory.

popup menu—A control item, typically in a dialog box, with a distinct visual appearance. It may or may not have a title. Menu items appear when the user clicks the popup control.

port—See *graphics port.*

Power Mac—A Macintosh computer using a Motorola PPC chip.

preflight—A memory management strategy that determines whether adequate memory is available before making a memory request.

preprocessor directive—A statement used to issue a command to a compiler before it compiles code.

printer driver—The code that translates QuickDraw commands and sends the results to a printer.

printing graphics port—A graphics port for drawing when printing.

printing loop—The code that controls page-by-page printing in an application.

process—A running task of any type, typically an open application but also includes desk accessories, the System, and some background processes.

pull-down menu—Menu that appears in the menu bar. It has a title. The menu items appear when the user clicks the title in the menu bar.

purge—To remove purgeable blocks from memory.

purgeable block—A block whose contents can be removed from memory in low-memory conditions.

QuickDraw—The Mac OS drawing routines.

QuickDraw global variables—QuickDraw's application-level globals that it uses to keep track of what's going on. Stored in your application's A5 world.

QuickDraw GX—Child of QuickDraw, they share the name only. A powerful and sophisticated object-based drawing environment.

R

radio button—A control item, a small circle with an adjacent title. Specifies a choice from a mutually exclusive set of options. When on, the control displays a black dot in the center of the button.

random access memory (RAM)—Memory whose contents can change.

read-only memory (ROM)—Memory whose contents cannot change.

recursive function—A function that calls itself.

region—A QuickDraw-defined arbitrary shape consisting of one or more closed contours.

relocatable block—A block of memory that can be moved by the Memory Manager.

ResEdit—A resource editing application from Apple Computer.

resource attributes—Features that tell the Resource Manager how to handle a resource, including whether the resource is locked, protected, and so forth.

resource—Data organized and stored in a structured format, typically intended for repeated use in an application.

resource fork—A structured data store accessed using the Resource Manager. See also *data fork*.

resource ID—A numerical value specifying an individual resource of a given type.

resource map—Contains the resource type, ID number, name, attributes, and location of every resource in a resource fork.

resource type—A four-character code identifying the nature of the resource.

resume event—Generated when an application is moving to the foreground.

RGB color—A data structure consisting of three values, one each for the colors red, green, and blue. QuickDraw uses the RGB (red, green, blue) color system.

S

Scrap—Area in memory where the System stores data for data exchange.

script system—Software components used to render a font onscreen according to the rules of grammar and syntax appropriate for the language.

scroll bar—A control item typically found in a document window that allows the user to scroll the view to see hidden parts of a document.

self-reference—See *self-reference*.

shared library—Compiled code that makes its function names and some data structures available for use by applications. Shared because more than one application may use a shared library simultaneously.

shell—See *application shell*.

signature—A resource that holds the application's unique creator type.

signed—A value that may be positive or negative. See also *unsigned*.

SIZE—Resource type that contains information about the application's memory requirements and operating features.

size box—See *grow box*.

snd—Resource type for sound data; actual type is 'snd ' with a trailing space.

sound channel—A string of sound commands treated as a first-in, first-out queue.

sound resource—Data stored in an 'snd ' resource.

source code—The text processed by a compiler to generate object code. More precisely, the instructions you write in a programming language to create software. See also *object code*.

stack—A last-in, first-out queue of stack frames.

stack frame—The data placed on the stack by a function call. The frame includes parameters, local variables, and return address.

submenu—A menu that appears when the user chooses a hierarchical menu item.

string—A series of characters. In C, an array of unsigned char containing characters.

struct—In C, a collection of variables that can be treated as a single unit, typically named and declared as a data type.

suspend event—Generated when an application is moving to the background.

synchronous sound—A sound that must complete playing before control returns to your application.

syntax—The rules governing the form and structure of a programming language.

syntax error—What happens when you don't follow the syntax rules.

System file—File that contains system-level resources, Toolbox patches, and other items necessary for the Mac OS.

system heap—The area of RAM occupied by the System code and resources.

T-V

tick—Approximately 1/60th of a second.

title bar—The bar across the top of a window that contains the name and (usually) a close box and zoom box.

Toolbox—The entire collection of Mac OS routines you use to make the Macintosh jump through hoops. In other words, these functions supply the basic implements you use to manage the user interface, print a page, write a file, or perform many other tasks. The Toolbox is the API for the Mac OS.

transfer mode—The Boolean-logic operation performed on a pixel based on the nature of the source pixel and the existing onscreen pixel.

trap dispatch table—On 68K Macs, when the CPU encounters an A-trap exception it calls the A-trap handler. That in turn uses the trap dispatch table to pass control to the appropriate Toolbox routine. Each Toolbox routine (or group of routines) has its own A-trap number.

typecast—See *type coercion*.

type coercion—Telling the compiler to treat data of one type as if it were data of another type.

typedef—The C keyword used to declare a new data type.

universal procedure pointer (UPP)— A data structure that incorporates all the information necessary for a callback routine to be called from either 68K or Power Mac code.

unlock—To allow a locked relocatable block to be moved again.

unsigned—A value that has no sign, hence is always positive. See also *signed*.

update event—Generated whenever some portion of a window needs to be redrawn.

update region—The area in a window in need of update.

UPP—See *universal procedure pointer*.

validate—To tell the System that a particular part of a window is valid.

variable—A named location in memory that holds a value or values that can change.

video device—A monitor. See also *graphics device*.

visible region—That part of a window visible on the Desktop.

volume—Part of a storage device formatted to store files. It may be an entire disk, or just part of a disk.

volume reference number—Assigned to each mounted volume by the File Manager so it can track volumes.

W-Z

WDEF—Resource type for a window definition function.

whizzy—That which is really cool.

WIND—Resource type for window data.

window—A viewing pane. In the Mac OS, the basic unit in which you view data.

window definition function—A code resource that defines the appearance and behavior of windows.

window list—System-maintained linked list of all open windows.

window origin—The coordinates at the top-left corner of the window, typically (0,0).

x-height—The height of the lowercase "x" in a font. More generally, the height of typical lowercase letters that have no ascenders or descenders.

zoom box—Item at the right side of the title bar in some windows. Clicking the zoom box causes the window dimensions to toggle between two states.

Index

C

X-Z

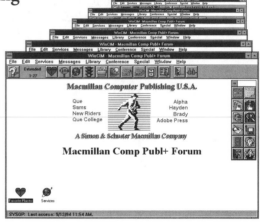

PLUG YOURSELF INTO...

MACMILLAN INFORMATION SUPERLIBRARY™

que   SAMS PUBLISHING   Hayden Books   que COLLEGE   NRP   alpha books   Brady   ADOBE PRESS

THE MACMILLAN INFORMATION SUPERLIBRARY™

Free information and vast computer resources from the world's leading computer book publisher—online!

FIND THE BOOKS THAT ARE RIGHT FOR YOU!

A complete online catalog, plus sample chapters and tables of contents give you an in-depth look at *all* of our books, including hard-to-find titles. It's the best way to find the books you need!

- **STAY INFORMED** with the latest computer industry news through our online newsletter, press releases, and customized Information SuperLibrary Reports.

- **GET FAST ANSWERS** to your questions about MCP books and software.

- **VISIT** our online bookstore for the latest information and editions!

- **COMMUNICATE** with our expert authors through e-mail and conferences.

- **DOWNLOAD SOFTWARE** from the immense MCP library:
    - Source code and files from MCP books
    - The best shareware, freeware, and demos

- **DISCOVER HOT SPOTS** on other parts of the Internet.

- **WIN BOOKS** in ongoing contests and giveaways!

TO PLUG INTO MCP: ➔ **WORLD WIDE WEB: http://www.mcp.com**

GOPHER: gopher.mcp.com

FTP: ftp.mcp.com

Home Page · What's New · Bookstore · Reference Desk · Software Library · Macmillan Overview · Talk to Us

1. Dave Mark, noted author, demystifies programming for those new to the Mac.

2. In-depth coverage of System Software Technologies, Object Oriented Programming, Visual Programming, Databasing ...

3. Bob Boonstra's monthly contest will challenge even the most experienced programmer!

4. Chris Espinosa talks about Apple – from the inside. Where it has been and where it is going.

5. Get information from the experts and Apple on how to make the transition to Power Macintosh.

6. Articles from industry leaders that will improve your code writing.

7. Workshop articles including languages from Assembly and C to Pascal, FORTRAN, and others.

8. Technical support for Symantec's products.

9. Impartial insider reviews of the latest development tools.

10. Legal issues specific to programming – from the release of new software to copyrights.

11. Interesting, not so conventional programming ideas.

12. Ideas to help you clean up, use shortcuts on, and organize your work.

13. Comments on the industry and pertinent notable events.

14. An open forum for developers to share their thoughts, dilemmas, solutions and opinions.

15. Recent releases, product updates, company mergers, shipping dates ...

16. Valuable developer tools and reference materials at discounted prices.

17. Your opportunity to share information or tips useful to other programmers – see it in print & get paid for it!

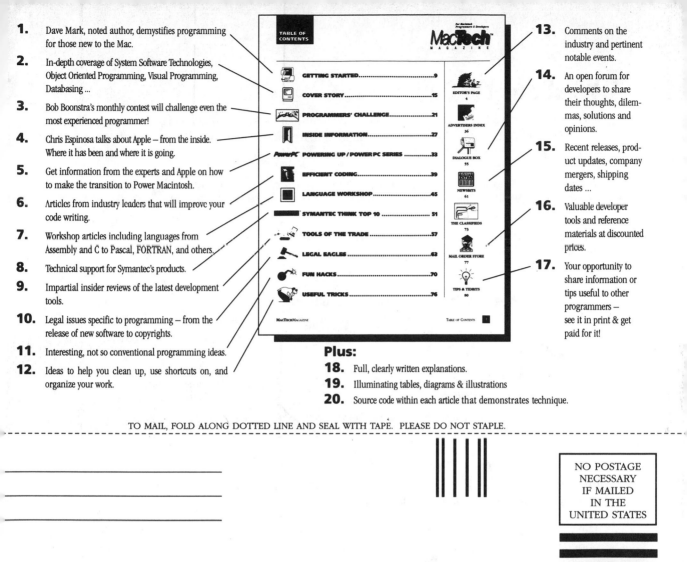

Plus:

18. Full, clearly written explanations.

19. Illuminating tables, diagrams & illustrations

20. Source code within each article that demonstrates technique.

TO MAIL, FOLD ALONG DOTTED LINE AND SEAL WITH TAPE. PLEASE DO NOT STAPLE.

NO POSTAGE
NECESSARY
IF MAILED
IN THE
UNITED STATES

BUSINESS REPLY MAIL
FIRST CLASS MAIL   PERMIT NO. 71745   LOS ANGELES, CA

POSTAGE WILL BE PAID BY ADDRESSEE

XPLAIN CORPORATION
P O BOX 250055
LOS ANGELES CA   90099-
3873

What's on the CD

The *Programming Starter Kit for Macintosh* CD contains a limited version of Metrowerks CodeWarrior. You can save files, but you cannot add or remove files from a project with this version. Chapter 2 introduces the CodeWarrior development environment.

The MPSK Code folder contains all the code you develop in the coding labs in this book. Chapter 2 explains when and how to use this code. Inside the MPSK Code folder are folders for each chapter that has a coding lab. In addition, the EasyApp Complete folder contains the final EasyApp application shell. This is provided for you to use in your own programming projects if you wish. The EasyPuzzle Complete folder contains the final EasyPuzzle application.

The Tools You Need folder contains a variety of software tools that developers rely on. You will use some extensively, others not at all. Although you do not use all the tools directly in this book, all are worthwhile. The MacErrors program is shareware. If you use it, please pay the authors.

The DUDemos folder contains software that demonstrates various elements of Macintosh programming. The EventDemo and HeapDemo applications are discussed in detail in the lab exercises. The QuickDrawDemo and ScrollDemo are provided for you to play with on your own.

The Extra PICTs folder contains images saved in PICT format. The program you develop in this book uses PICT images. These are provided for you in case you haven't got any PICT images hanging around to import into the puzzle.

The Commercial Demos folder contains demo versions of some software that is very useful or popular among developers. Information on all of these products can be found in their respective folders, and in Appendix D.

The develop Articles folder contains two articles that have appeared in Apple's *develop* magazine, one on window zooming and the other on asynchronous sounds. These topics are discussed in Chapters 8 and 14 respectively. With each article is the original code as published in *develop*. That code has been slightly modified and included in the projects you work with in this book.

Finally, the Glypha III folder contains the complete source code for this excellent arcade-style game for the Macintosh. This gives you a real-world example of how one programmer solves the problems you face when writing an application.